OCÉANO ATLÁNTICO

CUBA

La Habana

Santiago

PENÍNSULA DE YUCATÁN

REPÚBLICA DOMINICANA

San Juan

Ponce

PUERTO RICO

HAITÍ

Santo Domingo

JAMAICA

MAR CARIBE

Belmopan

BELICE

HONDURAS

Tegucigalpa

León

NICARAGUA

Managua

Lago de Nicaragua

Caracas

VENEZUELA

Río Orinoco

COSTA RICA

San José

Canal de Panamá

Panamá

PANAMÁ

Río Magdalena

Bogotá

COLOMBIA

BRASIL

P9-ECI-386

DESTINOS

A Telecourse Designed by
Bill VanPatten
University of Illinois at Urbana-Champaign

Martha Alford Marks

Richard V. Teschner
University of Texas, El Paso

Thalia Dorwick
Coordinator of Print Material for McGraw-Hill, Inc.

McGraw-Hill, Inc.
New York St. Louis San Francisco Auckland Bogotá
Caracas Lisbon London Madrid Mexico City Milan
Montreal New Delhi San Juan Singapore
Sydney Tokyo Toronto

DESTINOS

An Introduction to Spanish

Destinos
An Introduction to Spanish

8 9 0   DOC DOC   9 0 9 8 7 6 5

ISBN 0–07–002069–8 C
ISBN 0–07–067221–0 H

The senior editing supervisor was **Richard Mason**. The copyeditor was **Charlotte Jackson**. The editing assistant was **Eileen Burke**. The art director was **Francis Owens**. The text and cover designer was **Juan Vargas**. The production supervisor was **Diane Baccianini**. Production assistance was provided by **Edie Williams, Lorna Lo**, and **Anne Eldredge**. The illustrators were **Lori Heckelman** and **Allan Eitzen**. The photo researcher was **Judy Mason**. The compositor was **G & S Typesetters**. The printer and binder was **R. R. Donnelley & Sons**.

Library of Congress Cataloging-in-Publication Data

VanPatten, Bill.
   Destinos: An Introduction to Spanish / Bill VanPatten, Martha Alford Marks,
Richard V. Teschner.
     p. cm.
   Includes index.
   ISBN 0-07-002069-8
   1. Spanish language—Textbooks for foreign speakers—English.   I. Marks, Martha.
II. Teschner, Richard V.   III. Title.
PC4128.V36   1991   91-32511
468.2'421—dc20   CIP
0-07-911379-6 (Spanish for Business)   0-07-911383-4 (Spanish for the
0-07-91380-X (Spanish for Education)   Medical Professions)
0-07-911381-8 (Spanish for Tourism)   0-07-911384-2 (Spanish for Social Services)
0-07-911382-6 (Spanish for Law and
           Law Enforcement)

Grateful acknowledgment is made for use of the following:

Realia: *Page 125* © Quino/Quipos; *177* © Librerías Fausto; *180* © Quino/Quipos; *217* © *Diario las Américas*; *237* © *Casas y Jardines*, Editorial Contémpora; *291* Reprinted with permission of Gary G. Wiesman, M.D., F.A.C.S.

All photographs except those listed below are supplied courtesy of Olivia Tappan and Creative Television Associates (Boston).

Photographs: *Page 24* Museo del Prado; *27* © Stuart Cohen/Comstock; *36* (*top*) © Owen Franken/Stock, Boston; *36* (*bottom*) © Peter Menzel/Stock, Boston; *61* (*bottom left*) © Peter Menzel/Stock, Boston; *61* (*bottom right*) Bernard G. Silberstein/Monkmeyer Press; *80* © Jean Gaumy/Magnum Photos; *91* © Stuart Cohen/Comstock; *92* (*top*) © Mike

(*continued on page 556*)

HIGHLIGHTS OF THE VOCABULARY AND GRAMMAR TOPICS IN THE TEXTBOOK AND WORKBOOK

Note: Grammar topics are grouped by unit, not by the order of their introduction. Not all topics are included here.

	Vocabulario	*Gramática*
Lecciones 1–2 pages 2–25	cognates; family members	**ser**; articles and gender; possession

Un viaje a Sevilla (España) page 27

	Vocabulario	*Gramática*
Lecciones 3–6 pages 28–68	numbers (0–21); academic subjects; animals; days of the week; telling time	**hay**; **estar**; **ir**; present tense (regular verbs); subject pronouns; personal **a**; interrogatives; adjective agreement

Un viaje a Madrid (España) page 69

	Vocabulario	*Gramática*
Lecciones 7–11 pages 70–118	clothing; numbers (21–99); interrogatives; months; seasons; colors; descriptive adjectives	**saber**; **conocer**; present tense (irregular verbs, stem-changing verbs); reflexive pronouns; more on possession and adjectives; demonstratives; **ser** and **estar**

Un viaje a la Argentina page 119

	Vocabulario	*Gramática*
Lecciones 12–18 pages 120–188	numbers (100–1000); food groups; writing and written materials	preterite tense; object pronouns; more on using adjectives; verbs used reflexively and nonreflexively; **gustar** and verbs like it

Un viaje a Puerto Rico page 189

	Vocabulario	*Gramática*
Lecciones 19–26 pages 190–260	directions; more family members; weather; changes in states and conditions; parts of a house; domestic appliances; more descriptive adjectives	present and past progressive; imperfect; using imperfect and preterite together; **por** and **para**; affirmative and negative words; **tener** idioms; comparisons; **estar** + adjectives

	Vocabulario	*Gramática*
	UN VIAJE A MÉXICO: EL PUEBLO, LA CAPITAL page 263	
Lecciones 27–36 pages 264–365	parts of the body; medical situations; places in a city; stores; geographical features; professions; social life; giving advice	future; superlatives; present subjunctive and uses (noun and adjective clauses; adverbial conjunctions of time); commands; present perfect (indicative and subjunctive)
	UN VIAJE A MÉXICO: LA CAPITAL page 367	
Lecciones 37–52 pages 368–491	money; business; renting and buying; tourist needs; travel; restaurants; hotels; sports; relationships; pastimes	past subjunctive; conditional; *if*-clause sentences; subjunctive with certain conjunctions

Textbook Table of Contents

EPISODIOS 1–26   1

STUDY GUIDE: LECCIÓN 1   2

Lección 1   La carta   4
Preparación   5
¿Tienes buena memoria?   6
Vocabulario del tema: Los cognados   7
Un poco de gramática: Expressing *is/are*   9
Vocabulario   10

STUDY GUIDE: LECCIÓN 2   11

Lección 2   El secreto   14
Preparación   15
¿Tienes buena memoria?   16
Nota cultural: Las familias hispánicas   18
Vocabulario del tema: Los miembros de la familia   18
Conversaciones: Los saludos   21
Un poco de gramática: Expressing Possession   22
Nota cultural: La Guerra Civil española   23
Vocabulario   25

Note: Because of the repeating lesson structure, only certain sections of the lessons are listed from this point on. This is the repeating lesson structure for all except review lessons:

Preparación
¿Tienes buena memoria?
Vocabulario del tema
Conversaciones (not in all lessons)
Un poco de gramática
Nota cultural
Vocabulario

Additional **Notas culturales** appear as appropriate.

Un viaje a Sevilla (España)   27

Lección 3   El comienzo   28

Vocabulario del tema: Los números
del 0 al 21   32
Conversaciones: Más saludos   33
Un poco de gramática: Using Verbs to Talk
About Others   34

Lección 4   Perdido   38

Vocabulario del tema: En el Colegio de
San Francisco de Paula; Otras materias;
Los animales domésticos   41
Conversaciones: Las presentaciones   45
Un poco de gramática: Describing   46

Lección 5   La despedida   51

Vocabulario del tema: Los días de la semana;
¿Qué hora es?   55
Conversaciones: Las despedidas   59
Un poco de gramática: Using Verbs to Talk
About Group Activities   60

Lección 6   ¿Maestra?   64

Repaso de los Episodios 1–5   67

Un viaje a Madrid (España)   69

Lección 7   La cartera   70

Vocabulario del tema: La ropa; Los números
del 21 al 99   74
Conversaciones: Algo sobre la cortesía   78
Un poco de gramática: Expressing
knowing   79

Lección 8   El encuentro   82

Vocabulario del tema: Las palabras
interrogativas   87
Conversaciones: Los agradecimientos   88
Un poco de gramática: More About Verbs   90

Lección 9   Estaciones   94

Vocabulario del tema: Los meses y las
estaciones del año; Los colores   97

Conversaciones: Para decir que sí   99
Un poco de gramática: More About Talking
About Yourself   100

Lección 10   Cuadros   104

Vocabulario del tema: ¿Cómo son?
Los adjetivos descriptivos   107
Conversaciones: Más despedidas   109
Un poco de gramática: More About Talking
About Group Activities   110

Lección 11   La demora   114

Repaso de los Episodios 7–10   117

Un viaje a la Argentina   119

• • • • • • • • •

Lección 12   Revelaciones   120

Vocabulario del tema: Los números
de 100 a 1000   123
Conversaciones: Más sobre el tuteo   124
Un poco de gramática: Using Verbs to Talk
About the Past   126

• • • • • • • • •

Lección 13   La búsqueda   129

Vocabulario del tema: Los mariscos; El pescado;
Otros comestibles   133
Conversaciones: En una tienda   135
Un poco de gramática: More About Using Verbs
to Talk About the Past   136

• • • • • • • • •

Lección 14   En el extranjero   140

Vocabulario del tema: La carne; Otros
comestibles   143
Conversaciones: Cuando la conversación
es difícil...   146
Un poco de gramática: More About Using Verbs
to Talk About the Past   147

• • • • • • • • •

Lección 15   Culpable   150

Vocabulario del tema: Las frutas   155

Conversaciones: Para animar   156
Un poco de gramática: More About Using Verbs
to Talk About the Past   157

• • • • • • • • • •

Lección 16   Caras   161

Vocabulario del tema: Las legumbres y
las verduras   165
Conversaciones: Perdone Ud.   167
Un poco de gramática: More About Using Verbs
to Talk About the Past   168

• • • • • • • • • •

Lección 17   Inolvidable   173

Vocabulario del tema: El arte de escribir;
Las personas; Los medios de
comunicación   177
Conversaciones: Más saludos y despedidas   179
Un poco de gramática: More About Using Verbs
to Talk About the Past   180

• • • • • • • • • •

Lección 18   Estimada Sra. Suárez   184

Repaso de los Episodios 12–17   186

Un viaje a Puerto Rico   189

• • • • • • • • •

Lección 19   Por fin...   190

Vocabulario del tema: Las instrucciones   193
Un poco de gramática: Describing What Was
Happening While . . .   196

• • • • • • • • • •

Lección 20   Relaciones estrechas   200

Vocabulario del tema: Los parientes   205
Conversaciones: Cómo contestar
el teléfono   208
Un poco de gramática: More About Using
the Imperfect   208

Lección 21   El peaje   212

Vocabulario del tema: ¿Qué tiempo hace?   216
Un poco de gramática: More About the
   Imperfect   218

Lección 22   Recuerdos   221

Vocabulario del tema: Cambios de estado   225
Un poco de gramática: More About Using
   the Imperfect   227

Lección 23   Vista al mar   231

Vocabulario del tema: Las partes de una casa;
   Algunos aparatos domésticos   234
Un poco de gramática: Describing What
   Someone Was Doing   237

Lección 24   El don Juan   241

Vocabulario del tema: Para describir la
   personalidad   244
Conversaciones: Las reacciones   246
Un poco de gramática: Additional Uses of
   Some Preterite Forms   247

Lección 25   Reflexiones I   251

Repaso de los Episodios 1–18   253

Lección 26   Reflexiones II   257

Repaso de los Episodios 19–24   259

EPISODIOS 27–52   261

Un viaje a México: El pueblo, la capital   263

STUDY GUIDE: LECCIÓN 27   264

Lección 27   El rescate   266

Un poco de gramática: Another Way to Talk
   About the Future   271

STUDY GUIDE: LECCIÓN 28   273

Lección 28   Atrapados   276

Vocabulario del tema: Algunas partes
   del cuerpo   280
Conversaciones: Para saber qué pasó   282
Un poco de gramática: More About Talking
   About the Future   283

Lección 29   ¡Se derrumbó!   287

Vocabulario del tema: Los exámenes
   médicos   291
Conversaciones: Cómo decir que otra persona
   tiene razón   293
Un poco de gramática: Talking About What
   People Want Others to Do   294

Lección 30   Preocupaciones   298

Vocabulario del tema: En una ciudad   302
Conversaciones: Entre clientes y
   dependientes   305
Un poco de gramática: Expressing Your
   Feelings About Something   306

Lección 31   Medidas drásticas   310

Vocabulario del tema: Las tiendas y los comercios   313

Un poco de gramática: Another Way to Talk About the Future   315

Lección 32   Ha habido un accidente   320

Vocabulario del tema: El mundo y su forma   324

Un poco de gramática: Telling Someone to Do Something   326

Lección 33   Si supieras...   330

Vocabulario del tema: Profesiones y oficios   334

Un poco de gramática: Telling Someone to Do Something   337

Lección 34   Éxito   341

Vocabulario del tema: Relaciones sociales   345

Un poco de gramática: Talking About What Someone Has Done   348

Lección 35   Reunidos   352

Vocabulario del tema: Consejos y sugerencias   356

Un poco de gramática: Expressing Hope   358

Lección 36   ¿Qué estarán haciendo?   361

Repaso de los Episodios 27–35   363

Un viaje a México: La capital   367

Lección 37   Llevando cuentas   368

Vocabulario del tema: El dinero   372

Un poco de gramática: Talking About What You Wanted Someone to Do   374

Lección 38   Ocultando la verdad   379

Vocabulario del tema: El dinero y los negocios   383

Un poco de gramática: More About Talking About the Past   385

Lección 39   La misma sonrisa   388

Vocabulario del tema: Los bienes raíces   391

Un poco de gramática: More About Talking About the Past   393

Lección 40   Entre la espada y la pared   396

Vocabulario del tema: Para los turistas   400

Un poco de gramática: Talking About What You Would Do   402

Lección 41   ALGO INESPERADO   406

Vocabulario del tema: Hablando de
los viajes 410
Un poco de gramática: Quoting What
Someone Said 412

Lección 42   YO INVITO   416

Vocabulario del tema: En un restaurante 419
Un poco de gramática: Expressing What
Would Happen If . . . 422

Lección 43   SEREMOS CUATRO   426

Vocabulario del tema: En un hotel 430
Un poco de gramática: Talking About What
Had Happened Before . . . 431

Lección 44   UNA PROMESA Y UNA SONRISA   435

Vocabulario del tema: Hablando de los
deportes 438
Un poco de gramática: More About Talking
About What Had Happened 441

Lección 45   ¡ESTOY HARTA!   445

Vocabulario del tema: Las relaciones
interpersonales 448
Un poco de gramática: Talking About What
Someone Should Have Done 450

Lección 46   LAS EMPANADAS   454

Vocabulario del tema: Diversiones y
pasatiempos 459
Un poco de gramática: Expressing
If . . . , then . . . 462

Lección 47   TENGO DUDAS   465

Un poco de gramática: Expressing Relationships
Between Events 468

Lección 48   ASÍ FUE (I)   471

Repaso de los Episodios 3–11 473

Lección 49   ASÍ FUE (II)   475

Repaso de los Episodios 12–18 477

Lección 50   ASÍ FUE (III)   479

Repaso de los Episodios 19–26 481

Lección 51   ASÍ FUE (IV)   484

Repaso de los Episodios 27–36 486

Lección 52   SIEMPRE LO AMÓ   488

Cinco años después 491

Appendix 1:   ANSWER SECTION   492

Appendix 2:   VERB CHARTS   511

SPANISH-ENGLISH VOCABULARY   516

INDEX OF CHARACTERS   548

INDEX   552

PREFACE

Destinos: What Is It?

An old man has retired to his hacienda outside a small town close to Mexico City. With the wealth he has accumulated since leaving Spain at the end of its bloody Civil War, he is restoring the hacienda to its original sixteenth-century splendor. But his health has begun to fail, and now he hopes to live out the remainder of his years peacefully, in the tranquillity of the Mexican countryside.

Then a letter arrives—a letter in which a woman from Spain makes claims about the old man's past. Gathering his family around him, he reveals a secret, then announces that he must send someone to Spain to speak with the writer of the letter.

Enter Raquel Rodríguez, an attorney from Los Angeles who accepts the task of locating the letter writer and investigating her claims. What *is* the old man's secret? And what will Raquel discover on her unforgettable journey?

If all this sounds like a Friday night television show, you are only half right! This story is the premise for *Destinos: An Introduction to Spanish.* Consisting of fifty-two half-hour video episodes, *Destinos* is a television and video course that allows beginning language learners to hear Spanish and experience its cultural diversity while following a compelling story full of human emotions, the surprises that real life often offers, and the force of the human spirit.

Understanding Spanish

Adapting the format of the highly popular Hispanic *telenovela* (soap opera), *Destinos* is innovative in adopting a comprehension-based approach for the teaching of Spanish. The series of course allows students to develop speaking and writing skills, and abundant reading materials are also provided. But *Destinos* is especially suited to help learners develop good *listening comprehension skills.*

In each episode there are three kinds of Spanish. Two of them are specifically designed to be comprehensible to the beginner: the Spanish spoken by an off-screen narrator and that spoken by Raquel Rodríguez as she reviews the major highlights at the end of each episode. The purpose of this type of Spanish is to provide appropriate language for acquisition, that is, language that students can understand and from which they can learn.

In addition to this purposefully comprehensible Spanish, each episode also contains segments of more rapid conversational Spanish, that is, when the characters are speaking to each other. In most cases, actions and context will allow student viewers to follow this type of Spanish. Students are encouraged to follow along, get the general idea, and let comprehension develop over time. They are not asked to study and learn this type of Spanish, although they will often "pick up" words and phrases repeated in conversation (or emphasized in particular scenes). After watching the whole series, students should have achieved a level of comprehension far beyond that of most beginning students.

Another important feature of the Spanish of *Destinos* is captured in the review segments that Raquel usually provides toward the end of each show. Raquel's review is accompanied by sentences on-screen that allow students to see how major grammatical features work. Thus, students not only *hear* Spanish that they can understand; they also *see* Spanish that they can understand, which further promotes language learning.

The Goals of *Destinos*

If, in addition to watching the series, the student uses the Textbook along with the Workbook/Study Guides and the audiocassette program, he or she can expect to accomplish a great deal with *Destinos.*

- By the end of one year a student-viewer should be able to understand most Spanish spoken slower than normal pace, understand some Spanish spoken at normal pace, and develop skills and coping strategies for filling in the gaps of imperfect comprehension.
- In terms of speaking, students should be able to ask and answer questions on a variety of everyday topics, describe people and places, narrate recurring (present) events, and achieve some ability in narrating past events.
- Students should be able to perform many daily routines, such as making phone calls, greeting and departing, and so on.
- Students should be able to read almost any simple material, and will have gained some experience in reading materials written for the native-speaking reader.
- The writing skills that students develop will often be the same as the speaking skills, that is, the ability to describe and narrate in the present, and to some extent in the past, and so on.

In addition to gaining these language skills, students who use the *Destinos* materials will gain a wealth of cultural knowledge and awareness about the areas of the world in which Spanish is spoken.

The Student Textbook and Other Student Materials

The Textbook

The Textbook that accompanies the *Destinos* series contains fifty-two lessons, each corresponding to one episode of the series. Episodes 6, 11, 18, 25, 26, 36, and 48–51 are review shows in which characters in the series take stock of what has happened up to that point. In these lessons in the Textbook, students review the story line and other material presented thus far.

With the exception of these review lessons and of Lesson 52 (atypical because it is the last in the series), a typical lesson in the Textbook is divided into five main sections: **Preparación**, **¿Tienes buena memoria?**, **Vocabulario del tema**, **Conversaciones**, and **Un poco de gramática**.

- The purpose of **Preparación** is to refresh students' memory about where the story left off in the last episode and to preview story elements and conversations from the upcoming episode. In this section students make guesses about what might happen, listen to and read some of the conversations that they will see in the upcoming episode, and generally prepare themselves for watching it.
- In **¿Tienes buena memoria?** students are "tested" on what they understand about events and characters from the current episode, and they are encouraged to think about those characters and the situations in which they find themselves. For those using *Destinos* in a classroom setting, the activities in this section may serve as a springboard for continued discussion about the story and characters.
- **Vocabulario del tema** sections usually review and offer opportunities for using vocabulary presented during the episode. At times, these sections also present new vocabulary that ties in with some situation in which the characters are involved. As students work through these sections, they first use the vocabulary to refer to the episode or other people, and they work toward using the vocabulary to talk about themselves and their own lives.
- In many lessons **Conversaciones** sections allow students to listen to and work with everyday conversational tools—for example, how to answer the phone, how to indicate that you don't understand, how to express gratitude, and so on.
- **Un poco de gramática** sections preview a grammatical point that students will learn more about in the Workbook/Study Guides. Each preview usually offers a brief glimpse into a grammatical point, followed immediately by an activity in which students are generally not asked to reproduce the grammatical point but instead to see and understand it in context.

Each lesson continues with a **Nota cultural** that is relevant to the current episode. This is usually a review of and expansion upon some aspect of culture (art, history, social commentary, and so on). In some cases new cultural information is introduced that was not featured in the episode. Everyday cultural information (that is, habits and customs) is featured in briefer **Notas culturales** that occur as needed in each lesson. A reference **Vocabulario** list of active vocabulary for the lesson appears at the end.

The following materials appear at the end of the Textbook:

- an answer section for students to check their answers to many Textbook activities (Appendix 1)
- charts featuring the Spanish verb system (Appendix 2)
- a complete Spanish-English end vocabulary
- a brief reference index of the major characters in the series
- an index of the content of the Textbook.

The Workbook/Study Guides

There are two Workbook/Study Guides for students in the *Destinos* program: Workbook I (Lessons 1–26) and II (Lessons 27–52).

- Most lessons begin with a short reading or listening selection called **Más allá del episodio**. This contains information about characters and situations that goes beyond what appears in the episodes; for example, why some characters act the way they do. In some cases, background information about the story line is presented; for example, how a particular character came to live in a particular place or what was going on at the time another character did something.
- In **Gramática** the Workbook/Study Guides expand on the grammatical and structural features of Spanish previewed in the Textbook, allowing for more in-depth study of Spanish.
- Cognate study (**¡Aumenta tu vocabulario!**) and pronunciation sections (**Pronunciación**) are included in Workbook/Study Guide I. Workbook/Study Guide II features sections on reading authentic materials, called **¡A leer!**, and review sections called **Repaso**.
- Both Workbook/Study Guides have composition sections called **Para escribir**.
- Students may monitor their progress by taking a Self-Test at the end of most lessons.

Some lessons contain **Notas culturales**, as needed, and most lessons end with a **Vocabulario** list of additional active vocabulary that supplements that of the Textbook.

As happens in the Textbook, the Workbook/Study Guide lessons that correspond to review episodes do not follow this repeating format. Rather, they consist of summary and review sections on grammar structures and of review activities that focus on vocabulary, knowledge of the story line, and self-expression.

Students will find the following materials at the end of the Workbook/Study Guides:

- an answer section for students to check their answers to many Workbook/Study Guide activities (Appendix 1)

- charts featuring the Spanish verb system (Appendix 2)
- an index of the content of the Workbook/Study Guides, integrated with that of the Textbook.

A Comment About Methodology

Instructors and students alike will want to take special note of the input-to-output nature of the Textbook and Workbook/Study Guide materials. Students see and hear language used before being asked to produce it. The **Preparación** and **¿Tienes buena memoria?** sections use written and spoken language that students respond to first by checking, marking true/false, selecting the best guess, supplying the name of a character, and so on. Only later in the course are they explicitly asked to talk or write about the episodes and characters in these sections. In the sections that deal with vocabulary and grammar, students first encounter input activities, ones in which the target item is seen or heard in a simple context. After several input activities, they engage in more productive use of the items.

Other Components of the Series

The following materials accompany the television series, student Textbook and Workbook/Study Guides:

For Students:

- an audiocassette program (Part I: Lessons 1–26; Part II: Lessons 27–52) designed to be used with the Textbook and Workbook/Study Guides (Reel-to-reel tapes are available upon request.)
- an optional software program (for IBM and Macintosh) by John Underwood (Western Washington University), featuring comprehension, vocabulary, and grammar activities that supplement those in the Textbook and Workbook/Study Guides
- professional supplements (medical, legal, education, social services, business, tourism) by Ralph Kite and Deni Heyck (Loyola University of Chicago), with accompanying cassette programs, for those wishing to learn Spanish for use in professional settings.

For Faculty:

- a Faculty Guide (with a Telecourse Guide insert) that offers, among other things, general suggestions for using the series, lesson-by-lesson suggestions and supplementary activities, additional Self-Tests, and sample examinations
- a videoscript (of the series episodes) and an audioscript (of the materials in the audiocassette program)
- video modules (with an accompanying Instructor's Guide) that highlight functional language, vocabulary presentations, and cultural information. (These may be used independently of the series.)

Additional materials may become available throughout the life of the series.

How to Use *Destinos*

In a traditional classroom setting *Destinos* may be used in a number of ways.

- The Textbook and video episodes may both be used in class. For example, the **Preparación** section could be an activity for the whole class, after which the class could view the episode together. On subsequent days the rest of the Textbook could be completed in class. Most of the material in the Workbook/Study Guides could be assigned for homework, with follow-up discussions and selected activities done in class.
- The Textbook only could be used in class. Students could view the episodes at home, in the media center, or in the language laboratory.
- *Destinos* is especially appropriate as a complete telecourse for the distance ("at-home") learner. Students watch each episode and complete all sections of the Textbook and Workbook/Study Guides, as indicated by the Study Guides preceding Lessons 1 and 2 and Lessons 27 and 28.

In all cases it is recommended that students watch each episode from beginning to end, without interruption. Students can replay and review selected segments (for pedagogical purposes, for enjoyment, and so on) once they are familiar with the content of an episode. The Faculty Guide provides more detailed suggestions for using the *Destinos* materials.

Where Else Can *Destinos* Be Used?

The *Destinos* materials can also be used:

- as a complete college-credit television course
- as the foundation for a classroom-based beginning Spanish course at the college level
- as an offering for adult or continuing education students
- as the foundation for a classroom-based first- and second-year Spanish course at the high-school level
- as a supplement to beginning, intermediate, or advanced courses, at all levels of instruction
- as a resource for informal learning
- as training materials for Spanish language classes in business and industry
- as an important addition to library video collections.

Acknowledgments

A project of this magnitude has a life of its own. So many people have helped with the television series and print materials that it is impossible to acknowledge the work and contributions of all of them in detail. Here are some of the highlights.

Members of the Advisory Board, The Annenberg/CPB Project and WGBH

Bill VanPatten, Series Designer
Associate Professor of Spanish
University of Illinois at Urbana-
Champaign

Thalia Dorwick
Publisher, Foreign Languages
McGraw-Hill, Inc.

Trisha R. Dvorak
Director, Language Laboratory and
the Literature, Science, and Arts
Media Center, University of
Michigan

Rose Lee Hayden
Vice President, Eagle Multimedia
Services

Martha Alford Marks
Language Proficiency Testing
Expert

Douglas M. Morgenstern
Senior Lecturer in Spanish, MIT and
Harvard University Extension
School

Eduardo Albert Peniche
Associate Professor of Foreign
Languages
Central Virginia Community
College

Joy Renjilian-Burgy
Coordinator of Language and
Literature Instruction
Wellesley College

Harry L. Rosser
Chairman, Department of Romance
Languages and Literature
Boston College

Carmen Salazar
Chairperson, Department of
Foreign Languages
Los Angeles Valley College

Richard V. Teschner
Professor of Spanish
University of Texas at El Paso

Thomas C. Wilson
Director, Open University of South
Florida

Cultural and Linguistic Consultants, The Annenberg/CPB Project and WGBH

Alejandro Benes
Series Executive Editor

Efraín Barradas
Associate Professor of Spanish
University of Massachusetts

Teresa Almendros Cook
Associate Professor of Spanish
Piedmont Virginia Community
College

Ester Gimbernat de González
Associate Professor of Hispanic
Studies
University of Northern Colorado

Samuel Saldívar
Professor of Spanish
United States Military Academy

Cultural and Linguistic Consultants, McGraw-Hill

Eduardo Cabrera
Laura Chastain

María José Ruiz Morcillo

The authors of *Destinos* would also like to extend special thanks to the following individuals and organizations:

- The Annenberg/CPB Project (Washington, D.C.), especially to Lin Foa and Lynn Smith, for financial and creative support of the television series on which this Textbook is based
- WGBH Boston and to Michele Korf, Beth Kirsch, and Betsy Ryles, for their guidance and support at different stages of the project's development, and especially to Michele, for always being there
- The staff at Creative Television Associates (Boston), especially Fred Barzyk, Al Potter, Olivia Tappan, and Erin Delaney, as well as the film and sound editors (Ricardo Camacho, Christian Picker, Miguel Picker, and Jean Boucicaut), for the role they all played in bringing the series to you; special thanks to Olivia, for being our on-location photographer, and to Erin, for providing living proof that an input-based approach really does work!
- Trisha R. Dvorak (University of Michigan), whose perceptive comments on manuscript for the print materials were instrumental in keeping them on course
- Alex Binkowski, for his work on the **¡A leer!** sections that appear in the Workbook/Study Guide II.
- Michèle Sarner and Ralph Kite, for their help with aspects of the original manuscript for the print materials
- María José Ruiz Morcillo, for her work on the **Más allá del episodio** sections of most lessons
- The editorial and production staff and associates at McGraw-Hill, especially Sharla Volkersz, Kathy Melee, Heidi Clausen, Lesley Walsh, Richard Mason, Diane Baccianini, Eileen Burke, Francis Owens, Fred Martich, Juan Vargas, Edie Williams, Charlotte Jackson, Kathy Kirk, and others, for their patience with a project that was complex beyond belief
- Seib Adams, June Smith, Eirik Børve, and Tim Stookesberry, also of McGraw-Hill, for their support of this project from the very beginning and for helping to create the "space" in which it happened.

Last but not least, a very special thank you to Liliana Abud ("Raquel"), whose professional skill as an actress and generosity as a human being helped to keep us going during long working days on the set and at the computer.

Destinos
An Introduction to Spanish

Episodes 1-26

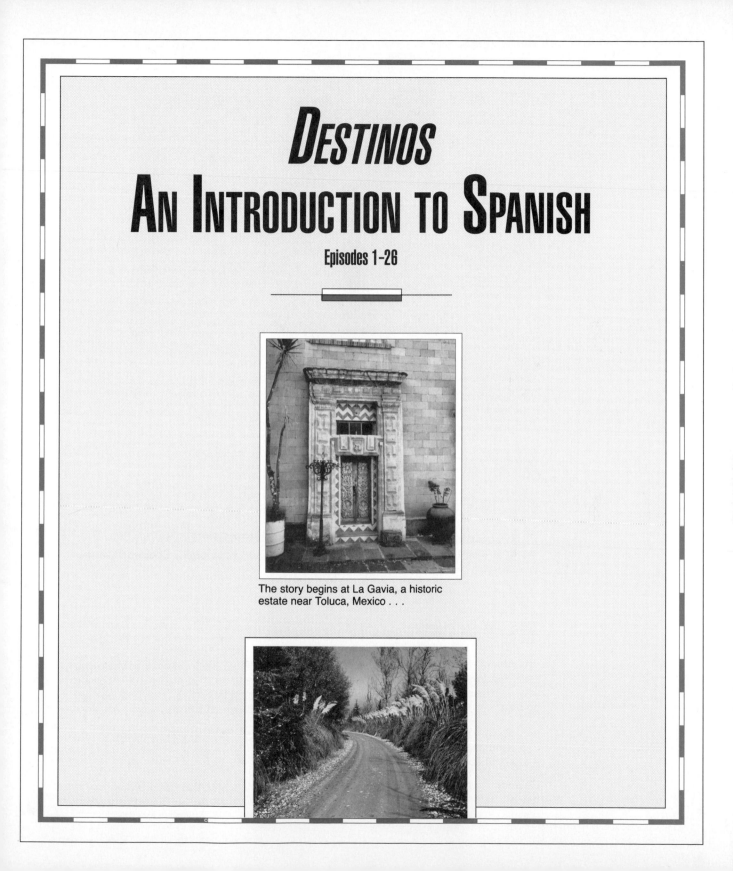

The story begins at La Gavia, a historic
estate near Toluca, Mexico . . .

STUDY GUIDE

LECCIÓN

Follow these simple steps as you work your way through **Lección 1** in the materials that accompany *Destinos*: the Textbook and the Workbook.

STEP 1   USING THE TEXTBOOK

BEFORE VIEWING . . .

Be sure to complete the preview section (called **Preparación**) in **Lección 1** before viewing **Episodio 1** (the video segment that corresponds to **Lección 1**). Check off the preview section here after you have completed it.

_____ **Preparación**

AFTER VIEWING . . .

The rest of the materials in **Lección 1** of the Textbook and the Workbook will help you better understand the video episode you have just seen and take you beyond it, giving you additional information about places and characters in the series. The Textbook will also help you to develop skill in using the Spanish language. In this lesson you will learn

- about cognates (words that look alike in English and Spanish and mean the same thing)
- about some simple Spanish verb forms.

Be sure to work through all parts of the lesson. When you see a cassette symbol in the margin, listen to the tape for **Lección 1**. Answers or hints for many activities are given in Appendix 1. Be sure to check your answers for each activity before going on to the next one.

Check off the following sections of the lesson here as you complete them.

_____ **¿Tienes buena memoria?**   _____ **Un poco de gramática**
_____ **Vocabulario del tema**

Now scan the words in the **Vocabulario** list to be sure that you understand the meaning of most of them.

· ·
STEP 2   USING THE WORKBOOK

Now turn to the Workbook and complete all the activities for **Lección 1**. Whereas the materials in the Textbook all had to do with the video episode, the materials in the Workbook will help you expand your knowledge of the Spanish language in general, as well as give you opportunities for self-expression in Spanish. In this lesson you will learn

- more about **ser** (one Spanish verb that means *to be*)
- more about cognates (how to pronounce them) and about false cognates.

Remember to listen to the tape for **Lección 1** when you see the cassette symbol, and to check your answers in Appendix 1.

Check off the following sections of the lesson here as you complete them.

_____ **Más allá del episodio**   _____ **Pronunciación**
_____ **Gramática**   _____ **¡Aumenta tu vocabulario!**

Now scan the words in the **Vocabulario** list to be sure that you understand the meaning of most of them.

· ·
STEP 3   WRAPPING THINGS UP

Now that you have worked through Steps 1–2, here are some of the things you have accomplished in Spanish.

- You can recognize many cognates, and you are aware that not every Spanish word that looks like an English word has exactly the same meaning.
- You know some basic information about one Spanish verb, **ser**.
- You have listened to, seen, and understood some spoken and written Spanish—in the video episode and on the cassette tape—and you have a sense of how much you are expected to understand when working with the *Destinos* materials.

After you have followed these steps in working your way through **Lección 1**, you will be ready to continue on with **Lección 2** in the Textbook.

1

LA CARTA*

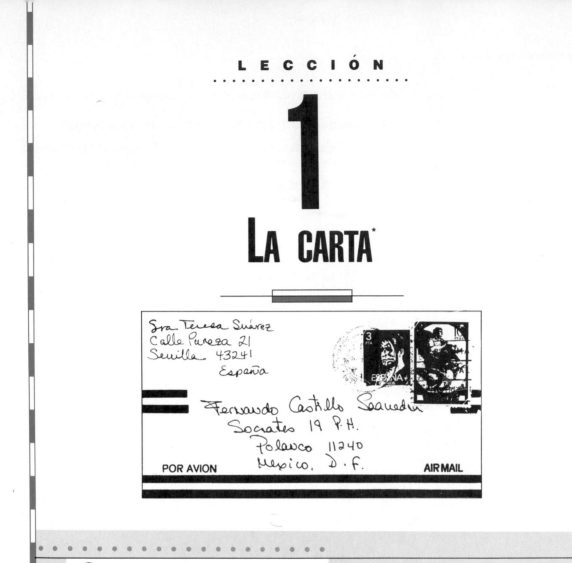

Sra. Teresa Suárez
Calle Pureza 21
Sevilla 43241
    España

Fernando Castillo Saavedra
Socrates 19 P. H.
  Polanco 11240
  Mexico. D. F.

POR AVION   AIR MAIL

OBJETIVOS

The materials in **Lección 1** of the Textbook and the Workbook will help you better under-stand the video episode and take you beyond it, giving you additional information about places and characters in the series. The Textbook will also help you to develop skill in using the Spanish language. In this lesson you will learn

- about cognates (words that look alike in English and Spanish and mean the same thing)
- about some simple Spanish verb forms.

Be sure to work through all parts of the lesson. When you see a cassette symbol in the margin, listen to the tape for **Lección 1**. Answers or hints for many activities are given in Appendix 1. Be sure to check your answers for each activity before going on to the next one.

* *The Letter*

BEFORE VIEWING . . .

Be sure to complete the preview section (called **Preparación**) in **Lección 1** before viewing **Episodio 1** (the video segment that corresponds to **Lección 1**).

PREPARACIÓN

You are about to watch **Episodio 1** from *Destinos*. At times you will hear narration in English that will explain things and help you follow along, and you will also hear a lot of Spanish. Even though you probably have never studied Spanish before, you will be able to understand much of what you hear because several kinds of Spanish are used. There is

- Spanish spoken directly to you by the narrator, which you will learn to understand with relative ease
- Spanish spoken directly to you by a special character, who will review the highlights of the video episode for you at the end of each show
- Spanish spoken by the characters to one another, which at first will be more difficult for you to understand.

As you watch the video episodes, especially at the beginning of the series, you should focus in particular on the Spanish spoken to you by the narrator and the special character. Just relax and listen, and you'll be surprised by how much you can understand. As for the Spanish spoken by the characters to each other, just try to get the gist (general idea) of it. As you continue with the series, you will find yourself understanding more and more of that type of Spanish.

Throughout the Textbook, the **Preparación** section is intended to start you thinking about the program and speculating about what may happen in the next video episode. So now, even before you watch the first episode, take a few moments to speculate about what it may be about. Look at the cover of this Textbook, at the opening page of the main text (on page 1), and at the **Lección 1** opening page (with its titles and visual material). Think about what the series title, *Destinos*, might mean. If you guessed either *destinies* or *destinations*, you were right. The title of the series is a play on both words. Now complete the following activities.

Actividad A.
Where do you think the first episode of *Destinos* will take place?

1. _____ in the United States
2. _____ in Argentina
3. _____ in Mexico
4. _____ in Spain

Actividad B.

What do you think the principal setting will be?

1. _____ a restaurant   3. _____ a university campus
2. _____ a hacienda (an estate)   4. _____ a hotel

Actividad C.

What do you think will set the story in motion?

1. _____ a letter   3. _____ a telegram
2. _____ a telephone call   4. _____ a crime

When you have finished watching **Episodio 1**, come back and see how accurate your first guesses were. Read through the activities again at that time and change your answers if you wish. Then check your answers in Appendix 1.

 AFTER VIEWING . . .

¿TIENES BUENA MEMORIA?

In this repeating section of the Textbook you will review important information from the episode that you have just watched.

Actividad A.   ¿Quiénes son? (*Who are they?*)

Now that you have watched **Episodio 1** of *Destinos*, look at the following photos and match them with the brief descriptions. As you do this activity, you will be reading brief, relatively easy sentences in Spanish. You should guess at the meaning of words you don't immediately understand.

a.

b.

c.

1. _____ Raquel es abogada. Vive (*She lives*) en Los Ángeles.
2. _____ Fernando es el paciente de Julio, el médico.
3. _____ Es una persona muy misteriosa.

Actividad B.   ¿Quién es don Fernando? (*Who is don Fernando?*)

The word **don** is a title of respect used with a man's first name. Which of the following statements describe don Fernando? Indicate **sí** or **no**, according to what you now know about the character.

	SÍ	NO	
1.	_____	_____	Es profesor de literatura.
2.	_____	_____	Es miembro de la familia Castillo Saavedra.
3.	_____	_____	Necesita (*He needs*) un doctor.
4.	_____	_____	Vive en La Gavia, una hacienda.
5.	_____	_____	Tiene (*He has*) una carta importante.

In statement 2 (and at various points in **Episodio 1**), did you notice that the full name of don Fernando's family has two words? You will learn more about this aspect of Hispanic names in **Lección 3**.

Actividad C.   ¡Un desafío! (*A challenge!*)

Raquel's story review at the end of **Episodio 1** contains a lot of information about the characters in *Destinos*. You will have the opportunity to hear and review this information again in upcoming episodes. For now, just focus on Raquel.

Listen again as Raquel describes herself. Then complete the sentences based on what you know about her.

1. _____ El nombre (*name*) completo de Raquel es
   a.   Raquel Gómez   b.   Raquel Rodríguez
2. _____ Raquel es
   a.   cubanoamericana   b.   mexicoamericana
3. _____ Raquel vive en
   a.   Los Ángeles   b.   Miami

Check your answers by listening to the cassette tape.

• •

VOCABULARIO DEL TEMA

This repeating section of the Textbook generally focuses on families of words explicitly presented in the video episode. However, since the concept of cognates is so important for your success in working with the *Destinos* materials, it is the topic of this first **Vocabulario del tema** section.

Los cognados

As you have already noticed both from the video episode and the Textbook, you can understand much of the Spanish you have heard because there are many words that are similar in Spanish and English. These words, called *cognates*, look—and often sound—alike in both languages.

Sometimes cognates exist because one language has "borrowed" words from the other. English has acquired many words from Spanish, such as *patio*, *rodeo*, *canyon*, and so on. Likewise, Spanish has acquired words from English: **automóvil**, **computadora**, **radio**, . . .

Other cognates exist because English and Spanish are both Indo-European languages. You have already guessed the meaning of **destinos**, the Spanish cognate of English *destinies* or *destinations*. You will practice this type of guessing constantly as you work with the video and text materials for *Destinos*. This strategy involves *inferring* the meaning of words from context (the words that surround the "guess" word). Another useful strategy is to simply *skip* over words you do not understand.

Actividad.   Más cognados

Some of the important words you have heard and used so far in **Lección 1** are cognates, and some are not. This activity will give you practice using both cognates and noncognate words.

Read the following sentences about **Episodio 1**. Then indicate which category the highlighted words belong to.

a.   Es un lugar (*place*).
b.   Es un concepto.
c.   Es una cosa (*thing*).
d.   Es una persona.

> MODELO: La Gavia es **una hacienda**. →
>   a.   (**una hacienda**) Es un lugar.

1. _____ La Gavia tiene **una historia** muy importante.
2. _____ Don Fernando es **el patriarca** de la familia Castillo Saavedra.
3. _____ Raquel es **abogada**.
4. _____ Raquel es **mujer**. Mercedes es **mujer** también.
5. _____ Don Fernando es **hombre**. Ramón es **hombre** también.
6. _____ Don Fernando tiene **una carta**.
7. _____ En la carta hay (*there is*) **un secreto**.

• •

UN POCO DE GRAMÁTICA

This repeating section of the Textbook presents information about Spanish grammar in an easy-to-understand fashion that you can put to use immediately to talk about the video episode, yourself, and others.

Expressing *is* and *are*

In this lesson you have heard and seen the Spanish equivalents of English *is* and *are*: **es** and **son**. Here are some examples of their use in context.

Mi historia **es** muy importante para la familia Castillo.	*My story is very important for the Castillo family.*
Juan **es** profesor de literatura.	*Juan is a literature professor.*
Dos personas en esta historia **son** importantes.	*Two people in this story are important.*

Actividad.   La familia Castillo

In **Episodio 1** you have heard the names of many people and places associated with the Castillo family. You will become increasingly familiar with them as you continue to watch episodes of *Destinos*. This activity is a first step in that process.

Identify the following people and places in as many ways as you can, using **es** or **son** and the phrases below. Several answers are possible for each item. Be alert to **-s** endings, which often signal plurality (more than one) in Spanish, just as in English.

MODELO: Raquel... abogada → Raquel **es** abogada.

1. Raquel
2. don Fernando
3. La Gavia

4. Raquel y Mercedes
5. Juan y Ramón

un lugar importante
una hacienda en México
un lugar histórico
mujeres hispanas
hombres mexicanos
de (*from*) los Estados Unidos
de México
de España

el patriarca de la familia
abogada
mexicoamericana
paciente de Julio (el doctor)
hijos (*sons*) de don Fernando
lugares en La Gavia
personas importantes en la
   historia

Have you completed the following sections of the lesson? Check them off here.

_____ **Preparación**   _____ **Vocabulario del tema**
_____ **¿Tienes buena memoria?**   _____ **Un poco de gramática**

   Now scan the words in the **Vocabulario** list to be sure that you understand the meaning of most of them. Then you will be ready to continue on with **Lección 1** in the Workbook.

VOCABULARIO

Note: This is a reference list of some words that appear frequently in **Lección 1** in the Textbook, and that are important for understanding and discussing the lesson. Be sure that you understand the meaning of most of them. Don't feel that you have to be able to use all of them right now. You will continue to work with them in upcoming lessons.

Las personas (People)

la abogada	lawyer
el doctor	doctor
el hombre	man
la mujer	woman
el patriarca	patriarch, male head of the family

Los lugares (Places)

| la hacienda | estate, hacienda |

Las cosas (Things)

| la carta | letter |

Los conceptos (Concepts)

| la historia | story; history |

Los verbos (Verbs)

es	is
son	are
tiene	he/she has
vive	he/she lives

Las palabras adicionales
   (Additional Words)

¿quién?	who?
de	of; from
en	in
muy	very
no	no
para	for
sí	yes
también	also
y	and

Palabras del texto

Note: These words are used in headings in the Textbook and in the structure of the *Destinos* materials. Be sure that you understand their meaning.

la actividad	activity	la lección	lesson	buena	a good
el desafío	challenge	el modelo	model	memoria	memory
el episodio	episode	el objetivo	objective	cierto/falso	true/false
la gramática	grammar	la preparación	preparation	¿tienes... ?	do you have . . . ?
el idioma	(Spanish)	el tema	theme, topic	un poco de...	a bit of . . .
(español)	language	el vocabulario	vocabulary		

LECCIÓN

Follow these simple steps as you work your way through **Lección 2** in the materials that accompany *Destinos*: the Textbook and the Workbook.

STEP 1   USING THE TEXTBOOK

BEFORE VIEWING . . .

Be sure to complete the preview section (called **Preparación**) in **Lección 2** before viewing **Episodio 2** (the video segment that corresponds to **Lección 2**). Check off the preview section here after you have completed it.

_____ **Preparación**

AFTER VIEWING . . .

The rest of the materials in **Lección 2** of the Textbook and the Workbook will help you better understand the video episode you have just seen and take you beyond it, giving you additional information about places and characters in the series. The Textbook will also help you to develop skill in using the Spanish language. In this lesson you will learn

- vocabulary to express family relationships
- greetings to people in Spanish
- ways to express possession (what belongs to you).

You will also learn information about Hispanic families and about the Spanish Civil War.

Be sure to work through all parts of the lesson. When you see a cassette symbol in the margin, listen to the tape for **Lección 2**. Answers or hints for many activities are given in Appendix 1. Be sure to check your answers for each activity before going on to the next one.

Check off the following sections of the lesson here as you complete them.

_____ **¿Tienes buena memoria?**   _____ **Conversaciones**
_____ **Vocabulario del tema**   _____ **Un poco de gramática**

Now scan the words in the **Vocabulario** list to be sure that you understand the meaning of most of them.

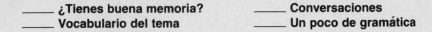

STEP 2   USING THE WORKBOOK

Now turn to the Workbook and complete all the activities for **Lección 2**. Whereas the materials in the Textbook all had to do with the video episode, the materials in the Workbook will help you expand your knowledge of the Spanish language in general, as well as give you opportunities for self-expression in Spanish. In this lesson you will learn

- how to express *a/an* and *the* in Spanish
- about the system of gender of Spanish nouns
- more about expressing possession
- how to pronounce the letters of the Spanish alphabet
- more about cognates.

Remember to listen to the tape for **Lección 2** when you see the cassette symbol, and to check your answers in Appendix 1.

Check off the following sections of the lesson here as you complete them.

_____ **Más allá del episodio**   _____ **Pronunciación**
_____ **Gramática**   _____ **¡Aumenta tu vocabulario!**

Now scan the words in the **Vocabulario** list to be sure that you understand the meaning of most of them.

STEP 3   TAKING THE SELF-TEST

Now that you have completed the Textbook and Workbook for **Lecciones 1** and **2**, take the Self-Test for those lessons. Remember to use the tape when you see the cassette symbol and to check your answers.

_____ **Self-Test**

• •

STEP 4   WRAPPING THINGS UP

Now that you have worked through Steps 1–3, here are some of the things you have accomplished in Spanish.

- You can use some basic greetings in Spanish.
- You can now talk simply about your own family and the families of others.
- You can give definite and indefinite articles for a variety of nouns, as well as their plural forms, and you know that all nouns in Spanish are either masculine or feminine.
- You know about several ways to express possession.
- You are familiar with the Spanish alphabet.
- You can recognize more common cognates.
- You have continued to work on listening skills with the video episode and the cassette tape, and you are comfortable focusing on what you do understand even when you don't comprehend every word.

After you have followed these steps in working your way through **Lección 2**, you will be ready to continue on with **Lección 3** in the Textbook.

LECCIÓN

2

EL SECRETO*

OBJETIVOS

The materials in **Lección 2** of the Textbook and the Workbook will help you better understand the video episode and take you beyond it, giving you additional information about places and characters in the series. The Textbook will also help you to develop skill in using the Spanish language. In this lesson you will learn

- vocabulary to express family relationships
- greetings to people in Spanish
- ways to express possession (what belongs to you).

You will also learn information about Hispanic families and about the Spanish Civil War.
    Be sure to work through all parts of the lesson. When you see a cassette symbol in the margin, listen to the tape for **Lección 2**. Answers or hints for many activities are given in Appendix 1. Be sure to check your answers for each activity before going on to the next one.

* *The Secret*

▬▬ **BEFORE VIEWING . . .**

Be sure to complete the preview section (called **Preparación**) in **Lección 2** before viewing **Episodio 2** (the video segment that corresponds to **Lección 2**).

Preparación

As you prepare to watch **Episodio 2** from *Destinos*, remember the three kinds
of Spanish you will hear: Spanish spoken directly to you by the narrator, Spanish
spoken to you by Raquel, and the Spanish that the characters speak to each
other. As you continue with the program, you will find that you understand
more and more of all three kinds of Spanish.

Actividad A.

At the end of **Episodio 1**, you saw don Fernando crush a letter in his hand.
Answer the following questions about the letter. As you read the questions, re-
member what you know about don Fernando and try to make logical guesses.
There are no right or wrong answers so far.

1. ¿De dónde (*From where*) es la carta?
    _____ de España
    _____ de los Estados Unidos
    _____ de la Argentina
    _____ de otra (*another*) parte de México

2. El narrador dice (*says*): «Don Fernando tiene un secreto importante. El
    secreto está en una carta... una carta importante.» ¿Cuál (*What*) es el se-
    creto de la carta? (¡OJO! tiene que ver con = *has to do with*)

    _____ El secreto tiene que ver con la vida privada (*personal life*) de don
          Fernando.
    _____ El secreto tiene que ver con asuntos legales (*legal matters*).
    _____ El secreto tiene que ver con la compañía de don Fernando.

Actividad B.

During **Episodio 1**, don Fernando says to Ramón, "Llama a tus hermanos. Y a tu
tío Pedro." If **llamar** means *to call*, can you guess who Ramón will be calling in
this episode?

Ramón va a llamar (*is going to call*)
_____ a otros médicos   _____ a una abogada
_____ a unos amigos   _____ a otras personas de la familia

When you have finished watching **Episodio 2**, come back and see how accurate your first guesses were. Read through Activities A and B again at that time and change your answers if you wish. Then check your answers in Appendix 1.

Actividad C.

Listen to the following phone call that Ramón will make to his brother Carlos during **Episodio 2**. Knowing that **Hoy vino...** means that someone *came to-day*, can you guess what Ramón is telling Carlos? (*Hint*: Remember what you saw in **Episodio 1**.)

Ramón le dice a Carlos que (*that*)

a. _____ hoy vino una abogada

b. _____ hoy vino el médico para ver (*to see*) a don Fernando

c. _____ hoy vino Juan

Listen to the conversation again. Knowing that **¿Puedes...?** means *Can you...?*, what do you think that Ramón is asking Carlos to do? What does Carlos answer?

Ramón desea que Carlos venga a (*come to*)

a. _____ un hospital

b. _____ la hacienda

c. _____ Los Ángeles

Carlos dice que _____ sí _____ no.

━━━▭━━ **AFTER VIEWING . . .**

· ·

¿TIENES BUENA MEMORIA?

Actividad A.   La familia de don Fernando

Today you met all of the known relatives in don Fernando's immediate family, plus a few other people. Review what you know about them by matching the people on the left with their descriptions on the right. Don't be discouraged if you can't get all of the items correct this time. You will be working with the same characters throughout the whole series. This is only your first chance to practice their names.

1. _____ Ramón   a. hijo de don Fernando; director de una compañía
2. _____ Pedro   b. esposa de don Fernando y madre de sus cuatro
3. _____ Juan   (4) hijos
4. _____ Carlos   c. hija de don Fernando; vive en La Gavia
5. _____ Mercedes   d. la esposa secreta de don Fernando
6. _____ Rosario   e. hijo de don Fernando; vive en La Gavia
7. _____ Carmen   f. hermano de don Fernando; profesor en México
                        g. hijo de don Fernando; profesor en Nueva York

¡Un desafío! ¿Tienes una memoria muy buena?

1. _____ Gloria   a. médico de la familia
2. _____ Pati   b. esposa de Carlos
3. _____ Consuelo   c. esposa de Juan
4. _____ Lupe   d. cocinera (*cook*)
5. _____ Maricarmen   e. hija de Consuelo y Ramón
6. _____ Julio   f. secretaria de Carlos
7. _____ Ofelia   g. antigua (*former*) estudiante de Pedro
8. _____ Raquel   h. esposa de Ramón

Check your answers by listening to the cassette tape.

Actividad B.   ¿Dónde vive?

Not all of the characters live and work with don Fernando. Complete each statement by indicating where each person lives and what he or she does for a living.

Los lugares: la Ciudad de México, La Gavia, Los Ángeles, Miami, Nueva York

Las profesiones: Es director de la Compañía Castillo Saavedra, S.A.*
                  Es administrador/administradora de la hacienda.
                  Es profesor de literatura en la universidad.
                  Es profesor de derecho (*law*) en la universidad.
                  Es abogada de derecho internacional.

MODELO: Carlos vive en _____ . Es _____ . →
           Carlos vive en Miami. Es director de la Compañía Castillo
           Saavedra, S.A.

1. Carlos vive en _____ . Es _____ .

2. Ramón vive en _____ . Es _____ .

———————————————————
*Castillo Saavedra, S.A. es la compañía de don Fernando. S.A. (Sociedad Anónima) significa *Inc.* en inglés.

3.　Mercedes vive en _____ . Es _____ .

4.　Juan vive en _____ . Es _____ .

5.　Pedro vive en _____ . Es _____ .

6.　Raquel vive en _____ . Es _____ .

Actividad C.　El secreto

At the family conference called by don Fernando, the patriarch revealed the information contained in the letter he received from Spain. Which of the following possibilities does he suggest? ¡OJO! There may be more than one right answer.

_____ Don Fernando tiene otra hacienda.
_____ Don Fernando tiene otra esposa.
_____ Don Fernando tiene otro hermano.
_____ Don Fernando tiene otro hijo.

Nota cultural: Las familias hispánicas

It is more typical of Hispanic families for many members of the extended family (all of the relatives, not just the immediate family) to live under the same roof. Widowed grandparents and unmarried aunts and uncles, in particular, may stay in the family home. Unmarried children tend to live with their parents much longer, in some cases for their whole lives. As is the case with Ramón, even married family members may still live under the same roof as their parents. This custom is changing somewhat in modern Hispanic society, especially in urban areas.

Regardless of whether it is a cause or a result of these living arrangements, there is a certain closeness in Hispanic families. How does this compare with *your* own experience?

VOCABULARIO DEL TEMA

This repeating section of the Textbook presents groups of vocabulary words presented in the video episode. Sometimes additional words—vocabulary from the same family or a new group of words—are presented only in the Textbook. Vocabulary lists presented in this section are always included on the cassette tape.

Los miembros de la familia	
los padres	parents
el padre/la madre	father/mother
los hijos	children
el hijo/la hija	son/daughter
los hermanos	brothers and sisters
el hermano/la hermana	brother/sister
los tíos	uncles and aunts
el tío/la tía	uncle/aunt
los esposos	husband and wife, spouses
el esposo/la esposa	husband/wife

Actividad A. ¿Cuál (*Which*) es mi familia?

Listen as the speakers on the cassette tape describe their family tree. Then select the drawing that best matches the description you heard. Look at the drawings in each group before you listen to the description.

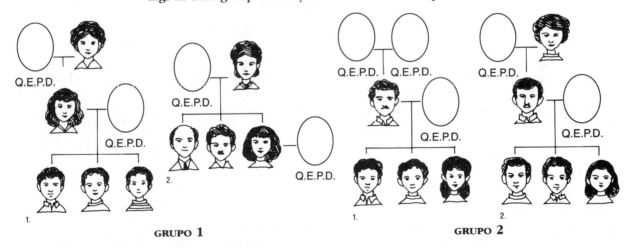

GRUPO 1   GRUPO 2

Actividad B. La familia de don Fernando

The following illustration represents two generations of the Castillo family. Work from top to bottom and from left to right. You will be indicating relationships among members of the same generation *and* between generations.

---

*Q.E.P.D. = Que en paz descanse (*May he/she rest in peace*)

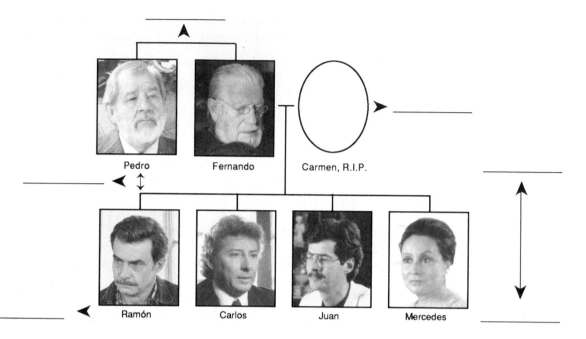

Pedro   Fernando   Carmen, R.I.P.

Ramón   Carlos   Juan   Mercedes

Actividad C.   ¿Quién es?

Look at the following photographs. The speaker on the cassette tape will ask you to identify each person by number. State that person's relationship to some-one else, referring back to the preceding photographs if necessary. You will then hear a factually correct statement on the tape. In some cases, more than one relationship is possible.

MODELO: (*you hear*)—¿Quién es la persona de la foto número uno?
(*you say*) —Es Juan, hijo de don Fernando.
(*you hear*)—Es Juan, hijo de don Fernando y hermano de Mercedes, Ramón y Carlos.

1 (uno)   2 (dos)   3 (tres)   4 (cuatro)

. . . .

CONVERSACIONES: LOS SALUDOS

This repeating section of the Textbook focuses on language useful for conversational exchanges with others: meeting and greeting people in Spanish, asking for directions, and so on.

 ## PASO (*STEP*) 1

In the video episode you saw and heard many people greet each other at different times of the day and under different social circumstances. It is important to know when different greetings are appropriate. You will learn many other ways to greet people in later lessons, and the Textbook and Workbook for *Destinos* will repeat the greetings you have heard in this episode, letting you listen to them again and use them.

Hola.	Hello (*used in almost any situation, but not usually to answer the phone*).
Buenos días.	Good morning.
Buenas tardes.	Good afternoon.
Buenas noches.	Good evening.

PASO 2

Here are three situations in which people will greet each other. Which greetings do you think they will use?

PASO 3

  Now listen to the brief greetings and find out whether you were right. How many different greetings did you hear in each conversation?

UN POCO DE GRAMÁTICA

Expressing Possession

In this lesson, you have heard and seen the possessive construction **de** + name.

la familia **de** Fernando	*Fernando's family*
la esposa **de** Ramón	*Ramón's wife*

You have also seen and heard the possessive adjectives **su** and **sus.** Note their multiple meanings in these phrases.

su padre	*his/her/their father*
sus hermanos	*his/her/their brothers*

Don't worry if you're confused about how to distinguish the meanings of these words. As with cognates, the context (surrounding information) will make the meaning of **su** and **sus** (and words like them) clear.

Actividad.   Parentescos (*Relationships*) famosos

Can you answer each of the following questions about famous relationships? Test your knowledge of the lives of famous people. As you do this activity, you may learn some things about the individuals mentioned.

¡OJO! Unos son fáciles (*easy*), otros son muy difíciles...

Before you begin, note the following information: **¿Quiénes?** is the plural form of **¿Quién? Fue** and **fueron** are the past tense forms of **es** and **son**, respectively.

FÁCILES

1. Rose Kennedy. ¿Quiénes fueron sus hijos? Fueron dos políticos muy importantes en la década de los 60 (sesenta).
2. Paloma Picasso. ¿Quién fue su padre, pintor muy famoso?
3. Caín y Abel. ¿Quién fue su madre?
4. John Kennedy, Jr. ¿Quién es su tío, senador demócrata de Massachusetts?
5. Franklin D. Roosevelt. ¿Quién fue su esposa, también muy activa en causas sociales?
6. Hansel. ¿Quién fue su hermana?
7. LaToya y Janet Jackson. ¿Quién es su hermano, cantante muy famoso?

UN POCO DIFÍCILES

8. Jane Fonda. ¿Quién es su hermano, también actor? ¿Quién fue su padre, un actor muy famoso?
9. Penélope. ¿Quién fue su esposo, héroe de la Guerra de Troya?
10. Rómulo. ¿Quién fue su hermano gemelo (*twin*), fundador de Roma?
11. Enrique VIII (octavo) de Inglaterra. ¿Quién fue su hija, una de las monarcas más importantes de Inglaterra?
12. Elizabeth Taylor. ¿Quién fue su quinto (*fifth*) esposo, actor ya muerto?
13. Martin Sheen. ¿Quiénes son sus dos hijos, también actores?

DIFÍCILES

14. Shirley MacLaine. ¿Quién es su hermano, actor y director de cine?
15. El príncipe Philip. ¿Quiénes son sus cuatro hijos?
16. Los señores Borden. ¿Quién fue su hija, una asesina notoria?
17. Isabella Rosellini. ¿Quién fue su madre, actriz muy famosa?

Nota cultural: La Guerra Civil española

As you know, don Fernando fought in the Spanish Civil War and left Spain soon after it ended. Look over the following information about this violent period in Spanish history. Remember to guess the meaning of as many words as possible.

La Guerra Civil española

¿Cuándo ocurre?
de 1936 a 1939

¿Quiénes son los adversarios?

Los republicanos contra los nacionales. La mayoría[1] de los republicanos eran[2] demócratas y los nacionales eran aliados de Hitler y Mussolini. El general

[1] *majority* [2] *were*

Francisco Franco era el líder de los nacionales. Se convirtió[3] en dictador de España después del[4] triunfo de los nacionales en 1939.

Acontecimientos[5] importantes

La Segunda República (1931–1936)
La rebelión de Franco (el 18 de julio de 1936)
El asesinato en Granada del poeta y dramaturgo Federico García Lorca (1936)
El bombardeo de Guernica (1937)
Fin de la Guerra Civil (el 1º de abril de 1939)

[3]Se... *He became*   [4]después... *after the*   [5]*Events*

Guernica de Pablo Picasso (en el Prado, Madrid)

Actividad.   ¿Y don Fernando?

Make predictions about don Fernando's life based on the information in the **Nota cultural**.

1.   On which side in the Spanish Civil War did Fernando probably fight?
2.   In what year did Fernando and Rosario probably become separated?
3.   When did Fernando probably leave Spain?

Have you completed the following sections of the lesson? Check them off here.

_____ **Preparación**   _____ **Conversaciones**
_____ **¿Tienes buena memoria?**   _____ **Un poco de gramática**
_____ **Vocabulario del tema**

Now scan the words in the **Vocabulario** list to be sure that you understand the meaning of most of them. Then you will be ready to continue on with **Lección 2** in the Workbook.

VOCABULARIO

Los miembros de la familia (Members of the Family)

los esposos	husband and wife, spouses
el esposo/la esposa	husband/wife
los hermanos	brothers and sisters
el hermano/	brother/
la hermana	sister
los hijos	children
el hijo/la hija	son/daughter
los padres	parents
el padre/la madre	father/mother
los tíos	uncles and aunts
el tío/la tía	uncle/aunt

Las personas (People)

el director	head, leader; director
el estudiante	student
el profesor	professor

Los saludos (Greetings)

Hola.	Hello.
Buenos días.	Good morning.
Buenas tardes.	Good afternoon.
Buenas noches.	Good evening.

Los conceptos (Concepts)

la compañía	company (*business*)
el matrimonio	marriage
el secreto	secret

Las palabras adicionales (Additional Words)

¿cuál?	which? what?
otro	other, another
pero	but
que	that
su/sus	his/her/their
ya	already
ya no	no longer
está muerto/muerta	is dead
ya murió	already died

Palabras del texto

la conversación	conversation
el paso	step

Un viaje a Sevilla (España)

La Catedral de Sevilla

FRANCIA

EL OCÉANO ATLÁNTICO

PORTUGAL

ESPAÑA

Madrid

Sevilla

EL MAR MEDITERRÁNEO

ÁFRICA

3

EL COMIENZO*

OBJETIVOS

The materials in **Lección 3** of the Textbook and the Workbook will help you better understand the video episode and take you beyond it, giving you additional information about places and characters in the series. The Textbook will also help you to develop skill in using the Spanish language. In this lesson you will learn

- how to express the Spanish numbers from 0 to 21
- what to say when you meet someone for the first time
- how to talk about what other people are doing.

You will also learn about the country of Spain and about Hispanic last names.

Be sure to work through all parts of the lesson. When you see a cassette symbol in the margin, listen to the tape for **Lección 3**. Answers or hints for many activities are given in Appendix 1. Be sure to check your answers for each activity before going on to the next one.

The Beginning

―――――□――― **BEFORE VIEWING...**

• •

PREPARACIÓN

Actividad A.

In **Episodio 1** of *Destinos* you met Raquel Rodríguez. Indicate whether the following statements about Raquel are **Cierto** (**C**) or **Falso** (**F**).

C   F   1. Raquel es hija de don Fernando.
C   F   2. Es abogada.
C   F   3. Vive y trabaja (*works*) en Los Ángeles.
C   F   4. Es mexicoamericana.
C   F   5. Cree (*She believes*) que Rosario vive en España.

Actividad B.

In **Episodio 2** you learned information about a trip Raquel will take. Because this episode is called **El comienzo**, it is a safe bet that her trip will start in this episode.

Where will Raquel go and for what reason? What information does she already have? ¡OJO! There may be more than one appropriate answer.

1. Raquel va a viajar a (*is going to travel to*)

    _____ España
    _____ la Argentina
    _____ Puerto Rico

2. Raquel va a buscar a (*is going to look for*)

    _____ Rosario, la primera (*first*) esposa de don Fernando
    _____ Carmen, la segunda (*second*) esposa de don Fernando
    _____ la persona que escribió (*wrote*) la carta
    _____ otro hijo de don Fernando

3. Raquel probablemente sabe (*knows*)

    _____ el nombre del hijo de Rosario y don Fernando
    _____ el nombre de la persona que escribió la carta
    _____ el nombre de la calle (*street*) donde la persona vive

Actividad C.

Listen to the following conversation that Raquel will have with the receptionist at her hotel in Spain. **¿Dónde está...?** means *Where is...?* Now that you know that, what does Raquel ask about?

Raquel pregunta (*asks*) dónde está

a. _____ Rosario
b. _____ la calle Pureza
c. _____ el hijo de Rosario y don Fernando

Listen to the conversation again. **¿Está lejos?** means *Is it far away?* Now that you know that, what information does the receptionist give to Raquel?

El recepcionista dice que la calle Pureza

a. _____ está lejos, un poco lejos
b. _____ no está lejos
c. _____ está en el Barrio de Triana (*Triana district*)
d. _____ no está en la ciudad

AFTER VIEWING . . .

• •

¿TIENES BUENA MEMORIA?

Actividad A.   Los nuevos personajes (*New characters*)

In **Episodios 1** and **2** you met the members of the Castillo family. Now you have gotten to know a few more characters. Can you match the names of some of the new characters with their photos?

a. Teresa Suárez
b. Elena Ramírez
c. Miguel Ruiz
d. Roberto, el taxista
e. Raquel Rodríguez

Now match the characters with the statements that describe them or what they do in the video episode. ¡OJO! More than one name may be possible for each statement.

1. _____ Busca a la señora Teresa Suárez.
2. _____ Entra en el Barrio de Triana con Raquel.

3. _____ Entra en la iglesia (*church*) de Santa Ana.
4. _____ Habla (__?__ *talks*) con dos chicos en la calle.
5. _____ Ya no vive en Sevilla.
6. _____ Su madre está en el mercado (*market*).
7. _____ Habla con Raquel en el mercado.
8. _____ Explica la historia de la carta.

Actividad B.   ¿De quién se habla? (*Who is being talked about?*)

Indicate whether the following statements refer to Elena Ramírez (**E**) or to Teresa Suárez (**T**), her mother-in-law (**su suegra**).

E   T   1. Vive en Madrid ahora (*now*).
E   T   2. Tiene dos hijos jóvenes (*young*).
E   T   3. Su hijo tiene esposa y dos hijos.
E   T   4. Está en el mercado cuando llega (*arrives*) Raquel a su barrio.
E   T   5. Es la abuela (*grandmother*) de Miguel y Jaime.

Actividad C.   ¿Cuánto saben? (*How much do they know?*)

Don Fernando's family knew nothing about the existence of Rosario. Based on what you have seen and heard in **Episodio 3**, do the following new characters have any information to give Raquel about the case?

a.   Es posible.
b.   No sabe nada. (*He/She doesn't know anything.*)
c.   Probablemente no sabe nada.

1. _____ Miguel Ruiz   3. _____ el esposo de Elena
2. _____ Elena Ramírez   4. _____ el taxista

Now listen to a brief excerpt from Raquel's conversation with Elena Ramírez and change any answers if necessary.

Nota cultural: Los apellidos hispanos

You have probably noticed in previous lessons that the Castillo family is sometimes called **la familia Castillo Saavedra** and sometimes just **la familia Castillo**. In most Hispanic countries people use two last names (**apellidos**). The first is the name of the father, the second that of the mother. It is correct to call a person by the first of the two names (the name of one's father) or by both names. Thus, both **la familia Castillo** and **la familia Castillo Saavedra** are authentic usages.

Miguel and Jaime, who are the sons of Miguel Ruiz and Elena Ramírez, have the last names **Ruiz Ramírez**. Elena's son, Miguel, is known either as **Miguel Ruiz** or as **Miguel Ruiz Ramírez**. It would not be correct to call him **Miguel Ramírez**.

A married woman can add the preposition **de** before her husband's last name. So **Teresa Suárez** could also be called **Teresa Suárez de Ruiz**. However, in Spain it is very common for a woman to use only her maiden name: **Teresa Suárez**, **Elena Ramírez**. Elena's full married name is **Elena Ramírez de Ruiz**.

VOCABULARIO DEL TEMA

Los números del 0 al 21 *

0 cero		
1 uno	11 once	21 veintiuno
2 dos	12 doce	
3 tres	13 trece	
4 cuatro	14 catorce	
5 cinco	15 quince	
6 seis	16 dieciséis [†]	
7 siete	17 diecisiete	
8 ocho	18 dieciocho	
9 nueve	19 diecinueve	
10 diez	20 veinte	

Uno is the number used in counting. As you know, **un** is used before masculine nouns, **una** before feminine ones. Note how **veintiuno** is used before nouns: **veintiún clientes**, **veintiuna oficinas**.

---

[*] The speaker on the cassette tape pronounces the Spanish letters *c* (before **e** or **i**) and *z* in these numbers the way they are pronounced in most of the Spanish-speaking world. Some of the speakers you have heard in the video episode—Jaime and the hotel clerk, for example—said the numbers with the pronunciation heard in most of Spain.

[†] The numbers 16 through 19 and 21 can be written as one word (as in the list) or as three: **diez y seis**, **diez y siete**, **diez y ocho**, **diez y nueve**, **veinte y uno**.

Actividad A.   ¿Cuál es el número?

You will hear the street numbers of five of the houses on **la calle Pureza**, but you will hear them out of order. Listen and indicate the order in which you hear them by writing the letters **a** through **e** next to the addresses.

_____ 16A   _____ 19A

_____ 17A   _____ 20A

_____ 18A

 ### Actividad B.

You will hear two segments from **Episodio 3** in which numbers play an important role. Listen to each segment, then answer the questions.

1. ¿Cuántos (*How many*) turistas hay en el grupo?
2. ¿Qué número tiene Juan?
3. ¿Qué número busca Raquel?

. . . .

CONVERSACIONES: MÁS SALUDOS

 ### Actividad.   El primer encuentro (*The first meeting*)

On the cassette tape you will hear three brief conversations in which people greet each other for the first time.

Paso 1

Listen to all of the conversations now, then answer the following questions.

1. What does a Spanish speaker say when he or she has just met someone for the first time?

   a. _____ Hola.
   b. _____ Mucho gusto.
   c. _____ ¿Qué tal?

2. What are two responses that the other speaker could make?

   a. _____ Mucho gusto.
   b. _____ Hola.
   c. _____ Igualmente.

Paso 2

Listen to the three taped conversations again. Pay attention to the various ways the speakers tell each other their names.

3. Based on what you have heard in the conversations, which of the following are acceptable ways for Raquel to identify herself?

a. _____ Me llamo Raquel Rodríguez. c. _____ Soy Raquel Rodríguez.

b. _____ Eres Raquel Rodríguez. d. _____ Raquel Rodríguez.

Paso 3

How would you introduce yourself, following one of the previous models?

UN POCO DE GRAMÁTICA

Using Verbs to Talk About Others

In this episode you have heard many verb forms used to tell what characters are doing at the moment. Most present-tense Spanish verbs used to talk about someone other than the speaker end either in **-a** or in **-e**. Note the verbs in this brief description of Raquel.

Raquel viv**e** en Los Ángeles. *Raquel lives in Los Angeles.*
Viaj**a** a España. *She is traveling to Spain.*

When talking about two or more people, an **-n** is added.

Raquel y el taxista preguntan a *Raquel and the taxi driver ask*
dos chicos dónde viven la *two boys where Mrs. Suárez*
señora Suárez y su familia. *and her family live.*

These forms are called *third-person* verbs. You will learn more about them in the Workbook. (Did you notice—in the sentence **Viaja a España**—that the subject of the verb does not have to be used?)

Actividad.   Fotografías

Identify the one sentence that best describes the action or situation you see in each photo.

1. _____ a. Raquel y el taxista trabajan
en la plaza.

_____ b. Raquel y el taxista hablan
en la plaza.

_____ c. Raquel y el taxista viven
en la plaza.

2. ____ a. Raquel tiene un mensaje (*message*).
    ____ b. Raquel escribe un mensaje.
    ____ c. Raquel busca un mensaje.

3. ____ a. El hombre entra en la tienda (*store*).
    ____ b. El hombre trabaja en la tienda.
    ____ c. El hombre escribe en la tienda.

4. ____ a. Toman un taxi para ir (*to go*)
              al barrio de Triana.
    ____ b. Llegan al barrio de Triana.
    ____ c. Hablan en el barrio de Triana.

Nota cultural: España, un país[1] de contrastes

Refresh your memory about the geography of Spain by listening to what the narrator told you at the beginning of **Episodio 3**. Try to associate the place names you hear with this map. Then, when the taped portion is over, continue on with the reading in the Textbook.

[1] nación

España es un país[1] de contrastes. Entre el norte y el sur hay una enorme diferencia. En el norte hay muchas montañas, bosques[2] y centros industriales. En el sur el terreno es más seco[3] y hay menos industria. También hay mucha influencia árabe en el sur, en Andalucía.

Datos[4] importantes

la capital: Madrid
el gobierno:[5] una monarquía constitucional, que preside el rey Juan Carlos I (primero)
la organización política: 17 comunidades autónomas[6]
el idioma[7] oficial: el español
   (el castellano)
otros idiomas: el catalán (Cataluña), el gallego (Galicia), el vascuence (el País Vasco)
la población: 39.000.000 (treinta y nueve millones) de habitantes

[1] nación   [2] *forests*   [3] más... *drier*   [4] Información
[5] *government*   [6] comunidades... regiones
[7] *language*

Los Pirineos, montañas entre Francia y España

Una zona agricultural, cerca de Córdoba

Actividad.   ¿Cuánto sabes (*How much do you know*) de España?

Based on the information provided in the preceding **Nota cultural**, are the following statements **Cierto** (**C**) or **Falso** (**F**)?

C   F   1. España es un país uniforme.
C   F   2. Hay mucha influencia árabe en el sur.
C   F   3. En España se habla sólo español.
C   F   4. Madrid está en el centro de la península.
C   F   5. España es una dictadura.

Have you completed the following sections of the lesson? Check them off here.

_____ **Preparación**   _____ **Conversaciones**
_____ **¿Tienes buena memoria?**   _____ **Un poco de gramática**
_____ **Vocabulario del tema**

   Now scan the words in the **Vocabulario** list to be sure that you understand the meaning of most of them. Then you will be ready to continue on with **Lección 3** in the Workbook.

• •

VOCABULARIO

Los verbos

busca	he/she looks for
cree	he/she believes
entra (en)	he/she enters
escribe	he/she writes
está	he/she is (*located*)
explica	he/she explains
habla	he/she speaks, talks
llega	he/she arrives
necesita	he/she needs
pregunta	he/she asks
tiene	he/she has
toma	he/she takes
trabaja	he/she works
viaja	he/she travels
visita	he/she visits

Las personas

los abuelos	grandparents
el abuelo/	grandfather/
la abuela	grandmother
el amigo/la amiga	friend
el chico/la chica	boy/girl, young kid
el señor (Sr.) *	gentleman, man; Mr.
la señora (Sra.) †	lady, woman; Mrs.
la señorita (Srta.)	young(er) lady, single woman; Miss ‡

Los conceptos

el apellido	last name
el comienzo	beginning
el nombre	(first) name

Los números

cero, uno, dos, tres, cuatro, cinco, seis, siete, ocho, nueve, diez, once, doce, trece, catorce, quince, dieciséis, diecisiete, dieciocho, diecinueve, veinte, veintiuno

Más saludos

me llamo...	my name is . . .
mucho gusto	pleased to meet you
igualmente	so am I (*pleased to meet you*)

Las palabras adicionales

ahora	now
con	with
a	to
al	to the (**a** + **el**) §
del	of the (**de** + **el**) §

---

* Note that the abbreviations for these words are capitalized but that the words themselves are not: **el señor Castillo, el Sr. Castillo**.

† **La señora** is used to refer to a married woman of any age and often to a middle-aged woman (whether or not her marital status is known).

‡ Note that there is no Spanish equivalent for English *Ms*.

§ Only the article **el** contracts with the words **a** and **de** to form the contractions **al** and **del**. Other articles do not contract: **a la iglesia, de los abuelos**.

4

PERDIDO*

· ·

OBJETIVOS

The materials in **Lección 4** of the Textbook and the Workbook will help you better understand the video episode and take you beyond it, giving you additional information about places and characters in the series. The Textbook will also help you to develop skill in using the Spanish language. In this lesson you will learn

- names of courses that you may be taking
- names for common household pets
- introductions of one person to another
- ways to describe in Spanish.

You will also learn about Sevilla and about the educational system in Hispanic countries.

　　　Be sure to work through all parts of the lesson. When you see a cassette symbol in the margin, listen to the tape for **Lección 4**. Answers or hints for many activities are given in Appendix 1. Be sure to check your answers for each activity before going on to the next one.

*Lost

━━━■━━ **BEFORE VIEWING . . .**

PREPARACIÓN

Actividad A.

In the last episode of *Destinos* you followed Raquel to Spain. What do you remember about her trip? Complete the following statements.

1. Raquel está ahora en... Barcelona / Sevilla / Madrid.
2. Tiene una carta escrita por (*written by*)... Teresa Suárez / Pedro Castillo / don Fernando.
3. Busca a... Miguel Ruiz / Elena Ramírez / Teresa Suárez.
4. En la calle, habla primero (*first*) con... dos chicos / dos esposos / dos taxistas.
5. Dicen (*They say*) que la señora Suárez vive ahora en... Barcelona / Málaga / Madrid.
6. Caminan (*They walk*) al mercado y Raquel habla con... Teresa Suárez / Elena Ramírez / Mercedes.
7. Elena es... la madre / la abuela / la hermana ...de los chicos.
8. Elena... tiene / no tiene / también desea ...información sobre (*about*) Rosario.

Actividad B.

What do you think will happen in this episode? Try to predict what will happen by answering the following questions.

1. In **Episodio 3** you learned that Teresa Suárez is currently living in Madrid. Do you think that Raquel will be able to make contact with her? If so, how?

   a. _____ Teresa Suárez no desea hablar con Raquel.
   b. _____ Raquel no habla con Teresa Suárez en este (*this*) episodio.
   c. _____ Raquel habla con Teresa por teléfono.

2. You also learned that Elena Ramírez knows nothing about the letter that señora Suárez wrote to don Fernando. Do you think her husband knows something?

   a. _____ El esposo de Elena no sabe nada (*knows nothing*).
   b. _____ El esposo sabe algo (*knows something*).

 ### Actividad C.

Listen to the following conversation that Raquel will have with Miguel Ruiz, Elena's husband. **Ya hablé** means *I already spoke*. Now that you know that, with whom did Miguel speak and what did he learn?

a. _____ Miguel habló (*spoke*) con Teresa Suárez.
b. _____ Miguel habló con Rosario.
c. _____ Miguel no sabe nada.
d. _____ Miguel sabe algo interesante.

Listen to the conversation again. **Vaya** means *go*. Now that you know that, how will Raquel and Teresa Suárez make contact?

a. _____ La señora Suárez desea hablar con Raquel por teléfono.
b. _____ La señora Suárez desea hablar con Raquel en Sevilla.
c. _____ La señora Suárez desea hablar con Raquel en Madrid.

▬ AFTER VIEWING . . .

· ·

¿TIENES BUENA MEMORIA?

Actividad A.   En este episodio

All of the following events took place during the two days shown in **Episodio** 4, but . . . in what order did they occur? Put them in order, from 1 to 3 or 4 in each group.

Por la noche (*In the evening*)

a. _____ Miguel revela su conversación con su madre.
b. _____ Raquel llama (*calls*) a Pedro Castillo por teléfono, y habla con él.
c. _____ Raquel decide viajar a Madrid, en tren.

Al día siguiente (*The next day*)

a. _____ La familia entra en una pastelería.
b. _____ Miguel padre compra un perro.
c. _____ Osito se escapa y se pierde (*he gets lost*).
d. _____ La familia lleva (*takes*) a Raquel al mercado de los animales.

Actividad B.   Los nuevos personajes (*New characters*)

In **Episodio** 4 several new members of the Ruiz family appeared, and you learned more about others. Can you match the characters with their photos?

a. Osito
b. Miguel hijo
c. Jaime
d. Miguel padre

1.   2.   3.   4.

Now indicate whether the following statements about some of the characters are **Cierto** or **Falso**.

Miguel padre

C   F   1. Trabaja en turismo, como guía.
C   F   2. Revela parte del secreto de Rosario.
C   F   3. Compra un animal para su hijo.

Jaime

C   F   4. Toma un fino (*sherry*) con Raquel y sus padres.
C   F   5. Acepta la responsabilidad de tener (*having*) un perro.
C   F   6. No le gusta (*He doesn't like*) la escuela.

Miguel hijo

C   F   7. Está en octavo (*8th*) grado.
C   F   8. Su materia favorita es ciencias naturales.
C   F   9. No le gusta estudiar.

• •

VOCABULARIO DEL TEMA

En el Colegio de San Francisco de Paula

LAS ASIGNATURAS DE MIGUEL

la historia
las matemáticas
las ciencias naturales
la religión
el español
el inglés
la educación física

LAS ASIGNATURAS DE JAIME

el español
la religión
las ciencias naturales
las matemáticas
las ciencias sociales
la educación física

COLEGIO DE SAN FCO. DE PAULA
SEVILLA   Departamento de Formación Religiosa
1º BUP   1ª Evaluación
Grupo B
Miguel Ruiz

1.- ¿Cuáles son los tres elementos característicos de la Religión Cristiana?

Fe, esperanza y caridad

2.- Define lo característico del Género Profético en los libros de la Biblia. ¿Conoces algún libro de este género?

Las predicciones para el futuro
Las Profecías de Isaías

Remember that the word **colegio** is a false cognate. It means *grade school* or *high school*. This **Colegio**, like many in Spain, is affiliated with a religious order.

Actividad A.   ¿Qué estudian los hermanos Ruiz?

What do you remember about the courses that Miguel and Jaime are taking? Indicate whether the following statements refer only to Miguel (**M**), only to Jaime (**J**), or to both boys (**2**). Try this without looking at the preceding list.

M   J   2   1. Estudia ciencias naturales.
M   J   2   2. Tiene un curso de ciencias sociales.
M   J   2   3. Estudia en un colegio religioso.
M   J   2   4. Toma inglés.
M   J   2   5. No estudia historia.

Actividad B.

You will hear a series of descriptions of what happens in different classes that Miguel and Jaime are taking. Match the descriptions with the following courses.

a. _____ las matemáticas   c. _____ la religión
b. _____ la educación física   d. _____ el inglés

Actividad C.   ¿Y tú?

What do grade school students typically study in your area? Imagine that you are describing to Miguel and Jaime what students study where you live by completing the following sentences.

Donde yo vivo, los chicos estudian _____, _____ y

_____ . No estudian _____ .

Otras materias

LAS ARTES LIBERALES *	LAS CIENCIAS NATURALES	LAS MATEMÁTICAS	OTRAS MATERIAS
el arte	la biología	el cálculo	el comercio
la filosofía	la química		las comunicaciones
las lenguas extranjeras			la contabilidad
la literatura	LAS CIENCIAS SOCIALES		los estudios agrícolas
	la sicología		la informática
	la sociología		

This list of subjects includes a number usually studied only at the college level. Most of them are easily recognizable cognates. Can you find the Spanish equivalents of *business* (Hint: *commerce*), *foreign languages*, *accounting* (Hint: *counting*), *chemistry*?

Many subjects have been listed here. You should learn primarily those that you are taking or that are of interest to you. If your major is not included in the list of courses, look it up in a dictionary or ask your instructor.

Note:* **el arte (*sing.*), but **las artes** (*pl.*). Other terms for *liberal arts* heard in the Hispanic world are **Filosofía y letras, Las letras, Las humanidades**. Ask your instructor which term to use.

Actividad D.

You will hear three Hispanic college students talk about what they are studying this term.

Paso 1

Listen and take notes on what they are studying.

ANITA   RAÚL   CELIA

_____   _____   _____

_____   _____   _____

_____   _____   _____

_____   _____   _____

_____   _____   _____

_____   _____   _____

Paso 2

Now answer the following questions based on the descriptions you just heard.

1. ¿Quién estudia ciencias?
2. ¿Quién estudia artes liberales?
3. ¿Quién no sabe todavía (*yet*) cuál es su campo (*what his field is*)?
4. ¿Quién tiene más cursos?

Nota cultural: En las universidades hispánicas

After completing their high-school degree (called **el bachillerato**), students in most Hispanic countries who enter the university must immediately select a major and follow a prescribed series of courses (with few electives). Courses tend to last for a full year, with obligatory examinations at the end of the course.

Observaciones del Profesor	Alumno _____
	Asignatura ____ NATURALEZA ____
	Curso 5º , Un. 4ª , Obj. 1.2.2.
	Fecha ____ – Noviembre ____
	Calificación [ ]

1.– ¿ Qué órganos forman el aparato circulatorio ?

2.– ¿ Qué elementos forman la sangre ?

3.– Las _____ son los vasos sanguíneos que conducen la sangre desde los órganos hasta el corazón.
Las _____ son los vasos sanguíneos que conducen la sangre desde el corazón a todos los órganos del cuerpo.

Actividad E.   ¿Y tú?

What courses are you and your friends taking this semester/quarter (**este semestre/trimestre**)? Answer by completing as many of the following sentences as necessary.

Yo tomo...
Mi amigo ___(*nombre*)___ toma...
Mi amiga ___(*nombre*)___ toma...
Otros amigos toman...

Actividad F.   Típicamente...

Now give the courses that are typically taken by certain groups of students at your school.

Los estudiantes de primer año (*freshmen*) toman...
Los estudiantes de ciencias toman...
Los estudiantes de artes liberales toman...
Los atletas toman...

Los animales domésticos

el perro	dog
el gato	cat
el pájaro	bird
el pez *	fish

Actividad G.   Animales de todo tipo

You will hear the narrator from **Episodio 4** describe **el mercadillo de animales** visited by Raquel and the Ruiz family. Listen specifically for the following information.

One type of fish that is sold there: _____

One type of bird that is sold there: _____

---

* The **-z** at the end of a word changes to **-c** when the plural is formed: **pez** → **peces**. This spelling change does not affect pronunciation.

Actividad H.   Más animales

Are animals part of your life in any way? Choose the sentences that best describe you, and complete them if necessary.

Tengo _____. Se llama (*Its name is*) _____.

No tengo ningún animal.

Los estudiantes de mi residencia (*dorm*) tienen _____.

En la casa (*house*) donde yo vivo, hay _____.

En la casa de mis padres (hijos), hay _____.

Mi hijo/a (esposo/a, amigo/a) desea tener (*to have*) _____.

. . . .

CONVERSACIONES: LAS PRESENTACIONES

Actividad.   Más sobre el primer encuentro (*More about meeting for the first time*)

On the cassette tape you will hear three brief conversations in which people make introductions. You will hear the following brief presentations used to indicate the person being introduced.

Éste es...   to introduce one male friend
Ésta es...   to introduce one female friend
Éstos son...   to introduce more than one male friend or a group of male and female friends
Éstas son...   to introduce more than one female friend

Paso 1

Listen to all of the conversations now and identify the form of introduction used in each one.

	éste es...	ésta es...	éstos son...	éstas son...
1.	____	____	____	____
2.	____	____	____	____
3.	____	____	____	____
4.	____	____	____	____

Paso 2

Listen to the four taped conversations again, then write the number of the conversation in which the following family members are introduced.

_____ hijas   _____ hijos   _____ esposo   _____ hermana

Paso 3
Using the previous models, how would you introduce the following people?

> su profesor(a) de español
> su padre/madre

· ·

UN POCO DE GRAMÁTICA

Describing

You have already learned that Spanish articles must reflect the gender and number of the nouns they accompany: **el perro**, **los perros**. Adjectives (words that describe nouns) are like articles in that they too must agree in gender and number with the noun they modify. Notice how adjectives are used in the following description of Osito, the lost dog from **Episodio 4**.

El perro de Jaime se llama Osito porque es pequeño y negro. Osito es un perro muy inteligente y cariñoso. En general, los perros son animales muy inteligentes. También son muy fieles. Algunas personas creen que los gatos son más listos, pero Jaime no está de acuerdo.

Jaime's dog is called Osito because he is small and black. Osito is a very intelligent and affectionate dog. In general, dogs are very intelligent animals. They are also very loyal. Some people think that cats are brighter, but Jaime doesn't agree.

Note the following patterns of adjective agreement:

> inteligente → inteligentes (+ **s**)
> fiel → fieles (+ **es**)

You will learn more about adjectives in the Workbook.

Actividad.   Los animales domésticos
Pets—and the pet industry supporting them—play an important role in the United States. This is one of the aspects of U.S. culture that strikes some Hispanics as unusual, because less importance is given to animals in many Hispanic settings. Here, however, animals tend to be treated like family members, and people often have strong opinions about their pets and animals in general.

Paso 1

Describe an animal you know or know about, forming complete sentences with elements from each column. (You can listen to the list of **Otros animales** and the adjectives on the cassette tape.)

Otros animales: el caballo (*horse*), el canario, el *hámster*, el loro (*parrot*), el lagarto (*lizard*), la serpiente, la tortuga

MODELO: El perro de mi hijo es cariñoso y fiel.

Mi _____	es	inteligente/tonto (*dumb*)
El _____ de mi		cariñoso/indiferente
(amigo, hijo,...)		fiel (*faithful*)
Garfield		(in)dependiente
Snoopy, Lassie, Benji		perezoso (*lazy*)
el señor Ed		cruel, egoísta
		bonito (*pretty*)/feo (*ugly*)
		(im)paciente
		hablador (*talkative*)
		furtivo (*sneaky*)
		pequeño/grande (*large*)
		lento (*slow*)/rápido

Paso 2

Now make generalizations about some of the following animals. Feel free to compare characteristics, as in the model. Use adjectives from **Paso 1**.

MODELO: En general, los perros son dependientes. Pero los gatos son independientes.

Animales: los perros, los gatos, los pájaros, los peces, los caballos, los lagartos, las serpientes, las tortugas

Nota cultural: Sevilla

In **Episodios 3** and **4**, many of the scenes you saw took place in Sevilla. Refresh your memory about Sevilla by listening to what the narrator told you at the beginning of **Episodio 3**. Try to associate the place names you hear with scenes you remember from the video episodes. Then complete the following activity.

Which of the following statements accurately describe Sevilla, based on what you now know?

C   F   1. Hay muchas iglesias en Sevilla.
C   F   2. No hay muchas tradiciones religiosas en la ciudad.
C   F   3. Es una ciudad de patios y jardines (*gardens*).
C   F   4. La ciudad tiene muchos monumentos históricos.
C   F   5. Sevilla no tiene barrios modernos.

After you have read the following passage about Sevilla, review this activity to see whether you wish to change any answers.

La Torre de la Giralda tiene 97 (noventa y siete) metros de alto.

Sevilla es una típica ciudad de Andalucía. Está situada a orillas del[1] río Guadalquivir. Tiene barrios modernos, pero muchas personas creen que las partes más interesantes de Sevilla son sus zonas históricas.

El barrio de Santa Cruz es la parte más antigua[2] de la ciudad. Es famoso por sus calles estrechas[3] y por los hermosos patios en el interior de las casas. En el pasado muchos judíos vivían[4] en este barrio.

Los monumentos más famosos de Sevilla son éstos:

- la antigua Catedral, de estilo gótico
- la tumba de Cristóbal Colón, que está en la Catedral
- la Giralda, una torre de la Catedral
- El Alcázar,[5] con su arquitectura de estilo árabe y sus bonitos jardines.

Sevilla es también muy famosa por sus procesiones de Semana Santa.[6] Muchas personas participan en estas procesiones. Las diferentes cofradías[7] desfilan[8] por las calles de la ciudad. Cargan[9] enormes pasos[10] que representan escenas de la vida[11] de Jesucristo. Algunos pasos tienen cruces o estatuas de la Virgen María o de Jesús.

En estas descripciones, se ve[12] la influencia de las tres culturas que convivían[13] en Sevilla en siglos anteriores: la cultura judía, la árabe y la cristiana.

---

[1] a... *on the banks of the*   [2] más... *oldest*   [3] *narrow*   [4] muchos... *many Jewish people lived*   [5] El... *Royal Palace*
[6] Semana... *Holy Week*   [7] *brotherhoods*   [8] caminan   [9] *They carry*   [10] *floats*   [11] *life*   [12] se... *one can see*
[13] *coexisted, lived together*

Actividad.   Un viaje a Sevilla

Based on the information provided in the preceding text, indicate what you would like to see if you went to Sevilla. Use the expression **Me gustaría** (*I would like*) plus an infinitive.

MODELO: Me gustaría visitar la Catedral y la Giralda.

Verbos útiles: visitar, caminar (en), entrar (en), fotografiar

---

Have you completed the following sections of the lesson? Check them off here.

_____ **Preparación**   _____ **Conversaciones**
_____ **¿Tienes buena memoria?**   _____ **Un poco de gramática**
_____ **Vocabulario del tema**

Now scan the words in the **Vocabulario** list to be sure that you understand the meaning of most of them. Then you will be ready to continue on with **Lección 4** in the Workbook.

• •

VOCABULARIO

Los verbos

aceptar	to accept
caminar	to walk
comprar	to buy
decidir	to decide
estudiar	to study
llamar	to call
llevar	to take (*something somewhere*)
sabe (algo)	he/she knows (something)
no sabe nada	he/she doesn't know anything

Los animales domésticos

el gato	cat
el pájaro	bird
el perro	dog
el pez (*pl.* peces)	fish

Los lugares

la casa	house, home
el colegio	grade/high school

Las materias (Courses)

la asignatura*	subject
el curso	course; class
el arte (*pl.* las artes)	art
la biología	biology
el cálculo	calculus

---

*As you saw in the video episode, this word is used in Spain to mean *school subjects*. **La materia** is also widely used in the Spanish-speaking world to mean *course* or *subject*.

las ciencias (naturales, sociales)	(natural, social) science
el comercio	business
la comunicación	communications
la contabilidad	accounting
la educación física	physical education
el español	Spanish
los estudios agrícolas	agriculture
la filosofía	philosophy
la informática	data processing
el inglés	English
la lengua (extranjera)	(foreign) language
la literatura	literature
las matemáticas	mathematics
la psicología	psychology
la química	chemistry
la religión	religion
la sociología	sociology

Repaso: la historia

Los adjetivos (Adjectives)

bueno/buenos	good
cariñoso/cariñosos	affectionate
negro/negros	black
perdido/perdidos	lost
primero/primeros	first

Las presentaciones (Introductions)

éste es... (*male*)	this is . . .
ésta es... (*female*)	this is . . .
éstos son... (*males; males and females*)	these are . . .
éstas son... (*females*)	these are . . .

Las palabras adicionales

al día siguiente	the next day
donde yo vivo	where I live
por teléfono	by telephone
porque	because
todavía	still, yet
(a Jaime) le gusta* + *inf.*	(Jaime) likes (*to do something*)
no le gusta + *inf.*	he doesn't like (*to do something*)

Palabras del texto

el repaso   review

In the **Vocabulario** section, this word introduces thematic vocabulary that has been listed in previous lessons of the Textbook or Workbook.

---

*Whenever you see or hear a form of the verb **gustar**, remember that the topic is someone's likes or dislikes. You will learn more about using **gustar** in upcoming lessons.

5

LA DESPEDIDA*

OBJETIVOS

The materials in **Lección 5** of the Textbook and the Workbook will help you better understand the video episode and take you beyond it, giving you additional information about places and characters in the series. The Textbook will also help you to develop skill in using the Spanish language. In this lesson you will learn

- how to express the days of the week in Spanish
- how to tell time
- how to say good-bye to someone
- how to talk about your activities with others.

You will also learn about Arabic influence in southern Spain.

Be sure to work through all parts of the lesson. When you see a cassette symbol in the margin, listen to the tape for **Lección 5**. Answers or hints for many activities are given in Appendix 1. Be sure to check your answers for each activity before going on to the next one.

* *The Farewell*

BEFORE VIEWING . . .

PREPARACIÓN

Actividad A.

Although Raquel has not yet unraveled the secret of the letter, she has accumulated some information and, being a lawyer, has kept careful records of it. How much do you remember about the details of the case?

Paso 1

In simple sentences, answer the following questions about Raquel's investigation.

1.   ¿Cómo se llama la persona que escribió la carta?
2.   ¿Dónde vive esa (*that*) persona?
3.   ¿Desea hablar con Raquel?
4.   ¿Adónde necesita ir (*to go*) Raquel para hablar con ella?
5.   ¿Sabe algo de Rosario la familia Ruiz?
6.   ¿Cómo debe ir Raquel a Madrid?

Now listen to the questions and answers on the cassette tape.

Paso 2

Now choose the appropriate words and phrases to complete the following paragraph.

1. No saben nada	Saben algo	4. compra un gato	compra un perro
2. personalmente	por teléfono	5. camina por (*through*)	
3. con otro hijo	con Rosario	se pierde en (*gets lost in*)	

En Sevilla, Raquel conoce[a] a los miembros de la familia Ruiz. _____[1] de Rosario, pero Miguel Ruiz habla con su madre _____.[2] Por eso[b] Raquel sabe que debe ir a Madrid para hablar con ella. Raquel no debe ir mañana,[c] porque la señora Suárez está en Barcelona, _____.[3] Por eso Raquel tiene un día libre[d] y pasa el tiempo con la familia. En la mañana,[e] todos visitan el mercadillo de los animales, donde Miguel padre _____[4] para su hijo Jaime. Pero Jaime no es muy responsable y el perro, que se llama Osito, _____[5] las calles del Barrio de Santa Cruz.

[a]*meets*   [b]*Por... For that reason*   [c]*tomorrow*   [d]*un... a free day*   [e]*morning*

Now listen to the completed paragraph on the cassette tape.

Actividad B.

At the end of **Episodio 4**, the entire Ruiz family disappeared along with Raquel into the narrow streets of el Barrio de Santa Cruz. What do you think will happen in this video episode? In each group, choose the statement that best expresses what you expect to see.

1. _____ Jaime encuentra (*finds*) a su perro.
   _____ Hay un accidente y Osito está muerto.
2. _____ Jaime se pierde también en el Barrio de Santa Cruz.
   _____ Raquel se pierde también.
3. _____ Raquel sale (*leaves*) para Madrid.
   _____ Raquel decide quedarse (*to stay*) en Sevilla otro día.

Actividad C.

Listen to the following conversation between Raquel and Elena Ramírez in the Barrio de Santa Cruz. **¿Dónde nos encontramos?** means *Where shall we meet?* Now that you know that, try to listen for the name of their meeting place.

1. Elena dice que van a encontrarse (*they are going to meet*) en

a. _____ otra calle
b. _____ un café
c. _____ La Giralda

Listen to the conversation again. Knowing that Raquel and Elena have arranged to meet, can you determine approximately at what time they will meet?
Hint: Listen for a number.

2. Elena y Raquel van a encontrarse aproximadamente

a. _____ a las dos
b. _____ a las once

━━━━ **AFTER VIEWING . . .**

• •

¿TIENES BUENA MEMORIA?

Actividad A.   Por la mañana (*In the morning*)

The events of the morning in Sevilla involve primarily three characters: Raquel, Jaime, and a new character, **el ciego**. Match those characters with the statements that describe them or indicate what they do in the video episode.
¡OJO! More than one name may be possible for each statement.

1. _____ Corre (¿_____? *runs*) por las calles del Barrio.

2. _____ Habla con un niño (*boy*) en la calle.

3. _____ Encuentra al perro en la Plaza de las Tres Cruces.

4. _____ Habla con el ciego.

5. _____ Vende (¿_____? *sells*) cupones de la lotería.

6. _____ Necesita estar en la Giralda a las once y media.

7. _____ Dice que tener un perro es una gran responsabilidad.

8. _____ Compra caramelos.

9. _____ Se pierde.

10. _____ Entra en la Catedral.

Actividad B.   Por la tarde y al día siguiente (*the next day*)

All of the following events took place after everyone was found in **Episodio 5**, but . . . in what order did they occur? Put them in order, from 1 to 7.

a. _____ Raquel compra un billete (*ticket*) en el Rápido (= un tren muy rápido).

b. _____ Desean visitar el Alcázar.

c. _____ Al día siguiente, llegan a la estación del tren.

d. _____ Desgraciadamente (*Unfortunately*), el Alcázar está cerrado (*closed*).

e. _____ Cenan (*They have dinner*) en un restaurante elegante.

f. _____ El tren sale (*leaves*) de la estación.

g. _____ Todos dicen adiós.

Actividad C.   ¡Un desafío!

Some of the events of **Episodio 5** have to do with a specific time. It is possible to understand the video episode without catching the specific hours mentioned, but . . . perhaps you did! Do you remember at what time the following events took place or were supposed to take place?

¿A qué hora... ?

1. _____ Deben encontrarse en la Giralda Raquel y Elena.

2. _____ Llegan al Alcázar.

3. _____ Raquel sale para Madrid.

a. A las doce.
b. A las once.
c. A la una.
d. A las once y media.
e. A las doce y media.
f. A la una y media.

VOCABULARIO DEL TEMA

Los días de la semana

lunes	Monday	**viernes**	Friday
martes	Tuesday	**sábado**	Saturday
miércoles	Wednesday	**domingo**	Sunday
jueves	Thursday		

Did you notice that the days of the week are not capitalized and that the week starts with Monday? Use the article **el** before the days of the week to express *on*: **el lunes** = *on Monday*.

lunes 14	*martes 15*	*miércoles 16*	*jueves 17*	*viernes 18*	*sábado 19*
8	8	8	8	8	
9	9	9	9	9	
10	10	10	10	10	
11	11	11	11	11	
12	12	12	12	12	
13	13	13	13	13	*domingo 20*
14	14	14	14	14	
15	15	15	15	15	
16	16	16	16	16	
17	17	17	17	17	

Actividad A.   Una semana decisiva

The video episodes of *Destinos* that you have seen thus far take place during a decisive week in the lives of don Fernando's family. Listen as the narrator relates the events of that week. Then identify the following actions by the day of the week on which each occurs, beginning with **el lunes**.

1. _____ Raquel va con la familia Ruiz al mercadillo de los animales.

2. _____ Raquel sale de México para Sevilla.

3. _____ Pedro habla con Raquel y Raquel acepta el caso.

4. _____ Raquel comienza su investigación en Sevilla.

5. _____ Los miembros de la familia llegan a La Gavia.

6. _____ Don Fernando habla con su familia. Revela el secreto.

7. _____ El doctor habla con don Fernando, en La Gavia.

Actividad B.   La semana de Miguel

The speaker on the cassette tape will tell you one special thing that Miguel typically does each day of the week. The days are mentioned out of sequence. Listen carefully and indicate on page 56 where Miguel is on each day.

Miguel está

a. _____ en casa

b. _____ en la iglesia

c. _____ con su padre

d. _____ en el mercado

e. _____ en casa de su abuela

f. _____ en casa de un amigo

g. _____ con su madre

Now listen as Miguel's week is described in sequence, with some additional information. How much more can you understand?

lunes	martes	miércoles	jueves	viernes	sábado	domingo

Actividad C.   Una semana típica

When do people typically participate in the following activities? Answer for each activity.   ¡OJO!**a** + **el** = **al**.

Muchas personas van (*go***) a... el lunes (martes...).**

1. la iglesia (la sinagoga, la mezquita)
2. una fiesta
3. la oficina
4. la universidad
5. el mercado (el supermercado)
6. un partido (*game*) de fútbol americano*

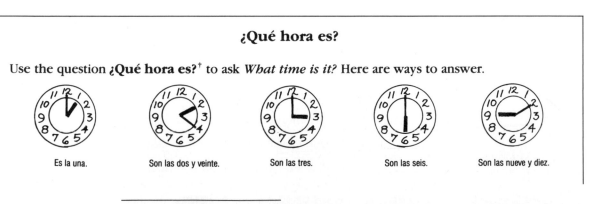

¿Qué hora es?

Use the question **¿Qué hora es?**[†] to ask *What time is it?* Here are ways to answer.

Es la una.   Son las dos y veinte.   Son las tres.   Son las seis.   Son las nueve y diez.

---

* The word **fútbol** is a false cognate; it means *soccer*. **Fútbol americano** (**norteamericano**) is the term generally used to designate *football*.

† The question you have heard in the episode, **¿Qué horas son?**, is a variation used primarily in Mexico and by those of Mexican descent in the United States.

Es la una menos diez.

Son las ocho y cuarto.

Son las diez y media.

Son las cinco menos cuarto.

Use **y** to express minutes between the hour and the half hour. Use **menos** to express minutes between the half hour and the next hour. The phrase **y cuarto** expresses the quarter hour and **y media** the half hour.

The time of day is indicated more precisely by adding the following phrases.

de la mañana	*in the morning*
de la tarde	*in the afternoon/evening*
de la noche	*in the evening/at night*

Son las ocho y media **de la mañana**.	*It's eight-thirty in the morning.*
Son las tres menos cuarto **de la tarde**.	*It's a quarter to three in the afternoon.*

To indicate that something happens at a particular hour, use the phrases **a la...** or **a las... .**

Raquel y Jaime llegan tarde a la Giralda, **a las doce**.	*Raquel and Jaime get to the Giralda late, at 12:00.*

Nota cultural: Hablando de la hora...
(*Talking about time . . .*)

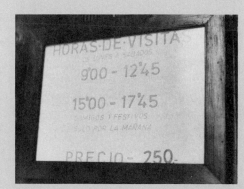

Although phrases in two languages may be roughly equivalent, cultural differences often make that correspondence less exact. For example, the Spanish phrase **de la tarde** does not exactly correspond to *in the afternoon*, the English equivalent offered above. Because lunch in Hispanic countries is generally served at 2:00 (or later) and dinner at 10:00 (or later), **la tarde** is often viewed as lasting until the dinner hour. Thus, in Spanish one speaks of **las ocho de la tarde**, which would be *8:00 in the evening* in English.

Another difference between English and Spanish time-telling systems is the more frequent use of the 24-hour clock in Hispanic countries. Note in the photo how the visiting hours for **La Giralda** are indicated. (When the time given is after 12:00 noon, simply subtract 12 to get the hour: 15:00 → 3:00 P.M.) Times in transportation schedules and TV listings are generally given using the 24-hour system.

Actividad D.   ¿Qué hora es?

You will hear a series of segments from **Episodio 5**. Listen carefully to them and try to catch the times of day you hear.

1. Raquel dice...
2. El ciego dice...
3. Los niños dicen...

Actividad E.   ¿Qué hora es?

Now it's your turn to answer the question. When you hear the number for each item, tell what time it is on the clockface shown. The speaker on the cassette tape will give you the correct answer.

MODELO: (*you see*)
(*you say*)   Son las cinco.
(*you hear*)   Son las cinco.

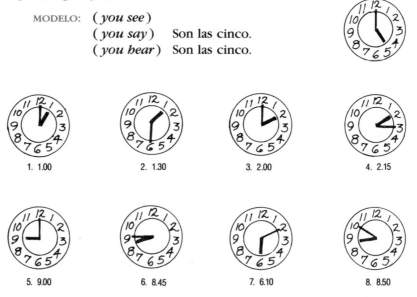

1. 1.00   2. 1.30   3. 2.00   4. 2.15

5. 9.00   6. 8.45   7. 6.10   8. 8.50

Actividad F.   Un día típico de Susan

Here are some of the things that Susan, a colleague of Raquel, does on a typical day. Look at the drawings and match them with the appropriate statements. Then complete the statements with the times of day.

1. _____ Toma algo en la cafetería a...
2. _____ Sale de la oficina a...
3. _____ Susan llega a la oficina, a...
4. _____ Trabaja hasta (*until*) muy tarde, hasta...
5. _____ Susan habla con un cliente a...
6. _____ Entra en su apartamento a...
7. _____ Escribe un reporte a...
8. _____ Cena con una amiga a...

Actividad G.　¿Y tú?

How does your schedule compare to Susan's? Using the preceding sentences as a guide, form as many sentences as you can about your own schedule, changing details as needed.

MODELO:　Llego a la universidad a la(s)…

CONVERSACIONES: LAS DESPEDIDAS

PASO 1

On the cassette tape you will hear three brief conversations in which people take leave of each other. As you listen to each conversation, indicate which **despedida** you hear by writing 1, 2, or 3 next to the appropriate expression.

_____ Hasta luego.　　　　　　_____ Hasta mañana.
_____ Adiós.

PASO 2

How would you say good-bye to these people in the following situations?

- to a friend you are going to see tomorrow
- to an acquaintance you may not see again
- to someone you just met and whom you hope to see again.

. . . .

UN POCO DE GRAMÁTICA

Using Verbs to Talk About Group Activities

You have already learned to use verbs to talk about what *you* and *I* are doing individually. To indicate what *we* are doing together, use the endings **-amos**, **-emos**, or **-imos**.

MIGUEL: Jaime y yo viv**imos** en el Barrio de Triana. Estudi**amos** en la escuela San Francisco de Paula. Mamá dice que deb**emos** estudiar más... y yo no comprendo. ¡Creo que Jaime necesita estudiar mucho más que yo!

MIGUEL: *Jaime and I live in the Triana District. We study at the St. Francis de Paula school. Mom says that we should study more . . . and I don't understand. I think that Jaime needs to study a lot more than I do!*

Actividad.   ¿Quiénes hablan?

Who might make the following statements?

a.   Ramón y Mercedes
b.   Miguel y Jaime
c.   Juanita y Carlitos

1. _____ A veces viajamos a Madrid para visitar a la abuela.
2. _____ Vivimos en La Gavia, con nuestro padre.
3. _____ Llamamos al médico cuando papá no está bien.
4. _____ Estamos en La Gavia hoy (*today*) pero no vivimos en la hacienda.
5. _____ Visitamos los sitios turísticos con Raquel.
6. _____ Maricarmen no sabe decir la hora (*tell time*) ¡pero nosotros sí sabemos!

Nota cultural: La España árabe

In previous episodes, you have learned a good deal about Sevilla and its cultural heritage. Do the following statements accurately describe Sevilla and the history of her region, based on what you now know?

C F 1. Andalucía es una región donde predomina la influencia árabe.
C F 2. Los árabes vivieron (*lived*) en España por mucho tiempo.
C F 3. En el arte árabe no se reproduce la figura humana.
C F 4. La Alhambra era (*was*) la residencia de los monarcas árabes. (¿Recuerdas *Tales of the Alhambra*, de Washington Irving?)

After you have read the following passage about the general cultural history of southern Spain, review this activity to see whether you wish to change any answers. The passage is included in the cassette tape program as well. You may wish to listen to it on the tape the first time you read it.

Es en Andalucía donde hay más influencia del arte árabe. Fiel al dogma del Corán, el arte árabe no reproduce nunca la figura humana. Se caracteriza por sus líneas curvas y sus complicados motivos geométricos.

En estas fotografías se ven algunos[1] de los monumentos más famosos de la cultura árabe en España. Identifica la foto que corresponda a cada descripción.

[1]*some*

1.

2.

_____ La Alhambra, de Granada, era residencia de los reyes[2] moros y un verdadero palacio del placer.[3] El Patio de los Leones es el sitio que los turistas visitan con más frecuencia.

_____ El Alcázar de Sevilla es un palacio árabe, construido en el siglo[4] XIV. Esta residencia de los monarcas es de estilo mudéjar. El arte mudéjar combina la ornamentación árabe y la arquitectura del arte cristiano.

_____ La Mezquita[5] de Córdoba es hoy una catedral cristiana. Este antiguo[6] templo del Islam tiene una infinidad de columnas de mármol[7] de formas diferentes.

¿Por qué[8] hay tanta influencia árabe en esta parte de España?

3.

Datos importantes sobre los siglos VIII–XV

- 711 (setecientos once): Los árabes invaden la Península Ibérica. Encuentran mucha oposición, pero después de[9] siete años, dominan toda la Península, con excepción del País Vasco y parte de Asturias.

- 1492 (mil cuatrocientos noventa y dos): Isabel de Castilla y Fernando de Aragón, los Reyes Católicos, conquistan Granada, el último reino[10] moro en territorio español. Es el fin de la dominación árabe en España… y el comienzo de la dominación española del Nuevo Mundo, con el primer viaje de Cristóbal Colón.

Una de las principales características de la dominación árabe en España es la tolerancia religiosa. Con unas excepciones, hay largos períodos de convivencia[11] pacífica. Cristianos, árabes y judíos viven y trabajan juntos.[12] En contraste, en 1492 los Reyes Católicos expulsan a los judíos. Los que[13] no desean convertirse al catolicismo están obligados a salir de España.

[2]*kings* [3]*pleasure* [4]*century* [5]*Mosque* [6]*former* [7]*marble* [8]*¿Por… Why?* [9]*después… after* [10]*último… last kingdom* [11]*living together* [12]*together* [13]*Los… Those who*

Actividad.   ¿Árabe, cristiano o judío?

Based on the passage you have just read, who would have made the following statements, **los árabes**, **los cristianos** or **los judíos**?

1. No debemos reproducir la figura humana en el arte.
2. Vivimos juntos con árabes y cristianos... y sin problemas.
3. Expulsamos a los judíos en 1492.

Have you completed the following sections of the lesson? Check them off here.

_____ **Preparación**   _____ **Conversaciones**
_____ **¿Tienes buena memoria?**   _____ **Un poco de gramática**
_____ **Vocabulario del tema**

Now scan the words in the **Vocabulario** list to be sure that you understand the meaning of most of them. Then you will be ready to continue on with **Lección 5** in the Workbook.

VOCABULARIO

Los verbos

cenar	to have dinner
comprender	to understand
correr	to run
vender	to sell
dice(n)	he/she says (they say)
encuentra(n)	he/she finds (they find)
se pierde	he/she gets lost
sale(n)	he/she leaves (they leave)
va(n)	he/she goes (they go)
vamos	we go

Las personas

el ciego	blind man
el niño/la niña	young boy/young girl

¿Qué hora es? (What Time Is It?)

Es la una.	It's one o'clock.
Son las dos (tres...).	It's two (three . . .) o'clock.
...y cuarto	. . . fifteen (quarter past . . .)
...y media	. . . thirty (half past . . .)

...de la mañana	A.M., in the morning
...de la tarde	P.M., in the afternoon
...de la noche	P.M., in the evening/at night
¿A qué hora... ?	At what time . . . ?
a la.../a las...	at . . .

Los días de la semana (Days of the Week)

lunes, martes, miércoles, jueves, viernes, sábado, domingo

Las despedidas

Adiós.	Good-bye.
Hasta luego.	See you later. Until later.
Hasta mañana.	See you tomorrow. Until tomorrow.

Las palabras adicionales

hoy	today
más	most

LECCIÓN

6

¿Maestra?*

OBJETIVOS

Part of this episode is a review. Be sure to work through all parts of the lesson. When you see a cassette symbol in the margin, listen to the tape for **Lección 6**. Answers or hints for many activities are given in Appendix 1. Be sure to check your answers for each activity before going on to the next one.

Teacher?

 **BEFORE VIEWING . . .**

Preparación

Actividad A.

In previous episodes of *Destinos* you have followed Raquel's investigation to Spain. What do you remember about her investigation and trip? Select the correct statement in each group.

1. _____ a. En Sevilla, Raquel habla con uno de los hijos de Teresa Suárez.
   _____ b. En Sevilla, Raquel habla con Teresa Suárez.
2. _____ a. Raquel sale de Sevilla para Madrid.
   _____ b. Raquel sale de Madrid para Sevilla.
3. _____ a. Raquel va en avión.
   _____ b. Raquel va en tren.

Actividad B.

What do you think will happen in this video episode? Try to predict what will happen by answering the following questions.

1. Raquel will speak to this person on the train. Who do you think he is?

   _____ Es reportero.
   _____ Es el conductor del tren.

2. What do you think this person wants?

   _____ Desea entrevistar (*to interview*) a Raquel.
   _____ Desea viajar con Raquel en su compartimiento.

Actividad C.

Here is part of a conversation that Raquel will have with someone on the train. Read through the conversation to get a general idea of what it is about.

—Aquí estoy en el rápido de Sevilla a Madrid. Conmigo está la ganadora del premio especial de la Organización Nacional de Ciegos.
—¿La lotería?
—Ud. estará muy contenta de su buena suerte.
—Perdone, pero no sé de qué habla.
—Esta maestra de primaria es la señora Díaz. Su clase de sexto grado le compró un cupón y...

 Now listen to the conversation on the cassette tape. **Su buena suerte** means *your good luck*. Now that you know that, can you guess the meaning of the words **ganadora** and **premio**?

1. La palabra **ganadora** significa

    a. _____ a person who lives in Granada
    b. _____ winner

2. La palabra **premio** significa

    a. _____ primary
    b. _____ prize

3. Based on your guesses so far, on the title of this video episode (called **¿Maestra?**), and on what you have learned in **Actividad C**, what do you think is happening?

    a. _____ El hombre cree que Raquel es otra persona.
    b. _____ El hombre sabe algo de don Fernando y busca más información, como Raquel.

AFTER VIEWING . . .

¿TIENES BUENA MEMORIA?

Actividad A.   Los nuevos personajes

The most important new character in this video episode appears to be the reporter. What do you remember about the interaction between him and Raquel? Complete the following statements. ¡OJO! There may be more than one right answer in some cases.

1. El reportero se llama... Federico Suárez / Alfredo Sánchez.
2. Alfredo cree que Raquel es... la ganadora de un premio / una reportera para la televisión / una maestra de primaria.
3. Alfredo... encuentra / no encuentra ...a la maestra de primaria durante este episodio.
4. Raquel... acepta / rechaza (*rejects*) ...el interés que tiene el reportero en el caso de don Fernando.
5. El reportero... desea investigar más / acepta la negativa de Raquel.

Actividad B.   En este episodio

All of the following events took place during the trip shown in **Episodio 6**, but . . . in what order did they occur? Put them in order, from 1 to 4 in each group.

En el compartimiento de Raquel

a. ＿＿＿ Raquel dice que no es la ganadora del premio.
b. ＿＿＿ Un reportero desea entrevistar a Raquel.
c. ＿＿＿ Raquel escribe en su computadora. Está sola.
d. ＿＿＿ Otro señor entra en el compartimiento.

Luego

a. ＿＿＿ Raquel dice que el caso es un secreto.
b. ＿＿＿ El tren llega a la estación.
c. ＿＿＿ El reportero pregunta mucho sobre el caso de Raquel.
d. ＿＿＿ Raquel y el reportero comen (*eat*) algo.

En la estación del tren

a. ＿＿＿ Raquel sale en taxi.
b. ＿＿＿ Ve el sobre (*envelope*) de la carta.
c. ＿＿＿ El reportero acompaña a Raquel a un taxi.
d. ＿＿＿ El reportero llama a su oficina.

● ●

REPASO DE LOS EPISODIOS 1 – 5

Actividad. Resumen

Complete the following summary of the first five video episodes of *Destinos* with words from the following lists. ¡OJO! Not all of the words will be used.

Nombres: Jaime, don Fernando, Teresa Suárez, Miguel, Rosario, Ramón

Miembros de la familia: el esposo, el hijo, el hermano, el tío

Lugares: México, España, La Gavia, Sevilla, Madrid

Verbos: toma, investiga, vende, vive, compra, encuentra, saben

Otras palabras: algo, nada, siempre

En México, un hombre muy viejo está gravemente enfermo. Se llama ＿＿＿＿＿＿.[1] Este señor recibe una carta y la carta tiene un gran secreto. El señor revela el secreto a su familia: que su primera esposa, ＿＿＿＿＿＿,[2] no murió en la Guerra Civil española.

Pedro, el ＿＿＿＿＿＿[3] de don Fernando, llama a Raquel Rodríguez. Raquel va a viajar a ＿＿＿＿＿＿,[4] a la ciudad de ＿＿＿＿＿＿,[5] para buscar a

_____,[6] la persona que escribió la carta. Pero la señora ya no _____[7]

allí.[a] Raquel habla con Elena Ramírez y con su _____,[8] Miguel Ruiz, quien

es también un _____[9] de Teresa Suárez. Ellos no _____[10] nada

de la historia de Rosario.

El domingo Raquel acompaña a la familia al mercadillo de los animales. Los hijos de

Miguel y Elena quieren un perro y su padre _____[11] uno. ¿Y qué pasa? El

perro se escapa y _____[12] se pierde en las calles de Sevilla buscándolo.[b]

Raquel corre por las calles también y finalmente _____[13] a Jaime. Los dos

hablan un poco con un hombre ciego que _____[14] cupones de la lotería.

Por fin Raquel y Jaime se reúnen con el resto de la familia. Al día siguiente Raquel

_____[15] un tren para Madrid. Allí vive la señora Suárez con otro hijo. Raquel

todavía no sabe _____[16] de Rosario.

[a] *there*   [b] *looking for him*

Have you completed the following sections of the lesson? Check them off here.

_____ **Preparación**
_____ **¿Tienes buena memoria?**
_____ **Repaso de los episodios 1–5**

Now scan the words in the **Vocabulario** list to be sure that you understand the meaning of most of them. Then you will be ready to continue on with **Lección 6** in the Workbook.

• •

Vocabulario

Las personas

el ganador/la ganadora	winner
el maestro/la maestra	grade-school teacher
el reportero/la reportera	reporter, journalist

Las cosas

el premio	prize

U n viaje a Madrid (España)

La Plaza Mayor de Madrid

FRANCIA

EL OCÉANO ATLÁNTICO

PORTUGAL

Madrid

ESPAÑA

EL MAR MEDITERRÁNEO

Sevilla

ÁFRICA

7

LA CARTERA*

DIA	COMUNICACION DE
HORA	
RECIBIDO POR:	

MENSAJE

☐ HA LLAMADO
☐ HA VENIDO

D. *Alfredo,*

¿Qué paso? ¡Lo busqué y no lo encontré!
Resulta que tengo que reunirme
con una persona. Por favor, deje
mi cartera en la recepción.
¿Me podría llamar esta noche?

Rafael Rodríguez.

OBJETIVOS

The materials in **Lección 7** of the Textbook and the Workbook will help you better understand the video episode and take you beyond it, giving you additional information about places and characters in the series. The Textbook will also help you to develop skill in using the Spanish language. In this lesson you will learn

- Spanish numbers from 21 to 99
- names for many articles of clothing
- ways to talk about who and what you know
- ways to make requests politely in Spanish.

You will also learn about the transition from dictatorship to democracy in today's Spain.
Be sure to work through all parts of the lesson. When you see a cassette symbol in the margin, listen to the tape for **Lección 7**. Answers or hints for many activities are given in Appendix 1. Be sure to check your answers for each activity before going on to the next one.

* The Wallet

BEFORE VIEWING . . .

PREPARACIÓN

a.   b.

Actividad A.

In the last episode of *Destinos* Raquel left Sevilla by train, on her way to Madrid to meet Sra. Suárez. What happened on the train? Indicate what you remember by identifying these two men.

1. _____ Viaja con Raquel en su compartimiento.
2. _____ Es reportero de la televisión.

Now indicate whether the following statements about **Episodio 6** are **Cierto** (**C**) or **Falso** (**F**).

C   F   1. El reportero cree que Raquel es otra persona.
C   F   2. El reportero no sabe por qué (*why*) Raquel está en España.
C   F   3. El señor que viaja en el compartimiento con Raquel se llama Alfredo Sánchez.
C   F   4. El reportero no tiene ningún (*any*) interés en el caso que investiga Raquel.

Actividad B.

What do you think will happen in this episode of *Destinos*? Indicate whether the following events are likely (**Probable**) or unlikely to happen (**Improbable**).

P   IMP   1. Raquel finalmente conoce a la Sra. Suárez.
P   IMP   2. El reportero sigue (*follows*) a Raquel porque quiere saber algo más del caso.
P   IMP   3. El reportero encuentra a la maestra que ganó (*won*) el premio de la lotería.
P   IMP   4. El reportero es persistente. Por fin Raquel le dice algo del caso que investiga.

Actividad C.

Here is one of the new characters you will meet in **Episodio 7**. As you look at the photo, listen to the brief description on the cassette tape. Then indicate who you think the man might be.

1. _____ Es el asistente que trabaja con el reportero.
2. _____ Es el recepcionista del hotel donde se aloja (*stays*) Raquel en Madrid.
3. _____ Es un hijo de la Sra. Suárez; vive en Madrid con ella.
4. _____ Es el hijo de don Fernando y Rosario.

Actividad D.

Here is part of a conversation that Raquel will have with a bellhop (**un botones**) at her Madrid hotel. Read through the conversation to get a general idea of what it is about.

BOTONES: ¡Qué pena lo de la cartera! Ojalá la encuentre pronto.

RAQUEL: Gracias. Un amigo está buscando el taxi ahora mismo. ¿Me puede hacer el favor de dejar un mensaje con el recepcionista?

BOTONES: Con mucho gusto, señorita.

RAQUEL: Cuando vuelva mi amigo, que me llame por teléfono.

BOTONES: ¿Y cómo se llama su amigo?

RAQUEL: Alfredo Sánchez. Bueno, realmente no es mi amigo. Es un reportero que conocí en el tren.

 Now listen to the conversation on the cassette tape. **Dejar** means *to leave*. Now that you know that, can you guess the meaning of the word **mensaje**?

La palabra *mensaje* significa

a. _____ messenger
b. _____ message

Based on your guesses so far, on the title of this video episode, and on what you have learned in **Actividad D**, what do you think will happen to Raquel?

a. _____ Raquel pierde (*loses*) su cartera.
b. _____ Raquel encuentra la cartera de otra persona, una persona muy importante para el caso.

AFTER VIEWING . . .

. . . .

¿TIENES BUENA MEMORIA?

Actividad A.   ¿Quién... ?

In **Episodio 7** you met some new characters and there is some confusion about who is who! Show that you know the characters by matching the following characters with their brief description.

1. _____ Federico Ruiz
2. _____ Alfredo Sánchez
3. _____ el Sr. Díaz

a.   un reportero
b.   otro hijo de la Sra. Teresa Suárez
c.   el botones que toma el mensaje de Raquel
d.   un maestro de primaria

Now match the following characters with the statements that describe them or that relate what they do in the episode. ¡OJO! More than one name may be possible for each statement.

a.   Federico Ruiz   d.   Raquel Rodríguez
b.   Alfredo Sánchez   e.   Teresa Suárez
c.   el Sr. Díaz

1.   _____ Pierde su cartera.
2.   _____ Encuentra la cartera perdida.
3.   _____ Busca a Raquel en el hotel.
4.   _____ Quiere conocer (*meet*) a Raquel.
5.   _____ Está alojado/a (*staying*) en el Hotel Príncipe de Vergara.
6.   _____ Espera (*Waits for*) a una persona en el hotel.

Actividad B.   ¿Qué pasa?

At this point, you know more about what happened this evening at the Hotel Príncipe de Vergara than some of the characters do! Answer the following questions about the slightly confusing events that happened in **Episodio 7**.

1.   ¿Por qué no recibe Raquel su cartera en este episodio?

    a.   _____ Porque Alfredo dice que no puede (*he can't*) llegar al hotel hasta mañana.

    b.   _____ Porque Raquel no puede encontrar a Alfredo y decide irse con Federico.

2.   ¿A quiénes confunde el botones cuando escribe la nota?

    a.   _____ Confunde a Alfredo Sánchez con Federico Ruiz.

    b.   _____ Confunde al Sr. Díaz con Alfredo Sánchez.

3.   ¿Qué confusión hay con el Sr. Díaz en la recepción?

    a.   _____ Creen que es una *señora*.

    b.   _____ No tienen su reservación.

Now listen to the answers on the cassette tape.

Actividad C.   ¡Un desafío!

Spain has a long and proud tradition of government by monarchy. You saw a number of famous Spanish monarchs in this video episode and you will learn more about the current Spanish monarchy later on in this lesson. Here are some of the names of the rulers from the video episode, in chronological order. Given what you know about Spanish history, can you match the names with the brief descriptions of them? ¡OJO! More than one name may be possible for each statement.

a.   Alfonso X, el Sabio (*The Wise*)   c.   Isabel de Castilla
b.   Fernando de Aragón   d.   Carlos I

1.   _____ Es esposo de una reina católica.
2.   _____ Cristóbal Colón habla con esta persona acerca de un proyecto especial.
3.   _____ Es un monarca español durante la época de la grandeza del Imperio español.
4.   _____ Conquistan a los árabes.
5.   _____ Es monarca cuando todavía hay muchos árabes en España.

• •

VOCABULARIO DEL TEMA

La ropa

la blusa	blouse	**la falda**	skirt
la bufanda	scarf	**el jersey**	sweater (*Spain*)
la camisa	shirt	**las medias**	stockings
la camiseta	T-shirt	**los pantalones**	pants
los calcetines	socks	**el suéter**	sweater
la corbata	necktie	**el vestido**	dress; suit
la chaqueta	jacket	**el zapato**	shoe
unas medias	a few pairs of stockings	**un par de...**	a pair of . . .
		zapatos	shoes
unos calcetines	a few pairs of socks	**pantalones**	pants

Of the two words that express *sweater*, **el suéter** is most widely used in the Spanish-speaking world. **El jersey** is used primarily in Spain.

Note the use of **unos/unas** to mean *a few*.

ROPA DE CABALLERO	LINGE DE MESSIEURS	GENTLEMEN'S LINEN	PTAS.
Camisa	Chemise	Shirt	450
Camiseta	Chemisette	Undershirt	250
Calzoncillo	Caleçon	Underpants	250
Calcetines	Chaussettes	Socks	225
Pañuelo	Mouchoir	Handkerchief	275

Actividad A.   ¿Qué ropa tiene Raquel?

Listen as Raquel lists the articles of clothing that she has brought with her on this trip. As she mentions each item, check it off in the following drawing and note how many of each item she has. ¡OJO! Some of the items depicted are not in Raquel's luggage. Look at the items before Raquel begins.

What does Raquel finally say about the amount of clothing she has with her?

_____ Tengo suficiente ropa.
_____ No tengo suficiente ropa.

Actividad B.   ¿Dónde está la ropa de Federico?

Listen as Teresa Suárez comments on the way her son takes care of his clothing. As she mentions each item, check it off in the following drawing. ¡OJO! Some of the items depicted are not in Federico's room. Look at the items before Sra. Suárez begins.

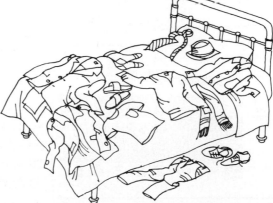

How do you think Sra. Suárez feels about the way her son takes care of things?

_____ Cree que Federico es muy ordenado (*neat*). Está muy contenta con él.
_____ No está muy contenta con él. Federico no es muy ordenado.

Actividad C. ¿Qué llevan?

What was Raquel wearing when she arrived at the hotel? What is Alfredo wearing in this photo? Describe their clothing as completely as you can.

Raquel lleva...

Alfredo lleva...

Actividad D. ¿Y tú?

¿Qué llevas en las siguientes situaciones?

MODELO: Vas a una fiesta informal. → Llevo pantalones y una camiseta.

Palabras útiles: una sudadera (*sweatshirt*), los pantalones cortos (*shorts*), los zapatos de tenis

1. Vas a una fiesta informal.
2. Vas a cenar en casa de unos amigos.
3. Vas a cenar en un restaurante elegante.
4. Vas a viajar en tren.
5. Estás en casa, estudiando (*studying*).
6. Corres en la mañana.
7. Limpias (*You're cleaning*) la casa/el apartamento.

Los números del 21 al 99

21 veintiuno*	30 treinta	70 setenta
22 veintidós	31 treinta y uno*	80 ochenta
23 veintitrés	32 treinta y dos	90 noventa
24 veinticuatro	33 treinta y tres	100 cien
25 veinticinco	...	101 ciento y uno
26 veintiséis	40 cuarenta	
27 veintisiete	50 cincuenta	
28 veintiocho	60 sesenta	
29 veintinueve		

---

*The numbers 21–29 can be written as one word (as in the list) or as three: **veinte y uno**, **veinte y dos**. From 31 to 99, compound numbers are written as three words only.

Express a year in this century by using the phrase **mil novecientos** (19–) followed by the appropriate numbers.

1993   mil novecientos noventa y tres

Actividad E.   ¿Cuál es el número?

The speaker on the tape will say a number. Circle the number you hear in each group.

1. 63   73   53
2. 41   81   91

3. 76   66   36
4. 55   45   95

Actividad F.   ¿Cuál es el teléfono?

Now the speaker will give a series of telephone numbers. As you listen, supply the missing numbers.

1. 3–____–33–____

2. ____–99–____–68

3. 7–36–____–____

4. ____–75–____–91

5. 5–____–25–____

6. 7–15–____–____

Actividad G.   ¿Cuándo… ?

The speaker will say a series of dates. All of them are from the twentieth century. Write what you hear, then match the dates with the appropriate historical event.

1. _____

2. _____

3. _____

4. _____

5. _____

a.   el comienzo de la Revolución mexicana
b.   el fin de la Segunda Guerra mundial
c.   el conflicto en Corea
d.   la Guerra Civil española
e.   la crisis del Golfo pérsico

Actividad H.   Números… y más números

You may not have to deal with as many numbers as does the hotel receptionist in Sevilla, but there are still many numbers that are personally important to you. Give the following numbers in Spanish.

1.   tu número de teléfono: el… (¡OJO! Follow the pattern for telephone numbers shown in **Actividad F**.)

2.   el número de teléfono de tu mejor amigo/a (*best friend*)

3.   el número de teléfono de tus padres/tus hijos

4.   la edad (*age*) de uno de tus padres: Mi padre/madre tiene

_____ años.

5.   ¿tu número de la suerte (*lucky*)?

CONVERSACIONES: ALGO SOBRE LA CORTESÍA

Actividad.   Necesito...

On the cassette tape you will hear four brief conversational exchanges in which people make a request or tell someone what they would like to do. You know several verbs to use to accomplish that task; for example, **Deseo...**, **Necesito...** However, stating your wishes in that way can seem very blunt or abrupt. The speakers on the tape will show you ways to be more polite.

Paso 1

Listen to all of the conversations now and indicate which of the expressions you hear in each.

_____ ¿podría... ?

_____ quisiera...

_____ ¿me permite... ?

_____ me gustaría...

Paso 2

Now listen to the conversations again and match the expressions with their probable meaning, as determined by the context of the conversations.

1.   _____ ¿podría... ?
2.   _____ quisiera...
3.   _____ ¿me permite... ?
4.   _____ me gustaría...

a.   I would really like to . . .
b.   May I please have . . . ?
c.   Could I please . . . ?

Note that expressions l, 2, and 4 were followed by infinitives in the conversations you just heard: **Me gustaría *pagar* con tarjeta de crédito.**

Paso 3

Following the model of the conversations you have heard, how would you make the following requests politely?

• May I please have your credit card?
• I would really like to talk with Raquel.
• Could I leave a message?
• May I use the telephone?

UN POCO DE GRAMÁTICA

Expressing *knowing*

Spanish speakers use **saber** to indicate that someone knows something and **conocer** to indicate knowing a person, meeting someone for the first time, or being familiar with a place.

Raquel no **sabe** dónde vive Rosario.	*Raquel doesn't know where Rosario lives.*
Sólo Teresa Suárez **conoce** a Rosario.	*Only Teresa Suárez knows Rosario.*

You will learn the irregular **yo** forms of these verbs (**sé**, **conozco**) in the Workbook.

Actividad.   ¿Qué sabe? ¿A quién conoce?

Indicate whether these statements are **Cierto** (**C**) or **Falso** (**F**). All are easy!

C   F   1. La Sra. Suárez sabe que Raquel busca información acerca de (*about*) Rosario.

C   F   2. Don Fernando conoce a la Sra. Suárez.

C   F   3. Teresa Suárez no conoce a Elena Ramírez.

C   F   4. Jaime y Miguel saben que su abuela ya no vive en la calle Pureza.

C   F   5. Raquel sabe la dirección (*address*) de Teresa Suárez en Madrid.

C   F   6. Miguel, Jaime y sus padres conocen a don Fernando.

C   F   7. Raquel no conoce al Sr. Díaz.

C   F   8. Alfredo Sánchez desea saber más acerca de don Fernando.

C   F   9. Raquel conoce España porque viaja allí con frecuencia.

C   F   10. El Sr. Díaz conoce Sevilla, pero no conoce Madrid muy bien.

Nota cultural: De la dictadura a la democracia

Refresh your memory about modern Spain by listening to what the narrator told you about the Spanish government in this video episode. Then reread the **Nota cultural** about **la Guerra Civil española** in **Lección 2**. Reviewing information you already know about a topic makes reading about it easier. Before reading, you may also want to take a quick look at the questions in the **Actividad** that follows this **Nota cultural**.

esde 1939 hasta 1975 España es gobernada por[1] el régimen dictatorial del general Francisco Franco. La muerte[2] del general Franco en 1975 abre las puertas[3] a la democracia. Dos días después de[4] su muerte, el 22 de noviembre, don Juan Carlos I (nombrado por Franco su sucesor) es proclamado Rey de España. Son días difíciles para todos, pero el deseo de libertad y democracia permite una transición política pacífica.

En 1977 se celebran las primeras elecciones democráticas desde[5] 1936. La principal tarea[6] del nuevo gobierno es redactar[7] una nueva Constitución, con la colaboración de todos los partidos[8] políticos. La Constitución se aprueba[9] popularmente en diciembre del 78. Adolfo Suárez es elegido el primer presidente de gobierno bajo la nueva Constitución. En 1982 los españoles votaron un gobierno socialista presidido por Felipe González, que también ganó las elecciones generales del 86 y del 89.

Así como en Inglaterra, el rey de España no tiene mucho poder[10] político. Más bien[11] es un símbolo de la larga historia política del país.[12] Pero, además de su papel[13] simbólico, el rey tiene algunos deberes. Por ejemplo, representa a España en muchas funciones nacionales e[14] internacionales.

Don Juan Carlos de Borbón y doña Sofía reinan en España con el respeto y la admiración de todo el pueblo.[15] En pocos años España se ha transformado de un país aislado[16] a un país europeo moderno. Desde el año 1986 forma parte de la Comunidad Económica Europea, afirmando así su nueva posición en el continente.

[1]gobernada... *governed by* [2]*death* [3]abre... *opens the doors* [4]después... *after* [5]*since* [6]*task* [7]escribir [8]*parties* [9]se... *is approved* [10]*power* [11]Más... *Rather* [12]nación [13]*role* [14]y [15]todo... *all the people* [16]se... *has transformed herself from an isolated country*

El rey don Juan Carlos y la reina doña Sofía

Actividad.   ¿Cuánto sabes?

Match the names on the left with the descriptions on the right.

1. _____ el régimen de Franco
2. _____ el gobierno actual de España
3. _____ don Juan Carlos
4. _____ Adolfo Suárez
5. _____ Felipe González
6. _____ doña Sofía
7. _____ el rey español

a. Reina de España y esposa de Juan Carlos
b. una monarquía constitucional
c. el primer presidente del gobierno bajo la Constitución del 78
d. una dictadura
e. Rey de España; nombrado por Franco su sucesor
f. papel político más simbólico que verdadero
g. presidente socialista de España

Have you completed the following sections of the lesson? Check them off here.

_____ **Preparación**   _____ **Conversaciones**
_____ **¿Tienes buena memoria?** _____ **Un poco de gramática**
_____ **Vocabulario del tema**

  Now scan the words in the **Vocabulario** list to be sure that you understand the meaning of most of them. Then you will be ready to continue on with **Lección 7** in the Workbook.

• •

VOCABULARIO

Los verbos

dejar	to leave (*something*) behind
esperar*	to wait (for)
llevar	to wear
conoce	he/she knows, meets (*a person*)
pierde	he/she loses
puede	he/she can

Repaso: sabe

La ropa (Clothing)

la blusa	blouse
la bufanda	scarf
los calcetines	socks
la camisa	shirt
la camiseta	T-shirt
la cartera	wallet
la corbata	necktie
la chaqueta	jacket
la falda	skirt
el jersey (*Spain*)	sweater
las medias	stockings
los pantalones	pants
el suéter	sweater
el vestido	dress; suit
el zapato	shoe
un par de...	a pair of . . .

Las personas

el botones	bellhop
el recepcionista	receptionist

Las cosas

el mensaje	message

Los números

treinta, cuarenta, cincuenta, sesenta, setenta, ochenta, noventa

mil novecientos...

La cortesía (Courtesy)

me gustaría + *inf.*	I would really like to (*do something*)
¿me permite... ?	may I please have . . . ?
¿podría + *inf.*?	could I please (*do something*)? is it possible for me to (*do something*)?
quisiera + *inf.*	I would really like to (*do something*)

Las palabras adicionales

acerca de	about
después de	after
¿por qué?	why?

---

*Note that *for* is included in the meaning of the verb **esperar** (just as **buscar** means *to look for*). Remember to use the personal **a** after this verb with specific persons. *Compare*: **Raquel espera el tren. Raquel espera *a* Jaime.**

8

EL ENCUENTRO*

OBJETIVOS

The materials in **Lección 8** of the Textbook and the Workbook will help you better understand the video episode and take you beyond it, giving you additional information about places and characters in the series. The Textbook will also help you to develop skill in using the Spanish language. In this lesson you will learn

- more about asking questions in Spanish
- more about the system of Spanish verbs
- expressions of gratitude in Spanish.

You will also learn about the differences between various areas of Spain.

Be sure to work through all parts of the lesson. When you see a cassette symbol in the margin, listen to the tape for **Lección 8**. Answers or hints for many activities are given in Appendix 1. Be sure to check your answers for each activity before going on to the next one.

*The Encounter

BEFORE VIEWING . . .

PREPARACIÓN

Actividad A.

In the last video episode of *Destinos*, you watched a "comedy of errors" that occurred at Raquel's hotel. Things were lost, everyone was looking or waiting for someone else, and identities were confused. To be sure that you have understood the details, match these statements with the characters who made them.

a. Raquel Rodríguez   b. Federico Ruiz   c. el Sr. Díaz   d. Alfredo Sánchez

1. «¡Huy! No encuentro mi cartera.»
2. «No se preocupe. José María y yo se la vamos a buscar.»
3. «Perdón. Hay un error. La tarjeta está a nombre de la Sra. Díaz.»
4. «Ya he conseguido (*managed to get*) su cartera.»
5. «Por ser tan amable, lo invito a tomar algo.»
6. «Mi madre está muy agradecida y quiere invitarla a cenar con nosotros en casa esta noche.»

¡Un desafío! Can you also indicate with whom each character is speaking?

Actividad B.

The title of this episode, **El encuentro**, refers to the fact that Raquel will finally talk to Teresa Suárez. What questions is Raquel likely to ask her? Indicate whether it is **Probable** (**P**) or **Improbable** (**IMP**) that Raquel will ask these questions.

P   IMP   1. ¿Por qué vive Ud. ahora en Madrid?
P   IMP   2. ¿Dónde está Rosario ahora?
P   IMP   3. ¿Cuándo murió el Sr. Ruiz, su esposo?
P   IMP   4. ¿Cómo sabe Ud. que don Fernando fue el esposo de Rosario?
P   IMP   5. ¿Cómo se llama el hijo de Rosario y don Fernando?

Now formulate two more questions that Raquel might ask Sra. Suárez. How do you think Sra. Suárez will answer all of these questions?

Actividad C.

In this activity you will learn about some key words and phrases that will enhance your understanding of **Episodio 8**.

Paso 1

Listen to the following excerpt from Raquel's conversation with Teresa Suárez.
Now read the following sentences as you listen to them on the cassette tape.

Don Fernando se casó con Rosario en 1935.
Don Fernando se casó con Carmen en 1942.
Teresa Suárez se casó con Juan Ruiz en 1941.

What do you think the phrase **se casó** means? If you guessed *got married,* you were right.

Paso 2

Look at this document, then answer the questions that follow.

This document is called **un certificado de nacimiento**. What kind of document do you think it is?

a. _____ an invitation to a function of some kind

b. _____ a letter

c. _____ a birth certificate

d. _____ a marriage license

Paso 3

As you know, Sra. Suárez is much older than Raquel. After Raquel has asked her questions, Teresa has a few of her own. Read this excerpt from their continuing conversation, and pay particular attention to the phrase **Cuando yo tenía su edad...**

SUÁREZ: ¿Es Ud. pariente de Fernando?
RAQUEL: No. Soy abogada. La familia de él me pidió que investigara el paradero de Rosario.
SUÁREZ: Así que tampoco es amiga cercana de la familia...
RAQUEL: Realmente no. Conozco bien a Pedro, el hermano de don Fernando.
SUÁREZ: Una señorita como Ud. tan atractiva, bien educada... ¡Y abogada! Eso era casi imposible cuando yo tenía su edad. Y ahora es tan corriente.

Paso 4

Now listen to the excerpt on the cassette tape. Then answer the following question.

What do you think Teresa means when she says **cuando yo tenía su edad**?

a. _____ When I met my husband . . .
b. _____ When I was your age . . .
c. _____ When I left my home . . .

──────　**AFTER VIEWING . . .**

¿TIENES BUENA MEMORIA?

Actividad A.　¿Quién lo hizo?

The following statements summarize the main events of **Episodio 8**. Who carried out each one? ¡OJO! More than one name may be possible for each statement.

¿Quién... ?

a.　Raquel
b.　Teresa
c.　Federico

1. _____ Finalmente conoce a la Sra. Suárez.
2. _____ Hace varias preguntas.
3. _____ Dice que Rosario vive en la Argentina.
4. _____ Dice que don Fernando está en el hospital.
5. _____ Tiene una carta de Rosario.
6. _____ Toma un fino (*sherry*) y cena.
7. _____ Cuenta (*tells*) la historia del perro perdido.
8. _____ Lleva a Raquel a su hotel.
9. _____ Llama a Elena Ramírez.
10. _____ Recibe un TELEX.

Actividad B.   ¿Quién lo va a hacer?

In **Episodio 8** the character made a number of plans for the near and distant
future. Indicate who is going to do each of the following by matching the names
on the left with the plans on the right.

1. _____ Raquel
2. _____ el Sr. Díaz
3. _____ Federico
4. _____ Alfredo Sánchez

a. Va a conseguir (*obtain*) un certificado de nacimiento.
b. Va a ver a Raquel mañana.
c. Va a darle una foto a la Sra. Suárez.
d. Va a visitar un taller de guitarras.
e. Tiene que viajar a la Argentina.
f. Va a visitar un museo famoso.
g. Va a darle una cartera a Raquel.

Nota cultural: La comida española

Tapas (Spanish *hors d'œuvres*) have recently
become popular in the United States. Consequently, you probably weren't surprised to see
a number of the characters in *Destinos* having
tapas. Olives (**las aceitunas**) and portions of
tortilla española are typical Spanish snacks;
others include **jamón serrano** (cured Spanish ham, similar to prosciutto) and **calamares
fritos** (fried squid rings).

Having a snack and a drink of some kind in
the late afternoon—a soft drink or mineral water, hot tea, an alcoholic beverage—is a
popular Hispanic custom. In this video episode and in a previous episode you have seen
some of the characters having **un fino** (a dry Spanish sherry), accompanied by the toast
¡Salud! (*To your health!*). As you will see, the specific food items and beverages for the
afternoon snack vary from country to country.

Finally, note that places like the bar (visited by Sr. Díaz and the reporter) and variations on them (**la Cervecería Giralda** from **Episodio 4**) do not have the negative connotations they can have in other cultures. You may recall that Miguel and Elena's children
accompanied their parents to the pub.

Actividad C.   ¿Qué más sabes ahora?

Raquel is finally finding out something about Rosario.

Paso 1

Indicate which of the following pieces of information Teresa Suárez gives Raquel.

1. _____ el nombre del segundo esposo de Rosario
2. _____ el número de teléfono de Rosario
3. _____ la fecha (*date*) en que Rosario se casó con Fernando
4. _____ la dirección (*address*) de Rosario en la Argentina
5. _____ el cumpleaños (*birthday*) de Rosario
6. _____ el nombre del hijo de Rosario y don Fernando.

Paso 2

Now listen to Raquel's review of the essential information she has learned. She will repeat some of the details, so you have two chances to catch them. Because Raquel is talking about the past, remember that she will use many past tense forms.

Paso 3

Now complete the following version of Raquel's review. Choose words and phrases from this list.

murió	la Argentina	un hijo	se casó
no murió	México	una hija	no se casó

La Sra. Suárez me cuenta la historia de Rosario. Rosario _____¹ durante la Guerra Civil española. Tampocoª murió don Fernando. Pero los dos creían que el otro había muerto.ᵇ Rosario sí tuvo _____² llamadoᶜ Ángel. Rosario y su hijo fueron a vivir a _____.³ Allíᵈ Rosario _____⁴ de nuevo.ᵉ Su segundo esposo se llama Martín Iglesias.

ªNeither ᵇhabía... *had died* ᶜnamed ᵈThere ᵉde... *again*

Vocabulario del tema

Las palabras interrogativas

¿cómo?	how?	¿dónde?	where?
¿cuál(es)?	which?	¿por qué?	why?
¿cuándo?	when?	¿qué?	what?
¿cuánto(s)?	how much? how many?	¿quién(es)?	who?

Most of these interrogative words should be familiar to you by now.

Note that interrogative words have an accent mark and that they are used with the inverted question mark (¿). You will learn more about using interrogatives in the Workbook.

Actividad.   Preguntas sobre *Destinos*

The speaker on the cassette tape will ask a number of questions about **Episodio 8**. Read the following answers before listening to his questions. Then, as you listen, write the number of the question next to its logical answer. In the speaker's questions you will hear the falling intonation that is typical of questions with interrogatives.

a. _____ Cerca de (*Close to*) Buenos Aires.

b. _____ Ángel.

c. _____ Es el segundo esposo de Rosario.

d. _____ Sóla una... ¡y la pierde!

e. _____ Unas cartas.

f. _____ Necesita hablar con Teresa Suárez.

g. _____ En casa de la Sra. Suárez.

h. _____ Sólo uno.

i. _____ De Guernica.

j. _____ Después de la guerra.

Now listen as the speaker asks the questions again. Give your answers and see whether you were right. The speaker will provide some additional information.

CONVERSACIONES: LOS AGRADECIMIENTOS

Actividad.   ¡Muchas gracias!

Knowing how to express and acknowledge gratitude is important in any language. You probably know the Spanish expressions **gracias** and **muchas gracias**. You will learn more about them in this activity.

Paso 1

On the cassette tape you will hear three brief conversations in which people express their gratitude. As you listen to each conversation, indicate how those individuals voice their appreciation by writing 1, 2, or 3 next to the appropriate expression.

_____ De nada.   _____ Hola.

_____ Adiós.   _____ No hay de qué.

Paso 2

Now listen to the first conversation again and to an additional conversation. This time pay attention to the word Raquel uses to express what she is thankful *for*.

Gracias _____ su (invitación, carta, amabilidad…).

_____ para

_____ por

_____ con

Paso 3

How would you tell someone you don't know well that you are grateful for the following things?

- his or her letter
- his or her invitation to dinner (**su invitación a cenar**)
- his or her kindness.

Nota cultural: Nos podemos tutear

As you know, Raquel uses **usted** with people she does not know well. In this video episode of *Destinos*, however, you heard one speaker "negotiate" for a less formal way of speaking. Do you remember who that was? As you listen, try to determine the word the speaker uses to describe informal use.

The words Federico used to express *using* **tú** *with each other* were **tutearse** or **tratarse de tú**. If someone asks you to do that, you will want to begin addressing him or her by using the second-person singular verb forms, just as Raquel shifts from **trabaja** to **trabajas**.

When everyone was in Teresa's kitchen, Federico tried to make Raquel feel at home with a frequently-used phrase: **Está en su casa**. Now that Federico and Raquel address each other with **tú**, he would say: **Estás en tu casa**.

Un poco de gramática

> ### More About Verbs
>
> You are already familiar with stem-changing verbs in Spanish.
>
> > Raquel **encuentra** a Jaime en el barrio de Santa Cruz.
> > Fernando **tiene** un hijo con Rosario.
>
> These verbs are called stem-changing because four forms have a vowel change in the stem. Note the infinitives of the previous verbs in the following sentences.
>
> > Raquel desea **encontrar** a Rosario.
> > Fernando quiere **tener** noticias de Rosario.
>
> **Querer** (**quiere**), another stem-changing verb, is a synonym of **desear**.
> You will learn more about stem-changing verbs in the Workbook.

Actividad.   El caso de Raquel

How do people feel about Raquel's investigation so far? Select the items that you think are true for each of the following persons. As you read the statements, note the stem changes (for example, **tiene** from **tener**).

1. Raquel

    _____ ya tiene suficiente información sobre Rosario.
    _____ quiere tener más información sobre Rosario.
    _____ puede regresar a Los Ángeles ahora.

2. Don Fernando

    _____ quiere hablar con la Sra. Suárez personalmente.
    _____ va a querer saber más acerca de su hijo Ángel.
    _____ no va a poder viajar a México.

3. Alfredo, el reportero,

    _____ no pierde ninguna (*any*) oportunidad para hacerle preguntas a
    Raquel.
    _____ quiere saber más sobre el caso de don Fernando.
    _____ ya no quiere encontrar a la maestra de primaria que ganó el premio.

Nota cultural: Las diferencias regionales en España

Before reading this **Nota cultural**, refresh your memory about modern Spain by listening to what the narrator told you about the cities of Madrid and Sevilla in this video episode. Then reread the **Nota cultural** in **Lección 3** about the contrasts that Spain presents, and the one in **Lección 5** about the Arab influence in Spain.

España se divide políticamente en 17 comunidades autónomas. Cada[1] autonomía tiene sus propias características geográficas y culturales.

Cataluña: en el norte

Cataluña es una de las zonas más prósperas de España. Es un centro industrial, agrícola y comercial muy importante. En Cataluña se habla otra lengua romance además del español: el catalán.

Barcelona es la ciudad catalana más grande y la segunda ciudad de España. La huella[2] del gran arquitecto Antoni Gaudí da un sabor[3] muy especial a esta ciudad cosmopolita.

[1] *each* [2] *influence* [3] *flavor*

La Catedral de la Sagrada Familia, una iglesia excepcional de Barcelona: obra de Gaudí

Castilla: el centro de la Península

En realidad hay dos comunidades con este nombre. Castilla-La Mancha es la zona más central del país. Tiene grandes extensiones de cereales[4] y molinos de viento.[5]

Castilla-León está llena de monumentos de gran interés histórico: la universidad de Salamanca (una de las más antiguas[6] de Europa), el acueducto romano de Segovia y otros.

El acueducto de Segovia: un monumento de la civilización romana que todavía funciona

Andalucía: en el sur

La variedad geográfica de Andalucía es impresionante. Hay dunas de arena[7] blanca, pueblecitos blancos. Tiene también las playas de la Costa del Sol, la Sierra Nevada y los mayores[8] desiertos del continente europeo (escenario de las famosas películas[9] del oeste de Clint Eastwood). ¿Y andaluces famosos? Entre ellos, Pablo Picasso, Diego Velázquez, el compositor Manuel de Falla y el poeta y dramaturgo Federico García Lorca.

Algunas autonomías en breve

- Valencia: Una zona agrícola muy rica, produce las famosas naranjas[10] valencianas.
- Asturias: Con sus montañas, valles y lagos, es la Suiza española.
- el País Vasco: La comunidad más industrializada y rica de España también atrae a los turistas a San Sebastián. Aquí se habla un idioma de origen desconocido.[11]
- Extremadura: En esta tierra de ganado[12] nacieron muchos de los exploradores del continente americano: Cortés, Pizarro, Balboa.
- las islas Canarias: Con su antiguo volcán, el Teide, son las islas Hawai del Océano Atlántico.

Olivares en una meseta de Andalucía

[4]*grains* [5]*molinos... windmills* [6]*más... oldest* [7]*sand* [8]*biggest* [9]*movies* [10]*oranges* [11]*unknown* [12]*cattle*

Actividad. ¿Dónde?

Where would you expect to find the following people and things in Spain?

1. personas bilingües
2. casas muy antiguas
3. monumentos romanos
4. granjas (*farms*)
5. playas con hoteles

6. un paisaje (*landscape*) impresionante
7. muchas fábricas (*factories*)
8. ranchos

Have you completed the following sections of the lesson? Check them off here.

_____ **Preparación**   _____ **Conversaciones**
_____ **¿Tienes buena memoria?**   _____ **Un poco de gramática**
_____ **Vocabulario del tema**

    Now scan the words in the **Vocabulario** list to be sure that you understand the meaning of most of them. Then you will be ready to continue on with **Lección 8** in the Workbook.

VOCABULARIO

Los verbos

se casó con	he/she married
cuenta	he/she tells
quiere	he/she wants

Los conceptos

la dirección	address
el encuentro	meeting
la guerra	war

Las palabras interrogativas
(Interrogative Words)

¿cuándo?	when?
¿cuánto(s)? ¿cuánta(s)?	how much? how many?

Repaso: ¿cómo?, ¿cuál(es)?, ¿dónde?,
¿por qué?, ¿qué?, ¿quién(es)?

Los adjetivos

segundo/a	second

Los agradecimientos (Thanks)

(Muchas) gracias.	(Many) thanks.
De nada.	You're welcome.
No hay de qué.	You're welcome (*formal*).

Las palabras adicionales

de nuevo	again
hacer preguntas	to ask questions

9

ESTACIONES*

OBJETIVOS

The materials in **Lección 9** of the Textbook and the Workbook will help you better understand the video episode and take you beyond it, giving you additional information about places and characters in the series. The Textbook will also help you to develop skill in using the Spanish language. In this lesson you will learn

- names for the months and seasons
- colors
- more ways to talk about what you are doing
- some ways to express agreement.

You will also learn about different kinds of Spanish music, including a special kind of singing group called **una tuna**.

Be sure to work through all parts of the lesson. When you see a cassette symbol in the margin, listen to the tape for **Lección 9**. Answers or hints for many activities are given in Appendix 1. Be sure to check your answers for each activity before going on to the next one.

*Seasons

━━━━▭━━━ **BEFORE VIEWING . . .**

. . . .

Preparación

Actividad A.

Episodio 8 was important in terms of the progress of Raquel's investigation. For the first time, Raquel has learned some concrete information about the case she is investigating. How much do you remember about the progress she made? Indicate whether the following statements are **Cierto** (**C**) or **Falso** (**F**). If Raquel still does not know a particular piece of information, indicate **no se sabe todavía** (**NSS**).

1. Raquel descubre que Rosario
   - C   F   NSS   a. no murió en la guerra.
   - C   F   NSS   b. no tuvo un hijo.
   - C   F   NSS   c. se fue a vivir a la Argentina.
   - C   F   NSS   d. nunca se casó de nuevo.
   - C   F   NSS   e. murió en la Argentina.
2. Al final del Episodio 8, Raquel
   - C   F   NSS   a. llama a Elena Ramírez.
   - C   F   NSS   b. necesita saber la dirección de Rosario en Buenos Aires.
   - C   F   NSS   c. quiere un certificado de nacimiento.
   - C   F   NSS   d. tiene la cartera perdida.
   - C   F   NSS   e. recibe una carta.

Actividad B.

At the end of the last video episode Raquel received a TELEX. What do you think the TELEX is about? Choose the description that best expresses your expectations.

```
GA
27063
0811:
27063 NHBAM E
#
27063 NHBAM E
27064 NHPVM E

   QUERIDA RAQUEL:
FERNANDO ESTA PEOR.ME URGE COMUNICARME CONTIGO.
LLAMAME AL HOSPITAL INGLES 3-95-72-83

            SALUDOS. PEDRO
```

1. _____ Es un TELEX de Pedro. Le dice a Raquel que don Fernando está muy mal. Ella debe llamar a la familia Castillo inmediatamente.
2. _____ Es un TELEX de la oficina de Raquel en Los Ángeles. Ella tiene que volver a la oficina lo más pronto posible (*as soon as possible*).
3. _____ Es un TELEX del hotel Doña María, en Sevilla. Tienen algunas cosas que Raquel dejó en el hotel.

AFTER VIEWING . . .

¿TIENES BUENA MEMORIA?

Actividad A.   ¿Quién lo hace?

Match the following events or actions from the video episode with the person or persons associated with them. ¡OJO! More than one character may be associated with each item.

a.   Teresa Suárez
b.   Raquel Rodríguez
c.   el Sr. Díaz

d.   Federico Ruiz
e.   Alfredo Sánchez

1.   _____ Va a un taller (*shop*) de guitarras para ver a Federico.
2.   _____ Le da algo a Raquel.
3.   _____ Escucha (*Listens to*) música.
4.   _____ Quiere saber más acerca de un caso interesante.
5.   _____ Revela la información correcta acerca de un caso.
6.   _____ Compra ropa.
7.   _____ Aprende (*Learns*) algo acerca de un caso.
8.   _____ Va a una agencia de viajes.

Nota cultural: Un café, por favor

When Raquel ordered coffee (**un café, nada más**), the waiter poured it immediately from the pot that he had in his hand. Raquel could also have ordered her coffee by saying **un café solo**.

The waiter had to return with Alfredo's order, which was somewhat different: **Y un café con leche, por favor**. In many parts of the Spanish-speaking world, very strong coffee (almost like *expresso*) is mixed with warm or hot milk (**leche**). The milk is served on the side and added by the customer, to his or her taste.

Actividad B.   Problemas nuevos y viejos

In **Episodio 9** a number of situations either escalated or were resolved or averted. Did you catch the most important details about them?

Acerca de don Fernando

C   F   1. Está en el hospital.
C   F   2. Ya murió.
C   F   3. Ahora está mucho mejor (*better*).

Acerca de «la maestra»

C F 4. La maestra que ganó el premio es maestro.
C F 5. El Sr. Díaz es el maestro.
C F 6. Alfredo ya no quiere saber la historia del cupón.

Acerca de Raquel

C F 7. No tiene reservación para la Argentina.
C F 8. No tiene ropa apropiada para la Argentina.

VOCABULARIO DEL TEMA

Los meses y las estaciones del año

el invierno winter **la primavera** spring **el verano** summer **el otoño** autumn

diciembre	**marzo**	**junio**	**septiembre**
enero	**abril**	**julio**	**octubre**
febrero	**mayo**	**agosto**	**noviembre**

Note that many Spanish speakers prefer the form **setiembre** (without the **p**). As you saw in **Episodio 9**, the seasons are reversed in the southern hemisphere.

ENERO					FEBRERO					MARZO				
L		7	14	21	28	L		4	11	18	25	L		4	11	18	25
M	1	8	15	22	29	M		5	12	19	26	M		5	12	19	26
M	(2)	9	16	(23)	30	M		6	13	20	27	M		6	13	20	27
J	3	10	17	24	31	J		7	14	21	(28)	J		7	14	21	28
V	4	11	18	25	V	(1)	8	15	22	V	1	8	(15)	22	29
S	5	12	16	26	S	2	9	16	23	S	2	9	16	23	30
D	6	13	20	27	D	3	10	17	24	D	3	10	17	24	31

Actividad A. ¿México o Chile?

As you watched **Episodio 9**, you answered questions about the seasons in Spain and Argentina. Now do the same for Mexico and Chile. First listen to a description of the seasons in the different hemispheres. Then answer the questions you hear.

¿Se refiere a México o a Chile?

1. ... 2. ... 3. ... 4. ...

Actividad B. ¿En qué mes... ?

Listen as the names of the following holidays are said by the speaker on the cassette tape. Then indicate in Spanish the name of the month in which the following events occur in the United States.

1. la celebración de la independencia de los Estados Unidos
2. el aniversario de la llegada (*arrival*) de Cristóbal Colón a América
3. el Día de Dar Gracias
4. el primer día del año
5. el Día del Padre
6. el Día de la Madre
7. el Día de San Valentín (el Día de los Enamorados [*Lovers*])
8. el Día de San Patricio
9. el Día del Trabajo (*Work*)
10. la Navidad y Chanuka

Actividad C.   ¿Qué estación asocias con… ?

Indicate the season with which you associate the following items. ¡OJO! More than one season may be appropriate for each.

1. las vacaciones
2. la agricultura
3. las flores (*flowers*)

4. el frío (*cold*)
5. el calor (*heat*)
6. el nacimiento de los pájaros

Los colores

amarillo	yellow	**morado**	purple
anaranjado	orange	**negro**	black
azul	blue	**rojo**	red
blanco	white	**rosado**	pink
gris	gray	**verde**	green
marrón, pardo	brown		

Remember that adjectives must agree in number and gender with the nouns they modify.

- Adjectives that end in **-o** have four forms: **rojo, roja, rojos, rojas**.
- Adjectives that end in **-e** or in most consonants have only a singular and a plural form: **verde, verdes**; **azul, azules**.

Actividad D.   Asociaciones

What colors do you associate with the following words and phrases?

> MODELO: la Navidad → el (color) verde, el (color) rojo…

1. el invierno
2. el verano

3. la primavera
4. el otoño

5. los peces tropicales
6. el perro Osito
7. Rosario

8. los gatos que traen mala suerte (*luck*)
9. el día de San Valentín
10. el día de San Patricio

Actividad E.　La ropa más apropiada

Describe the clothing you think is most appropriate for the following occasions or the following places. Specify colors whenever possible.

Palabras útiles: las botas, los guantes (*gloves*), los pantalones cortos (*shorts*), un sombrero, una gorra (*cap*), el pijama

1. un partido (*game*) de fútbol norteamericano en tu universidad, en noviembre
2. un partido de béisbol, en julio
3. una discoteca, en mayo
4. un baile de gala (*formal*), en junio
5. una clase de química, en septiembre
6. un viaje a Colorado en febrero, para esquiar (*ski*)
7. un viaje a Acapulco, en agosto
8. un día en casa, en enero
9. una fiesta de Halloween

Actividad F.　¿Y tú?

Describe four things that you are wearing today, being certain to specify the color(s) of each item. Then select two other people and describe what they are wearing.

1. Hoy llevo... Me gustaría llevar...
2. Mi amigo/a (profesor[a], esposo/a, hijo/a...) lleva...

. . . .

CONVERSACIONES: PARA DECIR QUE SÍ

Actividad.　¡De acuerdo!

It is important to know how to express agreement or disagreement. In this video episode you have heard several ways to express agreement, including one that is very typical of Spain.

Paso 1

On the cassette tape you will hear three brief conversations in which people agree to something. As you listen to each conversation, indicate how those individuals responded by writing the number of the conversation (1, 2, or 3) next to the appropriate expression.

    _____ Sí.   _____ Sí, vale.   _____ Claro.

    _____ Vale.   _____ De acuerdo.

Of these phrases for expressing agreement, **vale** (**sí, vale**) is most typically used in Spain, although it is understood in other parts of the Spanish-speaking world.

Paso 2

Now listen to the first conversation again. You might expect that the word **bueno** (*good*), used twice, serves to express agreement, but that is not the case. Listen and try to determine what function the word **bueno** performs in this conversation.

        _____ It helps speakers make a transition to a new topic.

        _____ It conveys the speaker's personal liking for a topic.

Paso 3

You now know several ways to express agreement in Spanish. Listen to the suggestions made to you by the speaker on the cassette tape and, if appropriate, express your agreement with them. If you are not interested, just say **Lo siento** (*I'm sorry*), **pero no puedo.**

1. ...   2. ...   3. ...

• •

Un poco de gramática

More About Talking About Yourself

When you are talking about someone else, you already know that **se** is used with some verbs.

> Raquel y la Sra. Suárez **se sientan** a hablar.
> El maestro **se llama** el Sr. Díaz.

To talk about yourself, use **me** with these verbs.

RAQUEL: **Me llamo** Raquel Rodríguez y soy una abogada muy dedicada. Nunca **me olvido** de mi cliente en México y siempre **pienso** en los detalles del caso. En este viaje no tengo mucho tiempo para pensar en mí... Y ahora... ¡otro viaje!

Did you notice in the example that stem-changing verbs also have a stem change in the **yo** form (**pienso**).

Actividad. ¿Quién habla?

Who might make the following statements?

a. Teresa Suárez	d. Alfredo Sánchez
b. Federico Ruiz	e. Manuel Díaz
c. Raquel Rodríguez	

1. _____ Me siento en el restaurante a hablar con Alfredo.
2. _____ Me acuerdo muy bien de Rosario porque era buena amiga mía.
3. _____ Pienso casarme con mi novia (*girlfriend*) pronto.
4. _____ Vuelvo a Sevilla en unos días.
5. _____ Me siento muy triste (*sad*) cuando pienso en la tragedia de don Fernando y Rosario.
6. _____ No puedo comprender qué pasó con la maestra...
7. _____ Quiero comprar esta blusa de color salmón, por favor.
8. _____ Empiezo a contarle la historia al reportero.

Nota cultural: La música española

In this video episode you learned about a special kind of Spanish musical group called **una tuna**. Refresh your memory about Spanish **tunas** by listening to an excerpt from **Episodio 9**. Then complete the following activity.

Which of the following statements accurately describe Spanish music, based on what you know now?

C   F   1. Toda la música española es folklórica, como las tunas.
C   F   2. A los españoles no les gusta la música importada de otras naciones.
C   F   3. El flamenco es de origen árabe y gitano (*gypsy*).
C   F   4. Existe en España un tipo de «*light opera*» como «*Oklahoma*».
C   F   5. La música preferida de los jóvenes es la ópera.

After you read the following passage about Spanish music, review this activity and see whether you wish to change any answers.

Toda la diversidad geográfica y cultural de España se refleja[1] en su música popular y en sus danzas. Probablemente el *folklore* español más conocido[2] en todo el mundo es el andaluz. El flamenco es una variedad de este *folklore*. El flamenco tiene profunda influencia oriental, árabe y gitana. Es una combinación de canciones[3] y bailes[4] que suele[5] acompañarse con palmas[6] y guitarras... y los famosos ¡*olé*!

[1]se... *is reflected*   [2]más... *best known*   [3]*songs*   [4]*dances*   [5]*is usually*   [6]*clapping hands*

Otro tipo de música muy típica de España es la zarzuela. Es un teatro lírico enteramente español de origen. La zarzuela, como una pequeña ópera, combina la declamación, el canto y la danza. Las zarzuelas reflejan las costumbres[7] o tradiciones de las diferentes zonas de España.

¿Te gusta la música clásica? Si dices que sí, probablemente reconoces los nombres de los siguientes grandes compositores de música clásica.

- Isaac Albéniz: la suite «Iberia», viaje musical por toda la Península
- Manuel de Falla: los ballets «El amor brujo»[8] y «El sombrero de tres picos»[9]

Y seguro que conoces los nombres de los siguientes cantantes líricos famosos internacionalmente: Montserrat Caballé, Plácido Domingo, Victoria de los Ángeles, José Carreras...

Pero no toda la música española es folklórica o clásica. El *rock* es la música más popular entre los jóvenes.[10] Y hay sitio para otros estilos. Hay canciones sociales, música melódica,[11] música con raíces[12] tradicionales, canciones románticas... El cantante español romántico de más fama internacional es Julio Iglesias. El grupo moderno más famoso desde hace años[13] es Mecano. Y el catalán Joan Manuel Serrat goza de fama mundial. A los jóvenes les gusta también la música importada, y hay para todos: Madonna, Durán-Durán, Ray Charles...

[7]*customs*   [8]El... *Love the Magician*   [9]El... *The Three-Cornered Hat*   [10]*young people*   [11]*easy-listening*   [12]*roots*
[13]desde... *for a number of years*

Actividad.   La música española y la norteamericana

What U.S. singers, groups, or works do you associate with the following types of Spanish music?

1. el *rock*
2. la canción social
3. la música melódica
4. la música con raíces tradicionales
5. la canción romántica
6. la zarzuela

Have you completed the following sections of the lesson? Check them off here.

_____ **Preparación**   _____ **Conversaciones**
_____ **¿Tienes buena memoria?**   _____ **Un poco de gramática**
_____ **Vocabulario del tema**

Now scan the words in the **Vocabulario** list to be sure that you understand the meaning of most of them. Then you will be ready to continue on with **Lección 9** in the Workbook.

VOCABULARIO

Los verbos

aprender	to learn
escuchar	to listen (to)
recibir	to get, receive

Los lugares

el taller	shop (*for manufacturing or repair*)

Los colores

amarillo/a	yellow
anaranjado/a	orange
azul	blue
blanco/a	white
gris	gray
marrón, pardo/a	brown
morado/a	purple
rojo/a	red
rosado/a	pink
verde	green

Repaso: **negro/a**

Las estaciones del año (Seasons of the Year)

la primavera	spring
el verano	summer
el otoño	autumn
el invierno	winter

Los meses del año: **enero**, **febrero**, **marzo**, **abril**, **mayo**, **junio**, **julio**, **agosto**, **septiembre**, **octubre**, **noviembre**, **diciembre**

Para decir que sí (Saying *Yes*)

claro	of course
de acuerdo	O.K.; I agree
vale	great; O.K.

10

CUADROS*

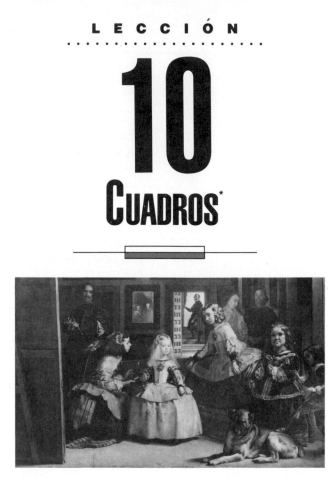

OBJETIVOS

The materials in **Lección 10** of the Textbook and the Workbook will help you better understand the video episode and take you beyond it, giving you additional information about places and characters in the series. The Textbook will also help you to develop skill in using the Spanish language. In this lesson you will learn

- ways to describe physical characteristics
- more ways to talk about what you are going to do with others
- one way to wish someone well.

You will also learn information about a number of well-known Spanish artists.

Be sure to work through all parts of the lesson. When you see a cassette symbol in the margin, listen to the tape for **Lección 10**. Answers or hints for many activities are given in Appendix 1. Be sure to check your answers for each activity before going on to the next one.

*Paintings

BEFORE VIEWING . . .

PREPARACIÓN

Actividad A.

During the last video episode of *Destinos*, several situations were "wrapped up" and others continued to develop. Indicate whether the following statements about the episode are **Cierto** (**C**) or **Falso** (**F**).

C F 1. Don Fernando está muy mal; está ahora en el hospital.
C F 2. Raquel pierde su cartera de nuevo.
C F 3. Raquel necesita comprar ropa porque en la Argentina es otoño.
C F 4. Alfredo convence a Raquel de que el caso de don Fernando debe presentarse en la televisión.
C F 5. Elena llama a Raquel para decirle que no puede obtener el certificado de nacimiento de Ángel Castillo.

Actividad B.

In this video episode you will see Raquel's last night and day in Madrid. Based on what you learned in the last episode and on your intuition, what do you think she will do?

Sí No 1. ¿Va a ver a Alfredo y al Sr. Díaz una vez más (*once more*)?
Sí No 2. ¿Va a conocer a la novia de Federico?
Sí No 3. ¿Va a despedirse de (*say goodbye to*) la Sra. Suárez?

El título de este episodio es «Cuadros». ¿Qué lugar crees que Raquel va a visitar en este episodio?

4. a. _____ la casa de un artista   c. _____ una galería de arte
   b. _____ un museo

Actividad C.

You have seen in other video episodes that Sra. Suárez has a tendency to comment on the actions of others. Listen to the advice she gives Raquel as they say good-bye. **El corazón** means *heart*.

Now that you have listened, what kind of advice do you think Sra. Suárez is offering?

1. La Sra. Suárez le da a Raquel consejos (*advice*) sobre
   _____ su vida profesional   _____ su vida personal

2. Parece que la Sra. Suárez cree que Raquel piensa demasiado (*too much*) en
   _____ su trabajo   _____ sus padres

3. La Sra. Suárez probablemente cree que Raquel debe buscar
   _____ más clientes   _____ un novio (*boyfriend*)

3. con barba/   4. de pelo corto, no largo/
   sin (*without*)   de pelo largo, no corto
   barba

Actividad D.

Look at the painting on the left of San Jerónimo by a Spanish artist and listen as it is described. The description contains some of the words and phrases for describing people that you will learn in this lesson. As you listen, indicate the word or phrase that you hear in each pair.

1. alto/bajo

5. ojos expresivos/ojos tristes

Now compare the painting of San Jerónimo with the painting on the right by another Spanish painter. What physical differences do you notice in the people in each painting? Keep these differences in mind when you listen to the narrator in the video episode describe the people in the painting.

2. delgado/gordito

 **AFTER VIEWING . . .**

¿TIENES BUENA MEMORIA?

Actividad A.   ¿Qué hicieron?

Indicate the statements that are true for each of the following characters you saw in **Episodio 10**.

Raquel
1. _____ por fin le da la foto de Miguel y Jaime a la Sra. Suárez.
2. _____ no ve al reportero y al Sr. Díaz otra vez (*again*).
3. _____ todavía no tiene el certificado de nacimiento de Ángel Castillo.

Federico
4. _____ tiene una novia que es pintora.
5. _____ no tiene la oportunidad de despedirse de Raquel.

La Sra. Suárez
6. _____ va con Raquel a la escuela de baile donde trabaja la novia de Federico.
7. _____ se despide de Raquel y le da un consejo.

 Now listen as the speaker on the tape gives the answers.

Actividad B.   ¡Un desafío!

If you have an excellent memory, perhaps you can remember the following details from **Episodio 10**.

1. Después de cenar con la Sra. Suárez, Federico y su novia, ¿cómo vuelve Raquel a su hotel?
2. ¿A qué hora debe salir el vuelo (*flight*) de Raquel para Buenos Aires?
3. Hay una maestra de primaria en el Prado. ¿De qué pintor le habla a la clase?
4. ¿A quién le escribe Raquel una tarjeta postal (*postcard*)?

• •

VOCABULARIO DEL TEMA

¿Cómo son? Los adjetivos descriptivos

alto/a	tall
bajo/a	short (*in height*)
de mediana estatura	average height

bonito/a	pretty, attractive (*said of women*)
guapo/a	pretty; handsome
feo/a	ugly, unattractive

corto/a	short (*in length*)
largo/a	long

grande	big	**joven**	young
pequeño/a	small	**nuevo/a**	new
		viejo/a	old

delgado/a	thin, slender
gordito/a	plump, fat

Tiene...	He/She has . . .	**Tiene...**	He/She has . . .
barba	a beard	**pelo largo**	long hair
pelo rubio	blond hair	**corto**	short hair
castaño	brown hair	**ojos claros**	light-colored eyes
negro	black hair	**oscuros**	dark eyes
blanco	white hair	**expresivos**	expressive eyes
canoso	gray hair		

Note that when **grande** comes before a masculine or feminine noun, it shortens to **gran** and means *great*: **El Greco es un gran pintor.**

Actividad A.   Retratos (*Portraits*) de El Greco y Velázquez

Listen again as the narrator describes these paintings by two famous Spanish painters. Then answer the questions that follow.

San Andrés y San Francisco
de El Greco

Las Meninas (Ladies in Waiting)
de Velázquez

Identifica en los cuadros a la figura que...

MODELO: es alta* → El pintor es alto.

1.   tiene barba
2.   tiene pelo rubio
3.   es delgada
4.   es baja

5.   es alta
6.   tiene pelo blanco
7.   es vieja
8.   tiene ojos expresivos

9.   es bonita
10.   tiene pelo largo

Actividad B.   ¿A quién se describe?

You will hear a series of descriptions on the cassette tape. Match the description with the following photos. First take a few seconds to scan the photos. You

a. _____

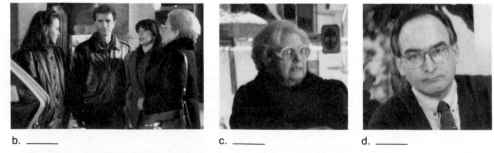

b. _____

c. _____

d. _____

---

*As you know, Spanish adjectives agree in number and gender with the nouns they modify. The adjectives in this activity agree with the feminine noun **la figura**; they are feminine for that reason. If you use them to modify a masculine noun (or to modify a plural noun), you will need to change the form of the adjective to make it agree.

e. _____ f. _____ g. _____

h. _____

should recognize all of these people, but you do not need to remember their names to do the activity.

Now that you have heard descriptions of the preceding people, try to invent your own descriptions. Give as many short sentences as you can about each photo. Use only words and phrases that you know.

Actividad C.   ¿Y tú?

Now briefly describe a member of your family and a friend. Then describe yourself. You may wish to look at workbook **Actividad E** (Section 27) for additional guidance.

• •

CONVERSACIONES: MÁS DESPEDIDAS

Actividad.   Adiós. Hasta luego.

You have already learned how to say good-bye to someone in everyday situations. In this video episode, because Raquel is getting ready to leave Madrid altogether, farewells of a different sort are in order. You will learn more about them in this activity.

Paso 1

Listen to Raquel's final conversation with Sra. Suárez, Federico, and María. Two of them will use approximately the same phrase to wish her well. See whether you can "catch" it. As you listen, try to remember what people were doing as they said good-bye.

Which of these expressions did you hear?

_____ Que lo pase/pases bien.
_____ Que tenga/tengas un buen viaje.
_____ Que le/te vaya bien.

You heard the second option in the excerpt, and you can probably guess that it means *Have a nice trip*. (The other expressions would have been appropriate in this situation as well, although they do not specifically refer to travel.)

Based on what you know about the Spanish verb system, what is the difference between the two verb forms used in this expression? If you said that one is the more formal form (equivalent to **usted**) and the other is familiar (equivalent to **tú**), you were right. Because Federico and Raquel use **tú** forms with each other, Federico told Raquel **Que tengas un buen viaje**. Both are forms of the verb **tener** that you will study later on in *Destinos*.

Paso 2

Now listen as Alfredo says good-bye to Raquel. What do you think he will say to her?

Because Alfredo and Raquel address each other more formally, Alfredo says **Que tenga buen viaje**.

Paso 3

How would you say good-bye to the following people in these situations?

- A good friend of yours is leaving for a vacation in the Caribbean.
- An elderly friend of your parents or grandparents is about to leave for a trip to Europe.

Nota cultural: Kissing Hello and Good-bye

In Spain, as well as in other parts of the Hispanic world, people frequently kiss hello and good-bye. This form of greeting is practiced by women with other women and by men with women, but not usually by men with other men.

As you have probably noticed in the video episode, in Spain the kiss is a double one. Women embrace lightly and touch cheeks, first one side, then the other, as they make a soft kissing sound. The same sequence can be followed by a man with a woman, depending on the closeness of the relationship between them. In this video episode, Raquel and Federico shake hands and embrace as they kiss, even though they do not know each other all that well.

In other parts of the Hispanic world a single kiss is more common. The question of whether or not to embrace is an individual one, depending on how comfortable one is with the other person.

UN POCO DE GRAMÁTICA

More About Talking About Group Activities

You have already learned to use stem-changing verbs and the pronouns **me**, **te**, and **se** with some verbs to talk about what others are doing.

Don Fernando, ¿**piensa** Ud. mucho en Rosario?

RAQUEL: **Me siento** a hablar con la Sra. Suárez.

Stem-changing verbs do not keep the stem change in the **nosotros** form.

FEDERICO: **Pensamos** ir a Los Ángeles algún día, Raquel. Bueno, si podemos, vamos a ir. Todo depende del dinero (*money*), ¿sabes?

Verbs that require reflexive pronouns use **nos** in the **nosotros** form.

MARÍA: Federico y yo vamos a **casarnos** este verano. ¡**Nos sentimos** muy felices!

You will learn more about these forms in the Workbook.

Actividad.   Parejas conocidas

You have met two of Sra. Suárez' three sons and seen them in the context of their significant relationships, Federico with María and Miguel with Elena and the children. Which of her sons might say the following, speaking for himself and his partner, Federico (F) or Miguel (M)? ¡OJO! Some of the statements may be appropriate for both.

F   M   1. Somos españoles.

F   M   2. Queremos casarnos pronto.

F   M   3. Podemos ver a mamá todos los días.

F   M   4. Pensamos visitar a mamá este verano.

F   M   5. No nos olvidamos nunca de llamar a mamá los domingos.

F   M   6. Queremos mucho a mi hermano menor (*younger*).

F   M   7. Recordamos una cena muy agradable con Raquel.

F   M   8. Nos sentamos a cenar con los niños todas las noches (*every night*).

Nota cultural: Los grandes maestros de la pintura española

The previous activities in this lesson have allowed you to listen again to information from the video episode about El Greco and Velázquez. Before beginning to read this **Nota cultural**, listen again to what you heard about Goya in the episode. Then go back to **Lección 2** and look at the painting *Guernica* by Pablo Picasso, another famous Spanish painter. In the activity that follows the **Nota cultural**, you will use all of the information you have to decide which of the four created works you have not seen previously in the *Destinos* materials.

Los pintores

- **Doménikos Theotokópoulos, El Greco**[1]
  Fechas: 1541 (Creta)–1614 (Toledo)

[1]El... *The Greek*

Obras[2]/*Estilo*: Temas religiosos, colores sombríos[3] y oscuros, forma alargada y estilizada de sus figuras.

- **Diego de Silva y Velázquez**

Fechas: 1599 (Sevilla)–1660 (Madrid)
Obras/*Estilo*: Uso de la luz[4] y de la perspectiva, muchos colores vivos, temas de la realidad, retratos de la familia real.[5]

- **Francisco de Goya y Lucientes**

Fechas: 1746 (Zaragoza)–1828 (Francia)
Obras/*Estilo*: Al principio,[6] retratos de la familia real, con espíritu crítico. En su período negro, formas grotescas. Precursor de la pintura moderna.

- **Pablo Ruiz Picasso**

Fechas: 1881 (Málaga)–1973 (Francia)
Obras/*Estilo*: Al principio, cuadros realistas, de las épocas azul y rosa. Luego, padre del «cubismo», estilo que trata de[7] presentar varias facetas del tema al mismo tiempo.[8] Enorme influjo[9] sobre el arte contemporáneo.

Goya y Picasso: ¿Tienen algo en común?
- Su obra es extensa y muy variada.
- En algunas de sus obras denuncian los abusos políticos y sociales de su época.
- Fueron testigos[10] de la crueldad de la guerra.
- Ofrecen una visión expresionista (no realista) de la realidad.
- Cultivaron el grabado[11] además de la pintura.
- Murieron en Francia.

[2]*Works* [3]*somber* [4]*light* [5]*royal* [6]Al... *At the beginning* [7]trata... *tries to* [8]al... *at the same time* [9]*influence* [10]*witnesses* [11]*etching*

Actividad.   ¿Quién es el artista?

Based on what you have seen and read (and also on what else you may know about art history), what Spanish artist is the creator of these works? Explain why you made your decision.

Have you completed the following sections of the lesson? Check them off here.

_____ **Preparación**   _____ **Conversaciones**
_____ **¿Tienes buena memoria?**   _____ **Un poco de gramática**
_____ **Vocabulario del tema**

Now scan the words in the **Vocabulario** list to be sure that you understand the meaning of most of them. Then you will be ready to continue on with **Lección 10** in the Workbook.

• •

VOCABULARIO

Los verbos

despedirse (i) (de)   to say good-bye (to)

Los adjetivos

alto/a	tall
bajo/a	short (*in height*)
bonito/a	pretty, attractive (*said of a woman*)
corto/a	short (*in length*)
delgado/a	thin, slender
feo/a	ugly, unattractive
gordito/a	plump, fat
grande (gran)	big; great
guapo/a	pretty; handsome
joven	young
largo/a	long
nuevo/a	new
pequeño/a	small
viejo/a	old

Más frases para las descripciones

Es de mediana estatura.   He/She is of average height.

Tiene...	He/She has . . .
barba	a beard
pelo rubio	blond hair
castaño	brown hair
negro	black hair
blanco	white hair
canoso	gray hair

pelo largo	long hair
corto	short hair
ojos claros	light-colored eyes
oscuros	dark eyes
expresivos	expressive eyes

Las personas

el pintor/la pintora	painter
el novio/ la novia	boyfriend/ girlfriend

El arte

el baile	dance
el cuadro	painting
el museo	museum
el retrato	portrait

Más despedidas

Que tenga (un) buen viaje.	Have a nice trip. (*form.*)
Que tengas (un) buen viaje.	Have a nice trip. (*fam.*)

Las palabras adicionales

otra vez	again
una vez más	one more time

LECCIÓN

11

LA DEMORA*

MENSAJE

Sr. D.

Srta

RODRIGUEZ

Habitación n.º 631

OBJETIVOS

Part of this video episode is a review. Be sure to work through all parts of the lesson. When you see a cassette symbol in the margin, listen to the tape for **Lección 11**. Answers or hints for many activities are given in Appendix 1. Be sure to check your answers for each activity before going on to the next one.

**The Delay*

 **BEFORE VIEWING . . .**

PREPARACIÓN

Actividad A.

As you know, the opening narration of each video episode consists of a summary of what happened in the previous episode. First read the following sentences that are based on the opening review in **Episodio 11**. Then indicate whether they are **Cierto** (**C**) or **Falso** (**F**), based on what you remember about that episode.

C   F   1. Raquel conoce a María, la novia de Federico.

C   F   2. Cena con ellos y con la Sra. Suárez, pero no se despide todavía.

C   F   3. Antes de salir para Buenos Aires, Raquel va al Museo del Prado.

C   F   4. Allí ve algunas obras de artistas españoles muy importantes: El Greco, Murillo y Picasso.

C   F   5. Al final de su visita al Museo del Prado, Raquel se encuentra con Alfredo y el Sr. Díaz.

C   F   6. Cuando Raquel vuelve a su hotel, hay un mensaje para ella, de la agencia de viajes.

C   F   7. Raquel trata de (*tries to*) comunicarse con la agencia de viajes. Por fin puede hablar con ellos.

C   F   8. Decide ir a la agencia para preguntar qué pasa con su reservación.

Now listen to the narration on the cassette tape and check your answers.

Actividad B.

Here is a message that the hotel receptionist will give to Raquel in this video episode. What problem is Raquel going to encounter, according to the message?

_____ La agencia perdió su billete (*ticket*).

_____ La agencia no puede confirmar su reservación.

If you were Raquel, what would you do? Keep in mind that Raquel is a bit tired from all of her traveling and from all of the experiences she has had in the last few days.

DIA _____   COMUNICACION DE _____
HORA _____
RECIBIDO POR: _____

M E N S A J E

☐ HA LLAMADO
☐ HA VENIDO

D. *Estimada Sta. Rodriguez :*
    Sentimos Mucho Informarle Que Hemos Tenido
Problemas en Reservar Su Asiento en el Vuelo **897** *Para*
Buenos Aires , Haga El Favor De Llamarnos lo
Mas Pronto Posible   *2-52-73-61*

     Roberto Ruiz
     Agencia Aguila

Yo creo que

a. _____ Raquel debe ir directamente al aeropuerto. Allí puede tomar un café y esperar su vuelo (*flight*).

b. _____ Raquel debe preguntarle al recepcionista si ella puede subir a (*go up to*) su habitación.

c. _____ Raquel debe visitar otros lugares interesantes o históricos, por ejemplo, otros museos.

AFTER VIEWING . . .

¿TIENES BUENA MEMORIA?

Actividad A.   En este episodio
All of the following events took place during Raquel's last few hours in Madrid, but . . . in what order did they occur? Put them in order, from 1 to 6.

Raquel

a. _____ Descansa (*She rests*) unas horas.

b. _____ Se entera de (*She finds out*) que hay una demora.

c. _____ Va a la agencia de viajes para resolver el problema.

d. _____ Se despierta cuando suena el teléfono.

e. _____ Va al aeropuerto y sale para la Argentina.

f. _____ Vuelve al hotel y sube a su habitación.

Actividad B.   ¡Un desafío!
¿Tienes una memoria muy buena? Can you recall any of these details from this video episode and previous ones?

1. ¿Cómo se llama el hotel de Raquel en Madrid?
2. ¿Cuál es el número de la habitación de Raquel?
3. ¿Qué cosa le da Raquel a la Sra. Suárez?
4. ¿Qué cosa le da la señora a Raquel?
5. ¿A qué hora sale el vuelo de Raquel para la Argentina? ¿Y cuál es el número del vuelo?

• •

Repaso de los episodios 7–10

Actividad A.   El sueño (*dream*) de Raquel: Primera parte

Complete the following summary of the first part of Raquel's dream with words from the following lists. ¡OJO! Some words will be used more than once. Others may not be used at all.

Verbos: buscar, conocer, creer, dar, deber, decir, empezar, encontrar, ir, llegar, poder, revelar, salir, tomar, volver

Cosas: el mensaje, la cartera, la corbata

Personas: el recepcionista, el botones, el reportero, el cliente

Otras palabras: porque, pero, pronto

Después de volver al hotel, Raquel sube a su habitación y toma una siesta. Mientras duerme,[a] _____[1] a soñar con lo que ha pasado desde que salió de Sevilla.[b]

Primero, toma el tren de Sevilla a Madrid. En el tren, _____[2] a dos señores. Uno se llama Alfredo Sánchez y es _____[3] de televisión. Alfredo _____[4] a una maestra para entrevistarla.[c] Alfredo _____[5] que Raquel es la maestra, pero Raquel le _____[6] que no, que está equivocado.[d] En el coche-comedor[e] del tren, Alfredo _____[7] a hacerle preguntas a Raquel acerca de su investigación, pero Raquel no _____[8] nada del caso.

Cuando por fin llega a su hotel en Madrid, Raquel descubre que ha dejado[f] su _____[9] en el taxi. Alfredo y su asistente _____[10] a buscarla. Por fin (ellos) la _____,[11] pero Raquel no está cuando ellos _____[12] al hotel.

Al día siguiente, Raquel y Alfredo se encuentran[g] en el hotel y Alfredo le _____[13] a Raquel el objeto perdido. Mientras _____[14] un café, Alfredo intenta convencer a Raquel una vez más de que el caso de don Fernando _____[15] ser muy interesante para un reportaje de televisión. _____[16] Raquel le dice que no, que ella _____[17] respetar el secreto profesional de su _____.[18]

[a]Mientras... *While she sleeps* [b]soñar... *to dream about what has happened since she left Sevilla* [c]*interview her* [d]*mistaken* [e]*dining car* [f]ha... *has left* [g]se... *meet*

Actividad B.   El sueño de Raquel: Segunda parte

Choose the appropriate completion for each sentence.

Raquel también sueña con la Sra. Suárez.

1. Raquel va a la casa de la Sra. Suárez porque
   a. _____ la Sra. Suárez la llama por teléfono y la invita.
   b. _____ el hijo de la Sra. Suárez va al hotel y la invita.
2. Durante la conversación con la Sra. Suárez, Raquel se entera de (*learns*) que, después de la guerra, Rosario se fue a vivir a
   a. _____ Sevilla.   c. _____ México.
   b. _____ la Argentina.
3. La Sra. Suárez también le dice a Raquel que Rosario
   a. _____ se casó de nuevo con un rico hacendado.
   b. _____ se casó de nuevo con un político importante.
4. Según (*According to*) Teresa Suárez, don Fernando y Rosario tuvieron (*had*)
   a. _____ un hijo.   b. _____ una hija.
5. Según la dirección que tiene Raquel, Rosario vive
   a. _____ cerca de Buenos Aires.
   b. _____ cerca de Bariloche.

 Now check your answers on the cassette tape.

Have you completed the following sections of the lesson? Check them off here.

_____ **Preparación**   _____ **Repaso de los Episodios 7–10**
_____ **¿Tienes buena memoria?**

Now scan the words in the **Vocabulario** list to be sure that you understand the meaning of most of them. Then you will be ready to continue on with **Lección 11** in the Workbook.

· ·

VOCABULARIO

Los verbos
subir (a)   to go up to (*a place*)

Los sustantivos
la demora   delay
el vuelo   flight

Las palabras adicionales
por fin   finally

Un viaje a la Argentina

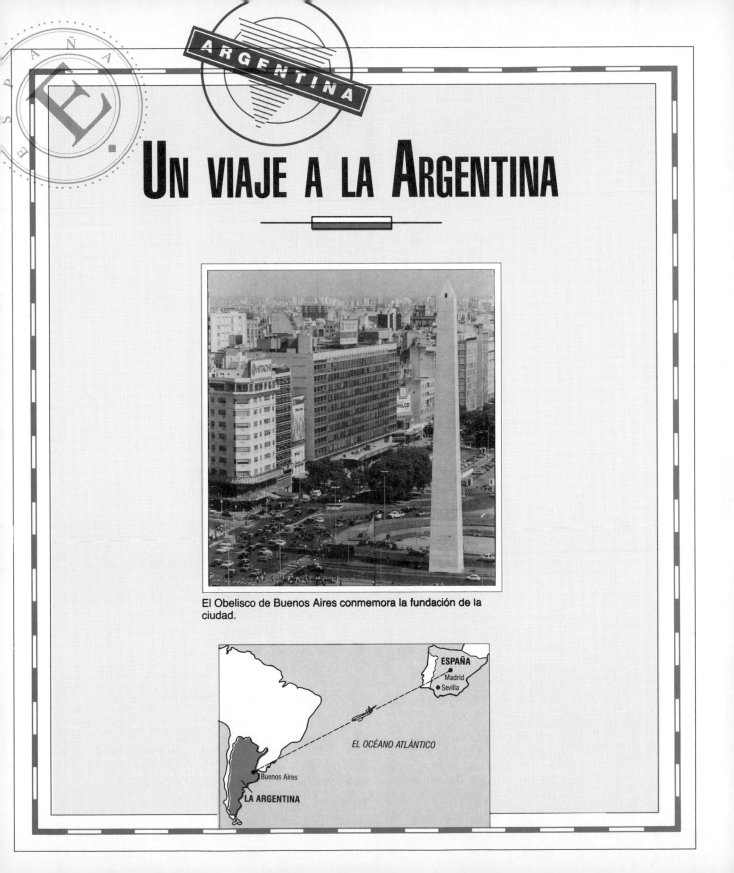

El Obelisco de Buenos Aires conmemora la fundación de la
ciudad.

ESPAÑA

Madrid
Sevilla

EL OCÉANO ATLÁNTICO

Buenos Aires

LA ARGENTINA

12
REVELACIONES*

OBJETIVOS

The materials in **Lección 12** of the Textbook and the Workbook will help you better understand the video episode and take you beyond it, giving you additional information about places and characters in the series. The Textbook will also help you to develop skill in using the Spanish language. In this lesson you will learn

- how to express the Spanish numbers from 100 to 1000
- how to talk about what other people did in the past
- how to talk with people you know by using the type of Spanish spoken in Argentina.

You will also learn about Argentina, both past and present.

Be sure to work through all parts of the lesson. When you see a cassette symbol in the margin, listen to the tape for **Lección 12**. Answers or hints for many activities are given in Appendix 1. Be sure to check your answers for each activity before going on to the next one.

Revelations

BEFORE VIEWING . . .

PREPARACIÓN

Actividad A.

In the last video episode of *Destinos* Raquel left Madrid by plane, on her way to Buenos Aires to continue her search for Rosario. Indicate whether the following statements about the events immediately preceding her departure are **Cierto** (**C**) or **Falso** (**F**).

C F 1. Raquel pierde su vuelo.
C F 2. Hay una demora y el vuelo no sale cuando debe.
C F 3. Raquel habla con don Fernando por teléfono.
C F 4. Raquel se duerme en su habitación.
C F 5. Piensa en el consejo (*advice*) de la Sra. Suárez.
C F 6. Sabe donde Rosario vive en la Argentina.

¡Un desafío! ¿Tienes una memoria excelente?   You have heard the following phrase in a previous video episode of *Destinos*. Identify it briefly by telling who said it and in what context.

7. «Hay que dedicarle tiempo al corazón.»

Actividad B.

Here are photographs of some of the places and events you will see in **Episodio 12**. What do you think is happening in each?

1. Raquel está en
    a. _____ un parque
    b. _____ un cementerio
    c. _____ una estancia

2. Toma una fotografía de
    a. _____ Rosario
    b. _____ un monumento
    c. _____ una tumba

3. Raquel toca a la puerta (*knocks on the door*) en
    a. _____ una estancia
    b. _____ una casa en Buenos Aires

4. La persona que contesta (*answers*) es
    a. _____ Martín Iglesias
    b. _____ Rosario
    c. _____ una persona desconocida (*unknown*)

AFTER VIEWING . . .

¿TIENES BUENA MEMORIA?

Actividad A.   ¿Quién es?

In **Episodio 12** you met these new characters. Identify them and tell where they work, then indicate why they are important to Raquel's investigation.

1. Este hombre se llama
    a. _____ Cirilo   b. _____ Francisco   c. _____ Esteban
2. Es
    a. _____ botones   b. _____ chofer   c. _____ gaucho
3. Trabaja en
    a. _____ el hotel   c. _____ la estancia
    b. _____ Buenos Aires   Santa Susana
4. Es un personaje importante porque
    a. _____ le dice a Raquel que Rosario se mudó (*moved*) a la capital y le da
             su dirección
    b. _____ le dice a Raquel que Rosario ya murió

5. Este hombre se llama
    a. _____ Enrique Casas   c. _____ Arturo Iglesias
    b. _____ Ángel Castillo
6. Es
    a. _____ profesor   c. _____ abogado
    b. _____ médico (psiquiatra)
7. Trabaja en
    a. _____ su casa   b. _____ el hotel   c. _____ la universidad
8. Es un personaje importante porque
    a. _____ quiere ayudar (*help*) a Raquel a buscar a Rosario
    b. _____ es hijo de Rosario y medio hermano de Ángel Castillo

Actividad B.   ¿Qué pasó?

Indicate whether the following events happen (**Sí ocurre**) or not (**No, no ocurre**) when Raquel reaches Buenos Aires.

Sí   No   1. En el hotel no hay habitación reservada para Raquel.
Sí   No   2. Raquel tiene mucha energía cuando llega. Va directamente a la es-
              tancia para buscar a Rosario.
Sí   No   3. Cuando Raquel llega a la estancia Cirilo contesta la puerta.
Sí   No   4. Raquel sabe que Rosario ya murió.
Sí   No   5. Arturo le cuenta a Raquel la triste (*sad*) historia de Martín, su
              padre y padrastro (*stepfather*) de Ángel.

Actividad C.   La historia de Ángel

As you know, Raquel has learned that Rosario has died. Her investigation must continue, however, and Arturo is willing to share information with her. The following events all form part of Ángel's story as told by Arturo, but . . . in what order did they occur? Put them in order, from 1 to 7. *Note*: All of the verbs are in the past tense.

a. _____ Martín murió de un ataque cardíaco.

b. _____ Ángel dejó los estudios y se dedicó a pintar.

c. _____ Ángel discutió (*fought*) con su padrastro.

d. _____ Martín, Rosario y el joven Arturo fueron a Buenos Aires para visitar a Ángel.

e. _____ Martín y Rosario supieron (*found out*) algo que no le gustó a Martín.

f. _____ Ángel se embarcó como marinero.

g. _____ Ángel se fue a la capital para estudiar ciencias económicas.

Now listen to Arturo's version of the story and check your answers.

· ·

VOCABULARIO DEL TEMA

<h3 align="center">Los números de 100 a 1000</h3>

100 cien, ciento	400 cuatrocientos	700 setecientos	1.000 mil
200 doscientos	500 quinientos	800 ochocientos	
300 trescientos	600 seiscientos	900 novecientos	

- **Cien** is used in counting. To express the numbers 101 to 199, **ciento** is used: **ciento uno**, **ciento dos**, **ciento setenta y nueve**, and so on.
- **Cien** also precedes a noun: **cien iglesias**. When the numbers 200 through 900 precede a noun, they must agree in gender: **doscientas casas**, **trescientas calles**. **Mil** precedes a noun, with no change: **mil años**.
- These numbers are also used to express the year.

  799   setecientos noventa y nueve
  1995   mil novecientos noventa y cinco

Actividad A.   ¿Hay una habitación disponible?

Listen as the hotel clerk tries to find out whether there is a room or suite available for Raquel today. Indicate the numbers you hear him say.

114   214   314   414   514   614   714   814   914

Actividad B.   Continúa la secuencia

You will hear three numbers in each group. Write down the numbers you hear in numerals, in the order you hear them.

> MODELO: (*you hear*) cien, doscientos, trescientos
> (*you write*) 100, 200, 300

1. _____   3. _____   5. _____

2. _____   4. _____   6. _____

Actividad C.   Hablando de la ropa

Here is the laundry list for men's clothing from the Hotel Príncipe de Vergara. Listen as the speaker on the tape names an article of clothing, then tell how much it costs—in **pesetas**—to have the item washed or cleaned. Remember to make numbers agree with the feminine noun **pesetas** when necessary.

ROPA DE CABALLERO	
Camisa	450
Camisetas	250
Pijama	600
Pantalón	500
Chaqueta	900
Traje completo	1500
Pantalón corto	400

> MODELO: (*you hear*) camisa
> (*you say*)   cuatrocientas cincuenta pesetas

1. ...   2. ...   3. ...   4. ...   5. ...   6. ...

Actividad D.   ¿En qué año?

You have heard and read about three of the following four dates in *Destinos*; they are events in Spanish history. Can you match the events with the year in which they occurred? Then find the event for the remaining date by process of elimination. It is an important date in Argentine history. After you make the match, express the years in Spanish.

1. _____ 1492   a.   La invasión de la Península Ibérica por los árabes
2. _____ 1939   b.   El fin de la Guerra Civil española
3. _____ 1808   c.   Empieza la lucha (*fight*) por la independencia de España
4. _____ 711   d.   Colón llega al Caribe

• •

CONVERSACIONES: MÁS SOBRE EL TUTEO

Actividad.   ¿Podemos tutearnos?

As you know, it is significant for two people to switch from addressing each other with the formal **Ud.** to using the familiar **tú**. You will learn more about that as well as find out about verb forms and pronouns used primarily in Argentina.

Paso 1

In **Lección 8**, you heard Federico ask Raquel to use **tú** forms with him. Listen to the conversation again, filling in the blanks as you listen.

RAQUEL: ¿En qué _____,[1] Federico?

FEDERICO: ¿Podemos tutearnos?

RAQUEL: De acuerdo. Es que nosotros usamos más _____.[2]

FEDERICO: Aquí es más común tratarse _____.[3]

RAQUEL: Está bien. ¿En qué _____,[4] Federico?

As you know, the phrases **tutearse** and **tratarse de *tú*** mean using familiar forms with each other. When Federico suggests doing that, Raquel agrees, but she points out that **usted** forms are more frequently used by the group with which she identifies most, Mexican-Americans (**nosotros**).

Paso 2

Now you will hear part of a conversation between Arturo and Raquel from this video episode. Arturo makes the same request, but some of the details are different. Listen for the pronouns that Arturo mentions.

Arturo proposes that he use **vos** with Raquel, as people do in Argentina, and also that Raquel use **tú** with him, as is usual in her variety of Spanish. **Vos** is the equivalent of **tú** in Argentina. It is used with its own verb forms. You can learn more about them in the **Nota cultural**.

Paso 3

Now you will hear three short exchanges between friends. Decide whether they take place in Spain or in Argentina.

1. España   la Argentina
2. España   la Argentina

3. España   la Argentina

Nota cultural: The *vos* forms

In some countries, particularly in Argentina, Uruguay, and most of Central America, the pronoun **vos** is used instead of **tú**. Most verb forms used with **vos** are the same as the **tú** verb forms. However, in the present tense the endings **-ás**, **-és**, and **-ís** are generally used: **trabajás**, **comés**, **vivís**. Stem vowels do not change: **podés**, **querés**, **dormís**.

Y vos, ¿qué **querés** hacer esta tarde?
¿**Vivís** en México?

Just as you heard **vosotros** forms in Spain, when Spaniards addressed each other, you will hear **vos** forms in the video episodes that take place in Argentina and whenever Argentine characters are talking. The **vos** forms will not, however, be practiced in the Textbook and Workbook.

UN POCO DE GRAMÁTICA

Using Verbs to Talk About the Past

Since the beginning of the *Destinos* series, you have been hearing verb forms that described things that happened in the past. In Spanish, as in English, there are a number of past-tense forms. In this section you will start to use forms of one of the Spanish past tenses, the preterite.

Most third-person singular preterite-tense Spanish verbs end in **-ó** (**-ar** verbs) or **-ió** (**-er** and **-ir** verbs). Note the verbs in this brief description.

> Rosario **vivió** en la estancia Santa Susana unos diez años. Luego se **mudó** a Buenos Aires.

-Ar and **-er** stem-changing verbs do not show the stem change in the preterite.

> Arturo **perdió** contacto con su hermano Ángel.

You will learn more about these verb forms in the Workbook. You will learn about the past-tense forms of **-ir** stem-changing verbs in a later lesson.

Actividad.   La investigación sigue

Match the logical answers with the following questions.

1. _____ ¿A qué ciudad viajó Raquel en este episodio?
2. _____ ¿Cómo viajó?
3. _____ ¿Con quién habló al llegar al hotel?
4. _____ ¿Qué clase de habitación le ofreció el recepcionista a Raquel?
5. _____ ¿Adónde llevó el chofer a Raquel al día siguiente?
6. _____ ¿Quién contestó la puerta de la estancia cuando Raquel tocó?
7. _____ ¿Con quién habló Raquel después?
8. _____ ¿Qué reveló Cirilo cuando habló con Raquel?
9. _____ ¿Esperó Raquel para hablar con otras personas?
10. _____ ¿A quién conoció en Buenos Aires?

a. A la estancia Santa Susana.
b. En avión.
c. A un hijo de Rosario.
d. Que Rosario ya no vive en la estancia.
e. Con el recepcionista.
f. Con Cirilo, un gaucho.

g. No. Volvió inmediatamente a Buenos Aires.
h. Una *suite*.
i. A Buenos Aires, la capital de la Argentina.
j. Un joven desconocido.

Nota cultural: La Pampa y los gauchos

Before you read this **Nota cultural**, refresh your memory about modern Argentina by listening to what the narrator told you about Argentina and Buenos Aires at the beginning of this video episode. As you listen, keep in mind the view of Buenos Aires that Raquel and Arturo enjoyed from the top of a tall building at the end of the episode.

Buenos Aires es una ciudad grande y cosmopolita. Tiene bulevares elegantes y edificios y monumentos hermosos.[1] Es la capital de la República Argentina y es también un puerto,[2] el puerto más grande de la Argentina. Algunas personas la llaman el París de Sudamérica. Sin embargo, las personas que llegan a la Argentina por primera vez quieren ver gauchos.

La verdad es que los gauchos dejaron de existir[3] hace muchos años.[4] Hoy día, los gauchos forman parte de la herencia folklórica argentina. Para ver a un gaucho, es necesario visitar una estancia modelo como en la que trabaja Cirilo. Allí se puede admirar la habilidad del gaucho con el lazo y su caballo.[5] También es posible ver sus juegos[6] típicos, como «el pato», el polo de los gauchos. Además hay canciones[7] y comida típicas de la vida gauchesca.

Los gauchos eran los héroes de La Pampa, y La Pampa es la región más importante de la Argentina. Tiene una posición central en el país y es también una región especialmente adecuada para el ganado.[8] La unidad básica de la agricultura y de la ganadería[9] en La Pampa es la estancia. Las estancias son grandes haciendas, con viviendas,[10] almacenes[11] y enormes extensiones de terreno dedicadas a la agricultura y a los pastos.[12]

Los amplios horizontes de La Pampa son la patria de un personaje ya mítico: el gaucho. Los gauchos eran jinetes[13] que cuidaban[14] el ganado. Vivían como nómadas, lejos de la civilización. Su vida era muy difícil y solitaria. Con frecuencia escapaban de un pasado no precisamente bueno.

[1]*beautiful* [2]*port* [3]*dejaron... disappeared* [4]*hace... many years ago* [5]*horse* [6]*games* [7]*songs* [8]*cattle* [9]*cattle raising* [10]*casas* [11]*storehouses* [12]*grazing* [13]*horsemen* [14]*cared for*

La figura de los gauchos sigue viva[15] en la literatura y en el *folklore* de la Argentina y el Uruguay. Aquí hay unos datos sobre «Martín Fierro», el poema nacional de la Argentina. Su héroe es un gaucho.

Autor: José Hernández

Obras: el poema «Martín Fierro» (1872), compuesto de 2000 versos; la segunda parte del poema, «La vuelta[16] de Martín Fierro» (1879)

Tema: la lucha[17] del héroe por la libertad contra adversidades, injusticias y prejuicios

[15]*alive* [16]*return* [17]*fight*

Actividad.   El gaucho y su *folklore*

Does the story of the Argentine gaucho remind you of a U.S. folk hero? What are the American equivalents for the following aspects of the gaucho and his history?

1. La Pampa   2. la estancia   3. el gaucho   4. «el pato»

Have you completed the following sections of the lesson? Check them off here.

_____ **Preparación**   _____ **Conversaciones**

_____ **¿Tienes buena memoria?**   _____ **Un poco de gramática**

_____ **Vocabulario del tema**

Now scan the words in the **Vocabulario** list to be sure that you understand the meaning of most of them. Then you will be ready to continue on with **Lección 12** in the Workbook.

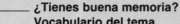

VOCABULARIO

Los verbos

ayudar	to help
contestar	to answer
mudarse	to move (*from one residence or city to another*)

Las personas

el medio hermano	half-brother
el padrastro	stepfather

Los adjetivos

desconocido/a	unknown

Las cosas

la puerta	door

Los lugares

la estancia	ranch
la habitación	room

Los conceptos

la revelación	revelation, unveiling

Los números: cien, doscientos, trescientos, cuatrocientos, quinientos, seiscientos, setecientos, ochocientos, novecientos, mil

El tuteo

vos	you (*fam. in Argentina and some other areas*)

13

LA BÚSQUEDA*

OBJETIVOS

The materials in **Lección 13** of the Textbook and the Workbook will help you better understand the video episode and take you beyond it, giving you additional information about places and characters in the series. The Textbook will also help you to develop skill in using the Spanish language. In this lesson you will learn

- the Spanish words for seafoods and for some other food items
- vocabulary and expressions that will allow you to interact with clerks in a store
- ways to talk about what you did in the past.

You will also learn about the regions of Argentina.

Be sure to work through all parts of the lesson. When you see a cassette symbol in the margin, listen to the tape for **Lección 13**. Answers or hints for many activities are given in Appendix 1. Be sure to check your answers for each activity before going on to the next one.

*The Search

BEFORE VIEWING . . .

PREPARACIÓN

Actividad A.
Listen to the review of **Episodio 12** that you will hear at the beginning of this video episode. Then, based on the review and on what you remember, indicate whether the following events took place (**Sí ocurrió**) or not (**No, no ocurrió**) in the previous episode.

Sí   No   1. No hay habitación para Raquel en el hotel de Buenos Aires.

Sí   No   2. En la estancia, un joven le dice a Raquel que Rosario murió hace años (*years ago*).

Sí   No   3. Un gaucho le dice que Rosario se mudó a la capital.

Sí   No   4. Con el chofer, Raquel busca un número en la calle Gorostiaga.

Sí   No   5. En una casa, Raquel conoce a un amigo de Rosario.

Sí   No   6. Arturo le da a Raquel la nueva dirección de Rosario y de su hermano Ángel.

Actividad B.
As you prepare to watch this video episode, think about its title, **La búsqueda**. What does the title **suggest** to you? What does a search for a person entail? Indicate the most logical completion for the following sentences.

1. Mientras (*While*) buscan a Ángel, Raquel y Arturo
    a. _____ hablan con muchas personas
    b. _____ hablan con pocas personas

2. Raquel y Arturo comienzan la búsqueda
    a. _____ en la estación central de policía de Buenos Aires
    b. _____ en el lugar donde Arturo vio a su hermano por última (*last*) vez

3. Las personas que van a saber algo de Ángel, probablemente, son
    a. _____ los dependientes (*clerks*) y dueños de negocios (*shop owners*)
    b. _____ los viejos marineros

Actividad C.
In this video episode, Raquel and Arturo will meet a man who is suspicious of strangers.

Paso 1
Listen to the conversation on the cassette tape, trying to get the gist of it. Then read the following version of it to see whether you missed anything. Then indi-

cate which of the following sentences is an accurate summary of the conversation you just heard.

a. ____*no*____ José cree que Héctor es el hermano de Arturo.

b. ____*yes*____ José no conoce a Ángel pero sí sabe el nombre de una persona que posiblemente lo conoció.

SEÑOR: Yo soy José, sí, señor.

ARTURO: Disculpe la molestia. Mario nos dijo que tal vez Ud. puede conocer a Ángel Castillo, mi hermano.

SEÑOR: ¿Ángel Castillo?

ARTURO: Sí, es mi hermano. Perdimos contacto hace muchos años. Tenía amigos acá. Pintaba. Le gustaban los barcos.[1]

SEÑOR: Lo siento. No lo conozco. ¿Ya hablaron con Héctor?

ARTURO: No. ¿Quién es?

SEÑOR: Sí. Tienen que hablar con Héctor. Él ha vivido siempre en este barrio. Conoce a todo el mundo.[2] Seguro que conoció a su hermano.

RAQUEL: ¿Y dónde podemos encontrar a Héctor?

[1]Le... *He liked boats.*　[2]todo... *everybody*

Paso 2

Now listen to the conversation again.

Paso 3

José is suspicious. For this reason, it is likely that he does not trust strangers. What do you think will happen after Raquel asks her question?

a. _____ José les da la dirección de Héctor en seguida.

b. _____ José piensa un momento y luego les da la dirección de Héctor.

c. _____ José les dice que él va a buscar a Héctor.

d. _____ José no quiere darles más información.

AFTER VIEWING . . .

• •

¿TIENES BUENA MEMORIA?

Actividad A.　¿Quiénes son? ¿Y qué hicieron?

Paso 1

As you probably predicted, Arturo and Raquel talk to a number of people in the course of their search for Ángel. Based on what you have seen in this video episode, who is the one person most likely to lead them eventually to Ángel?

a. _____ José, el marinero
b. _____ la dependienta de la tienda de comestibles (*grocery store*)
c. _____ Mario, el dueño de la tienda de antigüedades (*antiques*)
d. _____ el vendedor (*salesman*) de pescado
e. _____ Héctor, otro marinero
f. _____ doña Flora, la esposa de José
g. _____ Arturo

Paso 2

Now indicate which of the people in **Paso 1** made the following contributions to the search for Ángel.

1. _____ Mencionó a la señora del negocio de al lado (*next door*). ¿Por qué? Ella conoce a todo el mundo.
2. _____ Pensó en José. Llevó a Raquel y Arturo a la casa donde vive con su esposa.
3. _____ Encontró una foto de Ángel a los veinte años.
4. _____ Atendió a una clienta. Luego miró la foto varias veces pero no reconoció a Ángel.
5. _____ Mencionó dos lugares donde podían encontrar a José, en el bar o en el barco.
6. _____ Buscó a Héctor y sabe dónde va a estar mañana por la noche.

Paso 3

Select the statement that best describes what the next step in the search for Ángel will be.

a. _____ Héctor va a ir a la casa de Arturo.
b. _____ Arturo y Raquel van a buscar a Héctor en una fiesta.
c. _____ José va a hablar con Héctor para ver si conoce a Ángel.

Actividad B.   ¡Un desafío!

If you were able to answer most of the items in **Actividad A**, you "caught" enough to watch the next episode. But were you also able to take note of some of the details, such as the names of places and of some foods? Your ability to hear and remember details of this kind will increase as you work through the *Destinos* materials. How many details did you get from this video episode?

1. La parte de Buenos Aires donde Raquel y Arturo comenzaron la búsqueda se llama
   a. _____ la Boca   c. _____ Riachuelo
   b. _____ Recoleta

2. La última vez que Arturo vio a su hermano Ángel fue en la calle
   a. _____ Rivadavia   c. _____ Caminito
   b. _____ 9 de Julio

3. Arturo y Raquel almuerzan en un restaurante que se llama
    a. _____ la Boca   c. _____ la Vaca
    b. _____ la Barca

4. José les informó a Raquel y Arturo que mañana por la noche hay una fiesta
    en un bar-restaurante que se llama
    a. _____ Piccolo Navio   c. _____ Puerto Escondido
    b. _____ la Barca

5. Arturo invitó a Raquel a comer (*eat*) en su casa. Va a preparar
    a. _____ pescado   c. _____ pasta
    b. _____ unas brochetas

Nota cultural: ¿Cómo se dice... ?

As you have already learned, the names for some foods are different in different parts of the Spanish-speaking world. Listen again as Arturo and Raquel discuss what Arturo is going to prepare for dinner.

Did you notice that, as they discuss the main course, Arturo and Raquel use slightly different words to describe it? Arturo uses a more French pronunciation, **unas brochettes**, while Raquel uses the term more frequently used in most of the Spanish-speaking world, **las brochetas**. Neither term is more "correct" than the other; they are merely different. You will find out what **brochetas** are in the next video episode.

You should also note that neither Arturo nor Raquel is confused or upset by the difference in terminology. Spanish is an international language, and there are differences in pronunciation, in vocabulary, and in usage throughout the Spanish-speaking world. These differences do not generally make communication difficult.

VOCABULARIO DEL TEMA

Note: Many of the vocabulary sections in the video episodes from Argentina present food-related vocabulary. By the end of the Argentina episodes, you should be able to express which foods you like and dislike. If the words you need are not given, look them up in a dictionary or ask your instructor and make them part of your personal vocabulary. Don't try to learn all of the food vocabulary presented in the Textbook. Focus on those items you need to express your preferences and on those necessary for describing the story.

In the following list (and in those in subsequent Argentina episodes), the words on the left are from the video episode. Those in the right-hand column are additional vocabulary items for each category that you may want to learn.

Los mariscos

los calamares	squid	**el cangrejo**	crab
el langostino	prawn	**la langosta**	lobster
el mejillón	mussel	**la ostra**	oyster

El pescado

el lenguado	sole	**el atún**	tuna
el salmón	salmon	**la merluza**	hake

Otros comestibles

el aceite	oil
el arroz	rice
la ensalada	salad
la manteca (*Arg.*)	butter
la mantequilla	butter
el pan	bread

Remember that food vocabulary varies a good deal in the Spanish-speaking world. You may want to note these variations.

- **Mantequilla** generally means *butter*. For many Spanish speakers, **manteca** means *fat* or *lard*.
- Two frequently used words for *shrimp* are **la gamba** (in Spain) and **el camarón** (in Mexico and parts of Latin America).

Actividad A.   Los mariscos, el pescado y otros comestibles

Listen as the speaker on the cassette tape talks about some of her food preferences. She will use the phrases **me gusta…** and **me gustan…** as well as the verb **prefiero…** . Write the number of the sentence next to the appropriate drawing.

Actividad B.   ¿Cuánto cuesta?

Listen as the grocery clerk from **Episodio 13** tallies the prices of a number of items her customer has bought. As you listen, write down the price of each item. *Note:* The monetary unit of Argentina is **el austral** (from the adjective **austral**, which means *southern*).

El arroz, son __4__¹ australes; este pan, son __220__² aus-

trales; este otro pan, __47__³ australes; y este aceite, __17__⁴

australes. Total: __3__⁵ australes.

Now state the prices yourself, item by item. You will hear the correct answer on the tape.

Actividad C.   ¿Y tú?

What food items from the vocabulary list do you like or dislike? Indicate your preferences, using the following phrases.

> me gusta + *singular noun*
> me gustan + *plural noun*
>
> me gusta(n) mucho...
> no me gusta(n) nada...
>
> entre _____ y _____, prefiero...

• •

CONVERSACIONES: EN UNA TIENDA

Actividad.   Quiero...

You have already learned how to make requests politely. Sometimes, however, the language of everyday interactions is more direct. In this activity you will learn how to make very direct requests, using the phrases **déme** and **cóbreme**.

Paso 1

Listen to two exchanges from **Episodio 13** in which clients listen to what is available, then tell the clerk what they want to buy. Which of the two phrases do they use?

   Both clients used the phrase **déme...** , which, as you can probably guess from the context, means *give me*. Did you notice the units of weight used for fish? **Un kilo** and **medio kilo** are part of the metric system of weights used in most countries of the world except the United States.

Paso 2

Now you will hear one of the same clients conversing with a clerk in another store. Listen for the word **cóbreme** and see whether you can guess its meaning in context.

What is the meaning of **cóbreme**?

_____ Cover this for me.   _____ Ring this up for me.

If you chose the second phrase, you were right. **Cobrar** literally means *to charge*, so **cóbreme esto** means *charge me for this*, *ring this up*.

Paso 3
It is possible to use **por favor** with both **déme** and **cóbreme** to make the phrases sound less abrupt. How would you ask a clerk for the following items?

- a kilo of squid
- half a kilo of butter (two ways)

Now ask the clerk to ring up your purchases.

· ·

UN POCO DE GRAMÁTICA

More About Using Verbs to Talk About the Past

In **Lección 12** you learned to express what other people did in the past by adding **-ó/-ió** or **-aron/-ieron** to the stems of most verbs. To talk about your own actions in the past, add **-é** to the stems of most **-ar** verbs and **-í** to the stems of most **-er** and **-ir** verbs.

RAQUEL: Arturo volvió a su casa y yo **regresé** al hotel. **Llamé** a México y **hablé** con Pedro.

ARTURO: La última vez que **vi** a mi hermano fue aquí.

Remember that stem-changing verbs ending in **-ar** and **-er** do not have a stem change in the preterite. Note also that the first-person form of **ver** (**vi**) does not carry an accent mark.

Actividad.   Los primeros días en la Argentina
In the following sentences Raquel is relating what she has done since arriving in Argentina. Can you put the events in the correct order, from 1 to 8?

a.   __5__ Conocí a Arturo Iglesias.
b.   __1__ Llegué al hotel y por fin subí a una *suite*.
c.   __4__ Encontré la calle Gorostiaga y pregunté por el doctor en una casa.
d.   __2__ Fui a la estancia Santa Susana.
e.   __6__ Acepté una invitación a cenar en casa de Arturo.
f.   __3__ Hablé con Cirilo, un gaucho.

g. _____ Comencé la búsqueda con Arturo.

h. _____ Comí en la Barca con Arturo.

Nota cultural: La Argentina, país de contrastes

At the beginning of **Episodio 13** you saw a brief introduction to Argentina and to its incredible geographical variety. Listen to the introduction again. Try to remember the images you saw in the video episode and locate the places named on these maps.*

Now listen to a series of statements about Argentina. Are they **Cierto (C)** or **Falso (F)**? You will hear the answers on the cassette tape.

1. Ⓒ F   2. C Ⓕ   3. C Ⓕ
4. C Ⓕ   5. C Ⓕ

¿**C**ómo es la Argentina? Para contestar, muchos pensamos en los gauchos… en el tango… en Juan Perón y Evita (¿te acuerdas de la obra musical que se montó[1] en Inglaterra y los Estados Unidos?)… en el fútbol[2]… . Pero sobre todo pensamos en La Pampa. Es verdad que La Pampa ocupa la cuarta parte del territorio argentino y que da a la Argentina sus dos grandes riquezas:[3] la carne[4] y los cereales.

Pero la Argentina es mucho más que una inmensa llanura. Es también

- la selva[5] del norte, en la frontera con el Brasil
- las plantaciones de té de Misiones
- las viñas[6] de Mendoza (¡los vinos de la Argentina son fabulosos!)
- la impresionante cordillera de los Andes, con el Aconcagua, la cumbre[7] más alta de América, con sus 6.959 metros
- las famosas estaciones de esquí, como Bariloche

[1]*se… was produced*   [2]¡OJO! *soccer* (*football* = el fútbol americano) [3]*riches* [4]*meat* [5]jungla [6]*vineyards* [7]*peak*

La cordillera de los Andes

---

* As you look at the names on the maps and listen to the description of Argentina, note that the definite article is used with the names of some countries and not others: **la Argentina**, **el Brasil**, **el Uruguay**, **el Paraguay**; but: **Chile**, **Bolivia**, **Colombia** . . . . This isn't observed by all Spanish speakers.

- los glaciares y grandes lagos—entre ellos, el lago Argentino—de la Patagonia, donde termina el continente americano.

La Argentina es también una nación marítima por excelencia. Tiene 4.500 kilómetros de costa con su riqueza marina. ¿Sabías,[8] por ejemplo, que la península de Valdés es el único asiento continental[9] de elefantes marinos del mundo? Y, por supuesto,[10] está también la Tierra del Fuego, separada del continente por el estrecho de Magallanes. Su capital, Ushuaia, es la ciudad más austral del mundo.

Las cataratas del Iguazú

Todo esto ilustra el gran contraste que hay de una región a otra. ¿Cómo es posible que haya tanta variedad de climas y diversidad de paisajes[11]? Recuerda que la Argentina se extiende desde el Trópico de Capricornio hasta el Polo Sur. Aquí hay unas vistas más.

En las llanuras tropicales del noreste, entre la Argentina, el Brasil y el Paraguay, están las cataratas del Iguazú: unas 275 cascadas en medio de una vegetación exótica. Aunque la mayoría de los saltos[12] están en el lado argentino, las mejores vistas[13] se ven desde el Brasil: «Argentina pone el espectáculo[14] y Brasil cobra la entrada[15]», dicen allí.

La Cueva de las Manos

Los pueblos[16] que habitaron en lo que hoy es la Argentina, no llegaron a desarrollar[17] civilizaciones como la inca, maya o azteca. Sin embargo, crearon[18] culturas muy interesantes con bellas manifestaciones artísticas. Una de las expresiones artísticas más interesantes y antiguas está situada en la provincia de Santa Cruz en la Patagonia. Hace unos diez mil años, un pueblo de esta región cubrió de huellas de mano las paredes de una gruta.[19] Hoy se llama la Cueva de las Manos.

[8]*Did you know*   [9]asiento... *continental shelf*   [10]por... *of course*   [11]*landscapes*   [12]*falls*   [13]*views*   [14]pone... *puts on the show*
[15]*price of admission*   [16]*peoples*   [17]no... *didn't develop*   [18]*they created*   [19]cubrió... *covered the walls of a cave with handprints*

Actividad.   La Argentina y los Estados Unidos

Do the following aspects of Argentine geography remind you of places in the United States? Are there American equivalents for some of them?

1. La Pampa
2. las viñas de Mendoza
3. los Andes
4. Bariloche
5. el Aconcagua

6. la península de Valdés
7. Ushuaia (¿Cuál es la ciudad más norteña de los Estados Unidos?)
8. las cataratas del Iguazú

Have you completed the following sections of the lesson? Check them off here.

_____ **Preparación**	_____ **Conversaciones**
_____ **¿Tienes buena memoria?**	_____ **Un poco de gramática**
_____ **Vocabulario del tema**	

Now scan the words in the **Vocabulario** list to be sure that you understand the meaning of most of them. Then you will be ready to continue on with **Lección 13** in the Workbook.

VOCABULARIO

Los verbos

almorzar (ue)	to have lunch
comenzar (ie)	to begin
comer	to eat
preferir (ie)	to prefer
reconocer (reconozco)*	to recognize

Las personas

el/la dependiente	clerk
el marinero	sailor
todo el mundo	everybody

Los lugares

el barco	boat
el negocio	business; shop
la tienda	store

Los conceptos

la búsqueda	search
la (primera/última) vez	(first/last) time

Los mariscos (Seafood)

los calamares	squid
el cangrejo	crab
la langosta	lobster
el langostino	prawn
el mejillón	mussel
la ostra	oyster

El pescado (Fish)

el atún	tuna
el lenguado	sole
la merluza	hake
el salmón	salmon

Otros comestibles (Other Foods)

el aceite	oil
el arroz	rice
la ensalada	salad
la manteca (*Arg.*)	butter
la mantequilla	butter
el pan	bread

Las palabras adicionales

cóbreme...	charge me for . . . , ring . . . up for me
déme...	give me . . . , let me have . . .
me gusta(n) (mucho)...	I like . . . (a lot)
no me gusta(n) (nada)...	I don't like . . . (at all)
en seguida	immediately
hace... (años, horas...)	. . . (years, hours . . .) ago
luego	then, next; later

---

* Note that the first-person singular form of **reconocer** reflects the irregularity of **conocer** (**conozco**), from which it is derived.

14

EN EL EXTRANJERO*

OBJETIVOS

The materials in **Lección 14** of the Textbook and the Workbook will help you better understand the video episode and take you beyond it, giving you additional information about places and characters in the series. The Textbook will also help you to develop skill in using the Spanish language. In this lesson you will learn

- the Spanish words for some types of meat and for some other food items used to prepare **brochetas**
- some conversational strategies for dealing with talkative or inquisitive people
- some ways to talk about things you did with others in the past.

You will also learn about the national hero of Argentina.

Be sure to work through all parts of the lesson. When you see a cassette symbol in the margin, listen to the tape for **Lección 14**. Answers or hints for many activities are given in Appendix 1. Be sure to check your answers for each activity before going on to the next one.

*Abroad

BEFORE VIEWING . . .

PREPARACIÓN

Actividad A.

In the last video episode of *Destinos* Raquel and Arturo started their search for
Ángel. What do you remember about the search? Complete the following
statements.

1. Entre las cosas de su madre, Arturo encontró
    a. _____ una carta   c. _____ una foto... de Ángel
    b. _____ una pintura

2. En el barrio de la Boca, Raquel y Arturo hablaron con
    a. _____ pocas personas   c. _____ muchas personas
    b. _____ varias personas

3. Por fin encontraron a un marinero que
    a. _____ reconoció a Ángel   c. _____ les dio el nombre de
    b. _____ tenía la dirección de Ángel   otro marinero

4. Arturo invitó a Raquel a
    a. _____ cenar en su casa   c. _____ ir a un parque
    b. _____ ir al teatro

Actividad B.

In this video episode Raquel and Arturo will meet and talk with Héctor. Listen
to part of their conversation on the cassette tape, trying to get the gist of it.
Then read it to see whether you missed anything. Then listen to the conversation again.

RAQUEL: ¿Se quedó[1] a vivir en el extranjero?
HÉCTOR: Sí. No recuerdo bien qué país era... ¿saben? Creo que era Puerto Rico,
         pero no estoy seguro. Era un país en el Caribe... no sé si Puerto
         Rico, pero estoy seguro que era en el Caribe... Sí, posiblemente
         Puerto Rico.
RAQUEL: ¿Y la carta?
HÉCTOR: ¡Claro! ¡La carta! La tengo que buscar.
ARTURO: Es muy importante para mí.
HÉCTOR: Sí, comprendo. Mire, Ud. sabe dónde encontrarme. Necesito un par de
         días para buscar la carta.
ARTURO: Bueno, se lo agradezco muchísimo.[2]
HÉCTOR: No hay de qué. Ángel era mi amigo.

[1]Se... *He stayed*   [2]se... *I'm very grateful.* (*I thank you very much for it.*)

Para pensar...*

¿Qué importancia puede tener el Caribe en esta historia? ¿Qué no recuerda muy bien Héctor? ¿Y por qué está interesada Raquel en una carta que tiene Héctor?

━━━ **AFTER VIEWING...**

· ·

¿TIENES BUENA MEMORIA?

Actividad A.   ¿Cuánto recuerdas?

Listen to part of Raquel's story review once again if you think you need to, then answer the following questions about **Episodio 14**.

Paso 1

All of the following events happened in **Episodio 14**, but . . . in what order did they occur? Put them in order, from 1 to 6. The understood subject of most of the sentences is **Arturo y Raquel**.

a. _____ Fueron al Piccolo Navio.

b. _____ Tomaron café y miraron unas fotos.

c. _____ Se sentaron a cenar en el jardín.

d. _____ Comieron brochetas y hablaron.

e. _____ Raquel llamó a su madre por teléfono.

f. _____ Conocieron a Héctor y hablaron con él.

Paso 2

Raquel found out some things about Arturo in this video episode. What were they? Indicate whether the statements are **Cierto** (**C**) or **Falso** (**F**).

C   F   1. Arturo vive solo (*alone*).

C   F   2. Se casó una vez pero está divorciado.

C   F   3. Su esposa volvió a su país natal, el Perú.

C   F   4. Su profesión no es muy importante para él.

Actividad B.   El amigo de Ángel

So far, Héctor has been able to provide a little bit of information, and perhaps he might be of even more help later on. What do you remember about Héctor and the information he has given Arturo and Raquel? ¡OJO! More than one answer may be possible in some cases.

*****Para pensar...** means *Something to think about* . . . This repeating feature of the lessons, which can occur in any section, will suggest things for you to think about as you view the video episodes or work with the Textbook or Workbook.

1. Héctor se acuerda muy bien de Ángel porque Ángel
   a. _____ lo ayudó cuando era niño
   b. _____ vivió en el barrio
   c. _____ era su amigo

2. También dice Héctor que recibió una carta de Ángel
   a. _____ hace dos días
   b. _____ hace unas semanas
   c. _____ hace muchos años

3. Héctor cree que Ángel
   a. _____ se casó muy joven
   b. _____ se preocupaba mucho por su padre, don Fernando
   c. _____ se fue a vivir en el extranjero, en Puerto Rico

Nota cultural: Los brindis

As Arturo and Raquel have a glass of wine before dinner, they exchange a toast used throughout the Spanish-speaking world, with minor variations. You may have heard the toast on other occasions, and you can probably guess its general meaning.

¡Salud, dinero y amor! Y tiempo para disfrutarlos.*

A shorter toast is simply **Salud**, the equivalent of *To your health*. It is considered polite to use it even prior to drinking water, as in **Episodio 12** when Arturo brought up glasses of water for them both on the rooftop and began to tell Raquel about his city.

VOCABULARIO DEL TEMA

La carne

la carne de cerdo	pork	el bistec	steak
la carne de vaca	beef	el cordero	lamb
el chorizo	sausage	la chuleta	chop
el jamón	ham	de cerdo	pork chop
la panceta	bacon	de cordero	lamb chop
el pollo	chicken	la hamburguesa	hamburger
los riñones	kidney	el pavo	turkey
el tocino	bacon	la ternera	veal

---

*A frequent variation is: **Y tiempo para gozarlos**.

Otros comestibles

la cebolla	onion
el pimiento (morrón)	(red) pepper
el queso	cheese
el tomate	tomato
el vino	wine
el vino blanco	white wine
el vino tinto	red wine

Escalopines de Ternera con Setas a la Pimienta verde.- 1.800
Estofado de Rabo de Toro a la "Real Maestranza".- 1.600
Entrecot de Buey a la Bordalesa.- 1.800
Solomillo de Ternera al Estragón.- 1.950
Magre de Pato al Vino de Oporto.- 1.900
Salteado de Ternera a la Sevillana.- 1.600
Pollo con Champiñones al Ajillo.- 1.300

Note some variations frequently used in other parts of the Spanish-speaking world.

la carne de vaca = la carne de res (*Mex.*)
el chorizo = la salchicha (*Lat. Am.*)
el pavo = el guajolote (*Mex.*)

Actividad A.   La carne y otros comestibles

Listen as the speaker on the cassette tape talks about some of his food preferences. He will use the phrases **me gusta...** and **me gustan...** as well as the verb **prefiero...** . Write the number of the sentence next to the appropriate drawing.

Actividad B.   Las brochetas y otros comestibles

Listen as Arturo and Raquel talk about how **brochetas** are prepared, as well as some other dishes. Try to provide the missing words without looking back at the list of foods.

ARTURO: Preparo las brochettes con _____,¹ carne de

_____,² carne de cerdo, _____³ y panceta.

RAQUEL: ¿_____?⁴ ¿Qué es eso?

ARTURO: Creo que Uds. le llaman «_____».⁵

RAQUEL: Ah, sí.

ARTURO: Y también… _____⁶ morrón, _____,⁷

_____⁸ y ciruela, para darle el toque artístico y agridulce.

RAQUEL: En España probé unos _____⁹ deliciosos.

ARTURO: Sí, los jamones españoles tienen gran fama.

RAQUEL: La carne argentina también tiene gran fama, sobre todo la carne de vaca.

ARTURO: Si te gusta el _____,¹⁰ tengo una receta fabulosa: pollo a la inglesa. Se prepara* con limón y mayonesa.

Actividad C.   Las comidas (*meals*) especiales

Indicate which meats and other foods are most commonly served on the following special occasions.

1. Cuando hay una gran cena para celebrar algo especial, las carnes que preferimos en mi familia son _____ o _____.

2. Para celebrar el cuatro de julio, tradicionalmente se prepara una barbacoa (*barbeque*) de _____ o _____. Yo prefiero…

3. En los Estados Unidos, el clásico desayuno consiste en huevos (*eggs*), _____ y pan tostado. En otros países, no se come tanto; a veces sólo café o café con leche y pan.

4. Para celebrar el Día de Dar Gracias en los Estados Unidos, se prepara _____.

Actividad D.   ¿Y tú?

What food items from the list do you like or dislike? Express some of your preferences by completing the following sentences.

1. Para almorzar, prefiero _____.

2. Cuando ceno en casa, preparo _____.

3. Cuando voy a un restaurante muy elegante, me gusta pedir _____. Nunca pido _____. Otras cosas que siempre busco en el menú son…

4. Nunca como _____.

---

*Note the use of **se** before the verb in this sentence. **Preparo** expresses *I prepare*; **se prepara** in this context means *it is prepared*. You will hear and see the word **se** used frequently in this way throughout *Destinos*.

CONVERSACIONES: CUANDO LA CONVERSACIÓN ES DIFÍCIL...

Actividad. Hablando con los padres

Raquel's phone conversation with her mother was an affectionate one, but Raquel needed to "manage" the conversation a bit. You will learn some of her techniques in this activity.

Paso 1

As you listen to the conversation in its entirety, note which phrases Raquel uses in each of the following situations.

1. Her mother is making too much out of a situation.
   a. _____ No me hables así.
   b. _____ No te preocupes.
   c. _____ No es así, mamá.
   d. _____ No exageres, mamá.

2. Raquel wants to end the conversation.
   a. _____ Bueno, tengo que colgar.
   b. _____ Bueno, tengo que irme.

Check your answers in the Appendix. In this context, what do you think the verb **colgar** means?

Paso 2

Now listen to the conversation again just for fun. Even though Raquel is a mature adult and a professional, her mother asks the questions mothers typically ask when a child is far away from home. Listen for the phrases in the left-hand column, then indicate their meaning by selecting the answer from the right.

1. _____ Te echamos de menos.
2. _____ Me preocupo porque estás sola...
3. _____ Está bien, pero cuídate.
4. _____ ¿Comes bien?

a. Are you eating well?
b. OK, but take care of yourself.
c. We miss you.
d. I worry because you're alone.

Paso 3

What would you say in these situations to a friend who is away on a trip? You are talking with the friend on the phone.

1. You miss him/her.
2. He/She is worried because you're working too much.
3. He/She says you are working twenty-four hours a day.
4. You need to get off the phone now.

UN POCO DE GRAMÁTICA

More About Using Verbs to Talk About the Past

To talk about what you did in the past with others, add **-amos** to **-ar** verbs and **-imos** to **-er** and **-ir** verbs.

RAQUEL: Anoche **encontramos** a Héctor en el Piccolo Navio. Cuando lo **vimos**, se levantó para bailar. Por fin **hablamos** un poco con él. **Caminamos** con él hasta su casa. Nos **despedimos** de él y luego **volvimos** a la casa de Arturo.

RAQUEL: *Last night we found Héctor at the Piccolo Navio. When we saw him, he got up to dance. Finally we talked with him a bit. We walked to his house with him. We said good-bye to him and then we returned to Arturo's house.*

Did you notice that the present and preterite **nosotros** forms of most **-ar** verbs are identical, and that the same is true of most **-ir** verbs? Context will help you determine which tense is being used.

Actividad. Una tarde con Arturo

If Raquel made the following statements about the time she has spent with Arturo, would she be telling the truth? Indicate whether the statements are **Cierto** (**C**) or **Falso** (**F**), based on what has happened so far.

C F   1. Cenamos en casa de Arturo.
C F   2. Preparamos la cena juntos (*together*).
C F   3. Hablamos del pasado de Arturo.
C F   4. Vimos unas fotos que Arturo tomó.
C F   5. No hablamos de nuestros países.
C F   6. Nos llevamos muy bien. (*We got along very well.*)
C F   7. Regresamos a mi hotel.
C F   8. Llamamos a mi madre.
C F   9. Llegamos juntos al Piccolo Navio.
C F 10. Vimos a Héctor en seguida.
C F 11. Caminamos con él hasta su barco.
C F 12. Volvimos a la casa de Arturo.

Nota cultural: José de San Martín, héroe nacional de la Argentina

Before reading the following passage about José de San Martín and his role in Latin American history, review what you know about him by listening again to information from the video episode. Pay particular attention to the names of the countries.

El general José de San Martín fue uno de los líderes militares de la independencia de América. Fue el héroe de la independencia de la Argentina, Chile y el Perú.

San Martín nació[1] el 25 de febrero de 1778 en Yapeyú, un pueblo[2] de las antiguas misiones jesuitas. (Hoy está en la provincia argentina de Corrientes.) En 1786 viajó con sus padres a España. En Madrid estudió en un colegio para futuros militares. A los doce años entró como cadete en un regimiento del ejército[3] español. Más tarde luchó[4] en la guerra de independencia española contra Napoleón.

A pesar de[5] su educación española, San Martín no se consideró nunca español, sino[6] americano.* Regresó a la Argentina en 1812, muy animado por el espíritu de la guerra de la independencia de los Estados Unidos y de la revolución francesa. Muy pronto se puso al mando[7] de los movimientos independistas de Sudamérica. La independencia de la Argentina se proclamó en 1816. Pero aún quedaban[8] muchas colonias en el continente.

En el norte, actuó Simón Bolívar, el Libertador de Venezuela, Colombia y Ecuador. Desde el sur, el general San Martín dirigió[9] personalmente la lucha por la independencia. Su talento militar era excepcional. En 1817 salió de la Argentina y cruzó los Andes con un ejército de 5.200 hombres. En 1818 se declaró la independencia de Chile.

En 1820 San Martín organizó la expedición del Perú. Avanzó desde el sur y conquistó Lima en 1821. Bolívar avanzó desde el norte. Por fin se consiguió la independencia del Perú en 1824.

Después de una larga carrera militar, San Martín decidió volver a Europa. Se instaló[10] en Francia, donde murió en 1850.

El general José de San Martín siguió toda su vida esta máxima: «Serás[11] lo que debes ser, y si no, no serás nada.»

[1] *was born* [2] *village* [3] *army* [4] *he fought* [5] *A... In spite of* [6] *but rather* [7] *se... he took command* [8] *aún... there were still* [9] *directed* [10] *Se... He settled* [11] *You will be*

Actividad.   Sudamérica y los Estados Unidos

Da el nombre de

1.   dos libertadores de Sudamérica
2.   el héroe de la independencia de la Argentina
3.   un héroe de la independencia de los Estados Unidos
4.   un héroe argentino que fue militar
5.   un héroe estadounidense de la época moderna que fue militar

---

*Note the use of the word **americano** in this context. It does not mean American in the sense of *from the United States of America*, but rather American in the sense of *from the Americas, North and South America*.

Have you completed the following sections of the lesson? Check them off here.

_____ **Preparación**	_____ **Conversaciones**
_____ **¿Tienes buena memoria?**	_____ **Un poco de gramática**
_____ **Vocabulario del tema**	

Now scan the words in the **Vocabulario** list to be sure that you understand the meaning of most of them. Then you will be ready to continue on with **Lección 14** in the Workbook.

VOCABULARIO

Los verbos

llevarse (**bien/mal**)	to get along (well/badly)
pasar	to pass, spend (*time*); to happen
preparar	to prepare

Las carnes (Meats)

el bistec	steak
la carne de cerdo	pork
la carne de vaca	beef
el cordero	lamb
el chorizo	sausage
la chuleta	chop
de cerdo	pork chop
de cordero	lamb chop
la hamburguesa	hamburger
el jamón	ham
la panceta	bacon
el pavo	turkey
el pollo	chicken
los riñones	kidneys
la ternera	veal
el tocino	bacon

Otros comestibles

la cebolla	onion
el pimiento (**morrón**)	(red) pepper
el queso	cheese
el tomate	tomato
el vino (**blanco**, **tinto**)	(white, red) wine

Los adjetivos

divorciado/a	divorced
juntos/as	together
solo/a	alone

Más sobre la cortesía

No exageres.	Don't exaggerate. (*fam.*)
No te preocupes.	Don't worry. (*fam.*)
Tengo que colgar.	I have to hang up.

Las palabras adicionales

en el extranjero	abroad

Palabras del texto

para pensar…   something to think about

15

CULPABLE*

OBJETIVOS

The materials in **Lección 15** of the Textbook and the Workbook will help you better understand the video episode and take you beyond it, giving you additional information about places and characters in the series. The Textbook will also help you to develop skill in using the Spanish language. In this lesson you will learn

- how to express the names of many kinds of fruit in Spanish
- how to convince someone to do something
- how to form additional preterite-tense verb forms.

You will also learn about Buenos Aires and about one of Argentina's most important industries.

Be sure to work through all parts of the lesson. When you see a cassette symbol in the margin, listen to the tape for **Lección 15**. Answers or hints for many activities are given in Appendix 1. Be sure to check your answers for each activity before going on to the next one.

*Guilty

BEFORE VIEWING . . .

Preparación

Actividad A.
In the last video episode of *Destinos* Raquel and Arturo were finally able to make some progress in their search for Ángel. How much do you remember about **Episodio 14**? Complete the following statements.

1. En casa de Arturo, Raquel pasó una noche muy
    a. _____ aburrida (*boring*)   c. _____ triste (*sad*)
    b. _____ agradable

2. Al día siguiente, en la cantina Piccolo Navio, Raquel y Arturo conocieron a este hombre. Se llama
    a. _____ José   c. _____ Ángel
    b. _____ Héctor

3. Este hombre era (*was*) amigo de Ángel. Les dice a Raquel y Arturo que Ángel se fue a vivir a un país
    a. _____ del Caribe   c. _____ de África
    b. _____ de Europa

4. El hombre tiene algo que da la dirección de Ángel. Es
    a. _____ un telegrama   c. _____ una carta
    b. _____ un libro

5. Para buscarla, necesita
    a. _____ unos minutos   c. _____ una semana
    b. _____ un par de días

6. Al final de su conversación, este hombre le da algo a Arturo como recuerdo (*memento*) de su hermano Ángel. Es
    a. _____ una foto   c. _____ un poema
    b. _____ un cuadro

Para pensar...

¿Crees que hay una atracción mutua entre Raquel y Arturo? ¿Siente ella algo por él? Y él, ¿qué piensa de esta abogada norteamericana?

Actividad B.
In this video episode Arturo will express his concerns about Ángel's fate.

Paso 1

Listen to part of a conversation between Arturo and Raquel without looking ahead in this activity. Then answer the question. You should listen to this section of the cassette tape only once.

Which of the following statements best describes Arturo's mood in this conversation?

a. _____ Arturo está contento.

b. _____ Arturo está preocupado.

c. _____ Arturo está aburrido.

Paso 2

Now listen to the conversation again. A written version of it is provided to help you understand it. Then answer the questions. This time you may listen to the cassette tape as many times as you need to.*

RAQUEL: ¿En qué piensas?

ARTURO: En Ángel. ¿Qué quería de la vida? ¿Qué buscaba?

RAQUEL: ¿Te sientes bien? ¿Qué te pasa?

ARTURO: No te preocupes. No es nada.

RAQUEL: Ya verás. Pronto podrás hablar con tu hermano... Arturo, dime por favor qué es lo que te pasa.

ARTURO: Me tenés que perdonar, Raquel. Es que...

RAQUEL: ¿Sí... ?

ARTURO: Tengo un mal presentimiento... ¿Qué pasa si Ángel... ?

1. You should be able to understand the meaning of **¿Te sientes bien?** But what about **¿Qué te pasa?** What does Raquel want to know?
    a. _____ Where are you going?
    b. _____ What are you thinking about?
    c. _____ What's the matter?

2. The verb form **dime** is a command. Knowing that **me** means *me* or *to me* in English, what you do you think Raquel is saying when she uses this verb form? (*Hint*:   **Di** does not look very much like the infinitive from which it derives. Let the context in which **dime** is used be your guide.)

3. According to the context and to Arturo's mood, what do you think the word **presentimiento** means?
    a. _____ premonition
    b. _____ thought
    c. _____ headache

---

*Some of the verb forms used in this conversation between Raquel and Arturo are probably unfamiliar to you. However, you should be able to follow the conversation by focusing on the verb stems and making logical guesses about whether the action described by the verb is in the present, past, or future.

Para pensar...

¿Qué presentimiento tiene Arturo? ¿Qué quiere decir él cuando le dice a Raquel «¿Qué pasa si Ángel... ?» ¿A qué o a quién se refiere el título de este episodio?

AFTER VIEWING . . .

• •

¿TIENES BUENA MEMORIA?

Actividad A. ¿A quién se refiere?

Identify the character described in each sentence.

a. Ángel Castillo   c. Raquel Rodríguez
b. Arturo Iglesias   d. Héctor Condotti

1. __b__ Después de hablar con Héctor, está muy pensativo.
2. __d__ Va a buscar la carta que Ángel le escribió hace muchos años.
3. __c__ Probablemente tiene que hacer un viaje al Caribe.
4. __b__ Tiene vergüenza (*is embarrassed*) en el parque y no quiere andar en mateo (*ride in the carriage*).
5. __a__ Se fue a vivir al Caribe. Ahora tendrá* unos 52 años.
6. __b__ Se siente culpable porque nunca buscó a su hermano.

Actividad B. ¿Qué pasó?

The following paragraphs are a summary of what Raquel and Arturo did in **Episodio 15**. Complete the paragraph with phrases from the following list.

tuvieron (*they had*) un *picnic*
fue a la Cuadra
compró una bolsa de cuero
decidieron ir a un parque
llamó a Arturo
encontró la carta
no le gustó mucho

no le interesó mucho
recibió un regalo (*present*) de
   Arturo

---

*The phrase **tener... años** means *to be . . . years old*. **Tendrá** is a future form of **tener**. In this context it means *he is probably . . .*

Raquel visitó varias tiendas con Arturo y _____.¹ Más tarde, _____,²

un centro comercial. Allí compró una blusa y unos pantalones. Luego regresó a su hotel.

Mientras tanto,ª Héctor _____³ para decirle que _____.⁴ Pero no

puede ver a Arturo y Raquel hasta mañana. Esto _____⁵ a Raquel. Empieza

a ponerseᵇ un poco impaciente y quiere terminar pronto la investigación.

　　　Para pasar el resto del día, Raquel y Arturo _____,⁶ aunqueᶜ la idea

_____⁷ a Arturo. Pero lo pasaron muy bien.ᵈ Anduvieronᵉ en bote y en mateo

y también _____⁸ con la comida que Arturo llevabaᶠ en la canasta.ᵍ Por la

noche, Raquel _____,⁹ una linda chaqueta* de cuero. Parece que sí hay una

atracción entre Arturo y Raquel, ¿no?

ªMientras... *Meanwhile*　ᵇ*become*　ᶜ*although*　ᵈlo... *they had a good time*　ᵉ*They rode*　ᶠ*was carrying*　ᵍ*basket*

Now listen to the summary on the cassette tape and check your answers.

Actividad C.　¡Un desafío!

Can you remember the following details from **Episodio 15**?

1.　Un día después de su primera conversación con Héctor, Arturo y
　　Raquel pasan por una de las calles más conocidas de Buenos Aires,

　　la calle _____.

2.　Después Raquel y Arturo van a un gran parque de Buenos Aires, el Parque

　　del _____.

Nota cultural: Tiendas y parques

In this video episode Raquel and Arturo visit a number of well-known places in Buenos Aires. It is obvious from the video episode that Buenos Aires is a cosmopolitan city on a par with Paris, Madrid, New York, and other major cities and capitals. In addition to its wide boulevards and many public buildings, Buenos Aires is also home to

- **La calle Florida**, an elegant pedestrian mall with expensive shops, designer boutiques, and restaurants that serve many ethnic foods as well as the varieties of **parrillada** (*grilling*) for which Argentina is famous. Additional shopping options in Buenos Aires include **centros comerciales**, that is, shopping centers like **la Cuadra** (which

---

*In Argentina, a short jacket of the type Arturo buys for Raquel is called **una campera**. In México, it's **una chamarra**.

have begun to spring up in all major cities in the Spanish-speaking world), and smaller, less expensive **boutiques**, found in many neighborhoods.

- **El Rosedal**, the large park and recreational area in the center of Buenos Aires. It is similar to Central Park in New York, **el Parque Chapultepec** in Mexico City, and **el Retiro** in Madrid. All these parks are particularly crowded on the weekends. They are sites for family gatherings and picnics, and where young people can meet in groups or where couples can stroll. Why do you think Arturo was so reluctant to go there?

VOCABULARIO DEL TEMA

Las frutas

la banana	banana	**la cereza**	cherry	
el durazno	peach	**la ciruela**	plum	
la frutilla (*Arg.*)	strawberry	**la fresa**	strawberry	
la manzana	apple	**el limón**	lemon	
el melón	melon	**el melocotón**	peach	
la naranja	orange	**la pera**	pear	
la uva	grape	**la piña**	pineapple	
		el plátano	banana	
		la sandía	watermelon	
		la toronja	grapefruit	

apricot = el chabacán albaricoque

The names for fruits and vegetables are the most variable among all vocabulary groups in the Spanish-speaking world. Some specifically Argentine variations are noted in the preceding list. Additional words used in Argentina include **el pomelo** (= **la toronja**) and **el ananás** (= **la piña**).

Actividad A.   El espectáculo de Jaime Bolas

Listen again to Jaime's patter during his juggling act and indicate the fruits he mentions.

2 melón   ____   1 manzana   2 naranja

3 banana

Actividad B. En la canasta de Arturo

As you know, Arturo goes shopping for a picnic lunch. Listen again to the conversation he has with the fruit-store clerk. Then complete the following summary with as much information as you can remember.

Para el *picnic*, Arturo sorprendió a Raquel con una variedad de ~~frutas~~ .¹

Él recordó lo que dijo Raquel[a] en la calle Florida: «Ahora tengo ganas de[b] comer una

ensalada de fruta.»

Arturo fue al Paseo Natural y compró _____.² El dependiente también le

ofreció _____,³ pero no los compró. También compró ~~pan y caso~~ ,⁴

pero en otra tienda.

[a]lo... *what Raquel said* [b]tengo... *I feel like*

Actividad C. ¿Y tú?

What kinds of fruit do you like to eat? Listen as the speaker on the cassette tape talks about her preferences, then indicate whether you agree or disagree.

MODELOS: (*you hear*) A mí me gusta mucho la sandía.
             (*you say*) A mí *también* me gusta mucho (la sandía).
             or   A mí *no* me gusta (la sandía).

             (*you hear*) A mí no me gustan (los duraznos).
             (*you say*) A mí *tampoco* me gustan (los duraznos).
             or   A mí *sí* me gustan (los duraznos).

1. ...   2. ...   3. ...   4. ...   5. ...

CONVERSACIONES: PARA ANIMAR

Actividad. ¡Vamos!

As you noticed in the video episode, Arturo was not enthusiastic about Raquel's plans to spend the afternoon at Rosedal Park. In this activity you will focus on the ways in which Raquel was able to convince him to accompany her.

Paso 1

Listen to Raquel and Arturo's conversation about the buggy ride, trying not to look at the printed version of the conversation that follows.

Now indicate the words and expressions that Raquel used to urge Arturo on. Listen to the cassette tape again if you need to.

ARTURO: Ah no no no. Raquel, por favor, no...
RAQUEL: ¿No? Debe ser divertido¹... ¿Vamos?

¹*amusing, fun*

ARTURO: ¿En serio?

RAQUEL: ¡En serio! ¿No te gusta nada?

ARTURO: Bueno, está bien, si vos querés...

RAQUEL: ¿Qué pasa? ¿No te gusta? ¡Te da vergüenza! Mira lo rojo² que estás.

ARTURO: Raquel, todos nos están mirando.

RAQUEL: Anda, ¡vamos! ¡vamos! Debe ser divertido, ven...

²lo... *how red*

Paso 2

Now you will hear two brief conversations. A possible rejoinder for each is printed below, but it is incomplete. Complete each one with the expression you think is most appropriate.

1. ¡Sí,
   a. _____ vamos! Debe ser interesante.
   b. _____ vamos! Debe ser aburrida.

2. Pobrecito, pero... ¡Jaime es tu hijo también!
   a. _____ ¡Anda, vamos!   b. _____ De acuerdo.

· ·

UN POCO DE GRAMÁTICA

More About Using Verbs to Talk About the Past

Traer, **decir**, **estar**, **tener**, and **andar** belong to a group of Spanish verbs whose preterite forms are irregular. Here are some examples with first-person forms. Raquel is the speaker in each example.

No **traje** mucha ropa en este viaje. Por eso **tuve** que ir de compras varias veces.

I didn't bring a lot of clothes on this trip. That's why I had to go shopping several times.

Le **dije** a mi madre que conocí a un hombre muy simpático en Buenos Aires.

I told my mother that I met a very nice man in Buenos Aires.

Estuve en Buenos Aires sólo unos días. Entre otras cosas, **tuve** un *picnic* con Arturo en el Rosedal y **anduve** en mateo.

I was in Buenos Aires only a few days. Among other things, I had a picnic with Arturo in Rosedal and I rode in a carriage.

Did you notice the patterns of irregularity here?

- **Traer** and **decir** have a **j** in the stem of their preterite forms, while **estar**, **tener**, and **andar** have **uv** in the stem.
- All of these first-person forms, whether from **-ar**, **-er**, or **-ir** infinitives, end in *un*accented **e**.

See what other features you can spot in these irregular forms from the following activity, in which more than **yo** forms will appear. You will learn more about irregular preterite forms in the Workbook.

Actividad. ¿Qué dijo?

Complete the following brief excerpts from **Episodios 14** and **15** with the appropriate preterite forms.

1. RAQUEL: ¿Y tú? ¿Cuánto tiempo (estuviste/dijiste/trajiste) casado?
   ARTURO: Cinco años.
2. RAQUEL: Héctor (estuvo/tuvo/dijo) que Ángel se fue a vivir a un país del Caribe. Posiblemente a Puerto Rico.
3. RAQUEL: Arturo estaba muy pensativo porque (tuvo/estuvo/anduvo) un mal presentimiento.
4. RAQUEL: Primero, (anduvimos/tuvimos/trajimos) en mateo. Fue muy divertido para mí, pero para Arturo fue un escándalo. ¡Ja! Luego (estuvimos/tuvimos/anduvimos) en bote. Finalmente, (trajimos/tuvimos/anduvimos) un *picnic* muy especial.

Now check your answers by listening to the cassette tape.

Nota cultural: Buenos Aires, una ciudad europea en el Nuevo Mundo

At the end of **Episodio 12**, from the rooftop of a tall building Arturo pointed out some landmarks to Raquel. Listen again to his words, then complete the statement that follows.

La palabra *porteños* probablemente se refiere a

a. _____ personas que beben mucho vino   b. _____ personas que viven en un puerto

If you guessed *b*, you were correct. The word **porteños** is the name for people who live in the port city of Buenos Aires. Before reading the following passage about Buenos Aires, try to remember what you thought Buenos Aires would be like before you saw anything about the city in **Episodio 12**. Did you think Buenos Aires would be a modern or a colonial city? Would it be densely or sparsely populated? What would be the ethnic background of most of its inhabitants? You will find the answers to these questions in the reading passage.

«**B**uenos Aires… antes[1] morir que olvidarte»

Así dijo el famoso cantante[2] del tango Carlos Gardel, hablando[3] de su ciudad. Sin embargo,[4] cuando llegan a Buenos Aires, muchos visitantes se sienten un poco decepcionados. La ciudad es impresionante, pero no es exótica. No hay viejos monumentos históricos. No predomina el

[1]*rather* [2]*singer* [3]*talking* [4]*Sin… Nevertheless*

estilo colonial español. Y los habitantes de la ciudad podrían[5] ser de cualquier[6] nacionalidad. Uno tiene la impresión de estar en París, Londres, Milán o Madrid… en cualquier ciudad menos la capital de la Argentina, casi en el fin del mundo.

Dos factores importantes diferencian la Argentina de los demás países de la América Latina: su geografía y las características culturales de sus habitantes.

- Geográficamente la Argentina está aislada del resto de Hispanoamérica por los Andes al oeste y por el Brasil al norte. Por esta razón, la Argentina siempre miró más hacia[7] Europa que hacia sus vecinos. Y en Europa se sintió más cerca de Francia o de Inglaterra que de España.

- Además, la gran mayoría de los habitantes de la Argentina son descendientes de europeos. Desde mediados[8] del siglo XIX la Argentina recibió un gran número de emigrantes. Muchos de ellos eran europeos del área mediterránea, italianos y españoles, seguidos[9] a gran distancia por polacos, rusos, alemanes y gente de los países vecinos. Toda esta herencia étnica se refleja en la capital. Se puede decir que el porteño es «un italiano que habla español con acento napolitano y que se considera inglés o francés».

Esta gran capital es una metrópoli de unos nueve millones de habitantes, más del 30 por ciento del total de la población del país. Es uno de los centros financieros y comerciales más importantes del continente.

Pero al mismo tiempo[10] el nivel cultural y artístico que se respira en Buenos Aires es de excelente calidad. La ciudad tiene numerosos museos, galerías de arte, bibliotecas públicas, salas de cine y de teatro… Muy pocos teatros tienen el atractivo del Teatro Colón. En efecto, se dice que un artista no triunfa verdaderamente en Latinoamérica hasta que no triunfa en el Colón de Buenos Aires.

Hay que pasar unos días en Buenos Aires para tomarle el pulso a la ciudad. Andar por sus calles, hablar con su gente.[11] Siempre hay algo a la vuelta de la esquina[12] que llama la atención. La calle Rivadavia, que dicen que llega hasta la Patagonia (¿Es la más larga del mundo? ¿Y el Wilshire Boulevard?)… El obelisco blanco como el de Washington o la réplica del famoso Big Ben, regalo de Inglaterra… El barrio de San Telmo, donde viven muchos artistas y escritores, un barrio lleno de librerías, tiendas de antigüedades y artesanos[13]…. La Boca, cuyas[14] casas color pastel y restaurantes populares recuerdan el sur de Italia… En el centro, la animación de las calles peatonales[15] y las avenidas con sus *boutiques*.

Es con razón que los porteños, como Arturo Iglesias, se sienten muy orgullosos[16] de su ciudad.

Un monumento al general José de San Martín en Buenos Aires.

[5]*could* [6]*any* [7]*toward* [8]*the middle* [9]*followed* [10]al… *at the same time* [11]*people* [12]a… *just around the corner* [13]*craftspeople* [14]*whose* [15]calles… *pedestrian streets* [16]*proud*

Have you completed the following sections of the lesson? Check them off here.

_____ **Preparación**
_____ **¿Tienes buena memoria?**
_____ **Vocabulario del tema**

_____ **Conversaciones**
_____ **Un poco de gramática**

Now scan the words in the **Vocabulario** list to be sure that you understand the meaning of most of them. Then you will be ready to continue on with **Lección 15** in the Workbook.

VOCABULARIO

Los verbos

andar	to walk

Las frutas (Fruits)

la banana	banana
la cereza	cherry
la ciruela	plum
el durazno	peach
la fresa	strawberry
la frutilla (*Arg.*)	strawberry
el limón	lemon
la manzana	apple
el melocotón	peach
el melón	melon
la naranja	orange
la pera	pear
la piña	pineapple
el plátano	banana
la sandía	watermelon
la toronja	grapefruit
la uva	grape

Los adjetivos

aburrido/a	bored; boring*
culpable	guilty
divertido/a	fun

La ropa

la bolsa	purse, handbag

Los otros sustantivos

la canasta	basket
el recuerdo	memento
el regalo	present

Los conceptos

el presentimiento	premonition
la sorpresa	surprise

Para animar (To Encourage)

¡anda!	come on!
debe ser divertido...	it's probably fun . . .
¿vamos?	shall we go?
¡vamos!	let's go!

Las palabras adicionales

andar en mateo	to take a carriage ride
ir de compras	to go shopping
tener... años**	to be . . . years old
tener vergüenza**	to be embarrassed, ashamed

*Use **aburrido** with **estar** to express *bored* and with **ser** to express *boring*.

Note in each of these expressions that the Spanish verb **tener (*to have*) is used to express English *to be*. **Jaime tiene diez años** literally means *Jaime has ten years*, i.e., *Jaime is ten years old*. You will learn more about expressions of this kind in **Lección 21** of the Workbook/Study Guide.

16

CARAS*

OBJETIVOS

The materials in **Lección 16** of the Textbook and the Workbook will help you better understand the video episode and take you beyond it, giving you additional information about places and characters in the series. The Textbook will also help you to develop skill in using the Spanish language. In this lesson, you will learn

- how to express the names of many kinds of vegetables in Spanish
- how to excuse yourself or get someone's attention
- how to form additional preterite-tense verb forms.

You will also learn about other cities in Argentina.

Be sure to work through all parts of the lesson. When you see a cassette symbol in the margin, listen to the tape for **Lección 16**. Answers or hints for many activities are given in Appendix 1. Be sure to check your answers for each activity before going on to the next one.

Faces

BEFORE VIEWING . . .

. . . .

PREPARACIÓN

Actividad A.

In the last video episode of *Destinos*, Raquel and Arturo spent a lot of time together while waiting for Héctor to find Ángel's letter. Complete this summary of the episode with the following words and phrases.

5 la atracción mutua

2 un mal presentimiento

1 está pensativo

6 pasan mucho tiempo juntos

3 ya murió

4 calmar

7 noticias de Héctor

Al principio del episodio previo, Raquel nota que Arturo _está pensativo_.¹

Cuando ella le pregunta qué le pasa, Arturo le dice que tiene _____.²

—Arturo —dice Raquel— dime cuál es el mal presentimiento que tienes.

—Es que —contesta Arturo— algo me dice que Ángel _____.³

Raquel trata deª _____⁴ a Arturo. Y cuando están por salirᵇ para el hotel,

se dan cuenta deᶜ _____⁵ que sienten. Se besanᵈ y luego Arturo lleva a Raquel al hotel.

Al día siguiente los dos _____.⁶ Van de compras en la calle Florida y más tarde van al parque Rosedal. Lo pasan muy bien. Ahora, en este episodio, esperan

tener _____.⁷

ªtrata... *tries to* ᵇestán... *they are ready to leave* ᶜse... *they become aware of* ᵈSe... *They kiss*

Now listen to the cassette tape and check your answers.

Para pensar...

Ahora Raquel y Arturo están conscientes de su atracción mutua. ¿Crees que esta atracción va a convertirse en una relación seria?

Parece que Raquel tendrá que (*will have to*) hacer un viaje al Caribe para seguir con la búsqueda de Ángel. ¿Qué va a hacer Arturo?

Actividad B.

In this video episode Arturo will make an important decision.

Paso 1

Listen to part of a conversation between Arturo and Raquel without looking ahead in this activity. Then complete the statements according to what you understood. You should listen to this section of the cassette tape only once.

1. Raquel sale para Puerto Rico... pronto/en unos días.
2. Los dos están... muy serios/muy alegres (*happy*)... durante esta conversación.

Paso 2

Now listen to the conversation again. Read the following portion of it before listening. Then answer the questions. This time you may listen to the cassette tape as many times as you need to.

ARTURO: ¿Sabés? Ángel es el único pariente que tengo. ¿Ya decidiste cuándo te vas a ir?
RAQUEL: Debería tomar el primer vuelo... don Fernando está muy mal. Y no puedo tardarme mucho.
ARTURO: Hace unos pocos días que te conozco... y parece como si hiciera muchos años.
RAQUEL: Yo siento lo mismo.
ARTURO: Te voy a extrañar.
RAQUEL: Yo también a ti.

1. Arturo says, "Ángel es el único pariente que tengo." What do you think the word **pariente** means, according to the context?
   a. _____ friend
   b. __✓__ relative
   c. _____ enemy

2. Arturo says, "Hace unos pocos días que te conozco... y parece como si hiciera muchos años." What do you think he means?
   a. _____ I have known you for a few days, and I need more time to get acquainted.
   b. __✓__ I have known you for a few days, and it's as if I had known you for a long time.

3. A key word in this dialogue is the verb **extrañar**. Think about the context. Raquel has to travel to Puerto Rico to continue her search for Ángel. Given the mutual attraction that the two feel, when Arturo says to Raquel "Te voy a extrañar," and she responds "yo también a ti," what do you think they are saying to each other?
   a. _____ I'm going to forget you.
   b. __✓__ I'm going to miss you.
   c. _____ I'm going to follow you.

AFTER VIEWING . . .

¿TIENES BUENA MEMORIA?

Actividad A. ¿Quién lo dijo?

Identify the character who makes the following statements in **Episodio 16**.

a. Raquel Rodríguez
b. Arturo Iglesias
c. Héctor Condotti
d. el ama de casa (*housekeeper*)

1. _____ «Salgo mal en las fotos y la cámara lo sabe.»
2. _____ «Mira. Me gusta mucho esta foto. ¿La has visto? El fotógrafo debe ser muy imaginativo.»
3. _____ «Disculpe, doctor, lo llaman por teléfono. Un Sr. Héctor... »
4. _____ «Señorita, ¿está bien el señor?»
5. _____ «Otra vez... este presentimiento... algo me dice que Ángel ya murió.»
6. _____ «Yo también tengo una sorpresa para ti.... Pero me tienes que dar unos minutos para prepararla.»

Actividad B. ¿Qué pasó?

All of the following events happened in **Episodio 16**, but in what order did they occur? Put them in order, from 1 to 8.

a. _____ Héctor le da a Arturo la carta de Ángel.
b. _____ Raquel va al mercado para comprar legumbres y verduras.
c. _____ Arturo trata de tomar una foto con una cámara automática.
d. _____ Arturo lee la carta que Ángel le escribió a Héctor hace muchos años.
e. _____ Raquel encuentra una foto de una cara hecha de (*made of*) legumbres y verduras.
f. _____ Arturo le dice a Raquel que piensa viajar a Puerto Rico.
g. _____ Raquel le muestra (*shows*) dos caras de legumbres y verduras a Arturo.
h. _____ Arturo y Raquel van al puerto para buscar a Héctor.

Para pensar...

Arturo le dice a Raquel: «Tal vez (*Maybe*) yo podría ir a Puerto Rico y los dos continuar la búsqueda de Ángel.» ¿Por qué de repente (*suddenly*) quiere ir a Puerto Rico Arturo? ¿a causa de Ángel? ¿o a causa de Raquel?

Actividad C.   La carta de Ángel

Raquel and Arturo have finally found out some specific information about what happened to Ángel. Listen again as Arturo paraphrases the letter Ángel wrote to Héctor, then indicate whether the following statements about Ángel are **Cierto** (**C**) or **Falso** (**F**).

C   F   1. La carta de Ángel es de Ponce, Puerto Rico.
C   F   2. Ángel dice que ya no quiere ser marinero.
C   F   3. Ya no pinta.
C   F   4. Viajó a España.
C   F   5. Piensa volver pronto a la Argentina.

· ·

VOCABULARIO DEL TEMA

Las legumbres y las verduras

la aceituna	olive	**el apio**	celery
la cebolla	onion	**los guisantes**	peas
los chícharos (*Mex.*)	peas	**la calabaza**	squash
el chile	chili pepper	**el champiñón**	mushroom
los ejotes (*Mex.*)	string beans	**los frijoles**	beans
la lechuga	lettuce	**las judías verdes**	string beans
la papa (*Lat. Am.*)	potato	**el maíz**	corn
el tomate	tomato		
la zanahoria	carrot		

Cognados: el brécol/el brocolí, la coliflor, las espinacas, la patata (*Spain*)

Remember that the names for fruits and vegetables are the most variable among all vocabulary groups in the Spanish-speaking world. Some specifically Mexican and Latin American variations are noted in the preceding lists.

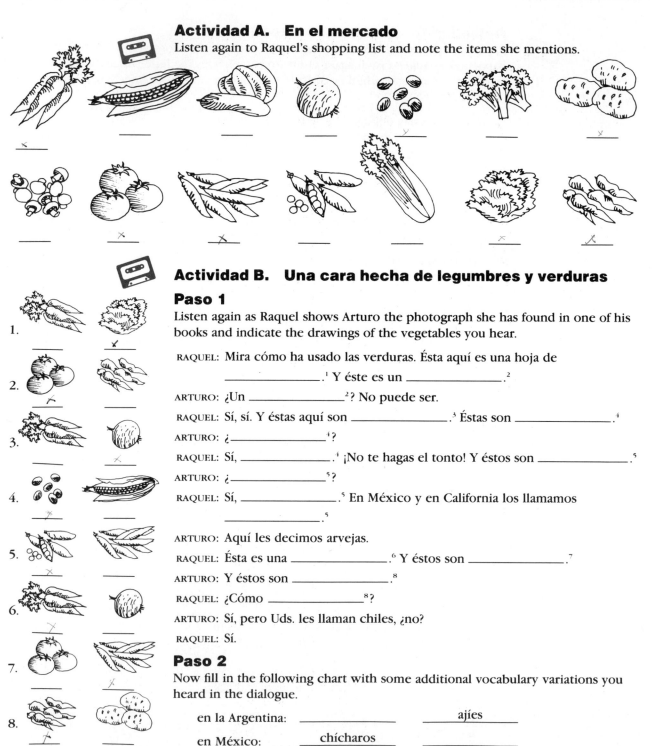

Actividad A.   En el mercado

Listen again to Raquel's shopping list and note the items she mentions.

Actividad B.   Una cara hecha de legumbres y verduras

Paso 1

Listen again as Raquel shows Arturo the photograph she has found in one of his books and indicate the drawings of the vegetables you hear.

RAQUEL: Mira cómo ha usado las verduras. Ésta aquí es una hoja de

_____.[1] Y éste es un _____.[2]

ARTURO: ¿Un _____[2]? No puede ser.

RAQUEL: Sí, sí. Y éstas aquí son _____.[3] Éstas son _____.[4]

ARTURO: ¿_____[4]?

RAQUEL: Sí, _____.[4] ¡No te hagas el tonto! Y éstos son _____.[5]

ARTURO: ¿_____[5]?

RAQUEL: Sí, _____.[5] En México y en California los llamamos

_____.[5]

ARTURO: Aquí les decimos arvejas.

RAQUEL: Ésta es una _____.[6] Y éstos son _____.[7]

ARTURO: Y éstos son _____.[8]

RAQUEL: ¿Cómo _____[8]?

ARTURO: Sí, pero Uds. les llaman chiles, ¿no?

RAQUEL: Sí.

Paso 2

Now fill in the following chart with some additional vocabulary variations you heard in the dialogue.

en la Argentina: _____ ajíes _____

en México: _____ chícharos _____

Actividad C.   ¿Y tú?

Indicate which vegetables and greens (and other things) you like to eat or combine with the following food items.

Palabras útiles: cocido/a (*cooked*), crudo/a (*raw*), frito/a (*fried*), al horno (*baked*), la mayonesa, la mostaza (*mustard*), la salsa (*dressing*), la salsa de tomate (*ketchup*), el puré de (papas, zanahorias...), la sopa de (legumbres, frijoles...)

1. Las legumbres que como con más frecuencia son _____ .

2. En cuanto a (*As for*) legumbres, ¡no me gusta(n) nada _____ !

3. Con el pollo, me gusta comer _____ . Prefiero el pollo

   _____ .

4. A una hamburguesa siempre le pongo _____ . También me gusta

   comer _____ con una hamburguesa.

5. A un sándwich de jamón le pongo _____ .

6. Mi sándwich favorito tiene _____ .

7. Una ensalada mixta (*tossed*) contiene _____ . Se toma con

   _____ .

8. Mi ensalada favorita contiene _____ .

• •

CONVERSACIONES: PERDONE UD.

Actividad.   ¡Perdón!

In this and in previous video episodes you have heard people apologize or request attention in a number of ways. In this activity you will review that information.

Paso 1

Listen to the following dialogues and complete them with the words you hear: **con permiso**, **disculpe**, or **perdone**.

1. —Esta maestra de primaria es la Sra. Díaz. Su clase de sexto grado le compró un cupón y...

   —_____ . Creo que se ha equivocado. Yo no soy la Sra. Díaz. Y tampoco soy maestra.

2. —Mostrame una foto tuya. De tu pasaporte, por ejemplo.

   —_____ , doctor, lo llaman por teléfono. Un Sr. Héctor...

3. —_____ . ¿Tiene Ud. la hora?

    —Sí, son las dos y cuarto.

    —Muchas gracias. Voy a buscar algo de comer. _____ .

Perdone (or **perdón**) and **disculpe** are used when asking for forgiveness or trying to get someone's attention. They can also be used to excuse onself when taking leave of others.

Paso 2

Now listen to two brief dialogues to identify the phrase used to ask permission to pass by or through a group of people.

    If you identified the phrase as **con permiso**, you were correct. Although one can also say **perdón** (or **perdone**) in this situation, the phrase **con permiso** (or just **permiso**) is generally used.

Paso 3

How would you express yourself in the following situations?

- You want to ask a stranger what time it is.
- You want to get a clerk's attention to buy half a kilo of tomatoes.
- You need to pass through a group of people to get to the back of a bus.

Un poco de gramática

More About Using Verbs to Talk About the Past

You have already encountered a number of verbs that have irregular preterite forms. Other verbs with irregular preterite forms include **querer**, **hacer**, **venir**, **poner**, **poder**, and **saber**. They use the same endings as the irregular verbs you learned in **Lección 15**. These examples are from Arturo's point of view.

Cuando Raquel **vino** a mi casa, **quise** tomar una foto de nosotros dos pero **no** lo **hice** bien.

When Raquel came to my house, I tried to take a photo of us two but I didn't do it well.

Raquel **puso** las verduras de forma que imitaban nuestras dos caras. ¡No lo **pude** creer!

Raquel arranged (placed) the vegetables so that they looked like our faces. I couldn't believe it!

¡Por fin **supimos** algo de Ángel!

We finally learned something about Ángel!

Can you identify the vowel common to the preterite stems of **querer**, **hacer**, and **venir**? And the vowel common to the preterite stems of **poner**, **saber**, and **poder**? You may also have noticed the slightly different meaning of some of these verbs in the preterite. You will learn more about these verbs in the Workbook.

Actividad.   ¿Quién fue?

Identify each of the following statements with the name of the person who might have made them: Raquel, Arturo, Ángel, or Héctor. ¡OJO! Some of the statements could possibly have been made by more than one person.

1. Vine a la Argentina en busca de una mujer.
2. No pude evitar (*avoid*) un mal presentimiento.
3. Hice dos caras con verduras.
4. Quise calmar a Arturo.
5. Vine a la Argentina hace muchos años.
6. Pude encontrar la carta de mi amigo.
7. Supe por fin la dirección de Ángel.
8. Puse fruta en una canasta.

Now listen to the cassette tape and check your answers.

MODELO: (*you see*) Vine a Buenos Aires en busca de Ángel y Rosario.
          (*you hear*) Raquel vino a Buenos Aires en busca de Ángel y Rosario.

Nota cultural: Otras ciudades argentinas

You have already learned a good deal about Buenos Aires, the political and economic capital of Argentina. In this video episode you learned a little bit about some other Argentine cities. Refresh your memory by listening to an excerpt from **Episodio 16** as you look at this map. Try to focus on the most important characteristics of each city. Then complete the following sentences.

1. Buenos Aires es importante porque es
   a. _____ una ciudad histórica   b. _____ un puerto
2. Córdoba es
   a. _____ una ciudad histórica   b. _____ un puerto importante
3. La ciudad de Mendoza es
   a. _____ un centro industrial   b. _____ un centro agrícola
4. Tucumán y Rosario son
   a. _____ ciudades importantes al norte de Buenos Aires
   b. _____ ríos que están en la parte central del país

¿**E**n qué ciudad vives? ¿Crees que esa ciudad es típica de las ciudades norteamericanas? Es probable que no. Los Estados Unidos son un país muy grande, con una variedad impresionante de paisajes,[1] centros industriales y costumbres[2] regionales. Además, muchas regiones tienen sus propios antecedentes[3] históricos: en el este y el sureste, la época colonial, la guerra de la independencia y la guerra civil; en Texas, la herencia mexicana, la República, la guerra con México; en California, también la herencia mexicana, la época de la búsqueda del oro[4]... Y así sucesivamente en muchos estados y regiones. Por eso no se puede decir que haya una ciudad ni una región típicas.

Lo mismo pasa en la Argentina, también un país muy grande con una gran variedad geográfica y demográfica. Ya sabes mucho de estos aspectos de la República Argentina y especialmente de Buenos Aires. Ahora vas a conocer otras ciudades argentinas. ¿Cuál te gustaría visitar?

- Córdoba y Rosario son las ciudades argentinas más importantes después de Buenos Aires. Córdoba cuenta con un millón de habitantes. Está situada en el centro del país. Fundada[5] en 1573, es una ciudad muy bella[6] con una rica herencia colonial. Su universidad, que se fundó en 1612, es la más antigua del país. En la actualidad, Córdoba es un centro industrial y comercial muy importante.

- La ciudad de Rosario está situada a orillas[7] del río Paraná. Su puerto tiene mucha actividad. Es también un centro industrial muy importante. Rosario es una ciudad moderna con muchos edificios altos, bellas plazas y hermosos parques.

- Al oeste de la Argentina, al pie[8] de la cordillera de los Andes, se encuentra la ciudad de Mendoza. Fue fundada en 1561 y durante un tiempo estuvo bajo la jurisdicción de Chile. Es famosa por su buena mesa[9] y sus buenos vinos. Hay muy pocos monumentos antiguos en Mendoza, porque casi toda la ciudad fue destruida[10] el siglo pasado por un terrible terremoto.[11] Es un centro agrícola importante, especialmente por el cultivo de la uva.

Viñas (*Vineyards*) cerca de Mendoza

[1] *landscapes* [2] *customs* [3] *beginnings, background* [4] *gold* [5] *Founded* [6] *bonita* [7] *a... on the banks* [8] *foot* [9] *food, cooking* [10] *destroyed* [11] *earthquake*

- Mar del Plata, en la costa atlántica, es uno de los puertos más importantes del país, y el primero entre los puertos de pesca.[12] El mar, los deportes[13] náuticos, las discotecas, los mariscos y su casino atraen cada año a millones de turistas. En verano (¡OJO! los meses de diciembre, enero y febrero en el hemisferio sur), sus playas están totalmente llenas de gente. Muchos argentinos celebran el Año Nuevo en las playas de Mar del Plata.

[12]*fishing*   [13]*sports*

Una de las playas en Mar del Plata

Actividad.   Ciudades argentinas y norteamericanas

Give one Argentine and one U.S. city that correspond to the following descriptions.

1. el centro político del país
2. un centro económico del país
3. un puerto muy importante del país
4. una ciudad histórica
5. un centro de producción del vino
6. una ciudad industrial
7. un puerto de pesca
8. una ciudad con muchas playas bonitas
9. una ciudad destruida por un terremoto
10. una ciudad con una universidad muy antigua

Have you completed the following sections of the lesson? Check them off here.

_____ **Preparación**   _____ **Conversaciones**
_____ **¿Tienes buena memoria?**   _____ **Un poco de gramática**
_____ **Vocabulario del tema**

    Now scan the words in the **Vocabulario** list to be sure that you understand the meaning of most of them. Then you will be ready to continue on with **Lección 16** in the Workbook.

VOCABULARIO

Los verbos

extrañar	to miss, long for
mostrar (**ue**)	to show
tratar de (+ *inf.*)	to try to (*do something*)

Las legumbres y las verduras
(Vegetables and Greens)

la aceituna	olive
el apio	celery
el brécol/brocolí	broccoli
la calabaza	squash
la coliflor	cauliflower
el champiñón	mushroom
los chícharos (*Mex.*)	peas
el chile	chile pepper
los ejotes (*Mex.*)	string beans
las espinacas	spinach
los frijoles	beans
los guisantes	peas
las judías verdes	string beans
la lechuga	lettuce
el maíz	corn
la papa (*Lat. Am.*)	potato
la patata (*Spain*)	potato
la zanahoria	carrot

Repaso: **la cebolla, el tomate**

Los lugares

el puerto	port

Las cosas

la foto*	photo

Otros sustantivos

la cara	face

Los adjetivos

pensativo/a	thoughtful, pensive

Perdone Ud.

con permiso	may I pass by?
disculpe	pardon me, excuse me
perdón, perdone	pardon me, excuse me

Las palabras adicionales

tal vez	perhaps

---

*Even though it ends in **-o**, the noun **foto** is feminine because it is derived from **la fotografía**.

17

INOLVIDABLE*

OBJETIVOS

The materials in **Lección 17** of the Textbook and the Workbook will help you better understand the video episode and take you beyond it, giving you additional information about places and characters in the series. The Textbook will also help you to develop skill in using the Spanish language. In this lesson, you will learn

- how to talk about written communication of all kinds
- more about how to talk about the past.

You will also learn about the cultural and political history of Argentina.

Be sure to work through all parts of the lesson. When you see a cassette symbol in the margin, listen to the tape for **Lección 17**. Answers or hints for many activities are given in Appendix 1. Be sure to check your answers for each activity before going on to the next one.

* Unforgettable

 **BEFORE VIEWING . . .**

PREPARACIÓN

Actividad A.

What happened in the last video episode of *Destinos*? Indicate whether the following brief narratives contain information that is **Cierto** (**C**) or **Falso** (**F**). Can you correct the false information?

C F 1. Raquel y Arturo lo pasaron muy bien cuando Arturo trató de sacar una foto de los dos y tuvo problemas con la cámara.

C F 2. Héctor llamó a Arturo por teléfono. Quería (*He wanted to*) pasar por (*by*) su casa para darle la carta de Ángel.

C F 3. Cuando leyó la carta de Ángel, Arturo supo que Ángel decidió quedarse (*to stay*) en Puerto Rico. Pensaba (*He intended*) volver a la Argentina para sus vacaciones.

C F 4. Raquel y Arturo sienten una atracción mutua. Les gusta mucho estar juntos.

Para pensar...

Arturo dice que quiere ir a Puerto Rico con Raquel, para continuar la búsqueda de Ángel. ¿Crees que realmente va a poder acompañarla en su viaje? ¿Crees que esto es una buena idea? ¿No está pasando todo muy rápido?

Actividad B.

In this video episode Arturo and Raquel will each make a "wish upon a star," **una estrella**. In this activity you will first hear their wishes individually, then have the chance to listen to the complete conversation.

Paso 1

Pedir un deseo means *to ask for a wish*. Based on everything you know about Raquel and her personality, what do you think she will wish for?

_____ Pide a las estrellas que pueda encontrar a Ángel en Puerto Rico.
_____ Pide a las estrellas que Arturo pueda acompañarla a Puerto Rico.

 Now listen to what Raquel actually says. Were you right?

Paso 2

Based on what you know about Arturo and on your observation of his behavior, what do you think he will wish for? Listen as he makes his wish.

　　　　Based on what you have heard Arturo say, which of the following do you think is the most appropriate title for this garden scene?

a. _____ La luna (*moon*)　　　　　c. _____ Declaración de amor
b. _____ El jardín por la noche

Paso 3

Now listen to the scene in its entirety.

Paso 4

Some of the verb forms used in this conversation between Raquel and Arturo are probably unfamiliar to you. You should be able to follow the conversation, however, by focusing on the verb stems. Can you give the infinitive for the following verb forms?

1. podamos　　2. esté　　3. pueda　　4. sea

Para pensar...

¿Qué van a hacer Arturo y Raquel después de esta conversación? ¿darse la mano (*shake hands*)? ¿abrazarse? ¿besarse (*kiss*)?

AFTER VIEWING . . .

· ·

¿TIENES BUENA MEMORIA?

Actividad A.　¿Quién lo dijo?

Paso 1

Arturo and Raquel talk about a lot of things in this video episode. Indicate which of the two, Arturo (**A**) or Raquel (**R**), made each of the following statements.

A　R　1. «Yo también les pido lo mismo. Que podamos encontrar a mi hermano y que él pueda conocer a su padre, don Fernando.»

A　R　2. «Por favor, déjame terminar. Lo que quiero decir es que... no es fácil decir estas cosas. Todo ha sido tan... tan rápido... Necesito tiempo para pensar.»

A　R　3. «Sabés, los argentinos somos más que la carne y el tango.»

A　R　4. «Cuando volvamos con Ángel de Puerto Rico, los tres podremos venir a ver un espectáculo.»

A　R　5. «¿Es posible que vuelvas entonces?»

Paso 2

Now indicate which of the preceding phrases expresses Raquel's answer to Arturo's declaration of his feelings. Is it an acceptance, a rejection, or something in between?

Actividad B.

In the last several video episodes you have learned information about Arturo and his half-brother Ángel. In this episode you learned more about Raquel. Listen again to Raquel's answers to Arturo's dinner table questions, then complete this summary with these words and phrases.

se fue a vivir	mucha gente interesante
en México	un estudiante joven
por un año entero	pasó los veranos
norteamericana	en la Universidad de California
don Pedro, hermano	Los Ángeles
de don Fernando	muy aburrida
muy contenta	

Raquel nació[a] en Los Ángeles, pero se siente tanto[b] mexicana como _nort_____.[1]

Ella siempre _P_____[2] en México con la familia mexicana de sus padres. Una vez fue a México _por un_____.[3] Le gustó mucho esa experiencia.

Raquel estudió _en la UdC_____.[4] Allí conoció a _un estudiante jov,[5] quien llegó a ser su novio.[c] Después de graduarse, él _se fue a vivir_[6] a Nueva York y ella se quedó en _Los Angeles_____.[7] Ahora ella está _m·_____[8] con su trabajo, porque viaja mucho y conoce a _mucha_____.[9]

[a] *was born* [b] *as much* [c] llegó... *became her boyfriend*

Now listen to the correct answers on the cassette tape.

Actividad C. «¡Somos más que la carne y el tango!»

In **Episodio 17** you heard a great deal about the history and culture of Buenos Aires. Summarize some of that information by matching the numbered names below with the descriptions below them.

1. _c_ el tango
2. _g_ el Teatro Colón
3. _b_ la Plaza de Mayo
4. _f_ Domingo Faustino Sarmiento
5. _e_ Jorge Luis Borges
6. _a_ *Ficciones* y *El Aleph*

a. son colecciones de cuentos de Borges
b. es famosa por las madres que protestan allí cada semana
c. era (*was*) la música de la gente (*people*) de Buenos Aires

    d.   son cuadros del Museo Nacional

    e.   un autor argentino que ganó (*earned*) fama mundial por sus obras literarias

    f.   un dictador militar de la Argentina

    g.   es famoso por sus espectáculos: conciertos, teatro, ballet...

    h.   era la música de la clase alta

    i.   una gran figura política y literaria de la Argentina

---

Nota cultural: Premios Nobel

Varios argentinos han ganado (*have won*) un premio Nobel. ¿Reconoces el nombre de alguno de ellos?

César Milstein, ganador del premio Nobel de Medicina

Carlos Saavedra Lamas, premio Nobel de la Paz en 1936;
Bernardo Houssay, premio Nobel de Medicina en 1947;
Luis Federico Lenoir, premio Nobel de Química en 1970;
Adolfo Pérez Esquivel, premio Nobel de la Paz en 1980;
César Milstein, premio Nobel de Medicina en 1984

¿Y el prestigioso premio Nobel de Literatura? No lo ha ganado todavía ningún argentino, aunque se sugirió con frecuencia el nombre de Jorge Luis Borges. Éstos son los escritores de lengua española que hasta la fecha (*until now*) han ganado este premio. ¿Los reconoces?

José Echegaray en 1904 (España); Jacinto Benavente en 1922 (España); Gabriela Mistral en 1945 (Chile); Juan Ramón Jiménez en 1956 (España); Miguel Ángel Asturias en 1967 (Guatemala); Pablo Neruda en 1971 (Chile); Vicente Aleixandre en 1977 (España); Gabriel García Márquez en 1982 (Colombia); Camilo José Cela en 1989 (España); Octavio Paz en 1990 (México)

VOCABULARIO DEL TEMA

El arte de escribir

el artículo	article
la comedia	play; comedy
el cuento	short story
el ensayo	essay
la novela	novel
la obra	work
la poesía	poetry
el poema	poem

LOS CINCO LIBROS MAS LEIDOS

FICCION	NO FICCION
1° "Noticias de la tarde" Arthur Hailey - Emecé - ₳72.000	1° "Las trampas de la fe" Octavio Paz - FCE - ₳96.000
2° "La inmortalidad" Milan Kundera - Tusquets - ₳96.000	2° "Los intelectuales" Paul Johnson - Vergara - ₳82.700
3° "El huevo de Fabergé" Robert Upton - Sudamericana - ₳57.850	3° "Historia de la vida privada" Duby/Ariés - Taurus - ₳158.000
4° "La ciudad de la alegría" Dominique Lapierre - Planeta - ₳87.200	4° "Más grandes que el amor" Dominique Lapierre - Planeta - ₳89.000
5° "Fénix Rojo" Larry Bond - Emecé - ₳88.000	5° "Soy Roca" Félix Luna - Sudamericana - ₳98.000

Las personas

el autor, la autora	author	**el/la novelista**	novelist
el escritor, la escritora	writer	**el/la periodista**	journalist

Los medios de comunicación

la computadora (*Lat. Am.*)	computer	**el periódico**	newspaper
la máquina de escribir	typewriter	**la revista**	magazine
el ordenador (*Spain*)	computer		

Actividad A.   ¿Quién era Borges?

The speaker on the cassette tape will tell you more about Jorge Luis Borges, the great Argentine writer. Write the number of each sentence next to the appropriate drawing.

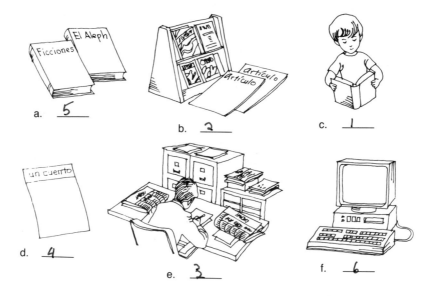

a. __5__

b. __2__

c. __1__

d. __4__

e. __3__

f. __6__

Actividad B.   Más sobre Borges

Paso 1

Refresh your memory about Borges by listening again to what you learned about him in **Episodio 17**.

Paso 2

Now complete the following description of Borges based on what you just heard and on the information you learned about him in **Actividad A**. You will also need to make some logical guesses.

Borges comenzó su carrera como _el periodista_ .[1] Trabajó para la _revista_ [2] *Nosotros* y también para el _periódico_ [3] *La Prensa*. Más tarde fue director de la Biblioteca Nacional y profesor de inglés en la Universidad de Buenos Aires.

Borges escribió poesías, pero sus obras más famosas son sus _novelas_ [4] y sus _ensayos_ .[5] En 1957 recibió un premio nacional por su libro *El Aleph*, una colección de _cuento_ .[6]

Este argentino fue un _autor_ [7] muy original. Sus temas favoritos eran la _realidad_ [8] y la fantasía. También estaba obsesionado por el tema del tiempo, un tiempo circular en que todo se repite.

Actividad C.   ¿Y tú?

Indicate the things you like to read (**leer**) and write. Scan the list of **Palabras útiles** before you begin.

Palabras útiles: la novela (de amor, de aventuras, de ciencia-ficción, de horror, histórica, policíaca), el trabajo para las clases, escribir a mano (*by hand*)

1. Me gusta leer _____ (tipo de libros).

2. Me gustan en particular las obras de _____ (escritor[a]). El/La _____ (obra) de él/ella que más me gusta es _____.

3. En cuanto a (*As for*) periódicos y revistas, leo _____. Mi revista favorita es _____. El periódico que prefiero es _____.

4. Escribo _____. Me gustaría escribir _____.

5. Para mis clases, tengo que escribir _____.

6. Cuando escribo trabajos para mis clases, prefiero usar/siempre _____.

CONVERSACIONES: MÁS SALUDOS Y DESPEDIDAS

Actividad.   Buenos días

In the video episodes that take place in Argentina you may have noticed some differences in the way people greet each other. You will learn more about those differences in this activity.

Paso 1

You will hear three brief conversations on the cassette tape. As you listen, complete them by indicating the words you hear.

1. CIRILO: ＿＿＿＿b＿＿＿＿, moza. Para mí es un gusto conocerla. ¿Así que Ud. anda buscando a la señora Rosario?
   RAQUEL: Sí. ¿Ud. la conoce?

   a. Hola   b. Buenas   c. Buenas tardes

2. ARTURO: Buenos días.

   DEPENDIENTE: ＿＿＿＿c＿＿＿＿.
   ARTURO: Estoy buscando a mi hermano, con el cual perdí contacto hace muchos años.

   a. Buenas   b. Buenas noches   c. Buen día

3. ARTURO: Te paso a buscar en quince minutos.
   RAQUEL: No, Arturo. Voy a tomar un taxi. Tengo... algunas cosas que hacer todavía.

   ARTURO: Está bien. ＿＿＿b＿＿＿.
   RAQUEL: Hasta luego.

   a. Adiós   b. Chau   c. Hasta luego

The greetings **Buen día**, **Buenos**, and **Buenas** are widely used in Argentina, along with the more standard **Buenos días** and **Buenas tardes/noches**. **Chau** is derived from the Italian word *ciao*. It has become popular with Spanish-speaking people throughout the world.

Paso 2

Now you will hear three short exchanges between friends. Decide whether they take place in Argentina or not.

1. <u>Sí</u>   No   2. <u>Sí</u>   No   3. Sí   <u>No</u>

Un poco de gramática

More About Using Verbs to Talk About the Past

The preterite forms of **-ir** stem-changing verbs have a stem change in the third-person singular and plural. As you read the following examples, note that the **-e** of the stem changes to **-i** and the **-o** to **-u**.

> Raquel y Arturo **prefirieron** cenar en casa. Arturo le **pidió** a Raquel que le contara algo de su pasado.
>
> *Raquel and Arturo preferred to have dinner at home. Arturo asked Raquel to tell him a bit about her past.*
>
> ¿**Murió** Ángel Castillo en Puerto Rico? Arturo tiene un mal presentimiento...
>
> *Did Ángel die in Puerto Rico? Arturo has a bad premonition . . .*
>
> You will learn more about using these verbs in the Workbook.

Actividad. ¿Quién lo hizo?

Identify the character described in each sentence.

a. Arturo Iglesias   b. don Fernando   c. Raquel Rodríguez   d. Rosario

1. _b_ Siguió la investigación de Raquel de España a la Argentina.
2. _d_ Murió hace unos años, en la Argentina.
3. _c_ Le pidió a Arturo que la llevara (*that he take her*) a la tumba de Rosario.
4. _a_ Se sintió culpable por no buscar a su medio hermano.
5. _c_ Se levantó y se vistió temprano para estar con Arturo.
6. _a_ Prefirió no andar en mateo, pero lo hizo.
7. _a_ Se despidió de Raquel en la entrada de su hotel y la besó.
8. _d_ Antes de salir para la Argentina, se durmió y soñó con (*dreamed about*) Rosario.

Nota cultural: Las madres de la Plaza de Mayo

In **Episodio 17** you learned about part of Argentina's history. Listen again as the narrator tells you about one of the results of that era. Then read the following narration to find out more details.

Desgraciadamente la violencia se conoce en todas partes del mundo. Los derechos[1] humanos son violados durante guerras civiles, guerras de independencia y revoluciones, bajo[2] dictaduras y otros regímenes represivos o simplemente cuando hay enfrentamientos[3] entre grupos étnicos o entre grupos con ideas diferentes sobre cualquier tema.

La Argentina vivió en los años 70 uno de los períodos más tristes de su historia. Gobernaba[4] entonces la viuda[5] del general Perón, María Estela, su segunda esposa. La situación política y

[1]*rights* [2]*under* [3]confrontaciones [4]*Was in power* [5]*widow*

social del país se iba deteriorando.[6] Finalmente en 1976 un golpe militar[7] terminó con el gobierno de María Estela de Perón.

Como sucede en numerosos regímenes autoritarios, la Argentina sufrió muchos abusos durante los años de esta dictadura militar. El más grave,[8] sin duda, fue la «desaparición»[9] de miles de personas sospechadas de actividades en contra del gobierno. Se les llama[10] «desaparecidos» porque no fueron arrestados ni tampoco hubo ninguna orden judicial[11] contra ellos. Simplemente desaparecieron. No se comunicaba oficialmente su paradero[12] ni tampoco se sabía si estaban vivos o muertos. Aunque la dictadura terminó hace muchos años, la gran mayoría de los «desaparecidos» siguen sin aparecer. Es como si, *oficialmente,* nunca hubieran existido.[13]

El Movimiento de las Madres de la Plaza de Mayo empezó para protestar en contra de esas desapariciones. Todos los jueves del año y en silencio, un grupo de madres y personas solidarias[14] marchan frente a la Casa Rosada.[15] Llevan las fotos de sus desaparecidos.

Para muchas personas, esta actitud ya no tiene sentido.[16] El régimen político ha cambiado[17] y piensan que el país debe aceptar la tragedia y olvidar el pasado. Pero, para las madres, «no hay olvido ni perdón». Además de las madres, muchos argentinos también denunciaron la violación de los derechos humanos. Ése es el caso de Adolfo Pérez de Esquivel, que en 1980 recibió el premio Nobel de la Paz. En esta fecha todavía gobernaba en la Argentina la dictadura militar.

Dice Arturo: «Es un episodio horrible en nuestra historia. Y no debemos olvidarnos de que estas cosas ocurren.» ¿Qué crees tú?

[6]se... *was deteriorating*   [7]golpe... *coup d'etat, military takeover*   [8]El... *The most serious (abuse)*   [9]*disappearance*   [10]Se... *They are called*   [11]ni... *nor was there any legal procedure*   [12]*whereabouts*   [13]Es... *It's as if they had never existed*   [14]*sympathetic (to the cause)*   [15]la... *the "Pink House," the Argentine equivalent of the White House*   [16]ya... *no longer makes any sense*   [17]ha... *has changed*

Have you completed the following sections of the lesson? Check them off here.

_____ **Preparación**   _____ **Conversaciones**
_____ **¿Tienes buena memoria?**   _____ **Un poco de gramática**
_____ **Vocabulario del tema**

Now scan the words in the **Vocabulario** list to be sure that you understand the meaning of most of them. Then you will be ready to continue on with **Lección 17** in the Workbook.

VOCABULARIO

Los verbos

besar	to kiss
leer	to read
quedarse	to stay, remain

El arte de escribir (The Art of Writing)

el artículo	article
la comedia	play; comedy
el cuento	short story
el ensayo	essay
la novela	novel
la obra	work
el poema	poem
la poesía	poetry

Las personas

el autor/la autora	author
el escritor/la escritora	writer
el/la novelista	novelist
el/la periodista	journalist

Los medios de comunicación
(Means of Communication)

la computadora (*Lat. Am.*)	computer
la máquina de escribir	typewriter
el ordenador (*Spain*)	computer
el periódico	newspaper
la revista	magazine

Más personas

la gente*	people

Los adjetivos

inolvidable	unforgettable

Los conceptos

el amor	love
el trabajo	work, job; paper, assignment (*for a class*)

Más saludos y despedidas

buen día (*Arg.*)	good day (*greeting*)
buenos, **buenas** (*Arg.*)	good day, good afternoon/evening
chau	good-bye

---

*Note that, even though its English equivalent is plural, this Spanish word is singular and takes a singular verb form: **La gente cree...**

18
ESTIMADA SRA. SUÁREZ*

OBJETIVOS

Part of this video episode is a review. Be sure to work through all parts of the lesson. When you see a cassette symbol in the margin, listen to the tape for **Lección 18**. Answers or hints for many activities are given in Appendix 1. Be sure to check your answers for each activity before going on to the next one.

Dear Mrs. Suárez

BEFORE VIEWING . . .

PREPARACIÓN

Actividad A.

Indicate whether the following events took place (**Sí ocurrió**) or not (**No, no ocurrió**) in the previous video episode of *Destinos*.

¿Qué pasó en el episodio previo?

Sí	No	1.	Raquel y Arturo bailaron.
Sí	No	2.	Arturo le hizo a Raquel una declaración de amor.
Sí	No	3.	Decidieron salir a cenar.
Sí	No	4.	Raquel le dijo a Arturo que él era muy importante para ella.
Sí	No	5.	Arturo habló más de su ex esposa.
Sí	No	6.	Raquel le dijo a Arturo que lo amaba (*loved*).

Al día siguiente, ¿qué hicieron Raquel y Arturo durante el día?

Sí	No	7.	Visitaron la casa de Jorge Luis Borges.
Sí	No	8.	Fueron a la ópera.
Sí	No	9.	Fueron a un parque.
Sí	No	10.	Comieron en un restaurante elegante.

Actividad B.

Look at the title of this lesson and at the photograph with which it begins. What do you think Raquel will do in this video episode?

a. _____ Llama por teléfono a la Sra. Suárez.

b. _____ Le escribe una carta a la Sra. Suárez.

c. _____ Le manda un telegrama a la Sra. Suárez.

If you selected *b*, you were correct. What might Raquel tell Sra. Suárez in her letter? Indicate all items that you think may be correct.

a. _____ las tristes noticias de Rosario

b. _____ de cómo pudo por fin encontrar a un hijo de Rosario

c. _____ de su relación con Arturo

d. _____ más noticias de don Fernando

e. _____ unos detalles de la búsqueda de Ángel en Buenos Aires

f. _____ la dirección de Ángel en Puerto Rico

g. _____ de sus compras en Buenos Aires

h. _____ de lo que (*what*) comió

AFTER VIEWING . . .

¿TIENES BUENA MEMORIA?

Actividad A.   Raquel se va

The following sentences describe what took place during Raquel's last hours in Argentina, but the words are out of order. Read all of the words in each group, then put them in the correct order to form complete sentences.

1. llevó / Raquel / a / aeropuerto / Arturo / al
2. se / los dos / entrada / en / despidieron / la
3. con / besaron / se / ternura (*tenderness*)
4. despedida / fue / triste / la
5. un / tuvo / poco / Raquel / esperar / que
6. carta / le / a / Sra. Suárez / escribió / una / la

Actividad B.   ¡Un desafío! ¿Tienes muy buena memoria?

Can you recall these details from this video episode?

1. ¿Le dio Arturo algo a Raquel en el aeropuerto?
2. ¿Le dijo Arturo adiós a Raquel?
3. ¿Cuándo piensa Arturo reunirse con Raquel en Puerto Rico?
4. ¿En qué piensa Raquel al despegar el avión (*while the plane is taking off*)?

REPASO DE LOS EPISODIOS 12–17

Actividad A.   La búsqueda de Raquel

The following summary of the first part of Raquel's search in Buenos Aires is adapted from her letter to Sra. Suárez. Complete it with phrases from the following list. ¡OJO! Not all of the phrases will be used.

se mudó a Puerto Rico
murió hace algunos años
era el hijo de Rosario y don
    Fernando
no me sirvió para nada
había muerto (*had died*)

perdió contacto con su hermano
se fue de la casa
se quedó en casa
me sirvió bastante (*a lot*)
ya no vivía allí

Estimada Sra. Suárez:

Ojalá que[a] cuando reciba esta carta se encuentre bien de salud.[b] Mi viaje a Buenos Aires ha resultado fructífero[c] gracias a su bondad en ayudarme, pues la dirección de la estancia _____.[1] Sin embargo,[d] me da mucha pena[e] tener que decirle que su buena amiga Rosario _____.[2]

En la estancia averigüé[f] que la familia Iglesias _____.[3] Un hombre me dio la dirección del hijo de Rosario. Fui a buscarlo, creyendo[g] que _____.[4] Imagínese Ud. la sorpresa que tuve al encontrarme con otro hijo de Rosario.

Fue durante esa conversación que el hijo, Arturo Iglesias que así se llama, me contó que Rosario _____.[5] En el cementerio conseguí pruebas[h] de la muerte de Rosario y allí Arturo me contó que Ángel Castillo _____[6] por una pelea[i] que tuvo con su padrastro. A causa de ese doloroso episodio, Arturo _____.[7] Al día siguiente, comenzamos juntos la búsqueda del paradero[j] de Ángel.

[a]Ojalá... *I hope that* [b]se... *you are well* [c]ha... *has had good results* [d]Sin... *Nevertheless* [e]me... *I'm very sorry*
[f]*I found out* [g]*believing* [h]*proof* [i]*fight* [j]*whereabouts*

Actividad B. La búsqueda de Arturo y Raquel
The following sentences from Raquel's letter describe her search with Arturo, but they are out of order. Put them in order, from 1 to 7.

a. _____ Finalmente dimos con (*we met up with*) un hombre [Héctor].
b. _____ En verdad, le estoy escribiendo (*writing*) esta carta desde el aeropuerto.
c. _____ Sabiendo (*Knowing*) que Ángel se quedó a vivir en Puerto Rico y con la dirección de su casa en San Juan, hice los preparativos para salir de Buenos Aires.
d. _____ Preguntamos por Ángel Castillo en varios lugares del barrio italiano, La Boca.
e. _____ Después de varios días, Héctor llamó a Arturo para decirle que había encontrado (*he had found*) la carta.
f. _____ Pero nadie se acordaba de Ángel.
g. _____ Ud. no tiene idea de lo difícil que nos fue (*how hard it was for us*) conseguir la información que buscábamos.

Now check your answers by listening to the cassette tape.

Actividad C.   Las actividades de Raquel

As you know, Raquel's visit to Buenos Aires involved more than just the search for Ángel. Here are the last paragraphs of Raquel's letter to Sra. Suárez, but some of the information has been changed. Read through the letter and indicate the incorrect information.

Tendría que decirle que mi estancia en Buenos Aires no ha sido nada más que[1] trabajo. En primer lugar, he tenido la oportunidad de conocer un poco el país. Pude hacer unas compras, pues como Ud. sabrá[2] en la Argentina hay muchos artículos de oro muy bonitos. Y, claro, también comí y comí y comí y comí… pero no me gustó.

Si me permite la confianza, quisiera decirle que no seguí sus consejos. El hermano de Arturo, Ángel, se ha hecho buen amigo mío.[3] Para decir la verdad, siento un amor muy especial por él. Resulta que Arturo me va a visitar en San Juan en un mes. Así concluye mi estancia en Buenos Aires.

Siento mucho la pelea que Ud. tuvo con su buena amiga tanto por Ud. como por[4] don Fernando. Ojalá[5] mi viaje a Puerto Rico tenga los resultados deseados, que encuentre a Rosario Castillo y que por fin se reúna con su madre.

Reciban Ud. y su familia un saludo cordial de
Raquel Rodríguez

[1]nada… solamente   [2]Ud. … *you probably know*   [3]se… *has become a good friend of mine*
[4]tanto… *as much for your sake as for*   [5]*I hope*

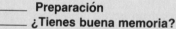 Now check your answers by listening to the cassette tape.

Have you completed the following sections of the lesson? Check them off here.

_____ **Preparación**   _____ **Repaso de los Episodios 12–17**
_____ **¿Tienes buena memoria?**

Now scan the words in the **Vocabulario** list to be sure that you understand the meaning of most of them. Then you will be ready to continue on with **Lección 18** in the Workbook.

VOCABULARIO

Los verbos
reunirse (con)   to be reunited (with), get back together (with)

Los adjetivos
estimado/a   dear (*often used in letters*)
triste   sad

Las palabras adicionales
sin embargo   nevertheless

Un viaje a Puerto Rico

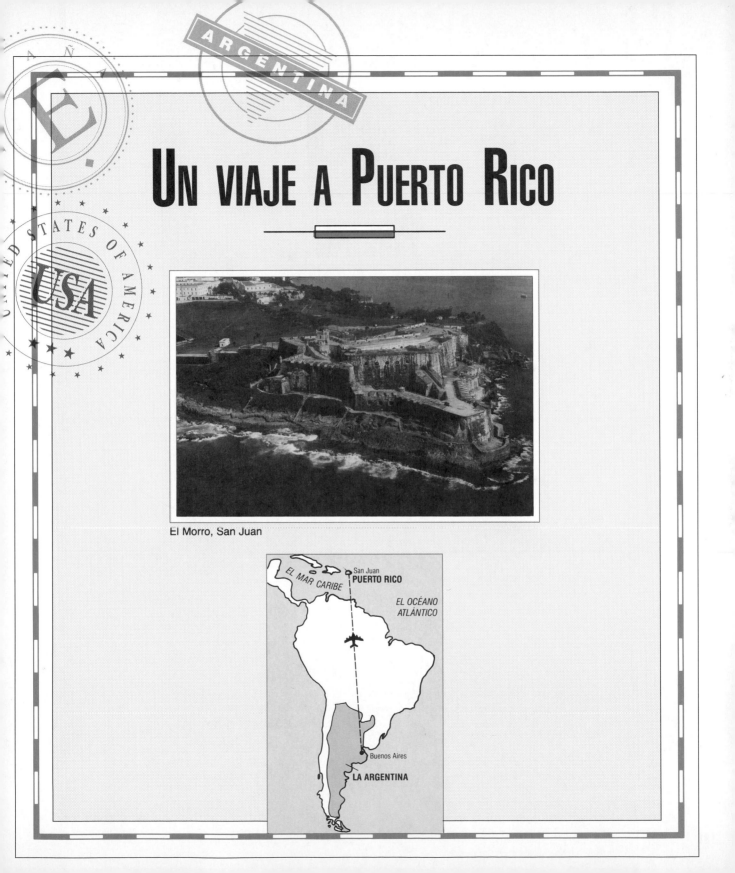

El Morro, San Juan

L E C C I Ó N

19

POR FIN...*

OBJETIVOS

The materials in **Lección 19** of the Textbook and the Workbook will help you better understand the video episode and take you beyond it, giving you additional information about places and characters in the series. The Textbook will also help you to develop skill in using the Spanish language. In this lesson, you will learn

- to understand directions in Spanish
- to talk about the past in another way.

You will also learn about the city of San Juan, Puerto Rico.

Be sure to work through all parts of the lesson. When you see a cassette symbol in the margin, listen to the tape for **Lección 19**. Answers or hints for many activities are given in Appendix 1. Be sure to check your answers for each activity before going on to the next one.

*Finally . . .

BEFORE VIEWING . . .

PREPARACIÓN

Actividad A.

Here are some photographs of scenes from **Episodio 19** of *Destinos*. What do they suggest to you?

1. Esta mujer es la vecina (*neighbor*) de Ángel Castillo. ¿Qué le está preguntando* Raquel? ¿Qué información le está dando a Raquel?

2. Raquel se encuentra en el Viejo Cementerio de San Juan. ¿Por qué está allí? ¿Qué o a quién anda buscando?

3. La mujer que está con Raquel se llama Ángela Castillo Soto. ¿Quién es? ¿Será (*Could she be*) pariente (*relative*) de Ángel Castillo?

2.

Actividad B.

In this video episode Raquel has a conversation with the woman in the first photograph in **Actividad A**.

Paso 1

In the conversation the woman will say the following: "Los dos están enterrados en el antiguo cementerio de San Juan." Read the line over a few times, so that you recognize it when you hear it.

Paso 2

Now listen to the dialogue on the cassette tape. You should be able to obtain a lot of information from it.

Paso 3

Now answer the following questions about the dialogue you just heard.

1. **Enterrados** means *buried*. Now that you know that, what two people do you think the woman is talking about? *Hint*: What two people would be of interest to Raquel at this moment?

2. The neighbor also says: "Nunca se repuso de la muerte de su esposa." The verb form **se repuso** comes from the infinitive **reponerse**, meaning *to get*

---

* As you can probably guess, the verb form **preguntando** is derived from **preguntar**. You have been seeing forms ending in **-ndo** since the beginning of the *Destinos* series. The **-ndo** form corresponds to English *-ing*: **preguntando** = *asking*. This form is used with forms of **estar** to express an action that is happening right now. You will learn more about these forms in upcoming lessons of *Destinos*.

over or *recover from* (*an illness*). Who is the woman describing in this sentence, a man or a woman? Do you think she is talking about Ángel or about someone who knew him well?

AFTER VIEWING . . .

. . . .

¿TIENES BUENA MEMORIA?

Actividad A.   Nuevos personajes

In this video episode of *Destinos* you have met some new characters. How much do you remember about them? Complete the following statements about the people shown in the photographs.

1.

4.

1.   Esta señora es la... esposa / vecina / viuda... de Ángel Castillo. [widow]
2.   La señora le dice a Raquel que Ángel... se mudó a otro país / volvió a España / murió hace poco.
3.   Le dice también que la esposa de Ángel era... anciana / escritora / maestra de primaria. [very old]
4.   Raquel descubre que esta señorita es la... hija / novia / viuda... de Ángel.
5.   Ángela llama a... unos parientes / unos amigos / sus hermanos... para que vengan (*they come over*) a conocer a Raquel.
6.   Hay otra sorpresa para Raquel al final del episodio. Ángela le dice que... ya sabe de don Fernando / tiene un hermano / ya conoce a Arturo.

Actividad B.   La primera tarde en San Juan

Raquel's investigation gets off to a quick start in Puerto Rico. She finds a member of Ángel's family quickly, and it appears that she will soon meet more family members. Complete this summary of part of her afternoon with Ángela with the following phrases. ¡OJO! Not all of the phrases will be used.

encontrar una foto de su padre	está en Nueva York
tomar una foto	van al cementerio
llamar a sus tíos	hablan más
mudarse	debe ser muy triste para Ángela
visitar un lugar de interés histórico	regresan al apartamento
mostrarle otros lugares interesantes	va a México

En el apartamento, Ángela le dice a Raquel que piensa _mudarse_.¹ «No quiero vivir sola en este apartamento», dice. Raquel queda sorprendida, porque el apartamento es muy bonito. Pero también comprende que el recuerdo de sus padres

debe ser muy.²

Ángela trata de _llamar a sus_,[3] pero no tiene suerte.[a] Mientras sigue intentando,[b] Raquel sale a _visita_,[4] la Casa Blanca. Luego Ángela se reúne con ella para visitar los jardines de la Casa Blanca y para _mostrarle_.[5] Van al Parque de las Palomas y a la Capilla de Cristo y finalmente _regr_.[6]

Allí es donde Raquel descubre que Ángela tiene novio. Pero no lo va a conocer pronto porque _está_.[7] Raquel también ve la foto de un joven atractivo. ¡Otro hijo de Ángel!

[a]*any luck* [b]sigue... *she keeps on trying*

Now check your answers by listening to the cassette tape.

Nota cultural: La inmediatez puertorriqueña

You may have noticed that Raquel and Ángela have already developed a warm, comfortable relationship. This is partly because they are both women, not so far apart in age, and partly because Raquel has given Ángela some startling but potentially exciting news about her family.

There is another factor at work as well. Most visitors to the island of Puerto Rico comment on how friendly and open the people are and how quickly comfortable relationships are established. One phrase that describes this phenomenon is **la inmediatez de la gente**, related to the adjective **inmediato** (*immediate*).

Raquel responds warmly to this characteristic of the islanders. But even here, as in other parts of the Spanish-speaking world that Raquel has visited previously, another person—Ángela—initiates the use of **tú** with her.

· ·

VOCABULARIO DEL TEMA

Las instrucciones

la bocacalle	intersection	**la esquina**	corner	**doblar**	to turn
el bloque (*P.R.*)	city block	**la ruta**	route, way	a la derecha	to the right
				a la izquierda	to the left
la calle	street	**bajar**	to go down	**seguir (i, i)**	to go straight
la cuadra	city block	**cruzar**	to cross	derecho	
las escaleras	steps, *ladder* *escalador*			**virar** (*P.R.*)	to turn

baje...	go down . . .	hacia	toward
camine...	walk . . .	hasta	until
doble...	turn . . .	por	through;
siga...	continue . . . ,		along
	follow . . .		
tome...	take . . .		
vire...	turn . . .		

As with the names for fruits and vegetables, the words used for giving directions and naming parts of a city vary from area to area.

- Whereas in Puerto Rico you would walk **dos bloques**, in Spain you would walk **dos manzanas**, and in Mexico, **dos cuadras**.
- In Puerto Rico you can **virar a la izquierda**. In most other areas of the Spanish-speaking world, you would **doblar** (**a la izquierda**). **Doblar** is also used in Puerto Rico.
- In Spain you would **seguir recto**, but in most of the Western Hemisphere you would **seguir derecho**.

Una calle del Viejo San Juan

For now, concentrate on learning the vocabulary listed here for giving directions. Note in particular the verb forms **baje...** , **camine...** , and so on. They are command forms, used to give people directions. You will learn more about giving directions in the second half of *Destinos*. In this lesson you will practice recognizing the meaning of commands when you see and hear them.

Actividad A.   Las instrucciones del taxista

As happens frequently in urban life, a road is closed off—**bloqueado**—due to construction work, and Raquel must reach Ángel's house on foot. Listen as the cab driver tells her how to get there and indicate in the following dialogue the words you hear.

EL TAXISTA: Mire. ¿Ve la _iz_¹?

RAQUEL: Sí.

EL TAXISTA: Tome a la _iz_².

RAQUEL: A la _____.²

EL TAXISTA: En el próximo bloque, vire a la _der_.³

RAQUEL: A la _____.³

EL TAXISTA: Camine _der_⁴ hasta que encuentre unas escaleras a la _izqu_.⁵

RAQUEL: A la _____.⁵

EL TAXISTA: Baje las escaleras y cuando encuentre la calle Sol... ¿cuál es el número que busca?

RAQUEL: El cuatro de la calle Sol.

EL TAXISTA: Entonces, creo que está a mano[a] _leta_.[6] Cuando encuentre la calle
Sol, si se pierde, pregunte. Todo el mundo conoce esa calle.

[a]*a... on the . . . side*

Actividad B. Otra ruta

Paso 1

Listen as Ángel's neighbor gives Raquel directions to the cemetery. As you listen,
fill in the missing words.

LA VECINA: Los dos están enterrados en el antiguo cementerio de San Juan.

RAQUEL: ¿El cementerio?

LA VECINA: Sí.

RAQUEL: ¿Podría decirme cómo llegar allí?

LA VECINA: Por supuesto. _Siga_ ¹ por esta calle. Entonces

vira ² a la izquierda. Luego va a encontrar una

bocalle ³ y vire a la _derecha_ ⁴ y allí está el Morro.

Al lado está el cementerio.

RAQUEL: _A lado Siso_ ⁵ por esta calle. Luego a la _iz_ ⁶ en-

cuentro una bocacalle. _derecha_ ⁷ a la derecha. Allí está el

Morro y al lado el cementerio.

Paso 2

Now that you have all of the words to the preceding dialogue, do you understand the directions? Select the appropriate visual representation for each part
of the directions.

1. _Siga a_ por esta calle. a. b. c.

2. Entonces _b_ a la izquierda. a. b. c.

3. Luego va a encontrar una _b_ ... a. b. c.

4. ...y vire a la _c_ y allí está el Morro. a. b. c.

Actividad C. ¿Dónde está la Plaza de San Martín?

Listen as a speaker from Argentina gives you directions to the Plaza de San
Martín from the corner of La Valle and la Avenida 7 de Julio. If you were there,
could you find the Plaza based on his directions? Listen to the passage all the
way through. Then listen step by step and indicate the directions you hear.

1. (a) b   c   a. ↑   b. ⌐←   c. ⌐→

2. a (b) c   a. ↑   b. ⌐←   c. ⌐→

3. (a) b   c   a. ↑   b. ⌐←   c. ⌐→

• •

UN POCO DE GRAMÁTICA

Describing What Was Happening While . . .

To describe an action that was taking place while something else was going on in the past, add **-aba** to the stem of all **-ar** verbs and **-ía** to the stem of almost all **-er** and **-ir** verbs.

Mientras **vivía** en San Juan, Ángel **pintaba** mucho.	*Ángel painted a lot while he was living in San Juan.*

Third-person plural forms have their characteristic final **-n**.

Mientras Ángel y su esposa **vivían** en el Viejo San Juan, no **sabían** que don Fernando **guardaba** un secreto.	*While Ángel and his wife were living in Old San Juan, they didn't know that don Fernando was keeping a secret.*

The past tense that you are learning to use is called the imperfect. Unlike the preterite, the imperfect signals that an action or event was in progress at a given point in the past. You will learn more about the forms and uses of the imperfect in the Workbook.

Actividad.   ¿Qué pasaba mientras... ?

What was happening when the following events took place in **Episodio 19**? Listen to the questions on the cassette tape, then select the correct answer and repeat it. You will hear the choices and the correct answer on the tape.

MODELO: (*you hear*)   Mientras el taxista le explicaba a Raquel cómo llegar a la calle Sol, ¿qué hacía Raquel?
a. Caminaba derecho.   b. Lo escuchaba con atención.   c. Miraba hacia el horizonte.
(*you say*)   Lo escuchaba con atención.
(*you hear*)   La respuesta correcta es *b*. Lo escuchaba con atención.

1. Mientras el taxista le daba instrucciones a Raquel, ¿qué más hacía Raquel?
    a. _____ Miraba un plano turístico.
    b. _____ Repetía las instrucciones.
    c. _____ Escribía las instrucciones.

2. Mientras Raquel tomaba una foto de la tumba de Ángel Castillo, ¿qué hacía Ángela?
    a. _____ La miraba.
    b. _____ Estaba en casa.
    c. _____ Ponía flores en varias tumbas.

3. Mientras Ángela llamaba a sus tíos, ¿qué hacía Raquel?
    a. _____ Escribía en su cuaderno.
    b. _____ Visitaba la Casa Blanca.
    c. _____ Miraba cuadros de Ángel.

4. Mientras esperaban a los tíos de Ángela, ¿qué hacían Raquel y Ángela?
    a. _____ Comían en un restaurante.
    b. _____ Tomaban algo y conversaban.
    c. _____ Dormían la siesta.

Nota cultural: San Juan, Puerto Rico

In **Episodio 19** you learned a little bit about the island of Puerto Rico as well as the city of San Juan. Listen again to the narrator's description as you look at this map. Then read the following narration to find out more about this capital city.

Los puertorriqueños quieren a la Isla donde viven. Es más que patriotismo. Se puede hablar de un verdadero amor al país y a sus lugares. Este amor se expresa en la forma de hablar de muchos puertorriqueños: «mi Isla», «mi Puerto Rico», «mi Viejo San Juan». De hecho[1] a esta última expresión se debe el título de una canción[2] famosa.

Muchas personas conocen San Juan como un centro turístico por excelencia. Pero pocas saben que es también una de las ciudades más antiguas[3] de América. Fue fundada en 1512 por Ponce de León, el explorador que buscaba en la Florida la fuente de la juventud.[4] Ponce de León fue también el primer gobernador español de la Isla. Así que[5] San Juan es a la vez una ciudad moderna y una ciudad histórica.

[1]*De... In fact* [2]*song* [3]*viejas* [4]*fuente... Fountain of Youth* [5]*Así... So*

La ciudad histórica

Ya anduviste con Raquel por las calles de adoquines azulados[6] que caracterizan el Viejo San Juan. El barrio tiene muchos atractivos: restaurantes, bares, galerías de arte, museos, monumentos históricos... Lo que más llama la atención es el estilo colonial del barrio; es decir, el estilo que caracterizaba la arquitectura de la Isla cuando Puerto Rico era todavía una colonia española.

Gran parte de la historia del barrio tiene que ver[7] con la presencia española en la Isla.

La Catedral del Viejo San Juan

- Uno de los edificios históricos más importantes es la Casa Blanca. La arquitectura de esta casa es típica de la época colonial. Fue construida para Ponce de León, quien nunca vivió en ella.

- La Catedral de San Juan es uno de los pocos ejemplos de arquitectura europea medieval en América. Es un edificio crema y blanco, simple pero imponente. Allí fue ordenado el primer obispo[8] de la Iglesia Católica en el Nuevo Mundo.

Cerca de este barrio colonial están dos viejas fortificaciones: San Cristóbal y San Felipe del Morro (llamado el Morro). Estas fortalezas protegían a la ciudad contra los ataques de los enemigos del Imperio español.

La ciudad moderna

San Juan es una ciudad capital del siglo XX. Tiene edificios altos (sobre todo en el distrito financiero), hoteles ultramodernos de gran lujo,[9] restaurantes internacionales, galerías de arte y exclusivas *boutiques* de moda. Sus residentes se quejan del[10] tráfico. ¡Y no hay que olvidar sus estupendas playas[11]!

Por eso San Juan es un lugar ideal para las vacaciones o para ir de compras. Pero San Juan es mucho más. Es también un centro cultural.

- ¿Eres aficionado[12] a la música clásica? Todos los años se celebra en San Juan el internacionalmente famoso Festival de Música Casals. Fue fundado en 1973 por el violoncelista español Pablo Casals y su esposa Marta Istomín (exdirectora del John F. Kennedy Center for the Performing Arts).

- Para los amantes[13] de la naturaleza y la historia, San Juan tiene un parque central muy atractivo, un museo arqueológico y un jardín botánico con más de 200 especies de plantas tropicales y subtropicales.

- Si quieres estudiar, en la ciudad vecina de Río Piedras se encuentra la Universidad de Puerto Rico, con 25.000 estudiantes. Allí han enseñado[14] muchos escritores famosos del mundo de habla española.

Si visitas San Juan, debes ir a la playa, eso sí. Pero... ¡no te debes perder las otras facetas de esta capital caribeña!

[6]adoquines... *bluish cobblestones* [7]tiene... *has to do* [8]*bishop* [9]*luxury* [10]se... *complain about the* [11]*beaches* [12]*fan* [13]*lovers* [14]han... *have taught*

La Universidad de Puerto Rico en Río Piedras

Actividad.   San Juan y otras ciudades

What does San Juan have in common with other large cities? Answer based on your own experience and on the reading passage.

Piensa en

1. la población
2. las partes de la ciudad
3. los aspectos culturales
4. los elementos modernos e históricos

Have you completed the following sections of the lesson? Check them off here.*

_____ **Preparación**   _____ **Vocabulario del tema**
_____ **¿Tienes buena memoria?**   _____ **Un poco de gramática**

Now scan the words in the **Vocabulario** list to be sure that you understand the meaning of most of them. Then you will be ready to continue on with **Lección 19** in the Workbook.

. . . .

VOCABULARIO

Los verbos

bajar	to go down
cruzar	to cross
doblar	to turn, *to fold*
virar (*P.R.*)	to turn, *de toca a ti – your Turn*
baje...	go down . . .
camine...	walk . . .
doble...	turn . . .
siga...	continue . . . , follow . . .
tome...	take . . .
vire...	turn . . .

Repaso: **seguir (i, i)**

En la ciudad

la bocacalle	intersection
el bloque (*P.R.*)	city block
la cuadra	city block
las escaleras	steps
la esquina	corner
la ruta	route, way

siga

Repaso: **la calle**

Las personas

el/la pariente	relative, family member
el/la vecino/a	neighbor

Los lugares

el apartamento	apartment
la isla	island

Las preposiciones

hacia	toward
por	through; along

Repaso: **hasta**

Las palabras adicionales

a la derecha	to the right
a la izquierda	to the left
derecho	straight *– continue straight*
mientras	while

---

*From this point on in the Textbook there will not be a **Conversaciones** section in each lesson. However, as you have probably noticed in viewing **Lección 19**, the vocabulary and strategies you have studied in previous **Conversaciones** sections are repeated in subsequent lessons because they occur frequently in natural conversation.

20

RELACIONES ESTRECHAS*

OBJETIVOS

The materials in **Lección 20** of the Textbook and the Workbook will help you better understand the video episode and take you beyond it, giving you additional information about places and characters in the series. The Textbook will also help you to develop skill in using the Spanish language. In this lesson, you will learn

- more vocabulary for talking about family members
- Spanish expressions to use when speaking on the phone
- more ways to use the imperfect to talk about the past.

You will also learn about the history of Puerto Rico.

Be sure to work through all parts of the lesson. When you see a cassette symbol in the margin, listen to the tape for **Lección 20**. Answers or hints for many activities are given in Appendix 1. Be sure to check your answers for each activity before going on to the next one.

*A Close Relationship

BEFORE VIEWING . . .

PREPARACIÓN

Actividad A.

Paso 1

Refresh your memory about the events of the previous video episode by listening to the narrator's summary of it, which you will hear again when you watch **Episodio 20**.

Paso 2

Now complete the following statements about the previous video episode based on what you have just heard and on what you remember.

1. La hija de Ángel / <u>Una vecina /</u> Una amiga... le dio a Raquel la triste noticia de la muerte de Ángel y de su esposa.
2. Ángela es... <u>la hija</u> / la esposa / la sobrina (*niece*)... de Ángel.
3. Cuando Raquel le dijo a Ángela que tenía un abuelo en México, Ángela... estaba furiosa / <u>estaba sorprendida</u> (*surprised*) / no lo creía.
4. Al final del episodio, Ángela y Raquel esperaban... <u>a los tíos</u> / a los hermanos / al novio... de Ángela.
5. Mientras esperaban, Ángela le dijo a Raquel que... <u>tenía un hermano tam-bién</u> / no quería ir a México con ella / vendía su apartamento.

Para pensar...

¿Cómo va a reaccionar la familia de Ángela cuando todos sepan las noticias? ¿Van a creer la historia? ¿Va a poder Ángela ir a México con Raquel?

Actividad B.

Paso 1

In this video episode you will meet one of Ángela's aunts, **la tía Olga**. Ángela calls her **la gruñona de la familia** (*the family grouch*). Listen to a conversation from **Episodio 20** between Raquel, Olga, and Ángela. You may follow along in the written text if you like.

RAQUEL: ...Y como don Fernando está gravemente enfermo en el hospital, es importante que Ángela vaya a México pronto.

OLGA: Creo que eso va a ser imposible.

ÁNGELA: ¿Por qué?

OLGA: Ángela, no conocemos a esa gente. Puede ser peligroso.
ÁNGELA: Titi Olga, por favor…

Paso 2

Now answer the following question.

> Olga dice que un viaje a México «puede ser peligroso». ¿Qué significa
> **peligroso**?
>
> a. ___✓___ dangerous   b. _____ exciting   c. _____ inconvenient

---

Para pensar…

¿Crees que la reacción de la tía Olga es razonable? Escucha con atención
(*carefully*) las preguntas que Olga le hace a Raquel en este episodio. Nota
también la reacción de Ángela a las preguntas de Olga. ¿Crees que su reacción es razonable?

Actividad C.

Paso 1

In this video episode you will hear Ángela read from a storybook that her father
wrote for her when she was a child. Listen to the beginning of the story, following along in your textbook as needed.
You should also look carefully at this
illustration from the storybook.

El pequeño coquí era tímido…
y se puso rojo con los elogios
de la princesa.

El coquí y la princesa

A nuestra hija Ángela, nuestra princesa…

Érase una vez un coquí. Le gustaba pintar.
Su padre y su madre querían mandarlo a la
escuela. Pero el pequeño coquí no quería
estudiar. Sólo quería pintar.

Paso 2

the drawing

1. Según (*According to*) el dibujo, ¿qué es un coquí?
    a. ___✓___ un animal anfibio pequeño y verde
    b. _____ un animal grande y feroz
    c. _____ un animal grande pero dócil

2. El coquí representa a una persona de esta historia. ¿A quién representa?
    ¡OJO! ¿A quién le pasó lo mismo (*the same thing*)?
    a. _____ a Arturo   b. ___✓___ a Ángel   c. _____ a don Fernando

3. ¿Qué significan las primeras palabras de la historia, «Érase una vez... »?
   a. _____ It was a cold and rainy   b. _____ Call me . . .
      night . . .   c. _✓_ Once upon a time . . .

AFTER VIEWING . . .

. . . .

¿TIENES BUENA MEMORIA?

Actividad A.   ¿Quiénes son?

Complete the following activity about some of the characters you met in this video episode.

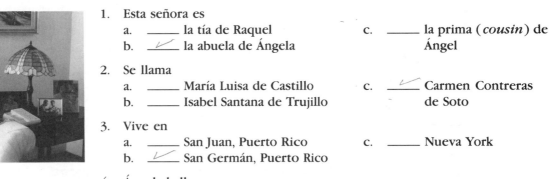

1. Esta señora es
   a. _____ la tía de Raquel   c. _____ la prima (*cousin*) de
   b. _✓_ la abuela de Ángela   Ángel

2. Se llama
   a. _____ María Luisa de Castillo   c. _✓_ Carmen Contreras
   b. _____ Isabel Santana de Trujillo   de Soto

3. Vive en
   a. _____ San Juan, Puerto Rico   c. _____ Nueva York
   b. _✓_ San Germán, Puerto Rico

4. Ángela la llama porque
   a. _✓_ quiere su permiso para ir a México
   b. _____ quiere pedirle dinero para viajar con Raquel
   c. _____ Raquel quiere conocerla

Now match Ángela's relatives with their names.

5. _d_ la abuela de Ángela   9. _f_ la tía Carmen
6. _a_ el tío Carlos   10. _e_ la madre de Ángela
7. _g_ el tío Jaime   11. _c_ Ángel Castillo, a los
8. _b_ la tía Olga   50 años

a.   b.   c.   d.   e.   f.   g.

Nota cultural: Las familias hispanas

Ángela is a young professional who lives alone and who is, for all intents and purposes, in charge of her own life. Yet a major topic of the family conference that takes place in her apartment concerns whether or not she should go to Mexico with Raquel to meet her paternal grandfather and to find out more about this "new" branch of the family. As you have learned, Ángela and Raquel will have to travel to San Germán to discuss the topic with Ángela's maternal grandmother.

It is very difficult to generalize about family customs in any culture. Depending on your particular situation, you may find the family unity shown in this video episode to be "normal" or "strange." It is fair to suggest, however, that Hispanic families are thought to be more close-knit than the average non-hispanic U.S. family. Hispanic young people often live at home longer than their typical non-hispanic U.S. counterparts, and the family is more often regarded as an important source of emotional support. You can read more about Ángela's family situation in the **Más allá del episodio** section of this lesson in the Workbook.

In Hispanic families, just as in families throughout the world, the use of terms of endearment to refer to family members is common. Ángela calls her Aunt Olga **titi** instead of **tía**. The use of the endings **-ito** or **-ita**, as appropriate, is also quite common: **abuelito**, **hermanita**, and so on.

Actividad B.   Yerno y suegra (*Son-in-law and mother-in-law*)

Ángel era el yerno de doña Carmen. ¿Cuánto recuerdas acerca de su relación?

1. Según Ángela, los dos
    a. __✓__ tenían unas relaciones muy estrechas *close*
    b. _____ no se llevaban bien
    c. _____ se toleraban el uno al otro

2. Según el episodio, doña Carmen
    a. _____ no guarda nada de Ángel
    b. _____ tiene algo que pertenecía (*belonged*) a Ángel
    c. _____ realmente no quería mucho a su yerno

Actividad C.   Llamadas de larga distancia

En este episodio, dos personas llamaron a México. ¿Cuánto recuerdas de sus llamadas?

1. ¿Quiénes llamaron a México?
    a. _____ Raquel y doña Carmen   c. __✓__ Ángela y Raquel
    b. _____ Raquel y el tío Jaime

2. ¿A quiénes llamaron? Y ¿pudieron hablar con ellos?

   <u>Raquel</u>   llamó a <u>Pedro Castillo</u>. Pudo/No pudo hablar con <u>él</u>/ella.

   <u>Ángela</u>   llamó a <u>su hermano</u>. Pudo/No pudo hablar con él/<u>ella</u>.

¡Un desafío! ¿Tienes una memoria excelente? Ahora, por una llamada, una persona sabe algo muy importante. ¿Recuerdas quién es? ¿Y qué sabe ahora?

Para pensar…

¿Quién llamaba a la habitación de Raquel al final del Episodio 20? ¿Era una llamada de México… con malas noticias?

- -

VOCABULARIO DEL TEMA

Los parientes

You already know the following names for family members. Be sure that you recognize the meaning of these words.

el abuelo, la abuela   **el hijo, la hija**
el esposo, la esposa   **el padre, la madre**
el hermano, la hermana   **el tío, la tía**

Here are the names for other members of the family.

los nietos	grandchildren	**los suegros**	in-laws
el nieto,	grandson,	**el suegro,**	father-in-law,
la nieta	granddaughter	**la suegra**	mother-in-law
los primos	cousins	**el yerno**	son-in-law
el primo, la prima	male/female cousin	**la nuera**	daughter-in-law
los sobrinos	nieces and nephews	**el cuñado**	brother-in-law
el sobrino, la sobrina	nephew, niece	**la cuñada**	sister-in-law

el padrastro, la madrastra	stepfather, stepmother
el hijastro, la hijastra	stepson, stepdaughter
el hermanastro, la hermanastra	stepbrother, stepsister
el medio hermano, la media hermana	half brother, half sister

Note that the masculine plural form (**los nietos**, **los primos**...) of the names for family members is used to refer to everyone in that category, both male and female. The most frequently used plural terms are indicated in the list of additional family members.

If you can't find in the above list the name for a family member that you need in order to describe your own family, look it up in a dictionary or ask your instructor.

Actividad A. Los parientes

Listen to the definitions provided by the speaker on the cassette tape. Can you provide the Spanish word that represents the relationship described? In each case the speaker describes how someone is related to him- or herself.

1. a. _____ los sobrinos   b. ✓ los nietos
2. a. ✓ los sobrinos   b. _____ los primos
3. a. _____ los sobrinos   b. ✓ los primos
4. a. _____ los cuñados   b. ✓ los suegros
5. a. ✓ los cuñados   b. _____ los yernos
6. a. _____ el hijastro   b. ✓ el hermanastro

Actividad B. La familia de Ángela

Paso 1

As you listen to Ángela describe her family, complete her family tree. Fill each box with the appropriate name and indicate family relationships using connecting lines. Some hints are given for you.

doña Carmen   (Q.E.P.D.)

Jamie   Olgo   Carmen   Oberolos

Ángel (Q.E.P.D.)   María Luisa (Q.E.P.D.)

Elenar   LaHoy   Sylvia

Ángela   Roberto

Paso 2

Now complete the following sentences based on the family tree you have just completed.

1. Doña Carmen y su esposo tuvieron _Cinco_ hijos.

2. María Luisa tenía _dos_ hermanos y _dos_ hermanas.

3. _Tres_ personas serían (*would be*) sobrinas de María Luisa si ella estuviera viva (*were alive*).

4. Doña Carmen tiene _cinco_ nietos en total.

5. Ángela tiene _un_ hermano y _tres_ primas.

6. _Ángel_ era el yerno de doña Carmen. Doña Carmen era _la suegra_ de Ángel. El _suegro_ de Ángel ya murió.

Actividad C.   Más parentescos (*relationships*)

Complete the sentences with the appropriate words for the family relationships described.

1. ¿Qué parentesco tienen Ángela y Roberto con Arturo? Son sus _los sobrinos_.

2. ¿Qué parentesco tienen Mercedes, Ramón, Carlos y Juan con Ángela y Roberto? Ellos son los _tíos_ de Ángela y Roberto.

3. ¿Qué parentesco hay entre Ángela y Maricarmen, la hija de Ramón y Consuelo? Ángela es la _prima_ de Maricarmen.

4. ¿Qué parentesco tiene Ángel con los hijos de don Fernando? Ellos son sus _medio hermanos_.

Actividad D.   ¿Y tú?

For each of the following family members, indicate whether or not you have one, how many there are, and what their names are. Can you also indicate where they live and how old they are?

MODELOS: No tengo (primas, suegra, ...).

Tengo un/una/varios/varias _____ . Se llama(n)

_____ y vive(n) en _____ . Mi

_____ tiene _____ años.

1. prima   2. suegra   3. abuelo   4. abuela   5. sobrino   6. cuñado/a
7. hermanastro/a   8. padrastro/madrastra

Conversaciones: Cómo contestar el teléfono

Actividad. ¡Brring! ¡Brring!

Because the action in *Destinos* takes place simultaneously at a number of locations throughout the Spanish-speaking world, you have heard a number of telephone conversations in this and in previous video episodes. In this activity you will focus on various ways to answer the phone.

Paso 1

Which of the following expressions do you think are acceptable to use when answering the phone in Spanish in different areas of the Spanish-speaking world? Indicate the ones that you think are appropriate.

1. Dígame. 2. Adiós. 3. Bueno. 4. Buenos días. 5. Buenas. 6. ¿Sí?
7. ¿No? 8. Hola. 9. Chau.

Paso 2

You will hear four brief excerpts from this and previous video episodes. Indicate the expressions you hear that appear in the previous list.

Did your predictions correspond to what you heard on the tape?

Paso 3

Now listen to the excerpts again. Do you recognize any of the characters or any characteristics about the type of Spanish they speak?

Here are the names of the speakers. Write the number of the conversation next to the appropriate name, then give the name of the country the speaker is from and the way he or she answers the phone.

Doña Carmen: 3   PR,   ¿Sí?

Arturo Iglesias: 1   Argentina Hola Sí Que tal

Teresa Suárez: 4   España   Si Dígame

Pedro Castillo: 2   Mex   Sí Bueno

Un poco de gramática

More About Using the Imperfect

In **Lección 19** you learned to talk about what someone else *was doing* by adding **-aba(n)** or **-ía(n)** to the stems of most verbs. To talk about yourself, use the singular form of the same endings.

RAQUEL: Mientras yo **tomaba** una fotografía,   *While I was taking a photograph,*
         Ángela Castillo llegó al cementerio.   *Ángela Castillo arrived at the*
                                                         cemetery.

         Mientras yo **visitaba** la Casa Blanca,   *While I was visiting The White*
         Ángela trató de hablar con sus tíos.   *House, Ángela tried to speak with*
                                                         her aunts and uncles.

Did you notice that the imperfect was used along with the preterite in the preceding sentences? You will learn more about the forms of the imperfect as well as about more of its uses in the Workbook.

Actividad.   ¿Quién lo diría?

Identify the person who would make the following statements.

a. Raquel Rodríguez   d. tía Olga
b. Ángela Castillo   e. Arturo Iglesias
c. doña Carmen, la abuela de Ángela

1. _b_ Mientras Raquel Rodríguez hablaba, yo la escuchaba atentamente.
2. _a_ Mientras Ángela llamaba a sus tíos, yo caminaba hacia la Casa Blanca.
3. _b_ No podía creerlo cuando Raquel me contó la historia de mi padre. ¡Estaba muy sorprendida!
4. _c_ Cuando hablaba con Ángela por teléfono, sabía que ella quería ir a México.
5. _e_ Mientras Raquel buscaba a Ángel en Puerto Rico, yo me preparaba para reunirme con ella.
6. _b_ Mientras Ángela me contaba algunos (*some*) detalles del caso, yo pensaba en un recuerdo que tengo de Ángel.
7. _d_ Mientras yo escuchaba la historia que nos contaba Raquel, tenía muchas dudas.

Nota cultural: Puerto Rico, la «Isla del Encanto»

Before reading the following passage about the past and present of Puerto Rico, think about what you have seen in the video episodes and about what you already know about the island. Then indicate whether the following are **Probable** (**P**) or **Improbable** (**I**).

P I   1. La población de la Isla es muy densa.
P I   2. La Isla tiene ríos y desiertos.
P I   3. El primer español que llegó a la Isla fue Ponce de León.
P I   4. Cuando llegaron los españoles, no había pueblos indígenas en la Isla.
P I   5. El oro (*gold*) fue muy importante en la historia de Puerto Rico.
P I   6. El inglés es la lengua oficial de la Isla.
P I   7. Puerto Rico está asociado con España políticamente.

After you have finished the reading, review this activity to check your answers. Are there any that you need to change?

Puerto Rico... la «Isla del Encanto»,[1] como la llaman los puertorriqueños y los que llegan a conocerla.[2] Es la más pequeña del archipiélago[3] que se llama las Antillas Mayores. A continuación[4] se presentan unos detalles acerca del presente y el pasado de esta isla tropical que tiene una relación especial con los Estados Unidos.

Datos importantes

Población: muy densa, más de tres millones de habitantes, en 9.000 kilómetros cuadrados[5]

Emigración: a Nueva York y otras ciudades del continente

Clima: cálido y soleado[6] casi todo el año

Geografía: playas, bosques,[7] colinas,[8] montañas, ríos abundantes, cascadas, áreas áridas, ...

EL OCÉANO ATLÁNTICO

un clima húmedo, con mucha vegetación

San Juan

PUERTO RICO

una autopista espectacular

LA CORDILLERA CENTRAL

la Punta, ▲ el pico más alto de la Isla

Ponce

El Yunque, un bosque tropical

un clima seco,[21] con áreas muy secas y cactus

EL MAR CARIBE

Historia

Cristóbal Colón llegó a la isla de Puerto Rico en 1493, en su segundo viaje a América. Le dio a la isla el nombre de San Juan. En aquel entonces[9] la isla estaba habitada por los indios taínos. La tribu era un pueblo pacífico y sedentario. Vivían de la pesca[10] y la agricultura. Se cree que llamaban a la isla Boriquén. (De allí[11] viene el nombre del himno nacional de Puerto Rico, «La Boriqueña».)

El explorador español Juan Ponce de León exploró la isla en 1508. Fundó la capital ese mismo año y la llamó Puerto Rico. (Más tarde se cambiaron[12] los nombres de la isla y de la capital.) Ponce de León fue nombrado gobernador de la isla al año siguiente.

Había poco oro en la Isla, pero el mito de su existencia atrajo[13] a muchos españoles. Obligaron a los taínos a buscar el oro. Entre el trabajo duro[14] de la búsqueda del metal precioso y las enfermedades[15] que contrajeron de los españoles, la mayoría de los indios murió en el siglo XVI.

Dentro de poco se extinguió el mito dorado[16] y el cultivo del jengibre,[17] del azúcar[18] y del tabaco lo sustituyó. Para trabajar en los campos, los españoles trajeron a la isla a esclavos africanos. Y para defender los cultivos de los ataques de los piratas, construyeron fortificaciones como El Morro. La isla ganó así fama como una de las rutas comerciales más importantes del imperio español.

Puerto Rico fue posesión española hasta finales del siglo XIX. Como resultado de la Guerra Hispanoamericana de 1898, la isla fue cedida a los Estados Unidos. Sus habitantes obtuvieron la ciudadanía[19] norteamericana en 1917. Años más tarde, los habitantes de la isla ganaron el derecho[20] a elegir a su propio gobernador.

A partir de 1952, Puerto Rico es un Estado Libre Asociado de la comunidad estadounidense. El idioma oficial de la Isla es el español, pero muchos puertorriqueños hablan inglés, idioma que también se enseña en las escuelas.

[1] *Enchantment* [2] *llegan... get to know her* [3] *grupo de islas* [4] *A... Here are* [5] *square* [6] *cálido... warm and sunny* [7] *forests* [8] *hills* [9] *En... At that time* [10] *fishing* [11] *De... From there* [12] *se... were transposed* [13] *attracted* [14] *hard* [15] *illnesses* [16] *el... the myth of the existence of gold* [17] *ginger* [18] *sugar* [19] *citizenship* [20] *ganaron... won the right* [21] *dry*

El Yunque es un bosque tropical en territorio estadounidense

Actividad.   Puerto Rico y los Estados Unidos

These areas of the world share a common history to some extent, starting with the arrival of explorers centuries ago. How many parallels can you find between the history of Puerto Rico and that of the United States? Think about these topics.

1. la geografía
2. la llegada de los españoles
3. la población indígena
4. la agricultura (y uno de los efectos importantes que tuvo en la historia)
5. un metal precioso
6. la importancia de una guerra
7. los idiomas que se hablan

Have you completed the following sections of the lesson? Check them off here.

_____ **Preparación**
_____ **¿Tienes buena memoria?**
_____ **Vocabulario del tema**

_____ **Conversaciones**
_____ **Un poco de gramática**

Now scan the words in the **Vocabulario** list to be sure that you understand the meaning of most of them. Then you will be ready to continue on with **Lección 20** in the Workbook.

VOCABULARIO

weather
nevaba
hacía
estaba

Los parientes

el cuñado, la cuñada	brother-in-law, sister-in-law
el hermanastro, la hermanastra	stepbrother, stepsister
el hijastro, la hijastra	stepson, stepdaughter
la madrastra	stepmother
la media hermana	half sister
los nietos	grandchildren
el nieto, la nieta	grandson, granddaughter
los primos	cousins
el primo, la prima	male/female cousin
los sobrinos	nieces and nephews
el sobrino, la sobrina	nephew, niece
los suegros	in-laws
el suegro, la suegra	father-in-law, mother-in-law
el yerno, la nuera	son-in-law, daughter-in-law

Repaso: **el medio hermano, el padrastro**

Los adjetivos

estrecho/a	close-knit
sorprendido/a	surprised

Cómo contestar el teléfono
(How to Answer the Phone)

Bueno. (*Mex.*)
Dígame. (*Spain*)
Hola. (*Arg.*)
¿Sí? (*P.R.*)

Las palabras adicionales

según   according to

Qué hacías – what were you doing

¿Qué hora era? – What time was it
eran las

Time in past is imperfect

21

EL PEAJE*

OBJETIVOS

The materials in **Lección 21** of the Textbook and the Workbook will help you better understand the video episode and take you beyond it, giving you additional information about places and characters in the series. The Textbook will also help you to develop skill in using the Spanish language. In this lesson, you will learn

- how to talk about the weather and climates in Spanish
- more about how to use the imperfect to talk about the past.

You will also learn about Puerto Rican cities other than San Juan and about the money used in Puerto Rico.

Be sure to work through all parts of the lesson. When you see a cassette symbol in the margin, listen to the tape for **Lección 21**. Answers or hints for many activities are given in Appendix 1. Be sure to check your answers for each activity before going on to the next one.

The Tollbooth

BEFORE VIEWING . . .

. . . .

PREPARACIÓN

Actividad A.

Paso 1

Refresh your memory about the events of the previous video episode by listening to the narrator's summary of it, which you will hear again when you watch **Episodio 21**.

Paso 2

Now answer the following questions about the previous video episode based on what you have just heard and on what you remember.

1. ¿Cuál era la actitud de los tíos de Ángela mientras escuchaban la historia de la investigación de Raquel?
   a. _____ Escuchaban sin gran interés.
   b. __✓__ Escuchaban con mucha atención.

2. ¿Cuál de los tíos tenía mucho que decir acerca de la historia de Raquel?
   a. _____ el tío Carlos
   b. __✓__ la tía Olga

3. En general, ¿cómo reaccionaban los tíos de Ángela ante las noticias?
   a. __✓__ Estaban preocupados.
   b. _____ Reaccionaban con indiferencia.

4. De los parientes de Ángela, ¿quién parecía ser el centro de la familia?
   a. _____ la tía Olga   b. _____ el tío Jaime   c. __✓__ la abuela

5. ¿Cómo eran las relaciones entre doña Carmen, la abuela, y su yerno, Ángel?
   a. _____ Eran problemáticas.
   b. __✓__ Eran muy estrechas.

6. ¿Con quién tiene que hablar ahora Raquel?
   a. _____ con la tía Olga
   b. __✓__ con doña Carmen

Actividad B.

In this video episode Raquel has the following conversation with an employee at a tollbooth on the highway. Listen, and follow along in the text if you like. As you listen, keep in mind that the word **taller** means *repair shop*.

RAQUEL: Perdone. Algo le pasó al carro. ¿Nos podría ayudar?
EMPLEADA: Me gustaría mucho, señorita, pero no puedo. ¿Por qué no llaman a un taller en Ponce?

Now answer the following questions.

1. ¿Qué problema tienen Raquel y Ángela en el camino a San Germán?
   a. _____ No funciona el carro.
   b. _____ Paran (*They stop*) porque necesitan gasolina.

2. ¿Hay talleres en la autopista (*highway*)?
   a. _____ No, pero los hay en una ciudad que está cerca.
   b. _____ Sí, junto al peaje.

AFTER VIEWING . . .

• •

¿TIENES BUENA MEMORIA?

Actividad A.   La historia sigue

The following statements are taken from Raquel's summary at the end of **Episodio 21**. Indicate the phrase that completes the statement or answers the question.

1. Esta mañana Ángela, su prima Laura y yo salimos de San Juan para ir a
   a. _____ Ponce   b. _____ San Germán   c. _____ Caguas

2. En ruta a San Germán aprendí muchas cosas interesantes. Por ejemplo, ¿es una peseta puertorriqueña igual a una peseta española?
   a. _____ No. Vale un dólar. Es una moneda (*coin*) norteamericana.
   b. _____ Sí. Son iguales. Una peseta puertorriqueña y una peseta española valen lo mismo.
   c. _____ No. Vale veinticinco centavos. Es una moneda norteamericana.

3. En Puerto Rico una banana es **un guineo**. En España se dice **plátano**. Otra fruta con un nombre diferente es
   a. _____ la manzana   b. _____ la naranja   c. _____ la pera

4. En camino a San Germán, cerca del peaje, tuvimos problemas con
   a. _____ la comida   b. _____ mi sombrero   c. _____ el carro

5. La mujer del peaje me dio un número de un taller para llamar. ¿En dónde estaba el taller?
   a. _____ En San Juan.   b. _____ En Caguas.   c. _____ En Ponce.

6. Luego vino el señor del taller y remolcó (*towed*) el carro a Ponce. En el taller, supimos que el carro
   a. _____ simplemente no tenía gasolina
   b. _____ estaba en muy malas condiciones
   c. _____ era imposible de reparar

7. Y aquí estamos, cansadas y listas para dormir. Ahora tendré que (*I'll have to*) esperar hasta mañana para conocer

    a. _____ al hermano de Ángela   c. _____ al dueño (*owner*) del

    b. ✓ a Carmen Contreras   taller

 Now check your answers by listening to the cassette tape.

Actividad B.   Un poco de historia. ¡Un desafío!

In this and in previous video episodes of *Destinos*, as well as in the lessons of the Textbook and Workbook, you have learned a great deal about Puerto Rico. Can you supply the missing information in the following paragraphs?

> **Lugares:** La Habana, Ponce, San Juan; Cuba, Puerto Rico
> **Fechas:** 1859, 1898, 1911
> **Otras palabras:** español, inglés; la batalla, la guerra

Por más de 400 años, Puerto Rico formó parte del vasto imperio _español_ .[1]

Para el imperio, _San Juan_ [2] era uno de los puertos más importantes de todas las Américas.

En _1898_ [3] estalló[a] la guerra entre los Estados Unidos y España. Al perder la _guerra_ ,[4] España tuvo que concederle el resto de su imperio a los Estados Unidos. Las Filipinas, _Cuba_ [5] y Puerto Rico pasaron a manos[b] norteamericanas.

En 1902 Cuba consiguió su independencia de los Estados Unidos. Las Islas Filipinas se independizaron en 1946, pero _Puerto Rico_ [6] siguió siendo[c] territorio norteamericano.

[a]empezó   [b]*hands*   [c]siguió... *continued to be*

Now check your answers by listening to the cassette tape.

Nota cultural: Los puertorriqueños, ciudadanos (*citizens*) de los Estados Unidos

When Raquel asks Ángela whether her passport is up to date, she has forgotten something of which many people are not aware: Puerto Ricans are U.S. citizens. They can travel back and forth freely from **la Isla** to the mainland, and, as U.S. citizens, they can go anywhere that other U.S. citizens are permitted to go without a passport, such as to Mexico.

    Another result of Puerto Rico's relationship to the United States is the use of U.S. currency . . . some with Spanish names! Can you remember the value in cents (*centavos*) of the following coins?

    una peseta   un vellón de 10   un vellón de 5   un chavo (un chavito)

VOCABULARIO DEL TEMA

¿Qué tiempo hace?

Hace (muy) buen tiempo.	The weather's (very) good.
Hace (muy) mal tiempo.	The weather's (very) bad.
Hace (mucho) frío.	It's (very) cold.
Hace (mucho) fresco.	It's (very) cool.
Hace (mucho) calor.	It's (very) hot.
Hace (mucho) sol.	It's (very) sunny.
Hace (mucho) viento.	It's (very) windy.
Está (muy) nublado.	It's (very) cloudy.
Está despejado.	It's clear (cloudless).

llover (ue): to rain: **nevar (ie):** to snow:

Llueve.
Está lloviendo. } It's raining.

Nieva.
Está nevando. } It's snowing.

La temperatura está a ＿＿ grados.   The temperature is ＿＿ degrees.

Note the following about describing the weather in Spanish.

- **Hacer** (*to do* or *to make*) is used to describe many weather conditions. The adverb **muy** modifies the adjectives **buen** and **mal** + **tiempo**. The adjective **mucho** is followed by nouns (**frío, fresco,** …) in a number of other expressions.
- The imperfect is generally used to talk about weather in the past: **Hacía mucho calor la semana pasada. La temperatura estaba a 38 grados.**

Actividad A.   En Ponce hace calor

Listen again as the narrator uses a number of terms to describe weather conditions. Complete the statements with the terms you hear.

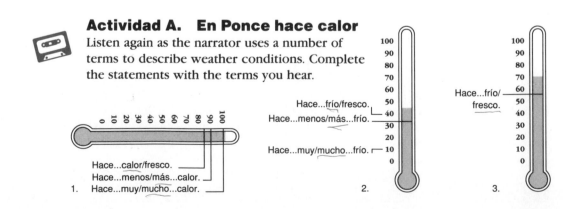

```
           0 10 20 30 40 50 60 70 80 90 100
```
Hace...calor/fresco. ＿＿＿＿
Hace...menos/más...calor. ＿＿＿＿
1. Hace...muy/mucho...calor. ＿＿＿＿

2.
```
100
90
80
70
60
50
40
30
20
10
0
```
Hace...frío/fresco. ＿＿＿＿
Hace...menos/más...frío. ＿＿＿＿
Hace...muy/mucho...frío. ＿＿＿＿

3.
```
100
90
80
70
60
50
40
30
20
10
0
```
Hace...frío/ fresco. ＿＿＿＿

Actividad B. En el mes de diciembre

In **Episodio 9** you learned that the seasons are reversed in the southern hemisphere. That is, when it is winter in Spain, it is summer in Argentina, and vice versa. In the Caribbean, of course, the weather conditions are fairly constant. Based on that information, indicate whether the following sentences are probably **Cierto** (**C**), **Falso** (**F**), or **Posible** (**P**).

En Buenos Aires

C (F) P 1. Hace frío en diciembre, con mucho viento.
C F (P) 2. Hace fresco en mayo.
(C) F P 3. Hace calor en enero, con mucho sol.

En Puerto Rico

(C) F P 4. Hace calor casi todo el año.
(C) F P 5. Hay un clima más o menos tropical.
C F (P) 6. Hace mucho viento a veces, especialmente en la playa.

En Madrid

(C) F P 7. Hace mucho frío en el mes de enero.
(C) F P 8. Hace calor en agosto.
(C) F P 9. Hace fresco en primavera.

Actividad C. ¿Qué tiempo hacía?

el 30 de marzo

NIEVE LLUVIAS LLOVIZNAS CALOR FRIO NUBLADO

You will hear a series of questions about weather conditions in different parts of the United States. Indicate what the weather was like in those places last March 30, based on the following map. If no particular weather condition is depicted, answer by saying **Hacía buen tiempo**. Take a few seconds to scan the map and its legend. You will hear the legend on the cassette tape. What known words can you associate with the unfamiliar words?

MODELO: (*you hear*) ¿Qué tiempo hacía en la Florida? ¿Llovía?
(*you say*) No, no llovía. Hacía buen tiempo.

1. *Nievando* 2. *llovía* 3. *30* 4. *frío* 5. ... 6. ...

Actividad D. ¿Y tú?

Describe the weather where you live according to the seasons. Use the following sentences as a guide.

Yo vivo en *Nuevo México*. Durante el otoño *hacía fresco*. También *está lloviendo*. No *frío*. El invierno es diferente/similar porque *hace sol* y *hace buen tiempo*. Durante la primavera *hace frío* y a veces *hace viento*. En verano generalmente *hace calor*. Yo prefiero el tiempo que hace en *otoño*.

Nota cultural: Hablando de la temperatura

In most Spanish-speaking countries, temperature is measured by *Celsius* degrees, rather than by *Fahrenheit*. The following chart gives approximate correspondences between the two scales.

Celsius	100°	37°	30°	20°	10°	0°
Fahrenheit	212°	98.6°	86°	68°	50°	32°

UN POCO DE GRAMÁTICA

More About the Imperfect

To describe what you *were doing* with others, add **-ábamos** or **-íamos** to the stems of regular verbs.

RAQUEL: Hacía mucho calor cuando **viajábamos** por las montañas. **Queríamos** llegar a San Germán esa noche, pero el carro no funcionaba bien.

Actividad.   ¿Qué hacíamos?

Form a summary of the events in **Episodio 21** by combining the numbered sentence beginnings with the lettered endings below. The first and last sentences of the summary, which is told from Raquel's point of view, are given for you.

1. Hacía muy buen tiempo cuando salimos de San Juan.
2. ___h___ Mientras Ángela manejaba (*was driving*),
3. ___e___ Todas esperábamos en el carro
4. ___a___ Laura y yo nos quedamos en el carro
5. ___f___ Mientras cruzábamos la Cordillera Central,
6. ___d___ Mientras salíamos del peaje,
7. ___b___ Mientras esperábamos al mecánico del taller,
8. ___g___ Estábamos muy preocupadas
9. ___c___ Cuando supimos que el mecánico no pudo reparar el carro ese día, nos preguntamos:
10. Encontramos un hotel, cenamos, nos acostamos y nos dormimos en seguida. ¡Estábamos muy cansadas!

a.   mientras Ángela compraba unos refrescos.
b.   tuvimos un *picnic*.
c.   ¿Dónde vamos a pasar la noche?
d.   el carro dejó de (*stopped*) funcionar.
e.   mientras el empleado llenaba el tanque.
f.   mirábamos el paisaje (*scenery*) impresionante.
g.   mientras el mecánico revisaba (*checked out*) el carro.
h.   Laura y yo tratábamos de doblar el mapa.

Nota cultural: Otras ciudades puertorriqueñas

In this video *episodio*, due to Raquel, Ángela, and Laura's unscheduled stop in Ponce, you learned a bit about that city. **Ponceños** (people who live in Ponce) and other Puerto Ricans are fond of saying that **Ponce es Ponce**, which probably implies that people do things their own way in this relatively small, attractive city. Listen again to what the narrator told you about Ponce and try to recall the images in the video episode. Then read this passage about Ponce and other cities on **la Isla** and indicate them on the map.

En la Isla, las poblaciones típicas y los vestigios coloniales alternan con edificios modernos y complejos de hoteles y casinos. Esta gran variedad de ambientes[1] atrae el turismo de todas partes del mundo. Aquí hay algunos lugares que visitar. ¿Cuál te interesa más? ¿Puedes encontrarlos todos en el mapa, según la lectura? ¿Y puedes identificar la siguiente foto?

- Una de las ciudades más importantes de Puerto Rico es Ponce, que está en la costa del Caribe. Es un antiguo centro agrícola, donde se cultiva la caña de azúcar[2] y el café. Ponce conserva su encanto provinciano. En el Parque Central está la Catedral de Guadalupe y el pintoresco[3] Parque de Bombas,[4] pintado de rojo y negro. Su museo de arte está entre los mejores del Caribe.

- Al oeste de la Isla se encuentra Mayagüez, ciudad que fundaron los españoles en un lugar ya habitado por los indios taínos. Además de ser una ciudad histórica, tiene modernas fábricas[5] y hoteles. Su zoológico es fascinante, sobre todo para los niños.

- Cerca de Mayagüez, en el suroeste, está La Parguera, una pintoresca aldea[6] de pescadores.[7] Uno de sus atractivos es la llamada «bahía fosforescente»: de noche, cuando la luna se oculta,[8] y se agita el agua, brilla[9] con la luz de unos

Barcos cerca de Fajardo, Puerto Rico

[1]*environments*   [2]*caña... sugar cane*   [3]*picturesque*   [4]*Parque... Fire Station*
[5]*factories*   [6]*village*   [7]*fishermen*   [8]*la... the moon is hidden*   [9]*it glows*

pequeños organismos marítimos unicelulares que viven en las aguas de la bahía. La Parguera tiene el mayor laboratorio marino de todo el Caribe.

• En la costa del norte, cerca de San Juan, está Arecibo. Se conoce por los carnavales, el ron y las piñas. Es también el centro de la industria farmacéutica. Y es famosa porque allí hay un observatorio con un enorme telescopio.

Actividad.   La Isla del Encanto

Based on what you have just read, where would you most likely find the following people, animals, and events?

1.   un estudiante de astronomía   2.   una hacienda   3.   viajes turísticos de noche, en bote   4.   un biólogo marino   5.   un estudiante de arte   6.   un tigre   7.   muchas personas que llevan máscaras y se divierten

Have you completed the following sections of the lesson? Check them off here.

_____ **Preparación**   _____ **Vocabulario del tema**
_____ **¿Tienes buena memoria?**   _____ **Un poco de gramática**

Now scan the words in the **Vocabulario** list to be sure that you understand the meaning of most of them. Then you will be ready to continue on with **Lección 21** in the Workbook.

VOCABULARIO

Los verbos

funcionar	to work, function (*machines*)
manejar	to drive
parar	to stop

En el camino

la autopista	highway; toll road
el carro	car
el peaje	tollbooth
el taller	repair shop (*automobiles*)

Los adjetivos

preocupado/a	worried

¿Qué tiempo hace? (What's the Weather Like?)

Hace (muy) buen tiempo.	The weather's (very) good.
Hace (mucho) calor.	It's (very) hot.
Hace (mucho) fresco.	It's (very) cool.
Hace (mucho) frío.	It's (very) cold.
Hace (muy) mal tiempo.	The weather's (very) bad.
Hace (mucho) sol.	It's (very) sunny.
Hace (mucho) viento.	It's (very) windy.
Está despejado.	It's clear (cloudless).
Está (muy) nublado.	It's very cloudy.
llover (ue)	to rain
Llueve./Está lloviendo.	It's raining.
nevar (ie)	to snow:
Nieva./Está nevando.	It's snowing.
La temperatura está a _____ grados.	The temperature is _____ degrees.

L E C C I Ó N

22

RECUERDOS*

*Éstas son
mis amigos del puerto...
los primeros en decirme que me dedicara a la pintura.*

OBJETIVOS

The materials in **Lección 22** of the Textbook and the Workbook will help you better understand the video episode and take you beyond it, giving you additional information about places and characters in the series. The Textbook will also help you to develop skill in using the Spanish language. In this lesson, you will learn

- how to describe changes in people's mood, condition, or state of being
- how to use the imperfect to talk about things you always used to do.

You will also learn about the economy of Puerto Rico.

Be sure to work through all parts of the lesson. When you see a cassette symbol in the margin, listen to the tape for **Lección 22**. Answers or hints for many activities are given in Appendix 1. Be sure to check your answers for each activity before going on to the next one.

* *Memories*

BEFORE VIEWING . . .

. . . .

PREPARACIÓN

Actividad.

In the previous video episode, Raquel and her traveling companions set off for San Germán, where Ángela's grandmother lives. Their trip was not uneventful, however. Complete the following summary of the previous episode. No words are given from which to choose, but you should be able to complete the paragraph easily. Read it through at least once before you fill in the blanks.

En camino a San Germán, Raquel, Ángela y Laura, la ___primera___¹ de Ángela, tuvieron dificultades con el ___carro___.² Llamaron a un ___teller___³ de reparaciones.ª Vino un hombre y remolcó el carro a Ponce. El mecánico les dijo que el carro no iba a estar listoᵇ hasta el ___día siguiente___.⁴ Raquel y sus dos compañeras tuvieron que pasar la noche en ___Ponce___.⁵

ª*repairs* ᵇ*ready*

 Now check your answers by listening to the cassette tape.

Para pensar...

Esto es un baúl. Contiene artículos personales de alguien. ¿De quién?

¿Qué hay en la caja que le está dando doña Carmen a Ángela? ¿Será (*Could it be*) algo relacionado con la historia de Ángel?

AFTER VIEWING . . .

. . . .

¿TIENES BUENA MEMORIA?

Actividad A.   Las preguntas de Raquel

Paso 1

Listen again as Raquel asks questions at the end of the video episode while she is waiting for the family to say good-bye. Select the correct answer from the choices provided. Raquel will give the correct answer on the cassette tape.

1. a. _✓_ Sí.   b. _____ No.
2. a. _____ Muy contenta. b. _✓_ Furiosa.
3. a. _✓_ En la iglesia.   b. _____ En el mercado.   c. _____ En el patio.

Paso 2

Now read the following statements and indicate whether they are **Cierto** (**C**) or **Falso** (**F**). Think both about what you have seen and heard in the video episode and what you know about the characters from other sources.

C (F) 1. Ángela estudió en la Universidad de Puerto Rico, en San Juan.

(C) F 2. Cuando la mamá de Ángela se enfermó, Ángela se quedó a vivir con la abuela.

(C) F 3. El padre de Ángela venía todos los fines de semana a San Germán.

C (F) 4. Pero en San Germán, Ángel no tenía interés en pintar.

Paso 3

Now listen again as Raquel gives the answers to the previous items. Then continue to answer her questions.

1. a. Poesías.   b. Recuerdos.   c. Fotografías.
2. a. Sí.   b. No.

Actividad B.   Doña Carmen, suegra de Ángel

You have seen doña Carmen in a previous video episode of *Destinos*. How much do you remember about her from before and from this episode? Complete the following statements about her.

1. Doña Carmen es la abuela... paterna / materna... de Ángela.
2. Doña Carmen y su esposo eran dueños (*owners*) de... una finca / una farmacia.
3. El esposo de doña Carmen... ya murió / está ahora en otra ciudad.
4. Doña Carmen vive ahora en San Germán con una... nieta / sirvienta.
5. Ángel era el... hijastro / yerno... de doña Carmen.
6. Los dos tenían relaciones... poco estrechas / muy estrechas.

7. Doña Carmen sugiere que Ángela examine las cosas de… su padre / su hermano.

8. Doña Carmen le tiene una sorpresa a Ángela:… un libro / una copa… de su abuela Rosario.

Nota cultural: La comida de Puerto Rico

Laura, Ángela's cousin, is still a growing girl who eats a lot. As her grandmother says, **¡Siempre tiene hambre esta chica!**

In this video episode, you saw the dessert course of a pleasant meal served in doña Carmen's house: **pasta de guayaba** (*guava paste*), which is served with cheese (**queso**). **La guayaba** is a tropical fruit from the West Indies, used in making preserves, jellies, and pastries of many kinds. Other fruits typical of Puerto Rican cuisine include **las piñas**, **los cocos**, **los mangos**, **los plátanos**, **la parcha** (*passion fruit*), and so on.

Bananas in particular appear in a number of dishes, including **el mofongo**, a type of fritter made with fried and baked bananas and served with a variety of sauces (shrimp or chicken, for example).

Actividad C.   Recuerdos de Ángel. ¡Un desafío!

Mi esposa, María Luisa. Recuerdo de ella su ternura, su voz, sus ojos y su hermoso pelo negro.

As you saw in this video episode, Ángela and Raquel found one of Ángel's sketchbooks among his belongings in the trunk in his old room. Can you select the phrase that best completes each page of Ángel's "**Recuerdos**"?

1. __d__ Mi madre me contaba de los horrores de la Guerra Civil. Mi padre…
2. __h__ Éstos son recuerdos…
3. __a__ El mar. La primera vez…
4. __i__ Éste es mi hermano Arturo, o por lo menos el recuerdo de él. …
5. __b__ Mi madre, …
6. __e__ Éstos son mis amigos del…
7. __c__ Mi esposa, María Luisa. …
8. __g__ Mis hijos…
9. __f__ El mar. …

a. que vi el mar fue en ruta a la Argentina.
b. ¡cuánto la extraño! A veces siento su presencia.
c. Recuerdo de ella su ternura, su voz, sus ojos y su hermoso pelo negro.
d. murió y yo nunca lo conocí.
e. puerto… los primeros en decirme que me dedicara a la pintura.
f. Mi inspiración… y mi destino final.
g. ahora lo más importante de mi vida, Ángela y Roberto.
h. de mi dura infancia.
i. Nos llevábamos como perros y gatos. Me gustaría verlo otra vez. Pero es imposible. Es muy tarde.

Now listen again as Ángela reads the pages aloud and see if your answers were correct.

VOCABULARIO DEL TEMA

Cambios de estado

Many Spanish verbs can be used with reflexive pronouns to express a change of state or condition. For example, the verb **casarse** expresses a change from single to marital status. Here are some additional verbs that express changes.

acostumbrarse	to become accustomed	**enfermarse**	to get sick
adaptarse	to adapt	**enojarse (con)**	to become angry (with)
alegrarse (de)	to become happy (about)	**molestarse**	to get irritated
cansarse	to get tired	**quedarse** + *adj*.	to become + *adj*.
divorciarse (de)	to get divorced (from)	**reponerse**	to get better; to get over (*an illness*)
enfadarse (con)	to become angry (with)		

Two other verbs that you already know are often used with adjectives to express similar changes: **ponerse**, **volverse**.

> Don Fernando **se** va a **poner** muy contento.
> A veces la gente **se vuelve** loca por las grandes tragedias.

- **Ponerse** means *to become*, *to get*, but in a physical or emotional sense: to become sick, sad, red (in the face), and so on.
- **Volverse** expresses *to become*, *to get* when the change is drastic and permanent. It is frequently combined with the adjective **loco** (*crazy*).

Actividad A. Ángela y Raquel

Paso 1

You now know even more about Ángela Castillo, and you have seen Ángela and Raquel interact over a number of video episodes. What have you observed about them? Start by indicating which of the following statements describe Ángela.

1. __✓__ Se molesta fácilmente… y con frecuencia.
2. _____ No es muy enérgica y se cansa rápidamente.
3. _____ Quiere casarse y tener una familia grande.
4. __✓__ No se acostumbra fácilmente a vivir en ciertas situaciones o lugares nuevos.
5. _____ A veces se pone muy pensativa.

Paso 2

Now indicate which of the same statements you think apply to Raquel.

1. _____   2. _____   3. _____   4. _____   5. ✓ _____

Paso 3

Would you say that Raquel and Ángela are similar or very different? Listen to a brief description of them on the cassette tape and see whether your observations were accurate.

Actividad B.   Adivinanzas (Guesses)

Most of the characters you have met or heard about so far in *Destinos* have undergone changes of one kind or another. Identify the characters described by each of the following statements. ¡OJO! Some statements may apply to more than one character.

1. Se casó dos veces.
2. Se divorció y ahora vive solo/a.
3. Se enfermó y murió.
4. Se acostumbró a vivir en otro país.
5. Se enfadó con un pariente.
6. Se molestó por una cosa pequeña.
7. Nunca se repuso de la muerte de su esposo/a.
8. Se alegró al saber (*upon learning*) cierta noticia.
9. Se puso muy triste al saber cierta noticia.
10. Se quedó muy sorprendido/a.

Actividad C.   ¿Y tú?

Which of the following statements are true for you? Change the statements that do not describe you to make them true for you.

1. _____ Me molesto por cualquier (*any*) cosa.
2. _____ Cuando me enfado con alguien, no digo nada. Me quedo callado/a (*silent*).
3. _____ Me enfermo fácilmente y con frecuencia... de gripe (*flu*), de resfriados (*colds*), ...
4. _____ No me adapto fácilmente a nuevas situaciones o lugares.
5. _____ Cuando me enfermo, me repongo rápidamente.
6. _____ Me vuelvo loco/a cuando los otros no hacen lo que (*what*) deben hacer.
7. _____ No pienso casarme.
8. _____ Me canso fácilmente. No tengo la energía de Ángela y Raquel.

Actividad D.   ¿Y tú? La última vez...

Describe the last time you became very angry, very sad, or very happy.

> MODELO: La última vez que me enojé fue porque/cuando...
>
> La última vez que me puse triste, estaba en _____.

La última vez que me alegré mucho fue porque/cuando...
La última vez que me molesté, estaba en...

UN POCO DE GRAMÁTICA

More About Using the Imperfect

The imperfect tense is also used to talk about habitual or repeated events in the past. How often the event or action occurred is not expressed.

DOÑA CARMEN:

Éramos dueños de una gran finca de caña. A veces **empleábamos** más de doscientos hombres para los trabajos.	*We were the owners of a large sugarcane plantation. At times we used to employ more than two hundred men to get the work done.*
El padre de Ángela **venía** todos los fines de semana.	*Angela's father would come every weekend.*

You will learn more about using the imperfect in this way in the Workbook.

Actividad. Hablando del pasado

As they sat on the patio of the house in San Germán, doña Carmen and Ángela talked about what used to happen. Only five of the following events were mentioned (**Sí se mencionó**). Can you find them? For the events that were not mentioned (**No se mencionó**), do you think it is likely that they happened?

Sí	No	1. Toda la familia se reunía en esta casa los domingos.
Sí	No	2. Doña Carmen preparaba todas las comidas.
Sí	No	3. Era una familia grande. Por eso se sentaban en dos mesas.
Sí	No	4. Ángel recitaba las poesías de su esposa después de comer.
Sí	No	5. El abuelo iba a los campos (*fields*) todos los días de la semana.
Sí	No	6. Empleaban a muchos hombres en la finca de los abuelos.
Sí	No	7. Poco a poco iban vendiendo la finca, en parcelas.
Sí	No	8. Ángela venía a la casa con frecuencia cuando era estudiante.
Sí	No	9. Cuando su esposa se enfermó, Ángel venía a San Germán todas las semanas.
Sí	No	10. Ángel pintaba mucho allí.
Sí	No	11. Vendía sus pinturas en una tienda en el centro de San Germán.

Nota cultural: La economía de Puerto Rico

Before reading the following selection about the economy of modern-day Puerto Rico, consider what you have already learned about the island. For what reason would many people from other countries come to visit it? If you thought of the tourist industry, you were correct. It is one of the mainstays of the present-day Puerto Rican economy. Now listen again as the narrator tells you about the history of San Germán. His description includes information about another important aspect of the economy of the Island.

Cuando ya había desaparecido[1] el mito del oro de América, los españoles empezaron la obra de sacarle a[2] su vasto territorio otro tipo de riqueza. Así es que, casi desde el principio, Puerto Rico fue un país agrícola. En la actualidad,[3] la agricultura sigue siendo importante para la economía puertorriqueña, junto con el desarrollo[4] industrial que ha traído[5] el siglo XX. Y, por fin, existe el turismo, una de las industrias más importantes del Puerto Rico moderno. Veamos estos tres aspectos de la economía puertorriqueña.

La agricultura

Por muchos años, el azúcar fue el producto más importante de Puerto Rico. Existían grandes fincas de caña, como la de doña Carmen y su esposo, y Puerto Rico era un gran exportador de azúcar. En la década de los años 40, el gobierno trató de diversificar la economía de Puerto Rico, para que la Isla no dependiera tanto de un solo producto. Pero muchos todavía siguen con el cultivo de la caña.

El café también figura en la economía de la Isla desde muy temprano. En 1738 se empezó a cultivar en Puerto Rico un café aromático, de un suave sabor.[6] Este café era muy apreciado en las cortes reales de España y de otros países europeos. Actualmente las exportaciones anuales de café superan[7] los 70 millones de dólares.

¿Y otros productos? Hay plantaciones de arroz, de frutas tropicales—sobre todo de bananas—y algo de ganadería.[8]

Plantación de bananas en Puerto Rico

La industria

Para la economía de la Isla, la industria moderna es lo que era la agricultura en siglos pasados. Hay más de dos mil fábricas[9] en la Isla, y Puerto Rico es hoy un gran productor de farmacéuticos, petroquímicas y productos metalúrgicos. Es necesario mencionar también la industria relacionada con la agricultura: ingenios[10] de azúcar, manufactura del tabaco y de textiles.

---

[1]había... *had disappeared*   [2]sacarle... *extracting from*   [3]En... *Currently*   [4]*development*   [5]ha... *has brought*
[6]suave... *soft flavor*   [7]*exceed*   [8]*cattle raising*   [9]*factories*   [10]*mills*

Y, por fin, sería imposible hablar de la industria puertorriqueña sin mencionar uno de sus productos más famosos: el ron. Famoso por su calidad, el ron puertorriqueño se produce cerca de San Juan. ¿No has visto[11] algunos anuncios[12] de la campaña publicitaria que se hace actualmente al ron puertorriqueño, con personajes como Raúl Julia, el excelente actor de cine y teatro?

La industria por excelencia

En las últimas décadas, Puerto Rico se ha convertido en[13] uno de los lugares más visitados del Caribe. La Isla ofrece al turista complejos hoteleros, casinos, restaurantes, y también campos de golf y facilidades para practicar todos los deportes acuáticos como el buceo[14] y el *surf*. Estos complejos modernos se encuentran sobre todo en San Juan—en las famosas playas de Isla Verde y Condado—, pero hay también hoteles y paradores[15] modestos en la capital y por todas partes de la Isla.

Nota al pie[16]

Con este retrato optimista de la economía de la Isla, no se quiere dar a entender[17] que Puerto Rico no tenga problemas económicos. De hecho, la tasa de desempleo[18] es alta, y muchos puertorriqueños emigran a las grandes ciudades industriales del este de los Estados Unidos—en Nueva York, Nueva Jersey y Pensilvania—en busca de trabajo.

[11]¿No... *Haven't you seen*   [12]*ads*   [13]se... *has become*   [14]*snorkeling*   [15]*inns*   [16]Nota... *Footnote*   [17]no... *one does not imply*   [18]tasa... *unemployment rate*

Actividad.   Opiniones

The following questions ask for your opinions or ideas about Puerto Rico. Answer as best you can, making inferences when necessary.

1. En la actualidad, ¿se puede decir que la economía de Puerto Rico es más diversa que antes?
2. ¿En qué sentido se puede decir que Puerto Rico depende de ingresos (*income*) externos?
3. Si Puerto Rico depende del turismo, ¿qué cosas pueden tener un efecto negativo en esa industria?

Have you completed the following sections of the lesson? Check them off here.

_____ **Preparación**   _____ **Vocabulario del tema**
_____ **¿Tienes buena memoria?**   _____ **Un poco de gramática**

Now scan the words in the **Vocabulario** list to be sure that you understand the meaning of most of them. Then you will be ready to continue on with **Lección 22** in the Workbook.

VOCABULARIO

Los verbos

acostumbrarse	to become accustomed
adaptarse	to adapt
alegrarse (de)	to become happy (about)
cansarse	to get tired
divorciarse (de)	to get divorced (from)
enfadarse (con)	to become angry (with)
enfermarse	to get sick
enojarse (con)	to become angry (with)
molestarse	to get irritated
reponerse	to get better; to get over (*an illness*)

Los lugares

la finca	farm; ranch; hacienda
el mar	sea

Las personas

el/la dueño/a	owner

Las cosas

la caña de azúcar	sugar cane
la hoja	leaf; sheet

Los conceptos

el recuerdo	memory
quedarse + *adj.*	to become + *adj.*
volverse (ue) loco/a	to go crazy

Repaso: ponerse + *adj.*

LECCIÓN

23

VISTA AL MAR*

OBJETIVOS

The materials in **Lección 23** of the Textbook and the Workbook will help you better understand the video episode and take you beyond it, giving you additional information about places and characters in the series. The Textbook will also help you to develop skill in using the Spanish language. In this lesson, you will learn

- ways to express in Spanish the parts of a house and some appliances
- another way to describe what someone is doing right now.

You will also learn about Puerto Ricans who live and work in the continental United States.

Be sure to work through all parts of the lesson. When you see a cassette symbol in the margin, listen to the tape for **Lección 23**. Answers or hints for many activities are given in Appendix 1. Be sure to check your answers for each activity before going on to the next one.

*A View of the Sea

BEFORE VIEWING . . .

Preparación

Actividad A.

In the last video episode of *Destinos* Raquel and Ángela spent time with doña Carmen, Ángela's grandmother. Do you remember the most important things that happened? Select the best answer for the following questions.

1. ¿Cómo reaccionó la abuela cuando Ángela le dijo que quería ir a México a conocer a don Fernando?
    Estaba _____.   a. a favor   b. en contra   c. indiferente

2. ¿Qué encontró Ángela entre las cosas de su padre?
    Encontró _____.   a. un álbum de fotografías   b. un libro de poesías
    c. unas hojas con sus recuerdos

3. ¿Qué le dio la abuela a Ángela?
    Le dio _____.   a. un retrato de Rosario   b. la copa de bodas
    de Rosario   c. una carta de Rosario

Actividad B.

As you know, Ángela wants to sell her parents' apartment in El Viejo San Juan. What kind of house or apartment do you think she will want to move into?

Ángela va a querer...

a.   _____ una casa antigua, en el Viejo San Juan, similar a la casa de sus padres
b.   _____ un apartamento en un edificio (*building*) muy moderno con una vista panorámica al mar
c.   _____ un apartamento pequeño pero cómodo, cerca de la universidad (donde trabaja su novio)

Para pensar...

¿Ha hablado (*Has... spoken*) Ángela con su hermano, Roberto, sobre la venta de la casa de sus padres? ¿Debe vender la casa sin consultar con él?

Actividad C.

This is one of the people that Raquel will meet during this video episode of *Destinos*. Look at the photograph carefully and consider the setting, then answer the following questions.

¿Quién es esta persona? ¿Por qué aparece en este episodio?

a. ✓ Ángela necesita pedirle permiso a su jefa (*boss*) para ausentarse de su trabajo. Quiere ir a México con Raquel por una o dos semanas.

b. _____ Además de ser su jefa, también es una buena amiga de Ángela y por eso quiere consultar con ella lo que (*what*) debe hacer en este caso.

c. _____ Ángela quiere renunciar (*quit*) a su trabajo en el banco. Raquel la acompaña para darle apoyo (*support*).

Para pensar...

Además de su jefa, hay otra persona importante en la vida de Ángela que vas a conocer en este episodio: su novio. ¿Qué tipo de persona será (*will he probably be*)? ¿Será alto? ¿rubio? ¿extrovertido? ¿tímido? ¿Qué imagen tienes de él en este momento?

AFTER VIEWING . . .

¿TIENES BUENA MEMORIA?

Actividad A.   ¿Relaciones serias?

Part of the video episode you have just seen focused on Raquel's activities. Can you complete this summary of the episode without consulting the choices that follow?

Esta tarde Raquel está en la facultadª de la Universidad de Puerto Rico. Está esperando a Ángela, y ella *está* _____.¹ su novio Jorge.

Ángela y Raquel regresaron de San Germán *ayer por la noche* _____.² Tan pronto comoᵇ Raquel llegó a su habitación, hizo una llamada de larga distancia *a BA* _____.³ Afortunadamente Arturo estaba en casa y los dos pudieron hablar un rato. Arturo le sorprendió a Raquel cuando le dijo que *la quería mucho* _____.⁴

Ahora Raquel está un poco perpleja. Arturo le gusta mucho, eso sí. Pero Raquel *no sabe si* _____.⁵ quiere tener relaciones serias en estos momentos.

ªcampus   ᵇTan... *As soon as*

1. está hablando afuera (*outside*) con / está tratando de llamar a
2. ayer por la mañana / ayer por la noche
3. a Buenos Aires para hablar con Arturo / a México para hablar con Pedro
4. la quería mucho / ya no la quería como antes
5. no sabe si / está segura que

Now listen to part of Raquel's story review again and check your answers. Raquel's words are not identical to the written summary, but they are close enough to allow you to follow along with ease.

Actividad B.   La vida de Ángela

The rest of **Episodio 23** focused on events and decisions in Ángela's life. Can you answer these questions about Ángela without referring to the list of **Frases útiles** that follows?

1. ¿Dónde trabaja Ángela?
2. ¿Con quién tenía que hablar allí?
3. ¿Con quién quería hablar en la universidad?
4. ¿Qué hacía esta persona cuando Raquel y Ángela llegaron?
5. ¿Qué le mostró Ángela a esta persona?

Frases útiles: en una tienda/un banco, con una amiga/su jefa/su profesor/su novio, tomar/dar una clase, una copa/unas hojas

Now listen to the second half of Raquel's story review and check your answers. **¡Un desafío!** What two questions does Raquel ask and leave unanswered at the end of her review?

• •

VOCABULARIO DEL TEMA

Las partes de una casa

el baño	bathroom	**el balcón**	balcony	**la escalera**	stairway
la cocina	kitchen	**el jardín**	garden	**el piso**	floor
el comedor	dining room	**el patio**	patio	**la planta baja***	ground floor
el cuarto	bedroom	**la terraza**	terrace	**la puerta**	door
la sala	living room			**la ventana**	window
		el estacionamiento	parking		
		la vista (a)	view (of)		

---

*See the **Nota cultural** at the end of this section for an explanation of how floors of a building are named in Spanish.

Algunos aparatos domésticos

la estufa   stove
el horno (de microondas)
   (microwave) oven
la lavadora   clothes washer   **el estéreo**   stereo
el lavaplatos   dishwasher   **el radio**   radio
la nevera   refrigerator   **el televisor**   television set
la secadora   clothes dryer   **la videocasetera**   VCR

Note the following information about the use of these terms in Spanish.

- The names of most rooms of a house are the same throughout the majority of the Spanish-speaking world. The word for *bedroom* does vary widely, however. The following terms may be used: **la alcoba** (Spain), **el cuarto** (used in Puerto Rico and in several other countries), **el dormitorio** (very widely used), **la recámara** (Mexico). **La habitación** is also used to mean *bedroom*, but for many native speakers of Spanish this term means only a hotel room.

- The feminine terms **la radio** and **la televisión** refer to the media. Thus one can say: **Me gusta mirar la tele(visión) y me gusta escuchar la radio**. The masculine nouns **el radio** and **el televisor** refer to the actual radio or TV set. Not all speakers of Spanish use these terms consistently, however.

Apartamento Moderno
****
Sala/Comedor Aparte
Patio
Amplia cocina completa
Dos cuartos
Baño

a.

Se Alquila Apartamento
_____
2° Piso
Sala Grande, Comedor
Balcón/Terraza con vista al mar
Cocina completa
Dos cuartos
Tres baños

b.

Actividad A.   ¿Qué decide Ángela?

Listen again as Ángela, Raquel, and Blanca, the realtor, discuss the features of one of the apartments that Ángela is considering. Then indicate which of these two advertisements corresponds to the apartment. Take a few seconds now to scan both of them. As you listen to the conversation, you may want to check off features in the advertisements as you hear them, noting the number of each and any other factors, as appropriate.

Actividad B.   ¿Qué tiene el *Town House*?

Paso 1

Listen to the same three characters as they walk through the town house. Use the advertisement you didn't select in **Actividad A** to keep track of the features.

Paso 2

Now compare the features of the apartment (**Actividad A**) and the town house (this activity) by indicating whether the following statements are true (**Cierto**), false (**Falso**), or unable to be determined (**No se sabe**).

C   F   NSS   1. El apartamento tiene una vista hermosa al mar, el *town house* no.
C   F   NSS   2. Los dos tienen tres baños.
C   F   NSS   3. Los dos tienen estacionamiento.
C   F   NSS   4. Los dos tienen lavaplatos.
C   F   NSS   5. Los dos son de dos pisos.
C   F   NSS   6. La cocina del *town house* es más grande.
C   F   NSS   7. La sala y el comedor están juntos en el *town house*.
C   F   NSS   8. La estufa y la nevera son nuevas en los dos.

Actividad C.   ¿Dónde se encuentran?

Form sentences that describe where the following appliances are generally found—or not found.

Nunca		una estufa		un cuarto
Casi nunca		una nevera		una sala
Frecuentemente	se encuentra	un televisor	en	una cocina
Casi siempre		un teléfono		un balcón
Siempre		una lavadora		el garaje
		un estéreo		un baño

Actividad D.   ¿Y tú?

Describe where you live now and what you would like a future dwelling to contain. Follow these models.

MODELOS: Vivo ahora en un(a) _casa_. Tiene _tres cuartos_,

y _dos baños_, ... Los _cuartos_ (no) son grandes.

También tiene _una comedor_. No tiene _el garaje_.

El/La _casa_ (no) es moderno/a.

Me gustaría vivir en un(a) _casa_ con

una cocina larga. Debería (*It should*) tener _una vista hermosa_,

a la mountains, ... Si no tiene _un televisor_, eso no me

importa.

Nota cultural: Vivo en el segundo piso

Just as in the United States, a wide range of types of housing is available in the Spanish-speaking world. In large cities the most common type of housing is an apartment or condominium, often in a high-rise building. An option available depending on the country is a separate house (generally called **una casa** but also called **un chalet** in Spain). Of the dwellings you have seen so far, Teresa Suárez's apartment best typifies middle-class housing. Héctor's apartment (seen only from the outside) is typical of people of more modest means.

The apartments Ángela looks at in this video episode, while luxurious by some standards, are relatively typical of modern apartments in most parts of the world. Note that Ángela and the agent use the term *town house*; in other parts of the Spanish-speaking world **el condominio** or **la casa adosada** would probably be used.

Something that is quite different about Hispanic buildings is the way the floors are numbered. The ground floor is generally **la planta baja**. The next floor up (the second floor in the United States) is **el primer piso**; the next floor (the third floor in this country) is **el segundo piso**; and so on. (This usage does not occur in Puerto Rico.)

Look at this floor plan. Is it for the first floor (**la planta baja**) or the second floor (**el primer piso**)? How do you know?

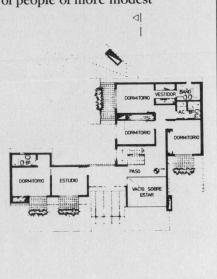

Un poco de gramática

Describing What Someone Was Doing

To describe what someone was doing at a given moment, use the imperfect of **estar** + the **-ndo** form of the verb.

Arturo **estaba hablando** con Raquel por teléfono.	*Arturo was talking on the phone with Raquel.*
Ángela, Raquel y la agente **estaban mirando** un apartamento.	*Ángela, Raquel, and the agent were looking at an apartment.*

This construction is called the past progressive. Like the present progressive, it places special emphasis on the ongoing nature of the action. You will learn more about these forms in the Workbook.

Actividad.   En este momento...

Think about the characters you saw at the end of **Episodio 23**. What were they doing? And what about the characters who were *not* shown at the end? What were *they* doing? Answer these questions by creating complete sentences with a word or phrase from each column. ¡OJO! More than one ending may be appropriate for some characters. First, listen to the list of endings.

1. Raquel	estaba	pensando en Raquel
2. Mercedes y Ramón	estaban	haciendo los preparativos para un viaje
3. Pedro		buscando la música que escuchó de repente
4. Jorge Alonso		abrazándose (*hugging each other*)
5. Arturo		leyendo una carta que le mandó Raquel
6. Laura, la prima de Ángela		comiendo—¡siempre tiene hambre!
7. Roberto		visitando a su padre en el hospital
8. Ángela		trabajando en una excavación
9. don Fernando		pensando en algo que le sorprendió mucho
10. Ángela y Jorge		pensando en sus «nuevos» nietos
		besando a su novia

Nota cultural: Los puertorriqueños en los Estados Unidos

In **Episodio 23** you learned about Puerto Ricans who live in the continental United States. Before you read this passage, refresh your memory about them by listening again to the narrator.

Los puertorriqueños forman uno de los grandes grupos de hispanos que viven en los Estados Unidos continentales. Son más de dos millones. Viven sobre todo en la costa este, principalmente en las zonas metropolitanas de Nueva York, Connecticut, Nueva Jersey y Pensilvania.

Personas y personajes

Después de la Segunda Guerra mundial y junto con[1] la expansión económica de los Estados Unidos en esa época, los puertorriqueños llegaron al continente en gran número en busca de trabajo y de oportunidades para una vida mejor. En los últimos años, muchos de ellos han decidido[2] volver a la Isla, por varias razones. Pero hay también muchos que se quedan a vivir en el

[1] junto... *together with*   [2] han... *have decided*

continente, y ellos, junto con la segunda y la tercera generaciones, forman parte integral de la economía y cultura de muchos estados. Muchos son bilingües y biculturales.

Muchos puertorriqueños hasta han encontrado[3] la fama en los Estados Unidos. ¿Puedes identificar a los siguientes puertorriqueños del pasado y del presente?

Marta Istomín	cantante[4] y guitarrista
José Ferrer y Raúl Julia	jugador de béisbol que murió
Piri Thomas	trágicamente en un accidente de
Rita Moreno	aviación
Roberto Clemente	solista de la Ópera Metropolitana
José Feliciano	de Nueva York
Justino Díaz	actores
	exdirectora del John F. Kennedy
	Center for the Performing Arts
	escritor

La situación política

Puerto Rico es un Estado Libre Asociado de los Estados Unidos, y los puertorriqueños son ciudadanos[5] estadounidenses desde 1917. Como tal[6] pueden ir y venir sin restricciones. Pero si viven en la Isla, no tienen derecho al voto en las elecciones presidenciales. (En cambio, sí pueden votar si residen en el continente.) Puerto Rico tiene representantes en el Congreso estadounidense—se les llama *resident commissioners*—pero con poder[7] limitado ya que tienen voz pero no voto.

En la actualidad, muchos puertorriqueños quieren que Puerto Rico se incorpore a los Estados Unidos como el estado número cincuenta y uno. Algunos prefieren que se independice. Otros desean que se mantenga el *status quo*.

[3]han... *have found*   [4]*singer*   [5]*citizens*   [6]Como... *As such (As citizens)*   [7]*power*

Actividad.   Opiniones

Answer the following questions about the Puerto Rican experience to the best of your knowledge.

1. Los puertorriqueños son ciudadanos de los Estados Unidos, pero se puede decir que su ciudadanía es «limitada». ¿En qué sentido es «limitada»?
2. Como sabes, muchos puertorriqueños llegan a los Estados Unidos continentales para vivir. Según lo que sabes de sus motivos, ¿con qué otros grupos los asocias? Explica tus respuestas.
   a.   con los peregrinos (*pilgrims*)
   b.   con los irlandeses del siglo XIX y del comienzo del siglo XX
   c.   con los vietnameses de los años ochenta
   d.   ¿——?

Have you completed the following sections of the lesson? Check them off here.

_____ **Preparación**
_____ **¿Tienes buena memoria?**

_____ **Vocabulario del tema**
_____ **Un poco de gramática**

Now scan the words in the **Vocabulario** list to be sure that you understand the meaning of most of them. Then you will be ready to continue on with **Lección 23** in the Workbook.

VOCABULARIO

Las partes de una casa
(Parts of a House)

el balcón	balcony
el baño	bathroom
la cocina	kitchen
el comedor	dining room
el cuarto	bedroom
el estacionamiento	parking
el jardín	garden
el patio	patio
el piso	floor
la planta baja	ground floor
la sala	living room
la terraza	terrace
la ventana	window
la vista (a)	view (of)

Repaso: **las escaleras, la habitación, la puerta**

Algunos aparatos domésticos
(Some Domestic Appliances)

el estéreo	stereo
la estufa	stove
el horno (de microondas)	(microwave) oven
la lavadora	clothes washer
el lavaplatos	dishwasher
la nevera	refrigerator
el radio	radio
la secadora	clothes dryer
el televisor	television set
la videocasetera	VCR

Las personas

el/la jefe/a	boss

24

EL DON JUAN*

OBJETIVOS

The materials in **Lección 24** of the Textbook and the Workbook will help you better understand the video episode and take you beyond it, giving you additional information about places and characters in the series. The Textbook will also help you to develop skill in using the Spanish language. In this lesson, you will learn

- vocabulary for talking about people's personality traits, both positive and negative
- some ways to express strong reactions, both positive and negative
- more ways to use the preterite.

You will also learn about a number of Puerto Rican musicians, artists, and literary figures.

Be sure to work through all parts of the lesson. When you see a cassette symbol in the margin, listen to the tape for **Lección 24**. Answers or hints for many activities are given in Appendix 1. Be sure to check your answers for each activity before going on to the next one.

* *The Don Juan*

BEFORE VIEWING...

PREPARACIÓN

Actividad A.

Here is the text of the summary of **Episodio 23** which you will hear at the beginning of this video episode. But some of the details have been changed. Read through the text and correct as many details as you can.

Hint: There are three incorrect details in each paragraph.

Al final de su estancia en San Germán, la abuela doña Carmen le da a Ángela un objeto muy especial... un regalo de su madre. Desde el hotel, Raquel manda un telegrama a Buenos Aires. Le cuenta a Arturo que Ángel ya murió... y que Ángel tenía dos hijas.

Ángela y Raquel hablan con la supervisora de la tienda donde Ángela trabaja. Le pide dos meses libres para ir a México a visitar a su abuelo, don Fernando. Don Fernando está muy enfermo y Ángela le explica a la supervisora que don Fernando va a enfadarse.

Raquel y Ángela hacen los preparativos para salir mañana para Los Ángeles. Luego van a la universidad para ver a Jorge, el hermano de Ángela. En un patio de la universidad, Ángela y Jorge hablan del viaje.

Now listen to the narration on the cassette tape to discover whether you found all of the incorrect information.

Para pensar...

Piensa en el título de este episodio. ¿Qué es un «don Juan»? ¿A quién se podría referir este nombre en este episodio?

Una palabra importante que vas a oír en este episodio es **mujeriego** (*womanizer*). ¿Hay un hombre mujeriego en este episodio?

Actividad B.

Listen to the following conversation between Ángela, Raquel, and Jorge on the cassette tape. Then answer the question about it. A written version of the conversation is provided to help you understand it.

JORGE: ¿Por qué no nos vamos a vivir a Nueva York?

ÁNGELA: No, gracias. Me gusta visitar esa ciudad, pero ¿vivir? No. Además, ¿no vas a formar una compañía de teatro acá en San Juan?

JORGE: Hay en San Juan un cine¹ que puede funcionar como teatro.

RAQUEL: Tiene que ser caro.²

JORGE: Sí, lo es. Pero es el mejor sitio. Perdónenme. Voy a cambiarme.

¹*movie theater* ²*expensive*

Piensa bien en lo que (*what*) Jorge quiere hacer, porque esto va a provocar un conflicto. ¿Cuál podría (*could*) ser el conflicto?

a. _____ Ángela cree que la idea de Jorge no es buena. Por eso pelean (*they quarrel*).

b. _____ Jorge le pide consejos sobre asuntos legales a Raquel, pero ella se niega a (*refuses to*) dárselos.

c. _____ Ángela quiere ayudarle a Jorge, pero Raquel cree que no es una buena idea.

▬ AFTER VIEWING...

. . . .

¿TIENES BUENA MEMORIA?

Actividad.   Las preguntas de Raquel

As usual, Raquel recapped the most important moments of the video episode in her review at the end of the show. Here is a series of statements based on her review. Can you complete them with a few essential details? Your answers need not be long or involved.

a. viajar a México en unos días

b. tutearla

c. Jorge las esperaba

d. estaba muy contento

e. lo esperaba un estudiante

f. el novio de Ángela

g. un don Juan

h. nadaban

i. hacía llamadas

j. se enojó con Raquel

1. Raquel fue con Ángela a la universidad para conocer a Jorge, el novio de Ángela. Para Raquel, fue una sorpresa cuando Jorge empezó a _____.

2. Por sus acciones, Raquel creía que Jorge era _____.

3. Cuando Ángela quería llevar a Raquel al museo de Oller, Jorge no quería acompañarlas porque _____.

4. Las dos mujeres vieron la colección de obras de Oller. _____ cuando salieron del museo. Todos fueron a unas tiendas cerca de la universidad, donde Raquel compró unos cassettes.

5. En el hotel, Jorge y Ángela _____ mientras Raquel _____. Habló con su madre y con Arturo.

6. Con su madre, Raquel habló sobre _____. Según su madre, Raquel no debe meterse (*get involved*) en la vida personal de otras personas. Efectivamente, cuando Raquel trató de hablar con Ángela, ésta (*the latter*) _____.

7. Con Arturo Raquel tuvo una conversación agradable porque Arturo _____. Raquel también se alegra, porque Arturo va a _____.

Now listen to Raquel's review and compare your answers with what she says.

Nota cultural: Más sobre la comida

In **Episodio 21**, on the road to San Germán, Ángela stopped the car to buy snacks at a small roadside store. Laura wanted **un pilón** (also called **un pirulí**), a fruit-based lollipop with seeds. Another popular Puerto Rican snack purchased by the characters in this video episode is **una piragua** (called a Sno Cone in parts of the United States), a small cone filled with chipped ice which is then flavored with a fruit syrup. Raquel and Ángela preferred **una piragua de frambuesa** (*raspberry*), while Jorge asked for **una piragua de tamarindo**, a tropical fruit popular in the Caribbean. Although Sno Cones are machine-made in the continental United States, in Puerto Rico **piragüeros** make them by hand and sell them from carts on the street.

Snack foods and treats are consumed all over the Spanish-speaking world and some places are famous for a particular food. Influenced by Italian culture, **heladerías** (*ice cream shops*) can be found on any street in Argentina, especially in Buenos Aires. In Spain **helados** of many kinds are also quite popular as a snack food, as are **patatas fritas** (*potato chips*). In Mexico street vendors routinely sell **chicle** (*chewing gum*) and **dulces** (*candy*) as well as **tacos.**

VOCABULARIO DEL TEMA

Para describir la personalidad

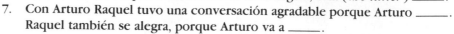

agresivo/a	aggressive	**desagradable**	disagreeable
alegre	happy	**desconfiado/a**	suspicious
cariñoso/a	affectionate	**egoísta**	selfish, egotistical
confiado/a	confident	**encantador(a)**	charming
chistoso/a	funny	**femenino/a**	feminine

grosero/a	crude, brutish	**optimista**	optimistic	
gruñón/	grouchy, irritable	**pesimista**	pessimistic	
gruñona		**sabio/a**	wise	
ingenuo/a	naïve, ingenuous	**simpático/a**	nice	
inocente	innocent	**terco/a**	stubborn	
macho	manly, macho	**trabajador(a)**	hard-working	
mujeriego	womanizer,	**triste**	sad	
	a "don Juan" type			

You already know some of the preceding adjectives that describe people, and others are easy-to-learn cognates. Is an adjective that you often use to describe people missing from the list? Ask your instructor how to say it in Spanish or look it up in a dictionary. Think in particular about words that you need to describe family and friends.

If you are describing someone's personality, use **ser** with these adjectives: **Arturo es encantador**. You can also say the following: **Esta persona es encantadora. Arturo es una persona encantadora.***

Actividad A.   ¿A quién se describe? (Parte 1)

Listen as the speaker on the cassette tape describes one quality of each of the following characters from *Destinos*. Identify the person referred to, following the model. You will hear a possible answer on the tape. ¡OJO! More than one person may be correct for some items.

> MODELO: (*you hear*)   Esta persona es trabajadora.
> (*you say*)   Es Raquel.
> (*you hear*)   Raquel es trabajadora.

Raquel Rodríguez   Jorge Alonso
Ángela Castillo   Arturo Iglesias
la tía Olga   Laura, la prima de Ángela
doña Carmen

1. ...   2. ...   3. ...   4. ...   5. ...   6. ...   7. ...   8. ...   9. ...   10. ...

Actividad B.   ¿A quién se describe? (Parte 2)

You will hear some additional descriptions of characters from *Destinos*, but this time the descriptions will be longer. Identify the person you think is being described.

1. ...   2. ...   3. ...   4. ...   5. ...   6. ...

---

*In these sentences the adjective is feminine because it agrees with the noun **persona**, even though Arturo is the person described.

Actividad C.   ¿Cómo son?

What can you say about the following movie, TV, literary, and political personalities? Describe each of them as fully as you can. Then choose at least two well-known personalities and describe them.

> MODELO: Lucy → Lucy es una persona muy inocente y alegre. Su esposo Desi es un poco macho a veces. Sus aventuras con Ethel son siempre chistosas.

1. Madonna
2. Ted Danson (Sam Malone en «Cheers»)
3. Romeo y Julieta
4. Miss Piggy y Kermit la Rana
5. Scarlett O'Hara y Rhett Butler
6. el presidente (el vicepresidente) de los Estados Unidos
7. Cleopatra
8. Cristóbal Colón
9. ¿   ?

Actividad D.   ¿Y tú?

Now select at least one family member and a good friend, and describe them. Try to describe them as much as you can in general terms as well as give interesting details about their personality.

> MODELO: Mi _____ es _____, _____ y
>
> _____. Tiene _____ años y vive en/con
>
> _____. Le gusta(n) _____, pero no le
>
> gusta(n) nada _____.

. . . .

CONVERSACIONES: LAS REACCIONES

Actividad.   ¡Ay de mí!

Throughout the previous video episodes of *Destinos* you have heard many characters use a number of typical expressions: **¡Ay!**, **¡Ay de mí!**, **¡Caramba!**, and so on. In this section you will learn additional expressions to use when reacting to what others have said or done.

Paso 1

Of all of the *Destinos* characters you have met so far, Ángela is one of the most expressive. In particular, she uses **¡Ay!** with great frequency.

Listen again to two brief exchanges that feature Ángela and indicate the reaction you hear in each.

a. _____ ¡Dios mío!   b. _____ ¡Por Dios!   c. _____ ¡Qué desastre!

d. _____ ¡Caray!

Paso 2

Another expression that is frequently used to express positive or negative reactions consists of **¡qué...** plus a noun, adverb, or adjective. The word **qué** appears in other types of expressions as well.*

Now listen to three additional brief exchanges. There is an expression with **qué** in each of them. Indicate the expression you hear.

1. _____   2. _____   3. _____

The meaning of the first expression you heard should be obvious to you. Of the other two, which do you think means "Come on. You can't put that one over on me . . . "? If you chose the second, you were correct. The remaining expression, loosely translated, means "So?" or "What does that have to do with anything?"

Paso 3

Can you invent **¡qué** plus noun or adjective expressions to use in these situations? The masculine form of the adjective is used: **¡Qué bueno/estupendo... !**

- A friend has just explained an innovative theory of the creation of the universe to you.
- You have just heard about a terrible plane crash.
- A friend has just won a big prize in the lottery.

UN POCO DE GRAMÁTICA

Additional Uses of Some Preterite Forms

Use the preterite forms of **saber** (**supe**, **supiste...**) to describe the moment when someone learned or found out something.

Al final de este episodio, Ángela **supo** que hubo un accidente en la excavación.	*At the end of this episode Ángela found out that there was an accident at the excavation site.*

Use the preterite forms of **conocer** (**conocí**, **conociste...**) to indicate that someone met someone else for the first time.

En San Juan Raquel **conoció** a Ángela Castillo.	*Raquel met Ángela Castillo in San Juan.*

You will learn more about these uses of the preterite in the Workbook.

---

*Remember that the word **¿qué?** is generally *not* used in Spanish to ask "What? What do you mean?" The word **¿cómo?** is generally used in that case.

Actividad.   ¿Dónde estaban? ¿Qué hacían?

Where were these people when the following events happened? And what were they doing? Answer the questions as fully as you can.

1. ¿Dónde estaba Raquel y qué hacía cuando
   a. conoció a Ángela?
   b. conoció a Arturo?
   c. conoció a Jorge?

2. ¿Dónde estaba Raquel y qué hacía cuando
   a. supo que Ángela tenía un hermano?
   b. supo que Ángel estaba muerto?
   c. supo que Jorge era un mujeriego?

3. ¿Dónde estaba Ángela y qué hacía cuando
   a. supo que su padre tenía familia en la Argentina?
   b. supo que su padre siempre añoraba a su familia?
   c. supo que Raquel se oponía a la idea del teatro de Jorge?

Nota cultural: El arte y la música en Puerto Rico

Throughout the Puerto Rican video episodes of *Destinos* you have caught glimpses of various aspects of the island's culture: popular and serious music, Jorge's interest in the theater, and works by a famous painter. The following reading will tell you more about music and the arts in Puerto Rico. Before you begin reading, listen again to Ángela's description of **El velorio** (*The Wake*) by Francisco Oller, as you look at this reproduction of it.

El mundo del arte

En Puerto Rico, Ángel Castillo encontró su verdadera inspiración como pintor. Lo inspiraba el colorido de la Isla, sus paisajes,[1] su gente… y sobre todo el mar. Pero eso pasó en la telenovela. En la realidad, el pintor puertorriqueño más famoso de todos es Oller.

Francisco Oller (1833–1917) fue uno de los primeros pintores americanos que se inspiró en el impresionismo francés. Estudió varios años en Madrid y París. Allí tuvo la oportunidad de conocer a pintores como Cézanne y Pissarro, quienes ejercieron gran influencia en su pintura. De regreso a Puerto Rico, Oller estableció la Academia Libre de Dibujo[2] y Pintura en 1868. Su obra incluye retratos, paisajes y naturalezas muertas.[3] A partir de 1884 abandonó la técnica

El velorio de Francisco Oller

[1] *landscapes* [2] *Drawing* [3] naturalezas… *still lifes*

impresionista y se dedicó a la creación de un arte de Puerto Rico para los puertorriqueños. Se inspiró mucho en escenas de la cultura popular, como se ve en *El velorio.*

El mundo musical

Así como otras artes, la música ha sido[4] siempre muy importante en la vida de los puertorriqueños. Los elementos africanos se mezclaron[5] con los hispánicos y los autóctonos[6] para crear una gran variedad de estilos populares. En los últimos años, «la salsa», derivada de la vieja rumba, se ha convertido en el ritmo más representativo de Puerto Rico y del Caribe en general. El cantante de salsa va acompañado por un coro, piano, bajo[7] y varios instrumentos de percusión. La salsa ha contagiado a medio mundo[8] con su cálido[9] ritmo.

Al mismo tiempo, la música clásica tiene mucha importancia en la Isla, especialmente debido a la figura de Pablo Casals. Considerado uno de los mejores violoncelistas del mundo, Casals nació en Cataluña en 1876. Organizó un Festival de música en Francia, país en donde se exilió después de la Guerra Civil española. En 1957 trasladó[10] la celebración del Festival, y su residencia, a la tierra natal de su madre, Puerto Rico. En la Isla, desarrolló[11] una gran actividad musical. Murió en Río Piedras en 1973, a los noventa y siete años.

Todos los años, durante el mes de junio, el Festival Casals de Puerto Rico ofrece las interpretaciones musicales de los mejores virtuosos. Este Festival es, sin duda, uno de los acontecimientos[12] más importantes del mundo para los amantes de la música clásica.

El mundo literario

En cuanto a la literatura, un tema que les ha interesado a varios escritores es el de la identidad puertorriqueña. Entre los escritores puertorriqueños que escriben o escribieron en la Isla y en el continente, se destacan[13] especialmente dos.

- Julia de Burgos (1914–1953), poeta que escribió obras sobre su identidad como mujer y la identidad de Puerto Rico como país.
- René Marqués (1911–1979), autor de teatro contemporáneo que se preocupó por la identidad puertorriqueña en relación con los Estados Unidos.

[4]ha... *has been* [5]se... *mixed* [6]los... *native ones* [7]*bass* [8]medio... *half the world* [9]*hot* [10]*he moved* [11]*he developed*
[12]*events* [13]se... *stand out*

Actividad.   ¿Probable o improbable?

Indica la oración que consideras más probable.

1. _____ Las obras de Oller son realistas.
   _____ Las obras de Oller son cubistas, como las de Picasso.
2. _____ La música de la salsa es buena para bailar.
   _____ La música de la salsa es buena para escuchar solamente.
3. _____ Julia de Burgos era una mujer muy tradicional.
   _____ Julia de Burgos tenía ideas feministas.

Have you completed the following sections of the lesson? Check them off here.

_____ **Preparación**	_____ **Conversaciones**
_____ **¿Tienes buena memoria?**	_____ **Un poco de gramática**
_____ **Vocabulario del tema**	

Now scan the words in the **Vocabulario** list to be sure that you understand the meaning of most of them. Then you will be ready to continue on with **Lección 24** in the Workbook.

• •

VOCABULARIO

Los verbos

comunicarse (con)	to get in touch, contact (with)
meterse (en)	to get involved (with, in)
nadar	to swim
oponerse (a)	to oppose

Para describir la personalidad
(To Describe Personality)

agresivo/a	aggressive
confiado/a	confident
chistoso/a	funny
desagradable	disagreeable
desconfiado/a	suspicious
egoísta	selfish, egotistical
encantador(a)	charming
femenino/a	feminine
grosero/a	crude, brutish
gruñón/ gruñona	grouchy, irritable
ingenuo/a	naïve, ingenuous
inocente	innocent
macho	manly, macho
mujeriego	womanizer, a "don Juan" type
optimista	optimistic
pesimista	pessimistic
sabio/a	wise
terco/a	stubborn
trabajador(a)	hard-working

Repaso: **alegre, cariñoso/a, simpático/a, triste**

Las reacciones (Reactions)

¡Caray!	Damn!
¡Dios mío!	My God!
¡Qué + noun/adjective/adverb!	What (a) . . . !/ How . . . !
¡Qué va!	Don't put me on!
¿Y qué?	So what? What do you want me to do?

25

REFLEXIONES I*

OBJETIVOS

This video episode is a review. Be sure to work through all parts of the lesson. When you see a cassette symbol in the margin, listen to the tape for **Lección 25**. Answers or hints for many activities are given in Appendix 1. Be sure to check your answers for each activity before going on to the next one.

*Reflections I

BEFORE VIEWING...

PREPARACIÓN

Actividad.

All of the following events happened in **Episodio 24**, but in a different order. Read through all of the statements, then put them in order from 1 to 5.

a. _____ Raquel, Ángela y Jorge hicieron unas compras en Río Piedras.

b. _____ Jorge y Ángela nadaban mientras Raquel hablaba por teléfono.

c. _____ Ángela y Raquel recibieron malas noticias.

d. _____ Raquel habló con Jorge, pero él no le cayó bien (*she didn't like him*).

e. _____ Raquel tenía una discusión muy fuerte (*nasty*) con Ángela.

Now listen to the review of **Episodio 24** that you will hear at the beginning of this video episode and check your answers. You will hear more information in the review than is given in the statements, so you will need to listen carefully.

Para pensar...

Las noticias sobre Roberto dejan a Raquel en *shock*. En ese trance (*condition*), comienza a recordar y reflexionar sobre su difícil investigación. ¿Qué acontecimientos (*events*) de su investigación recuerda? ¿Cuáles son los acontecimientos más importantes desde su salida de México hasta su llegada a Puerto Rico?

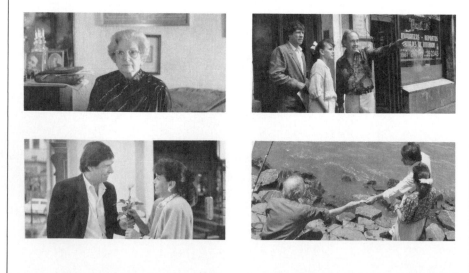

 **AFTER VIEWING . . .**

¿TIENES BUENA MEMORIA?

Actividad.   ¿Lo recuerda o no?

All of the following events have happened so far during Raquel's investigation, but did Raquel remember them as she thought back over the last few weeks? Indicate whether the following events were part of the review in **Episodio 25** (**Sí**) or not (**No**).

Sí   No   1. Raquel conoció a la familia de la persona que le escribió la carta a don Fernando.

Sí   No   2. Jaime y su perro se perdieron en las calles de Sevilla.

Sí   No   3. Raquel viajó a Madrid en tren.

Sí   No   4. Conoció a Teresa Suárez y habló con ella sobre Rosario.

Sí   No   5. En la Argentina, visitó una hacienda y conoció a un gaucho.

Sí   No   6. Supo que Rosario ya murió pero conoció a otro hijo de ella.

Sí   No   7. Pasó mucho tiempo con Arturo buscando a Ángel, el hijo de Rosario y don Fernando.

Sí   No   8. Raquel y Arturo se besaron por primera vez.

Sí   No   9. Héctor les dijo que Ángel se fue a vivir a Puerto Rico.

Sí   No   10. Arturo prometió ir a Puerto Rico para seguir la búsqueda.

REPASO DE LOS EPISODIOS 1–18

Actividad A.   Raquel habla con Teresa Suárez

You have now seen and heard several times the important conversation that takes place between Raquel and Teresa Suárez. It should be easier for you to understand most of it now. Here is part of the conversation, with all but the first of Teresa Suárez's lines missing. Complete the conversation with the appropriate lines from the list of possibilities on page 254.

RAQUEL: En su carta Ud. le dice que Rosario no murió en la guerra.

TERESA: Es verdad. Rosario no murió. _____.[1]

RAQUEL: Ay…

TERESA: _____.[2]

RAQUEL: También en su carta Ud. le dice que Rosario tuvo un hijo.

TERESA: _____.[3]

RAQUEL: ¿Y qué nombre le puso?

TERESA: _____ .[4]

RAQUEL: ¿Y dónde nació Ángel?

TERESA: _____ .[5]

RAQUEL: ¿Y dónde vive Rosario ahora?

TERESA: _____ .[6]

RAQUEL: ¿A la Argentina?

TERESA: _____ .[7]

RAQUEL: ¿Y sabe dónde se estableció Rosario?

TERESA: _____ .[8]

RAQUEL: ¿Se casó de nuevo?

TERESA: _____ .[9]

RAQUEL: Sí, sí. Lo comprendo. ¿Y con quién se casó?

TERESA: _____ .[10]

a. Después de la guerra se fue a vivir a la Argentina.
b. Sí. Todo este asunto es muy triste.
c. Ángel... Ángel Castillo.
d. Sí, sí. Como Ud. sabe, muchos españoles salieron del país después de la guerra.
e. Pues sí. Rosario era muy atractiva... muy simpática. Y como ella creía que Fernando había muerto...
f. Gracias a Dios, escapó de esa tragedia... pero ella creía que Fernando había muerto.
g. Muy cerca de Buenos Aires. La última carta que recibí de ella fue cuando se casó de nuevo.
h. Con un hacendado... un argentino llamado Martín Iglesias.
i. Sí.
j. En Sevilla, claro. Es allí donde conocí a Rosario.

Actividad B.   La búsqueda en la Argentina

In Argentina Raquel meets Arturo and the two search for Ángel, Arturo's half brother and the son of Rosario and don Fernando. Together they find Héctor Condotti, who once knew Ángel and who has some important information about him. The following narration about their meeting with Héctor contains some false information. Indicate the information you think is incorrect.
Hint: There are one or two incorrect details in each paragraph.

Después de conocer a Héctor en el Piccolo Navio, Raquel y Arturo lo acompañaron a su casa. En la calle le mostraron a Héctor un cuadro de Ángel y le preguntaron si conocía al artista. «Ángel», respondió Héctor. «Claro que lo recuerdo bien. Era mi amigo.»

En el camino, empezaron a hablar de Ángel. Cuando llegaron a la casa de Héctor, él los invitó a entrar. Héctor les dijo que creía que Ángel consiguió trabajo en un barco. En ese momento, su esposa lo llamó y Héctor subió a su apartamento.

Arturo y Raquel ya se iban, pero Héctor volvió con una foto de Ángel que le dio a Arturo. Muy conmovido,[1] Arturo le dio las gracias. Héctor también les dijo que creía que Ángel se quedó a vivir en el extranjero. No estaba seguro, pero creía que era en España.

Luego recordó una tarjeta postal que había recibido[2] de Ángel. Ésta debería[3] indicar la dirección de Ángel. Entonces Raquel y Arturo se fueron. Esa noche, los dos estaban muy pensativos, especialmente Arturo.

[1]*emotionally moved* [2]había... *he had received* [3]*would surely*

Now listen to the corrected narration on the cassette tape and see whether you found all of the incorrect information.

Actividad C.   «Hay que dedicarle tiempo al corazón.»

During Raquel's stay in Argentina, she and Arturo begin to feel a strong attraction for each other. But Raquel must leave Buenos Aires to continue the search for Ángel. They begin to say their good-byes on a pier, after receiving Ángel's letter from Héctor. Complete their conversation with items from the lists.

Verbos: decir, dejar, estar, extrañar, me gustaría, recordar, te gustaría
Sustantivos: la búsqueda, el extranjero, el tiempo, el trabajo, el primer vuelo
Adjetivos: muy bien, muy mal, regular
El tiempo: muchos años, unas semanas, unos pocos días

ARTURO: ¿Ya decidiste cuándo te vas a ir?

RAQUEL: Debería tomar _____.[1] Don Fernando está _____.[2]

Y no puedo tardarme mucho.

ARTURO: Hace _____[3] que te conozco... y parece como si hiciera[a]

_____.[4]

RAQUEL: Yo siento lo mismo.

ARTURO: Te voy a _____.[5]

RAQUEL: Yo también a ti.

ARTURO: Aunque... tal vez...

[a]como... *as if it had been*

RAQUEL: ¿Tal vez?

ARTURO: Tal vez... yo podría ir a Puerto Rico, y los dos continuar

_____⁶ de Ángel.

RAQUEL: ¿Quieres decir que iríasᵇ a Puerto Rico?

ARTURO: ¿_____⁷?

RAQUEL: ¡Claro que sí! Mucho. Pero, ¿tú puedes?

ARTURO: Creo que sí.

RAQUEL: ¿Y tu _____⁸? ¿tus pacientes?

ARTURO: Bueno, no sería fácil _____⁹ todo. Pero... yo quiero ir.

ᵇ*you would go*

Have you completed the following sections of the lesson? Check them off here.

_____ **Preparación**   _____ **Repaso de los episodios 1–18**
_____ **¿Tienes buena memoria?**

You are now ready to continue on with **Lección 25** in the Workbook.

26

REFLEXIONES II*

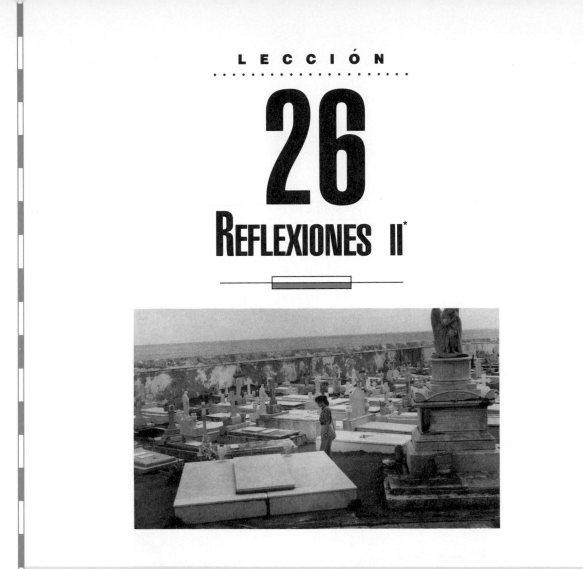

OBJETIVOS

This video episode is a review. Be sure to work through all parts of the lesson. When you see a cassette symbol in the margin, listen to the tape for **Lección 26**. Answers or hints for many activities are given in Appendix 1. Be sure to check your answers for each activity before going on to the next one.

Reflections II

BEFORE VIEWING . . .

PREPARACIÓN

Actividad.

Look at the following photographs of people Raquel met or heard about in Puerto Rico and match the photos with the names given. Then read the statements that accompany them and indicate which is correct. Then add one true statement of your own about the character. Your statement can be factual or it can be your own opinion about the character.

a. Jorge Alonso
b. los tíos de Ángela y Roberto
c. doña Carmen

d. Ángel, con su esposa y suegra
e. Ángela Castillo
f. Roberto Castillo

1. Es _____ .

   a. Es una joven tranquila que sigue siempre lo que le dice la razón (*reason*).
   b. Es una joven impaciente e ingenua... y muy enamorada.
   c. ¿ ?

1.

2. Es _____ .

   a. Su opinión es muy importante para Ángela... y para los otros parientes también.
   b. Nadie en la familia le hace mucho caso (*pays much attention to her*).
   c. ¿ ?

2.

3. Es _____ .

   a. Como en el estereotipo, este yerno no se llevó muy bien con su suegra.
   b. Este yerno era el hijo favorito de su suegra.
   c. ¿ ?

3.

4. Son _____ .

   a. Están ayudando a Ángela en esta época importante y difícil de su vida.
   b. No les importa la vida de Ángela en este momento.
   c. ¿ ?

4.

5. Es _____ .

   a. Estudia comercio y trabaja en un banco en México.
   b. Estudia arqueología y trabaja en una excavación en México.
   c. ¿ ?

5.

6. Es _____.

   a. Este hombre le gusta mucho a Raquel... tanto que casi no piensa más en Arturo.

   b. Raquel le gusta mucho a él, pero él no le cae muy bien a ella (*she doesn't like him very much*).

   c. ¿ ?

6.

AFTER VIEWING . . .

. . . .

¿TIENES BUENA MEMORIA?

Actividad.   ¿A quiénes conoció Raquel?

Complete the following paragraphs with the names of people Raquel met or heard about while in Puerto Rico.

Raquel conoció a _____¹ en el cementerio donde estaban enterrados Ángel y su esposa. Más tarde conoció a los cuñados de Ángel, incluyendo a la tía _____.² Ésta[a] no reaccionó bien al oír que su sobrina tenía otro abuelo en México.

   Raquel fue con Ángela y su prima _____³ a San Germán a ver a su abuela, doña _____.⁴ Al volver a San Juan, Ángela le presentó a Raquel a su novio, _____,⁵ quien acababa de regresar de Nueva York.

   Cuando estaban por salir para el aeropuerto Ángela y Raquel, el tío _____⁶ vino a darle a su sobrina unas malas noticias. Su hermano _____⁷ había tenido[b] un accidente en México.

[a]*The latter* [b]había... *had had*

Now listen to the paragraphs on the cassette tape and check your answers.

. . . .

REPASO DE LOS EPISODIOS 19–24

Actividad A.   ¿En qué orden?

All of the following events took place in **Episodios 19–24**, but in what order did they occur? Put them in order, from 1 to 13.

a. _____ En San Germán, doña Carmen le dio a Ángela una idea.

b. _____ Una vecina le dijo a Raquel: «Ángel Castillo murió hace poco.»

c. _____ Raquel y Ángela tenían que ir a San Germán.

d. _____ Doña Carmen también le dio a Ángela algo muy especial.

e. _____ Raquel conoció a los tíos de Ángela.

f. _____ Allí Ángela encontró unas hojas de su padre.

g. _____ Raquel trató de aconsejar a Ángela sobre sus relaciones con Jorge.

h. _____ Raquel tomaba una foto de la tumba de Ángel cuando Ángela apareció.

i. _____ Llegó el tío Jaime con unas malas noticias.

j. _____ Los tíos no sabían si Ángela debía hacer el viaje a México.

k. _____ ¿Por qué no revisaba (*look through*) lo que había entre las cosas de su padre?

l. _____ De regreso en San Juan, Raquel conoció al novio de Ángela.

m. _____ En San Juan, Raquel buscó una casa en la calle del Sol.

Be sure to check your answers in the Appendix, because the answers for this activity serve as the basis for the next one.

Actividad B.   ¿Y qué más?

The following sentences expand on the information given in the statements in **Actividad A**. Can you match these continuations with those statements? The first item is done for you.

a. _____ Era la copa de bodas de su abuela Rosario.

b. _____ Hubo un accidente en la excavación donde trabajaba Roberto.

c. _____ Pero Ángela se enfadó.

d. _____ También dijo que estaba enterrado en el cementerio del Viejo San Juan.

e. _____ Las hojas tenían sus recuerdos de la Argentina y de su vida en Puerto Rico.

f. __1__ Creía que Ángel Castillo vivía allí.

g. _____ Salieron en el carro de Ángela, con Laura, su prima.

h. _____ Fue al cuarto con Raquel y las dos encontraron un baúl.

i. _____ Raquel le contó la historia de su abuelo.

j. _____ No le gustó mucho.

k. _____ Debía ir al cuarto de su padre.

l. _____ Les contó la historia de Ángel Castillo.

m. _____ Creían que Ángela debía consultar con la abuela.

Listen to the pairs of statements on the cassette tape and check your answers. The number you hear will be that assigned to the statements in **Actividad A**.

Have you completed the following sections of the lesson? Check them off here.

_____ **Preparación**   _____ **Repaso de los episodios 19–24**

_____ **¿Tienes buena memoria?**

You are now ready to continue on with **Lección 26** in the Workbook.

Destinos
An Introduction to Spanish

Episodes 27–52

The story continues in a small town in the
central meseta of Mexico, in Mexico City,
and in the historic hacienda of La Gavia . . .

Un viaje a México: El pueblo, la capital

STUDY GUIDE

LECCIÓN

Follow these simple steps as you work your way through **Lección 27** in the materials that accompany *Destinos*: the Textbook and the Workbook.

STEP 1 USING THE TEXTBOOK

 BEFORE VIEWING . . .

Be sure to complete the preview section (called **Preparación**) in **Lección 27** before viewing **Episodio 27** (the video episode that corresponds to **Lección 27**). Check off the preview section here after you have completed it.

_____ **Preparación**

 AFTER VIEWING . . .

The rest of the materials in **Lección 27** of the Textbook will help you better understand the video episode you have just seen and take you beyond it, giving you additional information about places and characters in the series. The Textbook will also help you to develop skill in using the Spanish language. In this lesson you will learn

- another way to talk about the future in Spanish.

You will also learn information that will help you understand the background of Raquel's investigation and prepare you for future video episodes.

Be sure to work through all parts of the lesson. When you see a cassette symbol in the margin, listen to the tape for **Lección 27**. Answers or hints for many activities are given in Appendix 1. Be sure to check your answers for each activity before going on to the next one.

Check off the following sections of the lesson here as you complete them.

_____ **¿Tienes buena memoria?**   _____ **Un poco de gramática**

Now scan the words in the **Vocabulario** list to be sure that you understand the meaning of most of them.

STEP 2   USING THE WORKBOOK

Now turn to the Workbook and complete all the activities for **Lección 27**. Whereas the materials in the Textbook all had to do with the video episode, the materials in the Workbook will help you expand your knowledge of the Spanish language in general, as well as give you opportunities for self-expression in Spanish. In this lesson, you will learn

- the forms of regular verbs in the future in Spanish, plus one useful irregular verb.

In the **Repaso** sections, which begin in this lesson, you will practice narrating in the past with the preterite and the imperfect.

Remember to listen to the tape for **Lección 27** when you see the cassette symbol, and to check your answers in Appendix 1.

Check off the following sections of the lesson here as you complete them.

_____ **Gramática**   _____ **Repaso**

STEP 3   WRAPPING THINGS UP

Now that you have worked through Steps 1–2, here are some of the things you have accomplished in Spanish.

- You have learned another way to talk about your actions and those of others in the future.
- You have reviewed the major events of the first twenty-six video episodes of *Destinos*, while continuing to work on listening skills with the video episode and the cassette tape, and you have discovered that you can now understand a great deal more in the scenes that you saw earlier in the series.

After you have followed these steps in working your way through **Lección 27**, you will be ready to continue on with **Lección 28** in the Textbook.

27

EL RESCATE*

OBJETIVOS

The materials in **Lección 27** of the Textbook and the Workbook will help you better understand the video episode and take you beyond it, giving you additional information about places and characters in the series. The Textbook will also help you to develop skill in using the Spanish language. In this lesson, you will learn

- another way to talk about the future in Spanish.

You will also learn information that will help you understand the background of Raquel's investigation and prepare you for future video episodes.

Be sure to work through all parts of the lesson. When you see a cassette symbol in the margin, listen to the tape for **Lección 27**. Answers or hints for many activities are given in Appendix 1. Be sure to check your answers for each activity before going on to the next one.

*The Rescue

━━■━━　　**BEFORE VIEWING . . .**

• •

Preparación

Note: In this video episode you will watch a condensed version of Raquel's search for the truth about don Fernando's past. You will see highlights of the main events of **Episodios 1–26**, following Raquel's travels from Mexico to Spain, then on to Argentina, Puerto Rico, and back to Mexico (although not just yet to her exact point of departure!).

You may be surprised to realize how much more you can now understand from previous video episodes. What was challenging when you were watching **Episodio 5**, for example, may seem easier to you now. That is a measure of how much you have accomplished as you watched the first twenty-six video episodes and worked with the Textbook and Workbook.

Actividad A.

Antes de mirar el **Episodio 27**, trata de recordar algo de lo que (*what*) pasó en los episodios previos. ¿Puedes completar las respuestas a las siguientes preguntas?

Nombres: don Fernando Castillo Saavedra, Mercedes Castillo, Raquel Rodríguez, Rosario, Elena Ruiz, Teresa Suárez
Lugares: la Argentina, Córdoba, Costa Rica, Madrid, México, San Juan; el cementerio, la excavación, La Gavia, el puerto
Parientes: el hermano, el medio hermano, el hijo, la primera esposa

1. ¿Dónde comenzó esta historia? ¿Con qué comenzó? ¿Y con quiénes?

    La historia comenzó en una hacienda, ＿＿＿＿＿＿＿, en México. Co-

    menzó con una carta escrita por una mujer en España a ＿＿＿＿＿＿, el

    dueño de la hacienda. Don Pedro Castillo, ＿＿＿＿＿＿ de don Fer-

    nando, contrató a una abogada norteamericana, ＿＿＿＿＿＿, para

    hacer la investigación.

2. ¿A quién buscaba Raquel? ¿Por qué?

    Al principio Raquel buscaba a la persona que escribió la carta,

    ＿＿＿＿＿＿. La buscaba porque en la carta indicaba que sabía algo de

    Rosario, ＿＿＿＿＿＿ de don Fernando.

3. ¿A qué países viajó? ¿Qué ciudades visitó?

Raquel viajó a España, _____ y Puerto Rico. Visitó a Sevilla,

_____ , Buenos Aires, _____ , Ponce y San Germán.

4. ¿Dónde conoció a Ángela Castillo?

Raquel conoció a Ángela Castillo en _____ del Viejo San Juan, en

Puerto Rico.

5. ¿Adónde viajaron Ángela y Raquel? ¿Dónde está ahora el hermano de

Ángela? ¿Qué le pasó?

Viajaron a _____ . Roberto, el hermano de Ángela, está en

_____ , donde hubo un accidente.

6. ¿Quién es Arturo Iglesias? ¿Sabe algo de lo que le pasó al hermano de

Ángela?

Arturo es _____ de Ángel Castillo, el hijo de don Fernando y

_____ . No sabe nada de lo que le pasó a Roberto.

Para pensar...

1. ¿Qué crees que va a pasar con Roberto, el hermano de Ángela? ¿Lo van a
    sacar de la excavación vivo o muerto?
2. Al final del **Episodio 26**, Raquel quería llamar a Arturo, para decirle lo
    que pasaba con Roberto. ¿Crees que Raquel pudo comunicarse con
    Arturo? ¿Cómo va a reaccionar Arturo a las noticias de Roberto?

Actividad B.

Paso 1

Vas a escuchar una conversación entre Raquel y Ángela mientras manejan un
carro alquilado (*rented*) hacia el sitio de la excavación. Puedes leer el diálogo al
mismo tiempo que lo escuchas, si quieres. Después de escuchar, contesta la
pregunta.

ÁNGELA: Roberto siempre quiso venir a México. Se pasaba los días y las noches
         estudiando las civilizaciones prehispánicas.
RAQUEL: Roberto y tú son muy unidos, ¿verdad? En Puerto Rico me decías
         siempre que tu hermano era un encanto.
ÁNGELA: La verdad es que... pues, desde que se vino para México, nos hemos
         alejado un poco.

RAQUEL: Comprendo... con la distancia.

ÁNGELA: No, no es por eso. Es que... Bueno, yo nunca le he dicho esto a nadie, Raquel. Pues, la verdad es que siempre le he tenido un poco de envidia a Roberto.

¿De quién habla Ángela en esta conversación?

a. _____ de su novio, Jorge   c. _____ de su padre, Ángel

b. _____ de su hermano, Roberto

Paso 2

Ahora escucha la conversación otra vez. Al escuchar, piensa en el verbo **alejarse**. **Nos hemos alejado** significa *we've grown apart*. Después de escuchar la conversación otra vez, contesta las siguientes preguntas.

1. ¿Qué materia siempre le gustó a Roberto?
   a. _____ las civilizaciones prehispánicas   c. _____ la geografía mexicana
   b. _____ la historia de México

2. ¿Cómo son las relaciones entre Ángela y Roberto desde que él se va a vivir a México?
   a. _____ Se sienten más unidos.   c. _____ Nada cambió entre ellos.
   b. _____ Están un poco alejados.

3. ¿Qué secreto le revela Ángela a Raquel?
   a. _____ Le dice que no quiere a Roberto.
   b. _____ Le dice que Roberto no es realmente su hermano.
   c. _____ Le dice que siempre le ha tenido envidia (*she has always envied*) a Roberto.

Para pensar...

1. ¿Conoces a hermanos como Ángela y Roberto? ¿Son unidos o un poco alejados? ¿Tiene uno envidia al otro?

2. Imagina la conversación que va a tener Ángela con su hermano cuando lo vea. ¿Qué le va a decir?

AFTER VIEWING . . .

¿TIENES BUENA MEMORIA?

Actividad.   El repaso de Raquel

Los siguientes párrafos son del repaso que hace Raquel al final del **Episodio 27**, pero faltan unas palabras. ¿Puedes completar el repaso?

buscar a Roberto
empezó a mirar la lista de nombres
era más inteligente y responsable que ella
está desesperada
estaba bloqueado y no podíamos pasar
le tenía un poco de envidia
no sabe nada del accidente
que era un error
se llevaban muy bien
un poco culpable

¡Qué día tuvimos hoy! Primero Ángela y yo llegamos a la Ciudad de México. Estábamos cansadas. Pero también estábamos muy preocupadas. Aunque estábamos cansadas, teníamos que venir a este pueblo. Teníamos que _____ ,[1] el hermano de Ángela.

Mientras manejábamos, hablamos de Roberto. Ángela me decía que ella y su hermano _____.[2] Pero también me confesó que _____[3] a Roberto. Ángela le tenía envidia a Roberto porque sentía que él _____.[4] Pobre Ángela. Ahora se siente _____ _____.[5]

Bueno, por fin llegamos al sitio de la excavación. ¿Y qué pasó? El camino _____.[6] Entonces, vinimos aquí, al hospital.

Le preguntamos a la recepcionista si estaba Roberto Castillo, y ella nos dijo que no. Entonces Ángela _____[7] y ¿qué encontró? Encontró el nombre R. Castilla. Por un momento tuvimos esperanzas.[a] Pensamos _____ _____,[8] que debía ser R. Castillo. Pronto supimos que no. R. Castilla era Rodrigo Castilla.

¡Qué lástima! La pobre Ángela _____.[9] Y ahora estamos aquí. Quiero hablar con Arturo porque estará[b] esperándonos en el hotel y _____.[10] Pero no he podido[c] comunicarme con él.

[a]*hope* [b]*he is probably* [c]no... *I haven't been able*

 Ahora escucha la cinta para verificar tus respuestas.

• •

UN POCO DE GRAMÁTICA

Note: The grammar previewed in most **Un poco de gramática** sections is used in the sentences that appear on-screen during Raquel's story review. This **Un poco de gramática** section is an exception. However, the form described here has been used many times in previous video episodes of *Destinos*.

Another Way to Talk About the Future

To describe what another person will be doing in the future, add **-á** to most infinitives.

En unos días Raquel **estará** en la Ciudad de México.	*In a few days Raquel will be in Mexico City.*

To describe what more than one person will be doing, add **-án** to most infinitives.

Raquel y Ángela **llamarán** a los tíos en Puerto Rico.	*Raquel and Ángela will call the aunts and uncles in Puerto Rico.*

One useful verb that uses an irregular stem with these endings is **hacer**.

¿Qué **hará** Arturo si no puede comunicarse con nadie?	*What will Arturo do if he can't get in touch with anyone?*

You will learn more about these verb forms in the Workbook.

Actividad.   ¿Qué pasará en los siguientes episodios?

Indica lo que **no** quieres que pase.

1. Don Fernando
   _____ morirá sin conocer a sus nietos
   _____ no aceptará a Ángela y Roberto como sus parientes
   _____ estará muy contento de conocer a sus nietos
   _____ vivirá varios años más y pasará mucho tiempo con su nueva familia
   _____ morirá en paz... pensando en Rosario

2. Roberto

_____ morirá en la excavación

_____ será rescatado y estará más o menos bien

_____ se enfadará con su hermana por lo del apartamento

_____ insistirá en regresar a Puerto Rico en seguida, sin conocer a su abuelo y su tío

3. Raquel y Arturo

_____ no se verán más por un trágico accidente de coche en el que morirá Arturo

_____ se harán novios

_____ no se casarán a causa de la distancia

_____ se casarán y Raquel se mudará a la Argentina

_____ se casarán y Arturo se mudará a los Estados Unidos

_____ no verán a don Fernando

4. Los otros miembros de la familia Castillo

_____ no aceptarán a Ángela y a Roberto

_____ estarán muy contentos de conocer a sus nuevos parientes

_____ se verán involucrados (*involved*) en una serie de crisis familiares

_____ no aceptarán el testamento (*will*) de don Fernando

Have you completed the following sections of the lesson? Check them off here.

_____ **Preparación**   _____ **Un poco de gramática**
_____ **¿Tienes buena memoria?**

   Now scan the words in the **Vocabulario** list to be sure that you understand the meaning of most of them. Then you will be ready to continue on with **Lección 27** in the Workbook.

VOCABULARIO

Los adjetivos

unido/a   united, close

Los verbos

alejarse (de)   to draw away, grow apart (from)

Los conceptos

el rescate   rescue

Las palabras adicionales

lo que   what, that which
tenerle envidia (a alguien)   to envy (someone)

LECCIÓN

Follow these simple steps as you work your way through **Lección 28** in the materials that accompany *Destinos*: the Textbook and the Workbook.

STEP 1 USING THE TEXTBOOK

BEFORE VIEWING . . .

Be sure to complete the preview section (called **Preparación**) in **Lección 28** before viewing **Episodio 28** (the video episode that corresponds to **Lección 28**). Check off the preview section here after you have completed it.

_____ **Preparación**

AFTER VIEWING . . .

The rest of the materials in **Lección 28** of the Textbook will help you better understand the video episode you have just seen and take you beyond it, giving you additional information about places and characters in the series. The Textbook will also help you to develop skill in using the Spanish language. In this lesson you will learn

- vocabulary for talking about parts of the body
- a number of ways to ask what has happened
- more ways to talk about the future.

You will also learn about the geography and history of Mexico.

Be sure to work through all parts of the lesson. When you see a cassette symbol in the margin, listen to the tape for **Lección 28**. Answers or hints for many activities are given in Appendix 1. Be sure to check your answers for each activity before going on to the next one.

Check off the following sections of the lesson here as you complete them.

_____ **¿Tienes buena memoria?**   _____ **Conversaciones**
_____ **Vocabulario del tema**   _____ **Un poco de gramática**

Now scan the words in the **Vocabulario** list to be sure that you understand the meaning of most of them.

· ·

STEP 2   USING THE WORKBOOK

Now turn to the Workbook and complete all the activities for **Lección 28**. Whereas the materials in the Textbook all had to do with the video episode, the materials in the Workbook will help you expand your knowledge of the Spanish language in general, as well as give you opportunities for self-expression in Spanish. In this lesson you will learn

- more about the forms and uses of the future in Spanish
- how to express extremes in Spanish: the best, the worst, the biggest, and so on.

In the **Repaso** section you will continue to work with all of the forms of the past tense that you have learned so far.

Remember to listen to the tape for **Lección 28** when you see the cassette symbol, and to check your answers in Appendix 1.

Check off the following sections of the lesson here as you complete them.

_____ **Más allá del episodio**   _____ **Repaso**
_____ **Gramática**

Now scan the words in the **Vocabulario** list to be sure that you understand the meaning of most of them.

· ·

STEP 3   TAKING THE SELF-TEST

Now that you have completed the Textbook and Workbook for **Lecciones 27** and **28**, take the Self-Test for those lessons. Remember to listen to the tape for **Lección 28** when you see the cassette symbol, and to check your answers in Appendix 1.

_____ **Self-Test**

. . . .

STEP 4   WRAPPING THINGS UP

Now that you have worked through Steps 1–3, here are some of the things you have accomplished in Spanish.

- You know and can use the Spanish names for many parts of the body.
- You can use forms of the future to talk about what will happen.
- You can express extremes in Spanish.
- You can use a number of expressions to find out information about events that have happened.
- You have continued to work with various past-tense forms in Spanish, and your ability to talk about the past is growing.

After you have followed these steps in working your way through **Lección 28**, you will be ready to continue on with **Lección 29** in the Textbook.

28

ATRAPADOS*

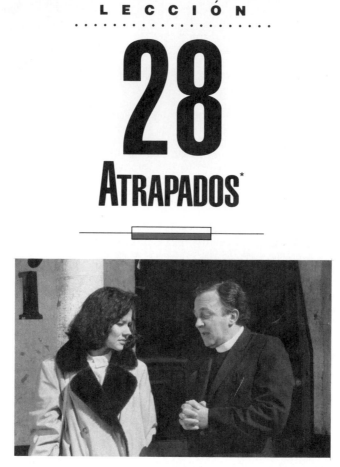

OBJETIVOS

The materials in **Lección 28** of the Textbook and the Workbook will help you better understand the video episode and take you beyond it, giving you additional information about places and characters in the series. The Textbook will also help you to develop skill in using the Spanish language. In this lesson, you will learn

- vocabulary for talking about parts of the body
- a number of ways to ask what has happened
- more ways to talk about the future.

You will also learn about the geography and history of Mexico.

Be sure to work through all parts of the lesson. When you see a cassette symbol in the margin, listen to the tape for **Lección 28**. Answers or hints for many activities are given in Appendix 1. Be sure to check your answers for each activity before going on to the next one.

Trapped

BEFORE VIEWING . . .

PREPARACIÓN

Actividad A.

Antes de mirar el **Episodio 28**, trata de recordar lo que pasó en los episodios previos y escucha el resumen del narrador al principio del episodio. Luego indica si los siguientes acontecimientos (*events*) ocurrieron (**Sí**) o no (**No**).

Sí   No   1. Raquel y Ángela llegaron al área de la excavación donde trabajaba Roberto.

Sí   No   2. Pudieron pasar en seguida al sitio del accidente.

Sí   No   3. Llevaron a Roberto de urgencia al hospital.

Sí   No   4. Arturo llegó a la casa de Pedro Castillo.

Sí   No   5. Raquel no lo estaba esperando.

Sí   No   6. Raquel quiso hablar con Arturo pero no pudo.

Actividad B.

En el **Episodio 28**, Raquel y Ángela pueden llegar a la excavación donde están atrapadas algunas personas. ¿Qué crees que pasará?

1. Roberto
   a. _____ morirá
   b. _____ estará atrapado, vivo, en la excavación

2. Arturo
   a. _____ seguirá sin saber lo que está pasando en la excavación
   b. _____ se enterará (*will find out*) del accidente por la televisión y saldrá en seguida para el pueblo

Actividad C.

Paso 1

En este episodio y a lo largo del resto de la serie, vas a ver con frecuencia a los miembros de la familia Castillo Saavedra. Los conociste a todos en los primeros episodios, pero ¿recuerdas ahora quiénes son? Escucha las siguientes descripciones de algunos de ellos e identifícalos.

a. Mercedes   d. Carlos   g. Carmen
b. Ramón   e. Maricarmen   h. Juan
c. Pedro   f. Pati   i. Consuelo

1. ...   2. ...   3. ...   4. ...   5. ...

Paso 2

Ahora completa el siguiente árbol de la familia, usando nombres de la lista y de la cinta del Paso 1.

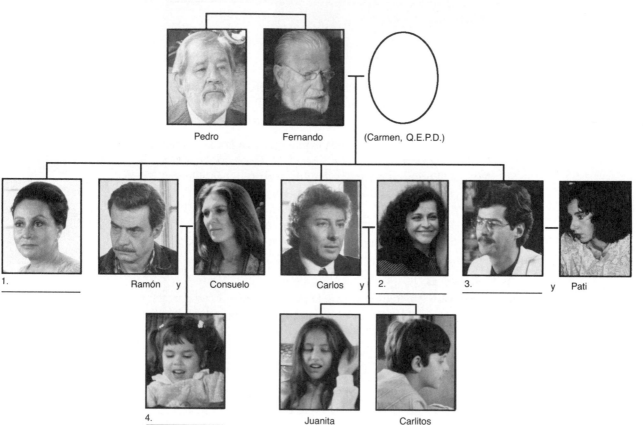

Pedro   Fernando   (Carmen, Q.E.P.D.)

1. _____   Ramón   y   Consuelo   Carlos   y   2. _____   3. _____   y   Pati

4. _____   Juanita   Carlitos

Actividad D.

Paso 1

Vas a escuchar una conversación entre el médico de don Fernando y sus hijos. Puedes leer el diálogo al mismo tiempo que lo escuchas, si quieres. Después de escuchar, contesta las preguntas del Paso 2.

DOCTOR: Su estado es muy delicado. Es necesario consultar a un especialista.

RAMÓN: ¿Y Ud. recomienda a alguien en particular?

DOCTOR: Conozco al mejor especialista en México, pero está de viaje. Está dando una serie de conferencias en Europa. No regresa hasta el fin de mes.

MERCEDES: ¿Y podemos esperar hasta entonces?

DOCTOR: No. Recomiendo que lo examine un especialista lo antes posible.

RAMÓN: ¿Y no hay otro, doctor? ¿Uno que sea de confianza?

DOCTOR: También conozco a otro muy bueno que radica[1] en la ciudad de Guadalajara. Tiene una clínica muy bien equipada en la Universidad de Guadalajara.

MERCEDES: ¿En Guadalajara? ¿Y aceptará venir a México?

DOCTOR: Eso no lo sé.

[1] vive, está situado

Paso 2

1. Según lo que dice el médico, ¿cómo está don Fernando?

   a. _____ mucho mejor   c. _____ igual que antes

   b. _____ muy mal

2. El médico recomienda a dos especialistas. ¿Es posible consultar al primero en este momento?

   _____ Sí.   _____ No.

3. Ramón quiere el nombre de un médico «que sea de confianza». ¿Qué puede significar esta frase?

   a. _____ one who can respect the confidentiality of the case

   b. _____ one in whom the family can have confidence

Actividad E.

En este episodio Carlos va a jugar (*play*) con sus hijos y su sobrina Maricarmen un juego muy divertido. Se llama «Simón dice» y, como seguramente lo sabes, en él se nombran muy rápidamente las partes del cuerpo. Lee las partes del cuerpo en la sección **Vocabulario del tema** en esta lección. Esto te ayudará a comprender más palabras, pero no necesitas saber los nombres del cuerpo para apreciar el juego porque lo más importante del juego es la frase «Simón dice».

AFTER VIEWING . . .

· ·

¿TIENES BUENA MEMORIA?

Actividad A.   En la excavación

Identifica al personaje a quien se refiere.

a. Raquel Rodríguez   d. Roberto Castillo

b. Ángela Castillo   e. el padre Rodrigo

c. Arturo Iglesias

1. _____ Le dio a Ángela noticias sobre su hermano.

2. _____ Se durmió sin ver las noticias de la televisión.

3. ____ Trató de llamar a Arturo, pero no pudo comunicarse con él.
4. ____ Todavía estaba vivo, aunque estaba atrapado en la excavación.
5. ____ Estaba angustiada, pero no podía hacer nada.
6. ____ Les recordó a todos que había que tener fe.
7. ____ Trató de apoyar (*support*) a su amiga tanto como pudo.

Actividad B.   En la capital

Al mismo tiempo que Ángela y Raquel siguen con angustia los acontecimientos de la excavación, los miembros de la familia Castillo tienen sus propios problemas. Completa las siguientes oraciones sobre lo que pasa en la capital.

1. El médico les dice a los miembros de la familia que hay que consultar a un especialista… en dos o tres semanas / en seguida.
2. El especialista está en… la capital / Guadalajara.
3. Pedro y Mercedes están muy preocupados… por don Fernando / por don Fernando y por otros asuntos familiares.

Para pensar…

En este episodio, Pedro y Mercedes hablan brevemente de tres asuntos que les preocupan en este momento. ¿Cuál crees que va a ser el resultado de cada uno de ellos?

1. ¿Qué le va a pasar a don Fernando? ¿Va a morir pronto? ¿sin conocer a sus nietos?
2. ¿Qué va a pasar entre Juan y Pati? ¿Cuáles son las dificultades que experimentan en esta época? ¿Las van a poder superar (*get through*)?
3. Y lo de la oficina en Miami, ¿en qué consiste? ¿Por qué no les ha dicho nada Carlos a sus hermanos y a su tío? ¿Es sólo porque don Fernando está enfermo?

VOCABULARIO DEL TEMA

Algunas partes del cuerpo

la boca	mouth	**la cabeza**	head	**la espalda**	back
el brazo	arm	**el corazón**	heart	**el estómago**	stomach

la mano	hand
la nariz	nose
los ojos	eyes
la oreja	ear
el pecho	chest
el pelo	hair
el pie	foot
la pierna	leg

Actividad A.   Con el médico

Escucha otra vez mientras el médico del pueblo examina en la clínica, cerca de la excavación, a un niño. Indica en el dibujo las partes del cuerpo que examina.

Actividad B.   Jugando con el Sr. Papa

Escucha otra vez mientras Pati y Maricarmen hablan del juguete que su prima le ha dado (*given*). Completa las oraciones con las partes del cuerpo apropiadas.

PATI: ¿Qué tienes allí, Maricarmen?

MARICARMEN: Es un juguete que Juanita me trajo de los Estados Unidos. Se llama Sr. Papa.

PATI: Ah, sí.

MARICARMEN: Sí. Aquí está todo lo que necesitas, Pati. Dos (orejas/ojos),[1] una nariz, (una boca/un corazón),[2] dos orejas, (un brazo/una boca)[3] con una mano, otro brazo con otra (nariz/mano)[4] y los pies.

PATI: Oye, Maricarmen, ¿y dónde están las piernas?

MARICARMEN: Pati, el Sr. Papa no necesita (pies/piernas)[5] sólo (piernas/pies).[6]

PATI: ¿Y el resto del (corazón/cuerpo)[7]? ¿No tiene espalda ni (pecho/pie)[8]?

MARICARMEN: No, Pati.

PATI: Y ¿por qué se llama el Sr. Papa?

MARICARMEN: Porque su (corazón/cabeza)[9] es una papa.

PATI: ¿No tiene (pelo/pierna)[10]?

MARICARMEN: No, Pati. Las papas no tienen pelo.

Ahora indica lo que significan las palabras que indicaste.

Actividad C.   Asociaciones

El Sr. Papa es un juguete norteamericano. ¿Con qué parte del cuerpo asocias los siguientes productos norteamericanos?

1. Desenex   2. Slim-Fast   3. Tylenol   4. Vicks VapoRub   5. Visine
6. Listerine   7. Q-Tips   8. Lady Clairol   9. Vaseline Intensive Care
10. Kleenex   11. Ben-Gay

Nota cultural: Hablando de la familia Castillo

You initially met the members of the Castillo family at La Gavia, the rural estate owned by don Fernando. In this video episode you have seen them in the urban environment of Mexico City. The following aspects of their life and lifestyle are worthy of note.

- Although Ramón and his family live at La Gavia, they also have a home in Mexico City. It is not uncommon for well-to-do Hispanic families—Mexicans, in this case—to have several residences. In Mexico wealthy people often have two residences in the same city. One is viewed as the primary residence; the other may be used for entertaining or as a place for out-of-town guests to stay (rather than in a hotel).
- Carlos' children have been exposed to a number of elements of U.S. culture, such as **Simón dice** and **el Sr. Papa**, because they have been growing up in Miami. Because they also spend as much time as is practical in Mexico, they are also quite comfortable in that country. At this stage of their lives, it is fair to describe them as bicultural, participating in the language, culture, and cultural values of both the English-speaking and the Hispanic worlds.

CONVERSACIONES: PARA SABER QUÉ PASÓ

Actividad.   ¿Qué pasa?

Esta frase ya forma parte del habla norteamericana, como equivalente de *What's happening?* Otra manera de hacer la misma pregunta es **¿Qué hay?** En español hay varias maneras de pedir detalles sobre lo que está pasando o lo que ya pasó.

Paso 1

Escucha la siguiente conversación entre Pati y Juan. Luego indica la frase que oíste.

_____ ¿Qué pasa?   _____ ¿Qué hay?

Paso 2

En la conversación anterior, la pregunta de Pati probablemente es un saludo. Pero se puede usar las mismas preguntas, en el pasado, como saludos o para pedir detalles sobre algo que ocurrió. Escucha la siguiente conversación e indica las frases que oíste.

a. _____ ¿Qué pasa?   c. _____ ¿Qué pasó?
b. _____ ¿Qué hay?   d. _____ ¿Qué hubo?

Como oíste, a veces se usan las dos preguntas seguidas (*one right after the other*).

Paso 3

¿Qué vas a decir?

1. Una amiga entra y te dice *¡Hola!* Le contestas...
2. Hay un ruido muy fuerte en la calle. Sales de tu casa y le dices a un vecino...
3. Te encuentras con un amigo que está muy triste. Le preguntas...

UN POCO DE GRAMÁTICA

More About Talking About the Future

The verbs **poder** and **tener** form the future with the irregular stems **podr-** and **tendr-**, respectively.

RAQUEL: **¿Podré** hablar con Arturo pronto? Si no, **tendré** que ponerme en contacto con él tan pronto como lleguemos a la capital.

RAQUEL: *Will I be able to speak with Arturo soon? If not, I'll have to get in touch with him as soon as we get to the capital.*

You will learn more about these and other verbs that use an irregular stem in the future in the Workbook.

Actividad.

¿Qué pasará en los próximos (*upcoming*) episodios de *Destinos*?

Paso 1

¿Qué podrán hacer los siguientes personajes? Indica con una **S** (sí) lo que crees que es posible y con una **N** (no) lo que crees poco probable que hagan.

1. _____ Ángela podrá hablar con su hermano.
2. _____ Los obreros (*workers*) no podrán rescatar a Roberto.
3. _____ Raquel podrá comunicarse con Arturo.
4. _____ El cspecialista podrá ir a la capital.
5. _____ Don Fernando podrá conocer a sus sobrinos muy pronto.
6. _____ Arturo y Raquel podrán pasar algún tiempo juntos.
7. _____ Juan y Pati podrán resolver sus dificultades.
8. _____ Don Fernando podrá regresar a La Gavia en buenas condiciones físicas.

Paso 2

¿Qué tendrán que hacer los siguientes personajes en los próximos episodios? Indica con una **S** lo que crees que es posible y con una **N** lo que crees poco probable que tengan que hacer.

1. _____ Roberto tendrá que pasar unos días en el hospital.
2. _____ Los hijos tendrán que llevar a don Fernando a Guadalajara.
3. _____ Arturo le tendrá que mandar un telegrama a Raquel.
4. _____ Raquel tendrá que tomar una decisión sobre sus relaciones con Arturo.
5. _____ Pedro tendrá que investigar la causa del problema que hay en la oficina de Castillo Saavedra, S.A., en Miami.
6. _____ Don Fernando tendrá que vender La Gavia para pagar los gastos (*expenses*) de su enfermedad.
7. _____ La tía Olga tendrá que viajar a México para resolver una disputa familiar.
8. _____ Raquel tendrá que volver a Los Ángeles sin terminar la investigación.

Nota cultural: México, a vista de pájaro*

Note: Throughout the first half of the Textbook a brief exercise before each extensive **Nota cultural** helped you review what you already knew about the topic—generally information from the video episode—before beginning the reading. Keep that strategy in mind as you work with the readings in the second half of the text. The first few **Notas culturales** will have a brief reminder.

Antes de leer, escucha una vez más lo que dice el narrador sobre México y trata de completar este mapa. En la lectura, hay más detalles para que lo completes.

Para mucha gente de los Estados Unidos, México es un país al sur, grande y tal vez desconocido... excepto por la música de sus mariachis y por sus hermosas[1] playas como las de Acapulco, Cancún y otras. Los que[2] se interesan por conocer a fondo[3] México se encuentran con una civilización compleja. México es ante todo una mezcla de lo autóctono[4] con lo español

[1]*beautiful* [2]Los... Las personas que [3]a... *in depth* [4]lo... *indigenous elements*

*a... *a bird's-eye view*

y otros elementos internacionales... de lo antiguo y lo moderno al mismo tiempo. A continuación se ofrece un fotografía de México a vista de pájaro.

México en cifras

Población: 90 millones de habitantes
Área: 76.605 millas cuadradas
Capital: México = Ciudad de México, el Distrito Federal, (el D.F.), a 7.575 pies de altura, en la meseta central con 21 millones de habitantes, la metrópoli más grande del mundo

México: una gran diversidad geográfica y cultural, pasado y presente

México es el único país de Latinoamérica situado en el continente de la América del Norte. Al norte, limita con[5] los Estados Unidos. El Río Grande (los mexicanos lo llaman el Río Bravo) sirve de límite natural desde Ciudad Juárez hasta el Golfo de México. Al sureste, México limita con Guatemala y Belice, en Centro América.

La diversidad geográfica y cultural de México es impresionante. De las siguientes características, ¿cuántas reconoces?

- un extenso litoral,[6] con hermosas playas como las de Acapulco y Cancún
- desiertos y regiones semiáridas, como el desierto de Sonora
- zonas de densa vegetación, como en Yucatán
- sierras altas
- la meseta central, el Altiplano Mexicano, donde está situada la capital
- ruinas precolombinas de las civilizaciones azteca y maya, en sitios como Uxmal y Chichén Itzá en Yucatán y Teotihuacán, cerca de la capital
- ciudades coloniales como Taxco o Guanajuato

En el D.F., hermosos edificios coloniales conviven[7] con edificios modernos, tiendas, teatros, cines y más. El mismo día se pueden visitar la Catedral Metropolitana de México, la más antigua de la América Latina, y la modernísima ciudad universitaria, la UNAM (Universidad Nacional Autónoma de México).

México... un país con un rico pasado y abierto al futuro, un país que busca mantener sus tradiciones y al mismo tiempo superar[8] los problemas del presente. En las siguientes lecciones de *Destinos*, llegarás a conocer este país más a fondo.

[5]limita... *borders on, has borders with* [6]*coastline* [7]*coexist*
[8]*to overcome*

Arte mosaico en la UNAM

Have you completed the following sections of the lesson? Check them off here.

_____ **Preparación**	_____ **Conversaciones**
_____ **¿Tienes buena memoria?**	_____ **Un poco de gramática**
_____ **Vocabulario del tema**	

Now scan the words in the **Vocabulario** list to be sure that you understand the meaning of most of them. Then you will be ready to continue on with **Lección 28** in the Workbook.

VOCABULARIO

Los verbos

enterarse (**de**)	to find out (about)
jugar (**ue**) (**al**)	to play (*a game*)
rescatar	to rescue

Las personas

el padre	priest, father

Algunas partes del cuerpo
(Some Parts of the Body)

la boca	mouth
el brazo	arm
la cabeza	head
el corazón	heart
la espalda	back
la mano	hand
la nariz	nose
los ojos	eyes
la oreja	ear
el pecho	chest
el pelo	hair
el pie	foot
la pierna	leg

Los conceptos

el acontecimiento	happening, event
el asunto	matter, affair, business
la esperanza	hope

Los adjetivos

atrapado/a	trapped

Para saber qué pasó
(To Find Out What Happened)

¿Qué hubo?	What happened?
¿Qué pasó?	

29

¡SE DERRUMBÓ!*

OBJETIVOS

The materials in **Lección 29** of the Textbook and the Workbook will help you better understand the video episode and take you beyond it, giving you additional information about places and characters in the series. The Textbook will also help you to develop skill in using the Spanish language. In this lesson, you will learn

- more vocabulary for talking about parts of the body, as well as vocabulary and expressions related to medical examinations and conditions
- ways to tell a person that he or she is right about something
- ways to talk about what people want others to do.

You will also learn about several Mexican traditions.

Be sure to work through all parts of the lesson. When you see a cassette symbol in the margin, listen to the tape for **Lección 29**. Answers or hints for many activities are given in Appendix 1. Be sure to check your answers for each activity before going on to the next one.

*It Collapsed!

▬▬▭▬ **BEFORE VIEWING . . .**

• •

PREPARACIÓN

Actividad.

En el último episodio de *Destinos*, viste lo que pasó en la excavación y también conociste de nuevo a varios miembros de la familia Castillo. Completa las siguientes oraciones según lo que ocurrió en el episodio.

1. Después de completar el examen de don Fernando, el doctor que lo atendía le dijo a la familia que don Fernando
   a. _____ podía volver a La Gavia
   b. _____ tenía que quedarse en la clínica una semana más
   c. _____ necesitaba ver a un especialista

2. En la familia Castillo
   a. _____ nadie sabía del accidente que ocurrió en la excavación donde trabajaba Roberto
   b. _____ todos sabían lo del accidente en la excavación
   c. _____ sólo Pedro sabía lo del accidente

3. Roberto
   a. _____ logró (*was able*) escapar del derrumbe
   b. _____ murió en el derrumbe
   c. _____ es una de las personas atrapadas en el derrumbe

4. Arturo
   a. _____ leyó la noticia del derrumbe en un periódico
   b. _____ vio la noticia del derrumbe en la televisión
   c. _____ se quedó dormido frente al televisor y no vio la noticia del derrumbe

▬▬▭▬ **AFTER VIEWING . . .**

• •

¿TIENES BUENA MEMORIA?

Actividad A.   En la excavación

Después de tomar un calmante, Ángela por fin se pudo dormir y Raquel también se durmió. Al despertarse, Raquel resume los acontecimientos más importantes que ocurrieron en la excavación. ¿Puedes completar el resumen?

1. teníamos pocas esperanzas
   teníamos muchas esperanzas
2. a un hombre y a una mujer
   a un profesor de Roberto
3. pero no fueron muchos los
   daños (*damage*)
   y se derrumbó todo otra vez
4. comenzó a salir
   comenzó a llorar (*cry*)
5. acostumbrarme al tiempo que
   hace aquí en la meseta
   comunicarme con la familia de
   don Fernando
6. Arturo
   Roberto

Pues, el calmante ha hecho[a] su efecto. Ángela está dormida. Pobre. Debe estar cansadísima… y con mucha razón. Han pasado[b] tantas cosas. Cuando volvimos al sitio de la excavación, _____.[1] Creíamos que sacaban a Roberto del túnel. ¿Y qué pasó? ¿Sacaron a Roberto? No sacaron a Roberto. Sacaron _____.[2]

Poco después, ocurrió algo inesperado. Ninguno de nosotros pensamos que esto ocurriría.[c] ¿Recuerdan qué pasó? Bueno, hubo un segundo derrumbe _____.[3]

Pues, esto fue demasiado para Ángela y _____.[4] Y tuvimos que traerla aquí. El doctor le dio un calmante. Poco después, entró el Padre Rodrigo con noticias.

Y aquí estamos. Ángela está dormida. Yo también tengo ganas de dormir, pero estoy muy preocupada. No he podido[d] _____.[5] ¿Sabrán ellos que estamos aquí? ¿Y cómo estará don Fernando?

Hmmm. Bueno, ya no puedo hacer nada más que esperar. Estoy muy cansada. ¡Ay! ¡Me olvidé de _____![6] Debe estar preocupadísimo.

[a]ha… *has had*   [b]Han… *Have happened*   [c]*would happen*   [d]No… *I haven't been able*

 Escucha la cinta para verificar tus respuestas.

Actividad B.   En la capital

Mientras Ángela y Raquel esperan noticias de Roberto, en casa de Pedro la vida sigue igual, con unos pequeños problemas. Las siguientes oraciones describen algunas de las cosas que pasan, pero hay un error en cada oración. Corrige las oraciones, cambiando solamente una palabra en cada una. Luego inventa una oración más sobre cada escena.

Por la noche

1. Juanita no se siente bien
2. Carlos y Gloria le toman la temperatura
3. también le dan una inyección
4. ¿_____?

Al día siguiente

5. toda la familia se reúne para cenar
6. Carlitos no está enfermo
7. Carlos le dice que el doctor le va a poner una inyección
8. Mercedes se pregunta por qué Arturo no ha llegado (*hasn't arrived*) todavía
9. Pedro le dice a la familia que anoche llamó Raquel
10. ¿——?

¡Un desafío! Durante el desayuno, se menciona que una persona llegó tarde a casa anoche. ¿Recuerdas quién era?

Para pensar...

1. ¿Crees que Ángela es una persona fuerte? En tu opinión, ¿quién es mas fuerte, Ángela o Raquel?
2. ¿Crees que es bueno ocultarle (*to hide*) a don Fernando lo del accidente de Roberto? ¿O deben decirle los hijos lo que está pasando?

Nota cultural: Dos tradiciones mexicanas

In this video episode you learned some information about two very important Mexican traditions, one secular and the other religious.

- Not only does Arturo miss news of the excavation on TV, but he also misses an advertisement for the **Ballet Folclórico de México**. The spectacular performances of this dance troupe reflect the music and traditions of native Mexican peoples: the Mayans, the Aztecs, and many other civilizations that constitute the country's rich indigenous heritage, of which all Mexicans are aware and proud. You will learn more about **el Ballet Folclórico** in **Lección 39**.

- In Mexico, a European heritage exists alongside the indigenous culture. Father Rodrigo promises Ángela that "**la Virgen cuidará a tu hermano**". The Virgin to whom he is referring is the Catholic **Virgen de Guadalupe**,* whose veneration started soon after the arrival in Mexico of the first Spanish priests and religious brothers. Today **la Virgen** is the patron saint not only of Mexico but also of all of Latin America. She is venerated as well by many Hispanic Catholics living in the United States. It is not a good idea to assume that all Hispanics are Catholic, however. In Mexico, for example, there are many Mexican Protestants and Jews, as well as members of other religious traditions.

---

*You will learn more about **la Virgen de Guadalupe** in the **Nota cultural** of this lesson.

VOCABULARIO DEL TEMA

Los exámenes médicos

Las enfermedades

la fiebre	fever
la fractura	fracture
el resfriado	cold

Los tratamientos

la aspirina	aspirin
la medicina	medicine
la pastilla	pill
la receta	prescription
el termómetro	thermometer

Las personas

el doctor/la doctora, el/la médico	doctor
el enfermero/la enfermera	nurse
el/la paciente	patient

Verbos y expresiones útiles

bajar	to bring down (*a fever*)
curar	to heal, cure
examinar	to examine
guardar cama	to stay in bed
ponerle (a alguien) una inyección	to give (someone) a shot
respirar	to breathe
sacar la lengua	to stick out one's tongue
sacar rayos X (*equis*)	to take X-rays
sentirse (ie, i) bien/mal	to feel well/bad
tomarle (a alguien) la temperatura	to take (someone's) temperature
doler (ue)	to hurt, be painful
Me duele (la garganta).	*My (throat) hurts.*
Le duelen (los pies).	*His (feet) hurt.*

R.F.C. MAAR 560224   CED. PROF. 162805

Dr. Alejandro Marroz R.
Médico Pediatra   Hospital Infantil
532-21-11
tels— 516-50-43

¿PROBLEMAS DE SINUSITIS?
¿DOLOR DE CABEZA?
¿FIEBRE?
¿OBSTRUCCION NASAL?

TODOS ESTOS SINTOMAS PUEDEN ESTAR RELACIONADOS A UNA ALERGIA Y/O PROBLEMAS DE SINUSITIS

ALLERGY/SINUS CENTER

OFFERING COMPLETE DIAGNOSTIC SERVICES, including
• ALLERGY SKIN TESTING
• RAST ALLERGY BLOOD TESTING
• FIBEROPTIC EXAMINATION OF NOSE & SINUS

ALSO COMPLETE ALLERGY/SINUS TREATMENT
• FUNCTIONAL ENDOSCOPIC SINUS SURGERY (OUTPATIENT)
• ALLERGY DESENSITIZATION

BOARD CERTIFIED OTORHINOLARYNGOLOGIST AND HEAD & NECK SURGEON

G. WIESMAN, M.D., F.A.C.S.

tener (*irreg.*)   to have

    Tienes (una fiebre alta).   *You have (a high fever).*
    Tienes (la lengua blanca).   *Your (tongue) is (white).*
    Tienes (el brazo) hinchado.   *Your (arm) is swollen.*

Note the following about the preceding health-related vocabulary.

- The terms **médico/doctor(a)** are not completely interchangeable. Both are used to speak about a doctor: **El médico/doctor vino a casa anoche**. But only **el doctor (la doctora)** can be used with the doctor's specific name: **Mi médico es la doctora Sánchez.**
- The verb **doler** is like **gustar**: the part of the body that hurts determines whether a singular verb form (**duele, dolía, dolió…**) or a plural one (**duelen, dolían, dolieron…**) is used.

Actividad A.   Carlitos tiene un resfriado

Escucha las oraciones de la cinta. ¿A qué foto o dibujo se refiere cada oración?

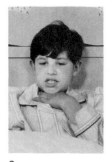    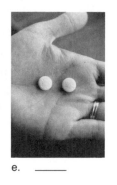 

a. _____   b. _____   c. _____   d. _____   e. _____   f. _____

Actividad B.

En la cinta, escucha otra vez el examen que les hace el médico a las dos personas rescatadas de la excavación donde está atrapado Roberto. Luego indica la información correcta para cada paciente.

Primer paciente: El hombre

1. Se siente… bien/mal.
2. Le duele… la garganta/la espalda.
3. Tiene/No tiene… fiebre.
4. El doctor… le da una aspirina/le pone una inyección.

Segundo paciente: La mujer

5. Tiene hinchado… el brazo/el pie.
6. También le duele… la cabeza/la pierna.

7. Según el médico, necesita... un termómetro/rayos X.
8. Tiene/No tiene... fiebre.

Actividad C.   ¿Y tú?

¿Cuáles de las siguientes oraciones describen tu propia experiencia? Indícalas.

1. _____ Cuando me duele la cabeza, no tomo aspirinas. Simplemente espero... y siempre se me pasa.
2. _____ Cuando algo me duele, tomo alguna medicina en seguida. ¡No aguanto (*I can't stand*) el dolor!
3. _____ Tengo por lo menos un resfriado cada año.
4. _____ Nunca me resfrío (*catch a cold*).
5. _____ Nunca he tenido (*I've never had*) una fiebre muy alta.
6. _____ Tomo varias medicinas todos los días.
7. _____ Trago (*I swallow*) las pastillas fácilmente.
8. _____ Creo que es peligroso que a uno le tomen muchos rayos X en un año.
9. _____ Ningún tratamiento médico me molesta para nada.
10. _____ Tengo miedo de las inyecciones.

Actividad D.   ¿Y tú?

Piensa en la última vez que te sentías mal o realmente estabas enfermo/a. Explica lo que pasó.

1. Una vez tuve/estaba...
2. Me dolía(n)...
3. Fui a ver a / Hablé con...
4. Él/Ella me dijo que...
5. También me dijo...
6. ¿   ?

• •

CONVERSACIONES: CÓMO DECIR QUE OTRA PERSONA TIENE RAZÓN

Actividad.   Sí, eso es.

En español como en inglés hay muchas maneras de decir que la persona con quien hablas tiene razón. En esta actividad vas a practicar algunas.

Paso 1

Escucha la siguiente conversación entre Mercedes, Pedro y Pati. Luego indica las frases que escuchaste.

_____ Claro.	_____ Sí, exacto.	_____ Definitivamente.
_____ Evidentemente.	_____ ¡Por supuesto!	_____ Sí, eso es.
_____ Absolutamente.	_____ ¡Así es!	

Si indicaste *Sí, exacto* y *¡Por supuesto!*, tuviste razón. Todas estas frases—y la frase *tener razón*, claro—pueden usarse para indicar que otra persona tiene razón.

Paso 2

Ahora escucha dos conversaciones más y trata de escribir las frases con que se expresa que la otra persona tiene razón.

Primera conversación: _____   Segunda conversación: _____

Paso 3

En la cinta, vas a escuchar tres preguntas de un amigo. Contéstalas afirmativamente con una de estas frases.

¡Por supuesto!   ¡Claro!   ¡Absolutamente!   Sí, exacto.

1. ...   2. ...   3. ...

Un poco de gramática

Talking About What People Want Others to Do

The following type of sentence is used to describe what someone wants another person to do.

Carlos **quiere que** Carlitos **se tome** la medicina. También **quiere que guarde** cama.	*Carlos wants Carlitos to take his medicine. He also wants him to stay in bed.*

The second half of each of these sentences contains an **-ar** verb, but with an **-e** ending. This is one form of a different verb system called the present subjunctive. It is formed by using the present-tense **yo** stem: **tom-** → **tome**.

To use an **-er** or **-ir** verb in this type of sentence, add an **-a** ending.

Carlitos no quiere que **venga** el médico.

Did you notice how the irregularity of the **yo** stem is reflected in this form? **Vengo** → **venga**, **pongo** → **ponga**, and so on. To form the third-person plural of the present subjunctive, add the characteristic **-n** ending to the **-a** or **-e**. You will learn more about these forms in the Workbook.

Actividad.   ¿Qué quieren?

Indica lo que quieren—¡o no quieren!—las siguientes personas. ¡OJO! Hay más de una respuesta posible en algunos casos.

1. _____ ¿Qué quiere el padre Rodrigo?
2. _____ ¿Qué quiere Consuelo?
3. _____ ¿Qué no quiere don Fernando? ¿Y qué quiere?

4. _____ Y Ángela, ¿qué quiere?
5. _____ ¿Qué no quiere Juanita, la hermana de Carlitos? ¿Y qué quiere?
6. _____ ¿Qué quiere Raquel?
7. _____ Y los hijos de don Fernando, ¿qué es lo que quieren?
8. _____ ¿Qué quiere Mercedes?

a. Quiere que, de alguna manera, Arturo se ponga en contacto con ella... porque ella no puede comunicarse con él.
b. Quiere que a ella también le den un poco de chocolate, no sólo a su hermano.
c. Quiere que rescaten a su hermano.
d. Quieren que su padre recupere la salud y que regrese a La Gavia.
e. Quieren que el especialista de Guadalajara se ponga en contacto con ellos de alguna manera.
f. No quiere que lo visiten más médicos... ni tampoco que le den más medicinas.
g. Quiere que Ángela y Raquel descansen un poco.
h. No quiere que Carlitos le pase el resfriado.
i. Quiere que Carlitos guarde cama... ¡y que le baje la fiebre!
j. Quiere que todos tengan fe en la Virgen.
k. Quiere que se resuelva de una vez (*once and for all*) el caso de su otra familia.
l. Quiere que llegue Raquel a la Ciudad de México.

Nota cultural: La Virgen de Guadalupe

Note: Remember that, throughout the first half of the Textbook, a brief exercise before each extensive **Nota cultural** reading helped you review what you already knew about the topic (usually information from the video episode) before beginning the reading. Keep that strategy in mind as you work with the readings in the second half of the text. The first few **Notas culturales** will have a brief reminder.

Antes de leer, escucha una vez más lo que el narrador dice sobre la Virgen de Guadalupe. Hay más información sobre la Virgen en la lectura.

Era el año 1531, pocos años después de la llegada de los primeros españoles a América. Un joven indio caminaba tranquilamente por el campo,[1] en lo que es hoy la capital de México. De repente, oyó una voz femenina que le decía: «Juan Diego, Juan Diego».

Era la Virgen María, quien es la madre de Jesucristo en la tradición[2] cristiana. La Virgen habló con Juan Diego. Le pidió que se construyera[3] un templo en su honor, en el mismo cerro[4] de Tepeyac. Juan Diego fue a ver al obispo de su pueblo, para contarle la increíble historia. Como era de esperar,[5] el obispo no le creyó. La madre de Dios no se le iba a aparecer a un pobre indio.

[1]*countryside* [2]*belief* [3]se... *be built* [4]en... *on that very hill* [5]era... *was predictable*

La Virgen persistió en su deseo de tener un templo en ese lugar. Hizo crecer un rosal[6] en el cerro, una región donde los rosales no crecían. Y se le apareció al joven otra vez. Le pidió al muchacho que le llevara al obispo unas rosas del rosal. Juan Diego las puso en una manta.[7] Al abrirla delante del obispo, apareció dibujada en la manta, junto a las rosas, la imagen de la Virgen.

Poco tiempo después se construyó en el sitio del milagro[8] una capilla. En el altar se colocó[9] la imagen de la Virgen indígena, Nuestra Señora de Guadalupe; también la llaman la Virgen Morena. Hoy día hay una catedral en este lugar, la Basílica de Guadalupe. Es un lugar sagrado[10] para todos los mexicanos católicos. Los pobres y los enfermos vienen a esta catedral a pedirle a la Virgen milagros.

En México y en las comunidades mexicoamericanas en los Estados Unidos, la imagen de la Virgen de Guadalupe está en todas partes: en calendarios, en pinturas, en casas privadas y sitios públicos… no sólo en las iglesias y las catedrales. Ricos y pobres la veneran.

Es fácil de explicar esta devoción del pueblo mexicano por la Virgen de Guadalupe. Para muchos mexicanos, la Virgen tiene un valor simbólico porque representa la raza indígena y demuestra el valor que la cultura indígena tiene ante los ojos de Dios. Pero no sólo los mexicanos y sus descendientes participan del culto a la Virgen. Desde 1910 la Virgen es también la santa patrona de toda Hispanoamérica.

[6]*rosebush* [7]*cloak* [8]*miracle* [9]*se… was placed* [10]*sacred, holy*

La Basílica de Guadalupe

Actividad. La historia de la Virgen de Guadalupe

1.   2.   3.   4.

5.   6.   7.   8.

En la página 296 hay ocho dibujos que narran la historia de la Virgen, pero un dibujo no pertenece a la narración que acabas de leer. ¿Puedes identificarlo?

Have you completed the following sections of the lesson? Check them off here.

_____ **Preparación**   _____ **Conversaciones**
_____ **¿Tienes buena memoria?**   _____ **Un poco de gramática**
_____ **Vocabulario del tema**

Now scan the words in the **Vocabulario** list to be sure that you understand the meaning of most of them. Then you will be ready to continue on with **Lección 29** in the Workbook.

VOCABULARIO

Los verbos

derrumbarse	to collapse, cave in
lograr	to manage to, be able
llorar	to cry
sacar	to take out, get out

Las enfermedades (Illnesses)

la fiebre	fever
la fractura	fracture
el resfriado	cold

Los verbos relacionados con la salud
(Health-related Verbs)

bajar	to bring down (*a fever*)
curar	to heal, cure
doler (ue)	to hurt, be painful
examinar	to examine
guardar cama	to stay in bed
ponerle (a alguien) una inyección	to give (someone) a shot
respirar	to breathe
sacar la lengua	to stick out one's tongue
sacar rayos X	to take X-rays
tomarle (a alguien) la temperatura	to take (someone's) temperature

Repaso: **sentirse (ie, i) bien/mal**

Los tratamientos (Treatments)

la aspirina	aspirin
el calmante	sedative
el examen	examination
la medicina	medicine
la pastilla	pill
la receta	prescription
el termómetro	thermometer

Otras partes del cuerpo

la garganta	throat
la lengua	tongue

Los adjetivos

hinchado/a	swollen
médico/a	medical

Las personas

el enfermero/la enfermera	nurse
el/la médico	doctor

Repaso: **el doctor/la doctora, el/la paciente**

Cómo decir que otra persona tiene razón
(How to Say That Someone Is Right)

¡Por supuesto!	Of course!
Sí, exacto.	Yes, that's exactly right.

LECCIÓN
· · · · · · · · · · · · · · · ·

30
PREOCUPACIONES*

· ·

OBJETIVOS

The materials in **Lección 30** of the Textbook and the Workbook will help you better understand the video episode and take you beyond it, giving you additional information about places and characters in the series. The Textbook will also help you to develop skill in using the Spanish language. In this lesson, you will learn

- the names for many places in a city
- additional ways to treat people, such as clients, with respect
- ways to use the subjunctive to discuss things about which you feel emotionally involved.

You will also learn about the Cuban-American community.

Be sure to work through all parts of the lesson. When you see a cassette symbol in the margin, listen to the tape for **Lección 30**. Answers or hints for many activities are given in Appendix 1. Be sure to check your answers for each activity before going on to the next one.

*Worries

BEFORE VIEWING . . .

Preparación

Actividad A.

A continuación tienes el texto del resumen del narrador que, como siempre, vas a escuchar al principio de este episodio, pero hay algunos detalles incorrectos. Indica la información equivocada. (Hay uno o dos detalles incorrectos en cada párrafo.)

En el episodio previo, cuando Raquel y Ángela llegaron al sitio de la excavación, ya sacaban a dos personas. Pero ninguna de las dos era el hermano de Ángela. Justo en ese momento, hubo otro derrumbe en la excavación. Roberto Castillo quedó atrapado de nuevo y murió. Ángela estaba desesperada.

Al día siguiente, en la Ciudad de México, la familia Castillo desayunaba y hablaba del derrumbe en la excavación. Mientras la familia desayunaba, Gloria hablaba con su hijo, quien estaba enfermo la noche anterior.

Muy contento porque ya sabía algo de Raquel, Arturo bajó a la recepción del hotel y preguntó por ella. Solo y sin amigos en esta ciudad grande, Arturo salió a la calle.

Ahora escucha la narración en la cinta para ver si encontraste todos los errores.

Para pensar...

Imagina que eres Arturo y que te encuentras en la situación que se describe al final del episodio previo. ¿En qué estás pensando? ¿Cuáles son tus preocupaciones? ¿Qué necesitas? ¿Qué vas a hacer para tratar de resolver algunas de tus preocupaciones?

Actividad B.

Paso 1

En este episodio, vas a ver otra vez a un personaje que apareció mucho antes, en uno de los primeros episodios de *Destinos*. Es Ofelia, la secretaria de Carlos en Miami.

Como muchas personas que viven en la Florida, Ofelia es cubana. Su dialecto del español y acento son diferentes de los de los otros personajes de la serie. Escucha parte de una conversación telefónica entre Carlos y Ofelia para familiarizarte con el acento de ella. Puedes escuchar la conversación varias veces, si quieres. Luego contesta la pregunta.

¿De qué le habla Ofelia a Carlos?

a. _____ De su familia.
b. _____ De un nuevo restaurante.
c. _____ De un nuevo cliente.

¿Notas la diferencia en su acento? ¿Cómo es diferente, por ejemplo, del acento de Carlos? ¿de Raquel?

Paso 2

En este episodio, el Padre Rodrigo sigue muy preocupado por el bienestar (*well-being*) de Ángela y Raquel. Les hace una sugerencia sobre algo que cree que ellas deben hacer. Escucha su conversación con ellas. Luego completa la oración.

El Padre Rodrigo les

a. _____ recomienda a las dos mujeres que vayan a un hotel en el pueblo
b. _____ recomienda que se queden con una persona religiosa

Como en inglés, la palabra **hermana** se refiere no solamente a un miembro de la familia sino también a las mujeres que dedican su vida al servicio de Dios en una comunidad religiosa.

AFTER VIEWING . . .

• •

¿TIENES BUENA MEMORIA?

Actividad A.   ¿Quiénes son?

Contesta las siguientes preguntas sobre dos mujeres que aparecen en este episodio. Una está relacionada con los asuntos de la capital; la otra, con los asuntos que ocurren en la excavación.

1. Esta mujer se llama
   a. _____ Pati   b. _____ Gloria   c. _____ Ofelia

2. Vive en... donde trabaja en la Compañía Industrias Castillo Saavedra, como secretaria de Carlos.
   a. _____ Los Ángeles   b. _____ Miami
   c. _____ Nueva York

3. Después de hablar con ella, Carlos
   a. _____ está preocupado   b. _____ está muy contento
   c. _____ empieza a llorar

Para pensar…

Sí, Carlos está muy preocupado después de hablar con Ofelia. ¿Crees que eran buenas o malas las noticias que Ofelia le dio?

4. La hermana María Teresa vive en el pueblo y trabaja
   a. _____ en la excavación
   b. ___✓___ en una escuela, con los niños del pueblo
   c. _____ en un hotel para turistas

5. La hermana les ofrece a Raquel y a Ángela
   a. ___✓___ un lugar donde descansar y refrescarse
   b. _____ algo de comer
   c. _____ un teléfono que funciona

Nota cultural: Aspectos de la vida religiosa

As you have seen in previous video episodes and continued to observe in this one, various aspects of religion and religious life play an important role in Hispanic countries, especially in rural areas. People who belong to religious orders—priests, nuns (sisters), monks (brothers)—are integral parts of the communities in which they live and work.

Here at the excavation site, for example, **el Padre Rodrigo** is a source of comfort to all who are involved with the accident, whether they are Catholic or not. And **la hermana María Teresa** unquestioningly offers support to Ángela and Raquel, opening the facilities of the church to them.

An important service offered by members of religious orders in some countries is education. In rural areas many schools are run by the Catholic Church. Do you remember that Jaime and Miguel Ruiz attended a religious school in Sevilla? Religion was one of the subjects that they both studied.

Actividad B.   En la excavación y en la capital

Los siguientes párrafos son un resumen de lo que pasó en este episodio. Complétalos con la forma correcta de las palabras y frases de las siguientes listas.

Lugares: la capital, la escuela del pueblo, el hotel, la iglesia del pueblo, Nueva York, Puerto Rico, el sitio de la excavación, la tienda del pueblo

Frases: le dejó un mensaje/una carta, descansar y almorzar, descansar y bañarse, durmió muy bien/muy mal, estaba ocupada la línea, no consiguió línea, hablando con alguien en la capital/Nueva York, llamar, tener noticias de Roberto/Arturo, tenía suficiente aire/comida

Ángela y Raquel pasaron la noche en la excavación. Ángela _durmió muy muy_ ¹ porque el doctor le dio un calmante. Tan pronto como se despertó, Ángela quería _Tener noticias_ ² Desgraciadamente, no había noticias. Ángela seguía muy preocupada, sobre todo porque pensaba que tal vez Roberto no _tenía suficiente_ ³

En una pequeña _la tienda del pueblo_ Raquel seguía tratando de comunicarse por teléfono con varias personas en la Capital. No pudo hablar con Pedro, porque _estaba ocupada la línea_ ⁵ (Raquel no lo sabía, pero en esa ocasión Pati estaba _con alguien en la_ ⁶) Pero Raquel sí pudo hablar con _el hotel_ ⁷ en México. Arturo no estaba en su habitación, pero Raquel _le dejó un mensy_ ⁸ (Cuando leyó el mensaje, Arturo estaba muy preocupado.) Por su parte, Ángela pudo hablar con sus tíos en _Puerto Rico_ ⁹

Después de hacer estas llamadas telefónicas, Raquel y Ángela fueron a _la escuela_ ,¹⁰ donde las esperaba la hermana María Teresa. Allí, pudieron _descansar y bañarse_ ¹

 Escucha la cinta para verificar tus respuestas.

Vocabulario del tema

Note: As in some previous lessons, the words on the left below and on page 303 are from the video episode. Those in the right-hand column on page 303 are additional vocabulary items for each category that you may want to learn.

En una ciudad

las afueras	suburbs; outskirts
el barrio, la zona	neighborhood
el centro	downtown
la colonia (*Mex.*)	neighborhood

el ayuntamiento	city hall	**la escuela**	school
el cine	movie theater	**el jardín (botánico)**	(botanical) garden
el edificio	building	**el (jardín) zoológico**	zoo
la iglesia	church	**el parque**	park
la plaza	plaza, square	**el rascacielos**	skyscraper
		el teatro	theater
el almacén	department store		
la farmacia	drugstore, pharmacy	**el banco**	bank
el hotel	hotel	**el centro comercial**	shopping center
el mercado	market	**el restaurante**	restaurant
el negocio	business		
la oficina	office		
el supermercado	supermarket		
la tienda	store		
la tienda de ropa para hombres	men's clothing store		
la tienda de ropa para mujeres	women's clothing store		

Actividad A.   El Distrito Federal

Paso 1

Escucha otra vez la descripción de la Ciudad de México. Mientras escuchas, indica en este dibujo con la letra **C** (**ciudad**) los diferentes lugares de la ciudad mencionados por el narrador.

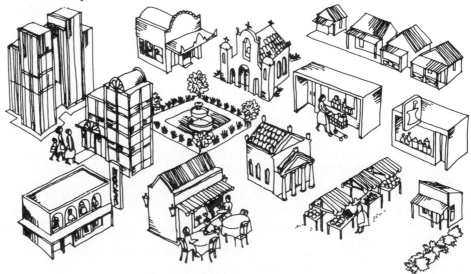

Paso 2

Ahora escucha otra vez la descripción de un pueblo típico. Mientras escuchas, indica en el mismo dibujo con la letra **P** (= **pueblo**) los lugares de la capital que también se encuentran en los pueblos o que solamente se encuentran en ellos. Con la letra **N** (= **no**) indica los lugares que no se encuentran en los pueblos.

¡Un desafío! ¿Recuerdas los sitios que Arturo quería encontrar en la capital? Le mencionó cinco lugares al agente de turismo.

Actividad B.   Lugares muy conocidos

Vas a escuchar una descripción breve de una serie de lugares. Pon el número del lugar junto al nombre apropiado de la siguiente lista.

> MODELO: (*oyes*)   Número uno: Un parque es un sitio donde hay mucho
> espacio, muchos árboles, muchas flores...
> (*escribes*)   __1__ el Rosedal
> (*dices*)   El Rosedal es un parque.
> (*oyes*)   El Rosedal es un parque.

a. _____ *the San Diego Zoo, the Bronx Zoo*

b. _____ la Torre Trump

c. _____ *Greenwich Village*

d. _____ *Macy's*

e. _____ La Barca

f. _____ La Cuadra

g. _____ *Radio City Music Hall*

h. _____ *A&P, Safeway, Lucky's...*

i. _____ el Rosedal

Actividad C.   ¿Y tú?

Lee la siguiente lista de lugares. Si hay alguno de éstos en tu ciudad, da el nombre que lleva cada uno. Si no los hay, di «No hay».

1. un restaurante muy elegante y muy caro
2. un rascacielos
3. un parque grande
4. un supermercado económico
5. un barrio elegante
6. un cine popular entre los estudiantes
7. un almacén económico, no muy caro
8. un centro comercial nuevo

Actividad D.   ¿Y tú?

¿Qué necesitas que haya en tu ciudad o pueblo? ¿Qué lugares son indispensables para ti? ¿Cuáles no te importa que haya o no haya? Contesta, completando las siguientes oraciones.

Tengo que vivir donde haya _____ y _____.

Me gusta vivir cerca de _____.

Cada semana voy al/a la _____. Por eso para mí es importante que haya uno/una cerca del lugar donde uno vive.

Nunca voy al/a la _____.

CONVERSACIONES: ENTRE CLIENTES Y DEPENDIENTES

Actividad. En una agencia

En este episodio Arturo habla con un agente en una oficina de turismo para pedir información sobre la Capital. El empleado y Arturo se tratan con el respeto y cortesía comunes en la mayoría de las conversaciones entre clientes y empleados. Algunas de las frases que usan en su conversación ya te son conocidas, pero hay unas nuevas.

Paso 1

Escucha otra vez el diálogo entre Arturo y el empleado. Luego complétalo con las frases que escuchaste. Estas frases necesarias son nuevas para ti; las otras ya te son conocidas.

A sus órdenes.   Mande Ud.

ARTURO: _____,[1] señor.

EMPLEADO: _____,[2] señor.

ARTURO: Es la primera vez que vengo a esta ciudad y no conozco nada. Quiero ir a varios lugares. Mire. Quiero ir a una farmacia, a una tienda de ropa para hombres, a un almacén, a un mercado o un supermercado.

EMPLEADO: _____,[3] señor. Podrá encontrar todo eso aquí en esta colonia. Estamos aquí. En esta calle, hay una tienda de ropa para hombres muy buena. Y en esta calle hay un almacén donde se vende de todo. Hay un mercado pequeño aquí, también hay un supermercado. A ver... sí, aquí. Si sale y va a la izquierda, en la esquina hay una farmacia.

ARTURO: _____[4]

EMPLEADO: _____[5]

Paso 2

¿Qué significan las frases nuevas?

- Sabes que **mandar** significa *to send*; también significa *to order* o *to command*. ¿Qué crees que significa **Mande Ud.**?
- **Orden** significa *order* (*a command*) o *order* (*sequence*). ¿Qué significa **a sus órdenes**?

Estas expresiones se usan típicamente en México; no se oyen en otros países hispanos. En otros lugares, es común decir **Dígame** (= **Mande Ud.**) o **No hay de qué** (= **A sus órdenes**).

En el diálogo, ¿en qué otras maneras Arturo y el empleado demuestran respeto mutuo?

Paso 3

¿Qué dices en las siguientes situaciones?

• Tu jefe te quiere dar una lista de cosas que hacer.
• Trabajas de noche en la recepción de un hotel. Acabas de darle información a un huésped y éste se despide de ti.

Un poco de gramática

<hr>

Expressing Your Feelings About Something

It is possible to express feelings or emotion about an event without using the subjunctive. But it is also common to use the subjunctive as the second verb in a sentence that starts out with an expression of emotion, feelings, or an attitude toward something.

Es lástima que Roberto todavía **esté** atrapado en el túnel.	*It's a shame that Roberto is still trapped in the tunnel.*
Carlitos **tiene miedo de que** el doctor le **ponga** una inyección.	*Carlitos is afraid that the doctor will give him a shot.*

As you do the following activity, notice other expressions of emotion used at the beginning of the sentence that "trigger" the subjunctive. And be on the lookout for the subjunctive forms of some irregular verbs. You will learn more about these aspects of the subjunctive in the Workbook.

Actividad.   ¿Cuáles son sus sentimientos?

Junta una frase del primer grupo con una del segundo para formar oraciones lógicas sobre los sentimientos de algunos personajes de *Destinos*... y para expresar algunos de los tuyos (*yours*). Hay más de una respuesta posible.

1. _____ Ángela tiene miedo de que
2. _____ Carlos siente (*regrets*) que
3. _____ Don Fernando siente que
4. _____ Mercedes tiene miedo de que
5. _____ Mercedes cree que es extraño (*strange*) que
6. _____ La madre de Raquel cree que es una lástima (*shame*) que su hija
7. _____ Yo creo que es extraño que
8. _____ Creo que es lástima que

    a.   haya problemas entre Juan y Pati
    b.   haya problemas en la oficina en Miami
    c.   no pueda conocer a sus nuevos nietos todavía
    d.   esté enfermo Carlitos, pero sabe que no es nada serio
    e.   no vayan a poder rescatar a su hermano
    f.   no esté casada todavía
    g.   Roberto no tenga suficiente aire
    h.   don Fernando se muera antes de conocer a sus nietos
    i.   Gloria llegue a casa tarde

Nota cultural: Los cubanos en los Estados Unidos

Los cubanos que viven en los Estados Unidos son en su mayoría[1] inmigrantes.* Viven dispersos por varias partes del país. El lugar donde hay una mayor concentración de ellos es en el sur de la Florida, sobre todo en Miami. En esa ciudad, especialmente en el barrio que se llama La Pequeña Habana, es marcada la presencia de la exuberante cultura cubana. Se nota en todo: en el fuerte café cubano; en los juegos de dominó de los ancianos; en los ritmos caribeños que se escuchan en la televisión y en la radio; en los nombres de las calles y de las tiendas; y en las personas.

Personas y personajes

Los cubanos comenzaron a llegar a los Estados Unidos en gran número hacia 1960. Fidel Castro ya había ganado[2] la revolución, y se perseguía a las personas que tenían una buena posición económica y social bajo la dictadura de Fulgencio Batista.

Por eso, los cubanos que inmigraron en aquel entonces[3] eran en su mayoría profesionales de las clases media y alta: abogados, médicos, ingenieros,[4] hombres de negocio.† Como refugiados políticos, llegaron con poco más que su cultura y educación. En algunos casos sus títulos universitarios no eran válidos en los Estados Unidos, y tuvieron que volver a la universidad a estudiar.

Veamos algo de la historia de dos cubanoamericanos, uno ya famoso y el otro… todavía no.

● Xavier Suárez: elegido alcalde[5] de la ciudad de Miami en 1985

Suárez nació en Cuba, el noveno[6] de catorce hijos. Llegó a los Estados Unidos a los once años, después de la invasión de la Bahía de Cochinos,[7] y pronto aprendió inglés. Como para

[1]en… *for the most part* [2]había… *had won* [3]en… *at that time* [4]*engineers* [5]*mayor* [6]*ninth* [7]Bahía… *Bay of Pigs*

---

*Como inmigrantes, los cubanoamericanos son diferentes a los mexicoamericanos y a los puertorriqueños. Como ya lo sabes, los puertorriqueños son ciudadanos de los Estados Unidos. Los antepasados de algunos mexicoamericanos fueron los dueños de territorios en Texas, California, Arizona, Nuevo México… Otros mexicoamericanos están en este país porque quieren vivir aquí. No vinieron como refugiados políticos como muchos cubanos.

†Ha habido otras olas de inmigración también: una, después de la invasión de la Bahía de Cochinos (*Bay of Pigs*) en 1961; otra, la llegada de los llamados «marielitos» en 1980.

muchos cubanoamericanos, la educación era muy importante para él. Por eso sacó un B.S. en ingeniería, un M.A. en administración pública y, por fin, el título de abogado en Harvard.

Aquí Suárez habla de una de sus primeras memorias en los Estados Unidos: «Yo fui a una iglesia el domingo y… no entendía nada de lo que decía el sacerdote[8] en el sermón. Nada. Nada. Y eso que estudié inglés como buen estudiante. ¡Vaya! Pensé que sabría[9] algo de lo que estaba diciendo. Nada. Nada. Nada. Dije 'Dios mío, ¿cómo yo voy a entender el idioma de este país?'»

Xavier Suárez y su familia

- Gustavo Medina: escritor, guionista[10]

Medina también nació en Cuba. Tenía nueve años cuando salió de Cuba con su familia en 1959, el mismo año en que cayó[11] el gobierno de Batista. Ya en los Estados Unidos, sacó un M.S. en psicología y luego trabajó de corrector de libros y de programas para computadoras. Después de alcanzar[12] éxito en este campo, decidió sacar un título en cinematografía. Ahora aspira a hacer televisión.

Aquí Medina habla de un tema que le interesa mucho: « …es el tema de ser un exiliado en un país extranjero… [Uno] no pertenece[13] a una cultura ni pertenece a otra, pero tiene que acomodarse[14] y es muy difícil a veces…. Para mí un tema importante en mi vida es cómo resolver ese aislamiento[15] que yo siento, en esta cultura y en otras culturas hispánicas. Por ejemplo, yo voy a la Argentina, voy a México, voy a Colombia, voy a Puerto Rico, y la gente me dice, «Ah, tú eres cubano». Sí, claro, pero no lo soy… Cuando estoy en Europa y la gente me oye hablar inglés, me dice, «*Oh, you are American.*» Entonces yo digo, «*No, not really. I'm from Cuba, but I'm not really anymore.*»

La situación política actual

Se habla mucho de los aspectos positivos de la presencia de los cubanos en la Florida, sobre todo en Miami. Pero hay que reconocer al mismo tiempo que presenta problemas. Algunos anglosajones guardan resentimiento hacia lo que ellos ven como la «dominación» latina de la ciudad. Para otros, sobre todo para los que no hablan español, el vivir constantemente en contacto con este idioma representa una molestia. La otra cara de la moneda[16] es la actitud de los cubanos a quienes no les gusta—o que no saben—hablar inglés.

También hay controversias entre la misma comunidad cubanoamericana. Algunos, sobre todo los más ancianos, se consideran todavía cubanos y les gustaría volver a vivir en Cuba. Para ellos, es antipatriótico renunciar a esa esperanza. Pero los jóvenes son cubano*americanos*, sobre todo los que nacieron aquí. Es cierto que les interesa Cuba y todo lo hispánico, pero se van forjando[17] sus vidas en este país. Para ellos, Cuba es algo que vive en el recuerdo de sus padres o abuelos; no es parte de su realidad. Otros, como Suárez y Medina, comparten ambas experiencias.

[8]*priest* [9]*would know* [10]*script writer* [11]*fell* [12]*achieving* [13]*belong* [14]*adjust* [15]*isolation* [16]La… *The other side of the coin*
[17]*creating*

Actividad.   La experiencia de un inmigrante

En tu opinión, ¿cuáles son las ventajas (*advantages*) y las desventajas de ser un inmigrante en otro país? Piensa no sólo en lo que acabas de leer sino también en lo que sabes de Ángel Castillo, quien siendo español, fue después argentino y luego emigró a Puerto Rico.

Have you completed the following sections of the lesson? Check them off here.

_____ **Preparación**   _____ **Conversaciones**
_____ **¿Tienes buena memoria?**   _____ **Un poco de gramática**
_____ **Vocabulario del tema**

Now scan the words in the **Vocabulario** list to be sure that you understand the meaning of most of them. Then you will be ready to continue on with **Lección 30** in the Workbook.

VOCABULARIO

Los verbos

descansar	to rest
sentir (ie, i)	to regret

En una ciudad

las afueras	suburbs, outskirts
el almacén	department store
el ayuntamiento	city hall
el banco	bank
el centro	downtown
el cine	movie theater
la colonia (*Mex.*)	neighborhood
el edificio	building
la farmacia	pharmacy
el hotel	hotel
el jardín (botánico)	(botanical) garden
el (jardín) zoológico	zoo
el parque	park
el rascacielos	skyscraper
el restaurante	restaurant
el supermercado	supermarket
el teatro	theater
la tienda de ropa para hombres/mujeres	men's/women's clothing store
la zona	neighborhood

Repaso: **el barrio, la escuela, la iglesia, el mercado, el negocio, la oficina, la tienda**

Otros lugares

el pueblo	town

Entre clientes y dependientes

A sus órdenes.	At your service.
Mande Ud.	How can I help you?

Las palabras adicionales

es extraño	it's strange
es (una) lástima	it's a shame

31
MEDIDAS DRÁSTICAS*

OBJETIVOS

The materials in **Lección 31** of the Textbook and the Workbook will help you better understand the video episode and take you beyond it, giving you additional information about places and characters in the series. The Textbook will also help you to develop skill in using the Spanish language. In this lesson, you will learn

- the names for various businesses and types of shops in Spanish
- the use of the subjunctive to talk about things that have not yet happened.

You will also learn about the Mexican-American community.

Be sure to work through all parts of the lesson. When you see a cassette symbol in the margin, listen to the tape for **Lección 31**. Answers or hints for many activities are given in Appendix 1. Be sure to check your answers for each activity before going on to the next one.

*Drastic Measures

BEFORE VIEWING . . .

PREPARACIÓN

Actividad A.

¿Recuerdas lo que hicieron estas personas en el **Episodio 30**? Haz oraciones completas tomando una frase de cada columna.

1. _____ Raquel
2. _____ Raquel y Ángela
3. _____ la Hermana María Teresa
4. _____ Pati
5. _____ Carlos

a. se enteró de que había problemas en el teatro en Nueva York
b. les dio a Ángela y Raquel dónde descansar y bañarse
c. le dejó un mensaje a Arturo
d. supo lo que pasa en la oficina en Miami
e. fueron a una iglesia
f. trató de comunicarse con Pedro y Arturo

Escucha la cinta para verificar tus respuestas.

Para pensar...

1. ¿Qué hará Pati ahora que sabe que hay problemas con la producción de la obra? ¿Se quedará con la familia o volverá a Nueva York?
2. En los episodios previos, se ha sugerido que la familia Castillo tiene problemas. En tu opinión, ¿cuáles son esos problemas?
3. ¿Por qué se puso preocupado Carlos cuando habló con Ofelia, su secretaria?

Actividad B.

Paso 1

Escucha parte de una conversación entre Juan y Pati. Es una discusión (*argument*) sobre algo. Después de escuchar, contesta la pregunta.

¿Cuál es el tema de la discusión entre Juan y Pati?

a. _____ el estado grave de la salud de don Fernando.
b. _____ los problemas que tiene Pati en el teatro
c. _____ el hecho de que (*the fact that*) Pati cree que Juan no comprende su situación como mujer profesional

Si indicaste la letra *c*, tuviste razón.

Paso 2

Lee las últimas líneas de la conversación que acabas de escuchar.

JUAN: ¿Pero por qué tienes que ir a Nueva York? ¿No lo puedes hacer desde aquí, por teléfono?

PATI: ¡Juan! ¡Estamos hablando de una obra de teatro! Lo que tú dices es como… como… pedirle a un doctor que cure a un enfermo por teléfono.

Paso 3

Ahora escucha toda la conversación de nuevo. Puedes leer las últimas líneas al mismo tiempo, si quieres. Luego contesta las preguntas.

1. ¿Qué quiere Juan que haga Pati?

   a. _____ Que vaya a Nueva York.   b. _____ Que se quede con él.

2. ¿Qué parece que va a hacer Pati?

   a. _____ Se va a quedar con Juan.   b. _____ Va a regresar a Nueva York.

 **AFTER VIEWING . . .**

¿TIENES BUENA MEMORIA?

Actividad A.   En la excavación

¿Son ciertas (**C**) o falsas (**F**) las siguientes declaraciones sobre lo que pasó en la excavación en este episodio?

C   F   1. Raquel y Ángela no saben nada de Roberto todavía.

C   F   2. Ángela no se siente mejor después de descansar en la iglesia.

C   F   3. La actitud de Ángela es pesimista en cuanto al rescate de Roberto.

 Ahora escucha el repaso de Raquel para verificar tus respuestas.

Para pensar…

Al final del episodio algo tuvo lugar (*took place*) en los Estados Unidos. ¿Recuerdas lo que pasó? Una persona llamó a los padres de Raquel. ¿Recuerdas quién era esa persona? La madre de Raquel dijo que era «el novio de mi hija».

1. ¿Ha hablado (*Has spoken*) Raquel alguna vez de un novio, del pasado o del presente?

2. ¿Qué efecto es posible que esta persona tenga en las relaciones que están formando entre Raquel y Arturo?

Actividad B.   En la capital

Contesta las siguientes preguntas sobre lo que está pasando en la familia Castillo en la Ciudad de México.

1.   ¿Sabe Pedro lo del accidente?
2.   ¿Quiénes se pelearon (*had a fight*)?
3.   ¿Quiénes hablaron con unos auditores?
4.   ¿Eran mínimas o drásticas las recomendaciones de los auditores?

Ahora escucha el repaso del narrador para verificar tus respuestas.

¡Un desafío! ¿Recuerdas las tres recomendaciones de los auditores?

VOCABULARIO DEL TEMA

Las tiendas y los comercios

la carnicería	butcher shop	**la barbería**	barber shop	**la papelería**	stationery store
la confitería	confectionery	**la droguería**	drugstore		
la farmacia	pharmacy	**la ferretería**	hardware store	**la peluquería**	beauty shop, hairdresser's
la panadería	bakery	**la frutería**	fruit store		
la pastelería	pastry shop	**la joyería**	jewelry store	**la pollería**	poultry shop
la pescadería	fish market	**la lavandería**	laundry	**la taquería**	taco stand
la zapatería	shoe store	**la librería**	bookstore	**la tortillería**	tortilla shop

Note the following about these store names.

- The names of many kinds of stores end in **-ería** in Spanish. Note that **la farmacia** is an exception.
- Many store names are derived from the names of the principal products sold in them or the service they perform. What product is sold in **una carnicería**? in **una librería**?

Where would **dulces** or **confites** (*candies*) be sold? Where would you have clothing washed (**lavar**)? What other store-product relationships can you find, based on words you know?

• Just as store names and products are related, so are the names for people who work there. In what store do these people work? **un carnicero**, **una peluquera**, **un panadero**, **una zapatera**.

Actividad A.   De compras con Lupe

Escucha otra vez mientras el narrador describe un día de compras con Lupe. Escribe los nombres de las tiendas que visita con los dibujos apropiados.

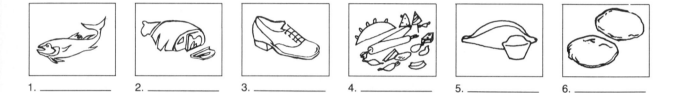

1. _____   2. _____   3. _____   4. _____   5. _____   6. _____

Ahora escucha otra vez la lección de ortografía (*spelling*) que Carlos le da a Juanita y trata de corregir lo que tú escribiste. Carlos y Juanita van a hablar de dos tiendas cuyos (*whose*) nombres no escribiste en la primera parte de esta actividad. Escribe esos nombres cuando los oigas.

7. _____   8. _____

Nota cultural: La educación bilingüe

The spelling errors made by Juanita are natural for her age and are also typical of anyone—native or nonnative—who is learning how to write in Spanish. Compared with English, the number of sound or written symbol pairs that cause learners difficulty in Spanish is quite minimal. Spanish-speaking children, like speakers of English, also pass through periods in which they have difficulty using irregular forms consistently, if at all, and it is not unusual to hear Hispanic children say **yo sabo** instead of **yo sé**. Children, like older learners, soon learn the correct forms.

In Miami, Juanita attends a bilingual school in which she receives instruction in both English and Spanish. The concept of bilingual education is currently being debated in the United States. It may be years before the debate is resolved, if ever.

Actividad B. ¿Adónde irás? (*Where will you go?*)

En la cinta vas a oír los nombres de una serie de
productos. Indica a qué tienda irás para comprarlas.

MODELO: (*oyes*) las bananas
(*dices*) Iré a una frutería.
(*oyes*) Debes ir a una frutería.

1. ...   2. ...   3. ...   4. ...   5. ...   6. ...
7. ...   8. ...   9. ...   10. ...   11. ...   12. ...

Actividad C. ¿Y tú?

Describe los comercios que hay en el lugar donde tú vives y también tus propias costumbres en cuanto a las compras. Completa solamente las oraciones que se relacionen con tus experiencias personales.

1. Por aquí (*Around here*) hay muchos/as _____, _____

   y _____.

2. No hay suficientes _____.

3. Casi nunca compro algo en un(a) _____.

4. Cuando necesito _____, siempre voy al/a la _____ que

   está en _____.

5. Casi siempre compro la comida en _____.

6. De joven, trabajaba en _____.

7. Hay un(a) _____ donde todos los estudiantes de la escuela superior se reúnen después de las clases.

8. Las tiendas están abiertas hasta las _____. Los supermercados

   como _____ están abiertos toda la noche.

UN POCO DE GRAMÁTICA

Another Way to Talk About the Future

As you know, it is possible to talk about future events by using the future forms, or forms of **ir** + **a** + an infinitive. But it is also common to use the subjunctive form of the verb when a sentence expresses future intent.

Ángela va a estar muy contenta **cuando rescaten** a Roberto.	*Ángela is going to be very happy when they rescue Roberto.*
Cuando hable otra vez con Raquel, Arturo le quiere decir muchas cosas.	*The next time he speaks with Raquel, Arturo wants to tell her lots of things.*

Did you notice that the subjunctive is used to express only the future event that directly follows **cuando**? You will learn more about this use of the subjunctive, as well as its use with other words such as **cuando**, in the Workbook.

Actividad.   ¿Qué pasará cuando... ?

Junta una frase del primer grupo con una del segundo para formar oraciones lógicas sobre lo que tú crees que va a pasar en los siguientes episodios de *Destinos*. En el segundo grupo, puedes inventar tus propias frases, si quieres.

1. Cuando encuentren a Roberto,
2. Cuando venga el especialista a ver a don Fernando,
3. Cuando la madre de Raquel le habla a Luis,
4. Cuando Pedro y Ramón hablen de las recomendaciones de los auditores,
5. Cuando Pati regrese a Nueva York,
6. Cuando Arturo y Raquel por fin se pongan en contacto,
7. Cuando Carlos hable con Ofelia otra vez,
8. Cuando don Fernando hable con Ángela (y con Roberto, si es que lo rescatan),

a. querrá saber / no querrá saber más detalles sobre los problemas
b. las van a aceptar/rechazar todas
c. Juan la va a divorciar/extrañar
d. los va a aceptar/rechazar como sus nietos
e. va a decirle que quiere / no quiere que hable con Raquel
f. estará vivo/muerto
g. dirá que hay / no hay esperanza
h. será en la capital / en La Gavia
i. ¿———?

Nota cultural: Los mexicoamericanos

La mayoría de los mexicoamericanos viven a lo largo de la frontera entre los Estados Unidos y México, de Texas a California. También hay una comunidad mexicana grande en Chicago. Pero la influencia mexicoamericana se nota por todas partes en este país. Son muy pocas las ciudades estadounidenses en donde no hay un restaurante mexicano. Y en todas las tiendas y mercados se venden productos típicamente mexicanos.

La influencia mexicana en muchos estados de los Estados Unidos es muy antigua. Hay que recordar que Texas fue territorio mexicano hasta 1836. Los actuales estados de Nuevo México, Arizona, Utah, Nevada, California, una parte de Colorado y de Wyoming fueron territorio mexicano hasta 1848. En aquella época, muchos mexicanos—y, con ellos, muchos descendientes de españoles que también vivían en ese territorio—prefirieron quedarse. Se hicieron ciudadanos americanos. En algunos casos sus descendientes todavía mantienen lazos muy estrechos[1] con la familia en México. Por otra parte mucha gente que hoy se considera mexicoamericana tiene raíces[2] familiares en España.

Luis Valdez

Personas y personajes

Los mexicoamericanos sobresalen[3] en una gran variedad de carreras y campos. ¿Puedes identificar a los siguientes mexicoamericanos del pasado y del presente?

Lee Treviño	actor de televisión y cine
Linda Ronstadt	fundador de la UFWA (United Farm Workers Association)
César Chávez	jugador de golf que ha ganado en muchas competiciones
Luis Valdez	política californiana, la primera hispana que fue elegida a
Gloria Molina	la Cámara de Diputados[4] del estado de California
James Edward Olmos	director de teatro y cine (*Zoot Suit* es una de sus
Richard «Cheech» Marin	películas)
	cómico popular, cuya pareja[5] fue Chong
	cantante popular que canta las canciones de sus antepasados mexicanos

Mitos y verdades de la comunidad mexicoamericana

Como en el caso de todo grupo «minoritario» en los Estados Unidos, hay ciertos estereotipos que se aplican a los mexicoamericanos que la mayoría acepta como verdades. ¿Cuánto sabes tú de este grupo? En tu opinión, ¿son ciertas o falsas las siguientes declaraciones?

[1]lazos... *very close ties*   [2]*roots*   [3]*excel*   [4]Cámara... *State Assembly*   [5]cuya... *whose partner*

1. La gran mayoría de los mexicoamericanos son bilingües. El español es su primer idioma.
2. Mexicanos… mexicoamericanos… no hay gran diferencia entre ellos.

La oración número uno es falsa. Todo depende de la generación y de la crianza[6] de la persona. Muchos mexicoamericanos mayores sí son bilingües y para ellos el español es su primer idioma. Pero hay muchos, sobre todo entre los muy jóvenes, que hablan español muy poco o no lo hablan en absoluto.[7]

Estos jóvenes, de apellido y tipo hispánico, ni son bilingües ni son, en muchos casos, biculturales, al punto que estudian español en la escuela como lengua extranjera. ¿Te acuerdas de Ritchie Valens, el cantante que hizo famosa la canción «La Bamba»? Su hermano nació en los Estados Unidos, como él, y hablaba español, pero Ritchie no lo hablaba para nada.

La segunda oración es también falsa. Aunque el típico mexicoamericano—si es que tal persona existe—comparte muchas costumbres con el mexicano típico, también hay muchas diferencias entre ellos. En cuanto a semejanzas, hay que citar la unidad familiar, característica primordial[8] de las dos culturas.* Además hay la religión católica y el culto a la Virgen de Guadalupe que, para los dos grupos, son muy importantes.

Por otro lado, la comida que se conoce en este país con el nombre de «mexicana» no siempre tiene mucho que ver con la verdadera comida mexicana de México. Aun cuando a algunos platos se les da el mismo nombre en los dos países, los ingredientes que llevan y el sabor[9] que tienen son distintos. Y hay algunos platos «mexicanos» que son realmente de origen estadounidense, como los burritos y las sopaipillas.[10] Muchos estadounidenses se sorprenden cuando llegan a conocer la gran variedad de la comida mexicana propia de México. ¡Es mucho más que tacos y enchiladas!

[6]*upbringing*   [7]en… *at all*   [8]*very important*   [9]*flavor*   [10]*dessert of New Mexican origin, similar to a cream puff but made with honey*

Actividad.   Hablando de los mexicoamericanos
Contesta las siguientes preguntas sobre los mexicoamericanos.

1. ¿Qué imagen tenías de los mexicoamericanos antes de leer esta **Nota cultural**? Y ahora, ¿qué piensas de ellos? ¿Tienes ahora diferentes opiniones de las que tenías?
2. ¿Puedes agregar (*add*) a la lista de mexicoamericanos famosos algunos otros nombres? Explica también por qué son famosos.

---

*Se debe notar que la famosa unidad de la familia hispánica, tanto en las comunidades hispánicas de los Estados Unidos como en México y en otros países del mundo hispánico, viene debilitándose (*weakening*) un poco con las costumbres y presiones del mundo moderno.

Have you completed the following sections of the lesson? Check them off here.

_____ **Preparación**	_____ **Vocabulario del tema**
_____ **¿Tienes buena memoria?**	_____ **Un poco de gramática**

Now scan the words in the **Vocabulario** list to be sure that you understand the meaning of most of them. Then you will be ready to continue on with **Lección 31** in the Workbook.

VOCABULARIO

Los verbos

pelearse   to fight

Las tiendas y los comercios
(Stores and Businesses)

la barbería	barber shop
la carnicería	butcher shop
la confitería	confectionery
la droguería	drug store
la farmacia	pharmacy
la ferretería	hardware store
la frutería	fruit store
la joyería	jewelry store
la lavandería	laundry
la librería	bookstore
la panadería	bakery
la papelería	stationery store
la pastelería	pastry shop
la peluquería	beauty shop, hairdresser's
la pescadería	fish market
la pollería	poultry shop
la taquería	taco stand
la tortillería	tortilla shop
la zapatería	shoe store

Los conceptos

la discusión	argument, (verbal) fight
la medida	measure, step

Los adjetivos

drástico/a   drastic

32

HA HABIDO UN ACCIDENTE*

OBJETIVOS

The materials in **Lección 32** of the Textbook and the Workbook will help you better understand the video episode and take you beyond it, giving you additional information about places and characters in the series. The Textbook will also help you to develop skill in using the Spanish language. In this lesson, you will learn

- vocabulary for talking about the natural world
- ways to give commands directly to someone whom you do not know well.

You will also learn about the civilization of the Aztecs.

Be sure to work through all parts of the lesson. When you see a cassette symbol in the margin, listen to the tape for **Lección 32**. Answers or hints for many activities are given in Appendix 1. Be sure to check your answers for each activity before going on to the next one.

* *There Has Been an Accident*

BEFORE VIEWING . . .

PREPARACIÓN

Actividad A.

Contesta las siguientes preguntas sobre lo que pasó en el episodio previo.

1. ¿Por qué se pelearon Pati y Juan?
    a. _____ Porque ella tiene que volver a Nueva York por su trabajo.
    b. _____ Porque él quiere regresar a Nueva York con ella.

2. ¿Qué descubrieron Pedro y Ramón?
    a. _____ Que la familia tiene graves problemas económicos.
    b. _____ Que el gobierno mexicano investiga las finanzas de la familia.

3. ¿Se enteraron de algo Ángela y Raquel?
    a. _____ Sí. Encontraron a Roberto, muerto.
    b. _____ No. En la excavación no hubo noticias.

Actividad B.

En el episodio previo apareció un nuevo personaje. ¿Recuerdas algo de él? Contesta estas preguntas.

1. ¿Cómo se llama este señor?
2. ¿Dónde vive ahora?
3. ¿Qué clase de relaciones había entre él y Raquel?

Para pensar...

Ya sabes que Luis es el antiguo (*former*) novio de Raquel. También sabes que ha vuelto (*he has returned*) a Los Ángeles. ¿Crees que todavía siente algo por Raquel? Y Raquel, ¿siente ella algo por él?

AFTER VIEWING . . .

¿TIENES BUENA MEMORIA?

Actividad A.   ¿Qué pasó?

Paso 1

Indica si las oraciones describen o no lo que pasó en cada sitio. ¿Puedes hacer un comentario sobre cada oración incorrecta?

En el sitio de la excavación…

Sí   No   1. Ángela y Raquel seguían esperando.
Sí   No   2. No hubo mucha actividad.
Sí   No   3. Por fin pudieron rescatar a Roberto.
Sí   No   4. Hubo otro derrumbe.
Sí   No   5. Roberto murió en el derrumbe.

En la capital…

Sí   No   6. Por fin los hermanos supieron lo del accidente.
Sí   No   7. Don Fernando se enteró del accidente también.
Sí   No   8. Ramón y Consuelo también tienen problemas.
Sí   No   9. Arturo le contó a Pedro todo lo que sabía.

En Los Ángeles…

Sí   No   10. Luis visitó a los padres de Raquel.
Sí   No   11. Luis les dijo que ellos debían ir a ver a Raquel a México.
Sí   No   12. El padre de Raquel no estaba muy convencido en cuanto al viaje.

Paso 2

Ahora, escucha otra vez el repaso que hacen Raquel y el narrador del fin de este episodio y corrige tus respuestas.

Para pensar…

María, la madre de Raquel, le ha sugerido a Luis que vaya a México. Así podrá ver a Raquel otra vez. ¿Crees que es buena idea que Luis vaya a México? ¿Qué revelan las acciones de María acerca de su personalidad?

Nota cultural: El español en los episodios en México

On network TV in the United States, one does not hear a strong regional accent, by and large, unless it is required by the role an actor is playing. Otherwise, the English spoken on prime time is a standard Midwestern form of English that most people who wish to work in the industry learn to speak, regardless of their city—or accent—of origin.

In the same way, the Spanish of many of the major Mexican characters in *Destinos* is not totally characteristic of Mexican Spanish. Most Mexican actors who work in movies, the theater, and in television are trained to speak a relatively accent-free variety of Spanish. In real life, the Spanish spoken in Mexico, like the English of the United States, has many varieties, according to the geographical area, ethnic background, and social class of the speaker.

Of the major Mexican characters, Lupe and Carlos in particular have pronounced accents, along with a number of actors who have small roles or make one-time appearances.

Something that is characteristic of Mexican and Mexican-American Spanish is the more frequent use of **Ud.** forms between adults (as compared to the more generalized use of **tú** found in some other countries). In this video episode, Luis addresses Raquel's mother as **Ud.** (even though he used to be her daughter's boyfriend!).

Actividad B.   ¿Quién sabe qué?

¿Tienes una idea muy clara de lo que sabe la mayoría de los personajes? Indica el verbo correcto para cada frase. ¡OJO! Hay información de algunos episodios previos.

1. Raquel... sabe/no sabe
   a. que Arturo llegó a México
   b. nada sobre el estado de don Fernando
   c. que sus padres hablaron con su antiguo novio

2. Arturo... sabe/no sabe
   a. lo del accidente en la excavación
   b. nada de Raquel
   c. que Raquel tuvo un novio en otra época

3. Don Fernando... sabe/no sabe
   a. que tiene dos nietos puertorriqueños
   b. lo del accidente en la excavación
   c. que hay problemas financieros en la Compañía Industrias Castillo Saavedra

4. La madre de Raquel... sabe/no sabe
   a. lo del accidente en la excavación
   b. mucho de las relaciones entre Arturo y Raquel
   c. la historia de los nietos puertorriqueños de don Fernando

Actividad C.   Una civilización indígena

Completa los siguientes párrafos sobre la civilización de esta tribu indígena de México.

En el centro de México había varias culturas indígenas. La más conocida era la (azteca/maya).[1] Pero los aztecas no eran originarios del centro de México. Eran del (este/norte),[2] de un lugar mítico llamado Aztlán.

En un (lago/río)[3] en el centro de la meseta, los aztecas fundaron la ciudad de Tenochtitlán. Eran una tribu fundamentalmente (pacífica/guerrera[a]).[4] Por eso, lograron (colonizar/conquistar)[5] todo el centro de México.

[a]*warlike*

• •

Vocabulario del tema

El mundo y su forma

la isla	island
la llanura	plain
la meseta	plain
la montaña	mountain
el paisaje	countryside, landscape
la pampa	pampa, grassland
la península	peninsula
la piedra	stone
la roca	rock
la selva	jungle
el valle	valley

el continente	continent	el campo	countryside
el mundo	world	el cañón	canyon
la tierra	earth	el cerro	hill
		la cordillera	mountain range
el árbol	tree		
el arbusto	shrub	la costa	coast
el bosque	forest	el desierto	desert
la flor	flower		
la hierba (yerba)	grass		

el arroyo	stream
el golfo	gulf
el lago	lake
el mar	sea
el océano	ocean
el río	river

Los puntos cardinales: el norte, el sur, el este, el oeste

Actividad A.   La geografía de algunos países hispánicos
En la cinta vas a escuchar la descripción de cuatro países hispánicos, pero no se da su nombre. ¿Puedes identificar el país que se describe?

1. ...   2. ...   3. ...   4. ...

Actividad B.   Hablando del paisaje
Vas a escuchar uno de los sustantivos de la primera columna. Di un nombre de la segunda columna que lo ejemplifica.

MODELO: (*oyes*)   una cordillera
          (*dices*)   los Andes
          (*oyes*)   Los Andes son una cordillera.

una cordillera, una montaña   el Titicaca
un golfo, un mar, un océano   Inglaterra (*England*)
un continente   el Atlántico
un desierto   Pike's Peak
una pampa   el Sahara
un cañón, un valle   los Andes
un lago, un río   el Nilo
una isla, una península   el Pérsico
                                    Sudamérica
                                    el Mediterráneo
                                    Napa
                                    Yucatán

1. ...   2. ...   3. ...   4. ...   5. ...   6. ...   7. ...   8. ...   9. ...   10. ...
11. ...   12. ...

¡Un desafío! ¿Puedes decir dónde quedan los lugares que acabas de identificar?
Es decir, ¿en qué país o estado, cerca de qué lugar, en qué hemisferio? etcétera.
Da todos los detalles que puedas.

Actividad C.   La geografía de los Estados Unidos
Indica qué se puede ver en los siguientes sitios. Da toda la información que
puedas.

1.   En Arizona se puede ver...
2.   En California hay...
3.   En la Cordillera Rocosa se puede ver...
4.   En la Florida hay...
5.   En Hawai hay...
6.   Cerca de Chicago hay...
7.   En el oeste medio hay...

Actividad D.   ¿Y tú?
Ahora describe el terreno y el paisaje en el lugar donde tú vives.

MODELO: Cerca de donde yo vivo, hay _____ , _____

y _____ . Me gusta(n) mucho _____

porque allí _____ . Es una lástima que no haya

_____ .

En cuanto a las plantas, hay (mucho/a/os/as) _____

y _____ . No hay _____ .

• •

UN POCO DE GRAMÁTICA

Telling Someone to Do Something

In Spanish, as you know, you must decide whether to address someone as **tú** or **Ud.** When you want to give a person a direct command (order), the same choice must be made.

 Ud. (and **Uds.**) commands are identical to the third-person subjunctive forms you have already learned. Here are some **Uds.** commands from previous video episodes.

HOMBRE DEL PUEBLO: ¡**Vengan**, **vengan**! Están a punto de rescatar a los hombres atrapados.
   PADRE RODRIGO: **Esperen** aquí. **No se muevan**. Voy a ver qué pasa.

 To form **Ud.** and **Uds.** commands, add to the **yo** stem of the present indicative the "opposite" vowel (**-e** for **-ar** verbs, **-a** for **-er/-ir** verbs). Add **-n** for **Uds.** commands. You will learn more about these commands in **Lección 32** of the Workbook. You will learn about **tú** commands in a later lesson.

Actividad.   Situaciones

A continuación hay una serie de situaciones o circunstancias que ocurren en este episodio y en episodios previos. ¿Puedes encontrar un mandato (en la página 327) apropiado para cada caso?

Situaciones

1. _____ Por fin Pedro puede comunicarse con Arturo, el día después que recibió su mensaje.
2. _____ Los auditores ofrecen sus recomendaciones.
3. _____ Don Fernando se despierta, preocupado, por la noche. Le habla una enfermera.
4. _____ Ángela y Raquel están muy cerca de donde están trabajando los obreros.
5. _____ Arturo ofrece tomar un taxi para ir a la casa de Pedro.
6. _____ El chofer de una ambulancia quiere pasar por donde está un grupo de espectadores.
7. _____ Luis quiere hacer planes para reunirse con Raquel y sus padres en México.
8. _____ Pedro sale para su cita con Arturo y no piensa regresar hasta muy tarde. Pero quiere saber las últimas noticias del sitio de la excavación.

Mandatos

a. Por favor, déjenme pasar, señores.
b. No, no. Quédese en el hotel. Yo paso por Ud.
c. Duérmase, por favor, señor. Tiene que descansar tanto como pueda.
d. Vendan La Gavia y cierren la oficina en Miami.
e. Por favor, vean Uds. las noticias esta noche.
f. Por favor, disculpe mi tardanza (*lateness*) en llamarlo.
g. Díganme, por favor, cuándo piensan Uds. hacer el viaje.
h. Siéntense allí, para no estorbar (*to be in the way*), ¿eh?

Nota cultural: La civilización de los aztecas

Entre todas las civilizaciones indígenas de América, la azteca era una de las más avanzadas. La conquista sangrienta[1] de esta civilización por los españoles, encabezados por el conquistador Hernán Cortés, puso fin a uno de los imperios más grandes de América.

La sociedad azteca

La sociedad azteca estaba muy bien organizada, con un complejo sistema de jerarquías y clases sociales. A continuación se ofrecen unos detalles de las costumbres y creencias de esta gran civilización.

- Las jóvenes aztecas se casaban a los dieciséis años. Los chicos se casaban más tarde, como a los veinte. En teoría, los hombres podían tener más de una esposa, pero la mayoría tenía solamente una.

- El oficio de curandera[2] era importante en la cultura azteca. Según sus creencias, algunas enfermedades eran causadas por un enemigo o por los dioses, como castigo.[3] Una curandera tenía que saber usar artes mágicas para averiguar la verdad.

- Para curar las enfermedades, los aztecas usaban más de doscientas hierbas medicinales. Hoy día se ha comprobado[4] la eficacia de algunas de ellas. Sirven para bajar la fiebre y contener las hemorragias.

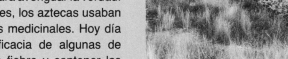

Hoy día en Teotihuacán se puede ver las ruinas de varios edificios ceremoniales de los aztecas. Entre ellos están las magníficas pirámides del Sol y de la Luna.

[1]*bloody* [2]*healer* [3]*punishment* [4]*se... has been shown, proven*

- Cuando los aztecas querían conquistar una ciudad, primero mandaban embajadores a ella. Les pedían tres cosas: hacer comercio con el imperio azteca, rendir culto[5] a los dioses aztecas y mandar regalos a Tenochtitlán todos los años. La ciudad tenía tres oportunidades para rendirse a estas demandas. Cada vez que una ciudad se negaba[6] a aceptar esas condiciones, los aztecas le mandaban un surtido de lanzas y escudos,[7] para que pudiera[8] defenderse en la batalla venidera.[9]
- Los dioses de los aztecas observaban constantemente a sus súbditos.[10] Se enojaban si no se celebraban los sacrificios y fiestas tal como debían.

La conquista por los españoles: ¿Por qué fue posible?

Aquí hay una teoría que contesta esta pregunta. Los aztecas creyeron en la profecía de la llegada de un dios blanco. Por eso cuando llegó Cortés en 1519 no ofrecieron resistencia, creyendo que era el dios que esperaban. El mismo emperador Moctezuma se sometió a los españoles. En dos años, el gran imperio azteca se convirtió en una colonia española. Moctezuma fue asesinado por algunos de sus hombres que se oponían a la conquista española. La destrucción de la ciudad de Tenochtitlán por los españoles en 1521 marcó el fin del imperio azteca.

Moctezuma era el emperador de los aztecas cuando llegaron los españoles. Según las cartas de Hernán Cortés, el emperador le dijo: «Por tanto vos sed cierto[11] que os obedeceremos y tendremos por señor… Y pues[12] estáis… en vuestra casa, holgad y descansad[13] del trabajo del camino y guerras que habéis tenido… »

[5]rendir… *to pay homage*   [6]se… *refused*   [7]un… *a supply of lances and shields*   [8](*the city*) *could*   [9]*upcoming*   [10]*subjects*   [11]Por… *For that reason, be certain*   [12]*since*   [13]holgad… *enjoy yourselves and rest*

Actividad.   Ahora, ¿cuánto sabes de los aztecas?
Según la **Nota cultural**, ¿son ciertas o falsas las siguientes afirmaciones?

1. Tenía poca importancia para los aztecas el concepto de las clases sociales.
2. La religión tenía mucha importancia para ellos.
3. Eran muy astutos en cuanto a sus relaciones con otras tribus.
4. En la sociedad azteca, los hombres tenían más poder (*power*) que las mujeres.

Have you completed the following sections of the lesson? Check them off here.

_____	**Preparación**	_____	**Vocabulario del tema**
_____	**¿Tienes buena memoria?**	_____	**Un poco de gramática**

Now scan the words in the **Vocabulario** list to be sure that you understand the meaning of most of them. Then you will be ready to continue on with **Lección 32** in the Workbook.

- -

VOCABULARIO

El mundo y su forma
(The World and Its Shape)

el árbol	tree
el arbusto	shrub
el arroyo	stream
el bosque	forest
el campo	countryside
el cañón	canyon
el cerro	hill
el continente	continent
la cordillera	mountain range
la costa	coast
el desierto	desert
la flor	flower
el golfo	gulf
la hierba (yerba)	grass
el lago	lake
la llanura	plain
la meseta	plain
la montaña	mountain
el océano	ocean
el paisaje	countryside, landscape

la pampa	pampa, grassland
la península	peninsula
la piedra	stone
el río	river
la roca	rock
la selva	jungle
la tierra	earth
el valle	valley

Repaso: **la isla, el mar, el mundo**

Los puntos cardinales (Cardinal Directions):
el norte, el sur, el este, el oeste

Los adjetivos

antiguo/a	former*
guerrero/a	warlike

Los verbos

estorbar	to be in the way

---

*Note: **Antiguo** has this meaning when it precedes a noun (**el antiguo novio**). It means *old* or *elderly* when it follows the noun (**una ciudad antigua**).

33

Sɪ SUPIERAS...*

OBJETIVOS

The materials in **Lección 33** of the Textbook and the Workbook will help you better understand the video episode and take you beyond it, giving you additional information about places and characters in the series. The Textbook will also help you to develop skill in using the Spanish language. In this lesson, you will learn

- the Spanish names for many careers and professions
- ways to give commands directly to someone whom you know well.

You will also learn about the Mayan civilization.

Be sure to work through all parts of the lesson. When you see a cassette symbol in the margin, listen to the tape for **Lección 33**. Answers or hints for many activities are given in Appendix 1. Be sure to check your answers for each activity before going on to the next one.

If You Only Knew . . .

BEFORE VIEWING . . .

PREPARACIÓN

Actividad A.
¿Recuerdas los acontecimientos más importantes del episodio previo? Completa las oraciones con la información correcta.

1. En el sitio de la excavación, Raquel y Ángela
   a. _____ decidieron regresar al pueblo
   b. _____ seguían esperando el rescate de Roberto

2. En la capital, Arturo por fin conoció a
   a. _____ Ramón
   b. _____ Pedro   c. _____ Carlos

3. Arturo le contó algunos detalles de la búsqueda de
   a. _____ Roberto
   b. _____ Ángel   c. _____ Rosario

4. En Los Ángeles, los padres de Raquel recibieron la visita de
   a. _____ un antiguo profesor de Raquel
   b. _____ un antiguo novio de Raquel
   c. _____ un colega de Raquel

5. La madre de Raquel le sugirió a Luis, el antiguo novio de su hija, que sería (*it would be*) buena idea
   a. _____ esperar en Los Ángeles para ver a Raquel
   b. _____ ir a México para verla
   c. _____ volver a Nueva York sin verla

 Ahora escucha la cinta para verificar tus respuestas.

Para pensar...

1. Como sabes, Raquel no sabe nada de lo que está pasando en Los Ángeles. ¿Crees que Luis irá a México para verla? ¿Qué pasará cuando Raquel lo vea después de tantos años? ¿Qué pasará si Luis y Arturo se conocen?
2. Al comienzo de este episodio, todavía no han rescatado a Roberto. En tu opinión, ¿en qué condiciones está él, después del segundo derrumbe?

Actividad B.

Paso 1

Escucha parte de una conversación entre Juan y Pati. Otra vez, discuten sobre algo. Debes leer la conversación al escuchar. Luego, contesta la pregunta.

JUAN: **Pati, ya te lo dije. ¡No puedes irte justo ahora!**

PATI: ¡No me grites así, Juan! Ya traté de explicarte los problemas de la producción en Nueva York. No entiendo por qué actúas como un niño mimado.

JUAN: ¿Cómo puedes hacerme esto?

PATI: ¿Ves? Todo te lo hacen a ti. Tus problemas son los más graves. A veces dudo que a ti te importen los demás.

JUAN: Me importa mi papá.

PATI: ¿Sí? Entonces, ¿por qué no estás más tiempo con él en el hospital? Te lo pasas aquí peleándote conmigo cuando él te necesita.

¿Cuál es el tema principal de la discusión entre Juan y Pati?

a. _____ el estado grave de la salud de don Fernando

b. _____ el hecho de que (*the fact that*) Pati cree que Juan es muy egoísta

c. _____ los problemas que tiene Pati en el teatro

Si indicaste la letra *b*, tuviste razón.

Paso 2

Ahora escucha toda la conversación de nuevo. Luego indica si las siguientes oraciones son ciertas (**C**) o falsas (**F**).

C   F   1. Juan todavía no quiere que Pati se vaya a Nueva York.

C   F   2. Pati se niega a explicarle a Juan los detalles de los problemas que tiene con la producción de la obra.

C   F   3. Pati insinúa que Juan debe pasar más tiempo en el hospital con su padre.

En esta conversación, Pati acusa a Juan de ser un «niño mimado», porque sólo piensa en sí mismo.

4. ¿Qué significa **mimado**?

   a. _____ memorable   b. _____ copy-cat   c. _____ spoiled

Para pensar...

Ya sabes que en este episodio Juan y Pati tendrán una gran discusión. ¿Cuál será el resultado de esa discusión? ¿Se irá Pati o se quedará? En tu opinión, ¿quién tiene razón, Juan o Pati? ¿A quién crees que va a apoyar la familia de Juan en esta discusión?

 **AFTER VIEWING . . .**

¿TIENES BUENA MEMORIA?

Actividad A.   En la excavación

Por fin hay buenas noticias en el sitio de la excavación. Completa las siguientes oraciones con la información correcta.

1.   Al principio, Ángela y Raquel... podían ver lo que pasaba muy bien / no sabían nada y tampoco podían ver bien lo que pasaba.
2.   Mientras esperaban, las dos mujeres empezaron a hablar de... las profesiones / la civilización maya.
3.   Ángela dijo que pensaba que Roberto tenía una profesión... fascinante/ peligrosa (*dangerous*).
4.   Raquel dijo que, de niña, pensaba en ser... abogada y médica / veterinaria y profesora.
5.   Ángela pensaba en ser... profesora y actriz / abogada y dentista.

 Ahora escucha la cinta para verificar tus respuestas.

Actividad B.   ¿Y Roberto?

¿Qué le pasó en este episodio? ¿Qué es lo que ahora se sabe de su condición? Contesta las siguientes preguntas.

1.   ¿Pueden por fin rescatar a Roberto?
2.   ¿Está consciente o inconsciente?
3.   ¿Parece estar bien o está muy lastimado (*injured*)?
4.   ¿Lo van a tratar en el sitio de la excavación? ¿O piensan llevarlo a otro sitio?

Actividad C.   En la capital

Completa el siguiente resumen de lo que pasaba en la Ciudad de México con los nombres de los personajes apropiados: Arturo, Pedro, Juan, Pati.

Mientras Raquel y Ángela esperaban en el sitio de la excavación, _____¹ hablaba con Pedro sobre el accidente y otras preocupaciones. Al mismo tiempo, en la casa de Ramón, _____² y _____³ seguían con su conflicto. _____⁴ quería regresar a Nueva York, pero para _____⁵ la familia es más importante que la profesión.

 Ahora escucha la cinta para verificar tus respuestas.

VOCABULARIO DEL TEMA

Profesiones y oficios

el abogado/la abogada	lawyer	**el arquitecto/la arquitecta**	architect
el actor/la actriz	actor, actress	**el/la artista**	artist
el ama* de casa	homemaker	**la azafata**	airplane stewardess
el/la dentista	dentist		
el enfermero/ la enfermera	nurse	**el camarero/la camarera**	waiter, waitress; airplane steward
el hombre/la mujer de negocios	businessman/ woman	**el carpintero/la carpintera**	carpenter
el ingeniero/ la ingeniera	engineer	**el/la dependiente**	clerk
		el/la electricista	electrician
		el escritor/la escritora	writer
el maestro/la maestra	teacher	**el hermano/la hermana**	brother/sister (*of a religious order*)
el/la médico	doctor		
el/la periodista	journalist		
el profesor/la profesora	teacher, professor	**el marinero/la marinera**	sailor
el/la programador(a) de computadoras	computer programmer	**el/la músico**	musician
		el piloto/la pilota	pilot
el veterinario/ la veterinaria	veterinarian	**el pintor/la pintora**	painter
		el/la plomero	plumber
		el/la psiquiatra	psychiatrist
		el reportero/la reportera	reporter
		el sacerdote (padre)	priest (father)
		el secretario/la secretaria	secretary

**EMPRESA MULTINACIONAL
REQUIERE
SECRETARIA BILINGÜE**

Para Gerencia General con experiencia de dos (2) años en el cargo o similares. Excelentes relaciones interpersonales y presentación personal. Magnífica remuneración.
Las interesadas llamar a los teléfonos 29961 al 67. Cartago.   *(16-Cisko-818)*

Nota cultural: Los nombres de las profesiones

In the Spanish-speaking world there is some variation in the words that should be used to refer to women who hold certain professions.

---

*Ama (**de casa**) is a feminine noun, but like **el agua**, it takes the masculine article **el**. All feminine nouns that begin with stressed **a** or **ha** take the masculine article (**el**) in the singular and the feminine article (**las**) in the plural: **las amas de casa, las aguas**. If a feminine noun begins with an *un*accented **a** or **ha**, the feminine article (**la**) is used: **la abogada, la actriz, la artista, la hamaca.**

The following patterns are generally followed:

- The feminine article is used with nouns that end in **-ista**: **el dentista** → **la dentista**.
- The feminine form of a noun is used:* **el pintor** → **la pintora**.
- The masculine and feminine articles are used with the same noun: **el/la médico**.
- The word **mujer** is used: **el hombre de negocios** → **la mujer de negocios**.

Some forms, especially **la pilota** in the preceding list, are not accepted by all Spanish speakers. If you want to be sure to use the correct word to describe a person's profession, listen to the form he or she uses and follow that example.

Actividad A.   Hablando de carreras

Paso 1

Escucha otra vez mientras Raquel y Ángela hablan de las profesiones. Mientras escuchas, indica en la siguiente tabla las profesiones que las dos mencionan, en las categorías indicadas.

ÁNGELA pensaba en estudiar para...   _____   _____

se hizo...   _____

EL PADRE DE ÁNGELA quería que ella fuera (*wanted her to be*)...

_____   _____

RAQUEL pensaba en estudiar para...   _____   _____

se hizo...   _____

LA MADRE DE RAQUEL quería que ella fuera...   _____

Paso 2

Ahora contesta las siguientes preguntas sobre las profesiones y las dos mujeres.

1. ¿Qué intereses compartían?
2. ¿Cuál de ellas siguió el consejo de su padre o de su madre?

Actividad B.   Comentarios del narrador

Escucha otra vez mientras el narrador habla de las profesiones. Escribe el nombre de las profesiones que escuchas. Luego escribe el número de cuatro de las profesiones mencionadas con el dibujo apropiado.

Aquí, en la excavación, hay ejemplos de varias de las profesiones de que hablaban Raquel y Ángela. Claro, está presente una _____.¹ También hay una

---

*The feminine form is usually avoided when it coincides with a word with the same form but a different meaning: **el músico** → **la músico** (not **la música** = *music*).

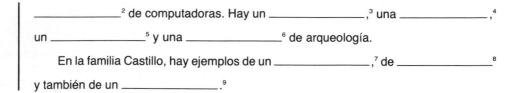

_____,² de computadoras. Hay un _____,³ una _____,⁴ un _____⁵ y una _____⁶ de arqueología.

En la familia Castillo, hay ejemplos de un _____,⁷ de _____⁸ y también de un _____.⁹

a.

b.

c.

d.

Actividad C.   Hablando de los personajes

¿Tienes una memoria muy buena? Vas a escuchar el nombre de un personaje de *Destinos*. Contesta con el nombre de la profesión que tiene.

> MODELO: (*oyes*)   Carlos
> (*dices*)   (Carlos) Es hombre de negocios.
> (*oyes*)   Es hombre de negocios.

Profesiones: el secretario, el sacerdote, el maestro, el marinero, el guía turístico, el reportero, el abogado, el psiquiatra, el pintor

Personajes de España: 1. ...   2. ...   3. ...

Personajes de la Argentina: 4. ...   5. ...

Personajes de México: 6. ...   7. ...   8. ...

Actividad D.   Situaciones

¿A quién necesitas en las siguientes situaciones? ¡OJO! Puedes mencionar a más de una persona.

1. Tuviste un accidente de automóvil.
2. Quieres construir una nueva casa.
3. Quieres comprar un perro y quieres saber si está sano.
4. Vas de pasajero en un avión y necesitas algo.
5. Te duele un diente (*tooth*).
6. Quieres dar una fiesta bailable para un amigo.
7. En el baño de tu casa o apartamento, hay agua por todo el piso (*floor*).
8. Quieres comprar algo en una tienda.

Actividad E.   ¿Y tú?

Completa las siguientes oraciones para describir las profesiones y oficios que tienen algo que ver con tu vida.

1.   De niño/a, pensaba en ser _____.

2.   Ahora pienso hacerme _____.

3.   Cuando era estudiante de secundaria, trabajaba de (*as a*) _____.

Ahora trabajo de _____.

4.   Mi padre/madre es _____.

5.   Uno de mis parientes tiene una profesión u oficio interesante: es

_____ y es _____.

UN POCO DE GRAMÁTICA

Telling Someone to Do Something

Tú commands are used to give a direct command to a person whom you address with **tú**. For most verbs the third-person singular *indicative* is the **tú** command. Pronouns are attached to the end of affirmative commands.

Espérame aquí.	*Wait for me here.*
Vuelve conmigo al pueblo.	*Go back to the town with me.*

Negative **tú** command forms are the same as the second-person singular subjunctive, but pronouns are placed in front of the verb.

No me esperes más.	*Don't wait for me anymore.*
No vuelvas a la excavación.	*Don't go back to the excavation.*

Some common irregular affirmative commands are **sal** (**no salgas**), **pon** (**no pongas**), **haz** (**no hagas**), and **di** (**no digas**).

You will learn more about **tú** commands as well as additional irregular forms in the Workbook.

Actividad.   Situaciones

A continuación hay una serie de situaciones o circunstancias posibles. ¿Puedes encontrar un mandato apropiado para cada caso?

Situaciones

1. _____ Ángela empieza a perder la esperanza.
2. _____ Pati sigue esperando que la comprenda su esposo.
3. _____ Juan sigue tratando de convencer a Pati de que no se vaya.
4. _____ Maricarmen no tiene sueño.
5. _____ Carlitos no quiere acostarse y se está portando mal.
6. _____ Un niño se acerca demasiado al borde (*edge*) de la excavación.
7. _____ Consuelo trata de consolar a Juan.
8. _____ Un hombre de rescate encuentra a Roberto.

Mandatos

a. ¡Sal de allí, niño! Es peligroso acercarte tanto.
b. Por favor, no te enojes. Trata de comprender mi punto de vista.
c. Ay, ¿no me escuchaste? Acuéstate ahora mismo. ¡Haz lo que te digo! No me digas que no.
d. ¡Ayúdame! ¡Necesito que alguien me ayude!
e. Explícame por qué te es tan importante esta producción.
f. Dime la verdad. ¿Pasa algo entre tú y Pati?
g. Pon tu fe en Dios. No pierdas confianza en Él.
h. Léeme un poco más, mami.

Nota cultural: La civilización de los mayas

Los mayas eran una familia de pueblos indios que habitaron durante unos 2000 años la península de Yucatán y partes de Guatemala, Honduras y El Salvador. Su origen es muy incierto.

La sociedad maya

- Se cree que los mayas no vivían en sus ciudades. La gente llegaba a las ciudades sólo para las fiestas y los días de mercado. Luego todo quedaba desierto porque la gente vivía en el campo, donde practicaban la agricultura.

- Por mucho tiempo se creyó que los mayas, como otras tribus de la región, usaban un sistema de agricultura rudimentaria basado en las milpas.[1] Ahora se sabe que cultivaban la tierra con un complicado sistema de campos[2] elevados en forma de terrazas. Este sistema avanzado para practicar la agricultura sirvió de base para que la civilización maya llegara a su apogeo.

- Los mayas hicieron grandes avances en aritmética y astronomía. Mientras en el resto de México y Centroamérica se usaba un calendario de 260 días, los mayas tenían un calendario

[1] *fields cultivated with slash-and-burn agriculture*   [2] *fields*

de 360 días. Su calendario empezaba en una fecha que corresponde al 13 de agosto de 3114 antes de Cristo[3] en el calendario gregoriano que usamos nosotros.

- En la cultura maya se empleaba un complejo sistema de escritura,[4] más avanzado que el de otros pueblos indígenas de la región. Los libros eran un elemento importante de su cultura y los escribientes[5] gozaban de una alta posición social. Desgraciadamente, al llegar los españoles a América, destruyeron[6] la gran mayoría de los libros y códices mayas.

- Por mucho tiempo no se pudo leer lo que quedaba de la escritura e inscripciones mayas. Se creía que los temas principales de estas obras eran la astronomía y la religión. Cuando por fin los arqueólogos pudieron desenredar[7] el misterio de ese sistema de escritura, descubrieron también una rica historia de dinastías: intrigas para heredar el trono, luchas entre herederos,[8] intentos de establecer la legitimidad de los reyes… historias muy parecidas a las que narró Shakespeare en algunas de sus obras.

- Una de las obras más importantes que dejaron los mayas se conserva hoy sólo en forma de una copia de una transcripción que se hizo de ella durante la época de los conquistadores españoles. Se llama el *Popol Vuh* (*Libro del Consejo*) y cuenta, entre otras cosas, la historia maya de la creación del mundo. Según el *Popol Vuh*, los dioses mayas tuvieron que hacer varios intentos antes de formar hombres que pudieran honrarlos tal como ellos querían. De uno de estos intentos fracasados nacieron los monos.[9]

> Y dicen que la descendencia de aquéllos son los monos que existen ahora en los bosques; éstos son la muestra[10] de aquéllos, porque de palo[11] fue hecha su carne por el Creador y Formador.
>
> Y por esta razón el mono se parece al hombre, es la muestra de una generación de hombres creados, de hombres formados que eran solamente muñecos[12] y hechos solamente de madera.[13]

Los mayas: ¿Por qué desaparecieron?

A partir del siglo X los mayas fueron desapareciendo de sus ciudades. Algunos creen que esto se debe a las constantes guerras e incursiones de los aztecas. Otros creen que las constantes guerras civiles y luchas dinásticas por fin debilitaron[14] la familia de pueblos mayas.

Realmente se ignora el motivo por el cual una civilización tan avanzada desapareció sin causas aparentes. Sigue siendo hasta hoy un verdadero enigma. Sus grandes ciudades y templos quedaron ocultados por las selvas de Yucatán hasta que, a mediados del[15] siglo pasado, algunos arqueólogos descubrieron sus ruinas. Hay que imaginar su sorpresa al encontrar, bajo la densa vegetación tropical, toda una civilización «perdida».

Chichén Itzá fue el mayor centro maya de Yucatán. En su apogeo, tenía explanadas, pirámides, terrazas y templos.

[3]antes... B.C.   [4]*writing*   [5]*scribes*   [6]*they destroyed*   [7]*untangle*   [8]*heirs*
[9]*monkeys*   [10]*remains*   [11]*sticks*   [12]*dolls*   [13]*wood*   [14]*weakened*
[15]a... *in the middle of the*

Actividad.   Los mayas y los aztecas

Compara los siguientes aspectos de las civilizaciones maya y azteca.

1. donde vivían   2. razones de la caída de su imperio   3. organización social

---

Have you completed the following sections of the lesson? Check them off here.

_____ **Preparación**   _____ **Vocabulario del tema**
_____ **¿Tienes buena memoria?**   _____ **Un poco de gramática**

Now scan the words in the **Vocabulario** list to be sure that you understand the meaning of most of them. Then you will be ready to continue on with **Lección 33** in the Workbook.

VOCABULARIO

Profesiones y oficios (Professions and Trades)

el actor, la actriz	actor, actress
el ama de casa	homemaker
el arquitecto, la arquitecta	architect
el/la artista	artist
la azafata	airplane stewardess
el camarero, la camarera	waiter, waitress; airplane steward
el carpintero, la carpintera	carpenter
el/la dentista	dentist
el/la electricista	electrician
el hermano, la hermana	brother/sister (*of a religious order*)
el hombre/la mujer de negocios	businessman/woman
el ingeniero, la ingeniera	engineer
el/la músico	musician
el piloto, la pilota	pilot
el/la plomero	plumber
el programador/la programadora de computadoras	computer programmer
el/la psiquiatra	psychiatrist
el sacerdote	priest
el secretario, la secretaria	secretary
el veterinario, la veterinaria	veterinarian

Los adjetivos

mimado/a	spoiled
peligroso/a	dangerous

Las palabras adicionales

sí mismo/a	oneself

Repaso: **el abogado, la abogada; el/la dependiente; el enfermero, la enfermera; el escritor, la escritora; el maestro, la maestra; el marinero, la marinera; el/la médico; el padre; el/la periodista; el pintor, la pintora; el profesor, la profesora; el reportero, la reportera**

34

ÉXITO*

. . . .

OBJETIVOS

The materials in **Lección 34** of the Textbook and the Workbook will help you better understand the video episode and take you beyond it, giving you additional information about places and characters in the series. The Textbook will also help you to develop skill in using the Spanish language. In this lesson, you will learn

- vocabulary for talking about interpersonal relationships of many kinds
- ways to talk about what has happened.

You will also learn about the social life typical of Hispanic young people.

Be sure to work through all parts of the lesson. When you see a cassette symbol in the margin, listen to the tape for **Lección 34**. Answers or hints for many activities are given in Appendix 1. Be sure to check your answers for each activity before going on to the next one.

*Success

341

BEFORE VIEWING . . .

PREPARACIÓN

Actividad A.

Completa las siguientes oraciones con las frases apropiadas.

1.   Después de mucho trabajo en el sitio de la excavación,
     a.   _____ no pudieron rescatar a Roberto
     b.   _____ finalmente rescataron a Roberto

2.   En casa de Pedro, Juan y Pati
     a.   _____ seguían discutiendo   b.   _____ se reconciliaron

3.   Juan quiere que Pati
     a.   _____ regrese a Nueva York   b.   _____ se quede en México
                                                          con él

4.   Pedro y Arturo decidieron tratar de averiguar (*find out*)
     a.   _____ lo que pasó en el sitio de la excavación
     b.   _____ dónde estaban Raquel y Ángela

Ahora escucha la cinta para verificar tus respuestas.

Actividad B.

Paso 1

Escucha parte de una conversación entre Juan y Ramón. Después de escuchar, contesta la pregunta.

¿Cuál es el tema principal de la conversación entre Juan y Ramón?

a.   _____ las relaciones que existen entre los hermanos Juan y Ramón, hijos de
           don Fernando
b.   _____ las relaciones que hay entre Juan y Pati
c.   _____ los problemas que tiene Pati en el teatro

Si indicaste la letra *b*, tuviste razón.

Paso 2

Ahora escucha la conversación de nuevo. Puedes leer las últimas líneas al mismo tiempo, si quieres. Recuerda el significado de la palabra **éxito**, el título de este episodio, y ten en cuenta (*keep in mind*) que **celoso** significa *jealous*. Luego contesta las preguntas.

RAMÓN: Bueno, yo en tu lugar me sentiría celoso.
 JUAN: ¿Celoso? ¿De quién?
RAMÓN: No es de quién... sino de qué. Mejor debo decir tendría envidia.

JUAN: Yo sé que Pati es muy inteligente... que tiene mucho talento. Es escritora, productora y directora y también profesora de teatro. Ramón, ¿crees que tengo envidia del éxito de mi esposa?

Ahora indica si las siguientes oraciones son ciertas (**C**) o falsas (**F**), según la conversación.

C   F   1. Ramón está de acuerdo con Juan.
C   F   2. Ramón insinúa que Juan tiene envidia del éxito de Pati.
C   F   3. Juan no lo quiere escuchar. Se niega a (*He refuses to*) pensar en lo que le dice Ramón.
C   F   4. Juan se pone a pensar en lo que insinúa Ramón.
C   F   5. Juan dice que su matrimonio es «un fracaso». ¿Qué significa «fracaso»?
             a. fricasse   b. fragile   c. failure

Para pensar...

Como sabes, la palabra **envidia** quiere decir *envy*. ¿Crees tú que Juan le tiene envidia a Pati? ¿Es egocéntrico Juan? ¿O es Pati la egocéntrica? ¿Son las relaciones entre Juan y Pati similares a las de alguna pareja que tú conoces?

 AFTER VIEWING . . .

¿TIENES BUENA MEMORIA?

Actividad A.   En la capital

Indica si los siguientes incidentes ocurrieron (**Sí**) o no (**No**) en el **Episodio 34**.

Sí   No   1. Después de su pelea con Juan, Pati salió corriendo al jardín.
Sí   No   2. El consejo de Mercedes es que Pati debe quedarse en México con Juan.
Sí   No   3. Mercedes recordó con afecto el día de la boda (*wedding*) de Pati y Juan.
Sí   No   4. Ramón le habló a Juan de una forma brutal sobre los problemas de su matrimonio.
Sí   No   5. Ramón le dice a Juan que es posible que él, Juan, tenga envidia de Pati.
Sí   No   6. Juan también le habló a Pedro, su tío, sobre los problemas que tiene en su matrimonio.

Actividad B.   Camino al Distrito Federal

Paso 1

Otra vez Raquel y Ángela se encontraron viajando juntas en un carro. Como ocurrió antes, pasaron el tiempo hablando de sus relaciones con varias personas. Indica todas las relaciones que mencionaron.

Las relaciones entre...

1. _____ Raquel y sus padres
2. _____ Raquel y su antiguo novio
3. _____ Raquel y Arturo
4. _____ Raquel y Jorge (el novio de Ángela)

5. _____ Ángela y Roberto
6. _____ Ángela y Jorge
7. _____ Ángela y sus tíos

Paso 2

Escucha el repaso de este episodio en la cinta para verificar tus respuestas.

Paso 3

Ahora describe lo que recuerdas de estas relaciones, haciendo oraciones con una palabra o frase de cada columna. Añade todos los detalles que puedas.

Ángela		admira a	Arturo
Raquel	(no)	es amigo/a de	Roberto
Jorge		es novio/a de	Jorge
Arturo		era novio/a de	Raquel
		quiere a	Ángela
		quiere casarse con	Luis
		recuerda a _____ con cariño	
		se separó de	
		trató de ligar con (*pick up*)	

Para pensar...

Al final del episodio, un camión se acercaba rápidamente al coche que manejaba Raquel. ¿Qué crees que va a pasar? ¿Va a haber (*Is there going to be*) otro accidente, un choque?

Nota cultural: Notas de interés lingüístico

Here are some notes of interest about some of the usages you have heard in this video episode.

- Did you notice the momentary difficulty that Arturo had in getting the desk clerk to pass him the newspaper? Arturo used the word **diario**, commonly used in Argentina to mean *newspaper*; the word **periódico** is more frequently used in other parts of the Spanish-speaking world. The two men do not focus at all on the brief misunderstanding; it is a normal incident in communication between speakers of a language that is used around the world.

- At the end of the flashback to Juan and Pati's wedding ceremony, the priest told the congregation: **Idos en paz**. (*Go in peace.*) The specific verb form used is a **vosotros** command (**ir → id**; **irse → idos**). As you know, **vosotros** forms are not generally used in Mexico. However, they survive in inscriptions on buildings, in documents that date back to the colonial era, and in religious services—like the wedding service—initiated in Mexico by the Spaniards. Even though the **vosotros** forms are not generally used in Mexico, their use in these situations does not cause any confusion.

Vocabulario del tema

Relaciones sociales

la amistad	friendship
el cariño, el afecto	affection
el amor (a primera vista)	love (at first sight)
la (primera) cita	(first) date
el noviazgo	engagement
la boda	wedding
el matrimonio	marriage
la luna de miel	honeymoon
el odio	hatred
el divorcio	divorce
el amigo/la amiga	friend
el compañero/ la compañera	companion; "significant other"

el novio/la novia	boyfriend, girlfriend; fiancé(e); groom, bride
la pareja	couple
el esposo/la esposa	husband, wife; spouse
el marido/la mujer	husband, wife
el matrimonio	married couple

llevarse bien/mal con	to get along well/badly with
tener envidia/celos (de)	to be envious/jealous (of)
tomarle cariño a alguien	to start to have affection for someone
enamorarse (de)	to fall in love (with)
estar enamorado/a (de)	to be in love (with)
casarse (con)	to get married (to)
odiar	to hate
divorciarse (de)	to divorce

Note the following about vocabulary used to describe marital relationships.

- Whereas the words **mujer** and **señora** can be used to mean *wife*, the words **hombre** and **señor** are never used to mean *husband*.
- The term **esposos** (in addition to meaning *husbands* or *husbands and wives*) can also mean *married couple*. **Maridos**, however, expresses only *husbands*.

Actividad A.   Las relaciones: ¿Cómo se desarrollan?

Escucha mientras el narrador define por medio de una serie de características las siguientes relaciones. Indica en la siguiente tabla la característica o características mencionadas que definen cada relación.

el cariño   un período de tiempo
el amor   una ceremonia

1. la amistad	4. el noviazgo
2. la familia	5. la boda
3. los novios	6. la luna de miel

Actividad B.   Juan y Pati

Pon en orden cronológico (del 1 a 10) los siguientes incidentes y aconteci-mientos tal como probablemente ocurrieron en las relaciones entre Juan y Pati.

a. _____ Los dos consiguieron puestos académicos al mismo tiempo, poco después de casarse.
b. _____ Tuvieron su primera cita al día siguiente.
c. _____ Se hicieron buenos amigos en seguida.
d. _____ Se casaron en La Gavia.
e. _____ Se conocieron en un teatro de Nueva York.
f. _____ Pasaron la luna de miel en Cancún.
g. _____ Pati empezó a tener mucho éxito en su carrera.
h. _____ Poco a poco Juan empezó a tenerle envidia a Pati.

i.　_____ No se enamoraron hasta mucho más tarde.

j.　_____ Empezaron a pelear por pequeñas cosas.

Actividad C.

Paso 1

¿Qué opinas de las relaciones entre Raquel y Arturo? Vas a escuchar las siguientes oraciones. Indica las oraciones que crees que mejor describen sus relaciones.

1.　_____ Se han tomado mucho cariño.
2.　_____ Ya son novios.
3.　_____ Se enamoraron a primera vista.
4.　_____ Realmente no han tenido (*they haven't had*) una «primera cita» todavía.
5.　_____ Se van a casar algún día.
6.　_____ Les gusta estar juntos.
7.　_____ Se llevan muy, muy bien.
8.　_____ Raquel tiene celos de la ex esposa de Arturo.

Paso 2

Ahora vas a escuchar estas oraciones. Indica solamente las oraciones que, para ti, describen las relaciones entre Raquel y Ángela.

1.　_____ Raquel le tiene mucho cariño a Ángela.
2.　_____ Le tiene un poco de envidia a Ángela porque ésta (*the latter*) tiene novio.
3.　_____ Se llevan muy bien, aunque a veces se pelean.
4.　_____ Les gusta estar juntas.
5.　_____ Comparten confidencias, esperanzas, consejos...
6.　_____ Ángela tiene celos de Raquel porque sabe que Jorge trató de ligar con ella.
7.　_____ Sus relaciones van a durar mucho tiempo.
8.　_____ Raquel cree que Ángela no debe casarse con Jorge.

Paso 3

Ahora explica en qué se parecen (*are similar*) y en qué se diferencian las relaciones entre Raquel y Arturo, por una parte, y entre Raquel y Ángela por otra. Haz todas las oraciones que puedas. Piensa sobre todo en las oraciones que indicaste en los **Pasos 1** y **2**.

MODELO:　Entre Raquel y Arturo, _____, pero también entre

Ángela y Raquel _____.

Raquel _____ a Arturo, pero/y también

_____ a Ángela.

Actividad D.   ¿Y tú?

Indica si estás de acuerdo o no con las siguientes afirmaciones. Luego explica por qué.

Sí   No   1. El noviazgo es la etapa más romántica de las relaciones entre dos personas que se quieren.

Sí   No   2. El matrimonio es la etapa más difícil de las relaciones.

Sí   No   3. Es más fácil ser un buen hermano (una buena hermana) que ser un buen esposo (una buena esposa).

Sí   No   4. Pelearse no es bueno para un matrimonio.

Sí   No   5. El cariño y la amistad son más importantes para una pareja que el amor.

UN POCO DE GRAMÁTICA

Talking About What Someone Has Done

If you want to indicate that someone has done something, use the word **ha** with the past participle of another verb. The past participle of most verbs is formed by adding **-ado** to the stem of **-ar** verbs and **-ido** to the stems of **-er** and **-ir** verbs.

Pati **ha hablado** con Juan mil veces sobre este asunto. Ahora **ha perdido** la paciencia con él.	*Pati has talked with Juan about this matter a thousand times. Now she has lost patience with him.*

Some common irregular past participles are **dicho** (**decir**) and **hecho** (**hacer**). You will learn more about these verb forms in the Workbook.

Actividad.   ¿A quién se refiere?

Identifica a la persona a quien se refiere cada oración.

a.   Raquel   d.   Pati   f.   Ángela
b.   Ramón   e.   Juan   g.   Arturo
c.   Mercedes

1. _____ Ha decidido volver a Nueva York.
2. _____ Le ha dicho a Pati que comprende por qué ella se preocupa tanto por el trabajo.
3. _____ Ha conversado con Juan sobre los problemas matrimoniales de éste.

4. _____ Ha admitido que tiene envidia del éxito de su esposa.
5. _____ Le ha pedido perdón a Raquel por actuar tan mal con ella en Puerto Rico.
6. _____ Le ha confesado a Ángela que hay algo entre ella y Arturo Iglesias.
7. _____ Ha buscado la dirección de la universidad donde estudiaba Roberto.
8. _____ Ha decidido no decirle nada a Ángela sobre su novio.

Nota cultural: La vida social de los jóvenes

Las diversiones de los jóvenes hispánicos son numerosas. Pueden variar según la clase social y el lugar, pero algunas gozan de[1] gran aceptación popular en todas partes: el cine, el baile, las fiestas, los deportes y hablar… en las calles, los cafés, en las reuniones y en los clubes.

Fiestas y bailes

Tal vez se puede decir que las diversiones más populares son las fiestas y los bailes. Es muy común reunirse con los amigos en la casa de alguien para hablar y bailar hasta muy tarde. Los jóvenes también van con frecuencia a los clubes nocturnos y a las discotecas. En las grandes capitales del mundo hispánico, la vida nocturna es muy activa. Ya que, según la costumbre, se cena relativamente tarde, es posible que una noche de baile con los amigos no empiece sino hasta las once o las doce.

Un café en Oaxaca, México

Aun a los muy jóvenes, entre los quince y los dieciocho años, les gusta salir a bailar. Para ellos, en España se ha empezado a ver el fenómeno de las Discotecas «Sin», es decir en algunas discotecas una noche a la semana no se sirven bebidas alcohólicas. Los jóvenes vienen a estas discotecas solamente para escuchar música, bailar y conocer gente.

Amigos y novios

Como se ve, es muy frecuente entre los jóvenes hispánicos salir en grupos, con los «compas» (= los compañeros). Aun las parejas suelen salir con su grupo de amigos, tal vez despidiéndose más temprano para estar a solas.

Una diferencia interesante entre la cultura hispánica en general y la de los Estados Unidos se ve en la distinción que se hace entre las relaciones amistosas y las amorosas. Las palabras **amigo** y **novio** realmente no tienen un equivalente exacto en inglés. **Amigo/Amiga** sirven para definir las relaciones que en inglés se conocen por *friend* y *boy/girlfriend*. En cambio, los términos **novia/novio** solamente se aplican a los que tienen relaciones formales. También significan *fiancée/fiancé* y *bride/groom*.

[1]gozan… *enjoy*

La juventud: ¿Una cultura internacional?

¿Son realmente diferentes los jóvenes hispánicos y los de otras partes del mundo? Muchos creen que no. Actualmente[2] vivimos en una comunidad global. Las noticias, las ideas, las canciones, las modas[3]… todo se puede comunicar casi instantáneamente por medio de la televisión, la radio (sobre todo la música) y el cine. Los efectos de este fenómeno se notan—tal vez más que en otros grupos—en los jóvenes.

Si hace cuarenta años había gran diferencia entre, digamos, un joven español y un joven norteamericano de la misma edad, actualmente las diferencias no son tan marcadas. Están familiarizados con algunas de las mismas canciones y los mismos conjuntos[4] musicales, hablan de los mismos artistas de cine, quieren ver las mismas películas y se visten de una forma parecida—el estilo *punk* no es exclusivamente norteamericano.

Con todo, no se quiere decir que sean idénticos. Una de las grandes diferencias entre los jóvenes hispánicos y los norteamericanos es que el típico joven hispano, además de conocer su propia cultura, se interesa por la cultura estadounidense y de otros países; se informa de ellas por los medios de comunicación. El típico joven norteamericano, en cambio, sabe poco—y a veces también se interesa poco—por la cultura popular europea, mexicana o latinoamericana.

Mucha gente también cree que los jóvenes hispánicos son más filosóficos y más comprometidos[5] que los norteamericanos. Es decir, que se interesan más por las cuestiones éticas o políticas. Por eso los debates y las discusiones en los clubes y las cafeterías pueden durar hasta muy tarde… ¡y ser muy animados!

¿Qué opinas tú? Si tienes algunos amigos hispánicos, ¿qué opinan ellos?

[2]*Currently* [3]*fashion* [4]*(musical) groups* [5]*involved, with strong ideas about issues*

Actividad.   En tu ciudad

¿Adónde debe ir un joven hispano en tu ciudad si quiere hacer lo siguiente?

1.   ver una película reciente filmada en los Estados Unidos
2.   ver una película hispánica o europea
3.   bailar
4.   hablar con unos amigos hasta muy tarde
5.   hablar con otros jóvenes que se interesan en la política

Have you completed the following sections of the lesson? Check them off here.

_____ **Preparación**   _____ **Vocabulario del tema**
_____ **¿Tienes buena memoria?**   _____ **Un poco de gramática**

Now scan the words in the **Vocabulario** list to be sure that you understand the meaning of most of them. Then you will be ready to continue on with **Lección 34** in the Workbook.

• •

VOCABULARIO

Los verbos

averiguar	to find out
ligar con	to "pick someone up"

Las relaciones sociales
(Social Relationships)

el afecto	affection
la amistad	friendship
el amor	love
(a primera vista)	(at first sight)
la boda	wedding
el cariño	affection
el divorcio	divorce
la luna de miel	honeymoon
el noviazgo	engagement
el odio	hatred
la (primera) cita	(first) date

enamorarse (de)	to fall in love (with)
estar enamorado/a (de)	to be in love (with)
odiar	to hate
tener celos (de)	to be jealous (of)
tomarle cariño a alguien	to start to have affection for someone

Repaso: **el amor, casarse** (con), **divorciarse** (de), **llevarse bien/mal con, el matrimonio** (*marriage*), **tener envidia**

Las personas

el compañero/ la compañera	companion; "significant other"
el marido/la mujer	husband, wife
el matrimonio	married couple
el novio/la novia	fiancé(e); groom, bride
la pareja	couple

Repaso: **el amigo/la amiga, el esposo/la esposa, el novio/la novia** (*boy/girlfriend*)

Los conceptos

el éxito	success
el fracaso	failure

35

REUNIDOS*

OBJETIVOS

The materials in **Lección 35** of the Textbook and the Workbook will help you better understand the video episode and take you beyond it, giving you additional information about places and characters in the series. The Textbook will also help you to develop skill in using the Spanish language. In this lesson, you will learn

- additional vocabulary for making requests and recommendations
- ways to say that you hope something has happened.

You will also learn about a popular Mexican drink, **tequila**.

Be sure to work through all parts of the lesson. When you see a cassette symbol in the margin, listen to the tape for **Lección 35**. Answers or hints for many activities are given in Appendix 1. Be sure to check your answers for each activity before going on to the next one.

352

*Reunited

BEFORE VIEWING . . .

Preparación

Actividad A.

Completa las siguientes oraciones con la información apropiada.

1. Llevaron a Roberto... a un hospital en la capital / a una clínica en los Estados Unidos.
2. Raquel y Ángela salieron... con Roberto / en su propio carro.
3. Mientras manejaba Raquel, las dos mujeres hablaban... de sus novios / de problemas familiares.
4. En la capital, Juan y Pati... pudieron resolver sus dificultades / siguieron discutiendo sin resolver nada.
5. Arturo trataba de averiguar algo sobre... el paradero de Raquel / el accidente.

Ahora escucha la cinta para verificar tus respuestas.

Actividad B.

Paso 1

En este episodio, Carlos llama de nuevo a Miami. Al hablar con Ofelia, recibe noticias de cómo van las cosas en la oficina. Escucha la conversación entre Carlos y Ofelia y luego contesta la pregunta.

¿Cuál es el tema principal de la conversación entre Carlos y Ofelia?

a. _____ algunos problemas que hay con el personal de la oficina
b. _____ unos reportes que Carlos tiene que escribir
c. _____ los reportes de los auditores y sus recomendaciones

Si indicaste la letra *c*, tuviste razón.

Paso 2

Ahora escucha la conversación de nuevo. Puedes leerla al mismo tiempo, si quieres. La palabra **gerente** es sinónimo de **jefe**. Trata de no fijarte en las palabras que no entiendes. Luego contesta las preguntas.

CARLOS: ¿Ofelia? Habla Carlos. Mira, ¿no sabes algo más?
OFELIA: Sí, el gerente del banco que ha estado llamando muchas veces. Quiere hablar con Ud.
CARLOS: ¿No ha dicho para qué?
OFELIA: No, pero que quiere hablar con Ud. Yo le dije que andaba de viaje para México.
CARLOS: ¿Qué más?
OFELIA: Tengo una copia de los reportes de los auditores. No son muy buenos...

CARLOS: ¿Qué dicen?

OFELIA: Dicen que el balance general arroja fuertes pérdidas, que ponen en peligro las otras inversiones de la familia. Y pues... recomiendan cerrar la oficina.

1. Según los auditores, ¿están en buenas o malas condiciones las finanzas de la oficina de Miami?

2. La palabra **pérdidas** se relaciona con el verbo **perder**. ¿Qué significa?

   a. _____ profits
   b. _____ losses

Para pensar...

Al saber las noticias que le da Ofelia, Carlos está muy agitado. ¿Por qué? ¿Qué secreto está ocultando? ¿Debe contárselo a la familia? Imagina que tú eres Carlos. ¿Qué vas a hacer?

 AFTER VIEWING . . .

¿Tienes buena memoria?

Actividad A. En la capital

Ahora todos están por fin en la Ciudad de México. ¿Cuánto recuerdas de lo que pasó en el episodio? Contesta las siguientes preguntas. ¡OJO! A veces hay que elegir dos frases.

1. ¿Que pasó mientras manejaba Raquel?
   a. _____ De repente apareció un perro en el camino...
   b. _____ De repente apareció un camión (*truck*) en el camino...

   c. _____ ...y tuvieron un accidente.
   d. _____ ...pero no tuvieron un accidente.

2. Cuando Ángela y Raquel llegaron al hospital, ¿quiénes estaban allí para ver a Roberto?
   a. _____ Pedro y Mercedes   c. _____ Arturo y Pedro
   b. _____ Ramón y Carlos

3. Ángela no los vio. Entró directamente al cuarto de Roberto. ¿Cómo estaba Roberto cuando entró?
   a. _____ Estaba dormido (*asleep*)...   c. _____ ...y la saludó con cariño.
   b. _____ Estaba despierto...   d. _____ ...y no le habló.

4. ¿Qué hizo Arturo cuando vio a Raquel?
    a. _____ Gritó su nombre y le dio la mano.
    b. _____ Gritó su nombre y la besó.

5. ¿Cuál fue la reacción de Raquel?
    a. _____ Estaba un poco avergonzada (*embarrassed*)...
    b. _____ Estaba enojada con Arturo...

    c. _____ ...y se peleó con él.
    d. _____ ...pero no le dijo nada.

Ahora escucha la cinta para verificar tus respuestas.

Actividad B.   Idas y venidas (*Comings and Goings*)

Paso 1

En la cinta, escucha la segunda parte del repaso de Raquel.

Paso 2

Ahora describe los incidentes más importantes que ocurren en este episodio, haciendo oraciones con una palabra o frase de cada columna. Añade todos los detalles que puedas.

Pedro	se despidió de	Puerto Rico, Miami, Los
Raquel	saludó a	Ángeles, Nueva York
Arturo	conoció a	
Ángela	salió para	el hospital, el hotel,
Pati (no)	estaba (dormido/a) en	la casa de Pedro,
Ofelia	llamó a	la oficina
Carlos	fue a	
Roberto	le(s) contó algo a	Carlos, Carlos y Gloria,
	estaba preocupado/a por	toda la familia, Raquel,
	besó a	Pedro, Arturo, Juan,
		Ángela, Pati

Para pensar...

1. En la **Actividad B,** comentaste las actividades de casi todos los personajes principales menos las de don Fernando. Parece que todos se han olvidado de él. ¿Cómo estará don Fernando? ¿En qué estará pensando? ¿Crees que sus nietos le van a causar una buena impresión?

2. ¿Crees que Arturo les ha causado una buena impresión a los miembros de la familia Castillo? ¿Por qué sí o por qué no? Piensa en sus interacciones con todos hasta ahora. Y la familia, ¿le ha causado una buena impresión a Arturo? ¿Está contento de conocer a su «nueva» familia?

VOCABULARIO DEL TEMA

Consejos y sugerencias

el consejo	aconsejar	el requisito	requerir (ie)
	insistir (en)		rogar (ue)
el mandato	mandar	la sugerencia	sugerir (ie, i)
la recomendación	recomendar (ie)		

The preceding nouns and verbs express ways of influencing the behavior of others. You should be able to guess the meaning of almost all of them, except for **rogar** (*to beg*).

Actividad A.   ¿Mandato o sugerencia?

Indica si lo que dice la persona es una recomendación, una sugerencia, un mandato o un requisito.

1. Arturo, hablando con Pedro: «¿Por qué no dejamos a Roberto, para que descanse?»
2. La doctora, hablando con Arturo: «Hay que dejarlo dormir y no despertarlo.»
3. La doctora, hablando con una enfermera: «Está muy agitado. Déle un calmante.»
4. Ofelia, hablando con Carlos: «Recomiendan cerrar la oficina.»
5. Arturo, hablando con Pedro: «Bueno, es mejor que salgamos, para no despertarlo.»
6. Arturo, hablando con Raquel y Ángela: «¿Por qué no vamos al hotel?»
7. Raquel, hablando con su madre: «Mamá, no comiences.»
8. Consuelo, hablando con los niños: «Ahora todos a la cama, sin chistar (*fussing*).»

Actividad B.   En el episodio...

Completa las siguientes oraciones para describir los consejos y sugerencias del **Episodio 35.** ¡OJO! En algunos casos hay más de una respuesta.

1. ¿Qué sugiere Pedro en este episodio? Sugiere que
   a. _____ Carlos y Gloria le den las noticias sobre Roberto al resto de la familia
   b. _____ Pati no se vaya a Nueva York
   c. _____ Arturo despierte a Roberto

2. ¿En qué insiste la madre de Raquel? Insiste en que
   a. _____ Luis vaya a México
   b. _____ Raquel regrese a los Estados Unidos
   c. _____ Raquel la presente a la familia Castillo

3. ¿Qué recomiendan los auditores? (¿Tienes una memoria muy buena?) Recomiendan que
   a. _____ se cierre la oficina en Miami
   b. _____ Ramón sea nombrado director de la compañía
   c. _____ se venda La Gavia

4. ¿Qué requiere la médico? Quiere que
   a. _____ le den un calmante a Roberto
   b. _____ se saquen más rayos X
   c. _____ dejen descansar a Roberto hasta mañana

5. ¿Qué sugiere Arturo? Sugiere que
   a. _____ la familia prepare a don Fernando para conocer a sus nuevos parientes
   b. _____ todos regresen al hotel
   c. _____ Ángela no los acompañe a la casa de Pedro

Ahora escucha la cinta para verificar tus respuestas.

Actividad C.   ¿Y tú?

¿Qué consejos o sugerencias darías (*would you make*) en estos casos?
¡OJO! No te olvides de usar el subjuntivo. Si no quieres ofrecer un consejo, di
«No le aconsejo (sugiero...) nada porque _____.»

1. Un chico tiene problemas con sus padres. Se va de casa y no quiere volver. Tiene diecisiete años. ¿Qué recomendaciones le das a esta familia?

   Le aconsejo al chico que _____ .

   Les recomiendo a sus padres que _____ .

2. Una persona quiere dar una fiesta para todos sus amigos. Pero varios amigos suyos (*of his*) no se llevan bien. ¿Los invita a todos o no?

   Le sugiero que _____ .

   Les recomiendo a sus amigos que _____ .

3. La madre de una amiga tuya se mete en los asuntos de su hija. ¿Qué opinas tú?

   A mi amiga le sugiero que _____ .

   Le aconsejo a la madre que _____ .

• •

Un poco de gramática

Expressing Hope

Use the phrase **ojalá** (**que**) to indicate what you hope will happen. You can also use this expression followed by **haya**(**n**) (the present subjunctive equivalent of **ha**[**n**]) plus the past participle to describe what you hope *has* happened.

Ojalá que Pati **haya llegado** a Nueva York sin problemas.	*It's to be hoped that Pati has arrived in New York without any difficulty.*
Ojalá que don Fernando no se **haya enterado** del accidente.	*It's to be hoped that don Fernando hasn't found out about the accident.*

You will learn more about using these forms in the Workbook.

Actividad.   ¡Ojalá!

Identifica lo que cada personaje *no* pensaría (*would not think*) durante el **Episodio 35.**

Raquel

1. _____ Ojalá que Arturo les haya gustado a los miembros de la familia Castillo.
2. _____ Ojalá que Luis se haya decidido a venir a México a verme.
3. _____ Ojalá que Jorge me haya escrito una carta.

Arturo

4. _____ Ojalá que Raquel no haya perdido el interés por mí.
5. _____ Ojalá que mis pacientes no hayan buscado a otro médico durante mi ausencia.
6. _____ Ojalá que Ángel no haya muerto todavía.

Ángela

7. _____ Ojalá que Jorge haya empezado a salir con otra mujer.
8. _____ Ojalá que Roberto se haya despertado antes de que yo llegue.
9. _____ Ojalá que la familia Castillo me haya perdonado por no ir a su casa esta noche.

Carlos

10. _____ Ojalá que los auditores no hayan descubierto los problemas en la oficina.

11. _____ Ojalá que Gloria no haya salido esta noche.
12. _____ Ojalá que Ofelia ya haya encontrado otro trabajo.

Roberto, en sus sueños (*dreams*)

13. _____ Ojalá que Ángela se haya preocupado mucho por mí.
14. _____ Ojalá que hayan rescatado a mis compañeros también.
15. _____ Ojalá que no le hayan avisado a mi familia que ocurrió este accidente.

Nota cultural: El tequila

Al sentarse todos en la sala de la casa de Pedro, éste le pregunta a Arturo si ya ha probado el tequila. Esta bebida fuerte se asocia mundialmente con la cultura mexicana. Muchos creen que es la bebida favorita de las clases bajas. También se cree que se toma principalmente con el propósito de emborracharse.[1]

Sin embargo, para los mexicanos de las clases media y alta, como la familia Castillo, el tequila es una bebida fina. Se sirve solo, con sangrita[2] o con sal y limón como aperitivo o para celebrar las grandes ocasiones, como lo es la llegada de Arturo Iglesias a la casa de Pedro. El tequila que todos prueban en esta ocasión es añejo, es decir, es un tequila muy fino y muy viejo. Se aprecia[3] en la cultura mexicana como en otras culturas se aprecia un escocés[4] fino o el coñac.

La próxima vez que oigas hablar de las margaritas, piensa en los siguientes detalles de interés sobre esta bebida mexicana.

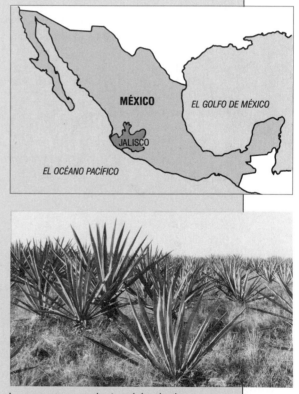

La agave es una planta originaria de México

- El tequila se destila del jugo[5] del mezcal, un tipo de agave originario de México. Se cultiva sobre todo en el estado de Jalisco.
- El tequila se conocía ya en la época prehispánica. Fue inventado por la tribu de los tiquila. En esa cultura sólo lo bebían los sacerdotes[6] y los ancianos.
- En la época de la llegada de los españoles, los aztecas usaban el tequila para curar la rigidez de las articulaciones.[7] Se aplicaba frotándolo[8] en cuerpo. También se usaba en ceremonias religiosas.
- El primer tequila mexicano fue producido por la familia de José Antonio Cuervo en 1795. Hoy día el tequila es reconocido internacionalmente, como lo son otras bebidas alcohólicas como el coñac y el champaña.

[1] *to get drunk* [2] *spicy tomato-based drink* [3] *Se... It is held in high regard* [4] *Scotch* [5] *juice* [6] *priests* [7] *rigidez... stiff joints* [8] *rubbing it*

Actividad. Bebidas nacionales

¿Con qué país, estado o ciudad asocias las siguientes bebidas? Debes prepararte para explicar el por qué de la asociación.

1. el té   2. el jerez   3. el vino   4. el champaña   5. la Coca-Cola
6. el café   7. la cerveza (*beer*)   8. el vodka

Have you completed the following sections of the lesson? Check them off here.

_____ **Preparación**   _____ **Vocabulario del tema**
_____ **¿Tienes buena memoria?**   _____ **Un poco de gramática**

Now scan the words in the **Vocabulario** list to be sure that you understand the meaning of most of them. Then you will be ready to continue on with **Lección 35** in the Workbook.

VOCABULARIO

Los verbos

aconsejar	to advise
insistir (en)	to insist (on)
mandar	to order
recomendar (ie)	to recommend
requerir (ie)	to require
rogar (ue)	to beg
sugerir (ie, i)	to suggest

Los conceptos

el mandato	order
la recomendación	recommendation
el requisito	requirement
la sugerencia	suggestion

Repaso: el consejo

En el camino

el camión (*Mex.*)   truck

Los adjetivos

avergonzado/a	embarrassed
dormido/a	asleep

Las palabras adicionales

ojalá (que)   It is to be hoped (that)

LECCIÓN

36

¿QUÉ ESTARÁN HACIENDO?*

OBJETIVOS

Most of this episode is a review. Be sure to work through all parts of the lesson. When you see a cassette symbol in the margin, listen to the tape for **Lección 36**. Answers or hints for many activities are given in Appendix 1. Be sure to check your answers for each activity before going on to the next one.

* *What Could They Be Doing?*

361

BEFORE VIEWING . . .

PREPARACIÓN

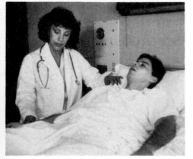

Actividad.

Los siguientes incidentes ocurrieron en el episodio previo. ¿Puedes dar el nombre del personaje o de los personajes apropiados que dijeron o hicieron estas cosas?

1. _____ por poco (*almost*) tienen un accidente en el camino.

2. _____ salió para Nueva York.

3. _____ le dio malas noticias a su jefe.

4. _____ llegó primero al hospital y vio a Roberto.

5. _____ dijo que Roberto no sufrió lesiones graves.

6. _____ conocieron a Ángela mientras estaban fuera del cuarto de Roberto.

7. _____ dormía durante todo el episodio.

8. _____ se besaron en el hospital (y también en el jardín en la casa de Pedro).

9. _____ llamó a Puerto Rico.

10. _____ habló con su madre.

11. _____ no quiso ir a la casa de Pedro.

12. _____ conoció a los miembros de la familia Castillo.

Para pensar...

En este episodio alguien le va a contar a otra persona lo que le ha pasado recientemente. Otras personas van a pensar en lo que les ha pasado a ellos. Piensa tú un momento en los **Episodios 27–35.** ¿Qué les ha pasado a estas personas?

Raquel	Ramón	Juan
Arturo	Pedro	Roberto
Mercedes	Carlos	Ángela

AFTER VIEWING . . .

¿TIENES BUENA MEMORIA?

Actividad.   ¿Qué pasó?

Contesta las siguientes preguntas sobre lo que pasó en este episodio.

1. Los miembros de la familia Castillo... se dan cuenta (*realize*) / no se dan cuenta... de la atracción entre Arturo y Raquel.
2. Raquel/Arturo... quería quedarse un poco más en el jardín antes de reunirse otra vez con los Castillo.
3. Arturo... sigue enamorado / ya no está enamorado... de Raquel.
4. En la sala... Consuelo/Gloria... habla sin parar mientras los demás piensan en sus propios problemas.

REPASO DE LOS EPISODIOS 27 – 35

Actividad A.   Lo que le pasó a Raquel

Pon los siguientes incidentes en orden cronológico (del 1 a 7), según los contaba Raquel.

a. _____ Raquel y Ángela fueron manejando del pueblo a la capital.
b. _____ Al llegar al pueblo, no pudieron pasar al sitio de la excavación.
c. _____ Raquel y Ángela fueron manejando de la Ciudad de México a un pueblo.
d. _____ Por fin sacaron a Roberto y lo llevaron a la capital.
e. _____ Estaban a punto de rescatar a Roberto cuando hubo otro derrumbe.
f. _____ En un hospital conocieron a un cura que las ayudó mucho.
g. _____ Al regresar al sitio de la excavación, supieron que Roberto estaba vivo.

Ahora escucha la cinta para verificar tus respuestas.

Actividad B.   ¿Y la familia Castillo?

Varios miembros de la familia Castillo reflexionaron sobre problemas importantes mientras Gloria hablaba sin parar. ¿Te acuerdas de la información más importante?

Juan

¿Cuál es el motivo principal del conflicto entre él y Pati?

a. _____ A Pati no le gusta la familia de Juan.

b. _____ Juan quiere que Pati pase más tiempo con él y con su familia.

c. _____ Pati no sabe manejar sus proyectos profesionales y por eso no puede pasar tiempo suficiente con Juan.

Para pensar...

Ya sabes que Ramón le sugirió a Juan que tal vez él, Juan, le tenga envidia a Pati, su mujer. ¿Crees que Juan tomó en serio la sugerencia de Ramón? ¿Qué va a hacer Juan?

Mercedes

Paso 1

¿Cuál es el problema esencial de ella?

a. _____ Sufre por la enfermedad de su padre y porque sabe que hay otros problemas familiares también.

b. _____ Les tiene envidia a Consuelo y a Pati, porque éstas están casadas y ella no.

c. _____ Les tiene envidia a sus hermanos porque éstos tienen carreras y ella no.

Paso 2

Indica si las siguientes oraciones son ciertas (**C**) o falsas (**F**) con relación a Mercedes.

C   F   1. Ha pasado la mayoría de su tiempo en el hospital.

C   F   2. También habló con Juan sobre sus problemas matrimoniales.

C   F   3. No sabe nada de lo que está pasando en la oficina en Miami. Pedro y Ramón no le han dicho nada del asunto.

Para pensar...

Algunas personas viven para sí mismas (*for themselves*). Otras viven para los demás. En tu opinión, ¿qué tipo de persona es Mercedes? ¿Por qué crees que es así? ¿Crees que es muy diferente de sus hermanos?

Pedro

Paso 1

¿De qué problema se entera él?

a. _____ Roberto y Ángela no son los verdaderos nietos de don Fernando.
b. _____ Don Fernando está arruinado económicamente por su enfermedad.
c. _____ Las finanzas de la compañía no están en buenas condiciones.

Paso 2

¿Qué recuerdas de la conversación que Pedro y Ramón tuvieron con los auditores? De las siguientes recomendaciones, ¿cuáles *no* fueron dadas por los auditores?

a. _____ vender La Gavia
b. _____ abrir otra oficina en la capital
c. _____ cerrar la oficina en Miami
d. _____ concentrarse en la producción de autos
e. _____ nombrar a Juan director de la compañía

Para pensar...

La situación económica de la compañía Castillo Saavedra realmente está grave. ¿Qué opinas tú? ¿Crees que Pedro y Ramón van a seguir las recomendaciones de los auditores? ¿Cuál es la causa de los problemas en la oficina de Miami? ¿Es culpa de Carlos? ¿O hay otra posibilidad?

Have you completed the following sections of the lesson? Check them off here.

_____ **Preparación**   _____ **Repaso de los Episodios 27–35**
_____ **¿Tienes buena memoria?**

You are now ready to continue on with **Lección 36** in the Workbook.

Un viaje a México: La capital

Un sector de la capital mexicana

37

LLEVANDO CUENTAS*

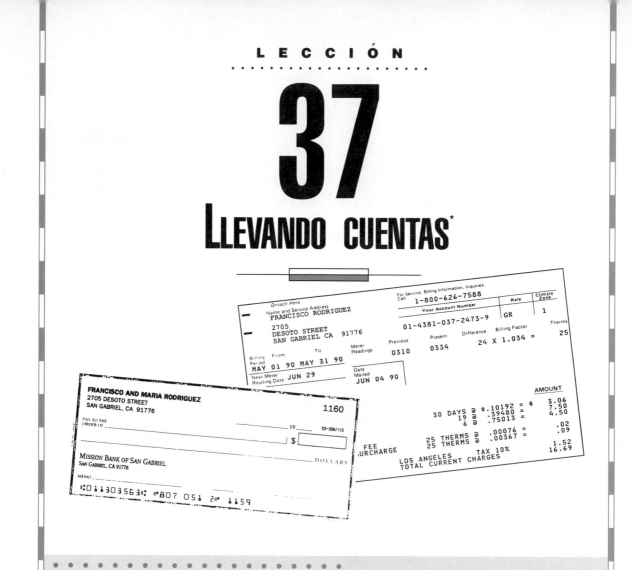

OBJETIVOS

The materials in **Lección 37** of the Textbook and the Workbook will help you better understand the video episode and take you beyond it, giving you additional information about places and characters in the series. The Textbook will also help you to develop skill in using the Spanish language. In this lesson, you will learn

- vocabulary related to money and financial matters
- ways to use subjunctive forms to talk about the past.

You will also learn about some important events in Mexican history.

Be sure to work through all parts of the lesson. When you see a cassette symbol in the margin, listen to the tape for **Lección 37**. Answers or hints for many activities are given in Appendix 1. Be sure to check your answers for each activity before going on to the next one.

* *Keeping the Books*

— **BEFORE VIEWING . . .**

PREPARACIÓN

Actividad A.

Al empezar esta serie de episodios de *Destinos*, varias situaciones están sin re-
solverse todavía. Otras están a punto de desarrollarse (*developing*). ¿Puedes dar
el nombre de la persona que está enfrentando (*facing*) las siguientes situaciones? ¡OJO! Más de una persona está involucrada (*involved*) en algunas situaciones, y algunos personajes no tienen sólo un problema que resolver, sino (*but
rather*) varios.

Personajes: Ángela, Arturo, Carlos, don Fernando, Gloria, Juan, Mercedes, Pati,
Pedro, Ramón, Raquel, Roberto

Situaciones

1. Le ha declarado su amor a una persona, pero esa persona todavía no le ha
    dado una respuesta.
2. Esta persona está muy pensativa porque alguien le ha dicho que es egoísta.
3. Tiene que tomar decisiones relacionadas con los problemas financieros
    causados por un pariente.
4. Su trabajo es la causa de que se separa de una persona querida.
5. Todavía piensa en una persona de su pasado… y en unos parientes que no
    ha conocido todavía.
6. Hay serios problemas financieros en la oficina que esta persona dirige.
7. Un pariente se mete mucho en la vida de esta persona, lo cual (*which*) le
    molesta mucho.
8. Aunque el esposo de una pareja es miembro de su familia, esta persona
    apoya (*supports*) a la esposa.
9. Alguien le ha declarado su amor a esta persona, pero no sabe qué hacer. Por
    un lado, está el amor. Pero por otro, está la familia…
10. Esta persona tuvo una pelea con otra persona que ahora está inconsciente a
    causa de un accidente.

Actividad B.

En este episodio, Mercedes le va a explicar a Arturo el significado de algunas
fiestas nacionales de México.

Paso 1

Primero, lee lo que Mercedes le va a decir sobre el 16 de septiembre.

MERCEDES: El 16 de septiembre se dio el grito de independencia. En ese día en el
           pueblo de Dolores, el padre Miguel Hidalgo supo que los españoles

habían descubierto los planes de independencia del grupo de patriotas. El padre Miguel Hidalgo era uno de estos patriotas. Entonces, en la madrugada de ese día, el padre tocó las campanas de la iglesia, llamando a todos los habitantes del pueblo. Cuando llegaron, Hidalgo les habló otra vez de la igualdad entre los hombres. Les habló de cómo los indígenas, mestizos y criollos deberían tener los mismos derechos que los españoles que gobernaban las colonias. Dijo que era el momento de ser una nación independiente. Y así empezó la lucha por la independencia. Por ese motivo, cada 16 de septiembre hay grandes celebraciones en todo el país.

Ahora escucha el pasaje en la cinta mientras lo lees otra vez al mismo tiempo.

Paso 2

Ahora escucha lo que Mercedes le dice a Arturo sobre el Cinco de Mayo. Luego contesta las preguntas.

1. En México, la celebración del Cinco de Mayo tiene que ver con (*has to do with*)...
    a. _____ una batalla contra tropas de los Estados Unidos
    b. _____ una batalla contra tropas francesas
    c. _____ una batalla contra tropas españolas

2. El Cinco de Mayo conmemora...
    a. _____ la valentía de los mexicanos en esa batalla
    b. _____ la independencia de México de España
    c. _____ el comienzo de la primavera

Paso 3

Ahora lee lo que Mercedes dice sobre el Cinco de Mayo. Luego escucha el pasaje otra vez, leyéndolo al mismo tiempo, si quieres. Vas a comprender más cada vez que lo repasas (*go over*).

MERCEDES: Como ya sabrás, Arturo, en 1861, los franceses invadieron México. Napoleón III siempre había soñado con poseer territorios en América. En esa época, Benito Juárez era presidente de México. Pero nuestro país estaba dividido. Había un gran conflicto entre los conservadores y los liberales. Llegaron las tropas francesas, y con la ayuda de los conservadores, Napoleón pudo instalar a Maximiliano de Austria como emperador de México. Pero el imperio de Maximiliano no duró mucho. Pues, las batallas con Juárez continuaban. En 1867, Maximiliano fue capturado y fusilado. Benito Juárez asumió su autoridad una vez más. Una de las batallas más importantes ocurrió el 5 de mayo de 1862 en la ciudad de Puebla. Allí, el general Zaragoza venció a las tropas francesas. Aunque la lucha contra los franceses duró varios años más, la batalla de Puebla representa el espíritu y la valentía con que los mexicanos luchaban. Cada año celebramos el Cinco de Mayo como un acontecimiento muy importante.

Para comprender un poco más

Note: On occasion boxes such as this one will present vocabulary that may help you understand certain conversations more completely. Can you guess the meaning of the boldfaced vocabulary items from their brief context?

atrasado/a	El vuelo de Raquel está **atrasado**. Debe llegar a las siete y media, pero no va a llegar hasta las ocho.
darle de alta	Don Fernando desea regresar a La Gavia. ¿Cuándo **le** van a **dar de alta** sus médicos?
una pesadilla	Carlitos se despertó porque tuvo **una pesadilla** y ahora no quiere estar solo.

  AFTER VIEWING . . .

. . . .

¿TIENES BUENA MEMORIA?

Actividad A.   ¿Qué pasó?

¿Puedes identificar a los siguientes personajes?

1. Esta persona habló de las fiestas nacionales de México.
2. Esta persona revisó sus asuntos económicos y llegó a la conclusión de que maneja muy mal el dinero.
3. Esta persona también revisó sus asuntos económicos y encontró que tenía suficiente dinero para hacer un viaje.
4. Esta persona llamó al hotel y dejó un mensaje para Raquel.
5. Esta persona ha comprado su pasaje para ir a México.

Actividad B.   ¿Quién lo dijo?

Identifica al personaje que hizo cada una de las siguientes declaraciones. ¿Puedes identificar también al personaje con quien hablaba?

Raquel	Pedro	Luis
Ángela	Mercedes	Carlitos
Arturo	Ramón	María Rodríguez
Roberto	Juan	(la madre de Raquel)

MODELOS: _____ está conversando con _____ .
_____ le(s) dijo esto a _____ .
_____ está hablando por teléfono con _____ .

1. Bueno, mi madre era una mujer... llena de vida, afectuosa. A veces tenía momentos de tristeza y yo no entendía por qué...
2. Ya verás las sorpresas que te esperan cuando despiertes, Roberto. Primero, conoceremos a nuestro abuelo, el padre de papá.
3. Tú eres el esposo de Raquel, ¿verdad?... Entonces, ¿son novios?... Porque sólo los novios o los esposos se besan en el jardín, ¿no es cierto?
4. Raquel se pondrá muy contenta de verte.... Será una completa sorpresa.... Yo creo que a ella también le gustará verte a ti.
5. Muy bien. Mañana le daré tus recibos (*receipts*) a mi secretaria y le diré que te haga un cheque.

Nota cultural: El español de María Rodríguez

The use of certain phrases by María, Raquel's mother, is in some ways typical of Mexican Americans and of Mexicans as well. Listen again as María works on the family's bills.

Did you note the following usages? Were you able to guess their meaning in context?

Anda, viejo.	**Anda** (also: **Ándale**, **Ándale pues**) is a common way to say *get going* or *get out of here* (in the literal and figurative sense). **Viejo** (also **vieja**) is an affectionate way to refer to one's spouse.
¡Híjole! ¡Caramba!	Frequently used interjections, roughly equivalent to English phrases such as *My God! Gosh!*

Para pensar...

Al final de este episodio, Raquel recibió un mensaje de Pedro. ¿Por qué quiere Pedro hablar con Raquel otra vez cuando acaba de verla en su casa? ¿Es posible que tenga que ver con don Fernando?

VOCABULARIO DEL TEMA

El dinero

los ahorros	savings		**los gastos**	expenses
la cuenta	account; bill		**los ingresos**	income

la cuenta corriente	checking account	**ahorrar**	to save
la cuenta de ahorros	savings account	**cargar**	to charge (*on a credit card*)
el cheque	check	**ganar**	to earn
el efectivo	cash	**gastar**	to spend
el recibo	receipt	**manejar**	
la tarjeta de crédito	credit card	**(bien/mal)**	to manage (well/badly)
		pagar	to pay
		sacar	to take out, withdraw (*from an account*)

Note that English *to save* and *to spend* have specific Spanish equivalents when they refer to money.

- **ahorrar** = to save (*money, time*)
  rescatar = to save, rescue (*a person or animal*)
  guardar = to save, keep (*things*)
- **gastar** = to spend (*money*)
  pasar = to spend (*time*)

Actividad A. María lleva cuentas

Escucha otra vez la descripción de la situación económica de los mayores. Indica con el número de la oración la foto o el dibujo a que corresponde cada oración.

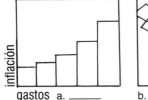

a. _____   b. _____   c. _____   d. _____   e. _____

Actividad B. Hablando de dinero

Escucha otra vez mientras algunos personajes hablan de dinero. Luego indica si las oraciones son ciertas (**C**) o falsas (**F**) para los personajes. ¿Puedes corregir las oraciones falsas?

Primera conversación

C   F   1. Ángela tiene mucho dinero en su cuenta de ahorros.
C   F   2. Sacó mucho dinero con su tarjeta de crédito.

C   F   3. No tiene ninguna dificultad en pagar la cuenta.
C   F   4. Maneja muy bien su dinero.

Segunda conversación

C   F   5. Raquel tiene preparada para Pedro una lista de los gastos de su viaje.
C   F   6. Usó poco su tarjeta de crédito en el viaje.
C   F   7. No le van a pagar los gastos pronto.
C   F   8. El jefe de Raquel se preocupa mucho por los gastos.

Actividad C.   ¿Y tú?

Paso 1

Para ti, ¿son ciertas o falsas las siguientes oraciones?

C   F   1. Por lo general, manejo muy bien el dinero.
C   F   2. Tengo una cuenta de ahorros y una cuenta corriente.
C   F   3. Casi todos los meses ahorro algún dinero.
C   F   4. Escribo unos ocho cheques todos los meses.
C   F   5. Casi nunca uso las tarjetas de crédito. Lo pago todo en efectivo o con cheque.
C   F   6. Casi nunca gasto más de lo que gano.
C   F   7. Por lo general, si no tengo dinero en efectivo para pagar algo, no me lo compro.
C   F   8. Mis ingresos siempre alcanzan para pagar mis gastos.

Paso 2

Ahora describe tus costumbres en cuanto al manejo del dinero, completando el siguiente párrafo.

Por lo general, manejo el dinero _____. Tengo _____. Gasto

_____. En cuanto a las tarjetas de crédito, _____. Mis

amigos/mi familia me dice(n) que _____.

· ·

UN POCO DE GRAMÁTICA

Talking About What You Wanted Someone to Do

You already know how to express your or someone else's wish that another person do something, using the present subjunctive.

Raquel **quiere que** Pedro le **pague** lo más pronto posible.   *Raquel wants Pedro to pay her as quickly as possible.*

> To express the same thing in the past, you can use the past subjunctive. It is formed by adding **-a** to the third-person plural of the preterite minus **-on**: **trabajaron** → **trabajar-** → **trabajara**, **pidieron** → **pidier-** → **pidiera**.
>
> María Rodríguez **quería que** Luis **viajara** a México.
>
> *María Rodríguez wanted Luis to travel to Mexico.*
>
> Carlos **quería que** su hijo **volviera** a la cama.
>
> *Carlos wanted his son to go back to bed.*
>
> You will learn more about the forms of the past subjunctive in the Workbook, and you will learn about its uses in this and subsequent lessons of the Textbook and Workbook.

Actividad.   El resumen de Raquel

Al final del **Episodio 37,** Raquel nos comentó, como siempre, algunos acontecimientos del episodio. ¿Recuerdas lo que nos dijo? Al leer, presta atención (*pay attention*) a las formas indicadas del pasado del subjuntivo.

1. La familia le pidió a Arturo que **hablara** de alguien. ¿De quién querían que **hablara**?

    Querían que Arturo **hablara**
    a. _____ de Rosario   c. _____ de Ángela y Roberto
    b. _____ de Ángel

2. Después seguimos conversando y la familia le dijo a Arturo que debería (*he should*) regresar a México. ¿Por qué le decían que **regresara** a México?

    Querían que Arturo **regresara** a México
    a. _____ para conocer a don   c. _____ para vivir con ellos
            Fernando
    b. _____ para conocer más el país

3. Después revisé las cuentas con Pedro. Le di los recibos de todos los gastos de mi viaje. Él prometió darme un cheque por los gastos y otro por mis servicios. Entonces, Pedro me pidió algo. Él quería que yo le **diera** algo importante. ¿Qué quería Pedro que yo le **diera**?

    Pedro quería que yo le **diera**
    a. _____ una foto de Rosario
    b. _____ información sobre Ángela y Roberto
    c. _____ los papeles de Rosario y Ángel

 Ahora escucha la cinta para verificar tus respuestas.

Nota cultural: Episodios en la historia de México

En este episodio, los miembros de la familia Castillo le explicaron a Arturo algunos episodios muy importantes de la historia de México. ¿Te acuerdas de las tres historias?

Lee los tres breves resúmenes que se dan a continuación y el siguiente bosquejo[1] de la historia de México. Luego trata de colocar las historias en su sitio en el bosquejo. Para terminar, hay una nota sobre la celebración de uno de estos episodios en los Estados Unidos. ¿Sabes cuál es?

Emiliano Zapata

1. Época de la Revolución mexicana, iniciada por Francisco I. Madero. Lucharon[2] en la Revolución Pancho Villa y Emiliano Zapata.
2. El padre Miguel Hidalgo dio el grito[3] que inició la lucha para independizarse. Según el Padre Hidalgo, indígenas, mestizos[4] y criollos[5] debían tener los mismos derechos que los españoles que gobernaban las colonias.
3. En la ciudad de Puebla el cinco de mayo las fuerzas mexicanas ganaron una batalla importante contra los invasores franceses.

Bosquejo esencial de la historia de México

–1521	*Época precolombina*: civilizaciones azteca, maya, olmeca, tolteca
1521–1821	*Época colonial*
1519	Llegada de Hernán Cortés.
1521	Destrucción de Tenochtitlán por Cortés y fundación de la Ciudad de México sobre sus ruinas. Se le dio al país el nombre de Nueva España.
1810	¿ ?
1810–1821	Guerras por la independencia.
1821	México se convierte en un país independiente.
1821–1910	*Época de consolidación del estado*
1836	El estado de Texas se separó de México tras una guerra de varios meses.
1846–1848	Guerra con los Estados Unidos en la que México perdió la mitad de su territorio: Nuevo México, alta California, Nevada, Utah, Arizona y partes de Colorado y Wyoming
1857	Benito Juárez llegó a ser el primer presidente mexicano de origen indígena
1861	La invasión de los franceses

Benito Juárez

[1] *outline* [2] *Fought* [3] *shout, cry* [4] *persons of Indian and Spanish extraction* [5] *persons born in Mexico but of Spanish heritage*

1862	¿ ?
1867	Se reestableció la república.
1876–1910	Dictadura de Porfirio Díaz. Gobernó favoreciendo las clases elevadas de la sociedad.
1910–	*Época moderna*
1910–1920	¿ ?
1917	Promulgación de una constitución que sirve de base a la reconstrucción del país.
1938	Nacionalización de las compañías petrolíferas.[6]
1964	Reforma agraria que introduce la modernización de la explotación del campo.
1973	Descubrimiento de nuevas reservas de petróleo que dan un gran impulso a la economía del país.

El Cinco de Mayo

La fiesta del Cinco de Mayo conmemora la batalla que dio la victoria a los mexicanos contra los franceses en Puebla, durante la época del imperio francés en México. Curiosamente, esta fiesta mexicana realmente se celebra en los Estados Unidos de una manera muy diferente de la forma en que se celebra en México.

En los Estados Unidos, muchos creen que el Cinco de Mayo es el Día de la Independencia de México, algo así como[7] el cuatro de julio. Pero el verdadero Día de la Independencia de México es el 16 de septiembre. El Cinco de Mayo es para los mexicanos lo que el Día de los Veteranos es para los estadounidenses: un día para celebrar la gran valentía nacional, pero *no* el Día de la Independencia.

En México las fiestas del Cinco de Mayo son primariamente patrióticas y se celebran de varias maneras en diferentes regiones del país. En los Estados Unidos, sin embargo, el Cinco de Mayo ha venido a ser[8] algo así como la celebración del orgullo[9] que siente por su raza de la comunidad mexicana y mexicoamericana. En muchas ciudades hay dos o tres días de fiestas, con canciones, bailes, comida típica, mercados, desfiles[10] y otros tipos de celebraciones. ¿Se celebra el Cinco de Mayo en tu comunidad?

[6]*oil, petroleum*   [7]algo... *something like*   [8]ha... *has come to be*   [9]*pride*   [10]*parades*

Have you completed the following sections of the lesson? Check them off here.

_____ **Preparación**	_____ **Vocabulario del tema**
_____ **¿Tienes buena memoria?**	_____ **Un poco de gramática**

Now scan the words in the **Vocabulario** list to be sure that you understand the meaning of most of them. Then you will be ready to continue on with **Lección 37** in the Workbook.

Vocabulario

Los verbos

desarrollar	to develop
enfrentarse (con)	to deal with, face (*a problem*)
resolver (ue)	to solve, resolve

El dinero

los ahorros	savings
la cuenta	account; bill
la cuenta corriente	checking account
la cuenta de ahorros	savings account
el cheque	check
el efectivo	cash
los gastos	expenses
los ingresos	income
el recibo	receipt
la tarjeta de crédito	credit card

ahorrar	to save
cargar	to charge (*on a credit card*)
ganar	to earn
gastar	to spend
llevar cuentas	to keep the books; to keep track of expenses
manejar (bien/mal)	to manage (well/badly)
pagar	to pay

Repaso: sacar

Las palabras adicionales

en cuanto a	as far as . . . is concerned

38

Ocultando la verdad*

· · · · · · · · · · · · · · ·

Objetivos

The materials in **Lección 38** of the Textbook and the Workbook will help you better understand the video episode and take you beyond it, giving you additional information about places and characters in the series. The Textbook will also help you to develop skill in using the Spanish language. In this lesson, you will learn

- more vocabulary related to financial matters and to business questions
- more ways to use the past subjunctive.

You will also learn about the Mexican economy and the economy of Latin America in general.

Be sure to work through all parts of the lesson. When you see a cassette symbol in the margin, listen to the tape for **Lección 38**. Answers or hints for many activities are given in Appendix 1. Be sure to check your answers for each activity before going on to the next one.

Hiding the Truth

BEFORE VIEWING . . .

PREPARACIÓN

Actividad A.

¿Qué pasó en el episodio previo? Indica si las siguientes afirmaciones son ciertas (**C**) o falsas (**F**).

C   F   1. La familia Castillo le pidió a Arturo que hablara un poco de su madre.

C   F   2. También le dijeron a Arturo que regresara a México para conocer al resto de la familia.

C   F   3. Arturo y Raquel salieron a bailar después de hablar con la familia.

C   F   4. En el hospital Ángela revisaba sus cuentas.

C   F   5. Al regresar por fin al hotel, Arturo le dio a Raquel un regalo, una foto.

C   F   6. Raquel recibió un telegrama urgente.

Ahora escucha la cinta para verificar tus respuestas.

Actividad B.

Ya sabes que la familia Castillo tiene problemas económicos. En este episodio, Ramón y Pedro le van a hablar de esos problemas a Mercedes. Luego van a hablar de posibles soluciones. Escucha una parte de su conversación y contesta las preguntas. Al escuchar, recuerda que **engañar** significa *to deceive*.

1. Cuando hablan de soluciones, Ramón habla de cerrar «la sucursal». ¿Qué significa esa palabra?

    a. _____ un tipo de investigación   b. _____ oficina de una compañía

2. Ramón también propone otra solución para los problemas financieros: «poner a otra persona a cargo». ¿Qué crees que significa esa frase?

    a. _____ darle la dirección (*management*) de la oficina a otra persona

    b. _____ cambiar el personal de la oficina, por ejemplo, la secretaria

---

Para pensar...

1. Según lo que sabes en este momento, ¿se te ocurre otra solución para los problemas financieros de la familia Castillo?

2. ¿Cuándo crees que los hermanos deben hablar con Carlos sobre estos asuntos? Antes de contestar, piensa en todas las preocupaciones que la familia tiene en este momento.

Para comprender un poco más

cabezón/cabezona　Juan es **cabezón.** A veces no escucha los consejos que le dan y sigue con lo suyo (*what he
wants to do*).

**caerle bien/mal
a alguien**　Arturo **les** quiere **caer bien** a los Castillo. Es
decir, quiere causarles una buena impresión.

AFTER VIEWING . . .

. . . .

¿TIENES BUENA MEMORIA?

Actividad A.　Lo que sabe Raquel

Esta noche, en el hotel, Raquel ha hablado con una serie de personas que le son
importantes de una forma u otra. ¿Puedes completar el siguiente resumen de sus
conversaciones?

Frases útiles:

>hablar de sí mismo / de nosotros, pasarlo bien/mal con, quedarse en Los
>　Ángeles, venir a México

>una carta para él, un mensaje para mí, una llamada telefónica

>con don Fernando / con Roberto, en mí / en mi familia

>si Ángela había regresado, si Roberto se había despertado

Me gusta mucho la foto que Arturo me dio. Yo siempre _____[1] Arturo. Es
muy amable y me hace sentir muy bien.

　　Cuando Arturo y yo regresamos al hotel, había _____[2] Pedro quería
que yo lo llamara a su casa. Otra vez olvidé la cartera. Ya que el mensaje era urgente,
Arturo y yo pensamos que tenía que ver _____[3] ¡Qué susto!ᵃ

　　Luego Arturo y yo fuimos a tomar algo. Al sentarnos, Arturo empezó a _____[4]
Yo le dije que había pensado en él, pero que *no* había pensado _____[5]

ᵃ¡Qué... *What a fright!*

Nuestra conversación fue interrumpida por _____.[6] Era mi madre, quien me

quería decir que ella y mi padre sí iban a _____.[7]

    Al subir a mi habitación, llamé a la recepción para saber _____,[8] pero

parece que no. Ojalá Roberto esté bien.

Ahora escucha la cinta para verificar tus respuestas.

Actividad B.   Lo que Raquel no sabe

Paso 1

Raquel no ha podido hablar con Ángela, así que no sabe nada sobre Roberto. ¿Te acuerdas de lo que pasó con Roberto en este episodio? ¿Se despertó o no?

Paso 2

Raquel tampoco sabe nada de las otras preocupaciones de la familia Castillo. ¿Puedes contestar las siguientes preguntas sobre esos problemas?

1. En cuanto al futuro de Juan y Pati, ¿son optimistas o pesimistas los hermanos?
2. ¿Qué le revelan Pedro y Ramón a Mercedes? ¿que Carlos ha sacado dinero de la compañía o que Carlos maneja mal el dinero?
3. ¿Qué ya no puede hacer Carlos? ¿ser director de la oficina u ocultar la verdad?

Para pensar...

1. En este episodio, Carlos le dijo a Gloria que no podía seguir ocultándole la verdad a su familia. ¿Qué «verdad» está ocultando Carlos? ¿Por qué crees que Carlos se enfadó con Gloria? ¿Es posible que ella tenga algo que ver con el dinero que ha sacado Carlos?
2. Al final del episodio, Carlos se enfadó muchísimo porque no encontró a Gloria en la casa. ¿Adónde crees que se fue? ¿Por qué se fue?

Nota cultural: La estructura familiar

In the Spanish-speaking world, as in many other cultures, the roles of men and women, and husbands and wives, are in a state of flux. In the Castillo family there are examples of a number of different roles:

- Ramón and Consuelo are a traditional couple. It appears that Consuelo is the primary caretaker of the children, and that Ramón is more involved with business matters.

- Juan and Pati are young urban professionals who do not have children yet, nor are there (apparently) any plans to have them.
- Carlos and Gloria are also somewhat nontraditional. Even though Carlos is a business executive, he takes great pleasure in spending time with his children; in fact, he appears to be more involved with child rearing than his wife is.

In short: No one image of the structure is typical for all Hispanic cultures. How would you describe Mercedes in this context? Raquel? María and Pancho (Raquel's parents)?

VOCABULARIO DEL TEMA

El dinero y los negocios

el auditor/la auditora	auditor	**andar bien/mal**	to be going well/badly
el dueño/la dueña	owner	**despedir (i, i)**	to fire (*an employee*)
el empleado/la empleada	employee	**dirigir (dirijo)**	to run (*a business*)
el jefe/la jefa	boss	**economizar**	to economize
el presupuesto	budget	**poner (a alguien)**	to put (someone)
		a cargo (de)	in charge (of)
la compañía	company		
la empresa	firm, company, business		
la oficina	office		
la sucursal	branch office		
S.A. (Sociedad Anónima)	Inc.		

Actividad A.   Preocupaciones financieras

Escucha otra vez mientras Pedro, Ramón y Mercedes hablan de los problemas económicos de Castillo Saavedra, S.A. Luego indica si las siguientes oraciones son ciertas (**C**) o falsas (**F**).

C   F   1. En la oficina de Miami, todo anda bien económicamente.
C   F   2. Hay irregularidades en el presupuesto.
C   F   3. Los ingresos son mayores que los gastos.
C   F   4. Mercedes no entiende el problema; dice que todo anda bien económicamente en los Estados Unidos.

C   F   5. En total Carlos ha sacado un millón de dólares.

C   F   6. El problema se encontraba en los libros de Carlos.

Actividad B. «Voy a cambiar.»

¿Te acuerdas de lo que decía Ángela mientras reflexionaba sobre sus problemas económicos? Completa el siguiente párrafo con las palabras apropiadas.

Sustantivos: los gastos, los ingresos, el presupuesto
Verbos: economizar, ganar, manejar

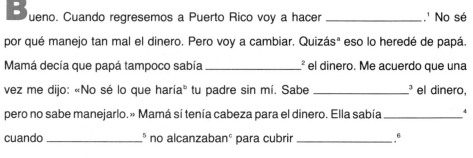

Bueno. Cuando regresemos a Puerto Rico voy a hacer _____.¹ No sé por qué manejo tan mal el dinero. Pero voy a cambiar. Quizás[a] eso lo heredé de papá. Mamá decía que papá tampoco sabía _____² el dinero. Me acuerdo que una vez me dijo: «No sé lo que haría[b] tu padre sin mí. Sabe _____³ el dinero, pero no sabe manejarlo.» Mamá sí tenía cabeza para el dinero. Ella sabía _____⁴ cuando _____⁵ no alcanzaban[c] para cubrir _____.⁶

[a]*Perhaps*   [b]*would do*   [c]*no... were not enough*

Ahora escucha la cinta para verificar tus respuestas.

Actividad C. Castillo Saavedra, S.A.

Imagina que te han puesto a cargo de esta compañía. ¿Qué vas a hacer para resolver la situación? Indica todas las posibilidades con que tú estás de acuerdo.

1.   _____ Cierro la sucursal de Miami.
2.   _____ Despido a la mitad (*half*) de los empleados.
3.   _____ Dejo a Carlos como director de la sucursal, pero hago que unos auditores lleven los libros.
4.   _____ Dejo a Carlos como director, pero yo mismo/a llevo control del presupuesto.
5.   _____ Despido a Carlos y dirijo la oficina.
6.   _____ Hablo con Ofelia para pedirle que vigile (*watch over*) las acciones de Carlos, pero no le digo nada a Carlos.

Actividad D. Hablando de negocios

¿Puedes dar el nombre de una compañía con una de las siguientes características?

1.   El apellido del dueño de la compañía es el nombre de la compañía.
2.   La compañía tiene sucursales en muchos países extranjeros.
3.   La empresa tiene una jefa.
4.   El director de la compañía es muy famoso.
5.   Es una empresa extranjera que tiene muchas sucursales en los Estados Unidos.

UN POCO DE GRAMÁTICA

More About Talking About the Past

The past subjunctive is used in most of the same contexts as the present subjunctive. The difference is that the time frame is the past.

Le **pidieron** a Arturo que les **hablara** de Rosario.	*They asked Arturo to talk to them about Rosario.*
Arturo **esperaba** que Raquel **pensara** mucho en él.	*Arturo was hoping that Raquel would think a lot about him.*
Ángela **quería** llegar al hospital antes de que Roberto **se despertara**.	*Ángela wanted to get to the hospital before Roberto woke up.*
No **había** nadie que **supiera** cuál era el problema de Gloria.	*No one knew what Gloria's problem was.*

You will learn more about the uses of the past subjunctive in the Workbook.

Actividad.   Reacciones de los hermanos

Al discutir la situación de la oficina en Miami, ¿cuáles son las recomendaciones y reacciones de Ramón, Mercedes y Pedro? Contesta, completando las siguientes oraciones.

1. Al principio, Mercedes no creía...
2. Mercedes recomendó...
3. Ramón no quería...
4. Ramón sugirió...
5. Ramón también sugirió...
6. Pedro no creía...
7. Pedro recomendó...

a. que tuvieran mucho cuidado antes de que hablaran con Carlos
b. que cerraran la sucursal
c. que hablaran pronto con Carlos
d. que Carlos tuviera la culpa de las irregularidades
e. que acusaran a Carlos
f. que debieran esperar más
g. que pusieran a otra persona a cargo

Nota cultural: La economía de Hispanoamérica

Tradicionalmente, el sistema económico de algunos países de Hispanoamérica se ha basado en un solo producto: el café, el banano, el azúcar, el tabaco… Esta situación es resultado de la explotación económica de los productos hispanoamericanos más valiosos[1] por los intereses internacionales.

Esta historia comenzó en la época colonial, cuando España explotaba el oro y la plata[2] de sus colonias americanas. Después de conseguir la independencia de España en el siglo XIX, las diez naciones hispanoamericanas—políticamente

El petróleo, el «oro negro» del lago Maracaibo, Venezuela

débiles—fueron lugares de fácil explotación económica para los países industrializados de Europa y para los Estados Unidos. El caso clásico es el banano centroamericano.

Actualmente los hispanoamericanos tienen una clara consciencia[3] de este pasado de explotación extranjera. Insisten cada vez más en su derecho[4] a manejar su propio destino económico. Por eso, cabe[5] hacer la siguiente pregunta: ¿Será algún día Hispanoamérica una de las regiones económicamente más importantes del mundo?

Cuando se considera la gran cantidad de recursos naturales que quedan aún por explotar, es muy fácil decir que sí. Un ejemplo de la riqueza natural que posee Hispanoamérica es el petróleo. Además, las tierras hispanoamericanas cuentan con grandes depósitos de cobre,[6] plata, hierro, plomo, estaño[7] y tungsteno. Todos éstos son productos que necesitará el mundo del futuro.

Será importante también el aprovechamiento[8] de la riqueza agrícola y pesquera.[9] Con sus vastos territorios cultivables y con la pesca—en especial a lo largo de la costa del Pacífico—las naciones hispanoamericanas, con un desarrollo apropiado, podrán producir suficiente comida para su propio consumo y también para la exportación.

Un vistazo a México

Tradicionalmente, México ha sido un país agrícola. Sus productos más importantes han sido el maíz, el café y el algodón.[10] Sin embargo, hoy en día la verdadera riqueza de México es la mineral. Es uno de los más importantes productores de plata del mundo. Además, desde 1973 México se ha convertido en un gran productor de petróleo. Sus principales depósitos se encuentran en la bahía de Campeche. La producción de gas natural es también considerable, y el comercio y la industria están en constante desarrollo.

MÉXICO

EL GOLFO DE MÉXICO

la bahía de Campeche

EL OCÉANO PACÍFICO

[1] *valuable* [2] oro… *gold and silver* [3] *awareness* [4] *right* [5] es apropiado [6] *copper* [7] hierro… *iron, lead, tin*
[8] *utilization* [9] *fishing* [10] *cotton*

Have you completed the following sections of the lesson? Check them off here.

_____ **Preparación**   _____ **Vocabulario del tema**
_____ **¿Tienes buena memoria?**   _____ **Un poco de gramática**

Now scan the words in the **Vocabulario** list to be sure that you understand the meaning of most of them. Then you will be ready to continue on with **Lección 38** in the Workbook.

VOCABULARIO

Los verbos

ocultar	to hide

El dinero y los negocios
(Money and Business)

la empresa	firm, company, business
el presupuesto	budget
la sucursal	branch office
S.A. (Sociedad Anónima)	Inc.

andar bien/mal	to be going well/badly
despedir (i, i)	to fire (*an employee*)
dirigir (dirijo)	to run (*a business*)
economizar	to economize
poner (a alguien) a cargo (de)	to put (*someone*) in charge (of)

Repaso: **la compañía, la oficina**

Las personas

el auditor/la auditora	auditor
el empleado/la empleada	employee

Repaso: **el dueño/la dueña, el jefe/la jefa**

Las palabras adicionales

caerle* bien/mal a alguien	to make a good/bad impression on someone

---

*Note the irregular first-person of **caer: caigo.**

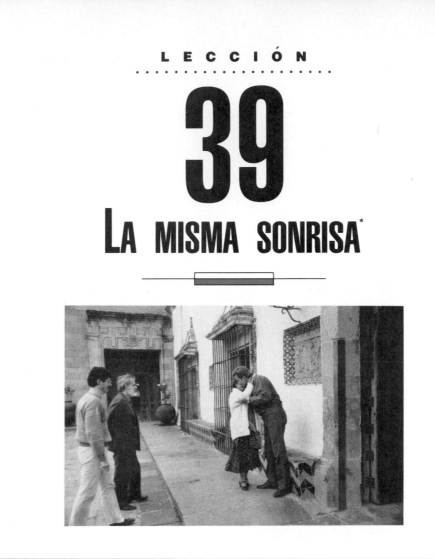

· · · · · · · · · · · · · · · · · · · ·

OBJETIVOS

The materials in **Lección 39** of the Textbook and the Workbook will help you better understand the video episode and take you beyond it, giving you additional information about places and characters in the series. The Textbook will also help you to develop skill in using the Spanish language. In this lesson, you will learn

- vocabulary related to real estate transactions
- more ways to use the past subjunctive.

You will also learn about the **Ballet Folclórico de México** and about Mariachi music.
    Be sure to work through all parts of the lesson. When you see a cassette symbol in the margin, listen to the tape for **Lección 39**. Answers or hints for many activities are given in Appendix 1. Be sure to check your answers for each activity before going on to the next one.

The Same Smile

—▭— **BEFORE VIEWING . . .**

• •

PREPARACIÓN

Actividad.

Aquí está el resumen del narrador que vas a escuchar al principio de este episodio. ¿Puedes completar las oraciones?

En el episodio previo,

1. Raquel y Arturo regresaron al hotel después de... ver a don Fernando en el hospital/una reunión en la casa de Pedro.
2. Había un mensaje para... Raquel/Arturo.
3. Ellos, alarmados, llamaron en seguida a... Puerto Rico/Pedro.

En el bar,

4. Arturo/Raquel... le preguntó a... Arturo/Raquel... si había pensado... en ellos/en su futuro.

Mientras tanto,

5. Pedro, Ramón y Mercedes hablaban de... los problemas que tienen Juan y Pati/los problemas económicos de la oficina en Miami.
6. Pedro y los demás no sabían que... Juan/Carlos... los escuchaba.

En casa de Ramón,

7. Carlos habló... seriamente/alegremente... con Gloria.
8. Más tarde, Carlos descubrió que... los niños habían desaparecido/Gloria había desaparecido.

 Ahora escucha la cinta para verificar tus respuestas.

Para pensar...

Las siguientes fotos representan algunas de las escenas que vas a ver en este episodio. ¿Quiénes son los personajes que se ven? ¿Qué te sugiere cada foto?

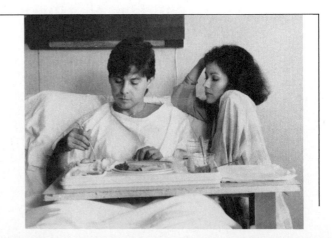

Para comprender un poco más

el boleto Si quieres ver una película o una obra de teatro, tienes que comprar **el boleto** para poder entrar.

 **AFTER VIEWING . . .**

¿TIENES BUENA MEMORIA?

 ### Actividad A. ¿Qué hicieron?
En la siguiente tabla se encuentran los nombres de los personajes principales de este episodio. Vas a escuchar una serie de oraciones. Escribe el número de cada oración junto a los nombres apropiados.

Raquel y Arturo	Carlos y Gloria
Ángela y Roberto	Juan, Ramón y Pedro

Actividad B. Encuentros

Paso 1

En este episodio, ¿recuerdas lo que decían Arturo y sus sobrinos puertorriqueños? Indica todos los temas de que hablaron en el episodio.

1. _____ El accidente en la excavación
2. _____ La condición de Roberto
3. _____ El parecido (*resemblance*) entre Roberto y su padre Ángel
4. _____ La esposa de Ángel
5. _____ Las cosas que trajo Arturo desde la Argentina
6. _____ La muerte del padre de Arturo
7. _____ El sentido de culpabilidad de Ángel
8. _____ El sentido de culpabilidad de Arturo

Paso 2

Antes de conocer a sus sobrinos, Arturo quería hablar con Raquel. ¿Te acuerdas de su breve conversación fuera del cuarto de Roberto? Escúchala una vez más, luego contesta las preguntas.

¿Cuál es el conflicto a que se refiere Arturo?

a. _____ Creía que Ángel tenía la culpa de la muerte de su padre.
b. _____ Se sentía culpable por no buscar a Ángel después de que éste (*the latter*) se fue.

Para pensar...

En este episodio, Juan pensaba en hacer una llamada telefónica, pero no lo hizo. ¿A quién pensaba llamar? ¿Por qué? ¿Qué le quería decir?

VOCABULARIO DEL TEMA

Los bienes raíces

el apartamento	apartment	**el precio**	price
la propiedad	property	**el préstamo**	loan
		la venta	sale
el alquiler	rent		
la oferta	offer	**el/la agente de bienes raíces**	real-estate agent

alquilar	to rent	**se alquila**	for rent
estar interesado/a en,	to be interested in	**se vende,**	for sale
interesarse en		**en venta**	
hacer una oferta	to make an offer		
aceptar la oferta	to accept the offer		
rechazar la oferta	to reject the offer		

The word **apartamento** is understood throughout most of the Spanish-speaking world to mean *apartment*. Other frequently-used words include **el departamento** (*Mexico and other Latin-American countries*) and **el piso** (*Spain*). In other parts of the Spanish-speaking world, the word **piso** means *floor*.

Actividad A.   En venta

En este episodio, se habla de vender dos propiedades. Escucha las conversaciones otra vez y luego contesta las preguntas.

Primera conversación

Indica si las siguientes oraciones son ciertas (**C**) o falsas (**F**).

C F 1. Una agente de bienes raíces llamó a la familia Castillo.
C F 2. El cliente que se interesa en comprar la propiedad es de la Argentina.
C F 3. Mercedes quiere aceptar la oferta inmediatamente.
C F 4. Pedro cree que es bueno saber cuál puede ser el precio.

Segunda conversación

Aquí está la conversación que acabas de escuchar. ¿Puedes encontrar la información equivocada?

TÍO JAIME: ¡Ah! Y hay algo muy importante. El hombre interesado en la casa ha hecho una oferta.
RAQUEL: ¿Para comprarla?
JAIME: Sí. Es una mala oferta. Ángela debe rechazarla. Pídale que se comunique conmigo.
RAQUEL: Por supuesto, yo se lo digo.
TÍO JAIME: Ah, y también hay que recordarle que lo hable con Roberto.
RAQUEL: Sí, por supuesto.
TÍO JAIME: Ángela, a veces, es un poco apresurada.
RAQUEL: Comprendo.

Actividad B.   ¿De quién se habla?

¿A cuál de los personajes de *Destinos* se refieren estas oraciones?

1. Son dueños del apartamento de sus padres.
2. Es el dueño de una hacienda histórica.
3. Una agente de bienes raíces tiene un cliente interesado en comprar su propiedad.
4. Hay una oferta para comprar su apartamento.
5. Tiene una oficina en su casa.
6. Debe consultar con un pariente antes de aceptar una oferta.
7. Vio varios apartamentos con una agente de bienes raíces.

Actividad C.   Se compra

Imagina que vives en un apartamento y que quieres comprar una casa. ¿En qué orden vas a hacer las siguientes cosas?

a. _____ Hago una oferta, que es rechazada por los dueños.
b. _____ Firmo todos los documentos legales y, más importante, escribo el cheque más grande de mi vida.
c. _____ Miro varias casas, sin poder decidirme.
d. _____ Pienso en todas las cualidades que quiero que la casa tenga.
e. _____ Hago otra oferta ¡y la aceptan!
f. _____ El antiguo dueño se va por fin de la casa.
g. _____ Por fin encuentro la casa ideal para mí/mi familia.
h. _____ Yo me mudo (Mi familia y yo nos mudamos) a la nueva casa.
i. _____ Me pongo en contacto con un agente de bienes raíces.
j. _____ Pido un préstamo en el banco.

Un poco de gramática

More About Talking About the Past

Use the past subjunctive in adjectival and adverbial clauses with time conjunctions when the time frame of the conversation is in the past.

Ángela llegó al hospital antes de que Roberto **se despertara**.	*Ángela arrived at the hospital before Roberto woke up.*
La agente de bienes raíces buscaba a alguien que **quisiera** comprar La Gavia.	*The real estate agent was looking for someone who wanted to buy La Gavia.*

You will learn more about this usage in the Workbook.

Actividad. Dificultades familiares
Completa las siguientes oraciones con las frases apropiadas.

1. Carlos tuvo que pedirle a Ramón su carro antes de que él
    a. _____ pudiera llevar a Juan al aeropuerto
    b. _____ pudiera buscar a Gloria
    c. _____ pudiera ir al hospital para ver a su padre

2. Carlos le prometió a Ramón que le explicaría (*he would explain*) lo que pasaba después de que
    a. _____ hiciera un viaje a Miami
    b. _____ hablara otra vez con Ofelia
    c. _____ encontrara a Gloria

3. Mientras los hermanos comentaban los problemas financieros de la familia, no había nadie que
    a. _____ supiera que Carlos los escuchaba
    b. _____ quisiera ayudar a Carlos
    c. _____ quisiera vender La Gavia

4. Arturo quería agradecerle a Raquel por su ayuda antes de que los dos
    a. _____ salieran para el Ballet Folclórico
    b. _____ entraran en el cuarto de Roberto
    c. _____ conocieran a don Fernando

5. En la capital, no había nadie que
    a. _____ supiera que un antiguo novio de Raquel venía a México con sus padres
    b. _____ entendiera lo que pasaba en la oficina de Miami
    c. _____ realmente quisiera que don Fernando conociera a sus sobrinos

---

Nota cultural: México, música y baile

Como muchos turistas que llegan a la capital, Raquel se interesa por ver el gran espectáculo del Ballet Folclórico. Esta obra, que se presenta en el elegante Palacio de Bellas Artes, es famosa en todo el mundo. Las funciones consisten en lujosas[1] imitaciones de fiestas típicas de diferentes regiones de México. También se presentan danzas de la tradición indígena, tal como se cree que se presentaban en la época precolombina.

El baile nacional de México

Entre todos los bailes que se presentan en el Ballet Folclórico, tal vez el más famoso sea el jarabe tapatío.[2] Es

El Palacio de Bellas Artes

[1] *lavish*   [2] jarabe... *Mexican Hat Dance* (tapatío = *from the state of Jalisco*)

derivado de bailes españoles. Se conocía ya en México en el siglo XVIII y fue prohibido durante los últimos años del dominio español, por su extrema desenvoltura.[3] Por su antigüedad y por su popularidad, es considerado el baile nacional de México.

La música de los mariachis

Ay, ay, ay, ay.
Canta y no llores
porque cantando,
se alegran,
cielito lindo,[4]
los corazones.

El Ballet Folclórico
de Guadalajara

Para muchos, la música que mejor ejemplifica a México es la de los mariachis. Estos músicos ambulantes se contratan para que den serenatas,[5] para que toquen en las fiestas o sencillamente para que les canten unas canciones a los clientes que están sentados en los cafés al aire libre. Cantan las canciones típicas del pueblo, con historias de la vida diaria y del amor.

[3] *liveliness, naturalness* [4] cielito... *Pretty Little Heaven (term of affection)* [5] *serenades*

Have you completed the following sections of the lesson? Check them off here.

_____ **Preparación**   _____ **Vocabulario del tema**
_____ **¿Tienes buena memoria?**   _____ **Un poco de gramática**

Now scan the words in the **Vocabulario** list to be sure that you understand the meaning of most of them. Then you will be ready to continue on with **Lección 39** in the Workbook.

Vocabulario

Los bienes raíces (Real Estate)

alquilar	to rent
estar interesado/a en, interesarse en	to be interested in
rechazar	to reject
se alquila	for rent
se vende, en venta	for sale
el/la agente de bienes raíces	real-estate agent
el alquiler	rent
la oferta	offer
el precio	price

el préstamo	loan
la propiedad	property
la venta	sale

Repaso: el apartamento

Sustantivos

la sonrisa	smile

Los adjetivos

mismo/a	same

40

ENTRE LA ESPADA Y LA PARED*

OBJETIVOS

The materials in **Lección 40** of the Textbook and the Workbook will help you better understand the video episode and take you beyond it, giving you additional information about places and characters in the series. The Textbook will also help you to develop skill in using the Spanish language. In this lesson, you will learn

- vocabulary useful to tourists traveling abroad
- ways to talk about what would happen.

You will also learn about Hispanic theater.

Be sure to work through all parts of the lesson. When you see a cassette symbol in the margin, listen to the tape for **Lección 40**. Answers or hints for many activities are given in Appendix 1. Be sure to check your answers for each activity before going on to the next one.

Between a Rock and a Hard Place

BEFORE VIEWING . . .

Preparación

Actividad A.

¿Puedes completar el siguiente resumen de lo que pasó en el episodio previo?

1. se acostó / desapareció
2. buscarla / dar un paseo
3. se sentía muy bien, con mucha hambre / estaba muy cansado y sin apetito
4. su abuelo / su tío
5. la posible venta de La Gavia / la enfermedad de don Fernando
6. se quedó en casa / regresó al hospital para estar con su padre

En el episodio previo, Carlos le dijo a Ramón que Gloria _____.[1] Después

de pedirle el carro a Ramón, Carlos salió a _____.[2]

   Mientras tanto, en el hospital, Roberto, ya despierto, _____.[3] Después

de comerse dos desayunos, Roberto conoció a _____.[4]

   En casa de Pedro, los hermanos también desayunaron y hablaron de _____.[5]

Luego, Ramón, Pedro y Juan salieron para la hacienda. Mercedes, como de costumbre,

_____.[6]

Actividad B.

Ya sabes que Pati se ha ido a Nueva York para resolver los problemas que tiene
con la producción de su obra. En este episodio, va a hablar de esos problemas
con su productor.

Paso 1

Escucha una parte de su conversación y luego contesta la pregunta.

   De las siguientes oraciones, ¿cuál describe mejor la conversación entre Pati
y el productor?

a. Es una conversación calmada. Pati y el productor se llevan bien y pueden
   resolver algunos asuntos.
b. Es una conversación animada. Es obvio que Pati y el productor tienen ideas
   diferentes sobre una serie de asuntos.

Paso 2

Escucha la conversación por lo menos una vez más y luego contesta las preguntas. Al escuchar, ten en cuenta que **patrocinadores** significa *sponsors* (*people
who give money to fund productions*).

1. Según el productor, ¿qué cosa importante tiene que hacer Pati?
   a. _____ hacer unos cambios en la obra
   b. _____ pasar más tiempo hablando con los patrocinadores
   c. _____ darle una entrevista a un reportero del periódico de la universidad

2. Según el productor, ¿qué pasará si Pati no sigue sus consejos?
   a. _____ La obra no tendrá éxito.   c. _____ La obra se cancelará.
   b. _____ Él buscará a otro director.

Para pensar…

En tu opinión, ¿cuál va a ser la respuesta de Pati a las demandas del productor? ¿Hará ella los cambios? ¿Qué sabes de Pati que te ayudará a determinar lo que hará?

Para comprender un poco más

me/le cansa	Algunas personas siempre se quejan de las mismas cosas. Realmente **me cansa** estar con ellas.
mandón/mandona	La mamá de Raquel es una persona muy **mandona**. Siempre les dice a todos lo que deben hacer.
me importa un comino	¡**Me importa un comino** lo que puedan decir los demás! ¡No me importa para nada!

 **AFTER VIEWING . . .**

¿TIENES BUENA MEMORIA?

Actividad A.   ¿A quién se refiere?
Indica al personaje descrito en cada oración.

a. Raquel   d. Carlos   g. la agente de bienes raíces
b. Arturo   e. Mercedes   h. Pati
c. Roberto   f. don Fernando i. el productor de Pati

1. _____ Le dan de alta (*They release him*) en el hospital.
2. _____ Lo tienen que llevar a otro hospital.
3. _____ No quiere hacer ningún cambio en un proyecto.
4. _____ Amenaza con cancelar un proyecto.
5. _____ Confiesa que su madre es un poco mandona a veces.
6. _____ Tiene un cliente que quiere comprar La Gavia.
7. _____ Tiene que ir de compras porque no tiene ropa.
8. _____ Va a ir con su padre a Guadalajara.
9. _____ Se sentó a hablar con su ayudante.
10. _____ No puede acompañar a su padre a Guadalajara.

Actividad B. Pati y su ayudante

Como sabes, después de hablar con el productor, Pati también habló largamente con Guillermo, su ayudante en el teatro. ¿Cuánto recuerdas de su conversación?

1. ¿Quién inició la conversación, Pati o Guillermo?
2. ¿De qué hablaron, de la obra o de Juan?
3. ¿Cree Guillermo que era necesario que Pati regresara a Nueva York, por la obra?
4. ¿Qué idea le dio Guillermo a Pati, que Juan tiene miedo o envidia de ella?

Para pensar...

Piensa un momento en la conversación entre Pati y su ayudante. ¿Qué tipo de relaciones existe entre ellos? ¿Crees que hace mucho tiempo que se conocen?

Actividad C. Raquel y sus padres

Durante este episodio, Raquel le habló a Ángela de sus relaciones con sus padres. ¿Recuerdas lo que dijo?

1. Según Raquel, su madre... es muy simpática / es un poco mandona.
2. Raquel... se lleva bien / trata de llevarse bien... con su madre.
3. En cambio, su padre... es muy machista / es una persona muy tranquila.

Para pensar...

¿Qué opinas de las relaciones entre Raquel y su madre? ¿Son parecidas a las relaciones que tienes (o tenías) tú con tu propia madre? ¿con tu padre? ¿Es muy común entre padres e hijos el tipo de tensión que describe Raquel?

VOCABULARIO DEL TEMA

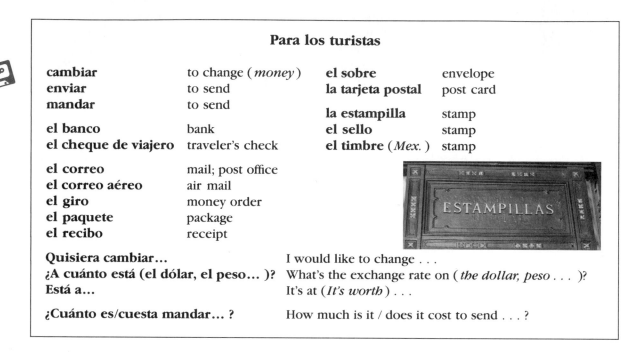

Para los turistas

cambiar	to change (*money*)	**el sobre**	envelope
enviar	to send	**la tarjeta postal**	post card
mandar	to send		
		la estampilla	stamp
el banco	bank	**el sello**	stamp
el cheque de viajero	traveler's check	**el timbre** (*Mex.*)	stamp
el correo	mail; post office		
el correo aéreo	air mail		
el giro	money order		
el paquete	package		
el recibo	receipt		

ESTAMPILLAS

Quisiera cambiar...   I would like to change . . .

¿A cuánto está (el dólar, el peso...)?   What's the exchange rate on (*the dollar, peso . . .*)?

Está a...   It's at (*It's worth*) . . .

¿Cuánto es/cuesta mandar... ?   How much is it / does it cost to send . . . ?

Actividad A.   Con Ángela y Raquel

Vas a escuchar otra vez tres breves conversaciones del episodio. Pon el número de la conversación con la foto a la que corresponde.

a. _____   b. _____   c. _____

Actividad B.   Más necesidades turísticas

Aquí hay dos conversaciones que has escuchado en este episodio, pero hay que poner las oraciones en un orden lógico. ¿Puedes hacerlo?

Primera conversación

Habla primero Ángela.

DEPENDIENTE	ÁNGELA
a. _____ Cómo no. ¿Cuántos?	d. _____ Gracias.
b. _____ Muy bien. Aquí tiene su recibo, señorita.	e. _____ ¿A cuánto está el dólar?
c. _____ A 2.900 pesos.	f. _____ Quisiera cambiar unos dólares, por favor.
	g. _____ Bueno. Quiero cambiar cien dólares entonces.

 Ahora escucha la cinta para verificar tus respuestas.

Segunda conversación

En esta conversación intervienen tres personas. Empieza a hablar primero Ángela.

ÁNGELA	DEPENDIENTE
a. _____ Gracias, Raquel. Pero yo tengo que mandar muchas postales a mi familia. ¿Venden sellos, ay, digo, timbres aquí?	d. _____ No, está aquí, cerquita. A la vuelta nada más.
b. _____ Necesito comprar sellos.	e. _____ Normalmente, sí, señorita, pero ahora no tenemos. Tendrá que ir al correo.
c. _____ ¿Y está muy lejos el correo?	

RAQUEL

f. _____ Ángela, aquí no se dice sellos. Se dice timbres. Yo guardé unos de antes. Mira.

Escucha la cinta para verificar tus respuestas.

Actividad C. ¿Cuánto cuesta... ? ¿A cuánto está?

¿Cuánto sabes del mundo real? ¿Puedes contestar las siguientes preguntas sobre los Estados Unidos?

¿Cuánto cuesta... ?

1. mandar una carta por primera clase
2. enviar una carta a Europa por correo aéreo
3. mandar un paquete por tercera clase
4. mandar un paquete a la Argentina por correo aéreo
5. comprar cheques de viajero
6. cambiar dinero en un banco
7. comprar un giro en el correo

¿Sabes a cuánto está... hoy?

8. el peso mexicano

9. la peseta española

10. el austral argentino

. . . .

UN POCO DE GRAMÁTICA

Talking About What You Would Do

To describe what would happen or what someone would do, add endings with **-ía** to most infinitives.

Ángela dijo que **compraría** sellos y que les **mandaría** postales a sus familiares.	*Ángela said that she would buy stamps and that she would send post cards to her relatives.*
CLIENTE: Sí, **estaría** interesado en comprar La Gavia.	CLIENT: *Yes, I would be interested in buying La Gavia.*
MARÍA: Luis, ¿**podrías** ir a México con nosotros?	MARÍA: *Luis, would you be able to come to Mexico with us?*
RAMÓN: Claro, **hablaríamos** con don Fernando antes de vender la hacienda.	RAMÓN: *Of course, we would speak with don Fernando before selling the estate.*

You will learn more about composing and using these forms in the Workbook.

Actividad.   ¿Quién lo diría?

¿Quién podría haber dicho las siguientes oraciones en este episodio o en episodios previos?

a. Carlos
b. Gloria
c. Mercedes
d. Ramón y Pedro
e. Arturo y Raquel

f. Pati
g. el productor de Pati
h. el ayudante de Pati
i. la agente de bienes raíces
j. el médico de don Fernando

1. _____ Ahora me gustaría seguir ensayando (*rehearsing*) con los actores.

2. _____ Los patrocinadores dijeron que algunas partes de la obra serían ofensivas para ciertas personas.

3. ____ Mi cliente haría construir aquí un lugar turístico.
4. ____ Yo hablaría con Juan de eso. Dile que entiendes su punto de vista, pero que...
5. ____ Señora, yo no esperaría. Su padre iría a Guadalajara muy bien en avión.
6. ____ Te acompañaríamos a Guadalajara, pero alguien tiene que quedarse aquí.
7. ____ No venderían la hacienda sin hablar primero con papá, ¿verdad?
8. ____ Gloria, me prometiste que no harías esto de nuevo.

Nota cultural: El teatro hispánico, una larga tradición

Como autora de su propia obra de teatro, Pati representa la continuación de una larga tradición literaria en el mundo hispánico. En esta tradición, hay de todo: teatro popular, para el público; teatro clásico (que sigue más o menos el estilo del teatro griego[1]); teatro experimental, de vanguardia; teatro de evasión, para las masas. A continuación[2] se encuentran tres ejemplos de esta tradición teatral.

Lope de Vega, español (1562–1635)

Lope fue el padre del teatro popular español. Contemporáneo de Shakespeare, fue el primero en romper[3] con la tradición del teatro clásico. Sus obras tenían como fin divertir y enseñar al público. Gracias a sus obras, el teatro se hizo popular en España. Su producción fue enorme: unas mil quinientas obras de teatro. Algunas de las mejores todavía se representan en todas partes del mundo.

Una de sus obras más conocidas es *Fuenteovejuna*,[4] que se basa en un acontecimiento histórico. El protagonista principal es todo el pueblo de Fuenteovejuna, en Andalucía. El pueblo entero se levantó[5] contra la tiranía de su Comendador,[6] quien había cometido numerosos abusos, y le dio muerte. Poco después un representante del rey llegó al pueblo para investigar el caso. «¿Quién mató al Comendador?» preguntó. Todos contestaron al mismo tiempo: «¡Fuenteovejuna, señor!»

Lope de Vega

Emilio Carballido, mexicano (1925–)

Carballido es sin duda una de las figuras cumbre[7] del teatro contemporáneo mexicano y de toda Hispanoamérica. Ha sabido representar e interpretar la realidad contemporánea, así que sus obras les hablan a las masas. Al mismo tiempo, se ha aprovechado de la temática[8] de la tragedia clásica y la ha adaptado al mundo contemporáneo.

En su pieza corta *El censo*, un empadronador[9] trata de recoger unos datos sobre un taller de costura[10] clandestino. Pero los empleados y Paco, el dueño, no se dejan contar fácilmente.

[1]*Greek*   [2]*A... Following*   [3]*breaking*   [4]*Sheep Well*   [5]*se... rose up*   [6]*Knight Commander*   [7]más importantes   [8]*characteristic themes or topics*   [9]*census taker*   [10]taller... *tailor shop*

EL EMPADRONADOR: (*Desesperado.*) Es como… Mire, la Nación se pregunta: ¿Cuáles son mis riquezas? Y hace la cuenta.[11] Como usted, ¿no le importa saber cuánto dinero hay en su casa?

PACO: No.

EL EMPADRONADOR: Pero… tiene que contar cuánto gastan, cuánto ganarán…

PACO: Nunca.

EL EMPADRONADOR: ¡Pero cómo no! Bueno, ustedes no, pero un país debe saber… cuánta riqueza tiene, debe publicarlo…

PACO: ¿Para que cuando lo sepan los demás países le caigan encima?[12] ¡Yo no voy a ayudar a la ruina de mi Patria!

El Teatro Campesino

Este teatro popular nació dentro de la huelga[13] contra los viñadores[14] de California. Al principio era un teatro de improvisación: algunos campesinos[15] improvisaron escenas de la huelga para enseñar y para llevar la huelga a otros. Los problemas trágicos de los campesinos pobres se presentaban con humor y sátira, y se utilizaban en sus espectáculos elementos de la tradición mexicana, como calaveras y esqueletos.[16] Los actores del Teatro Campesino viajaron a todas partes de los Estados Unidos para transmitir su mensaje político al público.

Luis Valdez

Ahora el Teatro Campesino es una compañía de teatro, todavía localizada en California. En la compañía, jóvenes actores, escritores y directores pueden aprender y practicar su arte. Luis Valdez, el fundador y director artístico del Teatro, ha escrito obras de teatro y películas, como, por ejemplo, *Zoot Suit*, una obra controvertida que tuvo mucho éxito, especialmente en California, y *La Bamba*, la historia de Ritchie Valens.

[11] *hace… it counts them*   [12] *¿Para… So that when other countries find out about it they will attack?*   [13] *strike*
[14] *grape-growers*   [15] *farm laborers*   [16] calaveras… *skulls and skeletons*

Have you completed the following sections of the lesson? Check them off here.

_____ **Preparación**   _____ **Vocabulario del tema**
_____ **¿Tienes buena memoria?**   _____ **Un poco de gramática**

   Now scan the words in the **Vocabulario** list to be sure that you understand the meaning of most of them. Then you will be ready to continue on with **Lección 40** in the Workbook.

Vocabulario

Para los turistas (For Tourists)

cambiar	to change (*money*)
enviar	to send

el correo	mail; post office
el correo aéreo	air mail
el cheque de viajero	traveler's check
la estampilla	stamp
el giro	money order
el paquete	package
el sello	stamp
el sobre	envelope
el timbre (*Mex.*)	stamp

Quisiera cambiar...	I would like to change . . .
¿A cuánto está (el dólar, el peso...)?	What's the exchange rate on (the dollar, peso . . .)?
Está a...	It's at (It's worth) . . .

¿Cuánto es/cuesta mandar... ?	How much is it / does it cost to send . . . ?

Repaso: **el banco, mandar, el recibo, la tarjeta postal**

Los adjetivos

mandón, mandona	bossy

Las palabras adicionales

darlo/la de alta	to release someone (*from an institution*)
entre la espada y la pared	between a rock and a hard place

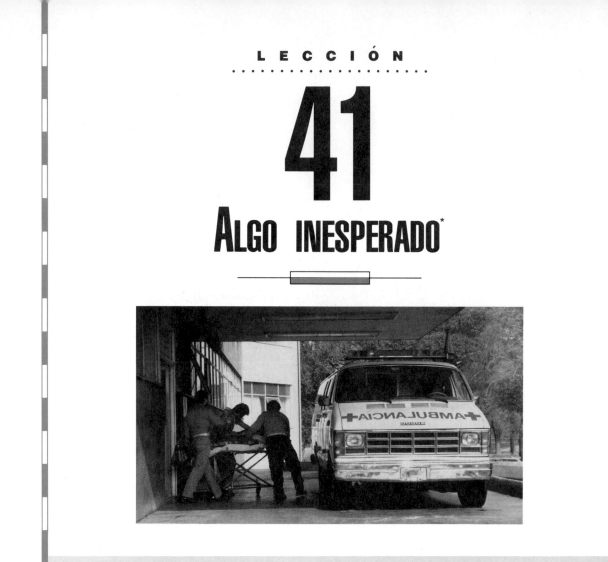

LECCIÓN

41

ALGO INESPERADO*

OBJETIVOS

The materials in **Lección 41** of the Textbook and the Workbook will help you better understand the video episode and take you beyond it, giving you additional information about places and characters in the series. The Textbook will also help you to develop skill in using the Spanish language. In this lesson, you will learn

- more travel-related vocabulary
- more about using the conditional.

You will also learn about the city of Guadalajara.

Be sure to work through all parts of the lesson. When you see a cassette symbol in the margin, listen to the tape for **Lección 41**. Answers or hints for many activities are given in Appendix 1. Be sure to check your answers for each activity before going on to the next one.

*Something Unexpected

▬ BEFORE VIEWING . . .

PREPARACIÓN

Actividad A.

¿Te acuerdas de lo que pasó en el **Episodio 40**? Indica si las siguientes oraciones son ciertas (**C**) o falsas (**F**).

C   F   1. A Roberto le dieron de alta en el hospital.
C   F   2. Antes de ir a conocer a don Fernando, Roberto quería ir al hotel para cambiarse de ropa.
C   F   3. En Nueva York Pati tenía problemas graves con el productor de su obra.
C   F   4. El productor quería que Pati hiciera unos cambios en la obra.
C   F   5. Más tarde Pati le contaba a su esposo los problemas que tenía en el teatro.
C   F   6. En México, le informaron a la familia Castillo que el especialista vendría a la capital para examinar a don Fernando.

Ahora escucha la cinta para verificar tus respuestas.

Actividad B.

En este episodio, Ángela y Roberto comienzan a hablar de la venta del apartamento en San Juan. Como sabes, el tío Jaime le dijo a Raquel por teléfono que había una oferta para comprarlo.

Paso 1

Escucha la conversación y trata de captar los puntos más importantes. Luego contesta las preguntas.

1. ¿Cuál es la reacción de Roberto?
   a. _____ Roberto está de acuerdo con la venta del apartamento.
   b. _____ Roberto se opone a la idea de venderlo.

2. ¿Cuál es el intento de Arturo?
   a. _____ Quiere calmar a sus sobrinos.
   b. _____ Trata de convencer a Ángela de su error.

Paso 2

Escucha la conversación otra vez y contesta las siguientes preguntas.

1. ¿Sabe Roberto por cierto que Ángela quiere darle dinero a Jorge, su novio?
2. ¿Qué les aconseja Arturo?
   a. _____ Que esperen, que dejen el asunto por el momento.
   b. _____ Que piensen bien lo que quieren hacer.
   c. _____ Que lo consulten con un abogado.

Para pensar...

1. ¿Has notado que Raquel no dijo nada durante la conversación? ¿Por qué crees que se queda callada (*silent*)?
2. ¿Qué opinas de la forma en que Arturo se comportaba (*behaved*) con sus sobrinos? Acaba de conocerlos. ¿Crees que es apropiado que les esté aconsejando de esta manera?

Para comprender un poco más

gruñón, gruñona	La tía Olga es la **gruñona** de la familia. Siempre se queja o encuentra defectos en todo.
rezongón, rezongona	No me gusta levantarme. Por eso por la mañana soy la persona más **rezongona** del mundo. Después de las diez, es otra cosa.

 AFTER VIEWING . . .

• •

¿TIENES BUENA MEMORIA?

Actividad A.   El repaso de Raquel

Al final de cada episodio de *Destinos*, has escuchado el repaso de Raquel. En esta actividad, vas a escuchar el repaso del **Episodio 41** otra vez, pero ¡ahora tú tienes que dar las respuestas!

Escucha las preguntas de Raquel con cuidado y contéstalas. Luego, como siempre, vas a oír la respuesta de ella. Tu respuesta no tiene que ser idéntica a la de Raquel, pero sí debe contener la misma información.

1. ...   2. ...   3. ...   4. ...

Actividad B.   La familia Castillo

Como sabes, al principio de este episodio, don Fernando sale para Guadalajara, acompañado por Mercedes. Pero había otros acontecimientos importantes también. ¿Puedes completar las siguientes oraciones?

Verbos: jugar al *bridge*, jugar por dinero (*to gamble*), llamar a Pati, llevar a don Fernando a Guadalajara, salir para el aeropuerto, vender La Gavia

Sustantivos: una enfermedad física, un vicio

Lugares: Guadalajara, Nueva York

Personas: don Fernando, Gloria, Pati

Adjetivos: culpable, preocupado

1. Carlos le revela a su familia su secreto: Gloria tiene.... Tiene que....
2. En este momento, Carlos se siente.... Cree que hablan de... por lo que él ha hecho con el dinero de la oficina en Miami.
3. Juan escucha parte de la confesión de Carlos, pero luego se levanta y.... Va a... para ver a....

Para pensar...

Algunas personas fácilmente llegan a ser adictas al juego. ¿Conoces tú a alguien que tenga este problema? ¿Conoces a alguien que tenga otro tipo de adicción? Habla con algunos amigos para ver lo que piensan de la adicción de Gloria.

Actividad C.   ¡Un desafío!

Hay varias acciones simultáneas en este episodio. ¿Cuántas recuerdas?

1. Tres personas o grupos de personas llegan en taxi o toman un taxi. ¿Quiénes son?

   _____ toma(n) un taxi para ir a _____.

   _____ llega(n) a _____ en taxi.

2. Dos personas toman el ascensor (*elevator*) del hotel al mismo tiempo. ¿Quiénes son?

Nota cultural: El regateo

Bargaining (**regatear, el regateo**) is a common custom in many Spanish-speaking countries, but only in certain locations: in markets, in some small shops and stalls, with street vendors who are selling objects (but not food). In other places—supermarkets, boutiques, department stores—prices are fixed (**los precios son fijos**) and one must pay the stated price. If objects in a store do not have a price written on a tag, it is possible that the seller will bargain. You can ask: **¿Son fijos los precios?** The worst that can happen is that the vendor will say yes.

In the video episode there is a brief example of the bargaining process. It can be as simple as giving a counter offer when a price is quoted. At times the seller will accept your offer. If not, he or she will make another offer, which you can accept, reject, or counter. If the price is not reduced to an acceptable level, you can walk away in the expectation that the seller might call after you to accept your last offer.

Bargaining can be fun, but you can also lose out on an item that you really want... unless you are prepared to take the seller's last offer!

VOCABULARIO DEL TEMA

Note: You have seen and heard a good deal of travel-related vocabulary throughout the previous video episodes of *Destinos*. Here is a listing of useful words and phrases.

Hablando de los viajes

la aduana	customs office
la agencia de viajes	travel agency
el billete (*Spain*)	ticket
el boleto (*Span. Amer.*)	ticket
...de ida	. . . one-way
...de ida y vuelta	. . . round-trip
la (primera, segunda) clase	(first, second) class
la clase turística	tourist class
el equipaje	luggage
la gira	tour
la maleta	suitcase
el mapa	(*road, geographical*) map
el pasaje	passage, fare; ticket
el pasaporte	passport
el plano	map (*of a city*)
la reserva (*Spain*)	reservation
la reservación	reservation
la sección de (no) fumar	(non)smoking section
el vuelo	flight

el/la agente de viajes	travel agent
el/la guía	guide
hacer/cancelar una reservación	to make/cancel a reservation
hacer la maleta	to pack one's suitcase
hacer una gira	to take a tour
tomar un (autobús, avión, barco, taxi, tren)	to take a (bus, plane, boat, taxi, train)

LA TAQUILLA SE CIERRA 10 MINUTOS ANTES DE LA HORA DE SALIDA DEL TREN

Actividad A. Juan se va, Luis ha llegado...

En *Destinos*, los personajes viajan mucho. Vas a escuchar una serie de descripciones de varios aspectos de los viajes. Pon el número de la descripción con la foto o el dibujo apropiado.

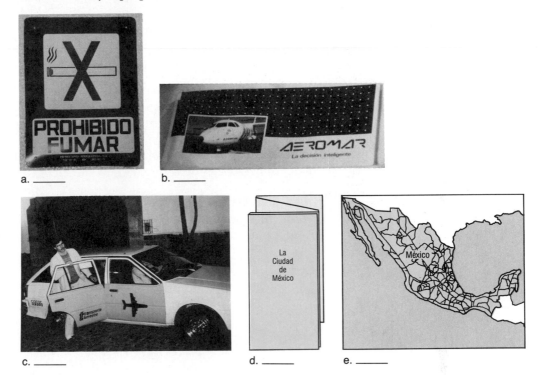

a. _____   b. _____

c. _____   d. _____   e. _____

Actividad B. Haciendo los arreglos

¿Cuánto sabes de arreglar un viaje? Completa los siguientes párrafos con las palabras apropiadas.

Para hacer un viaje en avión: Llamo a la (gira/agencia)[1] de viajes para (reservar/cancelar)[2] un (plano/billete)[3] de clase turística en un vuelo. Tomo (un barco/un taxi)[4] al aeropuerto, facturo[a] (el equipaje/el plano)[5] y espero en la sala, en la sección de no (pasar/fumar).[6]

Para ir de un país a otro: Al llegar a la frontera,[b] tengo que pasar por (la gira/la aduana).[7] Saco (el pasaporte/el plano)[8] y el agente de la aduana lo revisa. También tengo que abrir (el mapa/las maletas)[9] para que el inspector lo inspeccione todo.

Para ver las atracciones turísticas en una ciudad: Llamo a (la aduana / la agencia de viajes)[10] para reservar una plaza[c] en una (sección/gira).[11] (El barco/El

---

[a] *I check* [b] *border* [c] *seat*

autobús)[12] me recoge en el hotel y, con un grupo de viajeros, veo todo lo que hay que ver en la ciudad. No necesito comprar un (mapa/plano)[13] de la ciudad, porque nos dan uno en el autobús. Al fin de la gira, le doy una propina[d] al (agente/guía).[14]

[d]*tip (monetary)*

Actividad C. ¡Un desafío!
¿Puedes contestar las siguientes preguntas sobre los viajes en *Destinos*?

1. ¿Cuántas veces ha pasado Raquel por la aduana?
2. ¿Cuáles son los medios de transporte que ha usado Raquel en todos sus viajes? (¡OJO!)
3. ¿Cuántas maletas lleva Raquel en este viaje?
4. ¿En qué lugar tuvo que pasar por una agencia de viajes Raquel?
5. ¿Cuál de los personajes de la serie es guía turístico? (¡Es de España!)

Actividad D. Un viaje ideal
Si el dinero no fuera un impedimento, ¿adónde te gustaría viajar? Completa las siguientes oraciones para describir brevemente el viaje que harías.

Me gustaría ir/viajar a...   Iría en... , con...   Llevaría...   Al llegar, ...

UN POCO DE GRAMÁTICA

Reporting Events Projected in the Past

Use the conditional to quote indirectly what someone said in the past.
Note the verb forms used in this pair of sentences. The future is used to tell what *will* happen, the conditional to tell what *would* happen.

Mercedes le **dice** a don Fernando que **conocerá** a sus nietos pasado mañana.	*Mercedes tells don Fernando that he will meet his grandchildren the day after tomorrow.*
Mercedes le **dijo** a don Fernando que **conocería** a sus nietos en dos días.	*Mercedes told don Fernando that he would meet his grandchildren in two days.*

You will learn more about this use of the conditional in the Workbook.

Actividad.   Preocupaciones y decisiones

Completa el siguiente resumen de algunas partes de este episodio con los verbos apropiados.

El médico de don Fernando le dijo a Mercedes que el especialista no (tendría/podría)[1] venir a la capital para examinarlo. Desgraciadamente el paciente (tomaría/tendría)[2] que ir a Guadalajara. Mercedes empezó en seguida las preparaciones para el viaje.

Poco tiempo después de la salida de don Fernando, Ángela y Roberto llegaron al hospital con Arturo y Raquel. Los jóvenes pensaban que allí (harían/podrían)[3] conocer a su abuelo. Pero al llegar, descubrieron que ya no estaba allí. (Más tarde, en el hotel, por un mensaje de Pedro, supieron que don Fernando [estaría/regresaría][4] a la capital en un par de días.)

Luego, al almorzar con Raquel y Arturo, Ángela le explicó a Roberto que (guardaría/sería)[5] buena idea vender el apartamento de sus padres en San Juan. Pero Roberto se opuso y los dos empezaron a discutir el asunto. Arturo les dijo que (deberían/tendrían)[6] que hablar del asunto más tarde.

Mientras tanto, en el hospital de Guadalajara, don Fernando también almorzaba. Le aseguró a Mercedes que él mismo (tendría/tomaría)[7] un avión de regreso a la capital si no lo llevaran a casa pasado mañana. También se quejó mucho de la comida «incomible», y su enfermera le prometió que le (podría/guardaría)[8] unos tamales si se portara bien.

Nota cultural: Toluca y Guadalajara

De su cuarto en el hospital de la capital llevan a don Fernando… no a Toluca, para después ir en coche a La Gavia, sino a otro hospital, en la Universidad de Guadalajara. ¿Cómo son estas dos ciudades, de momento tan importantes para el señor Castillo?

Toluca

Esta ciudad es la capital de estado más alta de México. Por su altitud, en un valle a los pies del volcán Xinantécatl (= *Nevado*), su clima es seco

MÉXICO

EL GOLFO DE MÉXICO

Guadalajara

México, D.F.

Toluca

EL OCÉANO PACÍFICO

y frío, con una temperatura promedia[1] anual de 12°C (53°F). Según un viejo dicho,[2] en Toluca sólo hay dos estaciones al año: invierno y la estación del tren.

A pesar de su clima áspero,[3] Toluca tiene sus encantos. Es un centro industrial y comercial que ofrece a sus habitantes algunas de las ventajas de una metrópoli sin todas las desventajas. Su calendario de fiestas típicas es largo, y larga es también su tradición culinaria. Hay otro dicho que llama a esta ciudad «Toluca, ciudad choricera[4] y dulcera[5]». La industria choricera se remonta[6] a la época de los españoles, como también algunos de sus dulces típicos: yemitas,[7] mazapanes,[8] frutas cristalizadas…

Pero don Fernando no ha regresado a Toluca, para luego seguir el camino bien conocido a la hacienda. Lo han llevado en avión a otra ciudad señorial.

Guadalajara

Guadalajara es la segunda ciudad de México y capital del estado de Jalisco. Situada a 580 kilómetros al noroeste de la capital, cuenta con una población de unos tres millones y medio de habitantes.

Guadalajara es una hermosa ciudad colonial que, a pesar de las construcciones modernas, ha sabido mantener una atmósfera muy agradable. Pasear por la ciudad es una delicia, pues entre otras cosas tiene un clima templado, muy excepcional, durante todo el año. La ciudad también recibe el nombre de «ciudad de las rosas» y está llena de flores, árboles y fuentes.

Además de ser un importante y moderno núcleo económico para el país, Guadalajara es un centro histórico y cultural.

- La Universidad de Guadalajara se fundó en 1792.
- Fue uno de los principales núcleos independentistas. Allí el padre Hidalgo proclamó la abolición de la esclavitud en 1810.
- Se considera cuna[9] de los mariachis, los famosos conjuntos musicales; del rodeo mexicano o «charreada»;* y del jarabe tapatío.

[1]*average* [2]*saying* [3]*harsh* [4]*of the* chorizos (*sausages*)
[5]*of sweets* (*candy*) [6]*dates back* [7]*candied egg yolks*
[8]*marzipan* (*almond-based candy*) [9]*birthplace* (*cradle*)
[10]empuñando… *brandishing a torch*

En el centro histórico de Guadalajara, hay una hermosa catedral que fue construida durante los siglos XVI-XVIII. Está rodeada de cuatro plazas.

En una escalera del Palacio de Gobierno, José Clemente Orozco pintó al Padre Hidalgo empuñando una tea.[10] Su figura es a la vez inspirada y amenazante.

---

*The members of mariachi bands wear costumes typical of Mexican **charros**, skilled horsemen who perform in the rodeos.

Have you completed the following sections of the lesson? Check them off here.

_____ **Preparación**   _____ **Vocabulario del tema**
_____ **¿Tienes buena memoria?**   _____ **Un poco de gramática**

  Now scan the words in the **Vocabulario** list to be sure that you understand the meaning of most of them. Then you will be ready to continue on with **Lección 41** in the Workbook.

VOCABULARIO

Hablando de los viajes

la aduana	customs office
la agencia de viajes	travel agency
el/la agente de viajes	travel agent
el billete (*Spain*)	ticket
el boleto (*Span. Amer.*)	ticket
...de ida	. . . one way
...de ida y vuelta	. . . round-trip
la (primera, segunda) clase	(first, second) class
la clase turística	tourist class
el equipaje	luggage
la gira	tour
el/la guía	guide
la maleta	suitcase
el mapa	(*road, geographical*) map
el pasaje	passage, fare; ticket
el pasaporte	passport
el plano	map (*of a city*)
la reserva (*Spain*)	reservation
la reservación	reservation
la sección de (no) fumar	(non)smoking section
hacer/cancelar una reservación	to make/cancel a reservation
hacer la maleta	to pack one's suitcase
hacer una gira	to take a tour
tomar un (autobús, avión, barco, taxi, tren)	to take a (bus, plane, boat, taxi, train)

Repaso: **el vuelo**

Los lugares

el ascensor	elevator

Las condiciones

el vicio	bad habit

Los adjetivos

inesperado/a	unexpected

Las palabras adicionales

jugar (ue) (a las cartas) por dinero	to gamble (at cards)

42

YO INVITO*

OBJETIVOS

The materials in **Lección 42** of the Textbook and the Workbook will help you better understand the video episode and take you beyond it, giving you additional information about places and characters in the series. The Textbook will also help you to develop skill in using the Spanish language. In this lesson, you will learn

- how to order a meal in a restaurant
- how to express *What would happen if . . .* in Spanish.

You will also learn about Mexican food.

Be sure to work through all parts of the lesson. When you see a cassette symbol in the margin, listen to the tape for **Lección 42**. Answers or hints for many activities are given in Appendix 1. Be sure to check your answers for each activity before going on to the next one.

* *My Treat*

BEFORE VIEWING . . .

PREPARACIÓN

Actividad A.

Paso 1
Escucha el repaso que va a presentar el narrador al principio del **Episodio 42**.

Paso 2
Ahora contesta las siguientes preguntas sobre el **Episodio 41**.

1. ¿Sí o no? ¿Han llegado Ángela y Roberto a un acuerdo sobre la venta del apartamento?
2. ¿Cierto o falso? Ángela y Roberto no pueden conocer a su abuelo todavía.
3. En casa de Pedro, Carlos
   a. _____ confesó que había sacado fondos de la oficina
   b. _____ admitió que tenía problemas en manejar el dinero

Para pensar...

Cuando Raquel baje para ir a cenar con Arturo, se va a encontrar con Luis y con Arturo. ¿Qué harías tú en esta situación? ¿Cómo le presentarías a Luis a Arturo? ¿Invitarías a Luis a cenar?

Actividad B.

Paso 1

Luis les va a hablar a Raquel y Arturo de su vida profesional. Escucha una parte de lo que les dice y luego contesta la pregunta.

Según lo que acabas de escuchar, Luis es una persona

a. vanidosa   b. discreta   c. sencilla (*simple*)

Paso 2
Escucha la conversación una vez más. Puedes leerla al mismo tiempo, si quieres. Luego completa las oraciones.

RAQUEL: Y tú, Luis, ¿qué has hecho durante todos estos años? ¿Sigues trabajando en la misma compañía?

LUIS: No. Al poco tiempo de estar en Nueva York, encontré una mejor oferta de trabajo. Así que renuncié a mi antiguo puesto y me fui a esta nueva compañía. Me ha ido muy bien; no me puedo quejar. Soy ahora vice-presidente de la compañía.

1. En su vida profesional, Luis ha tenido... mucho/poco... éxito.
2. La intención de Luis al decir esto es irritar/impresionar... a Raquel.

AFTER VIEWING . . .

¿TIENES BUENA MEMORIA?

Actividad A.   En este episodio

¿Te acuerdas de los acontecimientos más importantes de este episodio? Completa el siguiente resumen.

Personas: Arturo, Luis, Raquel
Verbos: esperaba a Pati, había salido a tomar algo, hablaba con Pati, hablando mucho, pagando la cuenta, salieron a cenar

Cuando Raquel bajó en el ascensor para reunirse con Arturo, para su gran sorpresa

_____¹ estaba allí también. _____² invitó a Luis a acompañarlos,

y los tres _____.³ Raquel terminóª _____.⁴ Más tarde, poco

antes de acostarse Raquel, sonóᵇ el teléfono. ¿Quién seríaᶜ?

    En Nueva York, Juan _____⁵ en su apartamento, pero ella no regresó.

Después de ensayarᵈ con los actores, _____⁶ con su asistente.

ªended up   ᵇrang   ᶜ¿Quién... *Who could it be?*   ᵈrehearsing

Actividad B.   Momentos importantes

¿Recuerdas estas escenas? Escúchalas en la cinta y escribe la letra de la foto a que corresponde.

a.

b.

c.

1. _____
2. _____
3. _____
4. _____
5. _____

Actividad C.   ¿Qué recuerdas?

Raquel, Arturo y Luis hablaron mucho durante la cena. Indica quién hizo cada acción.

a.   Raquel   b.   Arturo   c.   Luis

1. _____ Habló de su trabajo y de cómo le ha ido bien en todo.
2. _____ Tuvo que defenderse de una crítica a su profesión.
3. _____ Recordó una conversación previa y se dio cuenta de quién era la otra persona.
4. _____ Pagó la cuenta. No dejó que otras personas la pagaran.
5. _____ Jugaba con algo que llevaba y dijo que era un regalo.

Para pensar...

1. Después de esta cena, ¿qué impresión tienes de Luis? ¿Cómo es su personalidad? ¿Crees que Raquel todavía siente algo por él? Y Arturo, ¿qué estará pensando esta noche?
2. Al final del episodio, el teléfono suena en la habitación de Raquel. ¿Quién será?

VOCABULARIO DEL TEMA

```
LAS TORTUGAS                  Nº  4830
TORTAS A LA PLANCHA
            PRESIDENTE MASARYK 249 A1-A2
COL. POLANCO                  TEL  531.47.96
C. P. 11560                   MEXICO, D. F.

         NOTA DE CONSUMO

  CONSUMO $   35.700

  TOTAL  $

  Reg. Fed. de Caus   TOR-811204-V93
  Cédula de Emp.   1083702
```

En un restaurante

el camarero/la camarera (el mesero/la mesera, el mozo/la moza)	waiter, waitress
el/la cliente	customer, client
la cuenta	bill, check
la orden	order
la propina	tip
el antojito (*Mex.*)	appetizer
el aperitivo	appetizer
el plato principal	entrée
el postre	dessert

la copa	wine goblet
el pimentero	pepper shaker/grinder
el plato	plate
el salero	salt shaker
la servilleta	napkin
la taza	cup
el vaso	glass

los cubiertos	silverware	invitar	to invite (*with the intention of paying*)
la cuchara	spoon	**ordenar** (*Mex.*),	to order (*a meal*)
el cuchillo	knife	**pedir (i, i)**	
el tenedor	fork	**tomar**	to have something to eat/drink

¿Me pasa el salero/el pimentero, por favor?

Will you pass me the salt/pepper shaker, please?

¿Me trae la cuenta / otra servilleta, por favor?

Will you bring me the check / another napkin, please?

Note the following about the preceding vocabulary and expressions.

- **Camarero** is the most widely accepted term for *waiter*. The term **mesero** is used primarily in Mexico.
- The term **ordenar** is widely used in Mexico. In other parts of the Spanish-speaking world, **pedir** is more common.
- To refer to hors d'oeuvres, use the terms **los antojitos** or **la botana** in Mexico, but **tapas** in Spain. You will hear other words in other parts of the Spanish-speaking world.

Actividad A.   ¿En qué consiste una cena?

Paso 1
Pon las siguientes oraciones en orden numérico (del 1 al 7), según ocurren cuando uno come fuera.

a. _____ Después de comer, el cliente pide la cuenta.

b. _____ Luego les pregunta si quieren pedir el plato principal.

c. _____ El camarero les pregunta a los clientes si quieren tomar algo.

d. _____ Para terminar, les sirve a los clientes el café y el postre, si es que ellos quieren.

e. _____ Luego les pregunta si van a tomar un plato para empezar.

f. _____ Después de servir la comida, un buen camarero quiere saber si todo está bien o si los clientes necesitan algo.

g. _____ Si la propina está incluida, el cliente deja una propina adicional cuando el servicio ha sido muy bueno.

Paso 2
Ahora escucha la cinta para verificar tus respuestas. ¡OJO! Las oraciones que oirás no son idénticas a las del **Paso 1**.

Actividad B.   En un restaurante
Empareja las siguientes oraciones con el dibujo que sugieren.

1. Mesero, me trae otra copa de vino tinto, por favor.
2. Mozo, faltan dos cubiertos en esta mesa.
3. Me pasas el salero y el pimentero, por favor.

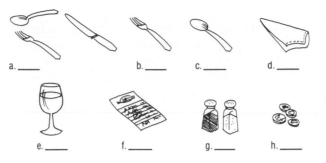

a. ____　　　　b. ____　c. ____　　　d. ____

e. ____　　　f. ____　　　g. ____　　h. ____

4. Ese camarero es muy bueno. Vamos a dejarle una buena propina. ¿Te parece?
5. Todo estaba excelente. ¿Nos trae la cuenta, por favor?
6. Este tenedor está sucio. ¿Me trae otro, por favor?
7. Necesito otra cuchara, por favor.
8. Dejé caer la servilleta. ¿Me trae otra, por favor?

Actividad C.　¿Y tú?

Indica solamente las oraciones que te describen a ti.

1. Siempre dejo de propina la menor cantidad de dinero posible.
2. Si no me ha gustado el servicio, no dejo ninguna propina.
3. Siempre pongo la servilleta en mis rodillas (*knees*), no importa donde sea: un restaurante elegante, McDonald's...
4. Creo que la costumbre de incluir la propina en la cuenta es buena.
5. Cuando como pollo frito, uso tenedor y cuchillo.
6. Creo que no es bueno llevarse la comida a la boca con las manos.
7. Casi ninguno de mis amigos invita a nadie a comer. Cuando comemos juntos, compartimos la cuenta.
8. Si faltan cubiertos en la mesa, los "robo" de otra mesa.

Nota cultural: En un restaurante hispánico

The customs related to eating out in the Hispanic world do not vary as greatly as the names for different food items. You may wish to note the following.

- In Spain and in other parts of the Spanish-speaking world, the term **servicio** (which often appears on a restaurant check) refers to the waiter. **El servicio está incluido** means that the tip has been included in the bill.
- When the tip is included, it is customary to leave the waiter any small change that is returned to the table (unless service has been really awful). Only if the service has been especially good or if the waiter has had to do something extraordinary does one add a substantial amount to the tip.

- Raquel orders a bottle of red wine with a direct command to the waiter: **Traiga una botella de vino tinto**. However, one should not limit oneself to direct commands only, because in many places this would seem abrupt or even impolite. Note the examples given in the **Vocabulario del tema** section: **¿Me trae (un tenedor), por favor?** A request can also be made with a direct statement: **Me trae (un tenedor), por favor**.

- When Hispanic friends go out, it is customary for one of them (the person who says **Yo invito**) to pay the check. When the check is shared, the occasion is referred to as going out **a la americana**.

UN POCO DE GRAMÁTICA

Expressing What Would Happen If...

Here are two questions that Raquel asked herself during the story review.

RAQUEL: ¿Cómo sería mi vida **si**...

RAQUEL: *What would my life be like if* . . .

todavía **estuviera** con Luis?
yo **viviera** en Nueva York?

I were still with Luis?
I lived in New York?

Did you notice the verb forms used in each part of the sentences? The past subjunctive follows the word **si** (*if*) and the conditional is used in the other part of the sentence. You will learn more about sentences like these in the Workbook.

Actividad.   ¿Qué pasaría si... ?

Indica todas las frases que te parecen posibles en los siguientes contextos. No hay respuestas correctas. En la mayoría de los casos, todo depende de lo que tú crees.

1. Mercedes estaría muy contenta si
    _____ se muriera don Fernando
    _____ Pati y Juan resolvieran sus problemas matrimoniales
    _____ don Fernando no fuera tan gruñón
    _____ no se hablara de vender La Gavia
    _____ pudieran curar a su padre

2. Si Raquel todavía estuviera con Luis,
    _____ estarían casados
    _____ no estaría muy contenta
    _____ todavía trabajaría dc abogada
    _____ ahora viviría en Los Ángeles otra vez
    _____ su madre estaría muy alegre

3. Si don Fernando se muriera ahora, en Guadalajara,
    _____ Ángela y Roberto nunca lo conocerían
    _____ no se enteraría de todos los detalles de la investigación de Raquel
    _____ estarían muy contentos todos
    _____ Ramón y Pedro venderían La Gavia
    _____ Juan tendría que regresar a México sin hablar con Pati

Nota cultural: La comida mexicana... dentro y fuera de México

Hace mucho tiempo que[1] la comida mexicana es[2] muy popular en los Estados Unidos. En casi todas las ciudades hay restaurantes que la sirven. Una de las grandes cadenas[3] de «comida rápida» se especializa en lo que se conoce en este país como platos mexicanos, y en las cafeterías y restaurantes de todas partes se sirven nachos y tacos.

Pero ¡cuidado! Toda comida que se conoce por el nombre de «mexicana» no lo es necesariamente...

La comida mexicana en México

La cocina[4] mexicana es muy rica y variada. Su origen se remonta[5] a antes de la llegada de los españoles. Los indios ya cultivaban el maíz, que servía de base para la preparación de una gran variedad de platos.

Después de la llegada de los españoles, la cocina de México cambió, ya que se introdujeron nuevos productos como frutas y cereales. La fusión de las dos cocinas dio como resultado la mayoría de los platos que se comen hoy en día. En la época del emperador austríaco Maximiliano (1861–1867), la cocina local se vio influida otra vez, ahora por la cocina francesa. Esto explica en parte la frecuente presencia de las crepas en los menús mexicanos.

La base de la comida mexicana es la tortilla. Es un tipo de pan que se hace por lo general de maíz o de harina[6] de trigo. Las tortillas no sólo se sirven como acompañantes de la comida principal, como el pan, sino que también se usan para hacer varios otros platos. Por ejemplo:

*   la enchilada: carne picada[7] bien condimentada[8] y envuelta[9] en una tortilla enrollada;[10] se sirve con una salsa de ají[11] (enchiladas verdes)
*   el taco: una tortilla rellena de carne picada, lechuga, tomate y queso blanco; se sirve a menudo con una salsa picante.[12]

[1]Hace... *For a long time* [2]*has been* [3]*chains* [4]*cuisine, cooking* [5]se... *dates back* [6]harina... *flour* [7]*chopped* [8]*seasoned* [9]*wrapped* [10]*rolled* [11]*chile* [12]*hot, spicy*

- Pero hay otros platos—menos conocidos en los Estados Unidos—que también son típicos de la cocina mexicana.
- el mole poblano: una salsa hecha, entre otras cosas, de chocolate y ajíes; se sirve a veces con pollo o guajolote[13]
- el filete de guachinango relleno de huitlacoche[14]

En total, la cocina mexicana ofrece una cantidad de platos apetitosos y llenos de color: antojitos, sopas, carnes y pescados que varían según las regiones. Pero si tú pides en un restaurante mexicano un burrito o, de postre, unas sopaipillas, el mesero probablemente no va a conocer esos platos. ¿Por qué? Porque no son comida mexicana auténtica.

La comida mexicana en los Estados Unidos

No es extraño que la comida mexicana haya influido mucho en la cocina del suroeste de los Estados Unidos. Esta región perteneció a México en una época, y con el cambio de gobierno no se cambiaron las costumbres de los habitantes.

Tampoco es de extrañar[15] que los habitantes de esta región—texanos, nuevomexicanos, etcétera—hayan hecho sus propios inventos muy a la mexicana. Un buen ejemplo son los burritos, un plato de origen texano. Hoy día los burritos (tortillas enrolladas y rellenas de frijoles, queso, pollo o carne) se encuentran hasta en la sección de comida congelada[16] de los supermercados en los Estados Unidos.

Otro plato de invención texana es la fajita: una tortilla de maíz rellena de carne en escabeche[17] preparada rápidamente en una parrilla. Al principio la palabra fajita se refería al tipo de carne que se usaba, el llamado *skirt steak*. Ahora, en los Estados Unidos, la palabra *fajita* ha venido a significar una manera de preparar algo; es decir, cortado en largas fajas.[18] Por eso se puede hablar de fajitas de pollo, de cerdo, de salmón…

Ahora las fajitas son populares en todas partes de los Estados Unidos… ¡y también en el norte de México! Así que representan una manera en que la cultura mexicoamericana ha influido en la cocina de México.

[13] *turkey* [14] el… *fillet of red snapper filled with, among other ingredients, a mushroom that grows on corn stalks*
[15] Tampoco… *Nor is it strange* [16] *frozen* [17] *marinade* [18] *strips*

Have you completed the following sections of the lesson? Check them off here.

_____ **Preparación**   _____ **Vocabulario del tema**
_____ **¿Tienes buena memoria?**   _____ **Un poco de gramática**

Now scan the words in the **Vocabulario** list to be sure that you understand the meaning of most of them. Then you will be ready to continue on with **Lección 42** in the Workbook.

VOCABULARIO

En un restaurante (In a Restaurant)

el/la cliente	customer, client
la cuenta	bill, check
el mesero/la mesera, el mozo/la moza	waiter, waitress
la orden	order
la propina	tip
el antojito (*Mex.*)	appetizer
el aperitivo	appetizer
el plato principal	entrée
el postre	dessert
los cubiertos	silverware
la cuchara	spoon
el cuchillo	knife
el tenedor	fork

la copa	wine goblet
el pimentero	pepper shaker/grinder
el plato	plate
el salero	salt shaker
la servilleta	napkin
la taza	cup
el vaso	glass
ordenar (*Mex.*), **pedir (i, i)**	to order (*a meal*)
¿Me pasa... , por favor?	Will you please pass me . . . ?
¿Me trae... , por favor?	Will you please bring me . . . ?
yo invito	(it's) my treat

Repaso: **el camarero/la camarera**

LECCIÓN
· · · · · · · · · · · · · · · · · ·

43

SEREMOS CUATRO*

OBJETIVOS

The materials in **Lección 43** of the Textbook and the Workbook will help you better understand the video episode and take you beyond it, giving you additional information about places and characters in the series. The Textbook will also help you to develop skill in using the Spanish language. In this lesson, you will learn

- vocabulary related to staying in hotels
- ways to express what you had done.

You will also learn about women in the Hispanic world.

Be sure to work through all parts of the lesson. When you see a cassette symbol in the margin, listen to the tape for **Lección 43**. Answers or hints for many activities are given in Appendix 1. Be sure to check your answers for each activity before going on to the next one.

*There Will Be Four of Us

━━━━━   **BEFORE VIEWING . . .**

Preparación

Actividad A.

Paso 1
Identifica a las personas a quienes se refieren las siguientes oraciones.

a. Raquel   c. Arturo   e. Juan
b. Pati   d. Luis

1. _____ Esperaba a *alguien* en un apartamento en los Estados Unidos.
2. _____ Durante una cena, se encontraba entre *dos personas que se obser-*
   vaban con atención.
3. _____ Durante una cena, observaba a *un posible rival.*
4. _____ Le sorprendió la llegada de *una persona de su pasado.*
5. _____ Se enteró del papel (*role*) de *otra persona* en el viaje de *alguien* a
   México.

Paso 2
Ahora escucha la cinta para verificar tus respuestas. ¿Puedes sustituir la información indicada por el nombre de una persona o personas?

Para pensar...

La madre de Raquel la ha puesto en una situación complicada... difícil. Si tú
fueras Raquel, ¿qué harías?

1. ¿Llamarías a tu mamá para hablar con ella? ¿Qué le dirías?
2. ¿Hablarías con Arturo en seguida? ¿O esperarías que él no supiera quién
   era Luis?

Actividad B.
En este episodio varios personajes van a hablar con un agente de viajes en una
agencia. Si quieres, lee brevemente el vocabulario relacionado con los hoteles
en la sección **Vocabulario del tema** en esta lección. No tienes que aprender el
vocabulario de memoria antes de ver el episodio.

Para pensar...

Al final del **Episodio 42**, alguien llamó a Raquel por teléfono. En tu opinión,
¿quién fue?

Para comprender un poco más	
la censura	En algunos países los escritores no pueden decir siempre lo que piensan porque hay un sistema de **censura** oficial.
se hace tarde	En un momento Raquel ve que **se le hace tarde**. Se va en seguida para no llegar tarde.

AFTER VIEWING . . .

¿TIENES BUENA MEMORIA?

Actividad A.   ¿A quién se refiere?
Indica a qué personaje se refiere cada oración.

a.	Raquel	d.	Juan	g.	Roberto
b.	Arturo	e.	Ángela	h.	don Fernando
c.	Luis	f.	Mercedes		

1. _____ Llamó a Raquel por teléfono después de llegar a su habitación.
2. _____ Le prometió a Luis reunirse con él mañana... a solas.
3. _____ Asustó (*Frightened*) a su esposa en su apartamento.
4. _____ Le iban a hacer un examen médico.
5. _____ Hizo reservaciones para cuatro personas en un hotel de Cozumel.
6. _____ Hizo reservaciones para dos personas en un hotel de Zihuatanejo.
7. _____ Hizo reservaciones para tres o cuatro personas en un hotel de Guadalajara.
8. _____ Hizo una llamada y se sorprendió cuando una mujer desconocida contestó el teléfono.

Actividad B.   Detalles
Completa las oraciones con la información apropiada.

1. Juan le confiesa a Pati que no está muy contento con su carrera porque
    a. _____ quiere trabajar en el teatro y no ha tenido éxito
    b. _____ no tiene una posición estable en la universidad
    c. _____ los libros que ha escrito no le han producido suficiente dinero

---

Para pensar…

¿Qué va a pasar con Juan y Pati, ahora que Juan le ha confesado a ella lo que realmente le pasa? ¿Es posible que se separen por un tiempo? ¿que se divorcien? ¿O crees que ahora se podrán reconciliar?

---

2. Cuando piensa en Luis, Raquel recuerda el momento en que
    a. _____ se conocieron en una fiesta
    b. _____ Luis le dijo que se iba a Nueva York
    c. _____ se besaron por primera vez

3. En la agencia de viajes, Arturo
    a. _____ sólo hizo las reservaciones; no compró los billetes
    b. _____ lo arregló todo, sin haber hablado con Raquel
    c. _____ llamó a Raquel al hotel para consultarla

4. En la agencia de viajes, Luis
    a. _____ sólo hizo las reservaciones; no compró los billetes
    b. _____ lo arregló todo, sin haber hablado con Raquel
    c. _____ llamó a Raquel al hotel para consultarla

Para pensar…

Arturo y Luis (y también Raquel) han ido a la misma agencia de viajes, pero no hicieron la misma cosa. ¿Qué diferencias de su personalidad revelan las acciones de Arturo y Luis en esta situación? ¿Cómo crees que Raquel va a reaccionar cuando sepa lo que los dos han hecho?

---

5. Hoy Ángela, Roberto y Arturo piensan
    a. _____ hacer una gira por México
    b. _____ ir a Guadalajara a conocer a don Fernando
    c. _____ hablar más del asunto del apartamento

• •

VOCABULARIO DEL TEMA

En un hotel

el baño privado	private bath
(con ducha)	(with shower)
la cabaña	bungalow; cabana
la habitación	(single/double) room
(individual/doble)	
el hotel de (cinco)	(five)-star hotel
estrellas	
el plan económico/	economy/deluxe plan
de lujo	
la tarifa	rate, price
el buceo	snorkeling
la cancha de tenis	tennis court

la piscina	swimming pool
la playa (privada)	(private) beach
alojarse (en)	to stay (at)
	(*accommodations*)
confirmar	to confirm
hacer una reservación	to make a reservation
(para el próximo	(for next weekend)
fin de semana)	

Actividad A.   Los planes de Arturo y Luis

Vas a escuchar otra vez la conversación entre Arturo y el agente de viajes, luego la conversación entre Luis y el mismo agente.

Paso 1

Primero, lee las siguientes oraciones. En el **Paso 2**, vas a indicar a quién se refieren, a Luis (**L**) o a Arturo (**A**).

L   A   1. Quiere información sobre un hotel con cabañas.
L   A   2. Le interesa conocer una playa.
L   A   3. Hace reservaciones, pero no las paga todavía.
L   A   4. Lo arregla todo porque no piensa consultar con nadie.
L   A   5. Hace reservaciones para dos personas.
L   A   6. Hace reservaciones para cuatro personas.
L   A   7. Pide tres habitaciones.
L   A   8. Parece que quiere solamente una habitación.
L   A   9. Quiere ir a Cozumel.
L   A   10. Le interesa ir a Zihuatanejo.
L   A   11. No le interesan los planes económicos.

Paso 2

Ahora escucha las conversaciones y completa el **Paso 1**.

Actividad B.   Lo que planea Raquel

Escucha otra vez la conversación entre Raquel y el mismo agente de viajes.
Luego contesta las preguntas.

1. ¿Adónde quería viajar Raquel, a Guadalajara o a Toluca?
2. ¿Cuántas personas van a viajar en total, dos, tres o cuatro? (¡OJO!)
3. ¿Cómo quería Raquel que viajaran, en avión o en tren?
4. ¿Quiere o no quiere que le recomienden un hotel?
5. ¿Compró Raquel los pasajes o solamente quería informarse?

Actividad C.   En el hotel

Lee las siguientes descripciones y da la palabra que se describe.

1. un deporte que se hace en el agua, con un equipo (*equipment*) especial
2. sinónimo de **precio**
3. un lugar donde se nada (dos respuestas, por lo menos)
4. una habitación para una sola persona
5. un lugar donde se descansa y se toma el sol (dos respuestas)
6. un plan para una persona que tiene mucho dinero
7. un lugar donde se practica un deporte que se juega con una raqueta y zapatos especiales
8. un lugar donde se alojan personas que pagan mucho dinero

Actividad D.   ¿Y tú?

Imagina que vas a una agencia de viajes para planear un viaje. Decide adónde
quieres ir. Luego completa las oraciones para indicar las preguntas que le harías
al agente.

1. Quiero información sobre _____, por favor.
2. ¿Cuál es la manera más _____ de llegar a _____?
3. ¿Me puede informar sobre los horarios de _____?
4. Quiero alojarme en _____. ¿Qué posibilidades hay?
5. En _____, me interesa _____ (actividades). ¿Qué me puede decir de eso?

. . . .

UN POCO DE GRAMÁTICA

Talking About What Had Happened Before...

To describe what had already happened before another event took place,
use the imperfect of **haber** (**había**, **habías**, ...) with the past participle
(the form that ends in **-do**).

> Raquel ya **había cenado** con Luis y Arturo cuando volvió a su habitación.
>
> *Raquel had already eaten dinner with Luis and Arturo when she returned to her room.*

Remember that a few past participles are irregular: **hecho** (**hacer**), **dicho** (**decir**), and so on.

Actividad.   ¿Qué había pasado?

Paso 1

Las siguientes oraciones se basan en el repaso del final de este episodio. ¿Puedes completarlas?

1. Cuando Raquel salió del ascensor, descubrió que
   a. _____ sus padres habían llegado
   b. _____ Luis había llegado

2. Raquel apenas se había (*had barely*) preparado para acostarse cuando
   a. _____ alguien tocó a la puerta
   b. _____ alguien llamó por teléfono

3. En Nueva York, cuando Pati llegó a casa, todavía no sabía que
   a. _____ Juan había llegado de México
   b. _____ su obra había sido cancelada

4. Cuando Juan habló con Pati, le dijo que
   a. _____ don Fernando le había dicho algo en el hospital
   b. _____ él había comprendido algo en La Gavia

Paso 2

Aquí hay algunas preguntas más que se parecen (*resemble*) a las que Raquel o el narrador hacen en los repasos. Indica las respuestas.

1. Raquel no sabía que Luis iba a México. ¿Por qué no?
   a. _____ Porque su mamá no le había dicho nada.
   b. _____ Porque Luis no le había dicho nada.

2. Luis no sabía que Arturo también planeaba un viaje. ¿Por qué no?
   a. _____ Porque había ido a otra agencia de viajes.
   b. _____ Porque Arturo ya había salido cuando Luis entró en la agencia.

3. Raquel no se fue a Nueva York con Luis hace varios años. ¿Por qué no?
   a. _____ Porque todavía no había terminado sus estudios.
   b. _____ Porque Luis no se lo había pedido.

Nota cultural: La mujer en el mundo hispano

La situación de la mujer en la sociedad hispana, igual que la de la mujer en los Estados Unidos, ha cambiado mucho en este siglo. Hoy en día, la posibilidad de quedarse en casa y ocuparse de la familia todavía existe. Además, en los países menos desarrollados[1] económica y socialmente, hay mujeres que todavía trabajan en el campo (a veces, al lado de los hombres). Pero muchas mujeres ahora tienen a su disposición otras alternativas.

La voz del presente

El cambio se ha notado mucho en los últimos treinta años, y ahora se puede hablar de varias generaciones de mujeres que han recibido un mejor trato en general y han tenido más oportunidades. Escuchemos la voz[2] de una mujer peruana que ha tenido éxito en los Estados Unidos como directora de un instituto lingüístico.

> [Mi padre] no quería que fuéramos al colegio. Porque él no tuvo buena educación. Mi madre… ella quería que estudiáramos, y realmente somos productos de mi madre porque ella tenía un carácter muy fuerte. No podíamos faltar[3] [a la escuela]. Teníamos que hacer tarea. Ella es la que nos ha empujado[4] a entrar a la universidad. Mi papá decía: «¿Para qué van a estudiar si realmente me van a ayudar en el campo?» Mi madre decía: «No, mis hijos tienen que hacer algo más.»

Cuando la estructura social y económica del país lo permite,* muchas mujeres han tenido éxito en el mundo profesional. Trabajan en grandes empresas y ocupan puestos que hace poco estaban reservados a los hombres. Hoy día es común ver a mujeres ejecutivas, abogadas, profesoras universitarias, periodistas, médicas o arquitectas. Al mismo tiempo, muchas se interesan o intervienen activamente en la vida económica y política de su comunidad.

El pasado en el presente

Al mismo tiempo, hay mucho por hacer todavía. Ya en el siglo XVII una monja[5] mexicana, Sor Juana Inés de la Cruz, escribió los siguientes versos:[6]

> Hombres necios[7] que acusáis
> a la mujer sin razón,
> sin ver que sois la ocasión
> de lo mismo que culpáis[8]…

¿Cuáles crees que son los papeles[9] de esta pareja española? ¿Quién trabaja fuera de casa? ¿Quién cuida a los niños? Hoy día es difícil contestar estas preguntas. Hace cincuenta años hubiera sido[10] más fácil.

[1] *developed* [2] *voice* [3] *skip classes, not attend* [4] nos… *pushed us* [5] *nun, sister* [6] *lines (of poetry)* [7] *stupid* [8] la… *the cause of what you criticize* [9] *roles* [10] hubiera… *it would have been*

---

*En los países menos industrializados, la posición de la mujer media (*average*) no ha cambiado tan radicalmente como ha pasado en países como España, la Argentina y Chile.

Así denunció la actitud intransigente y represiva de los hombres de su época y del hombre en general. Otra poeta famosa, la argentina Alfonsina Storni (1892–1938), siguió esa temática con una voz más moderna:

Hombre pequeñito, hombre pequeñito,
Suelta[11] a tu canario que quiere volar…
Yo soy el canario, hombre pequeñito,
Déjame saltar.[12]

Para algunas mujeres hispanas de esta década, el grito de estas dos autoras todavía conserva su vigencia.[13]

[11]*Set loose, Free*   [12]*fly away*   [13]*vigor*

Have you completed the following sections of the lesson? Check them off here.

_____ **Preparación**   _____ **Vocabulario del tema**
_____ **¿Tienes buena memoria?**   _____ **Un poco de gramática**

Now scan the words in the **Vocabulario** list to be sure that you understand the meaning of most of them. Then you will be ready to continue on with **Lección 43** in the Workbook.

Vocabulario

En un hotel

el baño privado (con ducha)	private bath (with shower)
el buceo	snorkeling
la cabaña	cabin
la cancha de tenis	tennis court
la habitación (individual/doble)	(single/double) room
el hotel de (cinco) estrellas	(five)-star hotel
la piscina	pool
el plan económico/ de lujo	economy/deluxe plan
la playa (privada)	(private) beach
la tarifa	rate, price
alojarse (en)	to stay (at) (*accommodations*)
confirmar	to confirm
hacer una reservación (para el próximo fin de semana)	to make a reservation (for next weekend)

44

UNA PROMESA Y UNA SONRISA*

OBJETIVOS

The materials in **Lección 44** of the Textbook and the Workbook will help you better understand the video episode and take you beyond it, giving you additional information about places and characters in the series. The Textbook will also help you to develop skill in using the Spanish language. In this lesson, you will learn

- vocabulary for talking about sports
- some additional ways to use the past perfect.

You will also learn about the work of some extraordinary muralists.

Be sure to work through all parts of the lesson. When you see a cassette symbol in the margin, listen to the tape for **Lección 44**. Answers or hints for many activities are given in Appendix 1. Be sure to check your answers for each activity before going on to the next one.

A Promise and a Smile

BEFORE VIEWING . . .

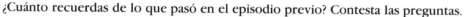

PREPARACIÓN

Actividad.

¿Cuánto recuerdas de lo que pasó en el episodio previo? Contesta las preguntas.

1. ¿Quién llamó a Raquel por la noche después de cenar con Arturo y Luis?
2. ¿Qué quería esa persona? ¿Quería ver a Raquel o sólo quería hablar con ella por teléfono?
3. ¿Qué le prometió Raquel a esa persona?
   a. _____ Reunirse con él en cinco minutos.   b. _____ Verla* al día siguiente.
4. ¿Quién fue a la agencia de viajes para pedir información, Arturo o Luis? ¿Y cuál de los dos compró pasajes para dos a un lugar romántico?
5. ¿Sabe Raquel algo de lo que pasó en la agencia de viajes?

Ahora escucha la cinta para verificar tus respuestas.

Para pensar…

1. En el episodio previo, Raquel recordó una conversación que tuvo con Luis hace unos años. ¿Recuerdas de qué hablaron en esa conversación? ¿Qué noticias le dio Luis a Raquel en aquel entonces (*back then*)?
2. Si tú fueras Raquel, ¿le recordarías a Luis esa conversación en la presente situación? ¿Cómo influiría en ti esa conversación al pensar en él ahora? ¿al pensar en Arturo?

Para pensar…

Al final del episodio previo, Ángela llamó a Puerto Rico, al apartamento de Jorge, su novio. Para su gran sorpresa, una mujer contestó al teléfono. ¿Quién era esa mujer? ¿Crees que por fin Ángela va a comprender por qué a los demás (*other people*) no les gusta Jorge?

---

*La is used as the object pronoun because the grammatical referent is **persona**.

━━ AFTER VIEWING . . .

¿TIENES BUENA MEMORIA?

Actividad.

¿Qué pasó en el episodio? Indica si las siguientes oraciones son ciertas (**C**) o falsas (**F**).

Raquel y Luis

C F 1. Luis sorprendió a Raquel con dos boletos para un viaje romántico a Zihuatanejo.

C F 2. Raquel mostró mucho interés en el viaje que le propuso Luis.

Ángela, Roberto y Arturo

C F 3. Ángela se enfadó con Jorge porque había una mujer en el apartamento de él.

C F 4. Roberto llevó a su hermana y a su tío a ver un poco la Ciudad de México.

C F 5. Al volver los tres al hotel, fueron con Raquel a La Gavia a ver a don Fernando, quien había regresado de Guadalajara.

La familia Castillo

C F 6. Para el final del episodio, Gloria todavía no había regresado.

C F 7. Los niños de Carlos no saben bien lo que pasa con su mamá. (¡OJO! Piensa también en los episodios previos.)

C F 8. Cuando Juan se levantó, vio que Pati estaba por salir. Se abrazaron y después ella se fue a dar unas clases.

C F 9. Al hojear (*page through*) una revista, Juan encontró un anuncio para un hotel. Se le ocurrió que él y Pati deberían pasar unas vacaciones juntos.

C F 10. Ramón le dijo a la agente de bienes raíces que la nueva oferta de su cliente estadounidense no le interesa a la familia.

Para pensar...

1. Como sabes, cuando Luis le dio a Raquel los pasajes para el viaje de vacaciones con él, ella se molestó. ¿Qué piensas de la reacción de ella? ¿Crees que tenía razón o que debería haber reaccionado de otra manera? ¿Cómo va a influir este incidente en lo que Raquel le va a decir a su mamá?

2. Ahora que has visto este episodio, ¿puedes explicar el significado del
   título, «Una promesa y una sonrisa»? ¿Significa lo que tú creías que sig-
   nificaba antes de ver el episodio?

VOCABULARIO DEL TEMA

Hablando de los deportes

el baloncesto/básquetbol	basketball
el béisbol	baseball
el buceo	snorkeling, scuba diving
el esquí (acuático/ alpino/nórdico)	(water/downhill/cross-country) skiing
el fútbol	soccer
el fútbol americano	football
el golf	golf
la natación	swimming
la navegación	sailing
la pesca	fishing
el tenis	tennis
el vólibol	volleyball
el/la atleta	athlete
el campeón, la campeona	champion
el entrenador/ la entrenadora	coach
el jugador/la jugadora	player
el barco	boat
la cancha	court
la caña de pescar	fishing pole
el equipo	team; equipment
el estadio	stadium

el gimnasio	gymnasium
la pelota	ball
la piscina	swimming pool
la pista	track
correr	to run
esquiar	to ski
hacer ejercicio (aeróbico)	to do (aerobic) exercise
jugar (ue) (a)	to play (*a game or sport*)
montar a caballo	to ride horseback
nadar	to swim
practicar un deporte	to play a sport

Note the use of **a** (**jugar al golf**, **al tenis...**) with **jugar**. Not all Spanish speakers observe
this usage.

Actividad A.　¿Practicabas algún deporte?

Paso 1

Escucha otra vez la conversación entre Carlos y Juanita. Luego contesta las preguntas en el **Paso 2**.

Paso 2

1. ¿A qué jugaba Carlos de niño, al básquetbol o al fútbol?
2. Indica cuáles de los siguientes deportes o actividades son parte de la educación física que se da en la escuela de Juanita en Miami.

_____ el tenis　　　　　　　　_____ nadar

_____ el béisbol　　　　　　　 _____ el buceo

_____ el fútbol　　　　　　　　_____ el esquí acuático

_____ el baloncesto

_____ correr

3. ¿Qué deporte quiere aprender Juanita? ¿el tenis, el esquí o el buceo? (¿También recuerdas por qué le interesa este deporte?)

Actividad B.　Cosas relacionadas con los deportes

¿Puedes dar el nombre del deporte que se identifica con las siguientes personas y objetos?

1. los zapatos Nike
2. Joe Montana
3. una piscina
4. Jane Fonda y la música
5. un equipo de nueve hombres
6. una raqueta y una pelota
7. el viento
8. el tiempo frío y la nieve
9. una máscara y el oxígeno

Actividad C.　¡Un desafío! La historia de los deportes

¿Cuántas de las siguientes preguntas puedes contestar?

1. Los Juegos Olímpicos modernos empezaron a celebrarse en el siglo XIX. ¿En qué país del mundo antiguo se habían celebrado antes?

   a. _____ Grecia　　　　b. _____ Turquía　　　　c. _____ Babilonia

2. Antes de 1968, año en que se celebraron los Juegos Olímpicos en la Ciudad de México, ¿habían tenido lugar (*taken place*) ya en otro país de habla española?

   Sí _____　　　No _____

3. El famoso actor Johnny Weismuller, quien hizo el papel (*role*) de Tarzán en muchas películas, había participado en los Juegos Olímpicos. ¿Cuál era su deporte?

   a. _____ el béisbol　　　b. _____ la natación　　　c. _____ la gimnasia

4. En 1984, la Unión Soviética se negó a (*refused to*) participar en los Juegos Olímpicos de Los Ángeles. ¿Qué nación había hecho lo mismo antes (en 1980), cuando los Juegos Olímpicos tuvieron lugar en Moscú?

   a. _____ España   b. _____ los Estados Unidos   c. _____ el Canadá

5. ¿Qué deporte habían inventado los aztecas que después se desarrolló y se hizo popular en los Estados Unidos y otros países?

   a. _____ el golf   b. _____ el baloncesto   c. _____ correr

Actividad D. ¿Y tú?

Contesta las preguntas según tu propia experiencia.

1. ¿Practicas algún deporte? ¿Cuál? ¿Dónde lo practicas? ¿Cuándo lo practicas? ¿Con quién? ¿Es necesario tener equipo especial para practicar este deporte?
2. ¿Qué deporte no te gusta para nada? Explica por qué no te gusta.
3. ¿Qué deporte no practicas pero te gusta verlo en la televisión o en el estadio? ¿Por qué te interesa este deporte? ¿Tienes un equipo favorito? ¿un jugador favorito/una jugadora favorita?
4. Si tuvieras mucho tiempo/dinero, ¿qué deporte te gustaría aprender? ¿Qué tendrías que hacer/comprar para practicarlo? ¿Adónde tendrías que ir?

Nota cultural: Los deportes en el mundo hispánico

In addition to being a matter of individual taste, preferences in sports are also a matter of social class and location. Many families, like their counterparts in the United States, like to go into the countryside to have a picnic or a cookout and to play sports like soccer, volleyball, or badminton. In urban areas, jogging is becoming more common, as are the oriental martial arts such as kung fu and tai chi.

With regard to team sports, soccer is definitely one of the favorite sports in the Spanish-speaking world. Games are not telecast as often as they are in the United States, but **la Copa Mundial de fútbol** (the World Soccer Cup) is a major television event that few fans miss. In addition to international competition, many countries have leagues, and fans are fiercely loyal to their city's team.

In the Caribbean, baseball is without question the leading sport, and many Hispanic baseball players come to the United States to play in the major and minor leagues.

Finally, although not as popular as it once was, **la corrida de toros** (*bullfighting*) is still the favorite sport of many people, especially in Spain (where the bull is killed) and in Mexico (where it is not). The question of whether bullfighting is a sport or an art is still debated by some. Nevertheless, it seems fair to say that younger generations are less taken with this sport than their parents and grandparents have been.

Representación de jugadores hispanos en las grandes ligas	
República Dominicana	33
Puerto Rico	21
Venezuela	13
Cuba	5
México	4
Panamá	3
Nicaragua	1
Honduras	1

UN POCO DE GRAMÁTICA

More About Talking About What Had Happened

You have learned that the imperfect of **haber** + **-do** can be used to express past events.

Juanita ya **había aprendido** a nadar cuando empezó el primer grado.
Juanita had already learned to swim when she started first grade.

De niño, Carlos **había jugado** al fútbol en la escuela.
As a child, Carlos had played soccer in school.

You now have four verb forms that can be combined to describe the past or narrate in the past.

the preterite: Raquel **viajó** a España porque
the imperfect: don Fernando **quería** saber la verdad de su pasado.
the past perfect: **Había viajado** al extranjero antes, y ahora
the conditional: le **gustaría** viajar más, especialmente por Sudamérica.

In the Workbook you will review how these four verb forms function. For now, continue to use the imperfect of **haber** + **-do** to talk about an event in the past that had occurred prior to another event.

Actividad.　El repaso de Raquel

¿Puedes completar el siguiente resumen del repaso de Raquel? Usa las frases útiles.

Frases útiles: hecho reservaciones para cuatro/tres personas
comprado esos boletos sin consultar a mi mamá/consultarme
comprado dos boletos para Zihuatanejo/Cozumel
conseguido información sobre una gira/un hotel
ido al Museo de Antropología/a la Universidad
llamado a Puerto Rico/a Guadalajara
pasado por la Catedral/el Estadio Olímpico
prometido que saldría con él/hablaría con él

Parece que los tres lo pasaron muy bien en su excursión. Según Ángela, vieron unos murales impresionantes. Antes de ver los murales, habían _____.[1]

Y también habían _____.[2]

Mientras tanto, Luis me llamó. Yo le había _____ [3] hoy. Por eso bajé a la cafetería y almorcé con él. Al final de la comida, me contó una sorpresa. Él había _____ [4] y también había _____ .[5] Mi reacción fue negativa. Él no debió haber _____ .[6]

Ahora escucha la cinta para verificar tus respuestas.

Nota cultural: El arte mural y los muralistas

(*Una sugerencia*: Antes de leer esta sección, te conviene ver una vez más los murales que se encuentran en las **Lecciones 32** [pág. 328] y **41** [pág. 414] de este libro. También debes pensar en los cuadros de estas páginas.)

Por horribles que sean, las guerras tienen la capacidad de servir de inspiración a las mentes creadoras: novelistas, pintores, dramaturgos y, ahora en el siglo XX, cineastas.[1] La Revolución mexicana no fue una excepción. La época de esta guerra civil, de 1910 a 1920, fue uno de los períodos más sangrientos[2] de toda la historia de México. Ha inspirado muchas novelas y películas famosas, pero sobre todo inspiró a tres pintores a utilizar y popularizar la pintura mural. Ellos convirtieron este arte en un gran instrumento social.

¿Por qué la pintura mural?

En los países donde el índice de analfabetismo[3] es muy alto, el artista puede servir de maestro a su pueblo. Desde el principio, el arte muralista se destinó a las masas.

- Por una parte, los artistas querían compartir con el pueblo la historia de los grandes acontecimientos de la Revolución y sus héroes, así como[4] los ideales de la Revolución.
- Por otra parte se buscaba enseñarles a las grandes masas las maravillas de la historia de la raza indígena: la grandeza de las civilizaciones azteca, maya, tolteca…

El campesino que ignoraba la palabra escrita podía mirar los dibujos, interpretar las figuras y así aprender. ¿Quién no se inspira al ver al *Padre Hidalgo*, en el mural de Orozco, en

En *Hispano-América* Orozco pinta al campesino revolucionario con las fuerzas que lo oprimen:[5] los banqueros, los soldados… Es toda una alegoría.

[1] *people who work in the movie industry*   [2] *bloody*   [3] *índice... level of illiteracy*   [4] *así... as well as*   [5] *oppress*

Guadalajara? No queda duda[6] sobre la fuerza y verdad de su mensaje.

Las grandes figuras del arte mural mexicano

- Diego Rivera (1886–1957)

Para este artista, quien se declaraba comunista, la historia de México no es más que una lucha de clases sociales: por una parte, el campesino, el obrero, el indio y el soldado; por otra, los militares, el clero[7] y los capitalistas. Más que ningún otro pintor, fue capaz de poner en alto[8] la herencia india mexicana.*

- José Clemente Orozco (1883–1949)

Este muralista pensaba que los artistas no debían tener convicciones políticas. Sin embargo sus murales expresan la tristeza de la guerra y denuncian los errores del sistema capitalista y de los militares.

- David Alfaro Siqueiros (1896–1974)

Hay que participar en los murales y cuadros de Siqueiros. En ellos se destacan[9] con frecuencia los brazos y las manos, símbolos de la dignidad del hombre trabajador.

El arte mural en los Estados Unidos

Estos grandes pintores no sólo crearon en México sus obras maestras. La obra de Orozco que se reproduce con esta Nota se pintó, y se encuentra todavía, en Dartmouth College. Pero Rivera no tuvo tanta suerte. Un fresco que pintó para el Centro Rockefeller en 1932 provocó manifestaciones anticomunistas. Esta obra fue destruida, pero luego se recreó[10] en la capital.

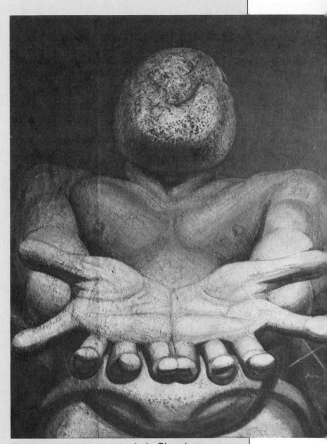

En *Nuestra imagen actual*, de Siqueiros, una figura anónima suplica[13] la devolución[14] de una identidad humana.

Hoy día todavía se puede afirmar que la tradición de la pintura mural sigue vigente[11] en los Estados Unidos. En los barrios mexicoamericanos de Los Ángeles, Chicago, San Diego, San Francisco y otras ciudades, se ven murales pintados por una nueva generación de muralistas. En ellos hay una temática basada en la experiencia de lo que es ser latino en los Estados Unidos.

Uno de los mayores proponentes del estilo mural es la profesora Judy Baca, de la Universidad de California en Irvine. Para ella, como para los maestros mexicanos de este arte, un mural es ante todo[12] comunicación, un lenguaje visual que puede unir a un pueblo. En su proyecto más famoso, *Great Wall of Los Angeles*, hay escenas de la historia de California.

[6]No... *There is no doubt*   [7]*clergy*   [8]poner... *putting on display*   [9]se... *stand out*   [10]se... *it was recreated*
[11]*vital, alive*   [12]ante... *above all else*   [13]*begs for*   [14]*return*

* En los últimos años, la fama de Diego Rivera ha crecido en los Estados Unidos por otra razón: fue el esposo de la pintora mexicana Frida Kahlo.

Have you completed the following sections of the lesson? Check them off here.

_____ **Preparación**	_____ **Vocabulario del tema**
_____ **¿Tienes buena memoria?**	_____ **Un poco de gramática**

Now scan the words in the **Vocabulario** list to be sure that you understand the meaning of most of them. Then you will be ready to continue on with **Lección 44** in the Workbook.

VOCABULARIO

Hablando de los deportes
(Talking About Sports)

el baloncesto/básquetbol	basketball
el barco	boat
el béisbol	baseball
la caña de pescar	fishing pole
el equipo	team; equipment
el esquí (acuático/alpino/ nórdico)	(water/downhill/ cross-country) skiing
el estadio	stadium
el fútbol	soccer
el fútbol americano	football
el gimnasio	gymnasium
el golf	golf
la natación	swimming
la navegación	sailing
la pelota	ball
la pesca	fishing
la pista	track
el tenis	tennis
el vólibol	volleyball

el/la atleta	athlete
el campeón, la campeona	champion
el entrenador/la entrenadora	coach
el jugador/la jugadora	player
esquiar	to ski
hacer ejercicio (aeróbico)	to do (aerobic) exercise
montar a caballo	to ride horseback
practicar un deporte	to play a sport

Repaso: **el buceo, la cancha, correr, jugar (ue) (a), nadar, la piscina**

Las personas

los/las demás	others, other people

Los conceptos

la promesa	promise

45

¡ESTOY HARTA!*

OBJETIVOS

The materials in **Lección 45** of the Textbook and the Workbook will help you better understand the video episode and take you beyond it, giving you additional information about places and characters in the series. The Textbook will also help you to develop skill in using the Spanish language. In this lesson, you will learn

- vocabulary for talking about relationships with family and friends
- ways to use another perfect tense to talk about what someone should have done.

You will also learn about Hispanic families.

Be sure to work through all parts of the lesson. When you see a cassette symbol in the margin, listen to the tape for **Lección 45**. Answers or hints for many activities are given in Appendix 1. Be sure to check your answers for each activity before going on to the next one.

I'm Fed Up!

445

BEFORE VIEWING . . .

PREPARACIÓN

Actividad.

Contesta las siguientes preguntas según lo que recuerdas del episodio previo.

1. ¿Quiénes fueron a conocer la Ciudad de México?
    a. _____ Arturo, Raquel y Ángela   c. _____ Raquel, Luis y Arturo
    b. _____ Ángela, Arturo y Roberto

2. ¿Con qué sorprendió Luis a Raquel?
    a. _____ con su plan de mudarse a Los Ángeles
    b. _____ con su plan de casarse con ella lo antes posible
    c. _____ con su plan de pasar el fin de semana con ella en Zihuatanejo

3. ¿Qué pasó con don Fernando?
    a. _____ El especialista lo autorizó a volver a su casa.
    b. _____ El especialista quería hacerle otros exámenes.
    c. _____ Su condición mejoró muchísimo.

4. ¿Qué pasó con Gloria?
    a. _____ Regresó a casa por fin.
    b. _____ La seguían esperando todos.
    c. _____ Llamó para decir que regresaría pronto.

Ahora escucha la cinta para verificar algunas de tus respuestas.

Para pensar...

1. En este episodio, Juan va al teatro donde Pati está ensayando (*rehearsing*) con los actores. ¿Qué le va a decir Juan a ella? ¿Crees que él ha llegado a una conclusión sobre lo que él debería hacer?
2. También en este episodio, los padres de Raquel llegan a México. ¿Cuál ha sido la actitud de María, la madre de Raquel, hacia Arturo hasta ahora? (Recuerda que Raquel le ha hablado por teléfono varias veces.) ¿Crees que su actitud será igual cuando María y Arturo se conozcan por fin? ¿Y qué le va a decir Raquel a su madre en cuanto al viaje de Luis a México?

AFTER VIEWING . . .

· ·

¿TIENES BUENA MEMORIA?

Actividad A.   ¿Qué pasó en el episodio?

Paso 1
Indica si las siguientes oraciones son ciertas (**C**) o falsas (**F**).

Raquel

C   F   1. Raquel se enteró de que Luis es la causa de su situación difícil.
C   F   2. Raquel y su madre se enojaron la una con la otra.
C   F   3. Arturo habló con Raquel sobre un viaje a Cozumel, posiblemente con sus padres.
C   F   4. De momento, Raquel piensa que Luis es más considerado que Arturo.

Ángela y Roberto

C   F   5. No tenían ningún interés en las relaciones entre Arturo y Raquel.
C   F   6. Bajaron para ir a cenar con los padres de Raquel y los demás.

La familia Castillo

C   F   7. Las noticias sobre la salud de don Fernando eran buenas.
C   F   8. Juan decidió regresar a México sin Pati.
C   F   9. Gloria todavía no ha vuelto a casa.
C   F   10. Don Fernando regresará a La Gavia mañana.

Paso 2
Ahora escucha la cinta para verificar algunas de tus respuestas.

Paso 3
Ahora lee el siguiente párrafo para verificar las otras respuestas.

Ángela y Roberto tenían muchas ganas de saber lo que Arturo pensaba hacer con respecto a sus sentimientos por Raquel. Pero cuando se lo preguntaron, Arturo les dijo que sus planes eran un secreto. Cuando Ángela y Roberto llegaron a la habitación de Raquel, conocieron a los padres de ella. También vieron la manera en que María se portó (*behaved*): muy fría con Arturo... y muy emotiva con Luis. Más tarde, decidieron no salir a cenar con el grupo. ¿Crees que fue porque, como dijeron, tenían muchas cosas de que hablar? ¿O fue por otra razón?

Actividad B. ¡Un desafío!

Esta es una parte de la conversación que Raquel tuvo con su madre en la habitación de sus padres, pero faltan algunas frases. ¿Puedes completar la conversación?

1. yo soy el problema / sí, todo es mi culpa
2. lo que tú le dijiste a / lo que hiciste con
3. Lo insultaste. / No le hablaste.
4. Para mí, es un extraño. / Para mí, no es nadie.
5. quién puede ser algún día / quién es para mí

RAQUEL: El verdadero problema que tengo eres tú.

MADRE: Ah, _____.¹ Mira, ¡yo no vine de tan lejos para que mi propia hija me insultara!

RAQUEL: ¿Que yo te insulto? ¿Y qué fue _____² Arturo?

MADRE: No comprendo.

RAQUEL: ¿No comprendes? ¡Te portaste muy grosera con él! _____.³ Actuaste como si fuera un extraño, como si fuera nadie.

MADRE: _____.⁴

RAQUEL: ¡No importa quién es Arturo para ti! Lo que importa es _____.⁵ Arturo es mi amigo, e insultarlo a él es como insultarme a mí.

 Ahora escucha la cinta para verificar tus respuestas.

- -

VOCABULARIO DEL TEMA

Las relaciones interpersonales

Por un lado...	*Por otro lado...*
aceptar	**rechazar**
acusar	**perdonar**
alabar (to praise)	**insultar, ofender**
amar, querer (ie)	**odiar**
confiar*(en) (to trust)	**desconfiar* (de)**
culpar (to blame)	**disculpar** (to excuse; to make excuses for)
decir la verdad	**engañar, mentir (ie, i)**

_____

* Note the patterns of accentuation in these verbs: **confiar: confío, confías... confiamos...** ; **desconfiar: desconfío, desconfías... desconfiamos...**

llevarse bien (con)

prestar atención (a) (to pay attention [to])

respetar, estimar, venerar

ser amigo íntimo/amiga íntima de

ser unido/a

tratar (to deal with, treat)

actuar*/portarse + *adverb*

  actuar*/portarse amigablemente/hostilmente

llevarse mal (con), discutir (to argue),
    pelear(se) (con)

no hacer caso (de)

despreciar, desdeñar

ser distante de

ser desunido/a

no hacerle caso a alguien

to act + *adverb*

You already know the meaning of some of the preceding verbs and phrases. Others are easily recognizable cognates. Still others are "guessable" when seen in the context of the word(s) with which they are grouped. If you are unsure of the meaning of any of these verbs, check their meaning in the **Vocabulario** at the end of this lesson or in the Spanish-English dictionary at the back of the Textbook.

Actividad A.   Opiniones

Escucha las siguientes descripciones o predicciones. Luego indica si estás de acuerdo (**Sí**) con ellas o no (**No**).

La familia Castillo Soto

Sí   No   1. Ángela y Roberto no son muy unidos.

Sí   No   2. Ángela no hace caso de las opiniones y consejos de los demás.

Sí   No   3. En la familia de Ángela y Roberto, todos veneran a la abuela y respetan sus opiniones.

La familia Rodríguez

Sí   No   4. Raquel y su madre se llevan bien en general.

Sí   No   5. Como ocurre entre todas las madres e hijas, a veces Raquel y su madre discuten porque son de distintas generaciones y tienen diferentes ideas sobre algunas cosas.

Sí   No   6. Al fin y al cabo (*In the end*), Raquel va a disculpar a su madre.

Sí   No   7. María (la madre de Raquel) no le hace mucho caso a su esposo.

Sí   No   8. María se portó hostilmente con Arturo porque no le caen muy bien los argentinos.

La familia Castillo Saavedra

Sí   No   9. Los miembros de la familia Castillo se mantienen distantes los unos de los otros.

---

*Note the pattern of accentuation in this verb: **actuar: actúo, actúas... actuamos...**

Sí   No   10. Carlos trató de engañar a la familia por razones económicas.

Sí   No   11. Es obvio que Juan no quiere a Pati, pues le tiene envidia.

Sí   No   12. Gloria hace lo que hace porque los hermanos de Carlos no la aceptan.

Actividad B.   Tú y los demás

Para cada una de las siguientes oraciones, da una respuesta: **siempre**, **muchas veces**, **a veces**, **muy poco**, **nunca**.

1.   Me llevo muy bien con mi familia.
2.   Le he mentido a una persona a quien quiero mucho.
3.   Mis profesores me tratan amigablemente.
4.   Actúo de una forma cortés y considerada con los otros.
5.   Alabo a los demás por sus triunfos y éxitos.
6.   Los demás me prestan atención cuando hablo u ofrezco una opinión.
7.   Me peleo con un pariente.
8.   Me han acusado de ser desleal.
9.   Rechazo a los demás por sus opiniones políticas.
10. Me ha insultado un buen amigo/una buena amiga.

Actividad C.   ¿Y tú?

De las siguientes preguntas, contesta las que tengan algo que ver con tu vida.

1.   ¿Con quién(es) te llevas muy bien? ¿Por qué razón? ¿Qué han hecho Uds. juntos?
2.   ¿Hay alguien con quien te lleves muy mal? ¿Puedes explicar por qué? ¿Qué ha pasado entre Uds.?
3.   ¿Quiénes son tus amigos íntimos? ¿Hace mucho que los/las conoces? ¿Dónde conociste a tu mejor amigo/a? ¿En qué circunstancias?
4.   ¿Es tu familia muy unida? ¿Cuántas veces a la semana (al mes/al año) se ven? ¿Hay un pariente de quien *des*confías?
5.   ¿Qué días acostumbras pasar con tu familia? ¿Qué hacen Uds. cuando se reúnen?
6.   ¿En quién confías mucho? ¿A quién le confiesas tus secretos más íntimos?

. . . .

Un poco de gramática

> ### Talking About What Someone Should Have Done
>
> To express what someone should—or should *not*!—have done in the past, use the conditional of **deber** + the infinitive of **haber** + the -**do** form.

> Luis no **debería haber comprado** los pasajes sin consultar a Raquel primero.
>
> *Luis should not have bought the tickets without consulting with Raquel first.*
>
> Gloria no **debería haber estado** ausente tanto tiempo... y sin llamar.
>
> *Gloria should not have been away from home for so long . . . and without even calling.*
>
> You will learn more about using these forms in the Workbook.

Actividad. Más opiniones

¿Estás de acuerdo (**Sí**) o no (**No**)?

Sí   No   1. La familia no debería haber aceptado la opinión del médico de Guadalajara.

Sí   No   2. Luis no debería haber comprado los pasajes para ir a Zihuatanejo sin consultar a Raquel.

Sí   No   3. María (la madre de Raquel) no le debería haber sugerido a Luis la idea de ir a México.

Sí   No   4. Cuando María actuó fríamente con Arturo, él le debería haber dicho algo.

Sí   No   5. El papá de Raquel debería haber intervenido en la discusión entre su hija y su esposa.

Sí   No   6. Roberto y Ángela no se deberían haber quedado en el hotel. Deberían haber acompañado a su tío a cenar con los demás.

Sí   No   7. Juan no debería haber decidido regresar sin Pati.

Sí   No   8. Carlos debería haber hablado con la familia sobre Gloria.

Sí   No   9. Raquel le debería haber dicho a Luis que le acompañaría en el viaje.

Nota cultural: Facetas de la familia hispana

La familia Castillo tiene una vida privilegiada en el sentido económico. Pero también goza de[1] otra circunstancia envidiable: la unidad de la familia. Los nietos tienen la oportunidad de pasar mucho tiempo con su abuelo. Dos hijos de don Fernando viven con él en la hacienda, por lo menos parte del tiempo. Parece que todos los hermanos se llevan bien y que se apoyan en todo. En realidad, de lo único que culpan a Carlos cuando se descubre lo de la oficina en Miami es de no haber confiado en la familia.

¿Telenovela o realidad?

Esta visión de la familia modelo muy bien puede servir de fondo[2] para una telenovela, como *Destinos*. Pero no representa necesariamente una realidad compartida por la mayoría de la gente

[1]goza... *they enjoy*   [2]de... *as a background*

de habla española. Entre los hispanos, como en toda cultura, hay familias unidas y desunidas, familias grandes y chicas, familias cariñosas y violentas. En algunas familias, muchos parientes viven en una misma vivienda[3] (la llamada «familia extendida»). Pero hay también familias nucleares (sólo padres e hijos) y también familias donde hay sólo uno de los padres.

Escuchemos lo que nos dice un niño chileno «moderno» de su familia. El chico tiene siete años.

> Los papás siempre llegan muy tarde. Solamente los fines de semana salimos. Casi siempre vamos a andar en bicicleta en las mañanas y a veces jugamos o vamos al estadio. Y cuando vamos donde mis abuelitos, hacemos lo que queremos. Si queremos un helado, el tata[4] va a comprarlo al tiro. Y siempre que vamos, nos tiene pasteles y cosas ricas. Pero ahora los veo menos, porque voy poco. Antes iba todos los viernes, y ahora me invitan y me invitan, y yo les digo «cuando pueda».

¿Te fijaste en las diferencias entre lo que dice este chico y la familia del estereotipo? (Piénsalo un poco antes de seguir leyendo.)

Aquí, los padres llegan tarde (¿trabajan los dos fuera de casa?) y realmente pasan con los niños solamente los fines de semana. Los abuelos no viven con los hijos. Y ya hay cierta distancia entre el niño y sus abuelos, pues ya, a los siete años, no tiene tiempo para ellos.

¿Lo pasado, pasado?[5]

No era antes así—ni en las culturas hispanas ni en los Estados Unidos. En todas partes del mundo moderno se ha notado en los últimos años una serie de cambios en la estructura de la familia y en la calidad de la vida familiar. ¿El ideal norteamericano del pasado? La familia de Ozzie y Harriet. ¿La realidad del presente? Piensa en los programas en la televisión esta semana.

El ideal de otras épocas de la familia hispana se parece en algunos detalles al ideal de la familia que se tenía en los Estados Unidos. Veamos esto en las palabras de una chilena de mediana edad.[6]

> La mamá de mi papá, mi abuela paterna, vivía con nosotros. La familia nuestra era los tres niños y los tres adultos. Es muy común que—sea un tío o los abuelos—vivan en el mismo lugar. Las familias son mucho más grandes en este sentido, más extendidas. La familia es un núcleo muy importante dentro de la sociedad, a todo nivel, en la clase más alta y en la clase más baja también. Y también los tíos que no son tíos, son amigos que también son muy próximos a la familia…

En los países menos industrializados, en donde se conservan las tradiciones, es posible que este tipo de familia todavía exista y hasta sea común. En las grandes ciudades, sin embargo, para bien o para mal,[7] entre la gente joven el patrón[8] se parece más al de los países industrializados. ¿Cómo será la familia dentro de veinticinco años? No se sabe, pero seguramente seguirá cambiando.

---

[3]*dwelling*   [4]abuelo   [5]¿Lo… *Is the past gone forever?*   [6]de… *middle-aged*   [7]para… *for better or worse*
[8]*pattern, model*

Have you completed the following sections of the lesson? Check them off here.

_____ **Preparación**   _____ **Vocabulario del tema**
_____ **¿Tienes buena memoria?**   _____ **Un poco de gramática**

Now scan the words in the **Vocabulario** list to be sure that you understand the meaning of most of them. Then you will be ready to continue on with **Lección 45** in the Workbook.

VOCABULARIO

Las relaciones interpersonales
(Interpersonal Relationships)

acusar	to accuse
alabar	to praise
amar	to love
confiar (**en**)	to trust
culpar	to blame
desconfiar (**de**)	to distrust
desdeñar	to disdain, scorn
despreciar	to hold in low esteem
disculpar	to make excuses for
discutir	to argue
estimar	to hold in high esteem
insultar	to insult
mentir (**ie, i**)	to lie
no hacer caso (**de**)	to pay no attention (*to an issue*)
no hacerle caso a alguien	to ignore someone
ofender	to offend
perdonar	to pardon
prestar atención (**a**)	to pay attention (to)
respetar	to respect
tratar	to treat, deal with
venerar	to venerate

ser...	to be . . .
amigo íntimo/amiga íntima	a close friend
distante	distant
desunido/a	fragmented
actuar/portarse + *adverb*	to act + *adverb*
amigablemente/hostilmente	in a friendly/ hostile manner

Repaso: aceptar, decir la verdad, engañar, llevarse bien/mal (con), odiar, pelear(se) (con), querer (ie), rechazar, unido/a

Las palabras adicionales

estar harto/a (**de/con**)	to be fed up (with)

46

LAS EMPANADAS*

OBJETIVOS

The materials in **Lección 46** of the Textbook and the Workbook will help you better understand the video episode and take you beyond it, giving you additional information about places and characters in the series. The Textbook will also help you to develop skill in using the Spanish language. In this lesson you will learn

- ways to talk about hobbies and pastimes
- ways to talk about what would happen if . . . .

You will also learn about a popular park in Mexico City.

Be sure to work through all parts of the lesson. When you see a cassette symbol in the margin, listen to the tape for **Lección 46**. Answers or hints for many activities are given in Appendix 1. Be sure to check your answers for each activity before going on to the next one.

The Turnovers (pies)

BEFORE VIEWING . . .

PREPARACIÓN

Actividad A.

Completa las siguientes oraciones según lo que recuerdas del episodio previo.

1. En el episodio previo, Arturo le sugirió a Raquel que
   a. _____ fuera a Buenos Aires con él
   b. _____ ellos fueran a Cozumel con sus padres
   c. _____ invitaran a sus padres a cenar

2. Raquel estaba muy impresionada por
   a. _____ el interés que Arturo mostraba en sus padres
   b. _____ la fineza de Arturo al elegir un lugar tan bonito para su fin de semana
   c. _____ el interés que Arturo tenía en ella

3. En el hospital de Guadalajara, le dieron de alta a don Fernando,
   a. _____ pero su estado de salud no era bueno
   b. _____ porque su estado de salud había mejorado mucho
   c. _____ pero él no quería volver a La Gavia

4. Juan le dijo a Pati que había decidido volver a México y que
   a. _____ ella tenía que volver con él
   b. _____ ella tenía que elegir entre su carrera y su esposo
   c. _____ entendía por fin por qué ella tuvo que volver a Nueva York

5. Gloria volvió a casa de Ramón, y Carlos
   a. _____ se enojó mucho con ella
   b. _____ le dijo que era hora de hablar seriamente
   c. _____ le dijo que esta vez no pagaría sus deudas

Ahora escucha la cinta para verificar tus respuestas.

Actividad B.

Paso 1

¿Cuánto recuerdas de la llegada de los padres de Raquel? Indica solamente las oraciones que la describan.

1. _____ Raquel y sus padres conversaban en la habitación de Raquel cuando llegaron Ángela, Roberto y Arturo.
2. _____ Arturo actuó muy fríamente con sus padres.
3. _____ Cuando llegó Luis, la madre de Raquel ni lo saludó.

4. _____ Raquel se enojó con su madre y fue a su habitación para hablarle de su conducta.

5. _____ Arturo se sentía apenado (*distressed*); no quería intervenir entre Raquel y sus padres.

6. _____ Luis sospecha que Raquel está enamorada de (*in love with*) Arturo.

¿Puedes modificar las oraciones que no indicaste para que sean verdaderas?

Para pensar...

¿Recuerdas cómo reaccionó Arturo ante la conducta de María Rodríguez? En su lugar, ¿cómo te sentirías tú? ¿Te sentirías como ella? ¿Qué harías tú si fueras Arturo? ¿Buscarías a los padres de Raquel para hablar con ellos? ¿Tratarías de hablar primero con Raquel?

Para comprender un poco más...

fastidiar   A veces los niños **fastidian** a sus padres, sobre todo cuando hacen muchas preguntas... sólo por preguntar.

AFTER VIEWING . . .

¿TIENES BUENA MEMORIA?

Actividad A.   Raquel: Discusión, confesión

Hoy ha sido un día difícil e importante para Raquel. ¿Puedes completar el siguiente resumen de su repaso?

1. Le había hecho
   Le había comprado
2. disculparse con su hija
   empezar una conversación seria
3. cenar con ellos la otra noche
   venir a México
4. de las relaciones entre Raquel y Arturo
   del impacto que tuvo la investigación en la carrera de Raquel

5. Raquel se casara con Arturo
    Raquel se fuera a vivir a la Argentina
6. una llamada de Luis
    un mensaje de Luis
7. no lo quiere ver más en su vida
    sí está enamorada de Arturo

Esta mañana, la madre de Raquel vino a verla a su habitación. _____[1]
unas empanadas. Esto fue como una señal[a] para Raquel porque su madre las usaba
para _____.[2]

Mientras comían las empanadas, María le explicó a Raquel por qué había invitado a
Luis a _____.[3] En realidad lo hizo porque tenía miedo _____.[4]
No quería que _____.[5]

María no debía de haberse preocupado.[b] Raquel no quiere irse a vivir a la Argentina, pero todavía no ha hablado con Arturo de todo esto.

Al bajar a la recepción con su madre, Raquel recibió _____.[6] Él ha regresado a Los Ángeles. Para Raquel, es mejor así porque ahora no le tiene que decir
que _____.[7]

[a]*sign, signal*   [b]no... *needn't have worried*

Ahora escucha el repaso de Raquel otra vez en la cinta para verificar tus
respuestas.

Para pensar...

Raquel ha dicho algo muy importante al final de este episodio: «Estoy enamorada de Arturo.» Ahora ella tiene que tomar una decisión, ¿no? O, tal vez,
varias decisiones. ¿Cuáles son las alternativas que tiene? ¿Qué harías tú si
fueras ella?

Actividad B.   Las otras actividades

Mientras Raquel iba resolviendo algunos de sus problemas, los asuntos de los
otros personajes también se iban resolviendo. Describe cómo, haciendo oraciones completas con una frase de cada grupo.

1. _____ Ángela y Roberto decidieron que
2. _____ El padre de Raquel le dijo a Arturo
3. _____ Mientras paseaba con su esposo y su hija, María
4. _____ Por fin don Fernando
5. _____ Los otros miembros de la familia Castillo
6. _____ Al comentar con sus hermanos la posible venta de La Gavia, Mercedes les
7. _____ Raquel, Arturo y sus sobrinos

a. pudo regresar a La Gavia
b. que su esposa cambiaría... a su manera
c. llegaron a la hacienda también
d. dijo que tenía una idea
e. llegaron a La Gavia y conocieron a todos los de la familia
f. no iban a vender el apartamento por el momento
g. caminaba y hablaba muy amigablemente con Arturo

Actividad C.   Dos conversaciones muy importantes

Paso 1

En este episodio, el padre de Raquel le ofrece un consejo al amigo de su hija. Al mismo tiempo, la madre de Raquel está hablando con su hija. Escucha las dos conversaciones otra vez.

Paso 2

Ahora di si estás de acuerdo (**Sí**) o no (**No**) con las siguientes oraciones.

Sí   No   1. A Pancho le gusta mucho Arturo.
Sí   No   2. Parece que el padre de Raquel comprende bien a las personas.
Sí   No   3. Es dudoso que Arturo se sintiera aliviado después de hablar con Pancho.
Sí   No   4. Pancho quiere que Arturo y su esposa se lleven bien.

Sí   No   5. Ésta es la primera vez que Raquel y su madre han tenido una conversación seria.
Sí   No   6. Es probable que Raquel se mude a la Argentina.
Sí   No   7. Raquel siente que Luis se haya ido.
Sí   No   8. La madre de Raquel se va a portar mejor con Arturo en el futuro.

Vocabulario del tema

Diversiones y pasatiempos

al aire libre	outdoors
el tiempo libre/los ratos libres	free time
cocinar	to cook
coleccionar estampillas/monedas...	to collect stamps/coins . . .
coser	to sew
dar/hacer fiestas	to give/have parties
dar paseos, pasear	to take walks
hacer un *picnic*	to have a picnic
ir al cine/a una función de teatro	to go to the movies/to a show at the theater
ir a un parque/al campo	to go to a park/the country
jugar (ue) a las cartas/al ajedrez/ al póquer/juegos de salón	to play cards/chess/poker/parlor games
leer revistas/novelas...	to read magazines/novels . . .
mirar la televisión	to watch television
pasarlo bien con los amigos	to have a good time with friends
salir con los amigos	to go out with friends
salir de la ciudad	to get out of the city
sacar fotos/vídeos	to take photos/videos
trabajar en el jardín	to work in the garden
ver una película	to see a movie
visitar un museo/a los parientes	to visit a museum/ relatives
disfrutar (de), gozar (de)	to enjoy
divertirse (ie, i)	to have a good time
entretenerse	to entertain oneself
llevar una vida activa	to have an active life
llevar una vida sedentaria	to have a sedentary life

You already know many of the preceding words and phrases, especially the verbs in the second section. If a hobby or pastime of yours is not given here, find out how to say it in Spanish by looking it up in a dictionary or asking your instructor. You should pay particular attention to the names of activities that are important to you and to your friends and family.

Actividad A. El pasatiempo apropiado

Junta el objeto o concepto de la primera columna con los pasatiempos de la segunda. ¡OJO! Algunos conceptos admiten más de una asociación.

1. _____ las flores y las plantas
2. _____ las reuniones familiares y toda ocasión importante
3. _____ un rey y una reina
4. _____ un parque, una calle residencial tranquila
5. _____ objetos raros o especiales por alguna razón
6. _____ recetas para cocinar platos mexicanos, italianos...
7. _____ la barbacoa, el badmintón, las hormigas (*ants*)
8. _____ los dibujos animados, sobre todo el sábado por la mañana
9. _____ hacer su propia ropa
10. _____ historias de amor

a. cocinar
b. dar una fiesta
c. sacar vídeos
d. mirar la televisión
e. trabajar en el jardín
f. jugar al ajedrez
g. coser
h. hacer un *picnic*
i. leer novelas
j. coleccionar
k. dar un paseo

Actividad B. Cómo se divierten

Paso 1

Indica si las siguientes descripciones son apropiadas (**A**) o no (**NA**) para los personajes. Al hacer esta actividad, piensa en lo que sabes de cada personaje.

A NA 1. A Raquel le gusta trabajar en el jardín.
A NA 2. A Raquel no le gusta ir ni al teatro ni al cine.
A NA 3. A Arturo le gusta sacar fotos.
A NA 4. A Arturo le gustan mucho las diversiones típicas de los parques públicos.
A NA 5. A Arturo no le interesa mucho visitar museos.
A NA 6. A Pancho, el padre de Raquel, sí le gustan los museos.
A NA 7. Pero a Pancho no le gusta jugar a las cartas con sus amigos.
A NA 8. A la madre de Raquel le gustan los juegos de salón.
A NA 9. A don Fernando le encanta leer.
A NA 10. A don Fernando también le gusta jugar al póquer.

Paso 2

Ahora escucha la cinta para verificar tus respuestas. También debes tratar de captar un detalle importante de cada comentario que vas a escuchar.

1. _____
2. _____
3. _____
4. _____
5. _____
6. _____

7. _____   9. _____

8. _____   10. _____

Actividad C.   ¿Y tú?

Explica lo que te gusta hacer en tus ratos libres.

1. Cuando tengo tiempo libre, me gusta _____ porque...

2. Pienso que es aburrido/divertido _____ porque...

3. Cuando era niño/a, pasaba mucho tiempo en/con _____ .

4. Una cosa que nunca he aprendido a hacer—¡y que me gustaría mucho aprender!—es _____ .

5. Para mí, lo mejor de vivir en esta ciudad (en el campo) es que uno puede _____ .

6. Yo no estaría contento/a si no pudiera _____ .

Nota cultural: Las diversiones en el mundo hispánico

As with sports activities, preferences in hobbies and pastimes—alone, with friends, or with family—are highly individual and are also greatly affected by social class and location. It is fair to suggest, however, that activities such as going to the movies and watching television are universally popular in the Spanish-speaking world.

Many families, like their counterparts in the United States, simply enjoy going out to the country to have a picnic or a cookout and to play sports such as soccer, volleyball, or badminton.

Two activities that are not widely practiced in the United States but that are an intimate part of Hispanic cultures throughout the world include **el paseo** and café-sitting.

- Going out for a walk with the family is a common, regular pastime for Hispanics wherever and whenever the weather permits. Especially around the midday meal and in the late afternoon, before the evening meal, the streets of many Hispanic cities are filled with people out for a walk. Sometimes errands and tasks are completed during the walk. Hispanics who come to the United States are often struck by the absence of people in the streets, especially at those times when Hispanic customs tell them that the streets should be bustling with people.

- Hispanics often combine the pleasant custom of café-sitting with the **paseo**. They have a cup of coffee (or tea, a beer, mineral water, **un jerez** . . .), chat with their companions, and watch people walk by. This is a relaxing way to run into friends and enjoy the sun on a warm day. Many individuals make it their habit to have an after-lunch cup of coffee or drink (**copa**) at a local café or bar.

• •

UN POCO DE GRAMÁTICA

Expressing *If . . . , then . . .*

Use **Si (no) hubiera** + **-do** to express *If . . . , then . . .* statements such as the following.

Si Raquel **no hubiera ido** a Buenos Aires, nunca **habría (hubiera) conocido** a Arturo.

If Raquel had not gone to Buenos Aires, she never would have met Arturo.

Si Carlos **hubiera hablado** con la familia, tal vez **no habría (hubiera) sido** necesario cerrar la oficina en Miami.

If Carlos had spoken with his family, perhaps it would not have been necessary to close the Miami office.

Note that either the **habría** or **hubiera** form can be used in the "then" part of the sentence. You will learn more about these usages in the Workbook.

Actividad.   Especulaciones

¿Estás de acuerdo con las siguientes oraciones? Explica por qué sí o por qué no.

Sí   No   1. Si Luis no hubiera regresado a Los Ángeles, Raquel no habría tenido conflictos con su madre sobre Arturo.

Sí   No   2. Si Pancho hubiera intervenido antes, Luis no habría ido a México.

Sí   No   3. Si Carlos hubiera hablado claramente con Gloria, ésta no hubiera salido a jugar la última vez.

Sí   No   4. Si Pati se hubiera quedado en México, se habría cancelado la obra.

Sí   No   5. Si Ángela no hubiera hablado de darle dinero a Jorge, Roberto no se habría opuesto a la idea de vender el apartamento.

Sí   No   6. Si don Fernando no se hubiera enfermado, no habría pedido a Raquel que investigara el caso de Rosario.

Sí   No   7. Si Arturo hubiera buscado antes a su medio hermano, toda su vida habría cambiado.

Nota cultural: El Parque de Chapultepec... y algunas notas sobre la historia de Texas

En los pueblos del mundo hispánico, casi siempre hay una plaza central donde se reúne la gente para ver a sus amigos, hablar con ellos y pasear. En las grandes ciudades de todos los países hay muchas plazas, pero también suele haber[1] una zona verde que es un parque público, por ejemplo, el famoso Parque Central en Nueva York, el Parque del Retiro en Madrid, el Rosedal en Buenos Aires. En México, está el Parque de Chapultepec.

El Parque de Chapultepec es un inmenso bosque de cipreses, con colinas[2] y espacios abiertos donde se reúne la gente—familias con sus niños, parejas de novios, esposos jóvenes y viejos—, sobre todo los fines de semana. Los domingos por la tarde hay conciertos gratis al aire libre. Toda el área del parque es una importante zona ecológica. Hay zoológicos, lagos y otros lugares de distracción. Hay también varios museos. En el Museo de Arte Moderno hay obras de los grandes pintores mexicanos del siglo XX. Y el famoso Museo de Antropología está al lado del Parque.

Se cree que el área de Chapultepec es el lugar donde se estableció por primera vez el pueblo mexicano en el valle de México. Durante muchos años las fuentes termales[3] de la zona abastecieron[4] de agua a la ciudad. Hoy día la zona se encuentra en el centro de la Ciudad de México.

En el Parque, hay también un castillo que data de la época colonial. Es ahora un museo que, con la estatua de los Niños Héroes, nos recuerda un episodio triste en la historia de México. ¿Sabes lo que es? Para contestar esa pregunta, hay que saber un poco de la historia de… Texas.

La República de Texas y lo que causó

El actual estado de Texas, antes territorio mexicano, ganó su independencia de México, tras[5] varios meses de conflicto armado, en 1836. (La famosa derrota[6] de El Álamo fue un episodio de esa guerra.) Nueve años más tarde, en 1845, Texas quedó incorporado a los Estados Unidos. Esto desencadenó[7] una guerra entre los dos países. Cuando terminó la guerra, México se vio obligado a cederles a los Estados Unidos dos quintas partes de su territorio.

Los Niños Héroes

La campaña final de esta guerra tuvo lugar en lo que es hoy el Parque de Chapultepec. En la cima de la colina de Chapulín, había un antiguo castillo que era en esa época una academia militar. Las tropas norteamericanas lo atacaron y, después de tres días de lucha, lo capturaron. Los jóvenes cadetes que lo defendían no querían entregarles[8] a las tropas la bandera[9] mexicana. Por eso uno de esos jóvenes se envolvió[10] en la bandera y se tiró de una muralla[11] del castillo. Los demás jóvenes lo siguieron, prefiriendo la muerte a ser capturados. El monumento a los Niños Héroes conmemora su valentía.[12]

[1]suele… *there usually is* [2]*hills* [3]fuentes… *hot springs* [4]*supplied* [5]*after* [6]*defeat* [7]*set off* [8]*hand over* [9]*flag* [10]se… *wrapped himself* [11]se… *threw himself off a wall* [12]*bravery*

El monumento a los Niños Héroes

Have you completed the following sections of the lesson? Check them off here.

_____ **Preparación**	_____ **Vocabulario del tema**
_____ **¿Tienes buena memoria?**	_____ **Un poco de gramática**

Now scan the words in the **Vocabulario** list to be sure that you understand the meaning of most of them. Then you will be ready to continue on with **Lección 46** in the Workbook.

· ·

Vocabulario

Diversiones y pasatiempos (Diversions and Pastimes)

al aire libre	outdoors
el tiempo libre/los ratos libres	free time
cocinar	to cook
coleccionar estampillas/monedas...	to collect stamps/coins . . .
coser	to sew
dar/hacer fiestas	to give/have parties
dar paseos, pasear	to take walks
hacer un *picnic*	to have a picnic
ir al cine/a una función de teatro	to go to the movies/to a show at the theater
ir a un parque/al campo	to go to a park/the country
jugar (ue) a las cartas/al ajedrez/ al póquer/juegos de salón	to play cards/chess/poker/parlor games
mirar la televisión	to watch television
salir con los amigos	to go out with friends
salir de la ciudad	to get out of the city
sacar fotos/vídeos	to take photos/videos
trabajar en el jardín	to work in the garden
ver una película	to see a movie
entretenerse	to entertain oneself
gozar (de)	to enjoy
llevar una vida activa	to have an active life
llevar una vida sedentaria	to have a sedentary life

Repaso: **disfrutar de, divertirse (ie, i), leer revistas/novelas, pasarlo bien con los amigos, visitar un museo/a los parientes**

Los adjetivos

enamorado/a (de)   in love (with)

47

TENGO DUDAS*

OBJETIVOS

The materials in **Lección 47** of the Textbook and the Workbook will help you better understand the video episode and take you beyond it, giving you additional information about places and characters in the series. The Textbook will also help you to develop skill in using the Spanish language. In this lesson, you will learn

- one way to express relationships between events.

Be sure to work through all parts of the lesson. When you see a cassette symbol in the margin, listen to the tape for **Lección 47**. Answers or hints for many activities are given in Appendix 1. Be sure to check your answers for each activity before going on to the next one.

*I Have Doubts

BEFORE VIEWING...

PREPARACIÓN

Actividad.

Completa el siguiente resumen del episodio previo con las palabras y frases apropiadas.

1. iban a poder curar a
   ya no había nada que hacer para
2. pasar sus últimos días con su familia
   pasarlo bien con sus nietos
3. Tampoco le caía muy bien a Pancho
   Le caía muy bien a Pancho
4. se fuera a vivir a la Argentina
   nunca más volviera a Los Ángeles

5. caerle bien a Arturo
   conocer a Arturo
6. venderlo al regresar a San Juan
   no venderlo por el momento
7. conocer a su abuelo paterno
   hablar de la venta de La Gavia

En Guadalajara, el médico le dijo a Mercedes que _____¹ don Fernando. Por eso le dieron de alta. Don Fernando sabía que regresaba a La Gavia para _____.²

Mientras tanto, Arturo pudo hablar con Pancho, el padre de Raquel. _____,³ quien le dio un consejo sobre María, la madre de Raquel. Al mismo tiempo que hablaban los dos hombres, Raquel y su madre también estaban conversando. María pudo confesarle a su hija que temía que _____.⁴ Más tarde, todos dieron un paseo juntos y María empezó a _____.⁵

Cuando Ángela y Roberto hablaron del apartamento, decidieron _____.⁶ Por la tarde, fueron a La Gavia con Arturo y Raquel para _____.⁷

 Ahora escucha la cinta para verificar tus respuestas.

Para pensar...

1. Al final del episodio previo, Ángela y Roberto entraron al cuarto de don Fernando. ¿Qué les va a decir su abuelo? Si tú fueras uno de sus nietos, ¿qué le querrías decir a don Fernando?
2. ¿Crees que los otros miembros de la familia tendrán dificultades en aceptar a Ángela y Roberto?

Para comprender un poco más

el orfanato　Cuando los padres de un niño se mueren, éste generalmente va a vivir con otros parientes. Cuando eso no es posible, mandan al niño a **un orfanato**, donde vive con otros huérfanos como él.

 AFTER VIEWING...

• •

¿TIENES BUENA MEMORIA?

Actividad A.　¿Qué pasó con Raquel?

¿Puedes poner en orden cronológico los siguientes acontecimientos en que Raquel participó en este episodio?

a. _____ Arturo le contestó que él se iría a vivir a Los Ángeles.

b. _____ Raquel le dijo a Arturo que no podía irse a vivir a la Argentina.

c. _____ Hubo un encuentro emocionante entre don Fernando, Ángela, Roberto y Arturo.

d. _____ Raquel les dejó un mensaje a sus padres para decirles que no regresaba al hotel esta noche.

e. _____ Durante el paseo, Arturo le quería hablar de algo importante.

f. _____ Les dijo que iba a quedarse en La Gavia para cenar con la familia.

g. _____ Arturo y Raquel salieron a dar un paseo.

Ahora escucha la cinta para verificar tus respuestas.

Para pensar...

Arturo le ha dicho a Raquel que está dispuesto a irse a vivir a Los Ángeles. Raquel le dice que debería pensarlo más, pero él no quiere. «Quiero actuar», le ha dicho a Raquel. ¿Crees que es una buena decisión? ¿Qué harías si tú fueras Raquel? ¿Y cómo van a reaccionar los padres de Raquel?

Actividad B. ¿Y la familia Castillo?

Completa las siguientes oraciones para describir lo que pasó con los miembros de la familia Castillo en este episodio.

1. Al llegar a La Gavia, don Fernando
    a. _____ podía pasar un poco de tiempo con Arturo y sus nietos
    b. _____ estaba tan enfermo que no podía hablar con nadie

2. Los hermanos le dijeron a Carlos que
    a. _____ el problema de la oficina de Miami ya se había solucionado
    b. _____ no podían salvar la oficina en Miami

3. Mercedes les propuso a todos que
    a. _____ convirtieran La Gavia en un orfanato
    b. _____ vendieran la hacienda lo más pronto posible

4. Carlos le confesó a Arturo
    a. _____ su sentido de culpabilidad por lo de la oficina en Miami
    b. _____ lo del problema de Gloria

5. Roberto y Ángela discutieron sobre
    a. _____ el apartamento, otra vez
    b. _____ Jorge y sus relaciones con Ángela

6. Al final del episodio, don Fernando sorprendió a todos cuando les dijo que
    a. _____ él era culpable de la muerte de Rosario
    b. _____ tenía grandes dudas sobre la identidad de Ángela y Roberto

Para pensar...

¿Por qué tendrá don Fernando dudas? ¿Qué más podrán hacer Raquel y los demás para demostrarle que Ángela y Roberto son verdaderamente sus nietos?

. . . .

UN POCO DE GRAMÁTICA

Expressing Relationships Between Events

The Spanish conjunction **para que**, meaning *in order that* (*for*), *so that*, expresses the relationship between the events in each part of a sentence. It is always followed by the subjunctive.

Para que don Fernando no **tenga** dudas, Raquel le va a decir cómo llegó a conocer a Ángela y Roberto.	*So that don Fernando doesn't have any doubts, Raquel is going to tell him how she met Ángela and Roberto.*
Raquel viajó a cuatro países y superó muchos obstáculos **para que** don Fernando **pudiera** conocer a sus nietos.	*Raquel traveled to four countries and overcame many obstacles so that don Fernando could meet his grandchildren.*

Note in the two examples that the present subjunctive is used in present-tense contexts and the past subjunctive in past-tense contexts. You will learn more about conjunctions such as **para que** in the Workbook.

Actividad.   ¿Estás de acuerdo o no?

Expresa tu opinión, indicando si estás de acuerdo (**Sí**) o no (**No**). ¿Puedes explicar tu respuesta?

Sí   No   1. Para que Raquel y Arturo sean felices en Los Ángeles, la mamá de Raquel tendrá que cambiar mucho.

Sí   No   2. Para que Arturo esté contento en los Estados Unidos, tendrá que poder ejercer su profesión.

Sí   No   3. Para que Ángela y Roberto dejen de pelearse, Ángela tendrá que romper con Jorge.

Sí   No   4. Para que los dos lleguen a conocer bien a su nueva familia, tendrán que quedarse a vivir en La Gavia.

Sí   No   5. Para que Juan y Pati no se separen, Juan tendrá que buscar ayuda sicológica para superar sus problemas.

Sí   No   6. Para que pueda abrir un orfanato, la familia Castillo debería pedirle fondos al gobierno federal de México.

Have you completed the following sections of the lesson? Check them off here.

_____ **Preparación**   _____ **Un poco de gramática**
_____ **¿Tienes buena memoria?**

Now scan the words in the **Vocabulario** list to be sure that you understand the meaning of most them. Then you will be ready to continue on with **Lección 47** in the Workbook.

Vocabulario

Los verbos
superar   to overcome, conquer

Los lugares
el orfanato   orphanage

Los conceptos
la duda   doubt

Las conjunciones
para que   in order that (for), so that

L E C C I Ó N

48

Así fue* (I)

OBJETIVOS

All of this video episode is a review. Be sure to work through all parts of the lesson. Answers or hints for many activities are given in Appendix 1. Be sure to check your answers for each activity before going on to the next one.

That's How It Happened

BEFORE VIEWING . . .

. . . .

PREPARACIÓN

No es necesario hacer nada especial antes de ver el **Episodio 48**. Todo lo que ocurre lo has visto varias veces, pues son escenas de la investigación de Raquel en España. Raquel les va a contar a don Fernando y los demás lo que le pasó en esta parte de su viaje.

   Antes de ver el episodio, piensa en todos los episodios que has visto y escuchado hasta ahora. ¿Te es más fácil ahora entender lo que dicen los personajes cuando hablan? ¿Captas más detalles ahora que antes? Es probable que entiendas mucho más ahora en comparación con lo que pudiste comprender cuando miraste los episodios por primera vez.

Para pensar...

En tu opinión, ¿quiénes son los personajes más importantes de la investigación de Raquel en España? Cuando piensas tú en el viaje de Raquel a España, ¿a quién(es) recuerdas inmediatamente? ¿Qué acontecimientos o información son de gran importancia para su investigación?

**Algunos personajes
de España**

AFTER VIEWING . . .

REPASO DE LOS EPISODIOS 3–11

Actividad A.   Lo que pasó en España

Paso 1

De los siguientes acontecimientos, ¿cuáles son los que Raquel les menciona a los demás?

1. _____ su llegada al hotel en Sevilla
2. _____ cómo fue que no encontró a la Sra. Suárez en la calle Pureza
3. _____ su visita a una iglesia en el barrio de Triana
4. _____ cómo y dónde conoció a Elena Ramírez
5. _____ su conversación con Miguel Ruiz, hijo de Teresa Suárez
6. _____ el tiempo que pasó con la familia Ruiz y su aventura con Jaime y Osito, el nuevo perro del niño, cuando se perdieron en las calles del barrio de Santa Cruz
7. _____ cómo y dónde conoció a Alfredo Sánchez, el reportero
8. _____ el interés de Alfredo en el caso de don Fernando
9. _____ cómo perdió y luego recuperó su cartera
10. _____ la confusión de Alfredo sobre la maestra de Sevilla que había ganado un premio de la lotería
11. _____ cómo y dónde conoció a Federico Ruiz y luego a la Sra. Suárez
12. _____ la conversación que tuvo con Teresa Suárez
13. _____ la cena que tuvo con Federico y Teresa Suárez en su apartamento
14. _____ cómo y dónde se despidió de la Sra. Suárez
15. _____ su visita al Museo del Prado
16. _____ su llamada a Elena Ramírez para pedirle que le consiguiera el certificado de nacimiento de Ángel Castillo

Paso 2

¿Puedes explicar por qué Raquel omitió algunos acontecimientos? En tu opinión, ¿debería haberlos incluido en la narración que le hizo a don Fernando? ¿Por qué sí o por qué no?

Actividad B.   Ahora te toca a ti (*Now it's your turn*)

Paso 1

¿Puedes contar lo que le pasó a Raquel en su viaje a España? Siguiendo este modelo, haz una breve narración. No están incluidos todos los detalles de la **Actividad A**.

Cuando Raquel llegó a Sevilla, no tardó en buscar a la Sra. Suárez. Fue a

_____, pero _____. Conoció a dos chicos en la calle. Ellos

_____. Luego llevaron a Raquel al mercado para _____.

Elena no sabía nada del caso, pero le sugirió a Raquel que sería buena idea

_____. Esa noche Raquel _____, pero Miguel tampoco sabía

nada del caso. Sin embargo, le dijo a Raquel que había hablado con su madre, quien

había dicho que _____.

A los dos días, Raquel salió para Madrid. En el tren, _____. El reportero

_____. Como no tuvo éxito, se interesó en _____. Raquel, res-

petando la confidencialidad de su cliente, _____.

En su hotel en Madrid, Raquel bajaba de su habitación cuando _____.

La invitó a su casa a cenar y por fin Raquel _____. Ésta le contó la triste

historia de _____, quien al final de la Guerra Civil _____,

pensando que don Fernando había muerto. La Sra. Suárez también le dio a Raquel

_____. Ahora Raquel podía seguir con su investigación. Se preparó para

otro viaje, esta vez a Buenos Aires.

Paso 2
Ahora compara tu narración con la del Apéndice 1. ¿Son muy similares?

Have you completed the following sections of the lesson? Check them off here.

_____ **Preparación**   _____ **Repaso de los Episodios 3–11**

You are now ready to continue on with **Lección 48** in the Workbook.

49

ASÍ FUE* (II)

OBJETIVOS

All of this video episode is a review. Be sure to work through all parts of the lesson. Answers or hints for many activities are given in Appendix 1. Be sure to check your answers for each activity before going on to the next one.

* *That's How It Happened*

BEFORE VIEWING . . .

PREPARACIÓN

En este episodio, Raquel sigue contándoles a don Fernando y los demás de su investigación. Ahora les va a decir lo que pasó cuando estaba en Buenos Aires, Argentina.

Para pensar...

Seguramente que Raquel les va a hablar de la muerte de Rosario y de cómo llegó a saber del paradero de Ángel. ¿Crees tú que también les va a hablar de sus relaciones con Arturo? Ya sabes que Ángela está al tanto de todo (*knows all about it*), pero ¿crees que los demás se han dado cuenta de los sentimientos entre Raquel y Arturo?

**Algunos personajes
de la Argentina**

AFTER VIEWING . . .

REPASO DE LOS EPISODIOS 12–18

Actividad A. ¿Quién la ayudó?

Paso 1

En la Argentina, varios personajes hicieron algo para ayudar a Raquel en su investigación. ¿Puedes encontrar el nombre de la persona que la ayudó con lo siguiente?

a. José
b. Arturo
c. Héctor

d. Cirilo
e. Mario
f. doña Flora

g. el vendedor de pescado

1. _____ Le dijo a Raquel que Rosario ya había muerto.
2. _____ Le dio a Raquel información sobre dónde podía encontrar a Rosario y su hijo en Buenos Aires.
3. _____ Conocía a Héctor y les dijo a Raquel y Arturo que era posible que Héctor conociera a Ángel.
4. _____ Les dijo dónde podían encontrar a Héctor.
5. _____ Quiso ayudar a Raquel en su búsqueda.
6. _____ Reconoció al joven de la foto, Ángel a los veinte años.
7. _____ Tenía una carta con la dirección de Ángel en Puerto Rico.
8. _____ Pensó en José y habló con su esposa, doña Flora, para averiguar dónde podían encontrar a José esa tarde.

Paso 2

Mira otra vez las fotos en **Preparación**. No todos los personajes que ves allí figuran en el **Paso 1**. ¿Los mencionó Raquel en su narración?

Paso 3

Lee otra vez la sección **Para pensar…** en **Preparación**. ¿Tenías razón al contestar las preguntas? ¿Habló Raquel de sus relaciones con Arturo? ¿Por qué no?

Actividad B. Ahora te toca a ti (*Now it's your turn*)

Paso 1

¿Puedes tú contar lo que le pasó a Raquel en su viaje a la Argentina? Siguiendo este modelo, haz una breve narración. No están incluidos todos los detalles de la **Actividad A**.

Cuando Raquel llegó a Buenos Aires, alquiló un coche con un chofer para ir a la estancia Santa Susana, la dirección que Teresa Suárez _____. Tenía muchas esperanzas de encontrar a Rosario. Llamó a la puerta y _____.

Éste no sabía nada de Rosario, pero le dijo a Raquel que _____. Cirilo sí

_____ y _____. También se acordaba de _____.

Raquel regresó a Buenos Aires y buscó la dirección que Cirilo le había dado. Por fin,

en una casa en la calle Gorostiaga, _____. Raquel quedó muy sorprendida

al encontrar por fin a un miembro de la familia. Desgraciadamente, _____.

Arturo también le contó a Raquel que no sabía nada de Ángel porque _____.

Los dos fueron al cementerio donde estaba enterrada Rosario. Allí _____.

Más tarde Arturo le dijo _____. Con una foto de Ángel a los veinte años, los

dos _____. Preguntaron en varias tiendas, pero _____. Por fin,

Mario, el dueño de una tienda de antigüedades, dijo que era posible que un tal José lo

conociera. Encontraron a José en su barco. José _____. Más tarde les dijo

dónde y cuando podrían encontrar a Héctor.

En un bar llamado el Piccolo Navio, Raquel y Arturo encontraron a Héctor con sus

amigos. Al acompañarlo a casa, le mostraron la foto de Ángel. Héctor _____.

Pensaba que Ángel se había embarcado para _____. A los dos días Héctor

le dio a Arturo una carta de Ángel que tenía en su casa. La carta _____. Era

verdad: Ángel _____.

Ahora, para seguir su investigación, Raquel tenía que ir a Puerto Rico. Fue

_____. Se despidió de Arturo en el aeropuerto. Mientras esperaba su vuelo,

_____.

Paso 2

Ahora compara tu narración con la del Apéndice 1. ¿Son muy similares?

Have you completed the following sections of the lesson? Check them off here.

_____ **Preparación**   _____ **Repaso de los Episodios 12–18**

You are now ready to continue on with **Lección 49** in the Workbook.

50

Así fue* (III)

OBJETIVOS

All of this video episode is a review. Be sure to work through all parts of the lesson. Answers or hints for many activities are given in Appendix 1. Be sure to check your answers for each activity before going on to the next one.

That's How It Happened

BEFORE VIEWING . . .

· ·

Preparación

En este episodio, Raquel sigue contándoles a don Fernando y los demás los incidentes de su investigación. Ahora les va a decir lo que pasó cuando fue a Puerto Rico.

Para pensar...

Ya tienes una idea, más o menos, del tipo de información que Raquel está incluyendo en su narración para la familia Castillo. Piensa en lo que sucedió en Puerto Rico. ¿Qué incidentes o detalles crees que Raquel incluirá y qué omitirá en la narración de este episodio? ¿Qué omitirías tú y qué incluirías?

Algunos personajes de Puerto Rico

 **AFTER VIEWING . . .**

• •

REPASO DE LOS EPISODIOS 19 – 26

Actividad A.　¿Qué pasó en Puerto Rico?

Paso 1

Contesta las siguientes preguntas sobre los acontecimientos en Puerto Rico.

1.　¿Cómo se enteró Raquel de la muerte de Ángel? ¿Se lo dijo alguien o encontró la tumba por casualidad (*by chance*) mientras visitaba el cementerio?

2.　¿Cuándo supo Raquel que Ángela tenía un hermano? ¿cuando hablaban en el apartamento de Ángela, antes de la llegada de los tíos, o cuando los tíos hablaban con ella?

3.　¿Sabían los tíos algo del pasado de Ángel? ¿O fue la primera vez que oían los nombres de Rosario y don Fernando?

4.　Los tíos pensaron que era importante que Ángela hablara con alguien. ¿Con quién? ¿Con la abuela de Ángela o con su hermano?

5.　Camino a San Germán, Ángela, Raquel y Laura tuvieron problemas con el carro. ¿Pudieron llegar a San Germán esa noche o tuvieron que quedarse en Ponce?

6.　En casa de la abuela, ésta le recordó a Ángela que había algo relacionado con su padre que Ángela no había hecho. ¿A qué se refería la abuela, a limpiar el cuarto de Ángel o a leer su testamento (*will*)?

7.　¿Qué encontraron Ángela y Raquel entre las cosas de Ángel, unas fotos de su familia en Buenos Aires o unos dibujos que él había hecho con recuerdos de su pasado?

8.　¿Qué pasó justo cuando Raquel y Ángela salían para el aeropuerto? ¿Se pelearon o recibieron noticias importantes?

Paso 2

¿Qué partes de lo que le pasó en Puerto Rico omitió Raquel en su narración? Haz una lista de los personajes y situaciones omitidos.

Para pensar...

¿Notaste que Raquel no mencionó nada de Jorge, el novio de Ángela? ¿Por qué todavía no le ha dicho nada de lo que le pasó con Jorge en San Juan?

Actividad B. Ahora te toca a ti (*Now it's your turn*)

Paso 1

¿Puedes tú contar lo que le pasó a Raquel en su viaje a Puerto Rico? Siguiendo este modelo, haz una breve narración. No están incluidos todos los detalles de la **Actividad A.**

Cuando llegó a San Juan, Raquel fue directamente a la dirección que estaba en la carta de Héctor. Tocó a la puerta, pero _____. Desde su balcón, una vecina le dijo que _____. En el cementerio Raquel _____. Allí en el cementerio, Raquel se lo explicó todo.

Raquel y Ángela regresaron al apartamento donde vivía ella, que era el antiguo apartamento de sus padres. Desde allí Ángela _____ para que vinieran a conocer a Raquel. Mientras los esperaban, seguían hablando. Raquel supo que _____.

Cuando llegaron los tíos de Ángela, Raquel les contó la historia de don Fernando y les habló de su investigación. También les dijo que Ángela _____. La tía Olga, la gruñona de la familia, _____. Por eso Ángela llamó a _____ para pedirle consejo. Ésta quería que Ángela y Raquel fueran a verla a San Germán.

Al día siguiente Raquel y Ángela, acompañadas por Laura, la prima de Ángela, salieron para San Germán. En un peaje tuvieron _____. Se quedaron por la noche en Ponce y a la mañana siguiente _____.

En San Germán, almorzaron con la abuela y hablaron de Ángel y su esposa. La abuela le recordó a Ángela que _____. Allí, en un viejo baúl, Ángela _____. Eran _____. Al salir para San Juan, la abuela salió corriendo de la casa y _____.

De regreso en San Juan, Raquel y Ángela pasaron por el banco donde trabajaba Ángela para _____. También vieron unos apartamentos con una agente de bienes raíces, porque Ángela _____. Al día siguiente, cuando salían para el aeropuerto, llegó el tío Jaime con malas noticias: _____.

Paso 2

Ahora compara tu narración con la del Apéndice 1. ¿Son muy similares?

Have you completed the following sections of the lesson? Check them off here.

_____ **Preparación**　　　　　　　　　　_____ **Repaso de los Episodios 19–26**

You are now ready to continue on with **Lección 50** in the Workbook.

51

ASÍ FUE* (IV)

OBJETIVOS

All of this video episode is a review. Be sure to work through all parts of the lesson. Answers or hints for many activities are given in Appendix 1. Be sure to check your answers for each activity before going on to the next one.

*That's How It Happened

BEFORE VIEWING . . .

PREPARACIÓN

En este episodio Raquel concluye la narración de los incidentes de su investigación. Va a contarle a don Fernando lo que le ha pasado hasta ahora en México. ¿Hasta qué punto llega la narración de Raquel? ¿Cuáles son los acontecimientos más importantes para el caso?

Algunos personajes de México

AFTER VIEWING . . .

REPASO DE LOS EPISODIOS 27–36

Actividad A.   En el sitio de la excavación

Paso 1

Pon en orden cronológico (del 1 al 10) los siguientes sucesos.

a. _____ Se derrumbó todo otra vez.

b. _____ Por fin Raquel pudo dejarle un mensaje a Arturo en el hotel.

c. _____ Fueron al hospital para ver si Roberto era uno de los accidentados.

d. _____ Ángela se puso histérica y el médico le dio un calmante.

e. _____ Raquel y Ángela llegaron por primera vez al sitio de la excavación.

f. _____ Sacaron a varias personas de la excavación, pero ninguna era Roberto.

g. _____ Raquel y Ángela se fueron a la capital y en el camino por poco chocan con un camión blanco.

h. _____ Rescataron a Roberto y lo llevaron a México.

i. _____ Allí conocieron a un padre, quien les ayudó mucho durante su estancia en el pueblo.

j. _____ Conocieron a la hermana María Teresa, quien les dio donde descansar y refrescarse.

Paso 2

Imagina que eres don Fernando y que Raquel acaba de resumirte su investigación. ¿Estás satisfecho ahora con lo que ella ha dicho? ¿Todavía tienes dudas?

Actividad B.   Ahora te toca a ti (*Now it's your turn*)

Paso 1

¿Puedes tú contar lo que le pasó a Raquel en el sitio de la excavación? Siguiendo este modelo, haz una breve narración. No están incluidos todos los detalles de la **Actividad A**.

Tan pronto como llegaron a México, Raquel y Ángela alquilaron un auto y salieron para un pueblo cerca de la excavación donde trabajaba Roberto. En el camino, Ángela le habló a Raquel de _____ y le confesó que _____ .

Al llegar al sitio, no las dejaron pasar. Entonces _____ . Allí les dieron la lista de los accidentados. Por un momento, _____ .

En el hospital conocieron a un padre que las ayudó mucho a lo largo de su estancia en el pueblo. Por medio del padre, Ángela y Raquel pudieron _____. Tenían muchas esperanzas de que rescataran a Roberto pronto. Por fin sacaron a dos personas, pero _____. Antes de que pudieran sacar a otras personas, _____. Ángela comenzó a llorar y le tuvieron que dar un calmante. Por fin se pudo dormir, y Raquel _____.

Por la mañana, mientras seguían esperando el rescate de Roberto, Raquel y Ángela hicieron varias llamadas. Raquel _____. Y Ángela _____. Después fueron a la iglesia del pueblo, donde _____.

Por fin encontraron a Roberto... ¡y _____! Antes de que pudieran rescatarlo, sin embargo, _____. Pero lo pudieron sacar de todas formas. Lo examinaron en seguida; por suerte _____. Sin embargo _____. Raquel y Ángela salieron para México en su auto, y en el camino _____. Al llegar al hospital, Ángela entró al cuarto de Roberto corriendo. Arturo, quien estaba allí con Pedro, vio a Raquel y _____.

Paso 2
Ahora compara tu narración con la del Apéndice 1. ¿Son muy similares?

Have you completed the following sections of the lesson? Check them off here.

_____ **Preparación**   _____ **Repaso de los Episodios 27–36**

You are now ready to continue on with **Lección 51** in the Workbook.

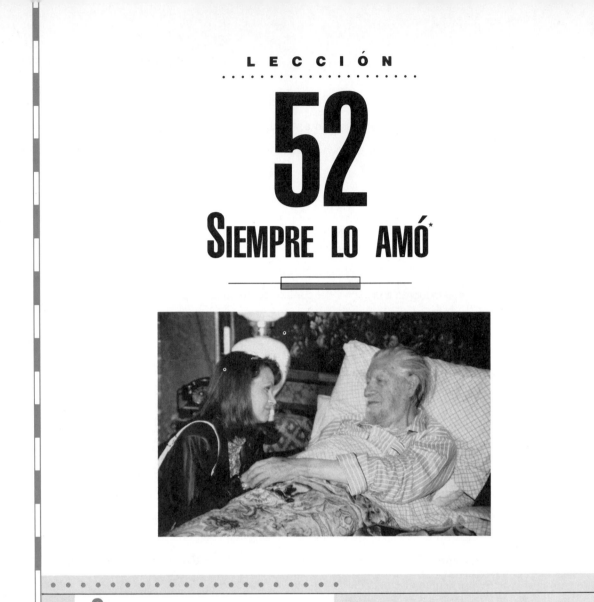

L E C C I Ó N
. . . .

52

SIEMPRE LO AMÓ*

OBJETIVOS

The materials in **Lección 52** of the Textbook will help you better understand the video episode. There is no corresponding Workbook lesson for this episode.

Be sure to work through all parts of the lesson. When you see a cassette symbol in the margin, listen to the tape for **Lección 52**. Answers or hints for many activities are given in Appendix 1. Be sure to check your answers for each activity before going on to the next one.

She Always Loved You

BEFORE VIEWING . . .

. . . .

PREPARACIÓN

Actividad.

En los **Episodios 48–51** de *Destinos*, has escuchado la narración de Raquel para don Fernando y no hubo información nueva. En este episodio la historia sigue. ¿Te acuerdas de lo que pasó en el **Episodio 47**? Completa las siguientes oraciones.

1. Ángela y Roberto por fin conocieron
   a. _____ al médico de don Fernando
   b. _____ a don Fernando

2. Raquel decidió quedarse en La Gavia esa noche porque
   a. _____ había una gran cena y todos querían que se quedara
   b. _____ no quería ver a sus padres

3. Mientras Arturo y Raquel daban un paseo en la hacienda, Arturo le pidió a Raquel que
   a. _____ se fuera a vivir a Buenos Aires con él
   b. _____ hablara con la madre de ella sobre él

4. Al oír la respuesta negativa de Raquel, Arturo le dijo que
   a. _____ él se iría a vivir a Los Ángeles
   b. _____ entendía por qué ella no quería hablar con su madre

5. Durante la cena, todos se sorprendieron cuando don Fernando se presentó y dijo que
   a. _____ tenía dudas sobre la identidad de Ángel y Arturo
   b. _____ tenía dudas sobre la identidad de Ángela y Roberto

 Ahora escucha la cinta para verificar tus respuestas.

Para pensar...

Don Fernando los sorprendió a todos cuando les dijo que tenía grandes dudas. ¿Qué otra(s) prueba(s) quiere? ¿Qué pueden hacer o decir Ángela y Roberto para que él esté seguro de su identidad?

AFTER VIEWING . . .

¿Tienes buena memoria?

Actividad.   En el episodio final

Paso 1

¿Puedes tú contar lo que pasó en el episodio final? Siguiendo este modelo, haz una breve narración.

Don Fernando tenía dudas de la identidad de Ángela y Roberto, y quería estar seguro de que eran sus nietos. Raquel le recordó a Ángela lo de la copa de bodas de Rosario, que _____ .

Al día siguiente, llegó la agente de bienes raíces. El deseo de su cliente de comprar La Gavia no fue realizado, porque _____ . Entonces Mercedes reveló su plan para fundar un orfanato en la hacienda. Todos quedaron sorprendidos cuando don Fernando reveló que _____ . Según don Fernando, Carlos y Mercedes _____ . Juan debería regresar a Nueva York, porque _____ .

Más tarde, en el cuarto de don Fernando, cuando todos estaban presentes, Ángela _____ . Cuando don Fernando la abrió, se puso muy emocionado. Entonces le pidió a Mercedes que le diera a Ángela una caja que él tenía allí en su cuarto, en un armario. Cuando Ángela la abrió, _____ . Así ya no había dudas: _____ .

Raquel y Arturo se despidieron de don Fernando y estaban para salir. Pero el patriarca quería hablar con Raquel a solas. Le dijo que no se le había escapado cómo _____ . Raquel le confesó que _____ . Entonces don Fernando le dio unos consejos: o ella _____ o él _____ , que no debían perder un amor verdadero. Se abrazaron una vez más.

Antes de salir, Raquel se volvió y le dijo a don Fernando que Rosario nunca dejó de pensar en él, que _____ . Con las dos copas reunidas, don Fernando se quedó en su cuarto a solas, pensando en el día en que, hace años, en un país lejano, dos jóvenes españoles las habían usado para celebrar el día de su boda.

quedó en su cuarto a solas, pensando en el día en que, hace años, en un país lejano,

dos jóvenes españoles las habían usado para celebrar el día de su boda.

Paso 2
Ahora compara tu narración con la del Apéndice 1. ¿Son muy similares?

• •

CINCO AÑOS DESPUÉS

Imagina que han pasado cinco años desde ese día en que Raquel se despidió de don Fernando. ¿Qué ha pasado? ¿En qué situación o condición están los varios personajes? ¿Qué ha pasado entre Arturo y Raquel, Juan y Pati, Carlos y Gloria y los demás? ¿Qué le ha pasado a don Fernando? ¿Y La Gavia? ¿Todavía pertenece a la familia Castillo? ¿Quién(es) vive(n) allí ahora?

Escribe una breve composición (100–200 palabras) con este título: «*Destinos*: Cinco años después».

APPENDIX 1: ANSWER SECTION

Note: In many of the **Preparación** sections, "prediction" activities encourage you to guess at the content of upcoming video episodes. The answers to these types of activities will be found not with the answers to other **Preparación** activities but at the end of the answers to the **¿Tienes buena memoria?** sections. This has been done to discourage you from checking your answers before you watch the video episode.

You should always go back and look at your answers to those activities *after* you have watched the video episode. If you are still unsure of an answer, that is the time to check it at the end of the **¿Tienes buena memoria?** section.

LECCIÓN 1

¿TIENES BUENA MEMORIA?

Actividad A. 1. c 2. b 3. a **Actividad B.** 1. No. Juan es profesor de literatura. La profesión de don Fernando no se sabe todavía (*is not known yet*). 2. Sí. 3. Sí. 4. Sí. 5. Sí. **Actividad C.** 1. b. El nombre completo de Raquel es Raquel Rodríguez. 2. b. Raquel es mexicoamericana. 3. a. Raquel vive en Los Ángeles.

Preparación. **Actividad A.** 3 **Actividad B.** 2 **Actividad C.** 1

VOCABULARIO DEL TEMA

Actividad. 1. b. Es un concepto. 2. d. Es una persona. 3. d. Es una persona. 4. d. Es una persona. 5. d. Es una persona. 6. c. Es una cosa. 7. b. Es un concepto.

UN POCO DE GRAMÁTICA

Actividad. *Possible answers:* 1. Raquel es de los Estados Unidos, es abogada, es mexicoamericana. 2. Don Fernando es de España, es el patriarca de la familia, es paciente de Julio (el doctor). 3. La Gavia es un lugar importante, es un lugar histórico, es una hacienda en México. 4. Raquel y Mercedes son mujeres hispanas, son personas importantes en la historia. 5. Juan y Ramón son hombres mexicanos, son de México, son hijos de don Fernando, son personas importantes en la historia.

LECCIÓN 2

PREPARACIÓN

Actividad A. 1. de España 2. El secreto tiene que ver con la vida privada de don Fernando. **Actividad B.** Ramón va a llamar a otras personas de la familia.

¿TIENES BUENA MEMORIA?

Actividad A. 1. e 2. f 3. g 4. a 5. c 6. d 7. b; 1. b 2. c 3. h 4. d 5. e 6. a 7. f 8. g **Actividad B.** 1. Carlos vive en Miami. Es director de la Compañía Castillo Saavedra, S.A. 2. Ramón vive en La Gavia. Es administrador de la hacienda. 3. Mercedes vive en La Gavia. Es administradora de la hacienda. 4. Juan vive en Nueva York. Es profesor de literatura en la universidad. 5. Pedro vive en la Ciudad de México. Es profesor de derecho en la universidad. 6. Raquel vive en Los Ángeles. Es abogada de derecho internacional. **Actividad C.** Don Fernando tiene otra esposa. Don Fernando tiene otro hijo.

Preparación. **Actividad C.** b. Ramón desea que Carlos venga a la hacienda.

VOCABULARIO DEL TEMA

Actividad B. Pedro y Fernando son **hermanos**. Pedro es el **tío** de Ramón, Carlos, Juan y Mercedes. Fernando y Carmen son **esposos**. Ramón, Carlos, Juan y Mercedes son **hermanos**. Fernando y Carmen son los **padres**. Ramón, Carlos, Juan y Mercedes son los **hijos**.

UN POCO DE GRAMÁTICA

Actividad. *If you answered with the names only of the people described, that is fine. But you should read the full sentences anyway when you check your answers for this activity.* 1. Sus hijos fueron Jack (John F.) Kennedy y Bobby (Robert) Kennedy. 2. Su padre fue Pablo Picasso. 3. Su madre fue Eva (*Eve*) (y su padre fue Adán [*Adam*]). 4. Su tío es Edward (Ted) Kennedy. 5. Su esposa fue Eleanor Roosevelt. 6. Su hermana fue Gretel. 7. Su hermano es Michael Jackson. 8. Su hermano es Peter Fonda. Su padre fue Henry Fonda. 9. Su esposo fue Ulises (*Ulysses*). 10. Su hermano fue Remo (*Remus*). 11. Su hija fue la reina Isabel (*Elizabeth*). 12. Su quinto esposo fue Richard Burton. 13. Sus hijos son Emilio Estevez y Charlie Sheen. 14. Su hermano es Warren Beatty. 15. Sus cuatro hijos son el Príncipe Charles, la Princesa Anne, el Príncipe Andrew y el Príncipe Edward. 16. Su hija fue Lizzie Borden. 17. Su madre fue Ingrid Bergman.

LECCIÓN 3

PREPARACIÓN

Actividad A.   1. Falso. Raquel no es miembro de la familia Castillo.   2 Cierto.   3. Cierto.   4. Cierto.   5. Cierto. Es lógico, ya que (*since*) la carta es de España.

¿TIENES BUENA MEMORIA?

Actividad A.   *Photos:* 1. c   2. b   3. d   *Statements:* 1. e   2. d   3. d, e   4. d, e   5. a   6. c   7. b   8. e   **Actividad B.**   1. T   2. E   3. T   4. E   5. T   **Actividad C.**   1. c   2. b   3. a   4. b

Preparación.   **Actividad B.**   1. España. This is the best answer based on what you know now. But don't rule out the possibility of other destinations in a series called *Destinos.*   2. Rosario, la primera esposa de don Fernando; la persona que escribió la carta; otro hijo de don Fernando. Three of the answers are possible. Raquel needs to find the letter writer in order to find out whether Rosario is alive and whether don Fernando has another child.   3. el nombre de la persona que escribió la carta; el nombre de la calle donde la persona vive. It is logical for Raquel to know this, because don Fernando has a letter from this person. The possible existence of a child is the mystery, thus no name is known.

Actividad C.   1. b   2. a, c

VOCABULARIO DEL TEMA

Actividad B.   1. Hay 10 turistas en el grupo.   2. Juan tiene el número 9.   3. Raquel busca el número 21.

CONVERSACIONES

Actividad.   *Paso 1*   1. b   2. a, c   *Paso 2*   3. a, c, d

UN POCO DE GRAMÁTICA

Actividad.   1. b   2. a   3. b   4. c

NOTA CULTURAL

Actividad.   1. Falso. España es un país de contrastes.   2. Cierto.   3. Falso. Otros idiomas que se hablan son el catalán, el gallego y el vascuence.   4. Cierto.   5. Falso. España es una monarquía constitucional.

LECCIÓN 4

PREPARACIÓN

Actividad A.   1. Sevilla   2. Teresa Suárez   3. Teresa Suárez   4. dos chicos   5. Madrid   6. Elena Ramírez   7. la madre   8. no tiene

¿TIENES BUENA MEMORIA?

Actividad A.   *Por la noche:* a. 1   b. 3   c. 2   *Al día siguiente:* a. 3   b. 2   c. 4   d. 1   **Actividad B.**   *Photos:* 1. d   2. b   3. c   4. a   1. Cierto.   2. Falso. Miguel no sabe nada.   3. Cierto.   4. Falso. Los chicos no toman un fino.   5. Cierto. Acepta la responsabilidad, pero... ¿realmente cumple con ella (*does he live up to it*)?   6. Cierto.   7. Cierto.   8. Cierto. Por eso (*That's why*) desea ponerle *Einstein* al perro.   9. Falso. Miguel es buen estudiante.

Preparación.   **Actividad B.**   1. b   2. a   **Actividad C.**   1. a, c   2. c

VOCABULARIO DEL TEMA

Actividad A.   1. los dos   2. Jaime   3. los dos   4. Miguel   5. Jaime   *Otras materias: business* = el comercio; *foreign languages* = las lenguas extranjeras; *accounting* = la contabilidad; *chemistry* = la química   **Actividad D.**   *Paso 2*   1. Celia   2. Raúl   3. Anita   4. Celia   **Actividad G.**   *Fish:* (peces) tropicales   *Birds:* canarios, loros (*parrots*), patitos (*ducklings*)

CONVERSACIONES

Actividad   **PASO 1**   1. éstos son...   2. éste es...   3. éstas son...   4. ésta es...   **PASO 2**   3. hijas   1. hijos   2. esposo   4. hermana

NOTA CULTURAL

1. Cierto.   2. Falso. En Sevilla, hay tradiciones judías, árabes y cristianas.   3. Cierto.   4. Cierto.   5. Falso. Hay barrios modernos, pero no son tan (*as*) interesantes como las otras partes de la ciudad, según (*according to*) algunas personas.

LECCIÓN 5

PREPARACIÓN

Actividad A.   *Paso 2*   1. No saben nada   2. por teléfono   3. con otro hijo   4. compra un perro   5. se pierde en   **Actividad C.**   1. c   2. b

¿TIENES BUENA MEMORIA?

Actividad A.   1. Jaime, Raquel   2. Jaime, Raquel   3. el ciego, Jaime   4. Raquel, Jaime   5. el ciego   6. Raquel   7. el ciego   8. Raquel   9. Jaime, Raquel. ¡OJO! Neither one is actually "lost," but they are not with each other, and the rest of the family

doesn't know where they are either!   10. Raquel   **Actividad B.**   a. 5   b. 1   c. 4   d. 2   e. 3   f. 7   g. 6   **Actividad C.**   1. d. A las once y media. Pero no todos llegan a las once y media.   2. c. A la una. Cierran (*They close*) el Alcázar a la una menos cuarto (12:45).   3. d. A las once y media. Llegan a la estación a las once y cinco.
Preparación.   **Actividad B.**   1. Jaime encuentra a su perro.   2. Jaime se pierde también en el Barrio de Santa Cruz. 3. Raquel decide quedarse en Sevilla otro día.

VOCABULARIO DEL TEMA

LOS DÍAS DE LA SEMANA   Actividad A.   1. el domingo   2. el viernes   3. el jueves   4. el sábado   5. el martes   6. el miércoles   7. el lunes

Actividad B.   el lunes: en casa de su abuela (visita a su abuela)   el martes: en casa (estudia mucho)   el miércoles: con su padre (trabaja, acompaña a su padre)   el jueves: en el mercado (camina con su madre)   el viernes: en casa de un amigo (cena)   el sábado: en casa con su madre ayuda [*he helps out*])   el domingo: en la iglesia (con la familia)   **¿QUÉ HORA ES?**
Actividad D.   1. las once y media   2. las ocho de la mañana, la una, las cuatro de la tarde, las ocho, las ocho y media de la tarde   3. las tres, las tres y cuarto, las cuatro, las cuatro y cuarto   **Actividad F.**   1. d. a las doce.   2. f. a las siete y media   3. a. a las ocho y cinco   4. e. hasta las siete y veinte   5. b. a las nueve   6. g. a las ocho y veinte   7. c. a las once y cuarto   8. h. a las nueve y diez

CONVERSACIONES
Actividad.   *Paso 1*   3. Hasta luego.   3. Adiós.   2. Hasta mañana.   *Paso 2*   Hasta mañana.   Adiós.   Hasta luego.

UN POCO DE GRAMÁTICA
Actividad.   1. b   2. a   3. a   4. c   5. b   6. c

NOTA CULTURAL
1. Cierto.   2. Cierto.   3. Cierto.   4. Cierto.   *Photos:*   2, 3, 1   **Actividad.**   1. los árabes   2. los judíos   3. los cristianos

LECCIÓN 6
PREPARACIÓN
Actividad A.   1. a   2. a   3. b

¿TIENES BUENA MEMORIA?
Actividad A.   1. Alfredo Sánchez   2. la ganadora de un premio, una maestra de primaria   3. no encuentra   4. rechaza 5. desea investigar más   **Actividad B.**   En el compartimiento de Raquel...   a. 3   b. 2   c. 1   d. 4   Luego...   a. 3   b. 4   c. 2 d. 1   En la estación del tren...   a. 3   b. 2   c. 1   d. 4
Preparación.   **Actividad B.**   1. Es un reportero.   2. Desea entrevistar a Raquel.   **Actividad C.**   1. b   2. b   3. a

REPASO DE LOS EPISODIOS 1–6
Actividad.   1. don Fernando   2. Rosario   3. hermano   4. España   5. Sevilla   6. Teresa Suárez   7. vive   8. esposo   9. hijo 10. saben   11. compra   12. Jaime   13. encuentra   14. vende   15. toma   16. nada

LECCIÓN 7
PREPARACIÓN
Actividad A.   *Fotos:* 1. b   2. a   1. Cierto.   2. Falso. Raquel le dice al reportero que investiga un caso para un cliente mexicano. 3. Falso. El reportero se llama Alfredo Sánchez.   4. Falso. El reportero tiene mucho interés en el caso.   **Actividad C.**   3

¿TIENES BUENA MEMORIA?
Actividad A.   1. b   2. a   3. d;   1. d   2. b   3. a, b   4. a, e   5. c, d   6. d   **Actividad C.**   *Hint:* If you have trouble doing this activity, reread the **Nota cultural** in *Lección 5.* It will give you an overview of the history of Spain. Then try to do the activity again, keeping in mind that the monarchs are listed *in chronological order.*   1. b   2. c   3. d   4. b, c   5. a
Preparación.   **Actividad B.**   *Note:* Now that you have seen the episode, you will know whether the events happened. For this reason, answers are given here as **Cierto** (C) or **Falso** (F).   1. F   2. C   3. F   4. F

VOCABULARIO DEL TEMA
Actividad A.   You should have indicated the following items of clothing: 2 blouses, 2 sweaters, 1 skirt, 1 dress, 2 pairs of shoes, a few pairs of stockings (number not specified), 1 pair of pants.   Raquel decide que *no* tiene suficiente ropa.   **Actividad B.** You should have indicated the following items of clothing: shirt, T-shirt, socks, tie, jacket, pants, scarf, sweater. La Sra. Suárez *no* está muy contenta con su hijo.   **Actividad C.**   Raquel lleva pantalones, una chaqueta, zapatos, medias...   Alfredo lleva pantalones, una chaqueta, una corbata, una camisa...   **Actividad E.**   1. 73   2. 81   3. 36   4. 45   **Actividad F.**   1. 3-45-33-60 2. 5-99-24-68   3. 7-36-64-85   4. 3-75-53-91   5. 5-59-25-44   6. 7-15-49-42   **Actividad G.**   1. 1910, a   2. de 1936 hasta 1939, d   3. 1991, e   4. de 1951 hasta 1953, c   5. 1945, b

CONVERSACIONES
Actividad.   PASO 1 3. ¿podría... ?   4. quisiera...   1. ¿me permite... ?   2. me gustaría...   **PASO 2** 1. c   2. a   3. b   4. a

UN POCO DE GRAMÁTICA
Actividad. 1. Cierto.   2. Falso. Don Fernando sólo tiene una carta de ella.   3. Falso. Teresa Suárez es su suegra (*mother-in-law*), la abuela de sus hijos.   4. Cierto.   5. Cierto.   6. Falso. No saben nada de él.   7. Falso. Raquel conoce al Sr. Díaz en el tren. Viajan en el mismo (*same*) compartimiento.   8. Cierto.   9. Falso. Éste es su primer viaje a España.   10. Cierto.

NOTA CULTURAL
Actividad. 1. d   2. b   3. e   4. c   5. g   6. a   7. f

LECCIÓN 8

PREPARACIÓN
Actividad A. a. Raquel Rodríguez (con el recepcionista)   d. Alfredo Sánchez (con Raquel)   c. el recepcionista (con el Sr. Díaz)   d. Alfredo Sánchez (con Raquel)   a. Raquel Rodríguez (con Alfredo)   f. Federico Ruiz (con Raquel)

¿TIENES BUENA MEMORIA?
Actividad A. 1. a   2. a, b   3. b   4. a   5. b. Teresa. Y ahora, Raquel tiene una carta para Rosario.   6. a, b, c   7. a   8. c   9. a   10. a   **Actividad B.** 1. a, c, d, e   2. f   3. b   4. b, g   **Actividad C.** *Paso 1* 1, 4, 6   *Paso 3* 1. no murió   2. un hijo   3. la Argentina   4. se casó
Preparación. **Actividad B.** 1. Improbable. Raquel desea saber información acerca de Rosario, no acerca de la Sra. Suárez.   2. Probable.   3. Improbable. Raquel no sabe nada de su esposo.   4. Probable. Pero Raquel no hace esta pregunta.   5. Probable.

Actividad C. *Paso 2* c   *Paso 4* b

CONVERSACIONES
Actividad.   PASO 1 De nada. 2   No hay de qué. 1, 3   **PASO 2** por

NOTA CULTURAL
Actividad. 1. Cataluña, el País Vasco   2. Castilla-León   3. Segovia (Castilla-León)   4. Extremadura   5. las islas Canarias, Andalucía   6. Andalucía, Asturias   7. el País Vasco   8. Andalucía, Extremadura

LECCIÓN 9

PREPARACIÓN
Actividad A. 1. a. Cierto.   b. Falso. Rosario sí tuvo un hijo.   c. Cierto.   d. Falso. Sí se casó de nuevo, con un hacendado argentino llamado Martín Iglesias.   e. No se sabe todavía.   2. a. Cierto.   b. Falso. Raquel ya sabe la dirección de Rosario.   c. Cierto.   d. Falso. Raquel no tiene la cartera todavía; el reportero tiene la cartera.   e. Falso. Raquel recibe un TELEX.

¿TIENES BUENA MEMORIA?
Actividad A. 1. b   2. e   3. b, d   4. b, e   5. c   6. b   7. b, e   8. b   **Actividad B.** 1. Cierto.   2. Falso. Está mal pero todavía vive.   3. Cierto.   4. Cierto.   5. Cierto.   6. Falso. Quiere saber toda la historia.   7. Falso. La agente tiene la reservación.   8. Cierto.
Preparación. **Actividad B.** La respuesta correcta es *1*.

VOCABULARIO DEL TEMA
Actividad B. 1. julio   2. octubre   3. noviembre   4. enero   5. junio   6. mayo   7. febrero   8. marzo   9. septiembre   10. diciembre   **Actividad C.** 1. el verano, el invierno (las vacaciones de Navidad), la primavera   2. la primavera, el otoño   3. la primavera   4. el invierno   5. el verano   6. la primavera   **Actividad D.** 1. el blanco, el gris...   2. el amarillo, el azul...   3. el rosado, el rojo, el verde...   4. el amarillo, el anaranjado, el rojo...   5. el anaranjado, el amarillo...   6. el negro   7. el blanco (el vestido de Rosario)   8. el negro   9. el rojo, el rosado   10. el verde

CONVERSACIONES
Actividad.   PASO 1 Sí. 1   Vale. 2   Sí, vale. 1   De acuerdo. 2   Claro. 3   **PASO 2** It helps speakers make a transition to a new topic.

UN POCO DE GRAMÁTICA
Actividad. 1. c ¡OJO! Manuel Díaz también está en el restaurante, pero no se sienta a hablar con Alfredo.   2. a   3. b   4. e   5. a, c   6. d   7. c   8. e

NOTA CULTURAL
1. Falso. Hay música de todos tipos en España.   2. Falso. Al contrario, les gusta mucho la música importada.   3. Cierto.   4. Cierto. Es la zarzuela.   5. Falso. Es el *rock*.

LECCIÓN 10

PREPARACIÓN
Actividad A. 1. Cierto. 2. Falso. El reportero le da a Raquel la cartera perdida. 3. Falso. Necesita comprar ropa porque es primavera en la Argentina. 4. Falso. Pero ahora el reportero puede hablar con «la maestra», el Sr. Díaz, sobre el premio de la lotería. 5. Falso. Raquel no sabe nada de esto todavía.

¿TIENES BUENA MEMORIA?
Actividad B. 1. en taxi 2. a las cinco 3. Goya 4. a su mamá y papá
Preparación. **Actividad B.** 1. sí 2. sí 3. sí 4. un museo (Pero no puedes saber eso sólo por el título. Todos los lugares son posibles.) **Actividad C.** 1. su vida personal 2. su trabajo 3. un novio **Actividad D.** You should have indicated the following words: **alto; delgado; con barba; del pelo corto, no largo; ojos expresivos**

VOCABULARIO DEL TEMA
Actividad A. Many answers are possible. Here is one answer for each item. 1. San Francisco tiene barba. 2. La princesa tiene pelo rubio. 3. El pintor es delgado. 4. Las Meninas son bajas. 5. San Andrés es alto. 6. San Andrés tiene pelo blanco. 7. San Andrés es viejo. 8. San Francisco tiene ojos expresivos. 9. La princesa es bonita. 10. La enana (*dwarf*) tiene pelo largo. **Actividad B.** a. 4 b. 6 c. 5 d. 1 e. 8 f. 2 g. 3 h. 7

UN POCO DE GRAMÁTICA
Actividad. 1. F, M 2. F 3. F 4. M 5. M 6. M 7. F, M. Federico y María cenan con Raquel en Madrid. Y Raquel también cena con la familia Ruiz en Sevilla. 8. M

LECCIÓN 11

PREPARACIÓN
Actividad A. 1. Cierto. 2. Falso. Raquel sí se despide de ellos. 3. Cierto. 4. Falso. Ve las obras de El Greco, Velázquez y Goya. 5. Cierto. 6. Cierto. 7. Falso. Llama, pero nadie contesta. 8. Cierto.

¿TIENES BUENA MEMORIA?
Actividad A. a. 4 b. 2 c. 1 d. 5 e. 6 f. 3 **Actividad B.** 1. Es el Hotel Príncipe de Vergara. 2. El número de su habitación es 631 (seiscientos treinta y uno; también, seis tres uno). 3. Raquel le da una foto de Jaime y Miguel con Osito. 4. La señora le da una carta para Rosario. 5. El vuelo 897 (ocho nueve siete) sale a las nueve.
Preparación. **Actividad B.** La agencia no puede confirmar su reservación.
b. Raquel debe preguntarle al recepcionista...

REPASO DE LOS EPISODIOS 7–10
Actividad A. 1. empieza 2. conoce 3. reportero 4. busca 5. cree 6. dice 7. empieza 8. dice 9. cartera 10. salen (van) 11. encuentran 12. llegan (vuelven) 13. da 14. toman 15. puede 16. Pero 17. debe 18. cliente **Actividad B.** 1. b 2. b 3. a 4. a 5. a

LECCIÓN 12

PREPARACIÓN
Actividad A. 1. Falso. Raquel está en el avión cuando sale el vuelo. 2. Cierto. 3. Falso. Raquel no habla con él. No habla con nadie de México en el Episodio 11. 4. Cierto. 5. Cierto. ¿Recuerdas el consejo? 6. Cierto. ¿Recuerdas la dirección? 7. Es el consejo de la Sra. Suárez.

¿TIENES BUENA MEMORIA?
Actividad A. 1. a 2. c 3. c 4. a 5. c 6. b 7. a 8. b **Actividad B.** 1. Sí. 2. No. Raquel está exhausta cuando llega. No sale para la estancia hasta el día siguiente. 3. No. Un joven desconocido contesta la puerta. 4. Sí. 5. Sí. **Actividad C.** a. 6 b. 2 c. 5 d. 3 e. 4 f. 7 g. 1
Preparación. **Actividad B.** 1. b 2. c 3. a 4. c

VOCABULARIO DEL TEMA
Actividad A. You should have indicated 314, 414, 514, 614, 714, and 814. **Actividad B.** 1. 200, 400, 600 2. 500, 600, 700 3. 100, 300, 500 4. 200, 220, 240 5. 150, 200, 250 6. 511, 512, 513 **Actividad D.** 1. d. mil cuatrocientos noventa y dos 2. b. mil novecientos treinta y nueve 3. c. mil ochocientos ocho 4. a. setecientos once

CONVERSACIONES
Actividad. PASO 1 1. trabaja 2. el usted (Ud.) 3. de tú 4. trabajas

UN POCO DE GRAMÁTICA
Actividad. 1. i 2. b 3. e 4. h 5. a 6. j 7. f 8. d 9. g 10. c

LECCIÓN 13

PREPARACIÓN

Actividad A. 1. Sí ocurrió. Pero el recepcionista le da a Raquel una suite. 2. No, no ocurrió. El joven no sabe nada de Rosario. 3. Sí ocurrió. 4. Sí ocurrió. 5. No, no ocurrió. Raquel conoce a un hijo de Rosario. 6. No, no ocurrió. Arturo le cuenta que Rosario ya murió y que perdió contacto con su hermano hace años.

¿TIENES BUENA MEMORIA?

Actividad A. *Paso 1* e *Paso 2* 1. d 2. c 3. g 4. b, d 5. f 6. a *Paso 3* b **Actividad B.** 1. a 2. c 3. b 4. a 5. b

Preparación. **Actividad B.** 1. a 2. b 3. b **Actividad C.** *Paso 1* b *Paso 3* c

VOCABULARIO DEL TEMA

Actividad A. 1. prawns, crab 2. squid, rice 3. salmon 4. tuna 5. salad, oil, bread 6. butter **Actividad B.** 1. 440 2. 220 3. 460 4. 1.050 5. 3.200 ¡OJO! What do you think of the shopkeeper's math?

UN POCO DE GRAMÁTICA

Actividad. a. 5 b. 1 c. 4 d. 2 e. 8 f. 3 g. 6 h. 7

LECCIÓN 14

PREPARACIÓN

Actividad A. 1. c 2. b 3. c 4. a

¿TIENES BUENA MEMORIA?

Actividad A. *Paso 1* a. 5 b. 3 c. 1 d. 2 e. 4 f. 6 *Paso 2* 1. Cierto. 2. Cierto. 3. Cierto. 4. Falso. Su profesión es muy importante para él (pero ya no es una obsesión). **Actividad B.** 1. c 2. c 3. c

VOCABULARIO DEL TEMA

Actividad A. 1. beef, steak 2. hamburger, ham, cheese 3. bacon 4. turkey, chicken 5. kidney, pork **Actividad B.** 1. riñones (riñoncitos) 2. vaca 3. chorizos 4. Panceta 5. tocino 6. pimiento 7. tomate 8. cebolla 9. jamones 10. pollo

CONVERSACIONES

Actividad. PASO 1 1. b, d 2. a colgar = *to hang up* PASO 2 1. c 2. d 3. b 4. a

UN POCO DE GRAMÁTICA

Actividad. 1. Cierto. 2. Falso. Arturo preparó la cena. 3. Cierto. 4. Cierto. 5. Falso. Arturo y Raquel sí hablaron de sus países. 6. Cierto. 7. Cierto. 8. Falso. Raquel llamó a su madre. 9. Cierto. 10. Cierto. 11. Falso. Raquel y Arturo caminaron con él a su casa. 12. Cierto.

LECCIÓN 15

PREPARACIÓN

Actividad A. 1. b 2. b 3. a 4. c 5. b 6. b

¿TIENES BUENA MEMORIA?

Actividad A. 1. b 2. d 3. c 4. b 5. a 6. b **Actividad B.** 1. compró una bolsa de cuero 2. fue a la Cuadra 3. llamó a Arturo 4. encontró la carta 5. no le gustó mucho 6. decidieron ir a un parque 7. no le interesó mucho 8. tuvieron un *picnic* 9. recibió un regalo de Arturo **Actividad C.** 1. Florida 2. Rosedal

Preparación. **Actividad B.** *Paso 1* b *Paso 2* 1. c 2. **dime** = *tell me* 3. a

VOCABULARIO DEL TEMA

Actividad A. You should have checked the apple, the orange, the banana, and the melon. **Actividad B.** 1. frutas 2. uvas, un melón, bananas, naranjas, manzanas 3. duraznos, frutillas (fresas) 4. pan, queso y vino

CONVERSACIONES

Actividad. PASO 1 You should have indicated: **Debe ser divertido...** ; **¿Vamos?; Anda, ¡vamos!**.

UN POCO DE GRAMÁTICA

Actividad. 1. estuviste 2. dijo 3. estuvo, tuvo 4. anduvimos, anduvimos, tuvimos

LECCIÓN 16

PREPARACIÓN

Actividad A. 1. está pensativo 2. un mal presentimiento 3. ya murió 4. calmar 5. la atracción mutua 6. pasan mucho tiempo juntos 7. noticias de Héctor

¿TIENES BUENA MEMORIA?

Actividad A. 1. a 2. a 3. d 4. c 5. b 6. a **Actividad B.** a. 4 b. 7 c. 2 d. 5 e. 1 f. 6 g. 8 h. 3 **Actividad C.** 1. Falso. Es de San Juan. 2. Cierto. 3. Falso. Dice que sigue pintando. 4. Cierto. 5. Falso. No quiere volver nunca más a la Argentina.

Preparación. **Actividad B.** *Paso 1* 1. pronto 2. muy serios *Paso 2.* 1. b 2. b 3. b

VOCABULARIO DEL TEMA

Actividad A. You should have marked the onions, peas, string beans, lettuce, tomatoes, carrots, potatoes, chile peppers, and olives. **Actividad B.** *Paso 1* 1. lechuga 2. tomate 3. cebollas 4. aceitunas 5. chícharos 6. zanahoria 7. ejotes 8. ajíes *Paso 2* en la Argentina: arvejas en México: chiles

CONVERSACIONES

Actividad. PASO 1 1. Perdone. 2. Disculpe. 3. Perdone. Perdone.

UN POCO DE GRAMÁTICA

Actividad. 1. Raquel 2. Arturo 3. Raquel 4. Raquel o Héctor 5. Ángel 6. Héctor 7. Arturo o Raquel 8. Arturo

NOTA CULTURAL

1. b 2. a 3. b 4. a

LECCIÓN 17

PREPARACIÓN

Actividad A. 1. Cierto. 2. Falso. Héctor sí llama a Arturo por teléfono, pero quiere hablar con ellos en el puerto de Buenos Aires. 3. Falso. Ángel sí decidió quedarse en Puerto Rico, pero no pensaba volver a la Argentina nunca más. 4. Cierto.

¿TIENES BUENA MEMORIA?

Actividad A. *Paso 1* 1. A 2. R 3. A 4. A 5. A *Paso 2* 2. Something in between. **Actividad B.** 1. norteamericana 2. pasó los veranos 3. por un año entero 4. en la Universidad de California 5. un estudiante joven 6. se fue a vivir 7. Los Ángeles 8. muy contenta 9. mucha gente interesante

Preparación. **Actividad B.** *Paso 1* Pide a las estrellas que pueda encontrar a Ángel en Puerto Rico. *Paso 2* c *Paso 4* 1. poder 2. estar 3. poder 4. ser

VOCABULARIO DEL TEMA

Actividad A. a. 5 b. 3 c. 1 d. 4 e. 2 f. 6 **Actividad B.** *Paso 2* 1. periodista 2. revista 3. periódico 4. ensayos 5. cuentos 6. cuentos 7. escritor (autor) 8. realidad

CONVERSACIONES

Actividad. PASO 1 1. b 2. c 3. b PASO 2 1. Sí. 2. Sí. 3. No.

UN POCO DE GRAMÁTICA

Actividad. 1. b 2. d 3. c 4. a 5. c 6. a 7. a 8. c

LECCIÓN 18

PREPARACIÓN

Actividad A. 1. Sí. 2. Sí. 3. No. Cenaron en casa de Arturo. 4. Sí. 5. No. Raquel habló de su ex novio. 6. No. Raquel le dijo que necesitaba (*she needed*) más tiempo. 7. Sí. 8. No. Pero sí fueron al Teatro Colón, donde presentan óperas. 9. Sí. 10. No. Por lo menos no se vio en el episodio. Sí comieron un helado en el parque.

¿TIENES BUENA MEMORIA?

Actividad A. 1. Arturo llevó a Raquel al aeropuerto. 2. Los dos se despidieron en la entrada. 3. Se besaron con ternura. 4. La despedida fue triste. 5. Raquel tuvo que esperar un poco. 6. Le escribió una carta a la Sra. Suárez. **Actividad B.** 1. Sí. Le dio un regalo (una pulsera de oro [*gold bracelet*]). 2. No. Le dijo «hasta pronto». 3. En un par de días. 4. Piensa en el deseo que les pidió a las estrellas: que la familia pueda reunirse definitivamente.

Preparación. **Actividad B.** a, b, c, e, g, h

Repaso de los episodios 12–17

Actividad A.   1. me sirvió bastante   2. murió hace algunos años   3. ya no vivía allí   4. era el hijo de Rosario y don Fernando   5. había muerto   6. se fue de la casa   7. perdió contacto con su hermano   **Actividad B.**   a. 3   b. 7   c. 6   d. 1   e. 5   f. 2   g. 4
Actividad C.   Correct wording: mi estancia en Buenos Aires ha sido más… , conocer un poco la ciudad, artículos de cuero… , y comí mucho, que seguí sus… , El hermano de Ángel, Arturo… , siento un afecto… , en un par de días, Siento mucho la muerte de… , que encuentre a Ángel Castillo… , con su padre

LECCIÓN 19

PREPARACIÓN

¿TIENES BUENA MEMORIA?

Actividad A.   1. vecina   2. murió hace poco   3. escritora   4. hija   5. unos parientes   6. tiene un hermano   **Actividad B.**   1. mudarse   2. debe ser muy triste para Ángela   3. llamar a sus tíos   4. visitar un lugar de interés histórico   5. mostrarle otros lugares interesantes   6. regresan al apartamento   7. está en Nueva York
Preparación.   **Actividad A.**   1. Raquel le está preguntando dónde está Ángel Castillo. La vecina le está diciendo que Ángel ya murió.   2. Está allí porque busca la tumba de Ángel Castillo.   3. Es hija de Ángel Castillo.   **Actividad B.**   *Paso 3*   1. Habla de Ángel Castillo y su esposa.   2. Describe a un hombre, a Ángel.

VOCABULARIO DEL TEMA

Actividad A.   1. esquina   2. izquierda   3. derecha   4. derecho   5. izquierda   6. derecha   **Actividad B.**   *Paso 1*   1. Siga   2. vire   3. bocacalle   4. derecha   5. Sigo   6. izquierda   7. Allí   *Paso 2*   1. a   2. b   3. c   4. c   **Actividad C.**   1. a   2. b   3. a

LECCIÓN 20

PREPARACIÓN

Actividad A.   *Paso 2*   1. Una vecina   2. la hija   3. estaba sorprendida   4. a los tíos   5. tenía un hermano también

¿TIENES BUENA MEMORIA?

Actividad A.   1. b   2. c   3. b   4. a   5. d   6. g   7. a   8. b   9. f   10. e   11. c   **Actividad B.**   1. a   2. b   **Actividad C.**   1. c   2. Raquel llamó a Pedro Castillo. Pudo hablar con él.   Ángela llamó a su hermano Roberto. No pudo hablar con él.
¡Un desafío! Ahora don Fernando sabe que tiene nietos (y que uno está en México).
Preparación.   **Actividad B.**   *Paso 2*   1. a
Actividad C.   *Paso 2*   1. a   2. b   3. c

VOCABULARIO DEL TEMA

Actividad B.   *Paso 2*   1. cinco   2. dos, dos   3. Tres   4. cinco   5. un, tres   6. Ángel, la suegra, suegro   **Actividad C.**   1. sobrinos   2. tíos   3. prima   4. hermanastros (medio hermanos)

CONVERSACIONES

Actividad.   **PASO 2**   Items checked should include *1, 3, 6, 8.*   **PASO 3**   Doña Carmen: 3, Puerto Rico, ¿Sí?   Arturo Iglesias: 1, la Argentina, Hola.   Teresa Suárez: 4, España, Dígame.   Pedro Castillo: 2, México, Bueno.

UN POCO DE GRAMÁTICA

Actividad.   1. d   2. a   3. b   4. c   5. e   6. c   7. d

NOTA CULTURAL

Actividad.   1. Probable.   2. Probable.   3. Improbable. Fue Cristóbal Colón.   4. Improbable. Había tribus indígenas que se llamaban los taínos.   5. Probable.   6. Improbable. El español es el idioma oficial, pero muchos hablan inglés.   7. Improbable. Puerto Rico es un Estado Libre Asociado con los Estados Unidos.

LECCIÓN 21

PREPARACIÓN

Actividad A.   *Paso 2*   1. b   2. b   3. a   4. c   5. b   6. b

¿TIENES BUENA MEMORIA?

Actividad A.   1. b   2. c   3. b   4. c   5. c   6. b   7. b   **Actividad B.**   1. español   2. San Juan   3. 1898   4. guerra   5. Cuba   6. Puerto Rico
Preparación.   **Actividad B.**   1. a   2. a

VOCABULARIO DEL TEMA

Actividad A. 1. calor, más, mucho 2. frío, más, mucho 3. fresco **Actividad B.** 1. Falso. Hace calor en diciembre porque es verano en la Argentina. 2. Es posible, porque es el fin del otoño. 3. Cierto. 4. Cierto. 5. Cierto. 6. Cierto. 7. Es posible. Por lo menos puede hacer frío. 8. Cierto. 9. Es posible. También puede hacer buen tiempo.

UN POCO DE GRAMÁTICA

Actividad. 2. h 3. e 4. f 5. a 6. d 7. b 8. g 9. c

LECCIÓN 22

PREPARACIÓN

Actividad. 1. prima 2. carro 3. taller 4. día siguiente (próximo día) 5. Ponce

¿TIENES BUENA MEMORIA?

Actividad A. *Paso 1* 1. a 2. b 3. a *Paso 2* 1. Falso. Ángela estudió en la Universidad Interamericana, en San Germán. 2. Cierto. 3. Cierto. 4. Falso. En San Germán, Ángel pintaba constantemente. *Paso 3* 1. b 2. a **Actividad B.** 1. materna 2. una finca 3. ya murió 4. sirvienta 5. yerno 6. muy estrechas 7. su padre 8. una copa **Actividad C.** 1. d 2. h 3. a 4. i 5. b 6. e 7. c 8. g 9. f

VOCABULARIO DEL TEMA

Actividad A. *Paso 1* 1, 5 *Paso 2* 5 **Actividad B.** *Possible answers:* 1. don Fernando, Rosario 2. Arturo 3. Martín Iglesias (padrastro de Ángel), Rosario, Ángel 4. Rosario, Ángel, don Fernando 5. Martín Iglesias, Ángel, la tía Olga, Ángela 6. Ángela 7. Rosario, Ángel,... 8. Raquel, Ángela 9. don Fernando, Raquel 10. Raquel, Arturo, Ángela, don Fernando, los hijos de don Fernando

UN POCO DE GRAMÁTICA

Actividad. 1. No. 2. No. 3. No. 4. No. 5. No. 6. Sí. 7. Sí. 8. Sí. 9. Sí. 10. Sí. 11. No.

LECCIÓN 23

PREPARACIÓN

Actividad A. 1. a 2. c 3. b

¿TIENES BUENA MEMORIA?

Actividad A. 1. está hablando afuera con 2. ayer por la noche 3. a Buenos Aires para hablar con Arturo 4. la quería mucho 5. no sabe si **Actividad B.** 1. Trabaja en un banco. 2. Tenía que hablar con su jefa (su supervisora). 3. Quería hablar con su novio. 4. Daba una clase. 5. Le mostró la copa de Rosario. **¡Un desafío!** ¿Qué va a decir don Fernando acerca de la copa? ¿Qué es esa música?

Preparación. **Actividad B.** b **Actividad C.** a

VOCABULARIO DEL TEMA

Actividad A. You should have selected *b.* **Actividad B.** *Paso 2* 1. Cierto. 2. Falso. El *town house* tiene solamente un baño. 3. Cierto. 4. No se sabe. Sólo sabes que el *town house no* tiene lavaplatos. 5. Falso. Sólo el *town house* es de dos pisos. 6. Cierto. 7. Falso. Están juntos en el apartamento. 8. No se sabe. Sólo sabes que las dos cocinas son modernas, pero no sabes si estos aparatos son nuevos.

UN POCO DE GRAMÁTICA

Actividad. 1. Raquel estaba buscando la música que escuchó de repente. 2. Mercedes y Ramón estaban visitando a su padre en el hospital. 3. Pedro estaba leyendo una carta que le mandó Raquel. 4. Jorge estaba besando a su novia. 5. Arturo estaba pensando en Raquel. También estaba haciendo los preparativos para un viaje. 6. Laura estaba comiendo—¡siempre tiene hambre! 7. Roberto estaba trabajando en una excavación. 8. Ángela estaba pensando en algo que le sorprendió mucho. 9. Don Fernando estaba pensando en sus «nuevos» nietos. 10. Ángela y Jorge estaban abrazándose.

LECCIÓN 24

PREPARACIÓN

Actividad A. *Paragraph one:* madre → padre; manda un telegrama → hace una llamada; hijos → hijas *Paragraph two:* de la tienda → del banco; meses → semanas; don Fernando va a enfadarse → es urgente *Paragraph three:* Los Ángeles → México; hermano → novio; del viaje → de la copa

¿TIENES BUENA MEMORIA?

Actividad. *Possible answers:* 1. b 2. g 3. e 4. c 5. h, i 6. f, j 7. d, a

Preparación. **Actividad B.** c

VOCABULARIO DEL TEMA

Actividad A.   1. Arturo es trabajador.   2. Jorge es muy macho.   3. Tía Olga es gruñona.   4. Ángela es ingenua.   5. Doña Carmen es sabia.   6. Jorge es agresivo.   7. Arturo es encantador.   8. Doña Carmen es cariñosa.   9. Laura es chistosa.   10. Raquel es simpática.   **Actividad B.**   1. Es Ángela.   2. Es Arturo.   3. Es doña Carmen.   4. Es la madre de Raquel.   5. Es la tía Olga.   6. Es Jorge.

CONVERSACIONES

Actividad.   **PASO 1**   1. d   2. a   **PASO 2**   1. ¡Qué interesante!   2. ¡Qué va!   3. ¿Y qué?

UN POCO DE GRAMÁTICA

Actividad.   1. a. Raquel estaba en el cementerio. Miraba la tumba de Ángel Castillo.   b. Estaba en la oficina de Arturo. Buscaba a Rosario.   c. Estaba en la universidad de Puerto Rico, en un salón de clase (*classroom*). Estaba con Ángela.   2. a. Raquel estaba en el apartamento de Ángela. Hablaba con Ángela.   b. Estaba en el Viejo San Juan, en la calle del Sol. Hablaba con una vecina.   c. Estaba en la universidad de Puerto Rico. Se quedó a solas (*alone*) con Jorge y hablaba con él.   3. a. Ángela estaba en el cementerio. Hablaba con Raquel.   b. Estaba en el cuarto de su padre, en casa de su abuela. Miraba en un baúl (*trunk*) las cosas de su padre.   c. Estaba en el patio del hotel donde se queda Raquel. Hablaba con Raquel.

LECCIÓN 25

PREPARACIÓN

Actividad.   a. 2   b. 3   c. 5   d. 1   e. 4

¿TIENES BUENA MEMORIA?

Actividad.   1. No.   2. No.   3. No.   4. Sí.   5. No.   6. Sí.   7. Sí.   8. Sí.   9. Sí.   10. Sí.

REPASO DE LOS EPISODIOS 1–18

Actividad A.   1. f   2. b   3. i   4. c   5. j   6. a   7. d   8. g   9. e   10. h   **Actividad B.**   *Paragraph one:* un cuadro → una foto; artista → hombre   *Paragraph two:* él los invitó a entrar → los tres se quedaron fuera para hablar   *Paragraph three:* una foto → un cuadro; España → Puerto Rico; tarjeta postal → carta   **Actividad C.**   1. el primer vuelo   2. muy mal   3. unos pocos días   4. muchos años   5. extrañar   6. la búsqueda   7. Te gustaría   8. trabajo   9. dejar

LECCIÓN 26

PREPARACIÓN

Actividad.   1. e   a. Falso.   b. Cierto.   2. c   a. Cierto.   b. Falso.   3. d   a. Falso.   b. Cierto.   4. b   a. Cierto.   b. Falso.   5. f   a. Falso.   b. Cierto.   6. a   a. Falso.   b. Cierto.

¿TIENES BUENA MEMORIA?

Actividad.   1. Ángela   2. Olga   3. Laura   4. Carmen   5. Jorge   6. Jaime   7. Roberto

REPASO DE LOS EPISODIOS 19–24

Actividad A.   a. 7   b. 2   c. 6   d. 10   e. 4   f. 9   g. 12   h. 3   i. 13   j. 5   k. 8   l. 11   m. 1   **Actividad B.**   a. 10   b. 13   c. 12   d. 2   e. 9   f. 1   g. 6   h. 8   i. 3   j. 11   k. 7   l. 4   m. 5

LECCIÓN 27

PREPARACIÓN

Actividad A.   1. La Gavia, don Fernando Castillo Saavedra, el hermano, Raquel Rodríguez   2. Teresa Suárez, la primera esposa   3. la Argentina, Madrid, San Juan   4. el cementerio   5. México, una excavación   6. el medio hermano, Rosario   **Actividad B.**   *Paso 2*   1. a   2. b   3. c

¿TIENES BUENA MEMORIA?

Actividad.   1. buscar a Roberto   2. se llevaban bien   3. le tenía un poco de envidia   4. era más inteligente y responsable que ella   5. un poco culpable   6. estaba bloqueado y no podíamos pasar   7. empezó a mirar la lista de nombres   8. que era un error   9. está desesperada   10. no sabe nada del accidente

LECCIÓN 28

PREPARACIÓN

Actividad A.   1. Sí.   2. No. No pudieron pasar. Tuvieron que ir al hospital de un pueblo cercano.   3. No. Ni se sabe todavía si Roberto es uno de los hombres atrapados.   4. No. Arturo llegó a un hotel en la Ciudad de México.   5. Sí.   6. Sí.   **Actividad C.**   *Paso 1*   1. d   2. b   3. a   4. f   5. c   *Paso 2*   1. Mercedes   2. Gloria (esposa de Carlos)   3. Juan (esposo de Pati)   4. Maricarmen (hija de Ramón y Consuelo)

PREPARACIÓN.   Actividad B.   1. b   2. a   **Actividad D.**   _Paso 2_   1. b   2. No.   3. b

¿TIENES BUENA MEMORIA?

Actividad A.   1. e   2. c   3. a   4. d   5. b   6. e   7. a   **Actividad B.**   1. en seguida   2. Guadalajara   3. por su padre y por otros asuntos familiares

VOCABULARIO DEL TEMA

Actividad A.   You should have indicated these body parts: eyes, nose, ears, both hands, arms, legs, heart, chest, back.
Actividad B.   1. ojos   2. una boca   3. un brazo   4. mano   5. piernas   6. pies   7. cuerpo   8. pecho   9. cabeza   10. pelo; 1. eyes   2. mouth   3. arm   4. hand   5. legs   6. feet   7. body   8. chest   9. head   10. hair   **Actividad C.**   1. los pies 2. todo el cuerpo   3. la cabeza   4. el pecho   5. los ojos   6. la boca   7. las orejas   8. el pelo   9. las manos   10. la nariz 11. los brazos, las piernas, la espalda, etcétera

CONVERSACIONES

Actividad.   PASO 1   ¿Qué hay?   **PASO 2**   d, c

LECCIÓN 29

PREPARACIÓN

Actividad.   1. c   2. a   3. c   4. c

¿TIENES BUENA MEMORIA?

Actividad A.   1. teníamos muchas esperanzas   2. a un hombre y a una mujer   3. y se derrumbó todo otra vez   4. comenzó a llorar   5. comunicarme con la familia de don Fernando   6. Arturo   **Actividad B.**   1. Juanita → Carlitos   2. Gloria → Consuelo (la esposa de Ramón)   3. una inyección → medicina   5. cenar → desayunar   6. no → todavía   7. inyección → receta (unas pastillas)   8. Arturo → Raquel   9. Raquel → Arturo   **¡Un desafío!** La persona que llegó tarde fue Gloria.

VOCABULARIO DEL TEMA

Actividad A.   a. 1   b. 3   c. 2   d. 6   e. 4   f. 5   **Actividad B.**   1. mal   2. la espalda   3. Tiene   4. y le pone una inyección   5. el brazo   6. la pierna   7. rayos X   8. No tiene

CONVERSACIONES

Actividad.   PASO 2   _Primera conversación:_ Sí, creo que sí.   _Segunda conversación:_ Sí, seguro.

UN POCO DE GRAMÁTICA

Actividad.   1. g, j   2. i   3. f, k   4. c   5. h, b   6. a   7. d, e   8. l

NOTA CULTURAL

Actividad.   4

LECCIÓN 30

PREPARACIÓN

Actividad A.   _Primer párrafo:_ murió → no se sabía nada de él   _Segundo párrafo:_ hablaba del derrumbe en la excavación → hablaba de varios asuntos; Gloria → Carlos   _Tercer párrafo:_ Muy contento porque ya sabía algo de Raquel → Muy preocupado porque no tenía noticias de Raquel

¿TIENES BUENA MEMORIA?

Actividad A.   1. c   2. b   3. a   4. b   5. a   **Actividad B.**   1. durmió muy bien   2. tener noticias de Roberto   3. tenía suficiente aire   4. tienda del pueblo   5. estaba ocupada la línea   6. hablando con alguien en Nueva York   7. el hotel   8. le dejó un mensaje   9. Puerto Rico   10. la iglesia del pueblo   11. descansar y bañarse

Preparación.   **Actividad B.**   _Paso 1_   b   _Paso 2_   b

VOCABULARIO DEL TEMA

Actividad A.   _Paso 1_   You should have written the letter _C_ on these places: the center of the town, the suburbs, the outskirts, the group of tall buildings, the office building, the hotel, the market, the supermarket, the pharmacy, the small shop, the large department store.   _Paso 2_   You should have written _P_ on the following parts of the drawing: the center, the plaza, the city hall, the church, the pharmacy, the shop, the market. You should have written _N_ on the following parts of the drawing: the group of tall buildings, the supermarket, the department store.
¡Un desafío! Arturo mencionó los siguientes lugares: una farmacia, una tienda para hombres, un almacén, un mercado, un supermercado.
Actividad B.   a. 4   b. 1   c. 5   d. 3   e. 2   f. 8   g. 9   h. 6   i. 7

CONVERSACIONES

Actividad.   PASO 1   1. Por favor   2. Mande Ud.   3. Muy bien   4. Muchas gracias.   5. A sus órdenes.   **PASO 2**   Mande Ud. = _How can I help you?_ (_Literally, Order, Give orders._) A sus órdenes = _At your service._ (_I am here to serve you in any way that I can._)   Arturo y el empleado usan mucho el título **señor** (_sir_). También se tratan de Ud.

Un poco de gramática
Actividad.   1. e, g   2. b, d, i   3. c   4. a, b, h   5. i   6. f

LECCIÓN 31

Preparación
Actividad A.   1. c, f   2. e   3. b   4. a   5. d   **Actividad B.**   *Paso 1*   c   *Paso 3*   1. b   2. b

¿Tienes buena memoria?
Actividad A.   1. Cierto.   2. Falso. Ángela se siente mucho mejor.   3. Falso.   Ángela es optimista. Es Raquel quien es
pesimista.   **Actividad B.**   1. Sí. Pedro lo sabe (porque Arturo se lo dijo por teléfono).   2. Juan y Pati se pelearon.   3. Ramón y
Pedro hablaron con los auditores.   4. Eran drásticas.
¡Un desafío! Que cierren la oficina en Miami. Que concentren en la producción de algo (el acero = *steel*). Que vendan La
Gavia (porque hace falta capital).

Vocabulario del tema
Actividad A.   1. la pescadería   2. la carnicería   3. la zapatería   4. la confitería   5. la tortillería   6. la panadería   7. (la) pastelería   8. (la) farmacia

Un poco de gramática
Actividad.   1. f   2. g   3. e   4. b   5. c   6. h   7. a   8. d

LECCIÓN 32

Preparación
Actividad A.   1. a   2. a   3. b   **Actividad B.**   1. Se llama Luis.   2. Vive ahora en Los Ángeles. (Acaba de mudarse para
allí.)   3. Eran novios. (La madre de Raquel lo llama «el novio de mi hija».)

¿Tienes buena memoria?
Actividad A.   *Paso 2*   1. Sí.   2. No. Hubo actividad. Llegaron más personas para ayudar con el rescate.   3. No. Pero casi
han sacado (*they've gotten out*) a Roberto.   4. Sí.   5. No se sabe todavía.   6. Sí.   7. No. Mercedes no quería contarle lo que
pasaba.   8. No. Están muy contentos en su matrimonio.   9. Sí.   10. Sí.   11. No. Al contrario, la madre de Raquel le dijo a Luis
que debía ir a México a ver a Raquel.   12. No. No se sabe todavía la actitud del padre de Raquel.   **Actividad B.**   1. a. sabe
b. no sabe   c. no sabe   2. a. sabe   b. no sabe   c. sabe (Raquel se lo dijo en la Argentina.)   3. a. sabe   b. no sabe   c. no sabe
(Aunque hay que admitir que es posible que, siendo dueño de la compañía, sepa algo del asunto, inclusive algo que Pedro y
Ramón no saben. Pero no se dice nada de esto en el episodio.)   4. a. no sabe   b. no sabe (Raquel le dijo algo, pero no se lo
contó todo.)   c. sabe   **Actividad C.**   1. azteca   2. norte   3. lago   4. guerrera   5. conquistar

Vocabulario del tema
Actividad B.   **¡Un desafío!** El Titicaca está en Sudamérica, entre Bolivia y el Perú.   Inglaterra está en el Océano Atlántico, al
oeste de Europa.   El Atlántico está entre América y Europa y África.   Pike's Peak está en los Estados Unidos, en Colorado.
El Sahara está en África, en el norte.   Los Andes están en Sudamérica, en el oeste.   El Nilo está en África, en Egipto.   El Golfo
Pérsico está entre Irán y Arabia.   Sudamérica está en el hemisferio sur.   El Mediterráneo está al sur de Europa y al norte de
África. Napa está en el norte de California.   Yucatán está en el sureste de México.

Un poco de gramática
Actividad.   1. f   2. d   3. c   4. h   5. b   6. a   7. g   8. e

LECCIÓN 33

Preparación
Actividad A.   1. b   2. b   3. b   4. b   5. b

¿Tienes buena memoria?
Actividad A.   1. no sabían nada y tampoco podían ver bien lo que pasaba   2. las profesiones   3. peligrosa   4. veterinaria y
profesora   5. profesora y actriz   **Actividad B.**   1. Sí, por fin pueden rescatarlo.   2. Está inconsciente.   3. Parece estar bien.
4. Piensan llevarlo a otro sitio, a un hospital en México.   **Actividad C.**   1. Arturo   2. Juan   3. Pati   4. Pati   5. Juan
Preparación.   **Actividad B.**   *Paso 2*   1. Cierto.   2. Falso. Ya trató de explicárselos.   3. Cierto.   4. c

Vocabulario del tema
Actividad A.   *Paso 1*   ÁNGELA pensaba en estudiar para profesora, actriz; se hizo programadora de computadoras.
EL PADRE DE ÁNGELA quería que ella fuera abogada, mujer de negocios.   RAQUEL pensaba en estudiar para profesora (de

historia), veterinaria; se hizo abogada.   LA MADRE DE RAQUEL quería que ella fuera abogada.   **Paso 2**   1. ambas querían ser profesoras   2. Raquel (Su madre quería que su hija fuera abogada.)   **Actividad B.**   1. abogada   2. programadora   3. médico   4. enfermera   5. ingeniero   6. profesora   7. hombre de negocios   8. profesores   9. ama de casa   *Los dibujos:* a. 3   b. 7   c. 1   d. 4   **Actividad D.**   1. un abogado   2. un arquitecto, un electricista, un ingeniero, un plomero   3. un veterinario   4. una azafata, un camarero   5. un dentista   6. un músico   7. un plomero   8. un dependiente

UN POCO DE GRAMÁTICA

Actividad.   1. g   2. b   3. e   4. h   5. c   6. a   7. f   8. d

LECCIÓN 34

PREPARACIÓN

Actividad A.   1. b   2. a   3. b   4. a

¿TIENES BUENA MEMORIA?

Actividad A.   1. Sí.   2. No. Mercedes cree que Pati debe regresar a Nueva York.   3. Sí.   4. No. Ramón le habló con tacto, con cariño.   5. Sí.   6. No. Juan sólo habló con Ramón.   **Actividad B.**   **Paso 1**   2, 3, 5, 6 (¡OJO! Raquel habla de Jorge en su repaso, pero no lo mencionó cuando hablaba con Pati en el carro.)   **Paso 3**   *Possible answers:* Ángela admira a Roberto. Es amiga de Raquel. Es novia de Jorge. Quiere a Jorge. Quiere casarse con Jorge. Recuerda a Roberto con cariño. Se separó de Roberto.

Raquel admira a Arturo. Es amiga de Ángela. Era novia de Luis. ¿Quiere a Arturo? ¿Quiere casarse con Arturo? Recuerda a Arturo y a Luis con cariño. Se separó de Arturo.

Jorge es novio de Ángela. ¿Quiere a Ángela? ¿Quiere casarse con Ángela? Trató de ligar con Raquel.

Arturo admira a Raquel. Es amigo de Raquel. Quiere a Raquel. ¿Quiere casarse con Raquel? Recuerda a Raquel con cariño. Se separó de Raquel.

Preparación.   **Actividad B.**   **Paso 2**   1. Falso. Ramón cree que Juan está exagerando.   2. Cierto.   3. Falso. Juan considera lo que Ramón le ha dicho (*has told him*).   4. Cierto.   5. Cierto; c

VOCABULARIO DEL TEMA

Actividad A.   1. el cariño   2. el cariño   3. el cariño, el amor   4. el amor, un período de tiempo   5. una ceremonia   6. un período de tiempo, el amor   **Actividad B.**   a. 7   b. 2   c. 3   d. 5   e. 1   f. 6   g. 8   h. 9   i. 4   j. 10

UN POCO DE GRAMÁTICA

Actividad.   1. d   2. c   3. b   4. e   5. f   6. a   7. g   8. a

LECCIÓN 35

PREPARACIÓN

Actividad A.   1. a un hospital en la capital   2. en su propio carro   3. de sus novios   4. siguieron discutiendo sin resolver nada   5. el accidente

¿TIENES BUENA MEMORIA?

Actividad A.   1. b, d   2. c   3. a, d   4. b   5. a, d   **Actividad B.**   **Paso 2**   *Possible answers:* Pedro se despidió de Pati. Les contó algo a Carlos y Gloria. Fue al hospital. Conoció a Ángela.

Raquel saludó a Arturo y a Pedro. Besó a Arturo. Llamó a Los Ángeles. Fue a la casa de Pedro. Conoció a toda la familia.

Arturo saludó a Raquel. Besó a Raquel. Conoció a Ángela en el hospital. Les contó algo a Raquel y Pedro. Fue a la casa de Pedro. Conoció a toda la familia.

Ángela conoció a Arturo. Llamó a Puerto Rico. No fue a la casa de Pedro y no conoció a toda la familia. Fue al hospital. Estaba preocupada por Roberto.

Pati se despidió de Pedro y Juan. Salió para Nueva York.

Ofelia le contó algo a Carlos.

Carlos llamó a Miami. Estaba preocupado por la oficina. Conoció a Arturo y a Raquel.

Roberto estaba dormido en el hospital.

Preparación.   **Actividad B.**   **Paso 2**   1. Están en malas condiciones.   2. b

VOCABULARIO DEL TEMA

Actividad A.   1. una sugerencia   2. un requisito   3. un mandato   4. una recomendación   5. una recomendación   6. una sugerencia   7. un mandato   8. un mandato

UN POCO DE GRAMÁTICA

Actividad.   Raquel: 2, 3; Arturo: 6; Ángela: 7, 8; Carlos; 12; Roberto: 15

LECCIÓN 36

PREPARACIÓN
Actividad. 1. Raquel y Ángela 2. Pati 3. Ofelia (la secretaria de Carlos) 4. Arturo 5. la médico (También Arturo les dijo esto a Pedro, Raquel y Ángela. También Ángela se lo dijo a su tío Jaime.) 6. Arturo y Pedro 7. Roberto 8. Raquel y Arturo 9. Ángela 10. Raquel 11. Ángela 12. Raquel y Arturo

¿TIENES BUENA MEMORIA?
Actividad. 1. se dan cuenta 2. Arturo 3. sigue enamorado 4. Gloria

REPASO DE LOS EPISODIOS 27–35
Actividad A. 1. c 2. b 3. f 4. g 5. e 6. d 7. a **Actividad B.** **Juan** b. **Mercedes.** *Paso 1* a *Paso 2* 1. Cierto. 2. Falso. Mercedes habló con Pati sobre sus problemas matrimoniales. 3. Cierto. **Pedro.** *Paso 1* c *Paso 2* b, d, e

LECCIÓN 37

PREPARACIÓN
Actividad A. 1. Arturo 2. Juan 3. Ramón, Pedro (Tal vez Mercedes también. No sabes hasta qué punto ella se interesa en los asuntos financieros de Castillo Saavedra, S.A.) 4. Pati 5. don Fernando 6. Carlos 7. Raquel 8. Mercedes 9. Raquel 10. Ángela

¿TIENES BUENA MEMORIA?
Actividad A. 1. Mercedes 2. Ángela 3. La madre de Raquel 4. Pedro 5. Luis. **Actividad B.** 1. Arturo les dijo esto a los miembros de la familia Castillo. 2. Ángela le dijo esto a Roberto. 3. Carlitos les dijo esto a Raquel y Arturo. 4. María Rodríguez está hablando por teléfono con Luis. 5. Pedro está conversando con Raquel.
Preparación. **Actividad B.** *Paso 2* 1. b 2. a

VOCABULARIO DEL TEMA
Actividad A. a. 7 b. 3, 4 c. 2, 5 d. 6 e. 1 **Actividad B.** *Primera conversación:* 1. Falso. No tiene casi nada en su cuenta de ahorros. 2. Cierto. 3. Falso. No sabe cómo va a pagar la cuenta. 4. Falso. Lo maneja muy mal. *Segunda conversación:* 5. Cierto. 6. Falso. La usó mucho. 7. Falso. La secretaria de Pedro le dará un cheque mañana. 8. Falso. Una secretaria en la oficina de Raquel se preocupa mucho por las gastos.

UN POCO DE GRAMÁTICA
Actividad. 1. a 2. b 3. c

LECCIÓN 38

PREPARACIÓN
Actividad A. 1. Cierto. 2. Falso. Le dijeron que regresara para las fiestas nacionales. 3. Falso. Regresaron al hotel. 4. Cierto. 5. Cierto. 6. Falso. Raquel recibió un mensaje de Pedro.

¿TIENES BUENA MEMORIA?
Actividad A. 1. lo paso bien con 2. un mensaje para mí 3. con don Fernando 4. hablar de nosotros 5. en mí 6. una llamada telefónica 7. venir a México 8. si Ángela había regresado **Actividad B.** *Paso 1* Sí, Roberto se despertó. *Paso 2* 1. Son optimistas. 2. Carlos ha sacado dinero. 3. Ya no puede ocultar la verdad.
Preparación. **Actividad B.** 1. b 2. a

VOCABULARIO DEL TEMA
Actividad A. 1. Falso. Hay irregularidades en esa oficina. 2. Cierto. 3. Falso. Los gastos son mayores que los ingresos. 4. Cierto. 5. Falso. Ha sacado cien mil dólares. 6. Falso. Los auditores hicieron sus propias cuentas. **Actividad B.** 1. un presupuesto 2. manejar 3. ganar 4. economizar 5. los ingresos 6. los gastos

UN POCO DE GRAMÁTICA
Actividad. *Possible answers:* 1. d 2. a 3. e 4. b 5. g 6. f 7. c

LECCIÓN 39

PREPARACIÓN
Actividad. 1. una reunión en la casa de Pedro 2. Raquel 3. Pedro 4. Raquel 5. los problemas económicos de la oficina en Miami 6. Carlos 7. seriamente 8. Gloria había desaparecido.

¿TIENES BUENA MEMORIA?
Actividad A. Raquel y Arturo: 3, 5, 6, 8 Carlos y Gloria: 1 Ángela y Roberto: 2 Juan, Ramón y Pedro: 4, 7 **Actividad B.** *Paso 1* 2, 3, 5, 6, 7 *Paso 2* b

VOCABULARIO DEL TEMA

Actividad A. *Primera conversación:* 1. Cierto.   2. Falso. Es de los Estados Unidos.   3. Falso. Quiere esperar para ver si su padre se mejora.   4. Cierto.   *Segunda conversación:* la casa → el apartamento; comprarla → comprarlo; Es una mala oferta → Es una buena oferta; Ángela debe rechazarla → Ángela debe decidir; ...que lo hable con Arturo → ....que lo hable con Roberto.
Actividad B.   1. Ángela y Roberto   2. don Fernando   3. la familia Castillo   4. Ángela y Roberto   5. Arturo   6. Ángela (que debe consultar con Roberto)   7. Ángela (con Raquel)   **Actividad C.**   a. 5   b. 8   c. 3   d. 1   e. 6   f. 9   g. 4   h. 10   i. 2   j. 7

UN POCO DE GRAMÁTICA

Actividad.   1. b   2. c   3. a   4. b   5. a

LECCIÓN 40

PREPARACIÓN

Actividad A.   1. desapareció   2. buscarla   3. se sentía muy bien, con mucha hambre   4. su tío   5. la posible venta de La Gavia   6. regresó al hospital para estar con su padre

¿TIENES BUENA MEMORIA?

Actividad A.   1. c   2. f   3. h   4. i   5. a   6. g   7. c   8. e   9. h   10. d   **Actividad B.**   1. Guillermo inició la conversación.   2. Pati quería hablar de la obra, pero Guillermo insistió en que hablaran de la vida de ella, de sus relaciones con Juan.   3. Sí, cree que era necesario.   4. Que Juan tiene celos de ella.   **Actividad C.**   1. es un poco mandona   2. trata de llevarse bien   3. es una persona muy tranquila
Preparación.   **Actividad B.**   *Paso 1*   b   *Paso 2*   1. a   2. c

VOCABULARIO DEL TEMA

Actividad A.   a. 3   b. 2   c. 1   **Actividad B.**   *Primera conversación:* 1. f   2. a   3. e   4. c   5. g   6. b   7. d   *Segunda conversación:* 1. b   2. f   3. a   4. e   5. c   6. d

UN POCO DE GRAMÁTICA

Actividad.   1. f   2. g   3. i   4. h   5. j   6. d   7. c   8. a

LECCIÓN 41

PREPARACIÓN

Actividad A.   1. Cierto.   2. Falso. Roberto no tenía ropa en el hotel porque la había dejado en la excavación. Quería ir de compras para comprar ropa.   3. Cierto.   4. Cierto.   5. Falso. Pati le hablaba a un amigo, su ayudante.   6. Falso. Le dijeron que don Fernando tendría que ir a Guadalajara.

¿TIENES BUENA MEMORIA?

Actividad A.   1. Arturo creía que sería mejor si yo entrara primero.   2. Cuando entré, vi que don Fernando no estaba. Luego una enfermera nos dijo que lo habían llevado a Guadalajara.   3. Ángela tenía que llamar a su tío Jaime.   4. A Roberto no le gustó.   **Actividad B.**   1. un vicio, jugar por dinero   2. culpable, vender La Gavia   3. sale para el aeropuerto, Nueva York, Pati   **Actividad C.**   1. Raquel, Arturo, Ángela y Roberto toman un taxi para ir al hotel. Luis llega al mismo hotel en taxi. Juan toma un taxi para ir al aeropuerto.   2. Luis y Arturo toman el ascensor al mismo tiempo.
Preparación.   **Actividad B.**   *Paso 1*   1. b   2. a   *Paso 2*   1. Sí, lo sabe.   2. *a* y *b* (¡OJO! *B* es también correcto porque Arturo les dice que no se dejen tentar por la primera oferta.)

VOCABULARIO DEL TEMA

Actividad A.   a. 3   b. 2   c. 1   d. 5   e. 4   **Actividad B.**   1. agencia   2. reservar   3. billete   4. un taxi   5. el equipaje   6. fumar   7. la aduana   8. el pasaporte   9. las maletas   10. la agencia de viajes   11. gira   12. El autobús   13. plano   14. guía   **Actividad C.**   1. cuatro veces: los Estados Unidos → España, España → la Argentina, la Argentina → Puerto Rico, Puerto Rico → México   2. seis: en avión, tren, taxi, coche particular (con Federico, con Arturo, etcétera), barco (en el Rosedal), mateo (cerca del Rosedal)   3. una   4. en Madrid   5. Miguel Ruiz (padre de Jaime y Miguel, esposo de Elena)

UN POCO DE GRAMÁTICA

Actividad.   1. podría   2. tendría   3. podrían   4. regresaría   5. sería   6. deberían   7. tomaría   8. guardaría

LECCIÓN 42

PREPARACIÓN

Actividad A.   *Paso 2*   1. No.   2. Cierto.   3. a

¿TIENES BUENA MEMORIA?

Actividad A.   1. Luis   2. Raquel   3. salieron a cenar   4. pagando la cuenta   5. esperaba a Pati   6. había salido a tomar algo
Actividad B.   1. b   2. c   3. a   4. c   5. b   **Actividad C.**   1. c   2. b   3. b   4. a   5. a

Preparación. Actividad B. *Paso 1* a ***Paso 2*** 1. mucho 2. impresionar

VOCABULARIO DEL TEMA

Actividad A. *Paso 1* a. 6 b. 3 c. 1 d. 5 e. 2 f. 4 g. 7 **Actividad B.** a. 2 b. 6 c. 7 d. 8 e. 1 f. 5 g. 3 h. 4

LECCIÓN 43

PREPARACIÓN

Actividad A. *Paso 2* 1. e, Pati 3. a, Arturo y Luis 3. c *or* d, Luis o Arturo 4. a, Luis 5. a, su madre, Luis

¿TIENES BUENA MEMORIA?

Actividad A. 1. c 2. a 3. d 4. h 5. b 6. c 7. a 8. e **Actividad B.** 1. b 2. b 3. a 4. b 5. a

VOCABULARIO DEL TEMA

Actividad A. *Paso 1* 1. L 2. A 3. A 4. L 5. L 6. A 7. A 8. L 9. A 10. L 11. A **Actividad B.** 1. Quería viajar a Guadalajara. 2. Iban a viajar tres, posiblemente cuatro. 3. Quería que viajaran en avión. 4. Sí, quiere que le recomienden un hotel, aunque tiene parientes en Guadalajara. 5. Solamente quería informarse. **Actividad C.** 1. el buceo 2. la tarifa 3. la playa, la piscina 4. la habitación individual 5. la playa, la piscina 6. el plan de lujo 7. la cancha de tenis 8. el hotel de cinco estrellas

UN POCO DE GRAMÁTICA

Actividad. *Paso 1* 1. b 2. b 3. a 4. b ***Paso 2*** 1. a 2. b 3. a

LECCIÓN 44

PREPARACIÓN

Actividad. 1. La llamó Luis. 2. Quería ver a Raquel. 3. b 4. Los dos fueron a la agencia de viajes. Luis hizo esas reservaciones. 5. No, Raquel no sabe nada de lo que pasó.

¿TIENES BUENA MEMORIA?

Actividad. 1. Cierto. 2. Falso. A Raquel no le interesaba el viaje que sugería Luis. 3. Falso. Ángela pareció aceptar la explicación que Jorge le ofreció. 4. Cierto. 5. Falso. Se encontraron con Raquel y Luis en el hotel. 6. Cierto. 7. Cierto. No saben los detalles, pero sospechan que hay algún problema. 8. Falso. Cuando Juan se levantó, Pati ya había salido. 9. Cierto. 10. Falso. Le dijo que hablaría con la familia sobre la oferta.

VOCABULARIO DEL TEMA

Actividad A. *Paso 2* 1. al fútbol 2. el béisbol, el fútbol, el baloncesto, correr, nadar 3. el tenis (Quiere hacerse rica y famosa.) **Actividad B.** 1. correr 2. el fútbol americano 3. la natación 4. el ejercicio aeróbico 5. el béisbol 6. el tenis 7. la navegación 8. el esquí (alpino-nórdico) 9. el buceo **Actividad C.** 1. a 2. No. 3. b 4. b 5. b

UN POCO DE GRAMÁTICA

Actividad. 1. ido al Museo de Antropología 2. pasado por el Estadio Olímpico 3. prometido que hablaría con él 4. comprado dos boletos para Zihuatanejo 5. conseguido información sobre un hotel 6. comprado esos boletos sin consultarme

LECCIÓN 45

PREPARACIÓN

Actividad. 1. b 2. c 3. b 4. b

¿TIENES BUENA MEMORIA?

Actividad A. *Paso 1* 1. Falso. Raquel se enteró del papel (*role*) de su madre en esta situación difícil. 2. Cierto. 3. Cierto. 4. Falso. Raquel piensa que Arturo es considerado y que Luis no lo es. 5. Falso. Se interesan mucho. Incluso se lo preguntaron a Arturo. 6. Falso. Dijeron que no querían salir a cenar. 7. Falso. Las noticias eran malas. 8. Cierto. 9. Falso. Gloria ya regresó. 10. Cierto. **Actividad B.** 1. yo soy un problema 2. lo que hiciste con 3. Lo insultaste. 4. Para mí, no es nadie. 5. quién es para mí

LECCIÓN 46

PREPARACIÓN

Actividad A. 1. b 2. a 3. a 4. c 5. b **Actividad B. *Paso 1*** 1, 4, 5, 6 2. La madre de Raquel actuó muy fríamente con Arturo. 3. Cuando llegó Luis, la madre de Raquel lo saludó con mucho cariño.

¿TIENES BUENA MEMORIA?

Actividad A. 1. Le había comprado 2. empezar una conversación seria 3. venir a México 4. de las relaciones entre Raquel y Arturo   5. Raquel se fuera a vivir a la Argentina   6. un mensaje de Luis   7. sí está enamorada de Arturo   **Actividad B.**   1. f   2. b   3. g   4. a   5. c   6. d   7. e

VOCABULARIO DEL TEMA

Actividad A.   1. e, k   2. b, c   3. f   4. k   5. j   6. a, h, j   7. h   8. d   9. g   10, d, i   **Actividad B.**   *Pasos 1 y 2*   Here are the answers, along with some details you may have caught.   1. A estar al aire libre, relajarse   2. A todo espectáculo artístico   3. A sacar vídeos   4. NA con Raquel, sí   5. A especialmente con los amigos   6. NA ni el teatro, ni cuando Raquel lo invita   7. NA especialmente el póquer   8. NA pocas amigas, Raquel es el centro de su vida   9. A la Guerra Civil española   10. NA el ajedrez, vida sedentaria

LECCIÓN 47

PREPARACIÓN

Actividad.   1. ya no había nada que hacer para   2. pasar sus últimos días con su familia   3. Le caía muy bien a Pancho   4. se fuera a vivir a la Argentina   5. conocer a Arturo   6. no venderlo por el momento   7. conocer a su abuelo paterno

¿TIENES BUENA MEMORIA?

Actividad A.   a. 5   b. 4   c. 1   d. 6   e. 3   f. 7   g. 2   **Actividad B.**   1. a   2. b   3. a   4. b   5. b   6. b

LECCIÓN 48

REPASO DE LOS EPISODIOS 3–11

Actividad A.   *Paso 1*   2, 4, 5, 7, 8, 9, 10, 11, 12, 14, 15, 16   **Actividad B.**   *Possible answer:* Cuando Raquel llegó a Sevilla, no tardó en buscar a la Sra. Suárez. Fue a *la calle Pureza*, pero *no encontró a la señora.* Conoció a dos chicos en la calle. Ellos *le dijeron que Teresa Suárez era su abuela pero que ahora vivía en Madrid.* Luego llevaron a Raquel al mercado para *conocer a su madre, Elena Ramírez.*

Elena no sabía nada del caso, pero le sugirió a Raquel que sería buena idea *reunirse con su esposo por la noche para ver si él sabía algo.* Esa noche Raquel *conoció a Miguel Ruiz, hijo de Teresa Suárez,* pero Miguel tampoco sabía nada del caso. Sin embargo, le dijo a Raquel que había hablado con su madre, quien había dicho que *Raquel fuera a Madrid para que hablara con ella personalmente.*

A los dos días, Raquel salió para Madrid. En el tren, *conoció a un reportero.* El reportero *buscaba a una maestra (y creía que Raquel era esa persona).* Como no tuvo éxito, se interesó en *el caso que Raquel investigaba.* Raquel, respetando la confidencialidad de su cliente, *no le dijo nada (¡aunque el reportero era muy persistente!).*

En su hotel en Madrid, Raquel bajaba de su habitación cuando *encontró a otro hijo de Teresa Suárez, Federico Ruiz.* La invitó a su casa a cenar y por fin Raquel *conoció a Teresa Suárez.* Ésta le contó la triste historia de *Rosario, quien al final de la Guerra Civil se fue con su hijo Ángel a la Argentina,* pensando que don Fernando había muerto. La Sra. Suárez también le dio a Raquel *la dirección de Rosario en la Argentina.* Ahora Raquel podía seguir con su investigación. Se preparó para otro viaje, esta vez a Buenos Aires.

LECCIÓN 49

REPASO DE LOS EPISODIOS 12–18

Actividad A.   *Paso 1*   1. b   2. d   3. a   4. a   5. b   6. c   7. c   8. e   **Actividad B.**   *Pasos 1 y 2*   *Possible answer:* Cuando Raquel llegó a Buenos Aires, alquiló un coche con un chofer para ir a la estancia Santa Susana, la dirección que Teresa Suárez *le había dado.* Tenía muchas esperanzas de encontrar a Rosario. Llamó a la puerta y *un joven contestó.* Éste no sabía nada de Rosario, pero le dijo a Raquel que *hablara con Cirilo, un gaucho.* Cirilo sí *recordaba a Rosario* y *le dijo a Raquel que Rosario y su hijo se habían mudado a la capital.* También se acordaba *del nombre de la calle.*

Raquel regresó a Buenos Aires y buscó la dirección que Cirilo le había dado. Por fin, en una casa en la calle Gorostiaga, *conoció a Arturo Iglesias, psiquiatra que es hijo de Rosario y medio hermano de Ángel.* Raquel quedó muy sorprendida al encontrar por fin a un miembro de la familia. Desgraciadamente, *Arturo le contó que Rosario había muerto y que hacía mucho tiempo que él no sabía nada de Ángel.* Arturo también le contó a Raquel que no sabía nada de Ángel porque *perdió contacto con él hace mucho tiempo.*

Los dos fueron al cementerio donde estaba enterrada Rosario. Allí *Raquel sacó una foto de la tumba para don Fernando.* Más tarde Arturo le dijo *que la quería ayudar con la búsqueda de Ángel.* Con una foto de Ángel a los veinte años, los dos *empezaron la búsqueda en La Boca, un barrio de Buenos Aires donde Arturo creía que Ángel tenía amigos.* Preguntaron en varias tiendas, pero *nadie lo conocía.* Por fin, Mario, el dueño de una tienda de antigüedades, dijo que era posible que un tal José lo conociera. Encontraron a José en su barco. José *no reconocía a Ángel, pero pensaba que era posible que Héctor lo conociera.* Más tarde les dijo dónde y cuándo podrían encontrar a Héctor.

En un bar llamado el Piccolo Navio, Raquel y Arturo encontraron a Héctor con sus amigos. Al acompañarlo a casa, le mostraron la foto de Ángel. Héctor *sí lo recordó, porque era su amigo.* Pensaba que Ángel se había embarcado para *Puerto*

Rico, pero no estaba muy seguro. A los dos días Héctor le dio a Arturo una carta de Ángel que tenía en su casa. La carta *tenía la dirección de Ángel*. Era verdad: Ángel *se había mudado a Puerto Rico*.

Ahora, para seguir su investigación, Raquel tenía que ir a Puerto Rico. Fue *de compras en Buenos Aires porque necesitaba ropa para su viaje al Caribe y, con Arturo, vio un poco de la ciudad*. Se despidió de Arturo en el aeropuerto. Mientras esperaba su vuelo, *le escribió una carta a la Sra. Suárez, dándole las malas noticias de la muerte de su amiga Rosario*.

LECCIÓN 50
REPASO DE LOS EPISODIOS 19–26
Actividad A.   *Paso 1*   1. Se lo dijo alguien, una vecina de la familia.   2. Raquel supo que Ángela tenía un hermano cuando hablaba con ella antes de la llegada de los tíos.   3. Fue la primera vez que oían los nombres de Rosario y don Fernando.   4. Pensaron que era importante que hablara con su abuela.   5. Tuvieron que quedarse en Ponce.   6. Ángela no había limpiado el cuarto de Ángel.   7. Encontraron unos dibujos que él había hecho con recuerdos de su pasado.   8. Recibieron noticias importantes. Supieron del derrumbe en el sitio de la excavación.   **Actividad B.   *Pasos 1 y 2***   Cuando llegó a San Juan, Raquel fue directamente a la dirección que estaba en la carta de Héctor. Tocó a la puerta, pero *no contestó nadie*. Desde su balcón, una vecina le dijo que *Ángel había muerto y que estaba enterrado en el cementerio del Viejo San Juan*. En el cementerio Raquel *conoció a Ángela Castillo Soto... la hija de Ángel Castillo*. Allí en el cementerio Raquel se lo explicó todo.

Raquel y Ángela regresaron al apartamento donde vivía ella, que era el antiguo apartamento de sus padres. Desde allí Ángela *llamó a sus tíos para que vinieran a conocer a Raquel*. Mientras los esperaban, seguían hablando. Raquel supo que *Ángela tenía un hermano, Roberto Castillo, que era estudiante de arqueología y estaba trabajando en una excavación en México*.

Cuando llegaron los tíos de Ángela, Raquel les contó la historia de don Fernando y les habló de su investigación. También les dijo que Ángela *iba a ir a México con ella a conocer a su abuelo*. La tía Olga, la gruñona de la familia, *no reaccionó bien a las noticias de Raquel*. Por eso Ángela llamó a *su abuela* para pedirle consejo. Ésta quería que Ángela y Raquel fueran a verla a San Germán.

Al día siguiente Raquel y Ángela, acompañadas por Laura, la prima de Ángela, salieron para San Germán. En un peaje tuvieron *problemas con el carro y por eso no pudieron llegar a San Germán*. Se quedaron por la noche en Ponce y a la mañana siguiente *recogieron el carro y empezaron el viaje de nuevo*.

En San Germán, almorzaron con la abuela y hablaron de Ángel y su esposa. La abuela le recordó a Ángela que *no había limpiado el cuarto de su padre*. Allí, en un viejo baúl, Ángela *encontró unos dibujos que su padre había hecho*. Eran *recuerdos de su vida en Puerto Rico y también de su vida en España y la Argentina*. Al salir para San Juan, la abuela salió corriendo de la casa y *le dio a Ángela otro recuerdo de su padre: la copa de bodas de Rosario, madre de Ángel y primera esposa de don Fernando*.

De regreso en San Juan, Raquel y Ángela pasaron por el banco donde trabajaba Ángela para *pedirle a su jefa permiso de ausentarse unas semanas*. También vieron unos apartamentos con una agente de bienes raíces, porque Ángela *quería vender el apartamento de sus padres y mudarse a otro sitio*. Al día siguiente, cuando salían para el aeropuerto, llegó el tío Jaime con malas noticias: *había habido un derrumbe en la excavación donde trabajaba Roberto*.

LECCIÓN 51
REPASO DE LOS EPISODIOS 27–36
Actividad A.   *Paso 1*   a. 5   b. 7   c. 2   d. 6   e. 1   f. 4   g. 10   h. 9   i. 3   j. 8   **Actividad B.   *Pasos 1 y 2***   *Possible answer:* Tan pronto como llegaron a México, Raquel y Ángela alquilaron un auto y salieron para un pueblo cerca de la excavación donde trabajaba Roberto. En el camino, Ángela le habló a Raquel de *sus relaciones con Roberto*, y le confesó que *le tenía un poco de envidia*.

Al llegar al sitio, no las dejaron pasar. Entonces *fueron al hospital del pueblo*. Allí les dieron la lista de los accidentados. Por un momento *pensaron que un tal R. Castilla era Roberto, pero no era así*.

En el hospital conocieron a un padre que las ayudó mucho a lo largo de su estancia en el pueblo. Por medio del padre, Ángela y Raquel pudieron *llegar al sitio de la excavación*. Tenían muchas esperanzas de que rescataran a Roberto pronto. Por fin sacaron a dos personas, pero *ninguno era el hermano de Ángela*. Antes de que pudieran sacar a otras personas, *hubo un derrumbe*. Ángela comenzó a llorar y le tuvieron que dar un calmante. Por fin se pudo dormir, y Raquel *pasó la noche a su lado*.

Por la mañana, mientras seguían esperando el rescate de Roberto, Raquel y Ángela hicieron varias llamadas. Raquel *no pudo ponerse en contacto con Arturo, pero sí le dejó un mensaje*. Y Ángela *pudo hablar con sus tíos en Puerto Rico*. Después fueron a la iglesia del pueblo, donde *una hermana muy amable les dio donde descansar y refrescarse*.

Por fin encontraron a Roberto... ¡y *estaba vivo*! Antes de que pudieran rescatarlo, sin embargo, *hubo un segundo derrumbe*. Pero lo pudieron sacar de todas formas. Lo examinaron en seguida; por suerte *no tuvo lesiones graves*. Sin embargo *era necesario llevarlo a un hospital en la capital*. Raquel y Ángela salieron para México en su auto, y en el camino *casi chocaron con un camión*. Al llegar al hospital, Ángela entró al cuarto de Roberto corriendo. Arturo, quien estaba allí con Pedro, vio a Raquel y *gritó su nombre y la besó*.

LECCIÓN 52

PREPARACIÓN

Actividad. 1. b   2. a   3. a   4. a   5. b

¿TIENES BUENA MEMORIA?

Actividad. *Pasos 1 y 2* Don Fernando tenía dudas de la identidad de Ángela y Roberto, y quería estar seguro de que eran sus nietos. Raquel le recordó a Ángela lo de la copa de bodas de Rosario, que *seguramente sería la prueba definitiva.*

Al día siguiente, llegó la agente de bienes raíces. El deseo de su cliente de comprar La Gavia no fue realizado, porque *don Fernando llegó y les dijo a todos que La Gavia no estaba en venta.* Entonces Mercedes reveló su plan para fundar un orfanato en la hacienda. Todos quedaron sorprendidos cuando don Fernando reveló que, *hace años, había establecido una fundación para hacer precisamente eso.* Según don Fernando, Carlos y Mercedes *administrarían el orfanato.* Juan debería regresar a Nueva York porque *allí estaba su vida y allí tenía su carrera.*

Más tarde, en el cuarto de don Fernando, cuando todos estaban presentes, Ángela *le dio la caja al patriarca.* Cuando don Fernando la abrió, se puso muy emocionado. Entonces le pidió a Mercedes que le diera a Ángela una caja que él tenía allí en su cuarto, en un armario. Cuando Ángela la abrió, *encontró otra copa igual.* Así ya no había dudas: *Ángela y Roberto eran sus nietos.*

Raquel y Arturo se despidieron de don Fernando y estaban para salir. Pero el patriarca quería hablar con Raquel a solas. Le dijo que no se le había escapado cómo *Arturo y ella se miraban.* Raquel le confesó que *lo que sentía por Arturo era serio.* Entonces don Fernando le dio unos consejos: o ella *tenía que irse a Buenos Aires* o él *tenía que ir a Los Ángeles*, que no debían perder un amor verdadero. Se abrazaron una vez más.

Antes de salir, Raquel se volvió y le dijo a don Fernando que Rosario nunca dejó de pensar en él, que *siempre lo amó.* Con las dos copas reunidas, don Fernando se quedó en su cuarto a solas, pensando en el día en que, hace años, en un país lejano, dos jóvenes españoles las habían usado para celebrar el día de su boda.

APPENDIX 2: VERB CHARTS

A. Regular Verbs: Simple Tenses

use To · *will* · *would* (handwritten annotations above IMPERFECT, FUTURE, CONDITIONAL columns)

INFINITIVE / PRESENT PARTICIPLE / PAST PARTICIPLE	INDICATIVE					SUBJUNCTIVE		IMPERATIVE
	PRESENT	IMPERFECT	PRETERITE	FUTURE	CONDITIONAL	PRESENT	IMPERFECT	
hablar hablando hablado	hablo hablas habla hablamos habláis hablan	hablaba hablabas hablaba hablábamos hablabais hablaban	hablé hablaste habló hablamos hablasteis hablaron	hablaré hablarás hablará hablaremos hablaréis hablarán	hablaría hablarías hablaría hablaríamos hablaríais hablarían	hable hables hable hablemos habléis hablen	hablara hablaras hablara habláramos hablarais hablaran	habla tú, no hables hable Ud. hablemos hablen
comer comiendo comido	como comes come comemos coméis comen	comía comías comía comíamos comíais comían	comí comiste comió comimos comisteis comieron	comeré comerás comerá comeremos comeréis comerán	comería comerías comería comeríamos comeríais comerían	coma comas coma comamos comáis coman	comiera comieras comiera comiéramos comierais comieran	come tú, no comas coma Ud. comamos coman
vivir viviendo vivido	vivo vives vive vivimos vivís viven	vivía vivías vivía vivíamos vivíais vivían	viví viviste vivió vivimos vivisteis vivieron	viviré vivirás vivirá viviremos viviréis vivirán	viviría vivirías viviría viviríamos viviríais vivirían	viva vivas viva vivamos viváis vivan	viviera vivieras viviera viviéramos vivierais vivieran	vive tú, no vivas viva Ud. vivamos vivan

B. Regular Verbs: Perfect Tenses

= compound tense (2 verbs) = helping verb (haber); I have spoken · I had spoken · I will have spoken · I would have spoken (handwritten annotations)

INDICATIVE					SUBJUNCTIVE	
PRESENT PERFECT	PAST PERFECT	PRETERITE PERFECT	FUTURE PERFECT	CONDITIONAL PERFECT	PRESENT PERFECT	PAST PERFECT
he has ha hemos habéis han	había habías había habíamos habíais habían	hube hubiste hubo hubimos hubisteis hubieron	habré habrás habrá habremos habréis habrán	habría habrías habría habríamos habríais habrían	haya hayas haya hayamos hayáis hayan	hubiera hubieras hubiera hubiéramos hubierais hubieran

Each perfect tense is followed by: hablado / comido / vivido

C. Irregular Verbs

INFINITIVE / PRESENT PARTICIPLE / PAST PARTICIPLE	INDICATIVE					SUBJUNCTIVE		IMPERATIVE
	PRESENT	IMPERFECT	PRETERITE	FUTURE	CONDITIONAL	PRESENT	IMPERFECT	
andar andando andado	ando andas anda andamos andáis andan	andaba andabas andaba andábamos andabais andaban	anduve anduviste anduvo anduvimos anduvisteis anduvieron	andaré andarás andará andaremos andaréis andarán	andaría andarías andaría andaríamos andaríais andarían	ande andes ande andemos andéis anden	anduviera anduvieras anduviera anduviéramos anduvierais anduvieran	anda tú, no andes ande Ud. andemos anden
caer cayendo caído	caigo caes cae caemos caéis caen	caía caías caía caíamos caíais caían	caí caíste cayó caímos caísteis cayeron	caeré caerás caerá caeremos caeréis caerán	caería caerías caería caeríamos caeríais caerían	caiga caigas caiga caigamos caigáis caigan	cayera cayeras cayera cayéramos cayerais cayeran	cae tú, no caigas caiga Ud. caigamos caigan
dar dando dado	doy das da damos dais dan	daba dabas daba dábamos dabais daban	di diste dio dimos disteis dieron	daré darás dará daremos daréis darán	daría darías daría daríamos daríais darían	dé des dé demos deis den	diera dieras diera diéramos dierais dieran	da tú, no des dé Ud. demos den
decir diciendo dicho	digo dices dice decimos decís dicen	decía decías decía decíamos decíais decían	dije dijiste dijo dijimos dijisteis dijeron	diré dirás dirá diremos diréis dirán	diría dirías diría diríamos diríais dirían	diga digas diga digamos digáis digan	dijera dijeras dijera dijéramos dijerais dijeran	di tú, no digas diga Ud. digamos digan
estar estando estado	estoy estás está estamos estáis están	estaba estabas estaba estábamos estabais estaban	estuve estuviste estuvo estuvimos estuvisteis estuvieron	estaré estarás estará estaremos estaréis estarán	estaría estarías estaría estaríamos estaríais estarían	esté estés esté estemos estéis estén	estuviera estuvieras estuviera estuviéramos estuvierais estuviera	está tú, no estés esté Ud. estemos estén
haber habiendo habido	he has ha hemos habéis han	había habías había habíamos habíais habían	hube hubiste hubo hubimos hubisteis hubieron	habré habrás habrá habremos habréis habrán	habría habrías habría habríamos habríais habrían	haya hayas haya hayamos hayáis hayan	hubiera hubieras hubiera hubiéramos hubierais hubieran	
hacer haciendo hecho	hago haces hace hacemos hacéis hacen	hacía hacías hacía hacíamos hacíais hacían	hice hiciste hizo hicimos hicisteis hicieron	haré harás hará haremos haréis harán	haría harías haría haríamos haríais harían	haga hagas haga hagamos hagáis hagan	hiciera hicieras hiciera hiciéramos hicierais hicieran	haz tú, no hagas haga Ud. hagamos hagan

C. Irregular Verbs (continued)

INFINITIVE / PRESENT PARTICIPLE / PAST PARTICIPLE	INDICATIVE					SUBJUNCTIVE		IMPERATIVE
	PRESENT	IMPERFECT	PRETERITE	FUTURE	CONDITIONAL	PRESENT	IMPERFECT	
ir / yendo / ido	voy	iba	fui	iré	iría	vaya	fuera	
	vas	ibas	fuiste	irás	irías	vayas	fueras	ve tú,
	va	iba	fue	irá	iría	vaya	fuera	no vayas
	vamos	íbamos	fuimos	iremos	iríamos	vayamos	fuéramos	vaya Ud.
	vais	ibais	fuisteis	iréis	iríais	vayáis	fuerais	vayamos
	van	iban	fueron	irán	irían	vayan	fueran	vayan
oír / oyendo / oído	oigo	oía	oí	oiré	oiría	oiga	oyera	
	oyes	oías	oíste	oirás	oirías	oigas	oyeras	oye tú,
	oye	oía	oyó	oirá	oiría	oiga	oyera	no oigas
	oímos	oíamos	oímos	oiremos	oiríamos	oigamos	oyéramos	oiga Ud.
	oís	oíais	oísteis	oiréis	oiríais	oigáis	oyerais	oigamos
	oyen	oían	oyeron	oirán	oirían	oigan	oyeran	oigan
poder / pudiendo / podido	puedo	podía	pude	podré	podría	pueda	pudiera	
	puedes	podías	pudiste	podrás	podrías	puedas	pudieras	
	puede	podía	pudo	podrá	podría	pueda	pudiera	
	podemos	podíamos	pudimos	podremos	podríamos	podamos	pudiéramos	
	podéis	podíais	pudisteis	podréis	podríais	podáis	pudierais	
	pueden	podían	pudieron	podrán	podrían	puedan	pudieran	
poner / poniendo / puesto	pongo	ponía	puse	pondré	pondría	ponga	pusiera	
	pones	ponías	pusiste	pondrás	pondrías	pongas	pusieras	pon tú,
	pone	ponía	puso	pondrá	pondría	ponga	pusiera	no pongas
	ponemos	poníamos	pusimos	pondremos	pondríamos	pongamos	pusiéramos	ponga Ud.
	ponéis	poníais	pusisteis	pondréis	pondríais	pongáis	pusierais	pongamos
	ponen	ponían	pusieron	pondrán	pondrían	pongan	pusieran	pongan
querer / queriendo / querido	quiero	quería	quise	querré	querría	quiera	quisiera	
	quieres	querías	quisiste	querrás	querrías	quieras	quisieras	quiere tú,
	quiere	quería	quiso	querrá	querría	quiera	quisiera	no quieras
	queremos	queríamos	quisimos	querremos	querríamos	queramos	quisiéramos	quiera Ud.
	queréis	queríais	quisisteis	querréis	querríais	queráis	quisierais	queramos
	quieren	querían	quisieron	querrán	querrían	quieran	quisieran	quieran
saber / sabiendo / sabido	sé	sabía	supe	sabré	sabría	sepa	supiera	
	sabes	sabías	supiste	sabrás	sabrías	sepas	supieras	sabe tú,
	sabe	sabía	supo	sabrá	sabría	sepa	supiera	no sepas
	sabemos	sabíamos	supimos	sabremos	sabríamos	sepamos	supiéramos	sepa Ud.
	sabéis	sabíais	supisteis	sabréis	sabríais	sepáis	supierais	sepamos
	saben	sabían	supieron	sabrán	sabrían	sepan	supieran	sepan
salir / saliendo / salido	salgo	salía	salí	saldré	saldría	salga	saliera	
	sales	salías	saliste	saldrás	saldrías	salgas	salieras	sal tú,
	sale	salía	salió	saldrá	saldría	salga	saliera	no salgas
	salimos	salíamos	salimos	saldremos	saldríamos	salgamos	saliéramos	salga Ud.
	salís	salíais	salisteis	saldréis	saldríais	salgáis	salierais	salgamos
	salen	salían	salieron	saldrán	saldrían	salgan	salieran	salgan

C. Irregular Verbs (continued)

	PRESENT	IMPERFECT	PRETERITE	FUTURE	CONDITIONAL	PRESENT SUBJ.	IMPERFECT SUBJ.	IMPERATIVE
ser siendo sido	soy eres es somos sois son	era eras era éramos erais eran	fui fuiste fue fuimos fuisteis fueron	seré serás será seremos seréis serán	sería serías sería seríamos seríais serían	sea seas sea seamos seáis sean	fuera fueras fuera fuéramos fuerais fueran	sé tú, no seas sea Ud. seamos sean
tener teniendo tenido	tengo tienes tiene tenemos tenéis tienen	tenía tenías tenía teníamos teníais tenían	tuve tuviste tuvo tuvimos tuvisteis tuvieron	tendré tendrás tendrá tendremos tendréis tendrán	tendría tendrías tendría tendríamos tendríais tendrían	tenga tengas tenga tengamos tengáis tengan	tuviera tuvieras tuviera tuviéramos tuvierais tuvieran	ten tú, no tengas tenga Ud. tengamos tengan
traer trayendo traído	traigo traes trae traemos traéis traen	traía traías traía traíamos traíais traían	traje trajiste trajo trajimos trajisteis trajeron	traeré traerás traerá traeremos traeréis traerán	traería traerías traería traeríamos traeríais traerían	traiga traigas traiga traigamos traigáis traigan	trajera trajeras trajera trajéramos trajerais trajeran	trae tú, no traigas traiga Ud. traigamos traigan
venir viniendo venido	vengo vienes viene venimos venís vienen	venía venías venía veníamos veníais venían	vine viniste vino vinimos vinisteis vinieron	vendré vendrás vendrá vendremos vendréis vendrán	vendría vendrías vendría vendríamos vendríais vendrían	venga vengas venga vengamos vengáis vengan	viniera vinieras viniera viniéramos vinierais vinieran	ven tú, no vengas venga Ud. vengamos vengan
ver viendo visto	veo ves ve vemos veis ven	veía veías veía veíamos veíais veían	vi viste vio vimos visteis vieron	veré verás verá veremos veréis verán	vería verías vería veríamos veríais verían	vea veas vea veamos veáis vean	viera vieras viera viéramos vierais vieran	ve tú, no veas vea Ud. veamos vean

D. Stem-changing and Spelling Change Verbs

INFINITIVE PRESENT PARTICIPLE PAST PARTICIPLE	INDICATIVE					SUBJUNCTIVE		IMPERATIVE
	PRESENT	IMPERFECT	PRETERITE	FUTURE	CONDITIONAL	PRESENT	IMPERFECT	
construir (y) construyendo construido	construyo construyes construye construimos construís construyen	construía construías construía construíamos construíais construían	construí construiste construyó construimos construisteis construyeron	construiré construirás construirá construiremos construiréis construirán	construiría construirías construiría construiríamos construiríais construirían	construya construyas construya construyamos construyáis construyan	construyera construyeras construyera construyéramos construyerais construyeran	construye tú, no construyas construya Ud. construyamos construyan
dormir (ue, u) durmiendo dormido	duermo duermes duerme dormimos dormís duermen	dormía dormías dormía dormíamos dormíais dormían	dormí dormiste durmió dormimos dormisteis durmieron	dormiré dormirás dormirá dormiremos dormiréis dormirán	dormiría dormirías dormiría dormiríamos dormiríais dormirían	duerma duermas duerma durmamos durmáis duerman	durmiera durmieras durmiera durmiéramos durmierais durmieran	duerme tú, no duermas duerma Ud. durmamos duerman

D. Stem-changing and Spelling Change Verbs (continued)

INFINITIVE / PRESENT PARTICIPLE / PAST PARTICIPLE	INDICATIVE					SUBJUNCTIVE		IMPERATIVE
	PRESENT	IMPERFECT	PRETERITE	FUTURE	CONDITIONAL	PRESENT	IMPERFECT	
pedir (i, i) / pidiendo / pedido	pido pides pide pedimos pedís piden	pedía pedías pedía pedíamos pedíais pedían	pedí pediste pidió pedimos pedisteis pidieron	pediré pedirás pedirá pediremos pediréis pedirán	pediría pedirías pediría pediríamos pediríais pedirían	pida pidas pida pidamos pidáis pidan	pidiera pidieras pidiera pidiéramos pidierais pidieran	pide tú, no pidas pida Ud. pidamos pidan
pensar (ie) / pensando / pensado	pienso piensas piensa pensamos pensáis piensan	pensaba pensabas pensaba pensábamos pensabais pensaban	pensé pensaste pensó pensamos pensasteis pensaron	pensaré pensarás pensará pensaremos pensaréis pensarán	pensaría pensarías pensaría pensaríamos pensaríais pensarían	piense pienses piense pensemos penséis piensen	pensara pensaras pensara pensáramos pensarais pensaran	piensa tú, no pienses piense Ud. pensemos piensen
producir (zc) / produciendo / producido	produzco produces produce producimos producís producen	producía producías producía producíamos producíais producían	produje produjiste produjo produjimos produjisteis produjeron	produciré producirás producirá produciremos produciréis producirán	produciría producirías produciría produciríamos produciríais producirían	produzca produzcas produzca produzcamos produzcáis produzcan	produjera produjeras produjera produjéramos produjerais produjeran	produce tú, no produzcas produzca Ud. produzcamos produzcan
reír (i, i) / riendo / reído	río ríes ríe reímos reís ríen	reía reías reía reíamos reíais reían	reí reíste rió reímos reísteis rieron	reiré reirás reirá reiremos reiréis reirán	reiría reirías reiría reiríamos reiríais reirían	ría rías ría riamos riáis rían	riera rieras riera riéramos rierais rieran	ríe tú, no rías ría Ud. riamos rían
seguir (i, i) (ga) / siguiendo / seguido	sigo sigues sigue seguimos seguís siguen	seguía seguías seguía seguíamos seguíais seguían	seguí seguiste siguió seguimos seguisteis siguieron	seguiré seguirás seguirá seguiremos seguiréis seguirán	seguiría seguirías seguiría seguiríamos seguiríais seguirían	siga sigas siga sigamos sigáis sigan	siguiera siguieras siguiera siguiéramos siguierais siguieran	sigue tú, no sigas siga Ud. sigamos sigan
sentir (ie, i) / sintiendo / sentido	siento sientes siente sentimos sentís sienten	sentía sentías sentía sentíamos sentíais sentían	sentí sentiste sintió sentimos sentisteis sintieron	sentiré sentirás sentirá sentiremos sentiréis sentirán	sentiría sentirías sentiría sentiríamos sentiríais sentirían	sienta sientas sienta sintamos sintáis sientan	sintiera sintieras sintiera sintiéramos sintierais sintieran	siente tú, no sientas sienta Ud. sintamos sientan
volver (ue) / volviendo / vuelto	vuelvo vuelves vuelve volvemos volvéis vuelven	volvía volvías volvía volvíamos volvíais volvían	volví volviste volvió volvimos volvisteis volvieron	volveré volverás volverá volveremos volveréis volverán	volvería volverías volvería volveríamos volveríais volverían	vuelva vuelvas vuelva volvamos volváis vuelvan	volviera volvieras volviera volviéramos volvierais volvieran	vuelve tú, no vuelvas vuelva Ud. volvamos vuelvan

Spanish-English Vocabulary

The Spanish-English Vocabulary contains all the words that appear in the Textbook and Workbook/Study Guides I and II (and their corresponding audiocassette materials), with the following exceptions: (1) most close or identical cognates that do not appear in the chapter vocabulary lists; (2) most conjugated verb forms; (3) diminutives ending in **-ito/a**; (4) absolute superlatives ending in **ísimo/a**; (5) most adverbs ending in **-mente** (if the corresponding adjective is listed); and (6) most vocabulary that is glossed in the Text and Workbook/Study Guides. Only meanings that are used in the Textbook and Workbook/Study Guides are given.

The gender of nouns is indicated, except for masculine nouns ending in **-o** and feminine nouns ending in **-a**. Stem changes and spelling changes are indicated for verbs: **dormir (ue, u)**; **llegar (gu)**; **seguir (i, i) (g)**.

Words beginning with **ch, ll,** and **ñ** are found under separate headings, following the letters **c, l,** and **n,** respectively. Similarly, **ch, ll,** and **ñ** within words follow **c, l,** and **n,** respectively. For example, **coche** follows **cóctel, calle** follows **calor,** and **añadir** follows **anuncio.**

The following abbreviations are used:

adj.	adjective	*m.*	masculine
adv.	adverb	*Mex.*	Mexico
approx.	approximately	*n.*	noun
Arg.	Argentina	*obj. (of prep.)*	object (of a preposition)
C. Am.	Central America	*pers.*	personal
conj.	conjunction	*pl.*	plural
def. art.	definite article	*poss.*	possessive
d.o.	direct object	*p.p.*	past participle
f.	feminine	*P.R.*	Puerto Rico
fam.	familiar	*prep.*	preposition
form.	formal	*pron.*	pronoun
gram.	grammatical term	*refl. pron.*	reflexive pronoun
inf.	infinitive	*s.*	singular
interj.	interjection	*Sp.*	Spain
inv.	invariable form	*sub. pron.*	subject pronoun
i.o.	indirect object	*U.S.*	United States
irreg.	irregular	*v.*	verb
L.A.	Latin America		

A

a to; at (*with time*); **a base de** on the basis of; **a bordo** aboard, on board; **a cargo (de)** in charge (of); **a causa de** because of, on account of; **a continuación** following, below, immediately after; **a dieta** on a diet; **a diferencia de** unlike; **a favor** in favor; **a fondo** completely, thoroughly; **a la vez** at the same time; **a la vuelta** around the corner; **a la(s) ...** at (*hour*); **a lo mejor** maybe; **a más tardar** at the latest; **a menos que** unless; **a menudo** often; **a nombre de** in the name of; **a orillas de** on the banks of; **a partir de** starting from; **a pesar de** in spite of; **a punto de** at the point of; about to; **¿a quién?** to whom? **a ratos** at times; **a sus órdenes** at your service; **a través de** through, across; **a veces** at times, sometimes; **a ver** let's see, let's have a look

abandonar to abandon

abanico fan

abastecer (zc) to supply, provide

abierto/a (*p.p. of* **abrir**) open(ed)

abogado/a lawyer

abolición *f.* abolition

abrazarse (c) to embrace

abrigador(a) heavy, warm (*of a coat*); sheltering

abril *m.* April

abrir (*p.p.* **abierto/a**) to open

absoluto/a absolute; **en absoluto** (not) at all

abuelo/a grandfather, grandmother, *pl.* grandparents

abundante abundant

abundar to abound, be plentiful
aburrido/a: ser (*irreg.*), **aburrido/a** to be boring; **estar** (*irreg.*) **aburrido/a** to be bored
aburrirse (de) to get bored (*with*)
abuso abuse
acá here
acabar to finish; **acabar de** + *inf.* to have just (*done something*)
academia academy
académico/a academic
acatarrarse to catch a cold
accidentado/a *person involved in an accident*
accidente *m.* accident
acción *f.* action
aceite *m.* oil
aceituna olive
acento accent
aceptación *f.* acceptance
aceptar to accept
acerca de *prep.* about, concerning
acercarse (qu) (a) to approach, draw near
acero steel
aclaración *f.* clarification
acoger (j) to welcome, bring in, receive
acomodarse (a) to adapt oneself (to)
acompañar to accompany
aconsejable advisable
aconsejar to advise
acontecimiento event
acordarse (ue) (de) to remember
acostar (ue) to put to bed; **acostarse** to go to bed
acostumbrarse (a) to get accustomed to
actitud *f.* attitude
actividad *f.* activity
activo/a active
actor *m.* actor
actriz *f.* (*pl.* **actrices**) actress
actual current
actualidad present time; **en la actualidad** at this time, nowadays
actualmente currently
actuar to act, perform; **actuarse** to behave
acuático/a *adj.* aquatic, related to water; **esquí** (*m.*) **acuático** water skiing
acueducto aqueduct
acuerdo agreement; **de acuerdo** OK, I agree; **estar** (*irreg.*) **de acuerdo (con)** to agree, be in agreement (with)
acusación *f.* accusation
acusar to accuse
Adán Adam
adaptar(se) to adapt
adecuado/a adequate; suitable
adelantarse to get ahead
además (de) besides, in addition (to)
adicción *f.* addiction
adicional additional

adicto/a addict
adiós good-bye
adivinanza riddle, puzzle
adjetivo *n.* adjective; **adjetivos posesivos** (*gram.*) possessive adjectives; **adjetivos demostrativos** demonstrative adjectives
administración *f.* administration; **administración de empresas** business administration
administrador(a) administrator
admiración *f.* admiration
admirar to admire
admitir to admit
adolescente *m., f.* adolescent
adonde where
¿adónde? (to) where?
adoquín *m.* cobblestone
adorar to adore
aduana *s.* customs
adulto/a adult
adversario adversary
adversidad *f.* adversity
aéreo: (por) correo aéreo (by) airmail
aeróbico: ejercicio aeróbico aerobic exercise
aeropuerto airport
afectar to affect
afectivo/a emotional
afecto affection
afectuosamente affectionately
afectuoso/a affectionate
aficionado/a fan, enthusiast
afirmación *f.* affirmation
afirmar to affirm
afirmativamente affirmatively
afortunadamente fortunately
africano/a *n., adj.* African
afuera *adv.* outside
afueras suburbs, outskirts
agave *f.* agave (*Mexican plant from which tequila is made*)
agencia agency; **agencia de viajes** travel agency
agente *m., f.* agent; **agente de bienes raíces** real estate agent; **agente de viajes** travel agent
agitado/a upset, worried; shaky; excited
agosto August
agradable agreeable, pleasant
agradar to be pleasing
agradecer (zc) to thank
agradecido/a grateful
agraria: reforma agraria agrarian reform
agravarse to worsen
agregar (gu) to add
agresivo/a aggressive
agrícola *m., f.* agricultural; **estudios agrícolas** agricultural studies
agricultura agriculture
agridulce bittersweet
agua *f.* (*but* **el agua**) water; **agua mine-**

ral mineral water; **pasar por agua** to boil (*eggs*)
aguacate *m.* avocado
aguantar to put up with, endure, tolerate
águila *f.* (but **el águila**) eagle
ahí there
ahora now; **ahora mismo** right now; **justo ahora** right now, just now
ahorrar to save (*money, time*)
ahorros savings; **cuenta de ahorros** savings account
aire *m.* air; (**estar** [*irreg.*]) **al aire libre** (to be) outdoors
aislado/a isolated
aislamiento isolation
ajedrez *m.* chess; **jugar (ue) (gu) al ajedrez** to play chess
ajeno/a distant, detached
ají *m.* pepper, chili
al (*contraction of* **a+el**) to the; **al** + *inf.* upon, while, when + *verb form;* **al anochecer** at nightfall, dusk; **al borde de** on the edge of; **al comienzo** at the beginning; **al contrario** on the contrary; **al día siguiente** the next day; **al fin y al cabo** after all, when all is said and done; **al final** in the end; **al final de** at the end of; **al horno** baked; **al menos** at least; **al (mes, año, ...)** per (month, year, . . .); **al mismo tiempo** at the same time; **al parecer** apparently; **al pie de** at the bottom of; **al poco tiempo** shortly after; **al principio** at first, at the beginning; **al terminar ...** when . . . is/was over; **al tiro** immediately
alabar to praise
alargado/a elongated, lengthened
alarmado/a alarmed
alcalde *m.* mayor
alcanzar (c) to reach; to amount to
alcázar *m.* fortress; castle
alcoba bedroom
alcohólica: bebida alcohólica alcoholic beverage
aldea village
alegoría allegory
alegrarse (de) to be glad, happy (about)
alegre happy
alegría happiness; happy nature
alejarse (de) to go far away (from); to separate (from); to draw away, grow apart (from)
alemán, alemana *n., adj.* German
Alemania Germany
alérgico/a allergic
aleta rudder
alfabeto alphabet
álgebra *f.* (*but* **el álgebra**) algebra
algo something, anything
algodón *m.* cotton
alguien someone; **caerle** (*irreg.*) **bien/**

mal a alguien to like (not like), make a good/bad impression on someone; **darle** (*irreg.*) **de alta a alguien** to release someone (*from an institution*); **poner ·** (*irreg.*) **a alguien a cargo (de)** to put someone in charge (of)

algún, alguno/a some; any; **alguna vez** ever

aliado/a *n.* ally; *adj.* allied

alianza wedding ring

alicantino/a from Alicante (*region of Spain*)

aliviar to alleviate, relieve

alma *f.* (*but* **el alma**) soul

almacén *m.* department store; storehouse

almorzar (ue) (c) to have lunch

almuerzo lunch

alojado/a *adj.* staying, lodged (*at a hotel*)

alojarse to stay, lodge

alpino: esquí (*m.*) **alpino** downhill skiing

alquilado/a rented

alquilar to rent

alquiler *m.* rent

alta: darle (*irreg.*) **de alta a (alguien)** to release (someone) (*from an institution*)

alternar to alternate

alternativa alternative

altiplano high plateau

altitud *f.* altitude

alto *n.* height; **de alto** in height

alto/a *adj.* tall; high; loud; **clase** (*f.*) **alta** upper class; **alta cocina** haute cuisine; **en voz alta** out loud

altura height

allá there; **más allá de** *prep.* beyond

allí there

ama (*f.* [*but* **el ama**]) **de casa** homemaker; housekeeper

amabilidad *f.* kindness

amable nice, kind

amaestrar to train

amante *m., f.* lover

amar to love

amarillo/a yellow

ambición *f.* ambition

ambicionar to desire

ambicioso/a ambitious

ambiental environmental

ambiente *m.* atmosphere; **medio ambiente** environment

ambos/as both

ambulancia ambulance

ambulante: músicos ambulantes strolling musicians

amenaza threat

amenazante threatening

amenazar (c) to threaten

ameno/a pleasant, agreeable

América Latina Latin America

americano/a *n. adj.* American; **fútbol** (*m.*) **americano** football

amigablemente amicably, in a friendly way

amigo/a friend; **amigo/a íntimo/a** close friend; **mejor amigo/a** best friend; **salir** (*irreg.*) **con los amigos** to go out with friends

amistad *f.* friendship

amistoso/a friendly

amor *m.* love; **amor a primera vista** love at first sight

amoroso/a affectionate, loving; amorous

amplio/a ample

analfabetismo illiteracy

análisis *m.* analysis

analizarse (c) to analyze

ananás *m. s.* pineapple (*Arg.*)

anaranjado/a orange (*color*)

anciano/a elderly person

¡anda! *interj.* move it!; go on!

Andalucía Andalusia

andaluz, andaluza (*pl.* **andaluces**) Andalusian

andar (*irreg.*) to walk; to go; **andar bien/mal** to be going well/badly; **andar buscando** to be looking for; **andar en barco** to take a boat ride; **andar en bicicleta** to go for a bicycle ride; **andar en bote** to take a rowboat ride; **andar en mateo** to take a carriage ride

anfibio: animal (*m.*) **anfibio** amphibian

anglosajón, anglosajona *n., adj.* Anglo-Saxon

angustia anguish

angustiado/a anguished

animación *f.* animation, liveliness

animado/a lively, animated, spirited; **dibujos animados** cartoons

animal *m.* animal; **animal anfibio** amphibian; **animal doméstico** pet

animar to encourage

ánimo strength

aniversario anniversary

anoche last night

anochecer: al anochecer at nightfall, dusk

anónimo/a anonymous; **sociedad** (*f.*) **anónima** incorporated; stock company

ansiedad *f.* anxiety

ansioso/a anxious

Antártida Antarctica

ante before, in the presence of; with regard to; **ante todo** above all

antecedentes (*m.*) **históricos** *pl.* historical record; background

antemano: de antemano beforehand

antepasado ancestor

anterior previous, preceding

antes *adv.* before, formerly; **antes de** *prep.* before (*in time*); **antes (de) que** *conj.* before; **antes de Cristo** b.c.; **lo antes posible** as soon as possible

anticipación: con anticipación in advance

anticipar to anticipate

anticomunista *m., f.* anticommunist

antigüedad *n. f.* antique; **tienda de antigüedades** antique store

antiguo/a former; old, ancient

antipatriótico/a unpatriotic

antojito appetizer (*Mex.*)

antropología anthropology

anual annual

anuncio announcement, advertisement

añadir to add

añejo/a old, aged

año year; **al año** per year; **hace muchos años** many years ago; **de primer año** *adj.* freshman; **tener** (*irreg.*) ... **años** to be ... years old; **una vez al año** once a year

añorar to long for

apacionado/a *n.* admirer

aparato apparatus, appliance; **aparato doméstico** household appliance

aparecer (zc) to appear

aparente apparent

apariencia appearance

apartamento apartment

apellido surname, last name

apenado/a grieved

apenas scarcely

apéndice *m.* appendix

aperitivo appetizer

apetito appetite

apetitoso/a: plato apetitoso appetizing dish

apio celery

aplicar (qu) to apply

apoderarse (de) to take possession (of)

apogeo height, summit

apoyar to support

apoyo support

apreciado/a esteemed

apreciar to appreciate, esteem

aprender to learn; **aprender a** + *inf.* to learn to (*do something*)

apresurado/a in a hurry

aprieto difficulty, fix

aprobar (ue) to approve, confirm; **aprobarse** to be approved

apropiado/a appropriate

aprovechamiento use; exploitation

aprovechar to take advantage of

aproximadamente approximately

aptitud *f.* aptitude

apuntar to note, write down

apuro difficulty, jam

aquel, aquella *adj.* that (*over there*); **aquél, aquélla** *pron.* that one (*over there*); **en aquel entonces** back then, at that time, in those days

aquello that, that thing, that fact

aquellos/as *adj.* those (*over there*); **aquéllos/as** *pron.* those (ones) (*over there*)

aquí here

árabe *n. m., f.* Arab; *adj.* Arabic
arador *m.* plowman
árbol *m.* tree
arbusto shrub
arcilla (bruta) (unworked) clay
archipiélago archipelago
área *f.* (*but* **el área**) area
arena: duna de arena sand dune
argentino/a Argentine
árido/a arid, dry; barren
aritmética arithmetic
armado: conflicto armado armed
    conflict
armario closet
aromático/a aromatic
arqueología archeology
arqueólogo/a archeologist
arquitecto/a architect
arquitectura architecture
arreglar to arrange; to fix
arreglo arrangement
arrestado/a arrested
arrestar to arrest
arriba upstairs
arrogante arrogant
arrojar to indicate, show
arrollada: tortilla arrollada rolled
    tortilla
arroyo stream
arroz *m.* rice
arruinado/a ruined
arte *m.* (*but* **las artes**) art; **artes** (*f.*) **li-**
    berales liberal arts; **bellas artes** (*f.*)
    fine arts
artesano/a artisan, craftsperson
articulación *f.* joint
artículo article
artista *m., f.* artist
artístico/a artistic
arvejas peas
ascendencia descent
ascender (ie) to advance
ascenso promotion
ascensor *m.* elevator
asco: dar (*irreg.*) **asco a (alguien)** to dis-
    gust (someone)
asegurar to assure
asentir (ie, i) to assent, agree
asesinar to assassinate
asesinato assassination, murder
asesino/a assassin, murderer
así *adv.* so, thus; that way; therefore, con-
    sequently; **así que** *conj.* so, then
asiento seat; breeding ground; site;
    asiento de atrás back seat
asignatura (school) subject
asimilar to assimilate
asistente/a assistant
asistir (a) to attend
asociación *f.* association
asociar to associate
aspecto aspect
áspero/a harsh

aspiración *f.* aspiration
aspirar (a) to aspire (to)
aspirina aspirin
astronomía astronomy
astrónomo astronomer
Asturias *region of Spain*
asunto issue, matter
asustar to frighten
atacar (qu) to attack
ataque *m.* attack; **ataque cardíaco** heart
    attack
atención *f.* attention; **llamar la atención**
    to attract attention; **prestar atención**
    (a) to pay attention (to)
atender (ie) to attend to, take care of
atentamente attentively
atlántico/a Atlantic; **Océano Atlántico**
    Atlantic Ocean
atleta *m., f.* athlete
atmósfera atmosphere
atracción *f.* attraction; **atracción**
    turística tourist attraction
atractivo *n.* attraction
atractivo/a *adj.* attractive
atraer (*like* **traer**) to attract
atrapado/a trapped
atrás behind; **asiento de atrás** back seat
atrasado/a *adj.* late, arriving late
atreverse (a) to dare (to)
atún *m.* tuna
auditor (a) auditor
aumentar to increase; **aumenta tu vo-**
    cabulario increase your vocabulary
aumento increase
aun *adv.* even
aún *adv.* still, yet
aunque although
ausencia absence
ausente absent
austral *n. monetary unit of Argentina;*
    adj. southern
autobús *m.* bus
autóctono/a native
automático/a automatic
automóvil *m.* automobile, car
autonomía autonomy
autónomo/a autonomous
autopista highway; toll road
autor(a) author
autoritario/a authoritarian
autorizar (c) to authorize
avanzado/a advanced
avanzar (c) to advance, get ahead
avenida avenue
aventura adventure
avergonzado/a embarrassed
avería breakdown
averiguar (gü) to find out, ascertain
avión *m.* airplane
avisar to advice, notify; to warn
¡ay! *interj.* oh!
ayer yesterday
ayuda help, assistance

ayudante *m., f.* assistant
ayudar to help, assist
ayuntamiento city hall
azafata airplane stewardess
azteca *n., m., f., adj.* Aztec
Aztlán *legendary place of origin of the*
    Aztecs
azúcar *m.* sugar; **caña de azúcar** sugar
    cane; **ingenio de azúcar** sugar mill
azul blue
azulado/a bluish

B

bachillerato high school diploma
bahía bay; **Bahía de (los) Cochinos** Bay
    of Pigs
bailar to dance
baile *n. m.* dance; **baile de gala** formal
    dance
bajar to go down(stairs); to bring down
    (*a fever*); **bajar de peso** to lose weight
bajo *n.* bass; *prep.* under
bajo/a, *adj.* short (*in height*); low; **clase**
    (*f.*) **baja** lower class; **planta baja**
    ground floor, first floor
balcón *m.* balcony
baloncesto basketball
balsa raft
ballet *m.* ballet
banca banking
banco bank; bench
bandera flag
banquero/a banker
bañarse to bathe, take a bath
baño bath; bathroom, **baño privado (con**
    ducha) private bath, (with shower);
    traje (*m.*) **de baño** bathing suit
bar *m.* bar
barato/a inexpensive, cheap
barba beard
barbacoa barbecue
barbaridad: ¡qué barbaridad! *interj.*
    how awful!
barbería barber shop
barca boat, barge
barco boat; **andar** (*irreg.*) **en barco** to
    take a boat ride; **navegar (gu) en**
    barco to sail
barrera barrier
barril *m.* barrel
barrio district; neighborhood
basarse to be based; **basarse en** to base
    one's ideas or opinions on
base *f.* base; basis; **a base de** on the
    basis of
básico/a basic
básquetbol *m.* basketball
bastante enough; a great deal; rather,
    quite
bastar to be enough
batalla battle
baúl *m.* trunk

bebé *m.* baby
beber to drink
bebida *n.* drink, beverage; **bebida alcohólica** alcoholic beverage
béisbol *m.* baseball
belleza beauty
bello/a beautiful; **bellas artes** *f.* fine arts
besar to kiss
beso kiss
biblioteca library
bicicleta: andar (*irreg.*) **en bicicleta** to ride a bicycle
bien *adv.* well; **andar** (*irreg.*) **bien** to be going well; **caerle** (*irreg.*) **bien a (alguien)** to like, make a good impression on (someone); **llevarse bien (con)** to get along well (with); **manejar bien** to manage well; **muy bien** very well; **pasarlo bien** to have a good time; **por bien o por mal** for better or worse; **sentirse (i, i) bien** to feel well
bien *n., m.* good; *pl.* goods; **agente** (*m., f.*) **de bienes raíces** real estate agent; **bienes raíces** *pl.* real estate
bienestar *m.* well-being
bienvenido/a welcome
bilingüe bilingual; **educación** (*f.*) **bilingüe** bilingual education
bilingüismo bilingualism
billete *m.* ticket (*Sp.*); **billete de ida y vuelta** round-trip ticket
biología biology
biólogo/a biologist
bistec *m.* steak
blanco/a white
bloque *m.* city block (*P.R.*)
bloqueado/a blocked, closed off
blusa blouse
boca mouth
bocacalle *f.* intersection (*of a street*)
boda wedding
bohemio/a bohemian
boleto ticket (*L.A.*)
bolsa purse, handbag
bomba *traditional Puerto Rican dance*
bombardeo bombing
bondad *f.* goodness; kindness
bonito/a pretty, attractive
borde: al borde de on the edge of
bordo: a bordo aboard, on board
Borinquen *f. aboriginal and poetic name of Puerto Rico*
borinqueño/a *n. adj.* Puerto Rican
borrar to erase
bosque *m.* forest; **bosque tropical** tropical forest
bosquejo outline
botana appetizer (*Mex.*)
botánico/a botanical; **jardín** (*m.*) **botánico** botanical garden
bota boot
botar to throw away

bote *m.* rowboat; **andar** (*irreg.*) **en bote** to take a rowboat ride
botella bottle
botones *m. s.* bellhop
brazalete *m.* bracelet
brazo arm
brécol *m.* broccoli
breve brief
brevísimamente very briefly
brillante brilliant
brillar to shine
brindar to (drink a) toast
brindis *m. s.* toast
brocolí *m.* broccoli
brocheta brochette, skewer
broma joke; **en broma** as a joke, jokingly
brujo/a magician
bruta: arcilla bruta unworked clay
buceo snorkeling; scuba diving
buen, bueno/a *adj.* good; **buen día** good day (*greeting*) (*Arg.*); **buena suerte** good luck; **buenas noches** good evening/night; **buenas tardes** good afternoon; **buenos, buenas** good day, good afternoon/evening; **buenos días** good morning; **hace buen tiempo** it's good weather; **bueno** (*when answering the telephone*) hello (*Mex.*); **bueno** *adv.* all right
bufanda scarf
bufete *m.* lawyer's office
bulevar *m.* boulevard
burlarse (de) to ridicule, make fun (of)
busca search; **en busca de** in search of
buscar (qu) to look for, seek; **andar** (*irreg.*) **buscando** to be looking for; **en busca de** in search of
búsqueda search, quest

C

caballero gentleman
caballo horse; **montar a caballo** to ride horseback
cabaña cabin
caber (*irreg.*) to fit; to go; to be possible; **no cabe duda** there is no doubt
cabeza head; **dolor** (*m.*) **de cabeza** headache; **me/le duele la cabeza** I/he/she/you (*form.*) have/has a headache
cabezón, cabezona stubborn, hardheaded
cabezonería stubbornness
cabo end; **al fin y al cabo** after all, when all is said and done
cacahuete *m.* peanut
cada *inv.* each, every; **cada vez más** more and more
cadena chain
cadete *m.* cadet
caer (*irreg.*) to fall; **caerle bien/mal a (alguien)** to like (not like), make a good/bad impression on (someone)

café *m.* (cup of) coffee; **café**, coffee shop; **café con leche** *strong coffee served with warm or hot milk;* **café solo** black coffee
cafeína caffeine
cafetería cafeteria
calabaza squash
calamar *m.* squid; **calamares fritos** fried squid rings
calavera skull
calcetines *m.* socks
calculador(a) calculating
calcular to calculate
cálculo calculus
calendario calendar; **calendario gregoriano** Gregorian calendar
calidad *f.* quality
cálido: clima (*m.*) **cálido** hot climate
caliente hot
califato (*region governed by an Islamic leader*)
calmado/a quiet, calm
calmante *m.* sedative
calmar to calm
calor *n. m.* heat; **hace un calor de mil demonios** it's a hellishly hot day; **hace (mucho) calor** it's (very) hot; **tener** (*irreg.*) **(mucho) calor** to be (very) hot
callado/a silent, quiet
calle *f.* street; **calle peatonal** pedestrian mall
cama bed; **cama matrimonial** double bed; **guardar cama** to stay in bed
cámara camera
camarero/a waiter, waitress
camarón *m.* shrimp (*Mex. and parts of L.A.*)
cambiar (de) to change; **cambiarse de ropa** to change one's clothes; **quisiera cambiar ...** I would like to change . . . (*money*)
cambio change; exchange; **en cambio** on the other hand
caminar to walk
camino street, road; way; **camino a** on the way to; **a lo largo del camino** along the way
camión *m.* truck; bus (*Mex.*)
camisa shirt; **camisa de noche** nightshirt
camiseta T-shirt
campana bell
campanada ringing of a bell
campaña campaign
campeche *m.* logwood
campeón, campeona champion
campera short jacket (*Arg.*)
campesino/a farm worker, peasant; **teatro campesino** farm worker's theater
campo field; countryside; **campo de golf** golf course
cana gray hair

canal *m.* canal
canario canary; **Islas Canarias** Canary Islands
canasta basket
cancelar to cancel
cáncer *m.* cancer
canción *f.* song
cancha court; playing field; **cancha de tenis** tennis court
cangrejo crab
canoso/a grey-haired; **pelo canoso** gray hair
cansado/a tired
cansar to tire; **cansarse** to get tired
Cantábrico: Mar (*m.*) **Cantábrico** Bay of Biscay
cantante *m., f.* singer
cantar to sing
cantidad *f.* quantity, amount
cantina bar
canto song
caña cane; **caña de azúcar** sugar cane; **caña de pescar** fishing pole
cañón *m.* canyon
caos *m. s.* chaos
capacidad *f.* capacity
capaz (*pl.* **capaces**) capable, able
capilla chapel
capital *f.* capital (city); *m.* capital (*money*)
capitalista *m., f.* capitalist
capítulo chapter
Capricornio: Trópico de Capricornio Tropic of Capricorn
capricho whim; desire
captar to grasp; to depict; to pick up (*sound*)
capturar to capture
cara face; side; **la otra cara de la moneda** the other side of the coin
carácter *m.* character
característico/a *adj.* characteristic
caracterizar (c) to characterize
¡caramba! *interj.* my God! gosh!
caramelo caramel; candy
¡caray! *interj.* damn!
cárcel *f.* prison
cardíaco/a *adj.* cardiac, heart; **ataque** (*m.*) **cardíaco** heart attack
cardinales: direcciones (*f.*) **cardinal** points
carga load
cargar (gu) to carry; to charge (*on a credit card*)
cargo position; **poner** (*irreg.*) **a alguien a cargo (de)** to put (someone) in charge (of)
Caribe *n. m.* Caribbean
caribeño/a *n., adj.* Caribbean
cariño affection; **tomarle cariño a (alguien)** to start to have affection for (someone)

cariñoso/a affectionate
carisma *m.* charisma
carnaval *m.* carnival
carne *f.* meat; **carne de cerdo** pork; **carne de res** beef (*Mex.*); **carne de vaca** beef; **carne picada** ground meat
carnicería butcher shop
carnicero butcher
caro/a expensive
carpintero/a carpenter
carrera career, profession; course of study
carretera highway
carro car
carta letter; **jugar (ue) (gu) a las cartas por dinero** to gamble on cards
cartel *m.* sign
cartera wallet
casa house; home; **ama** (*f.* [*but* **el ama**]) **de casa** homemaker; **en casa** at home
casado/a married; **recién casado/a** recently married, newly wed
casar(se) (con) to marry (someone); to get married (to)
cascada cascade
casero/a home, homemade
casi almost
casino casino
caso case; **en caso de que** in case; **en todo caso** in any case; **hacer** (*irreg.*) **caso a** to pay attention to; **no hacer caso (de)** to pay no attention (to an issue); **no hacerle caso (a alguien)** to ignore (someone)
castaño/a brown, brunet(te)
castigo punishment
Castilla Castile (*region of Spain*)
castillo castle
casualidad: dar (*irreg.*) **la casualidad** to just happen; **por casualidad** by chance
catalán *m.* Catalan (*language of Cataluña* [*region of Spain*])
catalán, catalana *n., adj.* Catalonian
Cataluña Catalonia (*region of Spain*)
catarata waterfall
catarro: catarro común common cold
catecismo catechism
catedral *f.* cathedral
categoría category
catolicismo Catholicism
católico/a *n., adj.* Catholic
catorce fourteen
causa cause; **a causa de** because of, on account of
causar to cause, be the cause of; **causar una buena impresión** to make a good impression
cautivar to captivate
cautivo *n.* captive
cebolla onion
ceder to give up, hand over
ceiba silk-cotton tree
celebración *f.* celebration

celebrar to celebrate
célebre *m.* celebrity
celos jealousy; **tener** (*irreg.*) **celos (de)** to be jealous (of)
celoso/a jealous; **estar** (*irreg.*) **celoso/a (de)** to be jealous (of)
cementerio cemetery
cena dinner, supper
cenar to have dinner
censo census
censura censureship
centavo cent
céntrico/a central
centro center; downtown; **centro comercial** shopping center
Centroamérica Central America
cerámica ceramic
cerca *adv.* near, nearby, close; **cerca de** *prep.* near (to); **de cerca** from a short distance
cercano/a *adj.* close
cerdo pig; **carne** (*f.*) **de cerdo** pork; **chuleta de cerdo** pork chop
cereal *m.* cereal; grain
ceremonia ceremony
cereza cherry
cero zero
cerrado/a closed
cerrar (ie) to close
cerro hill
certificado certificate; **certificado de nacimiento** birth certificate
cervecería beer tavern, pub
cerveza beer
ciclo cycle
ciego/a *n.* visually impaired person, blind person; *adj.* visually impaired, blind
cielo heaven; sky
cien, ciento (one) hundred
ciencia science; **ciencia-ficción** science fiction; **ciencias económicas** economics; **ciencias naturales** natural sciences; **ciencias sociales** social sciences
científico/a scientist
cierto/a true; certain; **es cierto** it's certain, true; **por cierto** by the way, certainly
cifra figure, number
cigarrillo cigarette
cima summit, top
cinco five
cincuenta fifty
cine *m.* cinema, movie theater; **ir** (*irreg.*) **al cine** to go to the movies; **sala de cine** theater
cinematografía cinematography, filmmaking
cinematógrafo filmmaker
cinta tape
ciprés *m.* cypress tree
círculo circle
circunstancia circumstance

ciruela plum
cita date; appointment; **primera cita** first date
ciudad *f.* city; **Ciudad de México** Mexico City
ciudadanía citizenship
ciudadano/a citizen
civil: guerra civil civil war
civilización *f.* civilization
clandestino/a secret, clandestine
clarín *m.* bugle
claro/a clear; light (colors); **claro** *interj.* of course; **claro que sí** of course; **ojos claros** light-colored eyes
clase *f.* class; kind; **clase alta** upper class; **clase baja** lower class; **clase elevada** upper class; **clase media** middle class; **clase obrera** working class; **clase social** social class; **clase trabajadora** working class; **clase turística** tourist class; **dar** (*irreg.*) **una clase** to teach a class; **primera clase** first class; **salón** (*m.*) **de clase** classroom
clásico *n.* classic
clásico/a *adj.* classic(al)
cláusula (*gram.*) clause
clero clergy
cliente/a client
clima *m.* climate; clime; **clima cálido** hot climate
climático/a climatic
clínica clinic
cobrar to cover; to charge; **cóbreme** charge me (for)
cobre *m.* copper
cocido/a cooked
cocina kitchen; cooking
cocinar to cook
cocinero/a *n.* cook, chef
coco coconut
cocotero coconut palm tree
coche *m.* car
coche-comedor *m.* dining car (*on a train*)
cochinita pibil roast suckling pig
cochino: Bahía de (los) Cochinos Bay of Pigs
códice *m.* body of laws; manuscript volume
cofradía *f.* brotherhood
cognado *n.* cognate
coincidencia coincidence
cola line (*of people*)
colaboración *f.* collaboration
colección *f.* collection
coleccionar to collect
colega *m., f.* colleague
colegio grade or high school
colgar (ue) (gu) to hang up
coliflor *f.* cauliflower
colina hill
colmo last straw
colocar (qu) to place

colombiano/a Colombian
Colón: Cristóbal Colón Christopher Columbus
colonia colony; neighborhood (*Mex.*)
colonial colonial
colonizar (c) to colonize
color *m.* color; **color claro** pastel-colored; **de color salmón** salmon-colored
colorido *n.* coloring, color
columna column
combatir to fight
combinación *f.* combination
combinar to combine
comedia comedy; play
comedor *m.* dining room; **coche-comedor** (*m.*) dining car (*on a train*)
comendador *m.* commander
comentar to comment (on); to discuss
comentario comment; commentary
comenzar (ie) (c) to begin
comer to eat; **comerse** to eat up
comercial *adj.* commerical; **centro comercial** shopping center
comerciante *m., f.* merchant
comercio commerce, business
comestible *n. m.* food; *adj.* edible; **tienda de comestibles** food store
cometer to commit
cómico/a comical
comida food; meal; **comida congelada** frozen food; **comida rápida** fast food
comienzo *n.* beginning; **al comienzo** at the beginning
comino: me importa un comino I couldn't care less
como as (a); like; since; **como consecuencia** as a result; **como tal** as such; **tal como** just as, exactly the same as; **tan ... como** as . . . as; **tan pronto como** as soon as; **tanto/a/os/as ... como** as much/many . . . as
¿cómo? how?, how's that?, what?, I didn't catch that
comodidades *f.* comforts
cómodo/a comfortable
compañero/a companion; mate, "significant other"
compañía company (*business*)
comparación *f.* comparison
comparar to compare
compartimiento compartment
compartir to share
compas *m. pl. shortened form of* **compañeros**
compasión *f.* compassion
competición *f.* competition
complacer (zc) to please
complejo/a complex, complicated
completar to complete
completo/a complete, full; **por completo** completely
complicación *f.* complication

complicado/a complicated
componerse (*like* **poner**) (**de**) to be composed (of)
comportamiento behavior
comportarse to behave oneself
composición *f.* composition
compositor(a) composer
compra purchase; **hacer** (*irreg.*) **las compras** to shop; **ir** (*irreg.*) **de compras** to go shopping
comprar to buy
comprender to understand
comprensión *f.* comprehension, understanding
comprensivo/a understanding
comprobar (ue) to check
comprometido/a committed; involved
compromiso obligation, commitment
compuesto/a (*p. p. of* **componer**) composed
compulsivo/a compulsive
computación *f.* computer science
computadora computer (*L.A.*); **programación** (*f.*) **de computadoras** computer programming; **programador(a) de computadoras** computer programmer (*L.A.*)
común common; **catarro común** common cold; **en común** in common; **sentido común** common sense
comunicación *f.* communication; **medios de comunicación** means of communication, media
comunicarse (qu) (con) to communicate (with); to get in touch (with), contact
comunidad *f.* community
comunismo communism
comunista *n., m., f., adj.* communist
con with; **con anticipación** in advance; **con destino a** bound for; **con frecuencia** frequently; **con más frecuencia** most frequently, most often; **con permiso** may I pass by?; **¿con qué frecuencia?** how often?; **¿con quién?** with whom?; **con razón** understandably so; **con respecto a** with respect to; **con tal (de) que** so that
conceder to grant, concede
concentración *f.* concentration
concentrar(se) to concentrate
concepto concept
concesión *f.* granting, concession
conciencia moral conscience
concierto concert
conciliador(a) conciliatory
concluir (y) to conclude
conclusión *f.* conclusion
concreto/a concrete
concurso contest
condición *f.* condition; **buenas/malas condiciones** *pl.* good/bad shape, condition

condimentado/a: bien condimentado/a
well-seasoned
conducta conduct
conductor(a) conductor
conferencia lecture
confesar (ie) to confess
confesión *f.* confession
confiado/a confident
confianza confidence; **de confianza**
trustworthy, reliable
confiar (en) to trust (in); to confide (in)
confidencialidad *f.* confidentiality
confirmación *f.* confirmation
confirmar to confirm
confitería confectionery
conflicto conflict; **conflicto armado**
armed conflict; **en conflicto** in conflict
confundir to confuse
confusión *f.* confusion
confuso/a confused
congelado/a frozen; **comida congelada**
frozen food
congestión *f.* congestion
congresista *m., f.* congressperson, member of congress
congreso convention; congress
conjunción *f.* conjunction
conjunto ensemble, outfit: group, ensemble (*musical*)
conmemorar to commemorate
conmigo with me
conmovido/a moved (*emotionally*)
conocer (zc) to know, be acquainted with; to meet
conocido/a well-known
conocimiento(s) knowledge
conquista conquest
conquistador(a) conqueror
conquistar to conquer
consciencia awareness
consciente conscious
consecuencia consequence; **como consecuencia** as a result
conseguir (i, i) (g) to get, obtain, attain; to succeed in
consejero/a a counselor
consejo(s) advice
conservar to conserve, save, preserve
considerar to consider
consigo with himself, with herself; with it; with them
consistir (en) to consist (of)
consolar (ue) to console
consolidación *f.* consolidation, strengthening
constante constant
constar (de) to consist, be composed (of)
constitución *f.* constitution
constitucional constitutional
construcción *f.* construction
constructor (a) builder, manufacturer
construir (y) to build

consulta *s.* consulting hours
consultar to consult
consumidor(a) consumer
consumir to consume, use
consumo consumption
contabiladad *f.* accounting
contacto contact
contagiar to infect
contar (ue) to tell (about); to count;
contar con to have; to rely on; to have available
contemplar to contemplate; to look at, study
contemporáneo/a contemporary
contener (*like* **tener**) to contain
contenido *n. s.* contents
contentarse (con) to be content, satisfied (with)
contento/a happy, content
contestar to answer
contexto context
contigo with you (*fam.*)
continental continental; **desayuno continental** continental breakfast
continente *m.* continent
continuación *f.* continuation; **a continuación** below, immediately after, following
continuar to continue, go on; to follow
contra against; **en contra (de)** against
contradicción *f.* contradiction
contradictorio/a contradictory
contraer (*like* **traer**) to contract (*an illness*)
contrario: al contrario on the contrary
contraste *m.* contrast
contratar to hire
contrato contract
contribución *f.* contribution
contribuir (y) to contribute
controlar to control
controversia controversy; **de controversia** controversial
controvertido/a controversial
convencer (z) to convince
convencido/a convinced
conveniente convenient
convenir (*like* **venir**) to be suitable, convenient for; to be desirable; to be worth one's while
conversación *f.* conversation
conversar to converse
convertirse (ie, i) (en) to become; to change (into); to convert
convicción *f.* conviction
convivencia coexistence, living together
convivir to coexist, to live together
coñac *m.* cognac, brandy
cooperar to cooperate
copa goblet, wineglass; drink (*slang*)
copado/a taken, filled up
copia copy
coquetear to flirt

coquí *small tree frog indigenous to Puerto Rico which makes a characteristic musical sound*
coraje *m.* courage
Corán *m.* Koran
corazón *m.* heart
corbata necktie
cordero lamb; **chuleta de cordero** lamb chop
cordillera mountain range
coriza head cold
coro chorus
correcto/a correct, right
corredor *m.* corridor, hall
corregir (i, i) (j) to correct
correo mail; post office; **(por) correo aéreo** (by) airmail
correr to run; **correr riesgo** to run a risk
corresponder to correspond, match
correspondiente *adj.* corresponding
corriente common, ordinary; **cuenta corriente** checking account
corrupción *f.* corruption
cortado/a cut (up)
cortapisas *pl.* restrictions
corte *f.* court (*of law*)
cortés, cortesa courteous, polite
cortesía courtesy
corto/a brief, short (*in length*); **pantalón** (*m.*) **corto, pantalones** (*m. pl.*) **cortos** shorts
cosa thing; **cualquier cosa** anything
coser to sew
cosmopolita *m., f.* cosmopolitan
costa coast
costar (ue) to cost; **costarle trabajo (a alguien)** to be hard, take a lot of effort (for someone)
costumbre *f.* custom, habit; **como de costumbre** as usual; **es costumbre** it is customary
costura *n.* sewing
creación *f.* creation
creador(a) creator
crear to create
creatividad *f.* creativity
crecer (zc) to grow
crédito: tarjeta de crédito credit card; **dar** (*irreg.*) **crédito** to believe
creencia belief
creer (y) (en) to think, believe (in); **creer que sí/no** to think (not think) so; **ya lo creo** I should say so
crema cream (-colored)
crepa crepe
criado/a servant
crianza upbringing
criar to raise; **criarse** to grow up
criollo/a creole
crisis *f.* crisis
crisol *m.* crucible; melting pot
cristalizadas: frutas cristalizadas candied (crystallized) fruit

cristiano/a *n., adj.* Christian
Cristo Christ; **antes de Cristo** B.C.
Cristóbal Colón Christopher Columbus
crítica criticism
criticar (qu) to criticize
crítico/a critical
cronológico: en orden cronológico in chronological order
crudo/a raw
crueldad *f.* cruelty
cruz *f.* (*pl.* **cruces**) cross
cruzar (c) to cross
cuaderno notebook
cuadra city block
cuadrado/a *adj.* square
cuadro painting; picture
cual *relative pron.* whom, which; **con el cual** with whom; **el motivo por el cual** the reason why; **lo cual** which; **para lo cual** for which; **la razón por la cual** the reason why
¿cuál? what?, which?; **¿cuál (es)?** which one(s)?
cualidad *f.* quality
cualquier(a) whatever, whichever; any; **cualquier cosa** anything
cuando when
¿cuándo? when?
cuanto: en cuanto as soon as; **en cuanto a ... as** for, as far as . . . is concerned
cuánto/a how much, how many
¿cuánto/a? how much?; **¿cuántos/as?** how many?; **¿a cuánto está el dólar?** what is the exchange rate for the dollar?; **¿a cuánto estaba la temperatura?** how high was the temperature?; **¿cuánto tiempo hace que ... ?** how long has it been that . . .
cuarenta forty
cuartel *m.* barracks, quarters
cuarto *n.* fourth; quarter (*hour*); (bed)room
cuarto/a *adj.* fourth
cuatro four
cuatrocientos/as four hundred
cubano/a *n., adj.* Cuban
cubanomericano/a *n. adj.* Cuban American
cubierto *n.* place setting; *pl.* silverware
cubierto/a (*p.p. of* **cubrir**) (**de**) covered (with)
cubismo cubism
cubrir (*p.p.* **cubierto/a**) to cover
cuchara spoon
cuchillo knife
cuenta account; bill, check; calculation; **cuenta corriente** checking account; **cuenta de ahorros** savings account; **darse** (*irreg.*) **cuenta (de)** to realize, become aware (of); **hacer** (*irreg.*) **cuentas** to do the accounts; **llevar (las) cuentas** to keep the books; **por**

su propia cuenta on his/her/its/your (*form.*)/their own account; **revisar las cuentas,** to audit the accounts; **tener** (*irreg.*) **en cuenta** to keep in mind
cuentista *m., f.* storyteller
cuento short story
cuero leather
cuerpo body
cuestión *f.* question; problem; matter
cueva cave
cuidado care; **¡cuidado!** be careful; **con cuidado** carefully; **tener** (*irreg.*) **cuidado** to be careful
cuidar(se) to take care of (oneself)
culinario/a culinary
culpa fault; blame; **tener** (*irreg.*) **la culpa (de)** to be to blame for, to be guilty (of)
culpabilidad *f.* guilt; **sentido de culpabilidad** sense of guilt or responsibility
culpable *n. m., f.* guilty person; responsible person; *adj.* guilty, responsible
culpar to blame
cultivar to cultivate
cultivo cultivation
culto worship, cult; **rendir (i, i) culto (a)** to worship
cultura culture
cumbre *n.f.* peak; *adj.* top
cumpleaños *m. s.* birthday
cumplir to perform; to keep (a promise); **cumplir años** to have a birthday; **cumplir con** to live up to; to meet, fulfill
cuna birthplace
cuñado/a brother/sister-in-law
cupón *m.* ticket
cura *m.* priest; *f.* cure
curación *f.* cure, recovery
curandero/a healer; witch doctor
curar to heal, cure
curiosidad *f.* curiosity
curioso/a curious
curso course, class
curvas: líneas curvas curved lines
cuyo/a whose

CH

champán *m.* champagne
champaña *m.* champagne
champiñón *m.* mushroom
Chanuka Chanukah, Hanukkah
chapulín *m.* grasshopper (*L.A.*)
chaqueta jacket
charlar to chat
charrada charro dance
chau ciao, 'bye, good-bye
chavo money, "dough" (*P.R.*)
cheque *m.* check; **cheque de viajero** traveler's check
chequear to check

chico/a *adj.* little, small; *n.* boy, girl; *pl.* boys, girls; children
chícharos peas (*Mex.*)
chile *m.* chili pepper
chileno/a *n., adj.* Chilean
chimpancé *m.* chimpanzee
chino/a *n., adj.* Chinese
chismear to gossip
chistar: sin chistar without saying a word
chistoso/a funny
chocar (qu) (con) to run into, collide (with)
chocolate *m.* (hot) chocolate
chófer *m.* chauffeur, driver
choque *m.* accident, collision
choricero/a sausage maker or seller
chorizo sausage
chuleta chop; **chuleta de cerdo** pork chop; **chuleta de cordero** lamb chop

D

danza dance
dar (*irreg.*) to give; **darle asco (a alguien)** to disgust, to nauseate (someone); **dar una clase** to teach a class; **dar con** to meet up with; **dar crédito** to believe; **dar una fiesta** to give a party; **dar las gracias** to thank; **dar muerte a** to put to death; **dar un paseo** to take a walk; **darle de alta (a alguien)** to release (someone) (*from an institution*); **darse cuenta (de)** to realize, become aware (of); **darse la mano** to shake hands; **darse prisa** to hurry; **Día** (*m.*) **de Dar Gracias** Thanksgiving Day; **me da pena** I'm sorry
daño: hacerle (*irreg.*) **daño (a alguien)** to hurt (someone)
datar to date
dato fact
de *prep.* of; from; **de acuerdo** OK, I agree; **de alto** in height; **de antemano** beforehand; **de confianza** trustworthy, reliable; **de controversia** controversial; **de fondo** thoroughly; **de joven** as a youth; **de memoria** by heart; **de moda** fashionable; **de momento** for the moment; **de nacimiento** by birth; **de nada** you're welcome; **de niño/a** as a child; **de noche** at night, by night; **de la noche** in the evening, at night; **de nuevo** again; **de primer año** *adj.* freshman; **de prisa** quickly, in a hurry; **¿de quién?** whose?; **de regreso** *adj.* return (*flight*); **de regreso a** on returning to; **de repente** suddenly; **de (la) tarde** P.M., in the afternoon; **de todas formas** in any case; **de una vez** now, right away; **¿de verdad?** really?; **de vez en cuando** sometimes; **estar** (*irreg.*) **de**

acuerdo (con) to agree, be in agreement (with); **más allá de** *prep.* beyond; **más de** more than; **vivir de** to live off of, support oneself by

deber *v.* should, ought to; to owe; **deber + inf.** should, must, ought to (*do something*); **deberse a** to be due to

deber *n. m.* duty

debido/a proper; right

débil weak

debilidad *f.* weakness

debilitar to weaken, debilitate

década *f.* decade

decadencia decadence, decline

decente decent

decepcionado/a disappointed

decidir to decide; **decidirse** to make up one's mind

decir (*irreg.*) to say, tell; **decir la hora** to tell time; **decir la verdad** to tell the truth; **decir que sí/no** to say yes/no; **es decir** that is to say

decisión *f.* decision; **tomar decisiones** to make decisions

decisivo/a decisive

declamación *f.* declamation, speech

declaración *f.* declaration

declarar to declare; **declararse** to declare (one's) love

dedicar (qu) to dedicate; **dedicarse** to dedicate oneself

defender (ie) to defend; **defenderse** to defend oneself; to get along/by

defensa defense

definición *f.* definition

definido a definite

definir to define

definitivo/a final, definitive

dejar to leave (behind); to let, allow; to quit, **dejar de + inf.** to stop (*doing something*); **dejar de existir** to disappear

del (*contraction of* **de + el**) of the; from the

delante *adv.* ahead; **por delante** ahead (of one); **delante de** *prep.* in front of

deletrear to spell

deletreo *n.* spelling

delgado/a thin, slender

delicado/a delicate

delicia delight

delicioso/a delicious

demanda demand

demás: los/las demás the rest, the others, others, other people

demasiado *adv.* too, too much

democracia democracy

demócrata *n. m., f.* democrat

demográfico/a demographic

demonios: hace un calor de mil demonios it's a hellishly hot day

demora delay

demostrar (ue) to show, demonstrate

demostrativos: adjetivos demostrativos demonstrative adjectives

denominación *f.* denomination, name

densidad *f.* density

denso/a dense

dentista *m., f.* dentist

dentro de inside, within; **dentro de poco** very soon

denunciar to denounce; to expose

depender (de) to depend (on)

dependiente *adj.* dependent

dependiente/a *n.* clerk

deporte *m.* sport; **practicar (qu) un deporte** to play a sport

deportivo/a *adj.* sports

depósito deposit

depresión *f.* depression

deprimir to depress

derecha: a la derecha to the right; **a mano derecha** on the right(-hand) side

derecho *n.* law; right **derechos humanos** human rights; **derecho** *adv.* straight ahead; **seguir (i, i) (g) (todo) derecho** to continue straight (ahead)

derivado/a derived

derrota defeat

derrumbarse to collapse, cave in

derrumbe *m.* collapse; caving in

desafío challenge

desagradable disagreeable

desamparado/a abandoned

desaparecer (zc) to disappear

desaparecido/a *n.* person who has disappeared; *p.p.* disappeared

desaparición *f.* disappearance

desarrollar to develop

desarrollo development

desastre *m.* disaster

desayunar to have breakfast

desayuno breakfast; **desayuno continental** continental breakfast

descansar to rest; **que en paz descanse** may he/she rest in peace

descanso rest; relaxation

descendencia descent

descendiente *m., f.* descendant

descomponer (*like* **poner**) to break down

desconfiado/a suspicious

desconfiar (en) to distrust

desconocido/a unknown

describir (*p.p.* **descrito/a**) to describe

descripción *f.* description

descriptivo/a descriptive

descrito/a (*p.p. of* **describir**) described

descubierto/a (*p.p. of* **descubrir**) discovered

descubrimiento discovery

descubrir (*p.p.* **descubierto/a**) to discover

desde *prep.* from; **desde hace años** for a number of years; **desde luego** of course; **desde pequeño/a** since he/she was small; **desde que** *conj.* since

desdeñar to disdain, scorn

deseado/a desired

desear to want, wish; **desear (+ inf.)** to wish, want to (*do something*)

desechable disposable

desembarcarse (qu) to land; to disembark

desempeñar to play, fulfill (*a role*)

desempleo: tasa de desempleo unemployment rate

desencadenar to unchain; to let loose, free

desenredar to untangle, unravel

desenvoltura self-confidence, assurance; eloquence

deseo desire, wish

desesperado/a desperate

desfilar to file past; to parade

desfile *m.* parade

desgracia: por desgracia unfortunately

desgraciadamente unfortunately

desierto desert

desilusión *f.* disappointment

desilusionado/a disillusioned

desleal disloyal

desnudez *f.* nudity

desobediente disobedient

despedida *n.* farewell, leave-taking, goodbye; **regalo de despedida** going-away present

despedir (i, i) to fire (*an employee*); **despedirse (de)** to say good-bye (to), take leave (of)

despegarse (gu) to take off (*airplane*)

despejado clear (*weather*)

desperdiciado/a wasted

despertar (ie) (*p.p.* **despierto/a**) to wake (*someone up*); **despertarse** to awaken, wake up

despierto/a awake; alert

despreciar to hold in low esteem

después *adv.* later, afterwards; **después de** *prep.* after; **después de que** *conj.* after

destacarse (qu) to stand out

destilar to distill

destino destiny; destination; **con destino a** bound for

destrozar (c) to destroy

destrucción *f.* destruction

destruir (y) to destroy

desunido/a fragmented, disunited; separated

desventaja disadvantage

detalle *m.* detail; **con detalle** in detail

detective *m.* detective

detenidamente carefully

deteriorar to deteriorate

determinado/a specific

determinar to determine
detestar to detest
detrás de *prep.* behind
deuda debt
devoción *f.* devotion
devolución *f.* return
devolver (ue) to return (things to a place or to someone)
devorar to devour
devoto/a devout
día *m.* day; **al día siguiente** the next day; **buen día** good day (*greeting*) (*Arg.*); **buenos días** good morning; **Día de Dar Gracias** Thanksgiving Day; **Día de los Enamorados** Valentine's Day; **Día de la Independencia** Independence Day; **Día de la Madre** Mother's Day; **Día del Padre** Father's Day; **Día de los Reyes** Epiphany; **Día de San Patricio** St. Patrick's Day; **Día de San Valentín** Valentine's Day; **día de la semana** day of the week; **Día del Trabajo** Labor Day; **hoy día** today, nowadays; **todos los días** every day; **un par de días** a few days
¿qué diablos? what the devil?
diagnosis *f.* diagnosis
diagnóstico diagnosis
dialecto dialect
diálogo dialogue
diario/a daily; **vida diaria** *adj.* daily life; *n. m.* daily newspaper
dibujar to draw; **dibujarse** to take form
dibujo drawing; sketch; **dibujos animados** cartoons
diccionario dictionary
diciembre *m.* December
dictador *m.* dictator
dictadura dictatorship
dicho *n.* saying
dicho/a (*p.p. of* **decir**) said
diecinueve nineteen
dieciocho eighteen
dieciséis sixteen
diecisiete seventeen
diente *m.* tooth
dieta diet; **estar** (*irreg.*) **a dieta** to be on a diet
diez ten
diferencia difference; **a diferencia de** unlike
diferente different
difícil difficult, hard
dificultad *f.* difficulty
difunto/a defunct, dead
dignidad *f.* dignity
dilema *m.* dilemma
dinamismo dynamism
dinámico/a dynamic
dinastía dynasty
dinero money; **dinero en efectivo** cash
Dios *m. s.* God; **¡Dios mío!** *interj.* my

God!; **gracias a Dios** *interj.* thank God; **por Dios** *interj.* for heaven's sake
diplomático/a *n.* diplomat
diputado/a representative; congressman, congresswoman
dirección *f.* address; direction; **direcciones cardinales** cardinal points
directamente directly
director(a) director; head, leader
dirigir (j) to direct, run
discar (qu) to dial
disciplina discipline
disciplinado/a disciplined
discoteca disco(theque)
discreto/a discreet
discriminación *f.* discrimination
discriminar to discriminate
disculpar to excuse, make excuses for; **disculparse** to apologize; **disculpe** pardon me, excuse me
disculpas: pedir (i, i) disculpas to apologize
discurso speech
discusión *f.* discussion; argument, (*verbal*) fight
discutir to discuss; to argue; to fight (*verbally*)
diseño design
disfrutar (de) to enjoy
disgustar to dislike; **disgustarse** to get annoyed
disgusto quarrel
disiparse to disappear
disperso/a dispersed, scattered
disponible available
disposición: a su disposición at their service, at their disposal
dispuesto/a (a) ready, willing (to)
disputa dispute
distancia distance; **llamada de larga distancia** long-distance call
distante distant
distinguir (g) to distinguish
distinto/a distinct, different
distracción *f.* recreation
distrito district; **distrito federal** federal district
diversidad *f.* diversity
diversificar (qu) to diversify
diversión *f.* pastime, recreation
diverso/a diverse
divertido/a amusing, fun
divertir (ie, i) to entertain; **divertirse** to have a good time
dividirse to be divided
divino/a divine
divorciarse (de) to divorce, get divorced (from)
divorcio divorce
doblar to turn
doble double; **habitación** (*f.*) **doble** double room

doce twelve
dócil docile
doctor(a) doctor
doctrina doctrine
documento document, paper
dogma *m.* dogma
dólar *m.* dollar; **¿a cuánto está el dólar?** what is the exchange rate for the dollar?
doler (ue) to hurt, be painful; to ache; **me/le duela la cabeza** I/he/she/you (*form.*) have/has a headache
dolor *m.* pain; **dolor de cabeza** headache
doloroso/a painful
doméstico/a domestic; **animal** (*m.*) **doméstico** pet; **aparato doméstico** household appliance
dominación *f.* domination, dominion; rule
dominante dominant
dominar to dominate; to master
domingo Sunday
dominio dominion, domain
dominó *s.* dominoes
don *title of respect used with a man's first name;* **don** *m.* gift; **don de gentes** charm
donde where
¿dónde? where?; **¿de dónde?** from where?
doña *title of respect used with a woman's first name*
dorado/a golden
dormido/a asleep
dormir (ue, u) to sleep; **dormir la siesta** to take a siesta, nap; **dormirse** to fall asleep
dormitorio bedroom
dos two
doscientos/as two hundred
dosis *f.* dose
drama *m.* drama, play
dramático/a dramatic
dramaturgo/a playwright
drástico/a drastic
droga drug
droguería drugstore
ducha shower; **baño privado con ducha** private bath with shower
ducharse to take a shower
duda doubt; **no cabe duda** there is no doubt; **sin duda** no doubt, without a doubt
dudar to doubt; to hesitate
dudoso: es dudoso que it's doubtful that
dueño/a owner; **dueño/a de negocios** shop owner
dulce *adj.* sweet
dulces *n. m. pl.* sweets, candy; **dulce de leche** spread made from sweetened condensed milk
dulzura sweetness
duna de arena sand dune

durante during; for (*period of time*)
durar to last
durazno peach (*Arg.*)
duro/a hard; harsh

E

e and (*used instead of* **y** *before words beginning with* **i** *or* **hi**)
eclesiástico/a ecclesiastical
eclipse *m.* eclipse
ecológico/a ecological
economía economy
económico/a economic; economical; **ciencias económicas** economics
economista *m., f.* economist
economizar (c) to economize
echar to throw out; **echar de menos** to miss, long for
edad *f.* age; **edad mediana** middle age
edificio building
editor(a) editor; publisher
educación *f.* education; **educación bilingüe** bilingual education; **educación física** physical education
educado/a educated
efectivamente actually, in fact
efectivo cash; **(dinero) en efectivo** cash
efecto effect
eficacia efficiency
Egipto Egypt
egocéntrico/a egocentric, self-centered
egoísmo selfishness, egoism
egoísta *m., f.* egotistical, selfish
¿eh? *tag phrase with approximate English equivalent of* **okay?**
ejecutivo/a executive
ejemplificar (qu) to exemplify
ejemplo example; **por ejemplo** for example
ejercer (z) to exert; to practice (*a profession*)
ejercicio exercise; **ejercicio aeróbico** aerobic exercise; **hacer** (*irreg.*) **ejercicio** to exercise, get exercise
ejército army
ejote *m.* string bean (*Mex.*)
el the (*m. def. art.*)
él *sub. pron.* he; *obj. of prep.* him
elección *f.* election
electricista *m., f.* electrician
elefante *m.* elephant; **elefante marino** elephant seal
elegancia elegance
elegante elegant
elegido/a elected
elegir (i,i) (j) to select, choose
elemento element
elevado/a raised; elevated; **clase** (*f.*) **elevada** upper class
elogiar to praise
elogio praise
ella *sub. pron.* she; *obj. of prep.* her

ello *pron. neut.* it
ellos/as *sub. pron.* they; *obj. of prep.* them
embajador *m.* ambassador
embarazada pregnant
embarcarse (qu) to embark, board ship
embargo: sin embargo nevertheless
emborracharse to get drunk
emigración *f.* emigration
emigrado/a emigrant
emigrante *m., f.* emigrant
emigrar to emigrate
emoción *f.* emotion
emocionado/a moved, emotional
emocionante exciting
emotivo/a emotional
empadronador *m.* census taker
empanada turnover, pie
emparejar to match
empeñar to pawn
empeño undertaking
emperador *m.* emperor
empezar (ie) (c) to begin; **empezar a** + *inf.* to begin to (*do something*)
empleado/a employee
emplear to employ
empresa firm, company, business; **administración** (*f.*) **de empresas** business administration
empresario/a employer, contractor
empujar to urge; to push
empuñar to seize, grasp
en in, on, at; **en la actualidad** at this time, nowadays; **en aquel entonces** back then, at that time, in those days; **en broma** as a joke, jokingly; **en busca de** in search of; **en cambio** on the other hand; **en casa** at home; **en común** in common; **en conflicto** in conflict; **en contra (de)** against; **en cuanto a ... as** far as . . . is concerned; **en este momento, en estos momentos** right now, currently; **en fin** in short; after all; **en el fondo** deep down, at heart; **en forma** in good shape; **en general** generally, in general; **en ninguna parte** not anywhere, nowhere; **en punto** on the dot (*with time*); **en realidad** actually, really; **en seguida** right away, immediately; **¿en serio?** seriously?; **en teoría** in theory; **en venta** for sale; **en voz alta** out loud; **pensar (ie) en** to think about
enamorado/a *n.* sweetheart; **Día** (*m.*) **de los Enamorados** Valentine's Day; **estar** (*irreg.*) **enamorado/a (de)** to be in love (with)
enamorarse (de) to fall in love (with)
enano/a dwarf
encabezado/a (por) led (by)
encantado/a in seventh heaven
encantador(a) charming

encantar to enchant, charm; to love, like
encanto *n.* charm, enchantment; delight
encarcelado/a imprisoned
encima *adv.* above; over; overhead; moreover; **encima de** *prep.* on top of
encontrar (ue) to meet; to find; **encontrarse** to find (*oneself*); **encontrarse con** to meet with
encuentro meeting, encounter
encuesta poll, survey
enemigo/a enemy
energía energy
enérgico/a energetic
enero January
enfadado/a angry
enfadarse (con) to get angry (at, with)
enfermarse to get sick
enfermedad *f.* illness
enfermero/a nurse
enfermo/a *n.* sick person; *adj.* sick, ill
enfocar (qu) to focus
enfrentamiento confrontation
enfrentar to face, confront; **enfrentarse (con)** to deal with, face (*a problem*)
enfrente de *prep.* in front of
enfriarse to become cold
engañar to deceive
engaño deception
engordar to gain weight
enigma *m.* puzzle, mystery
enojado/a angry
enojarse (con) to get angry (at)
enorme enormous
enrollado/a rolled up
ensalada salad
ensayar to rehearse
ensayista *m., f.* essayist
ensayo *n.* essay; rehearsal
enseñar to teach; to show
entender (ie) to understand
enteramente entirely
enterarse (de) to find out (about)
entero/a entire, whole
enterrado/a buried, interred
entonces then, at that time; **en aquel entonces** at that time, back then, in those days
entrada entrance; price of admission
entrar (en/a) to enter, go (in)
entre between, among; **entre la espada y la pared** between a rock and a hard place
entregar (gu) to surrender; to hand over
entrenador(a) coach
entrenar to train
entretenerse (*like* **tener**) to amuse oneself
entrevista interview
entrevistar to interview
entrometerse to meddle
entrometido/a nosy
entusiasmar to cause enthusiasm

entusiasmo enthusiasm

enviar to send

envidia envy; **tenerle** (*irreg.*) **envidia (a alguien)** to envy (*someone*)

envidiable enviable

envidioso/a: estar (*irreg.*) **envidioso/a (de)** to be envious (of)

envolverse (ue) (*p.p.* **envuelto/a**) **(en)** to wrap oneself up (in)

envuelto/a (*p.p. of* **envolver**) wrapped

episodio episode

época epoch, period, era

equipado/a equipped

equipaje *m.* luggage

equipo team; equipment

equis: sacar (qu) rayos equis to take X rays

equivalente *m.* equivalent

equivocación *f.* mistake

equivocado/a mistaken

equivocarse (qu) to make a mistake

érase una vez once upon a time

error *m.* error

escabeche *m.* marinade

escala scale

escalera step, stair; stairway; ladder; *pl.* stairs, steps

escándalo scandal

escandaloso/a scandalous

escapada escapade

escapar(se) to escape

escaparate *m.* display window

escasez *f.* (*pl.* **escaseces**) lack, shortage

escena scene; stage

escenario scene

esclavitud *f.* slavery

esclavo/a slave

escocés *m.* Scotch (*whiskey*)

escoger (j) to choose

escondido/a hidden

escribir (*p.p.* **escrito/a**) to write; **escribir a mano** to write by hand; **máquina de escribir** typewriter

escrito/a (*p.p. of* **escribir**) written

escritor(a) writer

escritura *n.* writing

escrúpulo scruple

escuchar to listen (to)

escudo shield

escuela school; **escuela primaria** elementary school; **escuela secundaria** high school; **escuela superior** high school

escultor(a) sculptor

escultura sculpture

ese, esa *adj.* that; **ése, ésa** *pron.* that one

esencia essence

esencial essential

esforzarse (ue) (c) to strive, make an effort

esfuerzo effort

esmero great care

eso that, that thing, that fact; **por eso** for that reason, that's why

esos/as *adj.* those; **ésos/as** *pron.* those (ones)

espacial: transbordador (*m.*) **espacial** spaceship

espacio space

espada: entre la espada y la pared between a rock and a hard place

espalda back

España Spain

español *m.* Spanish (*language*)

español(a) *n.* Spaniard; *adj.* Spanish; **mundo de habla española** Spanish-speaking world

especial special

especialidad *f.* specialty

especialista *m., f.* specialist

especialización *f.* specialization; major

especializarse (c) (en) to specialize (in); to major (in)

especialmente especially

especie *f.* species; type

espectacular spectacular

espectáculo spectacle, show

espectador(a) spectator

especulación *f.* speculation

esperanza(s) hope

esperar to wait (for); to hope; to expect

espinaca(s) spinach

espíritu *m.* spirit; **espíritu de hierro** iron will

esplendor *m.* splendor

espontaneidad *f.* spontaneity

espontáneo/a spontaneous

esposo/a husband/wife; spouse; *m. pl.* husband and wife, spouses

esqueleto skeleton

esquí *m.* skiing; **esquí acuático** water skiing; **esquí alpino** downhill skiing; **esquí nórdico** cross-country skiing; **estación** (*f.*) **de esquí** ski resort

esquiar to ski

esquina corner (*of a street*)

estable *adj.* stable

establecer (zc) to establish; **establecerse** to establish oneself, get settled

establo *n.* stable

estación *f.* station; season; resort; **estación de esquí** ski resort; **estación de gasolina** gas station; **estación del tren** train station

estacionamiento parking lot

estadio stadium

estado state

Estados Unidos *pl.* United States

estadounidense *of or from the United States*

estallar to break out (*war*)

estampilla stamp

estancia ranch; stay, visit

estaño tin

estar (*irreg.*) to be; to be located; **¿a cuánto está el dólar (el peso)?** what's the exchange rate for the dollar (the peso)?; **está a** it's at (it's worth); **está nublado** it's cloudy, overcast; **estar a dieta** to be on a diet; **estar a punto de** to be about to; **estar al aire libre** to be outdoors; **estar al tanto** to be informed, up to date; **estar de acuerdo (con)** to agree, be in agreement (with); **estar de vuelta** to be back; to have returned; **estar enamorado/a de** to be in love with; **estar envidioso/a (celoso/a) (de)** to be envious (jealous) (of); **estar harto/a (de/con)** to be fed up (with); **estar listo/a** to be ready; **estar mal** to be ill; **estar por** (+ *inf.*) to be about to (*do something*); to be ready to (*do something*); **(no) estar seguro/a** (not) to be sure; **la temperatura está a ... grados** the temperature is . . . degrees

estatua statue

estatura height; **de estatura mediana** of average height

este *n. m.* east

este/a *adj.* this; **éste/a** *pron.* this one; **en este momento** right now, currently; **esta noche** tonight

estéreo stereo

estereotipo stereotype

estilizado/a stylized; slender

estilo style

estimado/a dear (*correspondence salutation*)

estimar to hold in high esteem

estímulo stimulus

esto this, this thing, this matter

estorbar to hinder; to get in the way of

estos/as *adj.* these; **éstos/as** *pron.* these (ones); **en estos momentos** right now, currently

estrecho *n.* strait

estrecho/a *adj.* narrow; close-knit; **relación** (*f.*) **estrecha(s)** close, intimate relationship

estrella star

estrenar to debut, perform for the first time

estricto/a strict

estructura structure

estudiante *m., f.* student

estudiar to study

estudio study; **estudios agrícolas** agricultural studies

estudioso/a studious

estufa stove

estupendamente stupendously

estupendo/a wonderful, marvelous, stupendous, great

estupidez (*pl.* **estupideces**) stupid remark or action

etapa stage

ético/a ethical
etiqueta: de etiqueta formal (*dress*)
étnico/a ethnic
Europa Europe
europeo/a *n., adj.* European
evasión *f.* escape, evasion
evidente evident
evitar to avoid
evolucionar to evolve, change
exacto *adv.* exactly, that's exactly right
exacto/a *adj.* exact
exagerar to exaggerate
examen *m.* exam; examination
examinar to examine
excavación *f.* excavation
excavar to excavate
excelencia: por excelencia par excellence
excelente excellent
excepción *f.* exception; **con excepción de** with the exception of
excepcional exceptional
excepto except
exceso excess
exclamar to exclaim
excluido/a excluded
exclusivo/a exclusive
excursión *f.* excursion, trip
excusa excuse
excusarse to excuse oneself
ex esposo/a ex-husband/wife
exhausto/a exhausted
exhibir to exhibit
exiliado/a *n.* exile, exiled person
exiliarse to be exiled
exilio exile
existencia existence
existir to exist; **dejar de existir** to disappear
éxito success; **tener** (*irreg.*) **éxito** to be successful
exótico/a exotic
expansión *f.* expansion
expedición *f.* expedition
experiencia experience; experiment
experimentar to experience
experto/a expert
explanada esplanade
explicación *f.* explanation
explicar (qu) to explain
explorador(a) explorer
explorar to explore
explotación *f.* explotation
explotar to exploit
exportación *f.* exportation, export
exportador(a) exporter
exportar to export
exposición *f.* exhibition, exposition; show
expresar to express
expresión *f.* expression
expresionista *adj.* expressionist

expresivo/a expressive
expulsar to expel
exquisito/a exquisite
extenderse (ie) to extend
extendido/a extended; **familia extendida** extended family
extensión *f.* extension, stretch, expanse
extenso/a extensive
exterior exterior, outer
externo/a external
extinguir (g) to die out
extranjero *n.* abroad; **en el extranjero** abroad
extranjero/a *n.* foreigner; *adj.* foreign; **lengua extranjera** foreign language
extrañar to miss, long for
extraño/a *n.* stranger; *adj.* strange; **es extraño** it's strange; **¡qué extraño!** how strange!
extraordinario/a extraordinary
extravagancia folly
extravío loss of one's way
extremo/a extreme
extrovertido/a extrovert
exuberante exuberant, abundant

F
fábrica factory
fabricar (qu) to manufacture, make
fabuloso/a fabulous
faceta facet
fácil easy
facilidad *f.* facility
fácilmente easily
factor *m.* factor
facturar to check (*luggage*)
facultad *f.* faculty, school
faja strip
fajita *tortilla filled with strips of marinated meat and condiments*
falda skirt
falso/a *adj.* false
falta lack; **hacer** (*irreg.*) **falta** to be lacking, needed; **hacerle** (*irreg.*) **falta a alguien** to need (*something*)
faltar to be missing, lacking; to be absent
fallar to fail
fallecimiento death
fama fame, reputation
familia family; **familia extendida** extended family; **familia nuclear** nuclear family
familiar *n. m.* relation, member of the family; *adj.* family, related to the family
familiarizarse (c) to familiarize oneself
famoso/a famous
fantasía fantasy
farmacéutico/a pharmaceutical
farmacia pharmacy, drugstore
fascinante fascinating
fascinar to fascinate

fascismo fascism
fastidiar to "drive up a wall"
fatal fatal; disastrous
fatiga fatigue
favor *m.* favor; **a favor** in favor; **por favor** please
favorecer (zc) to favor
favorito/a favorite
fe *f.* faith
febrero February
fecha date; **hasta la fecha** so far, to date, up until now
fechado/a dated
federal: distrito federal federal district
felicidad *f.* happiness
felicitaciones *f. pl.* congratulations
feliz (*pl.* **felices**) happy
femenino/a feminine
feminista *m., f.* feminist
fenomenal phenomenal
fenómeno phenomenon
feo/a ugly
feria fair
feroz (*pl.* **feroces**) ferocious
ferretería hardware store
ferrocarril *m.* railroad
ficción *f.* fiction; **ciencia-ficción** science fiction
fiebre *f.* fever; **bajar la fiebre** to bring down one's fever; **tienes una fiebre alta** you (*fam.*) have a high fever; **tener** (*irreg.*) **una fiebre** to have a fever
fiel loyal, faithful
fiesta party; holiday; festival; **dar** (*irreg.*) **una fiesta** to give a party
figura figure
figurar (en) to be important (in)
fijamente: mirar fijamente to stare
fijarse en to pay attention to, take notice of, concentrate on
fijo/a fixed
filete *m.* fillet
Filipinas: (Islas) filipinas Philippine (Islands)
filmado/a filmed
filosofía philosophy; **filosofía y letras** liberal arts
filosófico/a philosophical
filósofo/a philosopher
fin *m.* end; **al fin y al cabo** after all, when all is said and done; **en fin** in short; after all; **fin de semana** weekend; **por fin** at last, finally; **tener** (*irreg.*) **como fin** to have as a goal
final *n. m.* end; *adj.* final; **al final** in the end; **al final de** at the end of; **hasta finales de** until the end of
financiero/a financial
finanzas finances
finca farm, ranch
fineza class, good taste

fino sherry
fino/a fine; dry (*liquor*)
firma signature
firmar to sign
física *n.* physics
físico/a *adj.* physical; **educación** (*f.*) **física** physical education
flan *m.* baked custard, flan
flirtear to flirt
flojo/a slack, sluggish
flor *f.* flower
florecer (zc) to flower; to prosper, flourish
folclórico/a *adj.* folk
folklore *m.* folklore
folklórico/a *adj.* folk
fondo background; *pl.* funds; **a fondo** completely, thoroughly; **de fondo** thoroughly; **en el fondo** deep down, at heart
forjar to forge, make
forma form; **de todas formas** in any case; **en forma** in good shape
formación *f.* (professional) training; education
formado/a (por) formed, made up (of)
formador *m.* maker, former
formar to form; to make; to shape; **formar parte de** to be or form a part of
fortaleza fortress
fortificación *f.* fortification, fort
fosforescente phosphorescent
foto(grafía) *f.* photo(graph); **tomar/sacar (qu) una foto** to take a picture, photograph
fotografiar to photograph
fotográfico/a photographic
fracasado/a unsuccessful
fracasar to fail
fracaso failure
fractura fracture
frágil fragile
frambuesa raspberry
francamente frankly
francés *n. m.* French (*language*)
francés, francesa *n.* Frenchman, Frenchwoman; *adj.* French
Francia France
frase *f.* phrase; sentence
frecuencia frequency; **con frecuencia** often; frequently **con más frecuencia** most frequently, most often; **¿con qué frecuencia?** how often?
frecuentar to frequent, go regularly to
frecuente frequent
frecuentemente frequently
frente a opposite, facing; **en frente** opposite
fresa strawberry
fresco/a fresh; **hace (mucho) fresco** it's (very) cool (*weather*)
fríamente coolly, coldly

frijol *m.* bean
frío *n.* cold; **hace (mucho) frío** it's (very) cold (*weather*)
frío/a *adj.* cold; **tener** (*irreg.*) **(mucho) frío** to be (very) cold
frito/a fried; **calamares fritos** fried squid rings, **papas fritas** French fries (*L.A.*); **patatas fritas** French fries (*Sp.*)
frívolo/a frivolous
frontera border
frotación *f.* rubbing
fructífero/a fruitful
frustrado/a frustrated
fruta fruit; **frutas cristalizadas** candied (crystalized) fruit
frutería fruit store
frutilla strawberry (*Arg.*)
fue: se fue he/she went away
fuego fire
fuente *f.* fountain; source; **fuente de la juventud** fountain of youth
fuera *adv.* out, outside; **fuera de** *prep.* out(side) of
fuerte strong; nasty; hard
fuerza strength; *pl.* strength; forces
fumar to smoke; **sección** (*f.*) **de (no) fumar** (non)smoking section
función *f.* performance, show, function
funcionar to function, work (*machines*)
fundación *f.* foundation
fundador(a) founder
fundamentalmente fundamentally
fundar to found
funerario/a *adj.* funeral
furioso/a furious
furtivo/a sneaky
fusión *f.* fusion; merging
fútbol *m.* soccer; **fútbol (norte)americano** football
futuro *n.* future
futuro/a *adj.* future

G

gabinete *m.* cabinet
gala: baile (*m.*) **de gala** formal dance
galería gallery
gallego Galician (*language of Galicia [region of Spain]*)
gamba shrimp (Sp.)
gana: de buena gana willingly
ganadería cattle raising
ganado cattle; herd
ganador(a) winner
ganar to win; to earn; to gain
ganas: tener (*irreg.*) **ganas de** + *inf.* to feel like (*doing something*)
garaje *m.* garage
garganta throat
gas *m.* gas; heat
gasolina gasoline; **estación** (*f.*) **de gasolina** gas station

gastar to spend (*money*)
gastos expenses
gato/a cat
gauchesco/a *pertaining to gauchos*
gemelo/a twin
generación *f.* generation
general *n. m., adj.* general; **en general** generally, in general; **por lo general** generally, in general
generalización *f.* generalization
generoso/a generous
genial pleasant; congenial
gente *f. s.* people; **don** *m.* **de gentes** charm
geografía geography
geográfico/a geographic(al)
geométrico/a geometric
gerente *m., f.* manager
gigante giant, gigantic
gimnasia *s.* gymnastics
gimnasio gymnasium
gira tour
giro money order
gitano/a gypsy
globo globe
gobernador(a) governor
gobernar (ie) to govern, rule
gobierno government
golf: campo de golf golf course
golfo gulf
golpe *m.* blow (*injury*); **golpe militar** military coup
golpear to bang
gordito/a plump, fat
gordo/a fat
gorra cap
gótico/a Gothic
gozar (c) (de) to enjoy
grabado etching
gracias thank you; **dar** (*irreg.*) **las gracias** to thank; **Día** (*m.*) **de Dar Gracias** Thanksgiving Day; **gracias a Dios** *interj.* thank God; **muchas gracias** thank you very much
gracioso/a funny
grado grade; degree (*temperature*)
graduado/a *adj.* graduate
graduarse (en) to graduate (from)
gramática grammar
gran, grande large, big; great
grandeza greatness
granja farm
gratis *inv.* free (*of charge*)
grave grave, serious
Grecia Greece
grecorromano/a Greco-Roman
gregoriano: calendario gregoriano Gregorian calendar
griego/a *n. adj.* Greek
gripe *f.* influenza, flu
gris gray
gritar to shout

grito shout; cry
grosero/a crude, brutish
grotesco/a grotesque
grueso/a heavy (*clothing*)
gruñón, gruñona grouchy, irritable
grupo group
gruta grotto, cave
guachinango red snapper (*Mex.*)
guajolote *m.* turkey (*Mex.*)
guantes *m.* gloves
guapo/a handsome; pretty
guardar to save, keep (*things, a secret*); to have; **guardar cama** to stay in bed
guardia *m.* guard
guerra war; **guerra civil** civil war; **guerra mundial** world war
guerrero/a *adj.* warlike; *n.* warrior
guía *m., f.* guide; **guía turístico/a** tour guide
guineo banana (*P.R.*)
guionista *m., f.* scriptwriter
guisantes *m.* peas
guisar to cook
guitarra guitar
guitarrista *m., f.* guitarist
gurú *m.* guru
gustar to like; to be pleasing to; **me gustaría + *inf.*** I would really like to (*do something*); **(no) gustarle + *inf.*** to (dis)like to (*do something*); **no me gusta(n) nada ...** I don't like . . . at all
gusto pleasure; like, preference; taste; **mucho gusto** pleased to meet you

H
Habana: la Habana Havana
habanero/a from Havana
haber (*irreg.*) *inf. form of* **hay**; to have (*auxiliary*); to be; **va a haber** there's going to be
había there was, there were (*imperfect of* **hay**)
habilidad *f.* ability
habitación *f.* room; **habitación doble** double room; **habitación individual** single room
habitante *m., f.* inhabitant
habitar (en) to inhabit, live (in)
habla *f.* (*but* **el habla**) speech; language; **(mundo) de habla española** Spanish-speaking (world)
hablador(a) talkative
hablar to talk; to speak
hacendado/a wealthy rancher
hacer (*irreg.*) to do; to make; **¿cuánto tiempo hace que ... ?** how long has it been that . . . ?; **desde hace años** for a number of years; **hace un calor de mil demonios** it's a hellishly hot day; **hace (mucho) calor (fresco, frío, sol, viento)** it's (very) hot (cool, cold, sunny, windy) (*weather*); **hace**

muchos años many years ago; **hacer buen/mal tiempo** it's good (bad) weather; **hacer caso a** to pay attention to; **hacer las compras** to shop; **hacer las cuentas** to do the accounts; **hacer ejercicio** to exercise, get exercise; **hacerle daño (a alguien)** to hurt (someone); **hacer falta** to be lacking, needed; **hacer la maleta** to pack one's suitcase; **hacer una oferta** to make an offer; **hacer el papel (de)** to play the role (of); **hacer un *picnic*** to have a picnic; **hacer planes** to make plans; **hacer una reservación** to make a reservation; **hacer televisión** to work in television; **hacer un viaje** to take a trip; **hacerle preguntas (a alguien)** to ask (someone) questions; **hacerse** to become (*a member of a profession*); **hacerse tarde** to be getting late; **hacerse el tonto** to play dumb; **no hacer caso (de) ...** to pay no attention (*to an issue*); **no hacerle caso (a alguien)** to ignore (someone); **¿qué tiempo hace?** what's the weather like?; **se me hace tarde** it's getting late
hacia toward
hacienda estate, hacienda
hada *f.* (*but* **el hada**): **hada madrina** fairy godmother
hallazgo find; discovery
hamaca hammock
hambre *f.* (*but* **el hambre**) hunger; **tener** (*irreg.*) **hambre** to be hungry
hamburguesa hamburger
hámster *m.* hamster
harina flour
harto/a: estar (*irreg.*) **harto/a (de/con)** to be fed up (with)
hasta *prep.* until; **hasta la fecha** so far, to date; up until now; **hasta finales de** until the end of; **hasta luego** until later, see you later; **hasta mañana** until tomorrow, see you tomorrow; **hasta pronto** see you soon; **hasta** *conj.* even; **hasta que** *conj.* until; **¿hasta qué punto?** up to what point?
hay there is, there are; **no hay** there is not/are not; **no hay de qué** you're welcome (*form.*)
hecho fact; **de hecho** in fact
hecho/a (*p.p. of* **hacer**) made, done
helado ice cream
helicóptero helicopter
hemisferio hemisphere
hemorragia hemorrhage
heredar to inherit
heredero/a heir, heiress
herencia heritage; inheritance
herido/a wounded
hermanastro/a stepbrother, stepsister
hermano/a brother, sister (*family; reli-*

gious vocation); *m. pl.* brothers and sisters; **medio/a hermano/a** half brother, half sister
hermoso/a beautiful
héroe *m.* hero
hierba grass; herb
hierro iron; **espíritu de hierro** iron will
hijastro/a stepson, stepdaughter
hijo/a son, daughter; child; *m. pl.* children; **hijo/a único/a** only child
¡híjole! my God! gosh!
himno nacional national anthem
hinchado/a swollen
hipnotizar (c) to hypnotize
hipócrita *m., f.* hypocrite
hispánico/a *adj.* Hispanic
hispano/a *n., adj.* Hispanic
Hispanoamérica Spanish America
hispanoamericano/a Spanish American
histérico/a hysterical
historia history; story
histórico/a historic(al); **antecedentes (*m.*) históricos** *pl.* historical record, background
hoja leaf; sheet of paper
hojear to leaf through, glance through; to scan
hola hello, hi
holgar (ue) (gu) to rest, enjoy oneself
hombre *m.* man; **hombre de negocios** businessman; **tienda de ropa para hombres** men's clothing store
honestidad *f.* honesty
honesto/a honest
honrar to honor
hora hour; time; **¿a qué hora?** at what time?; **decir** (*irreg.*) **la hora** to tell time; **¿qué hora es?** what time is it?; **¿qué horas son?** (*Mex.*) what time is it?
horario schedule; timetable
horizonte *m.* horizon
hormiga ant
horno oven; **al horno** baked; **horno de microondas** microwave oven
horrorizar (c) to terrify; to horrify
horroroso/a horrible
hospital *m.* hospital; **hospital de urgencia** emergency hospital
hostilmente in a hostile manner
hotel *m.* hotel
hotelero/a *adj.* hotel
hoy today; **hoy día** nowadays
huelga *n.* strike (*labor*)
huella mark; print; trace; track; **huella de mano** handprint
huérfano/a *n., adj.* orphan
huésped(a) guest
huevo egg; **huevos pasados por agua** soft-boiled eggs; **huevos revueltos** scrambled eggs
humanidades *f.* liberal arts, humanities

I

humano/a human; **derechos humanos** human rights; **ser** (*m.*) **humano** human being
húmedo/a humid
humilde humble; relatively poor
humor *m.* mood; **de mal humor** in a bad mood

I

Ibérico/a: Península Ibérica Iberian Peninsula
ida *n.* departure; **billete** (*m.*) **de ida** one-way ticket; **pasaje** (*m.*) **de ida y vuelta** round-trip ticket (fare)
idealista *n. m., f.* idealist; *adj.* idealistic
idéntico/a identical
identidad *f.* identity
identificar (qu) to identify
idioma *m.* language
iglesia church
ignorar not to know; to be unaware of
igual equal; the same
igualmente likewise; so am I (*pleased to meet you*)
iluminar to illuminate
ilustrar to illustrate
imagen *f.* image
imaginación *f.* imagination
imaginar(se) to imagine
imaginativo/a imaginative
imitación *f.* imitation
imitar to imitate; to look like
impaciencia impatience
impaciente impatient
impacto impact
impedimento impediment, obstacle
impedir (i, i) to prevent
imperfecto (*gram.*) imperfect tense
imperio empire
impetuoso/a impetuous
implicar (qu) to mean
imponente *adj.* imposing
imponer (*like* **poner**) to impose
importación *f.* import
importado/a imported
importancia importance
importante important
importar to be important, matter; **me importa un comino** I couldn't care less
imposible impossible
impresión *f.* impression; **causar una buena impresión** to make a good impression
impresionado/a impressed; **quedar bien impresionado/a (con)** to have or be left with a good impression (by/with)
impresionante impressive
impresionar to impress, make an impression on
impresionismo Impressionism
impresionista *n, m., f., adj.* Impressionist

improbable improbable
impropio/a inappropriate
improvisación *f.* improvisation
improvisar to improvise
impuesto tax
impulsivo/a impulsive
impulso impulse; thrust
inapropiado/a inappropriate
inca *n. m., adj. m. f.* Inca
incapaz (*pl.* **incapaces**) incapable
incidente *m.* incident
incierto/a uncertain
incitar to cause, motivate
inclinación *f.* inclination
inclinar(se) to bend down
incluir (y) to include
inclusive including
incluso *adv.* even
incomible inedible
incómodo/a uncomfortable
incompatibilidad *f.* incompatibility
incomprensible incomprehensible
inconsciente unconscious
inconveniente *n. m.* difficulty
incorporado/a incorporated
incorporarse (a) to incorporate; to join
incorrecto/a incorrect
increíble incredible
incumplimiento breach (*of contract*)
incursión *f.* raid
indefenso/a defenseless
indefinido/a indefinite
indemnización *f.* compensation
independencia independence; **Día** (*m.*) **de la Independencia** Independence Day
independiente independent
independentista *adj. m., f.* pro-independence
independizarse (c) to become independent
indicado/a appropriate
indicar (qu) to indicate, point out
indicativo (*gram.*) indicative
índice *m.* rate
indiferencia indifference
indiferente indifferent
indígena *n., m., f.* native; *adj.* indigenous, native
indio/a Indian
indirecta *n.* insinuation
indirecto/a *adj.* indirect
individual: habitación (*f.*) **individual** single room
individuo *n.* individual
industria industry
industrial *n. m.* industrialist, manufacturer
industrialista *adj., m., f.* pertaining to or in favor of industrialism
industrializado/a industrialized
inesperado/a unexpected

inestable unstable
inexperto/a inexperienced
infancia childhood
infección *f.* infection
infinidad *f.* infinity
infinitivo (*gram.*) infinitive
inflación *f.* inflation
influencia influence
influenciado/a influenced
influir (y) (en) to influence
influjo influence
información *f.* information
informal informal
informar to inform; **informarse** to inquire, find out
informática data processing
ingeniería engineering
ingeniero/a engineer
ingenio de azúcar sugar mill
ingenuo/a naive, ingenuous
Inglaterra England
inglés *m.* English (*language*)
inglés, inglesa *n.* Englishman, Englishwoman; *adj.* English
ingrediente *m.* ingredient
ingresar to enter
ingresos *pl.* income, earnings
iniciar to initiate; to start
injusticia injustice
injusto/a unjust, unfair
inmediatamente immediately, right away
inmediatez *f.* immediacy; closeness
inmediato/a immediate; close
inmenso/a immense
inmigración *f.* immigration
inmigrante *n., m., f., adj.* immigrant
inmigrar to immigrate
inocente innocent
inolvidable unforgettable
inquieto/a restless
inscripción *f.* inscription
inseguro/a insecure
insinuar to insinuate, hint at; **insinuarse** to ingratiate
insistir (en) to insist (on)
inspeccionar to inspect
inspector(a) inspector
inspiración *f.* inspiration
inspirar to inspire
inspirarse (en) to be inspired (by)
instalarse to establish oneself, settle in
instantáneamente instantaneously
instante *m.* instant
instinto instinct
institución *f.* institution
institucional institutional
instituto institute
instrucciones *f.* directions, instructions
instructor(a) instructor
instrumento instrument
insultar to insult
integrar to integrate

íntegro/a integral
intelectual intellectual
inteligencia intelligence
inteligente intelligent
intención *f.* intention
intenso/a intense
intentar to try, attempt
intento intention; attempt
interacción *f.* interaction
interés *m.* interest
interesante *adj.* interesting
interesar to interest, be of interest; **interesarse (en)** to be interested (in)
interior *n. m.* interior
internacional international
internar to check into (*a hospital*)
interpretación *f.* interpretation
interpretar to interpret; to act a part
interrogativas: palabras interrogativas (*gram.*) interrogative words
interrumpido/a interrupted
intervenir (*like* **venir**) to intervene; to interfere
íntimo/a intimate; close; **amigo/a íntimo/a** close friend
intransigente intransigent, uncompromising
intriga intrigue
introducir (*irreg.*) to introduce, bring in
intuir (y) to sense
invadir to invade
invasión *f.* invasion
invasor(a) invader
invención *f.* invention
inventar to invent
invento invention
inventor(a) inventor
inversión *f.* investment
invertir (ie, i) to invest
investigación *f.* investigation
investigador(a) investigator
investigar (gu) to investigate
invierno winter
invitación *f.* invitation
invitar to invite (*with the intention of paying*)
involucrar to involve, implicate
inyección *f.* shot, injection; **ponerle** (*irreg.*) **una inyección** to give (someone) a shot, injection
ir (*irreg.*) to go; **ir a** + *inf.* to be going to (*do something*); **ir al cine** to go to the movies; **ir a una función de teatro** to go to a show at the theater; **ir a un parque** to go to a park; **ir de compras** to go shopping; **irse** to go away, leave (*for a place*); **va a haber** there's going to be; **¿vamos?** shall we go?; **¡vamos!** *interj.* let's go!
irlandés, irlandesa *n.* Irishman, Irishwoman; *adj.* Irish
ironía irony

irónico/a ironic
irregularidad *f.* irregularity
irresponsable irresponsible
isla island; **Islas Canarias** Canary Islands; **Islas Filipinas** Philippine Islands
Islam *m.* Islam
Italia Italy
italiano/a *n., adj.* Italian
izquierdo/a left (*direction*); **a la izquierda** to the left; **a mano izquierda** on the left(-hand) side

J

jamás never
jamón *m.* ham; **jamón serrano** cured Spanish ham
Japón *m.* Japan
japonés, japonesa, *n., adj.* Japanese
jarabe (*m.*) **tapatío** *popular Mexican dance known as Mexican hat dance in U.S.*
jardín *m.* garden; **jardín botánico** botanical garden; **jardín zoológico** zoo
jefe/a boss
jarro pitcher
jengibre *m.* ginger
jerarquía hierarchy
jerez *m.* sherry
jersey *m.* sweater (*Sp.*)
Jesucristo Jesus Christ
jesuita *n., m.* Jesuit; *adj., m., f.* Jesuit
jinete *m.* horseman
jornada laboral day's work
joven *n., m., f.* young person; *adj.* young; **de joven** as a young person
joya jewel
joyería jewelry store
jubilado/a *n.* retired person; *adj.* retired
jubilarse to retire (*from the work force*)
judía verde string bean
judicial judicial, legal; **orden** (*f.*) **judicial** legal procedure
judío/a *n.* Jew; *adj.* Jewish
juego game; gambling; **juego de salón** parlor game (*cards, chess, poker, etc.*); **Juegos Olímpicos** Olympic Games
jueves *m. s.* Thursday
jugador(a) player; gambler
jugar (ue) (gu) (a) to play (*a game or sport*); **jugar a las cartas** to play cards; **jugar (por dinero)** to gamble; **jugar al póquer** to play poker
jugo juice
juguete *m.* toy
julio July
junio June
juntarse to meet
junto a next to; **junto con** together with
juntos/as together
jurar to swear (*as in a court*)
jurídico/a legal
jurisdicción *f.* jurisdiction

justificar (qu) to justify
justo *adv.* just, exactly; **justo ahora** right now, just now
juventud *f.* youth; **fuente** (*f.*) **de la juventud** fountain of youth
juzgar (gu) to judge

K

karate *m.* karate
kerosén *m.* kerosene
kilo(gramo) kilogram (*approx. 2.2 pounds*)
kilómetro kilometer (*approx. .62 miles*)

L

la the (*f. def. art.*); **a la(s) ...** at (*hour*)
la *d.o.* you (*form. s.*), her, it (*f.*)
laboral work, having to do with the working world; **jornada laboral** day's work
laboratorio laboratory
lado side; **al lado de** beside, next to; **de al lado** next door; **por un/otro lado** on the one (other) hand
lagarto lizard
lago lake
lágrima tear
lamentablemente regrettably
lamentar to lament
langosta lobster
langostino prawn
lanza spear
lápiz *m.* (*pl.* **lápices**) pencil
largamente at length, for a long time
largo/a long; **llamada de larga distancia** long-distance call; **a lo largo de** during; **a lo largo del camino** along the way
las the (*pl. f. def. art.*); you (*pl. f. form. pers. pron.*), them (*pl. f. pers. pron.*); *pron.* those; **las demás** the rest, the others, others, other people
le *i.o.* to/for you (*form. s.*), him, her, it
lástima *n.* pity; **es (una) lástima** it's a shame
lastimado/a hurt
lata: ¡qué lata! what a pain!
latino/a Latin; **América Latina** Latin America
Latinoamérica Latin America
latinoamericano/a *n., adj.* Latin American
lavado *n.* wash
lavadora clothes washer
lavandería laundry, laundromat
lavaplatos *m. s.* dishwasher
lavar to wash
lazo lasso
le *i.o.* to/for you (*form. s.*), him, her, it
lección *f.* lesson
lectura *n.* reading
leche *f.* milk; **café** (*m.*) **con leche** *strong coffee served with warm or hot milk;* **dulce** (*m.*) **de leche** spread made from sweetened condensed milk

lechuga lettuce
leer (y) to read
legal legal
legitimidad *f.* legitimacy
legítimo/a legitimate
legumbre *f.* vegetable
lejos far away; **lejos de** *prep.* far from
lema *m.* slogan, motto
lencería linen goods
lengua language; tongue; **lengua extranjera** foreign language; **sacar (qu) la lengua** to stick out one's tongue
lenguado sole (*fish*)
lenguaje *m.* language
lentitud *f.* slowness, sluggishness
leña firewood
león *m.* lion
les *i.o.* to/for you (*form. pl.*), them
lesión *f.* injury, wound, lesion
letra letter (*of alphabet*); lyrics; *pl.* liberal arts; **filosofía y letras** liberal arts
levantar to lift, raise; **levantarse** to get up; to rise up, rebel
ley *f.* law
leyenda legend
liberación *f.* liberation
liberal: artes (*f.*) **liberales** liberal arts
libertad *f.* liberty; freedom
libertador(a) liberator
libre free; **estar** (*irreg.*) **al aire libre** to be outdoors; **ratos libres** free time, spare time; **tiempo libre** free time, spare time
librería bookstore
libro book; **libro de texto** textbook
líder *m.* leader
ligar (gu) con to pick (someone) up
ligero/a *adj.* light
limitado/a limited
limitar con to be bounded by
límite *m.* boundary; limit
limón *m.* lemon
limonada lemonade
limpiar to clean
lindo/a pretty
línea line; **líneas curvas** curved lines
lingüístico/a linguistic
lío problem, trouble
líquido liquid
lírico/a lyric, lyrical
lista list
listo/a estar (*irreg.*) **listo/a** to be ready, prepared; **ser** (*irreg.*) **listo/a** to be bright, smart
literario/a literary; **obras literarias** literary works
literatura literature
litoral *m.* seaboard, coast
lo *d.o.* you (*form. s.*), him, it (*m.*); **lo antes posible** as soon as possible; **lo cual** which; **lo más posible** as much as possible; **lo más pronto posible** as

soon as possible; **lo que** what, that which; **lo siento** I'm sorry
localizado/a located
locamente madly
loco/a: volverse (ue) loco/a to go crazy
lógico/a logical
lograr to manage to, be able
Londres London
loro parrot
los the (*pl. m. def. art.*); *d.o.* you (*form. pl.*), them (*m.*); *pron.* those; **los demás** the rest, the others, others, other people
lotería lottery
lucha fight
luchador(a) fighter
luchar to fight
luego then, next; later; **desde luego** of course; **hasta luego** until later, see you later
lugar *n. m.* place; **en primer lugar** in the first place, firstly; **tener** (*irreg.*) **lugar** to take place
lujo luxury
lujoso/a luxurious
luna moon; **luna de miel** honeymoon
lunes *m. s.* Monday
luz *f.* (*pl.* **luces**) light

LL

llama: se llama (he/she) is called, named
llamada *n.* call; **llamada de larga distancia** long-distance call; **llamada telefónica** telephone call
llamado/a named; so-called
llamar to call (out); to call (*by phone*); **llamar la atención** to attract attention; **llamarse** to be called, named
llano *n.* plain
llano/a *adj.* flat, level
llanura *n.* plain
llave *f.* key
llegada arrival
llegar (gu) to arrive; **llegar a ser** to become
llenar to fill (up)
lleno/a full, filled
llevar to take; to carry; to wear; to have spent (time); **llevar (las) cuentas** to keep the books; **llevar una vida . . .** to lead a . . . life; **llevarse bien/mal (con)** to get along well/badly (with)
llorar to cry, weep
llover (ue) to rain
llovizna drizzle
lluvia rain

M

macho male, manly, macho
madera wood
madrastra stepmother

madre *f.* mother; **Día** (*m.*) **de la Madre** Mother's Day
madrileño/a *n.* person from Madrid; *adj.* from Madrid
madrina: hada madrina fairy godmother
maduro/a mature
maestro/a teacher; master; **obra maestra** master work
mágico/a magical
magnífico/a magnificent
mago: Reyes (*m.*) **Magos** Magi, Wise Men
maíz *m.* corn
majestuoso/a majestic
mal, malo/a *adj.* bad; *adv.* badly; **andar** (*irreg.*) **mal** to be going badly; **caerle** (*irreg.*) **mal (a alguien)** to not like, make a bad impression on (someone); **de mal humor** in a bad mood; **estar** (*irreg.*) **mal** to be ill; **llevarse mal (con)** to get along badly (with); **mala suerte** bad luck; **manejar mal** to manage (*something*) badly; **pasarlo mal** to have a bad time; **por bien o por mal** for better or worse; **sentirse (ie, i) mal** to feel bad, ill
malabarista *m., f.* juggler
maleta suitcase; **hacer** (*irreg.*) **la maleta** to pack one's suitcase
maltratar to maltreat, abuse
mamá mom
mamacita mom
mami *f.* mom
mamut *f.* mammoth
mandar to send; to order
mandato order
¿mande? pardon me?, what did you say? (*Mex.*)
mando command; **ponerse** (*irreg.*) **a mando** to take command
mandón, mandona bossy
manejar to drive; **manejar (bien/mal)** to manage (*something*) (well/badly)
manera manner, way
manía mania
manifestación *f.* manifestation; demonstration
maniobra maneuver
mano *f.* hand; **a mano** close by, at hand; **a mano derecha/izquierda** on the right/left(-hand) side; **darse** (*irreg.*) **la mano** to shake hands; **escribir a mano** to write by hand; **huella de mano** handprint
manta blanket
manteca fat, lard; butter (*Arg.*)
mantener (*like* **tener**) to maintain, keep up; to support (*a family*)
mantequilla butter
manufactura *n.* manufacture
manzana apple; city block (*Sp.*)
mañana *adj.* morning; *adv.* tomorrow; **pasado mañana** the day after tomorrow; **por la mañana** in the morning

mapa *m.* map

máquina machine; **máquina de escribir** typewriter; **máquina tragamonedas** slot machine

mar *m., f.* sea; **Mar** (*m.*) **Cantábrico** Bay of Biscay

maravilla marvel

maravilloso/a marvelous

marcado/a (*p.p.* of **marcar**) marked, pronounced

marcar (qu) to mark

marco frame

marchar to march

margarita daisy; drink made with tequila

marido husband

marinero/a sailor

marino/a *adj.* marine; **elefante** (*m.*) **marino** elephant seal

marisco shellfish; *pl.* seafood

marítimo/a maritime

mármol *m.* marble

marrón brown

martes *m. s.* Tuesday

marxismo Marxism

marzo March

más more; most; plus; **a más tardar** at the latest; **cada vez más** more and more; **lo más posible** as much as possible; **lo más pronto posible** as soon as possible; más allá de *prep.* beyond; **más de** more than; **más o menos** more or less; **más tarde** later

masas *pl.* the masses, the people

máscara mask

masculino/a masculine

matemáticas mathematics

mateo carriage; **andar** (*irreg.*) **en mateo** to take a carriage ride

materia subject; **materia prima** raw material; *pl.* courses

materialista *n., m., f.* materialist; *adj.* materialistic

materno/a maternal

matrícula tuition

matricularse to matriculate; enroll

matrimonial marital; **cama matrimonial** double bed

matrimonio marriage; married couple

máxima maxim, saying

máximo *n.* maximum

máximo/a *adj.* maximum; greatest

maya *n., m., f.* Mayan; *adj.* Mayan

mayo May

mayonesa mayonnaise

mayor bigger; biggest; older; oldest; greater; main

mayoría majority

mayoritario/a pertaining to the majority

mazapán *m.* marzipan

me *d.o.* me; *i.o.* to/for me; *refl. pron.* myself; ¿**me permite . . . ?** could you give me . . . ?

mecánico mechanic

media thirty (*half past*) (*with time*)

mediados *pl.* middle; **a mediados de** halfway through

mediano/a average; middle; **de estatura mediana** of average height; **edad** (*f.*) **mediana** middle age

mediante by means of

medias stockings

medicina medicine

medicinal medicinal, curative

médico/a *n. m., f.* doctor; *adj.* medical

medida measure, step

medieval medieval

medio *n.* middle; means; medium; environment; culture; **medio ambiente** environment; **medios** (*pl.*) **de comunicación** means of communication, media; **medios** (*pl.*) **de transporte/transportación** means of transportation; **por medio de** by means of

medio/a *adj.* half; average; **clase** (*f.*) **media** middle class; **medio/a hermano/a** half brother, half sister; **Oriente** (*m.*) **Medio** Middle East

mediocre mediocre

medioeste Midwest

medir (i, i) to measure

Mediterráneo Mediterranean

mejillón *m.* mussel

mejor better; best; **a lo mejor** maybe; **mejor amigo/a** best friend

mejorar to improve; to raise; **mejorarse** to get better, improve

melocotón *m.* peach

melódico/a melodic; "easy listening"

melón *m.* melon

memoria memory; **de memoria** by heart

mencionar to mention

menino/a *young page of the royal family; young lady-in-waiting*

menor younger; youngest; least

menos less; least; minus; except; **a menos que** unless; **al menos** at least; **echar de menos** to miss, long for; **más o menos** more or less; **por lo menos** at least

mensaje *m.* message

mentir (ie, i) to lie

mentiroso/a *adj.* lying

menú *m.* menu

menudo: a menudo often

mercadillo market

mercado market

merluza hake (*fish*)

mermelada marmalade, jam

mes *m.* month; **al mes** per month

mesa table; food; cooking

mesero/a waiter, waitress

meseta plain, plateau

mestizo/a *n., adj.* mestizo

meta goal

metal *m.* metal

metalúrgico/a metallurgical

meterse (en) to get involved (with, in); to meddle (in)

metódico/a methodic

metro meter; subway

metrópoli(s) *f.* metropolis

metropolitano/a metropolitan

mexicano/a *n., adj.* Mexican

México Mexico; **Ciudad** (*f.*) **de México** Mexico City

mexicoamericano/a *n. adj.* Mexican American

mezcal *m.* mescal

mezcla mix

mezclar(se) to mix; to be mixed

mezquita mosque

mi(s) *poss.* my

mí *obj. of prep.* me; myself

microondas: horno de microondas microwave oven

miedo: tener (*irreg.*) **miedo (de)** to be afraid (of)

miedoso/a cowardly

miel *f.* honey; **luna de miel** honeymoon *f.*

miembro member

mientras *conj.* while; *adv.* meanwhile; **mientras tanto** meanwhile

miércoles *m. s.* Wednesday

migrar to migrate

mil (one) thousand; **hace un calor de mil demonios** it's a hellishly hot day

milagro miracle

militar *n.* soldier, military man; *adj.* military; **golpe** (*m.*) **militar** military coup

milpa corn field (*C. Am., Mex.*)

milla mile

millón *m.* million

mimado/a spoiled, overindulged

mimar to spoil

mimos *pl.* pampering

minero/a *adj.* mining

mineral mineral; **agua** (*f. but* **el agua**) **agua mineral** mineral water

mínimo/a minimal

ministerio ministry

minoritario/a *adj.* minority

minuto minute

mío/a(s) *poss.* my; mine; of mine; ¡**Dios mío!** *interj.* my God!

mirada look, glance

mirar to look (at); to watch; **mirar la televisión** to watch television

misión *f.* mission

mismo/a same; **ahora mismo** right now; **al mismo tiempo** at the same time; **sí mismo/a** himself, herself, itself

misterio mystery

misterioso/a mysterious

mitad *f.* half

mítico/a mythical

mito myth

mixto/a tossed

moda fashion, mode; **de moda** fashionable

modelo *n.* model
modelo *adj. m., f.* model
moderación *f.* moderation
moderar to moderate
modernismo modernism
modernización *f.* modernization
moderno/a modern
modesto/a modest
modificar (qu) to modify
modo way
mojarse to get wet, soaked
moldear to mold
mole (*m.*) **poblano** *casserole dish prepared with meat and chili sauce* (*Mex.*)
molestar to bother, annoy; **molestarse** to get irritated
molestia bother; **siento la molestia** I'm sorry to bother you
molino mill; **molino de viento** windmill
momento moment; **de momento** for the moment; **en este momento, en estos momentos** right now, currently; **por el momento** for the time being
monarca *m., f.* monarch
monarquía monarchy
moneda coin; **la otra cara de la moneda** the other side of the coin
monja nun
mono monkey
monótono/a monotonous
montaje *m.* production
montaña mountain
montañoso/a mountainous
montar to set up; **montar a caballo** to ride horseback
monte *m.* mount, mountain
monumento monument
moño bun (*of hair*)
morado/a purple
morir(se) (ue, u) (*p.p.* **muerto/a**) to die
moro/a *n.* Moor; *adj.* Moorish
morrón: pimiento morrón red pepper
mosaico mosaic
mostaza mustard
mostrar (ue) to show
motivo motif; motive; **el motivo por el cual** the reason why
motor *m.* motor
mover(se) (ue) to move
movimiento movement
mozo/a waiter/waitress; *f.* young lady
muchacho/a young boy/girl
mucho *adv.* much, a lot of
mucho/a *adj.* a lot of; *pl. many;* **muchas gracias** thank you very much; **muchas veces** often; **mucho gusto** pleased to meet you
mudarse to move (*from one residence or city to another*)
mudéjar Mudejar (*Mohammedan living under a Christian king in Spain*)

muerte *f.* death; **dar** (*irreg.*) **la muerte a** to put to death
muerto/a (*p. p. of* **morir**) dead; **naturaleza muerta** still life (*painting*)
muestra proof
mujer *f.* woman; wife; **mujer de negocios** businesswoman; **tienda de ropa para mujeres** women's clothing store
mujeriego/a womanizer
multinacional multinational
mundial world(wide); **guerra mundial** world war
mundo world; **mundo de habla española** Spanish-speaking world; **Nuevo Mundo** New World; **todo el mundo** the whole world; everybody
muñeco/a doll
muralista *m., f.* muralist
muralla wall
murmurar to murmur, whisper
museo museum; **visitar un museo** to visit a museum
música music
musical musical
músico/a musician; **músicos ambulantes** strolling musicians
musulmán, musulmana Moslem
mutilar to mutilate
mutuo/a mutual
muy very; **muy bien** very well

N
nacer (zc) to be born
nacimiento birth; **certificado de nacimiento** birth certificate; **de nacimiento** by birth
nación *f.* nation
nacional national; **himno nacional** national anthem
nacionalidad *f.* nationality
nacionalización *f.* nationalization
nada *pron.* nothing, not anything; *adv.* not at all; **de nada** you're welcome; **no me gusta(n) nada ...** I don't like ... at all
nadar to swim
nadie no one
napolitano/a Neapolitan
naranja *n.* orange (*fruit*)
nariz *f.* nose
narración *f.* narration
narrador(a) narrator
narrar to narrate
natación *f.* swimming
natal natal, native
nativo/a native
natural natural; **ciencias naturales** natural sciences; **recurso natural** natural resource
naturaleza nature; **naturaleza muerta** still life
náutico/a nautical

navegación *f.* sailing
navegar (gu) (**en barco**) to sail
Navidad *f.* Christmas
necesario/a necessary
necesidad *f.* necessity, need
necesitar to need
necio/a foolish
negar (ie) (gu) to refuse
negativa *n.* refusal
negativo/a *adj.* negative
negocio(s) business; shop; **dueño/a de negocios** shop owner; **hombre** (*m.*) **de negocios** businessman; **mujer** (*f.*) **de negocios** businesswoman
negro/a black
nene, nena baby
neoclásico/a neoclassic(al)
nervioso/a nervous
nevar (ie) to snow
nevera refrigerator
ni neither, nor; **ni ... ni ...** neither ... nor ...; **ni siquiera** not even
nieto/a grandson, granddaughter; *m. pl.* grandchildren
nieve *f.* snow
ningún, ninguno/a *adj.* no, none, not any; **en ninguna parte** not anywhere, nowhere
ninguno/a *pron.* not one, not any
niñez *f.* childhood
niño/a young boy, young girl; young child; *m. pl.* young children; **de niño/a** as a child
nivel *m.* level
no no; not; **¿no?** right?, don't they (you, *etc.*)?; **no hay** there is not/are not; **ya no** no longer
nocturno/a *adj.* night, nocturnal
noche *f.* night, evening; **buenas noches** good evening/night; **camisa de noche** night shirt; **de la noche** in the evening, at night; **de noche** at night, by night; **esta noche** tonight; **por la noche** in the evening
nómada *m., f.* nomad
nombrar to name; to appoint
nombre *m.* (first) name; **a nombre de** in the name of
nopal *m.* cactus
nórdico/a Nordic; **esquí** (*m.*) **nórdico** cross-country skiing
noreste *m.* northeast
normalidad *f.* normality
noroeste *m.* northwest
norte *m.* north
Norteamérica North America
norteamericano/a *n., adj.* North American; *adj.* from the United States; **fútbol** (*m.*) **norteamericano** football
norteño/a *adj.* northern
nos *d.o.* us; *i.o.* to/for us; *refl. pron.* ourselves
nosotros/as *sub. pron.* we; *obj. of prep.* us

nostalgia nostalgia
nota note; grade, mark (*in schoolwork*);
   nota al pie footnote; **sacar (qu)**
   buenas/malas notas to get good/bad
   grades
notar to note, notice; **notarse** to be noted
noticia piece of news; *pl.* news; **últimas**
   noticias latest news
noticiero news (program)
notorio/a notorious
novecientos/as nine hundred
novela novel; **leer (y) novelas** to read
   novels; **novela policíaca** detective
   novel, mystery
novelista *m., f.* novelist
noveno/a ninth
noventa ninety
noviazgo engagement, courtship
noviembre *m.* November
novio/a boyfriend, girlfriend; fiancé(e)
nube *f.* cloud
nublado/a cloudy, overcast; **está**
   nublado it's cloudy, overcast
nuclear: familia nuclear nuclear family
núcleo nucleus
nudo knot
nuera daughter-in-law
nuestro/a(s) *poss.* our
nueve nine
nuevo/a new; **de nuevo** again
Nuevo Mundo New World
nuevomexicano/a New Mexican
número number; **número de la suerte**
   lucky number
numeroso/a numerous
nunca never, not ever

O
o or
obedecer (zc) to obey
obelisco obelisk
obispo bishop
objetivo *n.* objective
objeto object
obligado/a obliged, obligated
obligar (gu) to oblige, force
obra work (*of art, literature, etc.*); play;
   obra de teatro play, dramatic work;
   obra literaria literary work; **obra**
   maestra master work
obrero/a *n.* (*manual*) worker; laborer;
   adj. working; **clase obrera** working
   class
observar to observe; watch
observatorio observatory
obsesión *f.* obsession
obsesionarse to be(come) obsessed
obstáculo obstacle
obtener (*like* **tener**) to obtain, get
obvio/a obvious
ocasión *f.* occasion
occidental western

océano ocean; **Océano Atlántico** Atlantic Ocean; **Océano Pacífico** Pacific
   Ocean
octavo/a eighth
octubre *m.* October
ocultado/a (*p.p. of* **ocultar**) hidden
ocultar to hide
ocupado/a busy
ocupar to occupy; **ocuparse** to occupy
   oneself
ocurrir to happen, occur; **ocurrirse** to
   come to mind
ochenta eighty
ocho eight
ochocientos/as eight hundred
odiar to hate
odio hatred
oeste *m.* west
ofender to offend
ofensa offense, affront
ofensivo/a offensive
oferta offer; **aceptar la oferta** to accept
   the offer; **hacer** (*irreg.*) **una oferta** to
   make an offer; **oferta de trabajo** job
   offer; **rechazar (c) la oferta** to reject
   the offer
oficial *adj.* official
oficina office
oficio occupation, job
ofrecer (zc) to offer
oído ear
oír to hear; to listen
ojalá (que) God willing; I hope
ojo eye; **¡ojo!** *interj.* watch out!, be careful!, pay close attention!; **ojos claros**
   light-colored eyes; **ojos expresivos** expressive eyes
ola wave
olímpico/a Olympic; **Juegos Olímpicos**
   Olympic Games
olivar *m.* olive grove
olmeca *n., m., f., adj.* Olmec
olvidar(se) (de) to forget (about)
olvido *n.* forgetting; oblivion
omitir to omit, leave out
once eleven
opción *f.* option
ópera opera
operador(a) operator
opinar to think, have an opinion
opinión *f.* opinion
oponer(se) (*like* **poner**) to oppose; to
   be opposed
oportunidad *f.* opportunity
oportuno/a opportune
oposición *f.* opposition
opresión *f.* oppression
oprimir to oppress
optimista *m., f.* optimist; *adj.* optimistic
opuesto/a (*p.p. of* **oponer**) opposed
oración *f.* sentence
orden *m.* order (*chronological*); *f.*
   order (*command*); **a sus órdenes** at

your service; **en orden** (*m.*) **cro-**
   nológico in chronological order;
   orden (*f.*) **judicial** legal procedure
ordenado/a orderly; ordained
ordenador *m.* computer (*Sp.*)
ordenar *m.* to put in order; to ordain; to
   order (*a meal*) (*Mex.*)
oreja ear
orfanato orphanage
organismo organism
organista *m., f.* organist
organización *f.* organization
organizar (c) to organize
orgullo pride
orgulloso/a proud
oriental oriental; eastern
oriente *m.* east; Orient; **Oriente Medio**
   Middle East
origen *m.* origin
originario/a *adj.* originating
orilla bank (*of a river*); **a orillas de** on
   the banks of
ornamentación *f.* ornamentation
oro gold
orquesta orchestra
ortografía spelling
os *d.o.* you (*fam. pl. Sp.*); *i.o.* to, for you
   (*fam. pl. Sp.*); *refl. pron.* yourselves
   (*fam. pl. Sp.*)
oscuro/a dark
ostra oyster
otoño autumn
otro/a other, another; **la otra cara de la**
   moneda the other side of the coin; **otra**
   vez again; **por otro lado** on the other
   hand
oxígeno oxygen

P
paciencia patience
paciente *n., m., f.* patient; *adj.* patient
pacífico/a peaceful; **Océano Pacífico** Pacific Ocean
padrastro stepfather
padre *m.* father; priest; *pl.* parents; **Día**
   (*m.*) **del Padre** Father's Day
paella *Spanish dish of rice, shellfish,*
   chicken, and meat
pagar (gu) to pay (for)
página page
país *m.* country, nation
País (*m.*) **Vasco** Basque region (*of Spain*)
paisaje *m.* countryside; landscape
pájaro bird
palabra word; **palabras interrogativas**
   (*gram.*) interrogative words
palacio palace
palmas applause
palo stick
paloma pigeon
palomitas popcorn
pampa pampa, grassland
pan *m.* bread; **pan tostado** toast

panadería bakery; pastry shop
panadero/a baker
panceta bacon (*Arg.*)
panorámico/a panoramic
pantalón, pantalones *m.* pants; **pantalón corto, pantalones cortos** shorts
pañuelo handkerchief, kerchief
papa potato (*L.A.*); **papas fritas** French fries
papá *m.* dad, father
papel *m.* paper; role; **hacer** (*irreg.*) **el papel (de)** to play the role (of)
papelería stationery store
paquete *m.* package
par *m.* pair; **un par de** a pair of; **un par de (días)** a few (days)
para *prep.* for, in order to; **no es para tanto** it's not that big of a deal; **para pensar** something to think about; **para que** *conj.* so that, in order that (for); **¿para quién?** for whom?; **para saber qué pasó** to find out what happened
parada *n.* stop; **parada de taxis** taxi stand
paradero whereabouts, location
parador *m.* inn
parar to stop
parcela plot, parcel (of ground)
parcial partial
parcha passion fruit
pardo/a brown
parecer (zc) *v.* to seem, appear; **parecerse a** to be similar to; to resemble; **al parecer** apparently
parecer *n. m.* appearance
parecido *n.* resemblance
parecido/a *adj.* (*p.p. of* **parecer**) similar
pared *f.* wall; **entre la espada y la pared** between a rock and a hard place
pareja couple
parentesco relationship, kinship
paréntesis *m., s., pl.* parenthesis, parentheses; **entre paréntesis** in parentheses
pariente *m.* relative, family member; **visitar a los parientes** to visit relatives
parlamentaria parliamentary
parque *m.* park; **parque zoológico** zoo
párrafo paragraph
parrilla grill
parrillada barbecue
parte *f.* part; **en ninguna parte** not anywhere, nowhere; **formar parte de** to be or form a part of; **por parte (de alguien)** on behalf of (someone); **por todas partes** all over; everywhere
participar to participate
participio (*gram.*) participle
particular *adj.* particular; private; *n.* matter
partido game, match; (political) party; side
partir: a partir de starting from
parto childbirth

pasado *n.* past
pasado/a *adj.* past, last (*in time*); **huevos pasados por agua** soft-boiled eggs; **pasado mañana** the day after tomorrow
pasaje *m.* passage, fare; ticket; **pasaje de ida y vuelta** round-trip fare
pasajero/a *adj.* passing; *n.* passenger
pasaporte *m.* passport
pasar to happen; to pass (*someone*); to come by; to pass, spend (*time*); **pasar por** to come by to pick up (*someone, something*); **pasar por agua** to boil (*eggs*); **pasarlo bien/mal** to have a good/bad time; **para saber qué pasó** to find out what happened
pasatiempo hobby
pasear to stroll, take a walk
paseo walk; drive; avenue; **dar** (*irreg.*) **un paseo** to take a walk
pasillo corridor
pasión *f.* passion
paso step; float (*in parade*); passing, passage; **al paso que** at the same time as
pastel *m.* pastel (*color, drawing*); pie
pastelería pastry shop; bakery
pastilla pill
pasto pasture; grazing
patata potato (*Sp.*); **patatas fritas** French fries
paterno/a paternal
patio patio; yard
patito duckling
pato duck
patria fatherland
patriarca *m.* patriarch (*male head of the family*)
Patricio: Día (*m.*) **de San Patricio** St. Patrick's Day
patriótico/a patriotic
patriotismo patriotism
patrocinador(a) sponsor; backer
patrón, patrona patron, patron saint
pavo turkey
paz *f.* peace; **que en paz descanse** may he/she rest in peace
peaje *m.* toll; tollbooth
peatonal *adj.* pedestrian; **calle** (*f.*) **peatonal** pedestrian mall
pecar (qu) to sin
peculiar peculiar; characteristic
pecho chest; breast
pedido *n.* order
pedir (i, i) to ask for, order; **pedir prestado/a** to borrow
pelea fight
pelear(se) (con) to fight (with)
película movie, film
peligro danger
peligroso/a dangerous
pelo hair; **pelo canoso/rubio** gray/blond hair; **tomarle el pelo (a alguien)** to tease someone

pelota ball
peluquería barber shop; hairdresser shop
peluquero/a barber; hairdresser
pena punishment; sorrow; **es una pena** it's a pity; **me da pena** I'm sorry; **(no) vale la pena** it's (not) worth the trouble; **¡qué pena!** *interj.* what a pity!
península peninsula; **Península Ibérica** Iberian Peninsula
pensar (ie) to think; to intend to (*do something*); **para pensar** something to think about; **pensar en** to think about
pensativo/a thoughtful, pensive
peor *adv.* worse; worst
pequeño/a small; **desde pequeño/a** since he/she was small
pera pear
percusión *f.* percussion
perder (ie) to lose; to miss; **perderse (ie)** to get lost
pérdida loss
perdidamente madly
perdón *m.* pardon; *interj.* pardon me, excuse me
perdonar to pardon; **perdone** *interj.* pardon me, excuse me
peregrino/a pilgrim
perezoso/a lazy
perfecto/a perfect
perfume *m.* perfume
periódico newspaper
periodismo journalism
periodista *m., f.* journalist
período period (*of time*)
perla pearl
permanente permanent
permiso permission; **con permiso** may I pass by?
permitir to permit, allow; **¿me permite . . . ?** could you give me . . . ?
pero *conj.* but
perplejo/a perplexed
perro/a dog
perro caliente hot dog
persecución *f.* persecution
pérsico/a *n. adj.* Persian
persistente persistent
persistir to persist
persona person
personaje *m.* character
personal *n. m.* personnel; *adj.* personal
personalidad *f.* personality
perspectiva perspective
pertenecer (zc) to belong
pesadilla nightmare
pesado/a boring, tedious
pesar to weigh
pesar: a pesar de in spite of
pesca *n.* fishing
pescadería fish market
pescadero/a fishmonger; fishwife
pescado (*caught*) fish

pescador(a) fisherman; fisherwoman
pescar: caña de pescar fishing pole
peseta *monetary unit of Spain;* **peseta puertorriqueña** quarter (*U.S. coin used as monetary unit of Puerto Rico*)
pesimismo pessimism
pesimista *n., m., f.* pessimist; *adj.* pessimistic
peso *monetary unit of Mexico;* weight; **bajar de peso** to lose weight
pesquero/a *adj.* fishing (*industry*)
petróleo petroleum
petrolífero/a *adj.* oil
petroquímico/a *adj.* petrochemical
pez *m.* (*pl.* **peces**) (*live*) fish
picada: carne (*f.*) **picada** ground meat
picante spicy, hot; **salsa picante** hot sauce
picnic m. picnic; **hacer** (*irreg.*) **un *picnic*** to have a picnic
pico point; peak
pie *m.* foot; **al pie de** at the bottom of; **nota al pie** footnote
piedra stone
pierna leg
pieza play, piece
pijama *m.* pajamas
pilón *m. frozen dessert similar to a Popsicle*
piloto/a pilot
pimentero pepper shaker/grinder
pimiento pepper; **pimiento morrón** red pepper
pincel *m.* paintbrush
pintar to paint
pintor(a) painter
pintoresco/a picturesque
pintura painting
piña pineapple
piragua *SnoCone*
pirámide *f.* pyramid
pirata *adj., m., f.* pirate
Pirineos Pyrenees
pirulí *m. frozen dessert similar to a Popsicle*
piscina swimming pool, pool
piso floor
pista track; trail
pistola gun
placer m. pleasure
plan m. plan; **hacer** (*irreg.*) **planes** to make plans
planchar to iron
planear to plan
planeta *m.* planet
plano (turístico) map (*of a city*)
plano/a flat
planta plant; **planta baja** ground floor
plantación *f.* plantation
plástico plastic
plata silver
plátano banana

platicar (qu) to talk, chat
plato plate; dish; **plato principal** entrée, main course; **plato apetitoso** appetizing dish
platónico/a platonic
playa beach
plaza plaza, square; place
plenamente fully
plomero *m., f.* plumber
plomo lead
población *f.* population
poblano: mole (*m.*) **poblano** *casserole dish prepared with meat and chili sauce (Mex.)*
pobre *n., m., f.* poor person; *adj.* poor
pobrecito/a poor little thing
pobreza poverty
poco *n.* **un poco de** a little; **dentro de poco** very soon
poco *adv.* little; **poco a poco** little by little; **por poco** almost, nearly
poco/a *adj.* little; *pl.* few, a few; **al poco tiempo** shortly after; **pocas veces** seldom
poder *v.* (*irreg.*) to be able, can; *n. m.* power
poderoso/a powerful
¿podría + *inf.*? could I (*do something*)?; is it possible for me to (*do something*)?
poema *m.* poem
poesía poetry
poeta *m., f.* poet
polaco/a *n.* Pole; *adj.* Polish
policía police
policíaco/a *pertaining to police;* **novela policíaca** detective novel, mystery
poliéster *m.* polyester
política *s.* politics
político/a *n.* politician; *adj.* political
polo polo; pole; **polo sur** South Pole
pollería poultry shop
pollo chicken
pomelo grapefruit (*Arg.*)
ponceño/a *person from Ponce (P.R.)*
poner (*irreg.*) to put, place; to put on; **poner (a alguien) a cargo (de)** to put (someone) in charge (of); **ponerle una inyección (a alguien)** to give (*someone*) a shot, injection; **ponerse + *adj.*** to become + *adj.* **ponerse a mando** to take command
popularidad *f.* popularity
popularizar (c) to popularize
póquer *m.* poker; **jugar (ue) (gu) al póquer** to play poker
por *prep.* by; in (*the morning, evening, etc.*); through; along; for; because of; per; **estar** (*irreg.*) **por** (+ *inf.*) to be about to (*do something*); to be ready to (*do something*); **pasar por** to come by to pick up (*someone, something*); **pasar por agua** to boil (*eggs*); **por**

bien o por mal for better or worse; **por casualidad** by chance; **por cierto** by the way; certainly; **por completo** completely; **por delante** ahead of one; **por desgracia** unfortunately; **por Dios** *interj.* for heaven's sake; **por ejemplo** for example; **por eso** for that reason, that's why; **por excelencia** par excellence; **por favor** please; **por fin** at last, finally; **por un lado** on the one hand; **por lo general** generally, in general; **por la mañana** in the morning; **por lo menos** at least; **por medio de** by means of; **por el momento** for the time being; **por otro lado** on the other hand; **por parte (de alguien)** on behalf of (*someone*); **por poco** almost, nearly; **por primera vez** for the first time; **por semana** in a week's (time); **por su propia cuenta** on his/her/its/your/ their own account; **por suerte** fortunately, luckily; **por supuesto** of course; **por la tarde/noche** in the afternoon (evening); **por teléfono** by telephone; **por todas partes** all over; everywhere; **por última vez** for the last time; **por lo visto** evidently; **terminar por + *inf.*** to finish or end up by (*doing something*)
porción *f.* portion
¿por qué? why?
porque because
portarse to behave; **portarse + *adj.*** to act + *adv.*
porteño/a *inhabitant of Buenos Aires*
portugués *n. m.* Portuguese (*language*)
portugués, portuguesa *n., adj.* Portuguese
poseer (y) to possess
posesión *f.* possession
posesivo: adjetivos posesivos (*gram.*) possessive adjectives
posibilidad *f.* possibility
posible possible; **lo antes posible** as soon as possible; **lo más posible** as much as possible; **lo más pronto posible** as soon as possible
posición *f.* position
positivo/a positive
postal *f.* postcard; **tarjeta postal** postcard
postguerra postwar period
postre *m.* dessert
postular to stand as a candidate for
práctica practice
practicar (qu) to practice; to carry out; to perform; **practicar un deporte** to play a sport
pragmático/a pragmatic
preceder to preceed
precio price
precioso/a precious; beautiful, lovely
precipitado/a hasty, hurried

precisamente precisely, exactly
preciso/a necessary
precolombino/a pre-Columbian
precursor(a) precursor
predecir (*like* **decir**) to predict
predicción *f.* prediction
predilecto/a favorite
predominar to predominate
preferencia preference
preferible preferable
preferido/a favorite
preferir (ie, i) to prefer
pregunta question; **hacerle** (*irreg.*) **preguntas (a alguien)** to ask (someone) questions
preguntar to ask (*a question*); **preguntarse** to wonder; to ask oneself
prehispánico/a *n., adj.* pre-Hispanic
prehistórico/a prehistoric
prejuicio prejudice
premio prize
prensa press (*newspapers*)
preocupación *f.* preoccupation, worry
preocupar(se) to worry
preparación *f.* preparation
preparar to prepare
preparativos preparations
preposición *f.* preposition
preposicional: pronombre (*m.*) **preposicional** (*gram.*) prepositional pronoun
presencia presence
presentación *f.* presentation; introduction
presentar to present; to introduce; **presentarse** to appear
presente *n. m. adj.* present
presentimiento presentiment, premonition
presentir (ie, i) to have a presentiment of
presidencia presidency
presidencial presidential
presidente *m., f.* president
presidido/a (por) presided (over)
presidir to preside over
presión *f.* pressure
prestado: pedir (i, i) prestado/a to borrow
préstamo loan
prestar atención (a) to pay attention (to)
prestigio prestige
prestigioso/a prestigious
presupuesto budget
pretérito (*gram.*) past; preterite (tense)
pretexto pretext, excuse
prevenir (*like* **venir**) to prevent
previo/a previous
primo/a: materia prima raw material
primaria: (escuela) primaria elementary school
primariamente primarily

primavera spring
primer, primero/a first; **amor** (*m.*) **a primera vista** love at first sight; **de primer año** *adj.* freshman; **en primer lugar** in the first place, firstly; **(por) primera vez** (for the) first time
primo/a cousin
primordial primordial, fundamental
princesa princess
principal main, principal; **plato principal** entrée, main course
príncipe *m.* prince
principio beginning; **al principio** at first; at the beginning
prisa haste; **darse** (*irreg.*) **prisa** to hurry; **de prisa** quickly, in a hurry; **tener** (*irreg.*) **prisa (por** + *inf.*) to be in a hurry (*to do something*)
prisión *f.* prison
prisionero/a prisoner
privacidad *f.* privacy
privado/a private, personal; **baño privado (con ducha)** private bath (with shower); **vida privada** personal life
privatización *f.* privatization
privatizar (c) privatize
privilegiado/a privileged
probabilidad *f.* probability; likelihood
probable probable
probar (ue) to try (on); to taste (*food*); to prove
problema *m.* problem
problemático/a problematic
proceder to originate
procesión *f.* procession
proclamar to proclaim
producción *f.* production
producir (zc) to produce
productivo/a productive
producto product
productor(a) producer
profecía prophecy
profesión *f.* profession
profesional *adj.* professional; **secreto profesional** confidentiality
profesor(a) teacher, professor
profundo/a profound
programa *m.* program
programación (*f.*) **de computadoras** computer programming
programador(a) programmer; **programador(a) de computadoras** computer programmer (*L.A.*)
progresar to advance, improve
prohibir to prohibit, forbid
promedio/a *adj.* average
promesa promise
prometer to promise
promulgación *f.* promulgation
pronombre *m.* (*gram.*) pronoun; **pronombre preposicional** (*gram.*) prepositional pronoun
pronto soon; **hasta pronto** see you soon;

lo más pronto posible as soon as possible; **tan pronto** como as soon as
pronunciación *f.* pronunciation
propiedad *f.* property
propietario/a proprietor, owner
propina tip
propio/a *adj.* own, one's own; **por su propia cuenta** on his/her/its/your/their own account
proponente *m., f.* proponent
proponer (*like* **poner**) to propose
propósito intention
prosperar to prosper
próspero/a prosperous
protagonista *m., f.* protagonist
proteger (j) to protect
protesta *n.* protest
protestar (por) to protest (about)
provincia province
provinciano/a provincial
provocar (qu) to provoke
próximo/a near; next
proyecto project
prueba(s) proof; test
psicología psychology
psicológico/a psychological
psiquiatra *m., f.* psychiatrist
psiquiatría psychiatry
publicar (qu) to publish
publicitario/a *adj.* advertising
público/a *n. m., adj.* public
pueblecito village, small town
pueblo people; town
puente *m.* bridge
puerta door; **tocar (qu) la puerta** to knock on the door
puerto port
puertorriqueño/a *n., adj.* Puerto Rican; **peseta puertorriqueña** quarter (*U.S. coin used as monetary unit of Puerto Rico*)
pues *interj.* well
puesto *n.* position, job
puesto/a (*p.p. of* **poner**) put, placed
pulso pulse; **tomar el pulso** to feel the pulse
punto point; (**estar** [*irreg.*]) **a punto de** (to be) at the point of; about to; **a tal punto que** to the point that; **en punto** on the dot (*with time*); **¿hasta qué punto?** up to what point?; **punto de vista** point of view
puntual punctual
puntualidad *f.* punctuality
puré *m.* purée

Q

que that, who; **lo que** what, that which; **para que** so that, in order that (for); **que en paz descanse** may he/she rest in peace; (**el mes, el año ...**) **que viene**

the coming, next (month, year ...); **ya que** since

¿qué? what?; which?; **¡qué + *noun/adj./adverb!* *interj.*** what a ... !; how ...!; **¡qué barbaridad!** how awful!; **¿qué diablos?** what the devil?; **¡qué pena!** what a pity!; **¿qué tal?** how are you (doing)?; how about ... ?; **¿qué tal si ... ?** what if....? **¡qué va!** don't put me on!; **¡qué vergüenza!** how embarrassing!; **¿y qué?** so what?; what do you want me to do?

quedar to be situated; **quedar + *adj.*** to be + *adj.;* **quedar bien impresionado/a** to be left with a good impression; **quedarse** to stay, remain; to be left; **quedarse + *adj.*** to become + *adj.*

quehacer *m.* chore

queja complaint

quejarse (de) to complain (about)

querer (*irreg.*) to wish, want; to love

querido/a (*p.p. of* **querer**) **(de)** *adj.* dear; loved (by)

queso cheese

quien who

¿quién(es)? who?, whom?; **¿a quién?** to whom?; **¿con quién? with whom?; ¿de quién?** whose?; **¿para quién?** for whom?

química chemistry

quince fifteen

quinientos/as five hundred

quinto/a fifth

quiosco kiosk

quisiera + *inf.* I would like to (*do something*); **quisiera cambiar ...** I would like to change ...

quizá(s) maybe, perhaps

R

racismo racism

radicar (qu) to live; to be located

radio *m.* radio (set); *f.* radio (broadcasting meduim)

raíz (*pl.* **raíces**) root; **(agente [*m., f.*] de) bienes** (*m. pl.*) **raíces** real estate (agent)

rana frog

rapidez *f.* rapidity

rápido/a rapid, fast; express, fast (*train*); **comida rápida** fast food

raqueta racket (*sports*)

raro/a rare, uncommon; odd, peculiar

rascacielos *m. s.* skyscraper

rasgo trait, feature

ratificado/a ratified, confirmed

rato while, short time; period of time; **a ratos** at times; **ratos libres** *pl.* spare time, free time

rayo ray; **rayos X** X rays; **sacar (qu) rayos X** to take X rays

raza race (*of human beings*)

razón *f.* reason, cause; reason, faculty of reasoning; **con razón** understandably so; **la razón por la cual** the reason why; **tener** (*irreg.*) **(toda la) razón** to be (absolutely) right

razonable reasonable

reacción *f.* reaction

reaccionar to react

real royal; real

realidad *f.* reality; **en realidad** actually, really

realista *n. m., f.* realist; *adj.* realistic

realización *f.* fulfillment

realizar (c) to carry out; to fulfill, accomplish

realmente really, truly; actually

rebelarse to rebel

rebelión *f.* rebellion

recámara bedroom (*Mex.*)

recepción *f.* front desk (*in a hotel*); reception

recepcionista *m., f.* receptionist

receta prescription; recipe

recibir to get, receive; to receive (*visitors*)

recibo receipt

recién casado/a recently married, newly wed

reciente recent; fresh

recitar to recite (*poem*)

recoger (j) to pick up; to go for

recomendable commendable; recommendable

recomendación *f.* recommendation

recomendar (ie) to recmmend

recompensa reward

reconciliarse (con) to be reconciled, come together; to make up (with)

reconocer (zc) to recognize; to acknowledge

reconocido/a (*p.p of* **reconocer**) acknowledged

Reconquista Reconquest (*struggle to end Moorish rule in Spain*)

reconstrucción *f.* reconstruction

reconstruir (y) to reconstruct

recordar (ue) to remember, recall; to recollect; **recordarle (algo) (a alguien)** to remind (someone) of (something)

recrear to recreate

recto/a straight; **seguir (i, i) (g) recto** to continue straight ahead

recuerdo memory; memento, souvenir

recuperar to recover, retrieve

recurrir(a) to resort (to)

recurso natural natural resource

rechazar (c) to reject; **rechazar la oferta** to reject the offer

rechazo rejection

redactar to write; to draw up

reemplazar (c) to replace

referirse (ie, i) (a) to refer (to)

refinado/a refined, polished

refinamiento class; refinement

reflejar to reflect; to show, reveal; **reflejarse** to be reflected

reflexión *f.* reflection

reflexionar (sobre) to reflect (on)

reflexivo/a reflective, thoughtful

reforma agraria land reform

refrescarse (qu) to refresh oneself

refresco soft drink

refugiado/a refugee

regalar to give (*as a gift*)

regalo gift, present; **regalo de despedida** going-away present

regañar to scold, reprimand

regatear to bargain

regateo *n.* bargaining

régimen *m.* regime

regimiento (*military*) regimen

región *f.* region

registrar to register

regla rule

reglamento regulation; rules

regresar to return, come or go back

regreso *n.* return; **de regreso** *adj.* return (flight); **de regreso a** on returning to

regular fair, average; common, ordinary

rehacer (*like* **hacer**) to remake, make over

reina queen

reinar to reign

reino kingdom

reír(se) (i, i) (de) to laugh (at); to laugh (over)

relación *f.* relation, relationship; **relación estrecha** close, intimate relationship

relacionar to relate; to associate

relajarse to relax

relativo/a *adj.* relative

religión *f.* religion

religiosidad *f.* religiousness

religioso/a religious

reloj *m.* watch

relleno/a stuffed, filled

remar to row

remolcar (qu) to tow

remontarse to go back (*to some date in the past*)

renacer (zc) to be reborn

rendir (i, i) culto (a) to worship; **rendirse** to surrender; to conquer

renunciar to renounce, give up (*right, claim*); to resign (*post, position*)

reparaciones *f.* repairs; **taller** (*m.*) **de reparaciones** repair shop

reparar to repair

repartición *f.* distribution

repasar to review

repaso *n.* review

repente: de repente suddenly

repentino/a sudden

repetir (i, i) to repeat

réplica replica, copy

reponerse (*like* **poner**) to recover (*from an illness*); to get better
reportaje *m.* article; report; special feature
reporte *m.* report
reportero/a reporter
reposo rest
representación *f.* representation; performance
representante *m., f.* representative
representar to represent; to act, perform; to show, express
reprochar to reproach
repugnar to disgust
requerir (ie, i) to require
requisito requirement
res: carne (*f.*) **de res** beef (*Mex.*)
rescatar to save, rescue
rescate *m.* rescue
resentido/a resentful; annoyed
resentimiento resentment
resentir (ie, e) to resent
reserva reservation (Sp.)
reservación *f.* reservation (*L.A.*); **hacer** (*irreg.*) **una reservación** to make a reservation
reservado/a reserved; reticent
resfriado *n.* cold
resfriarse to catch a cold
residencia dormitory; residence
residir to reside
resistencia resistance
resistir to resist, oppose
resolver (ue) (*p.p.* **resuelto/a**) to resolve; to solve
resonar (ue) to resound; to resonate
respaldo support, backing
respectivo/a respective
respecto: con respecto a with respect to
respetar to respect
respeto respect
respirar to breathe
responder to respond
responsabilidad *f.* responsibility
respuesta answer
restablecer (zc) to reestablish, reinstate
restaurante *m.* restaurant
restaurar to restore
resto *n.* rest
restricción *f.* restriction
resuelto/a (*p.p of* **resolver**) resolved
resultado result
resultar to result; to turn out to be
resumen *m.* summary
resumir to sum up, summarize
retrato portrait
reunión *f.* meeting, gathering
reunirse (con) to get (back) together (with); to be reunited (with)
revelación *f.* revelation; unveiling
revelar to reveal
revisar to check, inspect; **revisar las cuentas** to audit accounts

revista magazine
revolución *f.* revolution
revolucionario/a revolutionary
revuelto/a (*p.p. of* **revolver**) scrambled; **huevos revueltos** scrambled eggs
rey *m.* king; **Reyes Magos** Magi, Wise Men
rezar (c) to pray
rezongón, rezongona *n.* grouch, grumbler; *adj.* grouchy
ribera shore, bank
rico/a *n. m., f.* rich person; *adj.* rich; wealthy; tasty, delicious (*food*); abundant (*crops*)
ridículo/a ridiculous
riesgo: correr riesgo to run a risk
riguroso/a rigorous
riñón *m.* kidney
río river
riqueza richness; *pl.* riches
risueño/a smiling
ritmo rhythm
rivalidad *f.* rivalry
robar to steal
robot *m.* robot
roca rock
rock *m.* rock (*music*)
rocoso/a rocky
rodeado/a surrounded
rogar (ue) (gu) to beg
rojo/a red
romántico/a romantic
romper (*p.p.* **roto/a**) to break; **romper con** to break up with (*someone*)
ron *m.* rum
ropa clothing; **cambiarse de ropa** to change one's clothes; **tienda de ropa para hombres/mujeres** men's/women's clothing store
rosa rose; rose color
rosado/a pink
rosal *m.* rosebush or plant
rostro face
rubio/a blond(e); **pelo rubio** blond hair
ruido noise
ruina ruin
ruleta roulette
rumba rumba (*Cuban dance*)
ruso/a *n., adj.* Russian
ruta route, way
rutina routine

S
S.A. (sociedad anónima) Inc. (incorporated; stock company)
sábado Saturday
saber (*irreg.*) to know (*information*); **saber** + *inf.* to know how (*to do something*)
sabio/a *n.* wise person; *adj.* wise
sabor *m.* flavor
saborear to savor, taste
sabroso/a tasty

sacar (qu) to get out; to take out; to take out, withdraw (*from an account*); to get, receive (*grades*); **sacar buenas/malas notas** to get good/bad grades; **sacar una foto** to take a picture, photograph; **sacar la lengua** to stick out one's tongue; **sacar rayos X (equis)** to take X rays; **sacar vídeos** to take videos
sacerdote *m.* priest, clergyman
sacrificar (qu) to sacrifice
sagrado/a sacred
sal *f.* salt
sala living room; **sala de cine/teatro** theater
salchicha sausage
salero salt shaker
salida departure
salir (*irreg.*) to leave (*a place*), go out; to turn out; **salir con los amigos** to go out with friends; **salir de la ciudad** to get out of the city; **salirse con lo suyo** to get one's own way
salmón *m.* salmon; **de color salmón** salmon-colored
salón *m.* lobby; **juegos de salón** parlor games (*cards, chess, poker, etc.*); **salón de clase** classroom
salsa sauce, dressing; salsa (*style of music*); **salsa de tomate** ketchup; **salsa picante** hot sauce
saltar to jump; to fly off
salto waterfall
salud *f.* health; **¡salud!** *interj.* to your health!
saludar to greet
saludo greeting
salvar to save; to rescue
san, santo/a saint; holy; **Semana Santa** Easter (Holy) Week
sandía watermelon
sándwich *m.* sandwich
sangriento/a bloody
sano/a healthy; wholesome; sound
sátira satire
satisfacción *f.* satisfaction
satisfacer (*like* **hacer**) (*p.p.* **satisfecho/a**) to satisfy
se (*impersonal*) one; *refl. pron.* yourself (*form.*), himself, herself, yourselves (*form.*), themselves
secadora clothes dryer
sección *f.* section; **sección de (no) fumar** (non)smoking section
seco/a dry
secretario/a secretary
secreto secret; **secreto profesional** confidentiality
secuencia sequence
secundaria secondary; **(escuela) secundaria** high school
sed *f.* thirst; **tener** (*irreg.*) **(mucha) sed** to be (very) thirsty
seda silk

sede *f.* headquarters
sedentario/a sendentary
seductor(a) seducer; charmer
seguida: en seguida right away,
  immediately
seguido/a followed; in a row, running
seguir (i, i) (g) to follow; to continue; to
  keep on; **seguir (todo) derecho/recto**
  to continue straight (ahead); **seguir**
  vigente to continue to be viable
según according to
segundo *n.* second (*time*)
segundo/a *adj.* second
seguridad *f.* security; **seguridad social**
  social security
seguro *n.* insurance; **seguro social** social
  security
seguro/a *adj.* sure, certain; safe; **(no)**
  estar (*irreg.*) **seguro/a** (not) to be
  sure; **seguro que** of course, certainly
seis six
seiscientos/as six hundred
selva jungle
sello stamp (*Mex.*)
semáforo traffic light
semana week; **día** (*m.*) **de la semana**
  day of the week; **fin** (*m.*) **de semana**
  weekend; **por semana** in a week('s
  time); **Semana Santa** Easter (Holy)
  Week
semejante *adj.* similar
semejanza similarity
semestre *m.* semester
seminario seminary
senado senate
senador(a) senator
sencillo/a simple
sendero path
sensación *f.* sensation
sensible sensitive
sentar (ie) to seat, lead to a seat; **sen-**
  tarse to sit, sit down
sentido sense; **sentido común** common
  sense; **(no) tener** (*irreg.*) **sentido**
  (not) to make sense; **sentido de culpa-**
  bilidad sense of guilt or responsibility
sentimiento feeling
sentir (ie, i) to feel; to regret; to feel
  sorry about; **lo siento** I'm sorry; **sen-**
  tirse to feel; **sentirse bien/mal** to feel
  well/bad (*ill*); **sentirse solo/a** to feel
  lonely; **siento la molestia** I'm sorry to
  bother you
seña sign; signal, gesture
señal *f.* signal; sign
señor (Sr.) *m.* Mr., sir; gentleman, man
señora (Sra.) *f.* Mrs., lady, woman
señores (Sres.) *m. pl.* Mr. and Mrs.;
  gentlemen
señorial noble, majestic
señorita (Srta.) Miss; young lady, woman
separación *f.* separation
separar(se) to separate

septiembre *m.* September
séptimo/a seventh
ser (*irreg.*) to be; **es cierto** it's certain; **es**
  decir that is to say; **es una pena** it's a
  pity; **lograr ser** to manage to become;
  llegar (gu) a ser to become; **ser listo/**
  a to be bright, smart; **ser unido/a** to be
  united, close-knit, close
ser *n. m.* being; life; **ser humano** human
  being
serenata *n.* serenade
serenidad *f.* serenity
sereno/a calm, serene
serie *f.* series; (TV) series
serio/a serious; **¿en serio?** seriously?;
  tomar en serio to take seriously
serpiente *f.* snake, serpent
serrano: jamón (*m.*) **serrano** cured
  Spanish ham
servicio service
servilleta napkin
servir (i, i) to serve; to be suitable, useful;
  servir de to serve as, act as
sesenta sixty
sesión *f.* session; sitting
setecientos/as seven hundred
setenta seventy
severo/a severe
sevillano/a Sevillian (*of or from Seville*)
sexto/a sixth
si if
sí yes; **claro que sí,** *interj.* of course
sí mismo/a himself, herself, oneself, itself
sicología psychology
sicólogo/a psychologist
siempre always
siesta siesta, nap; **dormir (ue, u) la**
  siesta to take a siesta, nap; **tomar**
  una siesta to take a siesta, nap
siete seven
siglo century
significado meaning; significance
significar (qu) to mean
siguiente next, following; **al día**
  siguiente the next day
silenciar to silence
silencio silence
simbólico/a symbolic
simbolizar (c) to symbolize; to typify,
  represent
símbolo symbol
simio ape
simpático/a nice, pleasant
simpatizar (c) to get along well together
simplificado/a simplified
simultáneo/a simultaneous
sin *prep.* without; **sin chistar** without
  saying a word; **sin duda** no doubt, without a doubt; **sin embargo** nevertheless;
  sin que *conj.* without
sinagoga synagogue
sincero/a sincere
sino but (rather)

sinónimo synonym
sintético/a synthetic
siquiera: ni siquiera not even
sirviente/a servant
sistema *m.* system; **sistema solar** solar
  system
sitio site, place
situación *f.* situation
situar to situate; **situarse** to be located
sobre *n. m.* envelope; *prep.* about; on;
  sobre todo above all
sobresalir (*like salir*) to stand out, excel
sobrevivir to survive
sobrino/a nephew, niece; *pl.* nieces and
  nephews
social: ciencias sociales social sciences;
  clase (*f.*) **social** social class;
  seguridad (*f.*) **social** social security;
  seguro social social security
sociedad *f.* society; **sociedad anónima**
  (S.A.) incorporated; stock company
  (Inc.)
socio/a member; partner
socioeconómico/a socioeconomic
sociología sociology
sofá *m.* sofa
sofisticado/a sophisticated
soga rope
sol *m.* sun; **hace (mucho) sol** it's (very)
  sunny (*weather*); **tomar el sol** to
  sunbathe
solamente only
solar solar; **sistema** (*m.*) **solar** solar
  system
solas: a solas alone; in private
soldado soldier
soleado/a sunny
soler (ue) + *inf.* to tend to be, be in the
  habit of (*doing something*)
solicitar to ask for
solidario/a sympathetic (to a cause)
solista *m., f.* soloist
solitario/a solitary; lonely
sólo *adv.* only
solo/a *adj.* alone; sole; **café** (*m.*) **solo**
  black coffee; **sentirse (ie, i) solo/a** to
  feel lonely
soltar (ue) to let go, set free
soltero/a single
solterón bachelor
solución *f.* solution
solucionar to solve
sombrero hat
sombrío/a somber
someter to subject
sonar (ue) to sound; to ring
sonido sound
sonrisa smile
soñador(a) dreamy
soñar (ue) (con) to dream (about)
sopa soup
sopaipilla *fritter dipped in honey* (*Mex.*)
soportar to bear, put up with

sor *f.* sister (*used before the name of a nun*)
sorprendente surprising
sorprender to surprise; **sorprenderse** to be surprised
sorpresa surprise
sospechar to suspect
sospechoso/a suspicious
soviético/a *n.* Soviet, *adj.* Soviet (*of or from the Soviet Union*); **Unión** (*f.*) **Soviética** Soviet Union
su(s) *poss.* his, her, its, your (*form. s., pl.*), their
suave smooth, soft
súbdito/a citizen; subject
subir (a) to go up
subjuntivo (*gram.*) subjunctive
subrayar to underline
suceder to happen
sucesivamente successively
suceso event
sucesor(a) successor
sucio/a dirty
sucursal *f.* branch office
sudadera sweatshirt
Sudamérica South America
sudar to sweat
suegro/a father-in-law, mother-in-law; *m. pl.* in-laws
sueldo salary, pay
suelo floor, ground
sueño dream; sleep; **tener** (*irreg.*) **(mucho) sueño** to be (very) sleepy
suerte *f.* luck; **buena/mala suerte** good (bad) luck; **número de la suerte** lucky number; **por suerte** fortunately, luckily; **tener** (*irreg.*) **(buena) suerte** to be lucky, in luck; **tener** (*irreg.*) **mala suerte** to be unlucky
suéter *m.* sweater
suficiente enough, sufficient
suficientemente sufficiently, enough
sufrimiento suffering
sufrir to suffer
sugerencia suggestion
sugerir (ie, i) to suggest
suite *f.* suite
Suiza Switzerland
sumamente extremely
superar to get through; to overcome
superficie *f.* surface
superior: escuela superior high school
superlativo (*gram.*) superlative
supermercado supermarket
suplicar (qu) to implore, pray
supuesto: por supuesto of course
sur *m.* south; **polo sur** South Pole
sureste *m.* southeast
surgir (j) to come up, occur
surf *m.* surfing
suroeste *m.* southwest
surtido assortment

sustantivo (*gram.*) noun
sustituir (y) to substitute
sustituto/a *n., adj.* substitute
susto scare, fright
sutil subtle
sutileza subtlety
suyo/a(s) *poss.* your, of yours (*form. s., pl.*) his, of his; her, (of) hers; its; their, of theirs; **salirse con lo suyo** to get one's own way

T
tabaco tabacco
tabla table, list (*of figures, etc.*); board
tablavela windsurfing
taco taco (*tortilla filled with cheese, chicken, roast pork, etc.*) (*Mex.*)
taino/a *n. m. f.* Taino (*member of an extinct Indian people of the West Indies*); *adj.* Tainan
tajo cut; slash, gash
tal such (a); a certain (fellow) called; **como tal** as such; **con tal (de) que** so that; **¿qué tal?** how are you (doing)?; how about ... ?; **¿qué tal si ... ?** what if ... ?; **tal como** just as, exactly the same as; **tal vez** perhaps, maybe
talento talent
taller *m.* shop (*for manufacturing or repair*); repair shop (*automobiles*); **taller de reparaciones** repair shop
tamal *m.* tamale (*dish made of corn meal, chicken or meat and chili wrapped in banana leaves or corn husk*)
tamarindo tamarind (*tropical friut used to make juice*)
también also, too
tampoco neither, not either
tan as, so; **tan ... como** as ... as; **tan pronto como** as soon as
tanque *m.* (gas) tank
tanto *adv.* so much; **estar** (*irreg.*) **al tanto** to be informed, up to date; **mientras tanto** meanwhile; **no es para tanto** it's not that serious; **tanto como** as much as
tanto/a/os/as *adj.* as much/many; so much/many; **tanto/a/os/as ... como** as much ... as
tapas hors d'oeuvres (*Sp.*)
tapatío: jarabe (*m.*) **tapatío** *popular Mexican dance known as Mexican hat dance in U.S.*
taquería taco stand
tardanza delay, tardiness
tardar to be long; to be or take a long time; **tardar (en)** + *inf.* to be or take a long time (to) (*do something*); **a más tardar** at the latest
tarde *n. f.* afternoon, evening; **buenas**

tardes good afternoon; **de (la) tarde** P.M., in the afternoon; **por la tarde** in the afternoon
tarde *adv.* late; **hacerse** (*irreg.*) **tarde** to be getting late; **llegar (gu) tarde** to arrive late; **más tarde** later; **se me hace tarde** it's getting late
tarea task; (*school*) assignment
tarifa rate, price
tarjeta de crédito credit card
tarjeta postal postcard
tasa rate; **tasa de desempleo** unemployment rate
taxi *m.* taxicab; **parada de taxis** taxi stand
taxista *m., f.* taxicab driver
taza cup
te *d.o.* you (*fam. s.*); *i.o.* to, for you (*fam. s.*); *refl. pron.* yourself (*fam. s.*)
té *m.* tea
teatral theatrical
teatro theater; **ir** (*irreg.*) **a una función de teatro** to go to a show at the theater; **obra de teatro** play, dramatic work; **sala de teatro** theater; **teatro campesino** farm workers' theater
telefonear to telephone
telefónico/a *adj.* telephone; **llamada telefónica** telephone call
teléfono telephone; **por teléfono** by telephone
telegrama *m.* telegram
telenovela soap opera
(tele)visión *f.* television (*broadcasting medium*); **hacer** (*irreg.*) **televisión** to work in television; **mirar (la) televisión** to watch television
televisor *m.* television set
telón *m.* (*theater*) curtain
tema *m.* theme, topic
temática collection of themes
temer to fear, be afraid of
temor *m.* fear
temperatura temperature; **¿a cuánto estaba la temperatura?** how high was the temperature?; **la temperatura está a ... grados** the temperature is . . . degrees; **tomarle (a alguien) la temperatura** to take (someone's) temperature
tempestuoso/a tempestuous
templado/a temperate, moderate
templo temple
temporada period (*of time*)
temprano early
tender (ie) to tend, have a tendency
tenedor *m.* fork
tener (*irreg.*) to have; **(no) tener sentido** (not) to make sense; **que tenga (un) buen viaje** have a nice trip; **tener ... años** to be . . . years old; **tener un aire ...** to be like, resemble . . .; **tener**

(buena) suerte to be lucky, in luck; **tener celos (de)** to be jealous (of); **tener como fin** to have as a goal; **tener cuidado** to be careful; **tener la culpa (de)** to be to blame (for); to be guilty (of); **tener en cuenta** to keep in mind; **tenerle envidia (a alguien)** to envy (someone); **tener éxito** to be successful; **tener una fiebre** to have a fever; **tener ganas de** + *inf.* to feel like (*doing something*); **tener hambre** to be hungry; **tener lugar** to take place; **tener mala suerte** to be unlucky; **tener miedo** to be afraid; **tener (mucha) sed** to be (very) thirsty; **tener (mucho) calor/frío** to be (very) hot/cold; **tener (mucho) sueño** to be (very) sleepy; **tener prisa (por** + *inf.***)** to be in a hurry (*to do something*); **tener que** + *inf.* to have to (*do something*); **tener que ver con** to have to do with, be related to (*a topic*); **tener (toda la) razón** to be (absolutely) right

tenis *m.* tennis; **cancha de tenis** tennis court; **zapatos de tenis** tennis shoes

tensión *f.* tension

tenso/a tense

tentar (ie) to tempt

teñir (i, i) to dye, tint

teoría theory; **en teoría** in theory

terapia therapy

tercer, tercero/a *n., adj.* third

terco/a stubborn

termal *adj.* thermal

terminación *f.* end; ending

terminar to end, be over; **al terminar ...** when . . . is/was over; **terminar con** to finish (*something*); **terminar por** + *inf.* to finish or end up by (*doing something*)

termómetro thermometer

ternera veal

ternura tenderness

terraza terrace

terremoto earthquake

terreno terrain

terrible: ¡qué terrible! how terrible!

territorio territory

testamento will, testament

testigo *m., f.* witness

texano/a Texan

texto text; **libro de texto** textbook

ti *obj. of prep.* you (*fam. s.*); **contigo** with you

tiempo time; weather; (*gram.*) tense; **al mismo tiempo** at the same time; **al poco tiempo** shortly after; **¿cuánto tiempo hace que ... ?** how long has it been that . . . ?; **hace buen/mal tiempo** it's good (bad) weather; **¿qué tiempo hace?** what's the weather like?; **tiempo libre** free time, spare time;

todo el tiempo all the time, the whole time, all along

tienda store, shop; **tienda de antigüedades** antique store; **tienda de comestibles** food store; **tienda de ropa para hombres/mujeres** men's/women's clothing store

tierra land, earth

tigre *m.* tiger

timbre *m.* stamp (*Mex.*)

tímido/a timid

tinto: vino tinto red wine

tío/a uncle, aunt; *m. pl.* uncles and aunts

típico/a typical

tipo type, kind; guy

tiranía tyranny

tirano tyrant

tirar to throw out; **tirarse** to throw, cast oneself

tiro: al tiro immediately

titi *fam. form of* **tía**

título title; diploma, degree; **título universitario** university degree

tocar (qu) to touch; to play (*musical instrument*); **tocar la puerta** to knock on the door; **tocarle (a alguien)** to be someone's turn; to be coming (to someone)

tocino bacon

todavía still, yet

todo *n.* whole; all, everything; **ante todo** above all; **sobre todo** above all

todo/a *adj.* all, every; **de todas formas** in any case; **por todas partes** all over, everywhere; **todo el tiempo** all the time, the whole time, all along; **todo el mundo** the whole world; everybody; **todos los días** every day

tolerancia tolerance

tolerante tolerant

tolerar to tolerate

tomar to take; to have something to eat or drink; **tomar el aire** to get some fresh air, go for a walk; **tomar un autobús (barco, avión, taxi, tren)** to take a bus (ship, plane, taxi, train); **tomar decisiones** to make decisions; **tomar en serio** to take seriously; **tomar una foto(grafía)** to take a picture, photograph; **tomar el pulso** to feel the pulse; **tomar una siesta** to take a siesta, nap; **tomar el sol** to sunbathe; **tomarle (a alguien) la temperatura** to take (someone's) temperature; **tomarle cariño (a alguien)** to start to have affection for (someone); **tomarle el pelo (a alguien)** to tease someone

tomate *m.* tomato; **salsa de tomate** ketchup

tono tone

tontería foolishness; *pl.* nonsense

tonto/a *n.* fool; *adj.* stupid, dumb;

hacerse (*irreg.*) **el tonto** to play dumb

toque *m.* touch

tormenta tempest, storm

toro bull

toronja grapefruit

torre *f.* tower

tortilla *thin unleavened cornmeal or flour pancake* (*Mex.*); *egg and potato omelette* (*Sp.*); **tortilla arrollada** rolled tortilla

tortillería tortilla shop

tortuga turtle; tortoise

torturar to torture

tos *f.* cough

tostada slice of toast

tostado/a toasted; **pan** (*m.*) **tostado** toast

totalitario/a totalitarian

trabajador(a) *n.* worker; *adj.* hard-working; **clase** (*f.*) **trabajadora** working class

trabajar to work; **trabajar de** to work as; **trabajar de noche** to work at night

trabajo work; school paper, report; job; **costarle (ue) trabajo** to be hard, take a lot of effort; **Día** (*m.*) **del Trabajo** Labor Day; **oferta de trabajo** job offer

trabalenguas *m. s.* tongue twister

tradición *f.* tradition

tradicional traditional

traer (*irreg.*) to bring

tráfico traffic

tragamonedas: máquina tragamonedas slot machine

tragedia tragedy

trágico/a tragic

trago drink

traje *m.* suit; dress, costume; **traje de baño** bathing suit

tranquilidad *f.* tranquility

tranquilo/a calm, peaceful; quiet

transbordador (*m.*) **espacial** space ship; space shuttle

transcripción *f.* transcription

transformarse to be or become transformed

transición *f.* transition

transportación: medios (*pl.*) **de transportación** means of transportation

transporte: medio de transporte means of transportation

tras *prep.* after

trasatlántico/a transatlantic

trasladar(se) to move

trastorno upheaval; disturbance; disruption

tratamiento treatment

tratar to treat; to deal with; **tratar de** + *inf.* to try to (*do something*); **tratar de tú** to use informal address (**tú**) in conversation; **tratarse de** to be a question of

traumático/a tramatic

través: a través de through, across
travieso/a mischievous, naughty
trazar (c) to trace; to plan, design; to create, form
trece thirteen
treinta thirty
tremendo/a tremendous
tren *m.* train; **estación** (*f.*) **del tren** train station
tres three
trescientos/as three hundred
triángulo triangle
tribu *f.* tribe
trimestre *m.* (*school*) quarter
triste sad; **¡qué triste!** how sad!
tristeza sadness
triunfar to triumph
triunfo triumph
trono throne
tropas troops
tropical: bosque (*m.*) **tropical** tropical forest
Trópico de Capricornio Tropic of Capricorn
tu(s) *poss.* your (*fam. s.*)
tú *sub. pron.* you (*fam. s.*); **tratar de tú** to use informal address (**tú**) in conversation
tubo tube, pipe
tumba tomb
tumultuoso/a tumultuous
tuna *group of student serenaders*
túnel *m.* tunnel
tungsteno tungsten
turismo tourism
turista *n. m., f.* tourist
turístico/a *adj.* tourist; **atraccion** (*f.*) **turística** tourist attraction; **clase** (*f.*) **turística** tourist class; **guía** (*m., f.*) **turístico/a** tourist guide; **plano turístico** map (*of a city*)
tutear to use the informal address (**tú**) in conversation
tuteo use of the familiar form (*tú*) of address
tuyo/a(s) *poss.* your, of yours

U

u or (*used instead of* **o** *before words beginning with* **o** *or* **ho**)
últimamente lately
último/a last, final, ultimate; latest; **por primera vez** for the first time; **por última vez** for the last time; **última vez** last time; **últimas noticias** latest news
ultrafeminista ultrafeminist
un, uno/a one; a, an (*indefinite article*); *pl.* some, a few, several
UNAM Universidad Nacional Autónoma de México
unicelular *adj.* unicellular

único/a unique; only; **hijo/a único/a** only child
unidad *f.* unity; unit
unido/a united; close-knit, close; **ser unido/a** to be united, close-knit, close; **Estados Unidos** United States
Unión (*f.*) **Soviética** Soviet Union
unir(se) to unite; to join
universidad *f.* university
universitario/a *adj.* university; **título universitario** university degree; **zona universitaria** university campus, grounds
urbano/a urban; urbane
urgencia: de urgencia emergency; **hospital** (*m.*) **de urgencia** emergency hospital
urgente urgent
urna ballot box
usar *v.* to use
uso *n.* use
usted (Ud., Vd.) *sub. pron.* you (*form. s.*); *obj. of prep.* you (*form. s.*)
ustedes (Uds., Vds.) *sub. pron.* you (*form. pl.*); *obj. of prep.* you (*form. pl.*)
útil *adj.* useful
utilizar (c) to utilize, use, make use of
uva grape

V

va: ¡qué va! *interj.* don't put me on!
vaca cow; **carne** (*f.*) **de vaca** beef
vacaciones *f. pl.* vacation
vacilar to vacillate
vacío emptiness
vacuna vaccine
vago/a vague
vagón *m.* wagon
valenciano/a *n., adj.* Valencian
valentía bravery
Valentín: Día (*m.*) **de San Valentín** St. Valentine's Day
valer (*irreg.*) to be worth; **(no) vale la pena** it's (not) worth the trouble; **vale** great, OK
válido/a valid
valiente brave
valioso/a valuable, highly esteemed
valor *m.* worth, value; *pl.* values
valorar to value
valle *m.* valley
¿vamos? shall we go; **¡vamos!** *interj.* let's go!
vanguardia: de vanguardia avant-garde
vanidoso/a vain, conceited
variación *f.* variation, change
variado/a varied, diverse
variar to vary, change
variedad *f.* variety
varios/as various; several
vasco: País (*m.*) **Vasco** Basque region (*of Spain*)

vascuense *m.* Basque language
vaso (*drinking*) glass
vasto/a vast
vecino/a *n.* neighbor; *adj.* neighboring
vegetación *f.* vegetation
vegetariano/a *n.* vegetarian
veinte twenty
veintún, veintiuno twenty-one
vela sail
velada evening
velorio wake, vigil
vellón *m.* five-cent piece (*P.R.*); nickel (*U.S.*)
vendedor(a) salesclerk
vender to sell; **se vende(n)** for sale
venerar to venerate
venida arrival; return
venidero/a *adj.* coming, future
venir (*irreg.*) to come; **que viene** coming, next
venta sale; **en venta** for sale
ventaja advantage
ventana window
ver (*irreg.*) to see; **a ver** let's see, let's have a look; **tener** (*irreg.*) **que ver con** to have to do with; be related to (*a topic*)
verano summer
verbo verb
verdad *f.* truth; **¿de verdad?** really?; **decir** (*irreg.*) **la verdad** to tell the truth; **¿verdad?** right?
verdadero/a true, real
verde green; **judía verde** string bean (*Sp.*); **zona verde** open space; public park
verduras greens, vegetables
vergüenza shame; **¡qué vergüenza!** *interj.* how embarrassing! **tener** (*irreg.*) **vergüenza** to be embarrassed
verificar (qu) to verify; to check
versión *f.* version
verso verse
vértigo vertigo
vestido dress; suit
vestir(se) (i, i) to get dressed, to dress
veterinario/a veterinarian
vez *f.* (*pl.* **veces**) time, occasion; **a la vez** at the same time; **a veces** at times, sometimes; **alguna vez** ever; **cada vez más** more and more; **de una vez** now, right away; **de vez en cuando** sometimes; **en vez de** instead of; **érase una vez** once upon a time; **muchas veces** often; **otra vez** again; **pocas veces** seldom; **(por) primera vez** (for the) first time; **por última vez** for the last time; **tal vez** perhaps, maybe; **última vez** last time; **una vez** once; **una vez al año** once a year; **una vez más** one more time
viajar to travel

viaje *m.* trip; **hacer** (*irreg.*) **un viaje** to take a trip; **que tenga (un) buen viaje** have a nice trip

viajero/a traveler; **cheque** (*m.*) **de viajero** traveler's check

viajes: agencia de viajes travel agency; **agente** (*m., f.*) **de viajes** travel agent

vicepresidente/a vice-president

vicio bad habit, vice

vicioso/a vicious

víctima victim

victoria victory

vida life; **llevar una vida ...** to lead a . . . life; **vida diaria** daily life; **vida privada** personal life

vídeo: sacar (qu) vídeos to take videos

videocasetera VCR

videograbadora VCR

viejo/a *n.* old woman, old man; *adj.* old; **llegar (gu) a viejo/a** to get to be old

viene: que viene coming, next

viento wind; **hace (mucho) viento** it's (very) windy; **molino de viento** windmill

viernes *m. s.* Friday

vietnamés, vietnamesa *n., adj.* Vietnamese

vigencia force, effect

vigente in force; in vogue; **seguir (i, i) (g) vigente** to continue to be viable

vigilar to watch; to keep an eye on

vino wine; **vino blanco** white wine; **vino tinto** red wine

viña vineyard

viñador(a) grape grower

violación *f.* violation; rape

violado/a violated

violar to violate; to rape

violencia violence

violento/a violent

violincelista *m., f.* cellist

violinista *m., f.* violinist

virar to turn (*P.R.*)

virgen *f.* virgin; **Virgen María** Virgin Mary

visión *f.* vision

visita *f.* visit; visitor

visitante *m., f.* visitor

visitar to visit

víspera the night before

vista view (of); sight; **amor** (*m.*) **a primera vista** love at first sight; **punto de vista** point of view

vistazo glance

visto: por lo visto evidently

vitalidad *f.* vitality

vitamina vitamin

viudo/a widower/widow

vivido/a lived; experienced

vivienda dwelling, house; housing

vivir to live; **vivir de** to live off of, support oneself by

vivo/a alive, live, living

vocabulario vocabulary

vocación *f.* vocation

volar (ue) to fly

volcán *m.* volcano

vólibol *m.* volleyball

volumen *m.* volume

voluntad *f.* will, willingness

volver (ue) (*p.p.* **vuelto/a**) to return; **volver a** + *inf.* to do (*something*) again; **volverse** to become, turn into; **volverse loco/a** to go crazy

vos *sub. pron. s. and pl.* you (*substitute for* **tú**) (*Arg.*)

vosotros/as *sub. pron.* you (*fam. pl. Sp.*); *obj. of prep.* you (*fam. pl. Sp.*)

votar to vote

voto vote

voz (*pl.* **voces**) *f.* voice; **en voz alta** out loud

vuelo flight

vuelta return; **a la vuelta** around the corner; **billete** (*m.*) **/pasaje** (*m.*) **de ida y vuelta** round trip ticket (fare); **estar**

(*irreg.*) **de vuelta** to be back; to have returned; **pasaje** (*m.*) **de ida y vuelta** round trip fare

vuestro/a(s) *poss.* your (*fam. pl. Sp.*); of yours (*fam. pl. Sp.*)

X

X: rayos X X rays; **sacar (qu) rayos X** to take X rays

xenofobia xenophobia

xerografía xerography (*system for copying printed material*)

xilófono xylophone

Y

y and; **¿y qué?** so what?; what do you want me to do?

ya already; now; later, later on; right away, at once; at last; **ya lo creo** of course; **ya no** no longer; **ya que** since

yema yolk

yerba grass

yerno son-in-law

yo *sub. pron.* I

yucateco/a from the Yucatan peninsula

Z

zanahoria carrot

zapatería shoe store

zapatero/a shoemaker

zapato shoe; **zapatos de tenis** tennis shoes

zar *m.* czar

zarina czarina

zarzuela *Spanish musical comedy or operetta*

zona zone; neighborhood; **zona universitaria** university campus, grounds; **zona verde** open space; public park

zoológico: jardín (*m.*) **zoológico** zoo; **parque** (*m.*) **zoológico** zoo

zumo juice (*Sp.*)

zurdo/a left-handed

INDEX OF CHARACTERS

This index includes the names of most of the characters who appear in *Destinos*, alphabetized by their first name in most cases. Photographs are included for many characters as well, along with a brief description of them and a city in which they live.

Alfredo Sánchez, Madrid, España. A reporter who meets Raquel.

Ángel Castillo del Valle, Buenos Aires, Argentina. Son of Fernando Castillo Saavedra and Rosario del Valle.

Ángela Castillo Soto, San Juan, Puerto Rico. Daughter of Ángel Castillo and María Luisa Soto.

el Dr. Arturo Iglesias, Buenos Aires, Argentina. A psychiatrist and the son of Rosario and Martín Iglesias.

Blanca Núñez, San Juan, Puerto Rico. A real estate agent.

Carlitos Castillo, Miami, Florida. Son of Carlos and Gloria and grandson of don Fernando.

Carlos Castillo Márquez, Miami, Florida. One of don Fernando's sons and director of the Miami office of the family company.

Carlos Soto Contreras, San Juan, Puerto Rico. One of Ángela's uncles.

Carmen Contreras de Soto, San Germán, Puerto Rico. Ángela and Roberto's grandmother.

Carmen Márquez de Castillo, La Gavia, México. Second wife of don Fernando and mother of their four children, Ramón, Carlos, Mercedes, and Juan.

Carmen Soto, San Juan, Puerto Rico. One of Ángela's aunts.

el ciego, Sevilla, España. He sells lottery tickets.

Cirilo, Estancia Santa Susana, Argentina. A gaucho and ex-employee of Rosario.

Consuelo Castillo, La Gavia, México. Don Fernando's daughter-in-law, she lives at La Gavia with her husband Ramón and daughter Maricarmen.

Dolores Acevedo, San Germán, Puerto Rico. A longtime household employee of doña Carmen and her family.

Elena Ramírez de Ruiz, Sevilla, España. Daughter-in-law of Teresa Suárez and mother of Miguel and Jaime. Her husband is Miguel Ruiz.

Federico Ruiz Suárez, Madrid, España. Son of Teresa Suárez, Federico is a guitar maker.

Fernando Castillo Saavedra, La Gavia, México. Patriarch of the Castillo family, don Fernando initiates the investigation that is carried out by Raquel Rodríguez.

Flora, Buenos Aires, Argentina. Wife of José, a sailor.

Francisco (Pancho) Rodríguez Trujillo. *See* Pancho Rodríguez Trujillo.

Gloria Castillo, Miami, Florida. Carlos's wife and mother of Juanita and Carlitos.

Guillermo, New York, New York. Pati's assistant director at the university theater.

Héctor Condotti, Buenos Aires, Argentina. An experienced sailor and friend of Ángel.

Isabel Santiago, San Juan, Puerto Rico. A bank executive.

Jaime Ruiz Ramírez, Sevilla, España. Grandson of Teresa Suárez and son of Miguel Ruiz.

Jaime Soto Contreras, San Juan, Puerto Rico. One of Ángela's uncles.

Jorge Alonso, San Juan, Puerto Rico. Ángela's boyfriend and a professor of theater at the University of Puerto Rico.

José, Buenos Aires, Argentina. A sailor and friend of Héctor.

Juan Castillo Márquez, New York, New York. The youngest child of don Fernando and a professor of literature at New York University; married to Pati.

Juanita Castillo, Miami, Florida. Daughter of Carlos and Gloria.

el Dr. Julio Morelos, Toluca, México. The Castillo family physician.

Laura Soto, San Juan, Puerto Rico. One of Ángela's cousins and the daughter of tío Jaime.

Luis Villarreal, Los Angeles, California. The former boyfriend of Raquel.

Lupe, La Gavia, México. A household employee of the Castillo family at La Gavia.

Manuel Díaz, Sevilla/Madrid, España. A schoolteacher who meets Raquel.

Manuel Domínguez, New York, New York. The producer of Pati's current play.

María, Madrid, España. Federico's girlfriend, who teaches flamenco dancing.

María Luisa Soto de Castillo, San Juan, Puerto Rico. Daughter of doña Carmen and wife of Ángel Castillo.

María Orozco de Rodríguez, Los Angeles, California. Raquel's mother.

la Hermana María Teresa, un pueblo, México. A nun who gives Ángela and Raquel a place to rest and bathe.

Maricarmen Castillo, La Gavia, México. Daughter of Ramón and Consuelo.

Mario, Buenos Aires, Argentina. A storekeeper in the La Boca district.

Martín Iglesias, Buenos Aires, Argentina. Second husband of Rosario, stepfather of Ángel Castillo, and father of Arturo Iglesias.

Mercedes Castillo Márquez, La Gavia, México. Don Fernando's only daughter, who lives at La Gavia with her father.

Miguel Ruiz Ramírez, Sevilla, España. Grandson of Teresa Suárez and son of Miguel Ruiz.

Miguel Ruiz Suárez, Sevilla, España. Son of Teresa Suárez and father of Miguel and Jaime.

Ofelia, Miami, Florida. Carlos's Cuban-born secretary.

Olga Soto Contreras, San Juan, Puerto Rico. One of Ángela's aunts.

Osito, Sevilla, España. A dog purchased by Miguel and Elena Ruiz for their sons, Miguel and Jaime.

Pancho Rodríguez Trujillo, Los Ángeles, California. Raquel's father.

Pati Castillo, New York, New York. The wife of Juan and professor of theater at New York University, as well as a writer/director.

Pedro Castillo Saavedra, México, D.F., México. Law professor at the National University of México and brother of don Fernando.

Pepe, Sevilla, España. A barber in Sevilla.

Ramón Castillo Márquez, La Gavia, México. The oldest son of don Fernando. He runs Castillo Saavedra, S.A.

Raquel Rodríguez Orozco, Los Ángeles, California. A lawyer contracted by Pedro Castillo to conduct the investigation.

Roberto Castillo Soto, San Juan, Puerto Rico. Son of Ángel Castillo and María Luisa Soto.

Roberto García, Sevilla, España. A taxi driver from the Triana district.

el Padre Rodrigo, un pueblo, México. A priest who offers comfort to Raquel and Ángela.

Rosario del Valle de Iglesias, Buenos Aires, Argentina. First wife of don Fernando Castillo.

el Dr. Salazar, Guadalajara, México. A specialist who examines don Fernando.

Teresa Suárez, Madrid, España. Friend of Rosario who writes the letter to don Fernando that initiates the investigation.

Virginia López Estrada, México, D.F., México. A real estate agent.

INDEX

In this index, **Conversaciones** (functional expressions), **Notas culturales** (both specific and general), and vocabulary topics appear as groups; items in those lists are not cross-referenced. Abbreviations in the index are identical to those used in the end vocabulary. For irregular verbs not listed in this index, consult Appendix 2: Verbs.

a + el, 37, 56
accent marks, with interrogatives, 87–88
adjectives
  agreement of, 46, 98, 108n, 245n
  descriptive, 46, 107, 113, 244–245, 250
  gender of, 46, 98, 108n, 245n
  number of, 46, 98, 108n
  possessive (unstressed), 22
  with **ser** to describe personality, 245
age, expressing, 153
agreement
  of adjectives, 46, 98, 108n, 245n
  of articles, 46
  of possessive adjectives, 22
al, 37, 56
andar (*irreg.*), preterite, 157–158. *See also* Appendix 2.
apocopation of **gran**, 107
-ar verbs, 34, 60, 111. *See also* Appendix 2; subjunctive; *names of tenses and parts of verbs.*
articles
  definite, 46, 55
  indefinite, 74

bueno, as adverb, 100

cardinal numbers, 32, 37, 76, 81, 123, 128
cognates
  adjective, 244–245, 250
  defined, 8
commands. *See also* Appendix 2.
  defined, 194, 326, 337
  formal (**Ud., Uds.**), 194, 326
  informal (**tú**), 152, 337
conditional. *See also* Appendix 2.
  regular, 402
  used in softened requests and statements, 78
  uses of, 78, 402, 412, 422, 441
conditional sentences, 402, 422, 462
conjunctions
  of time, 393
  use of subjunctive after, 315–316, 393, 468–469

conocer (zc). *See also* Appendix 2.
  present, 79
  preterite, 247
  versus **saber**, 79
contractions
  al, 37, 56
  del, 37
contrary-to-fact conditions, 422, 462
Conversaciones: functional expressions
  agreement, expressing, 99–100, 103, 293–294, 297
  answering the telephone, 146, 208, 211
  courtesy, expressions of, 78, 81
  disagreement, expressing, 99–100
  doing business, 305–306, 309, 383, 387
  emotion, expressions of, 246–247, 250
  encouraging someone, 156–157, 160
  excusing oneself, 167–168, 172
  getting someone's attention, 167–168
  gratitude, expressions of, 88–89, 93
  greetings, 21, 25, 33, 37, 179–180, 183
  information, asking for, 282–283, 286
  introductions, 33, 37, 45
  leavetaking, 59–60, 63, 109–110, 113, 167–168, 179–180, 183
  managing a conversation, 146, 149
  pardon, asking for, 167–168, 172
  polite requests, 78, 81, 135–136, 139
  persuading someone, 156–157, 160
  ¡**qué** + noun/adjective/adverb!, 247, 250
  reacting to others, 246–247, 250
  requests, 78, 81, 135–136, 139
  saying that someone is right, 99–100, 103, 293–294, 297
  shopping, 135–136, 139, 305–306, 309

telephone calls, 146, 208, 211
using the familiar (**tú**) forms, 89, 109–110, 124–125
using **vos** forms, 125–126
counting, 32, 37, 76, 81, 123, 128
cuando, use of subjunctive after, 315–316

days of the week
  definite article used with, 55
  listed, 55, 63
de + name, to show possession, 22
deber
  conditional of, 450–451
  uses, 450–451
decir (*irreg.*). *See also* Appendix 2.
  command, 152, 337
  participle, 432
  preterite, 157–158
definite article
  agreement of, 46
  use with days of the week, 55
del, 37
describing, 46, 107, 113, 244–245, 250
descriptive adjectives, 46, 107, 113, 244–245, 250
doler (ue), used like **gustar**, 292
don, 7
¿**dónde?**, ¿**adónde?**, ¿**de dónde?**, 87

endings, personal. *See also* Appendix 2.
  for regular **-ar** verbs, 34, 60, 111
  for regular **-er** verbs, 34, 60
  for regular **-ir** verbs, 34, 60
-er verbs, 34, 60, 111. *See also* Appendix 2; subjunctive; *names of tenses and parts of verbs.*
estar (*irreg.*). *See also* Appendix 2.
  + **-ndo**, 191n, 237
  preterite, 157–158
formal commands, 194, 326. *See also* Appendix 2.
functional expressions. *See* **Conversaciones**.
future meaning, subjunctive used to express, 315–316

future tense. *See also* Appendix 2.
  irregular, 271, 283
  regular, 271
  uses of, 153n, 271, 412

gender, 46, 98, 108n, 245n
gran(de), 107
gustar
  doler used like, 292
  using, 49–50, 78, 134–135, 156

haber (*irreg.*). *See also* Appendix 2.
  as auxiliary, 348, 358, 431–432,
    441, 450–451, 462
  with **deber**, 450–451
hacer (*irreg.*). *See also* Appendix 2.
  command, 337
  future, 271
  imperfect, 216
  past participle, 432
  preterite, 168–169
  with weather expressions, 216
hope, expressing, 358

idioms with **tener**, 153, 292
if clauses, 422, 462
imperatives. *See* commands.
imperfect indicative. *See also* Appendix 2.
  English equivalents of, 196,
    208–209, 218, 227
  irregular, 227
  in past narration, 441
  regular, 196, 208–209, 218, 227
  uses of, 196, 208–209, 216, 218,
    227, 441
  versus preterite, 196, 208–209
imperfect subjunctive. *See* past
  subjunctive.
impersonal **se**, 145n
indefinite and nonexistent antecedents followed by subjunctive,
  393
infinitives. *See* Appendix 2.
informal (**tú**) commands, 152, 337.
  See also Appendix 2.
information questions, 87–88
interrogative words, 87–88, 93
intonation in questions, 88
irregular verbs. *See* Appendix 2; *individual verbs; names of tenses
  and parts of verbs.*
-ir verbs, 34, 60, 111. *See also* Appendix 2; subjunctive; *names of tenses and parts of verbs.*

jugar + **al** + sport, 438

maps
  Argentina (la); from Argentina to
    Puerto Rico, 189; cities in, 137
    (**Buenos Aires, Mendoza, Mi-
    siones, San Carlos de Barilo-
    che, Santa Cruz, Ushuaia**), 169
    (**Córdoba, Mendoza, Rosario,**

Tucumán); geography, 137, 159;
    la pampa, 127; and surrounding
    countries, 137
  España (Spain); **Andalucía** (An-
    dalusia), 61; artists' cities, 112
    (**Madrid, Málaga, Sevilla,
    Toledo, Zaragoza**); **Asturias,**
    62; **la Guerra Civil española**
    (Spanish Civil War), 23; geogra-
    phy, 35; **País Vasco (el)** (Basque
    country), 62; **Sevilla** (Seville),
    48; from Seville to Madrid, 69;
    from Spain to Argentina, 119
  México; Aztec civilization in, 327;
    la bahía de Campeche, 386;
    cities in, 284 (**Acapulco, Can-
    cún, Chichen Itzá, Ciudad
    Juárez, Guadalajara, Guana-
    juato, Teotihuacán, Uxmal**);
    geography of, 284; **Guadalajara,**
    413; **Jalisco**, 359; Mayan civiliza-
    tion in, 338; **Toluca**, 413
  Puerto Rico; cities in, 197
    (**Caguas, Mayagüez, Ponce,
    San Juan**), 210 (**Ponce, San
    Juan**), 219; geography and cli-
    mate, 210; **Ponce**, 219; **San
    Juan**, 197; from San Juan to Mex-
    ico City, 263

narration in the past, 441
nonexistent and indefinite antecedents followed by subjunctive,
  393
Notas culturales: country-specific
  cultural notes
  Argentina (la); **Buenos Aires,**
    154–155, 158–159; cities in,
    169–171 (**Córdoba, Mar del
    Plata, Mendoza, Rosario,
    Tucumán**); **los gauchos,**
    127–128; geography and climate
    of, 137–138; history of, 147–
    148, 181–182; **las madres de
    la Plaza de Mayo**, 181–182;
    Nobel prize winners of, 177; **la
    pampa**, 127–128; San Martín,
    José de, 147–148; using **vos**
    forms in, 125–126
  España (Spain); **Andalucía** (An-
    dalusia), 92; Arab presence in,
    61–62; art of, 111–112; **Castilla**
    (Castile), 92; **Cataluña** (Cata-
    lonia), 91; dictatorship of
    Francisco Franco, 79–80; fine
    arts of, 111–112; geography of,
    36; music of, 101–102; painters
    of, 111–112; political structure
    of, 36, 79–80; present-day con-
    stitutional monarchy in, 79–80;
    regional differences in, 91–92;
    Sevilla (Seville), 47–48; Spanish
    Civil War, 23–24; theater in, 403

  Estados Unidos (los) (United
    States [The]); Cuban Americans
    in, 307–308; Hispanic theater in,
    404; Mexican Americans, 317–
    318; Mexican cooking in, 424;
    mural art and muralists in, 442–
    443; Puerto Ricans in, 238–239
  México; Aztec civilization in, 327–
    328; **Ballet Folclórico**, 290,
    394–395; cooking in, 423; cul-
    tures of, 284–285; economy of,
    386; geography of, 284–285;
    Guadalajara, 413–414; history
    of, 376–377, 463; **los maria-
    chis**, 395; Mayan civilization
    in, 338–339; Mexico City (**el
    Parque de Chapultepec**),
    462–463; mural art and mu-
    ralists of, 442–443; music and
    dance of, 394–395; **los Niños
    Héroes**, 463; religion in, 290,
    295–296; **el tequila**, 359; Texas,
    Republic of, 463; theater in,
    403–404; **Toluca**, 413–414; **la
    Virgen de Guadalupe**, 295–
    296; war between U.S. and
    Mexico (1845), 463
  Puerto Rico; art and music
    of, 248–249; cities in (**Are-
    cibo, Mayagüez, La Parguera,
    Ponce**), 219–220; economy of,
    228–229; fine arts of, 248–249;
    foods of, 224, 244; geography
    and climate, 210; history and
    government of, 209–210, 238–
    239; literature of, 249; music and
    art of, 248–249; **Ponce**, 219;
    Puerto Ricans in the U.S., 238–
    239; **San Juan**, 197–198; as U.S.
    citizens, 215–216, 238–239;
    warmth of relationships in, 193
Notas culturales: general cultural
  notes
  afternoon snacks (**las tapas**), 86
  bargaining (**el regateo**), 409–410
  biculturalism, 282
  bilingualism, 314
  Celsius and Fahrenheit tempera-
    tures, 218
  coffee drinking, 96
  dining out, 421–422
  economy of Latin America, 386
  embracing, 110
  family life and relationships, 18,
    204, 282, 382–383, 451–452
  food and mealtimes, 57, 86,
    419–420, 425
  greeting and leavetaking, 110
  higher education, 43
  Hispanic surnames, 32
  hobbies and pastimes, 461
  housing, 236–237, 282

kissing hello and goodbye, 110
language differences, regional, 133, 154n, 322–323, 344–345, 372
language learning, 314
names, family, 32
names of professions, 334–335
Nobel prize winners in literature, 177
pastimes and hobbies, 461
regional language differences, 133, 154n, 322–323, 344–345, 372
religious life, 301
restaurant dining, 421–422
snacks (**las tapas**), 86, 244
social life, 349–350
sports, role of, 440
talking about time, 57, 63
temperature equivalents, Celsius and Fahrenheit, 218
theatrical traditions, 403–404
time of day, 57, 63
toasts (**los brindis**), 143
tú versus **usted**, 89
university life, 43
usted versus **tú**, 89, 109–110, 124–125
vos forms, using, 125–126
women and their roles, 433–434
youth, 349–350

nouns
de + noun, possession, 22
gender of, 46, 108n, 245n
plural of, 46, 108n, 206
number. *See* agreement.
numbers
cardinal, 32, 37, 76, 81, 123, 128
years, how to express, 77, 123

object pronouns, reflexive, 100, 111, 225
ojalá, 358
order. *See* word order.
orthographic changes. *See* spelling changes.

para que + subjunctive, 468–469
participle
past, 348, 358, 431–432, 441, 450–451, 462
present, 191n, 237
past narration, 441
past participle. *See also* Appendix 2.
formation of, 348
with **haber**, 348, 358, 431–432, 441, 450–451, 462
irregular, 432
past perfect indicative, 431–432, 441. *See also* Appendix 2.
past perfect subjunctive, 462. *See also* Appendix 2.
past progressive, 237. *See also* Appendix 2.

past subjunctive. *See also* Appendix 2.
formation of, 374–375
uses of, 78, 374–375, 385, 393
pedir (i, i), preterite, 180–181. *See also* Appendix 2.
pensar (ie), present, 100, 111. *See also* Appendix 2.
perder (ie), preterite, 126
perfect tenses. *See also* Appendix 2.
past perfect indicative, 431–432, 441
past perfect subjunctive, 462
present perfect indicative, 348
personal endings. *See also* Appendix 2.
of regular **-ar** verbs, 34, 60
of regular **-er** and **-ir** verbs, 34, 60
pluperfect subjunctive, 462. *See also* Appendix 2.
plural
adjectives, 22, 46
nouns, 46, 206
poder (*irreg.*). *See also* Appendix 2.
future, 283
preterite, 168–169
polite requests and statements with conditional and past subjunctive, 78, 81
poner (*irreg.*) *See also* Appendix 2.
command, 337
present subjunctive, 294
preterite, 168–169
reflexive, 225
¿por qué?, 87
possession with **de**, 22
possessive adjectives
agreement of, 22
unstressed, 22
present indicative. *See also* Appendix 2.
of **-ar** verbs, 34, 60, 111
English equivalents of, 237
of **-er** and **-ir** verbs, 34, 60, 111
of stem-changing verbs, 90, 100, 111
present participle. *See also* Appendix 2.
in past progressive, 237
in present progressive, 191n
present perfect indicative, 348. *See also* Appendix 2.
present progressive, 191n. *See also* Appendix 2.
present subjunctive. *See also* Appendix 2.
to express future, 315–316
formation of, 294
of irregular verbs, 294
meaning of, 294, 306, 315–316
preterite. *See also* Appendix 2.
English equivalents of, 247

of irregular verbs, 136, 157–158, 168–169, 247
meaning of, 247
in past narration, 441
of regular verbs, 126, 136, 147
of stem-changing verbs, 126, 136, 180–181
uses of, 126, 136, 147, 247, 441
versus imperfect, 196, 208–209
progressive forms
past, 237
present, 191n
pronouns
reflexive, 100, 111, 225
pronunciation
intonation in questions, 88

¡qué + noun/adjective/adverb!**, to express reactions, 247, 250
¿qué?
versus **¿cómo?**, 247n
versus **¿cuál?**, 87–88
querer (*irreg.*). *See also* Appendix 2.
present, 90
preterite, 168–169
questions
information, 87–88, 93
intonation in, 88
question words, 87–88, 93
quisiera, 78, 81

radical-changing verbs. *See* stem-changing verbs.
-ra forms of the past subjunctive, 374–375, 385, 393. *See also* Appendix 2.
reflexive
to express change of state, 225, 230
pronouns, 100, 111, 225
verbs, 100, 111, 225
regular verbs. *See* **-ar**, **-er**, **-ir** verbs and Appendix 2.
requests, making polite, 78, 81

saber (*irreg.*). *See also* Appendix 2.
present, 79
preterite, 168–169, 247
versus **conocer**, 79
salir (*irreg.*), command, 337. *See also* Appendix 2.
se
impersonal (*one*), 145n
reflexive pronoun, 100, 225
-self/-selves, 100, 225
ser (*irreg.*). *See also* Appendix 2.
with adjectives, 245
imperfect, 227
present, 9
preterite, 22
shall, in future tense, 271
shortened forms. *See* apocopation.
si clauses, 422, 462
softened requests and statements with

conditional and past subjunctive, 78, 81
spelling changes, in preterite, 126, 136, 157. *See also* Appendix 2.
stem-changing verbs. *See also* Appendix 2.
  present indicative of, 90, 100, 111
  preterite of, 126, 136, 180–181
subject, use and omission of, 34
subjunctive. *See also* Appendix 2.
  in adjectival clauses, 393
  in adverbial clauses, 393
  concept of, 294, 306
  English equivalent of present, 294
  formation of past, 374–375
  formation of pluperfect (past perfect), 462
  formation of present, 294
  used after certain conjunctions, 393, 468–469
  used after conjunctions of time, 315–316, 393
  used after expressions of feelings or emotion, 306, 385
  used after expressions of influence, 294, 374–375, 385
  used after nonexistent and indefinite antecedents, 385, 393
  used in conditional sentences, 422, 462
  used in softened requests and statements, 78
  used to express future, 315–316
  used with **ojalá (que)**, 358
  uses of past, 78, 374–375, 385, 393
su(s). *See* possessive adjectives.

telling time, 56–57, 63
tener (*irreg.*). *See also* Appendix 2.
  future, 153n, 283
  idioms with, 153n, 292
  present, 90
  preterite, 157–158
  subjunctive, 109–110
time of day (telling time), 56–57, 63
titles (of address), 7, 37
traer (*irreg.*), preterite, 157–158.
  See also Appendix 2.
tú. *See also* Appendix 2.
  commands, 152, 337
  versus **usted**, 89, 109–110, 124–125

unos/as, 74
usted(es). *See also* Appendix 2.
  commands, 193–194, 326
  versus **tú**, 89, 109–110, 124–125

venir (*irreg.*). *See also* Appendix 2.
  present subjunctive, 294
  preterite, 168–169
ver (*irreg.*), preterite, 136, 147. *See also* Appendix 2.

verbs, using, 34, 60. *See also* Appendix 2; commands; subjunctive; *names of tenses and parts of verbs.*
vocabulary
  academic subjects, 41–42, 49–50
  adjectives, 113, 244–245, 250
  advice, giving, 356, 360
  airport and air travel, 410, 415
  animals, 44, 47, 49
  appliances, 235, 240
  bank, at the, 372–373, 378, 383, 387, 400
  body, parts of the, 280–281, 286
  books and literature, 177–178, 183
  business matters, 372–373, 378, 383, 387
  cars and driving, 220
  change of state, expressing, 225, 230
  city streets, 193–194, 199, 302–303, 309
  clothing, 74, 81
  cognates, 8
  colors, 98, 103
  customs inspection, 410, 415
  dating and marriage, 225, 230
  days of the week, 55, 63
  description, 244–245, 250
  directions, 193–194, 199
  doctor's office, in the, 291–292, 297
  domestic life, 235, 240
  driving, 220
  entertainment, 459, 464
  family members, 19, 25, 205, 211
  fish and seafood, 134, 139
  floors of a building, 237
  food and drink, 134, 139, 143–144, 149, 155, 160, 165, 172, 420, 425
  fruits, 155, 160, 224
  furniture and appliances, 235, 240
  geographical terms, 324, 329
  giving directions, 193–194, 199
  health, physical fitness, 291–292, 297
  home appliances, 235, 240
  hotels, 430, 434
  house or apartment purchase, 391–392, 395
  house, parts of, 234–235, 240
  housing, 391–392, 395
  leisure activities, 459, 464
  literary terms, 177–178, 183
  meals, 134, 139, 143–144, 149, 155, 160, 165, 172, 419–420, 425
  meats, 144, 149
  money and finances, 372–373, 378, 383, 387, 400, 405

months and seasons, 97, 103
numbers, 32, 37, 76, 81, 123, 128
occupations, 334, 340
office, in the, 334, 340, 383, 387
pastimes, 438, 444, 459, 464
personal relationships, 345–346, 351, 448, 453
personality descriptions, 244–245, 250
pets, 44, 47, 49
post office, at the, 400, 405
professions and trades, 334, 340
real estate matters, 391–392, 395
recommendations, making, 356, 360
relationships, 345–346, 351, 448, 453
restaurant, 134, 139, 143–144, 149, 155, 160, 165, 172, 419–420, 425
road trips, 220
rooms of a house, 234–235, 240
seafood and fish, 134, 139
seasons and months, 97, 103
shopping, 313–314, 319
social relationships, 345–346, 351, 448, 453
sports, 438, 444
stores and businesses, 313–314, 319
subjects (academic), 41–42, 49–50
suggestions, making, 356, 360
textbook terms, 10
train, bus, and oceanliner, 410, 415
travel, 410, 415
university, 41–42, 49–50
vacation activities, 410, 415, 430, 434, 438, 444
vegetables, 165, 172
weather expressions, 216, 220
work, bosses, and employees, 334, 340, 383, 387
volver (ue). *See also* Appendix 2.
  command, 337
  reflexive, 225
vos forms (in South and Central America), 125–126
vosotros/as. *See* Appendix 2.

will, in future tense, 271, 412
word order, of perfect tenses, 348, 431–432, 441
would
  in conditional tense, 402, 412, 422
  in polite requests, 78, 81
written accent marks, with interrogatives, 87–88

years, how to express, 77, 123

About the Authors

Bill VanPatten is Associate Professor of Spanish at the University of Illinois, where he also directs the graduate program in Spanish. He received his Ph.D. in Spanish from the University of Texas at Austin in 1983. His areas of specialty are input and input processing in second language acquisition, the impact of instruction on second language acquisition, and the acquisition of Spanish syntax and morphology. He has published numerous articles and chapters in books, and he is also the co-author of several McGraw-Hill Spanish textbooks for the college level, including *Puntos de partida*, *¿Qué tal?*, and *¿Sabías que... ?* Professor VanPatten is the designer of *Destinos*, a telecourse for PBS television stations.

Martha Alford Marks received her Ph.D. in Spanish Literature from Northwestern University in 1978. She subsequently served on the faculties of Kalamazoo College and Northwestern University, where she coordinated the first- and second-year Spanish programs, supervised teaching assistants, appeared consistently on the Faculty Honor Roll, and won the 1982 Outstanding Teaching Award. Nationally known for her work as an ACTFL Oral Proficiency tester and trainer, Dr. Marks is also the co-author of several other McGraw-Hill Spanish textbooks for the college level, including *¿Qué tal?* and *Al corriente*.

Richard V. Teschner is Professor of Language and Linguistics at the University of Texas-El Paso, where he has taught since 1976. He received his Ph.D. in Spanish Linguistics from the University of Wisconsin-Madison in 1972. His publications range from bibliographies and textbooks (in particular, Spanish for native speakers) to numerous reviews, articles, and monographs. In 1988 he served as President of the American Association of Teachers of Spanish and Portuguese. He has also been Secretary-Treasurer, then President, of the Linguistic Association of the Southwest.

(*Credits continued from page iv*)
Mazzaschi/Stock, Boston; *92* (*bottom*) © Mark Antman/The Image Works; *104* and *106* (*top right*) "Las Meninas" by Diego Velázquez/Museo del Prado; *106* (*top left*) Museo del Prado/Más, Barcelona; *108* (*top left*) Museo del Prado/Scala/Art Resource; *108* (*top right*) Museo del Prado; *108* (*bottom left*) Museo del Prado/Más, Barcelona; *112* (*bottom left*) "The Sleep of Reason Brings Forth Monsters" by Francisco de Goya, Victoria and Albert Museum, London/Art Resource, New York; *112* (*bottom right*) "Los tres músicos" © Pablo Picasso, Museum of Modern Art, New York, Mrs. Simon Guggenheim Fund; *119* © Sergio Penchansky/Photo Researchers, Inc.; *137* © Alex Ocampo/DDB Stock Photo; *138* (*top*) © Hugh Rogers/Monkmeyer Press; *148* © Stuart Cohen/Comstock; *159* © Stuart Cohen/Comstock; *170* © J. Maisy/DDB Stock Photo; *171* © Georg Gerster/Comstock; *173* © Peter Menzel/Stock, Boston; *177* © Wide World Photos; *189* © Fritz Henle/Photo Researchers, Inc.; *198* (*bottom*) © Owen Franken/Stock, Boston; *210* © Owen Franken/Stock, Boston; *219* © Gary Conner/DDB Stock Photo; *228* © Owen Franken/Stock, Boston; *238* © Owen Franken/Stock, Boston; *248* Art Museum of the Americas/OAS; *261* © Peter Menzel; *285* © Ulrike Welsch; *296* © Peter Menzel/Stock, Boston; *308* Wide World Photos; *317* UPI/Bettmann Archive; *328* Menschenfreund/Monkmeyer Press; *339* © Peter Menzel/Stock, Boston; *349* © Hugh Rogers/Monkmeyer Press; *359* Frank Siteman/Stock, Boston; *367* © Peter Menzel/Stock, Boston; *376* (*top*) The Image Works; *376* (*bottom*) © Beryl Goldberg; *386* © Mark Antman/The Image Works; *395* © Peter Menzel/Stock, Boston; *403* Más, Barcelona; *404* UPI/Bettmann Archive; *414* (*top*) © Beryl Goldberg; *414* (*bottom*) © Peter Menzel/Stock, Boston; *433* © Peter Menzel/Stock, Boston; *442* "The Epic of American Civilization," panel #16, "Hispano-América", 1932–1934, by José Clemente Orozco. Courtesy of the Trustees of Dartmouth College, Hanover, New Hampshire; *443* "Nuestra imagen actual", 1947, by David Alfaro Siqueiros. Col. Museo de Arte Moderno INBA. Courtesy of the Unidad de Documentación e Investigación del Instituto Nacional de Bellas Artes, México, D.F.; *463* Odyssey/Frerck/Chicago.

Scenes of Fidel Castro and Cuban immigration to Florida (Episode 30), copyright © Louis Wolfson 2 Media History Center, Incorporated.

Readings: *Pages 307–308* Suárez quotation with permission from Xavier Suárez, and Medina quotation with permission from Gustavo Medina; *pages 403–404 El censo* by Emilio Carballido excerpted with permission from Editorial Grijalbo, S.A.

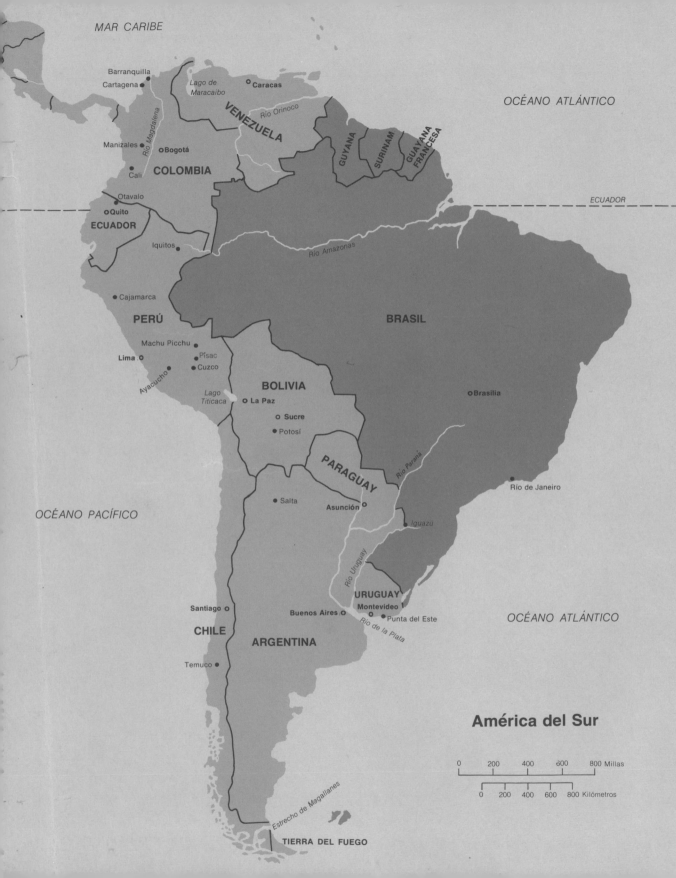

MAR CARIBE

OCÉANO ATLÁNTICO

Barranquilla
Cartagena
Lago de Maracaibo
○ Caracas
Rio Orinoco
VENEZUELA
GUYANA
SURINAM
GUAYANA FRANCESA

Manizales
Rio Magdalena
○ Bogotá
COLOMBIA
Cali

Otavalo
● Quito
ECUADOR

Iquitos

ECUADOR

Rio Amazonas

Cajamarca

PERÚ

BRASIL

Machu Picchu
Pisac
Lima ○
Cuzco
Ayacucho
Lago Titicaca
BOLIVIA
○ La Paz
● Sucre
Potosí
○ Brasilia

PARAGUAY
Rio Paraná

Salta
Asunción
Rio de Janeiro

OCÉANO PACÍFICO

Iguazú

Rio Uruguay

URUGUAY

Santiago ○
Buenos Aires ○
Montevideo
Punta del Este
OCÉANO ATLÁNTICO

CHILE
ARGENTINA
Rio de la Plata

Temuco

América del Sur

0   200   400   600   800 Millas

0   200   400   600   800 Kilómetros

Estrecho de Magallanes

TIERRA DEL FUEGO